SIRE LINES

UPDATED EDITION

Blood-Horse
CLASSICS LIBRARY

SIRE LINES

UPDATED EDITION

by Abram Hewitt

EP
ECLIPSE
PRESS

Lexington, KY

Library of Congress Cataloging-in-Publication Data

Hewitt, Abram S., 1901 or 2-1987.
    Sire lines / By Abram S. Hewitt. -- Updated ed.
        p. cm.
    ISBN-13: 978-1-58150-144-5 (hardcover)
    ISBN-10: 1-58150-144-7 (hardcover)
    1. Thoroughbred horse--Pedigrees. 2. Race horses--Pedigrees. I. Title.
    SF293.T5H44   2006
    636.1'3222--dc22

                                                    2006017906

Printed in the United States
Original edition published in 1977 by the Thoroughbred Owners and Breeders Association,
publisher of *The Blood-Horse*, in which magazine the material originally appeared in a series
of articles published from 1973 through 1976.

Distributed to the trade by
National Book Network
4501 Forbes Blvd., Ste 200, Lanham, MD 20706
1.800.462.6420

ECLIPSE
PRESS

a division of
Blood-Horse Publications
PUBLISHERS SINCE 1916

CONTENTS

5

CONTENTS

In this updated edition of *Sire Lines*, we have attempted to remain true to Abram Hewitt's original text, making factual changes where necessary. The foreword by Kent Hollingsworth, editor-in-chief of *The Blood-Horse* at the time the original *Sire Lines* was published, has been included. Updates have been made to the sire records of various stallions, particularly those that were still active at the time the original was published in 1977, with emphasis on those stallions whose tail-male lines remain extant in 2006 with significant descendants at stud. End notes in various chapters point out these updates as well as factual discrepancies and other items of interest. Each chapter contains the subject stallion's race record and a five-generation pedigree.

The Editors

FOREWORD

Before the war, which at this point probably should be specified as the Second German War, Joe Estes and Joe Palmer brightened the pages of *The Blood-Horse* with, at once, the funniest and most scholarly material written about Thoroughbreds. Fascinated by the mysteries of genetic probabilities in breeding a good racehorse, Estes set about resolving some of these statistically, while Palmer inquired of that which was before with a series of historical sketches on nineteenth-century stallions, searching for the meaning of "strength in the pedigree." Occasionally, a reader of equal sagacity and humor would toss a brick at Estes or Palmer, and this would be lateraled back and forth in the pages of *The Blood-Horse* to the edification and amusement of all.

Among the best of the prewar brick throwers was Abram S. Hewitt, a sixth-generation New Yorker graduated from Oxford in 1925 with honors in philosophy, politics, and economics. Hewitt obtained his law degree from Columbia and taught there before being appointed counsel in bankruptcy for the Kreuger and Toll collapse, the match conglomerate that involved some 450 companies and serious international political and financial consequence. Upon his return from Europe in 1933, Hewitt went to Washington with the New Deal, organized the Farm Credit Administration, and served as counsel for sundry initialed agencies.

At the same time, Hewitt directed considerable curiosity and not much money toward breeding Thoroughbreds in Virginia. This resulted in the importation of Tourbillon's sire, Ksar, who did nothing of consequence in this country except die after siring two crops. Then Hewitt bought Pilate when no one thought a scion of the Friar Rock line worth feeding, shortly after which Pilate's son Eight Thirty began running over horses with regularity. From Pilate, Hewitt bred $125,275-earner Prefect; $360,920-earner Royal Governor; and $409,275-earner Phalanx. Hewitt sold a half-interest in Phalanx to C.V. Whitney, in whose colors Phalanx raced to three-year-old championship honors in 1947. The best horse to carry Hewitt's colors was Some Chance, whom he bought from Calumet Farm for $15,000 and picked up $90,000 in purses. From a small band of broodmares, Hewitt bred a dozen stakes winners before dispersing his stock in 1950.

During the war, Hewitt served with the OSS and negotiated with German bankers he had met a decade earlier, operating out of Sweden and England. At the same time, he contributed to *The Blood-Horse* accounts of his visits to European racecourses and stud farms, while maintaining a sharp eye for a good horse.

"Well, there I was in England with no money at all except U.S. government funds, which I did not think, really, should be used to purchase yearlings. I was offered an opportunity, however, to buy a colt by Nearco out of Mrs. Rustom, by Blandford, for 500 pounds from the Aga Khan, and I did not see how I could turn it down. There was difficulty then about selling to a foreigner, and I could not get any British notes. So I went around to Tattersalls, explained this embarrassing situation whereby I had agreed to purchase this yearling and had no way to pay for it. They said that was all right, that I could go ahead, and pay them back by check after the war. Which I did. That was Rustom Sirdar. If I had been smart, or if Colonel Phil Chinn had been with me, he would have quickened to the situation and inquired of Tattersalls when they were holding their next sale."

After Phalanx, Hewitt turned his attention elsewhere, as a technical adviser for a few banks and security houses, and for a quarter-century we would encounter him only occasionally at Saratoga, Longchamp, Hialeah, or a Keeneland sale. He always seemed to have a horse in training in New York or Newmarket—and a new breeding theory. At Deauville he was found checking yearlings' heartbeats with a stethoscope, investigating the possibility of classic potential measured by the heart rather than the angle of the shoulder.

In 1973 Hewitt observed, "You know, Joe Palmer's *Names in Pedigrees* covered 51 stallions and stopped at the turn of the century. Wondered if you'd like to bring that series up to date, follow the male lines through today's pedigrees." Yes, we would. Thereupon Hewitt rummaged through his considerable store of personal knowledge and books and began a series of articles on sires here and abroad that have contributed to "strength in the pedigree" today. This series, comprising eighty-six articles that appeared in *The Blood-Horse* from 1973 through 1976, is presented here in a single volume, a tandem to Joe Palmer's *Names in Pedigrees* reprinted in 1974, to provide a century of the noteworthy in Thoroughbred breeding.

Kent Hollingsworth
Editor-in-Chief, The Blood-Horse
November 1977

CHAPTER ONE

ROCK SAND

S ir James Miller, breeder and owner of Rock Sand, was one of those favorites of Fortune who, from time to time, are dogged by good luck. Sir James was an army officer who inherited a fortune yielding an income of about 25,000 pounds a year above all his living expenses. Having inherited that tidy nest egg, he decided to test his fortunes on the Turf, and in 1890 he made an offer of 6,000 pounds to the famous trainer John Porter for the three-year-old colt Sainfoin.

The colt had won a race at Sandown Park in an impressive performance, and Porter, who owned him in partnership with Sir Robert Jardine, hesitated for a time to accept the offer. Porter did not think Sainfoin was likely to beat Surefoot in the Epsom Derby, so he accepted the offer, with the stipulation that the former owners receive half of the Derby stakes should Sainfoin win.

Although Porter's suspicion that Sainfoin could not win the Derby proved wrong, the trainer's overall assessment that the colt would not be a world beater was correct. After his victory in the 1890 Derby, Sainfoin's career on the Turf was not distinguished. Nor was he an overwhelming success at stud although he did sire Rock Sand, plus the dams of Phalaris and Hurry On—two of the best British sires of the 1920–30 period.

As a mate for Sainfoin, Roquebrune was purchased by Sir James at the dispersal of the Duchess of Montrose's stud. (Quite why that forceful lady continued to be called a duchess two husbands after the disappearance of the late duke, the writer never has been able to understand.) Roquebrune was by St. Simon and had been a high-class two-year-old winner at Royal Ascot. She was a half sister to Oaks and St. Leger winner Seabreeze. Their dam, St. Marguerite, by Hermit, won the One Thousand Guineas in a year of remarkable fillies who, among them, won all the classic races and filled the first three places in the St. Leger (Dutch Oven, Geheimniss, Shotover, etc.).[1] The next dam, Devotion, by Stockwell, also was a good race mare and broodmare. There can have been few mares with more solid credentials of high quality than Roquebrune possessed.

Barren previously, Roquebrune at the age of seven produced her first foal in 1900—the brown colt Rock Sand, by Sainfoin. When he came into training with George Blackwell at Newmarket, Rock Sand could not have looked a very dazzling prospect, as by all accounts he was in his slow paces one of the worst-actioned horses ever seen. It was not until he stretched out at full racing pace that he gave any idea that he was a colt of quality.

Perhaps it was that unattractive way of going that caused Rock Sand to be unquoted in the betting on a field of eight for the five-furlong Bedford Stakes at Newmarket on May 15, 1902. Nevertheless, Rock Sand won easily, by three lengths, with the great American rider Danny Maher up. His next start was for the six-furlong Woodcote Stakes, run at the Epsom Derby meeting on June 3. There Rock Sand started at odds-on, 10-11, and again won easily by three-quarters of a length.

For Rock Sand's next five races the competition was stiffer, and he did not have such an easy time. In the Coventry Stakes at Royal Ascot on June 12, a race of five furlongs and 136 yards, Rock Sand won, but only by a head. Second was Baroness La Fleche, a daughter of the wonderful race mare La Fleche, winner of the One Thousand Guineas, Oaks, St. Leger, Ascot Gold Cup, Champion Stakes, Cambridgeshire, etc. A month later, Rock Sand had an easier time in the Chesterfield Stakes at Newmarket, winning by two lengths in a field of seven at even money.

His remaining races all were among the most important two-year-old fixtures on the British calendar. For the Champagne Stakes at Doncaster on September 9, a party of only four turned out, and the field was without another first-class two-year-old. Rock Sand was 1-3 and won by a length from William Rufus, who was second in the following year's St. Leger. Fourth was Hammerkop, destined to win a Cesarewitch and to produce the Derby winner Spion Kop.

In the six-furlong Middle Park Stakes, known as the two-year-old Derby, Rock Sand came up against two colts of high quality [in a field of eight runners] and all carried even weights.[2] On that occasion, Rock Sand was ridden by W. Lane, while Maher, his usual partner, had the mount on Flotsam. The Duke of Portland's Greatorex, a son of the mighty Australian hero Carbine, was also in the field. Rock Sand started at even money, but Flotsam won by a head from Greatorex, with the favorite third, two lengths away.

Twelve days after suffering his first defeat, Rock Sand met Greatorex again in the seven-furlong Dewhurst Stakes, also at Newmarket. That time, Rock Sand carried 131 pounds and was giving Greatorex three pounds, and as a result of the

Middle Park form, Greatorex was favored at 11-10 with Rock Sand 6-4. Maher was back in the saddle, and Rock Sand beat Greatorex by more than three lengths.

Thus, Sir James' colt had run in virtually all the prestige races for two-year-olds and had won six of seven. He went into the winter a strong favorite for the Derby.

Rock Sand's three-year-old campaign opened on April 17 with an easy tune-up race of one mile, the Bennington Stakes at Newmarket. There were only three starters, and Rock Sand easily won by a length under 130 pounds.

In the season's first colt classic, the Two Thousand Guineas at one mile, Rock Sand was 6-4 in a field of eleven, and he beat his old rival Flotsam by one and one-half lengths. Third was Rabelais, two lengths behind the runner-up. (It is of some interest to note that Rabelais later became one of the most famous sires in France and was a male-line ancestor of the mighty Ribot. Yet, at that stage of his career, Rabelais' trainer, Richard Marsh, wrote that there was simply "nothing remarkable" about him. Rabelais, in fact, was a small colt who toed out and was markedly sickle-hocked.)

For the Derby, run on May 27 that year, there were only seven starters, and Rock Sand, with Maher aboard, went off at 2-3. An American observer, not familiar with Rock Sand's way of going at slow paces, remarked to trainer Blackwell as the hors-

ROCK SAND					
Sainfoin, 1887	Springfield, 1873	St. Albans, 1857	Stockwell, 1849	The Baron / Pocahontas	
			Bribery, 1851	The Libel / Splitvote	
		Viridis, 1864	Marsyas, 1851	Orlando / Malibran	
			Maid of Palmyra, 1855	Pyrrhus the First / Palmyra	
	Sanda, 1878	Wenlock, 1869	Lord Clifden, 1860	Newminster / The Slave	
			Mineral, 1863	Rataplan / Manganese	
		Sandal, 1861	Stockwell, 1849	The Baron / Pocahontas	
			Lady Evelyn, 1846	Don John / Industry	
Roquebrune, 1893	St. Simon, 1881	Galopin, 1872	Vedette. 1854	Voltigeur / Mrs. Ridgway	
			Flying Duchess, 1853	The Flying Dutchman / Merope	
		St. Angela, 1865	King Tom, 1851	Harkaway / Pocahontas	
			Adeline, 1851	Ion / Little Fairy	
	St. Marguerite,1879	Hermit, 1864	Newminster, 1848	Touchstone / Beeswing	
			Seclusion, 1857	Tadmor / Miss Sellon	
		Devotion, 1869	Stockwell, 1849	The Baron / Pocahontas	
			Alcestis, 1860	Touchstone / Sacrifice	

Rock Sand

MCCLURE COLLECTION

es were on their way to the post: "I suppose you know your horse is lame?"

"Oh, you've noticed that, have you?" Blackwell responded casually. "I think he has a chance all the same."

Rock Sand, as usual, showed different action in the race, and he won by two lengths from the French colt Vinicius, with Flotsam another two lengths away in third. The one-mile St. James's Palace Stakes at Ascot often has been used as the next race for a new Derby winner, and Rock Sand duly won it in a field of four, at the cramped odds of 7-100.

Up to this point, we have been tracing the record of a colt that had won ten of eleven starts, including three of the most important two-year-old events and the first two classics for which colts compete. On the face of it, are we not entitled to regard such a colt as a racer of the very highest caliber, fit to hold his own against all comers?

At any rate, the public thought so in 1903, for in the one and a quarter-mile Eclipse Stakes at Sandown Park on July 17, he was made a 5-4 favorite over exceptional competition. In the field of five were Ard Patrick (142 pounds), winner of the previous year's Derby, and Sceptre (139), winner of all the four other classics of Ard Patrick's year. Rock Sand, carrying 130 pounds, was receiving twelve pounds from Ard Patrick and nine from Sceptre, in actual weight.

In a hair-raising finish, Ard Patrick beat Sceptre a neck, with Rock Sand three lengths back. On that form, the three-year-olds of 1903 came out some distance behind the classic-aged group of 1902. Such is the value of weight-for-age races; they give a guide, such as nothing else can provide, to the relative merits of respective crops.

The St. Leger at Doncaster on September 9 was not of much interest, as Rock Sand was the only good colt in the field of five. At odds of 2-5, he won easily by four lengths from William Rufus, thus completing a sweep of England's Triple Crown classics.

Renewing their Eclipse Stakes rivalry, Rock Sand and Sceptre met again in the one and three-quarters-mile Jockey Club Stakes at Newmarket in October. The weights were more heavily in Rock Sand's favor than they had been at Sandown, he carrying 125 pounds to Sceptre's 140. In a field of five, Sceptre was 5-4 and Rock Sand 11-10, but Sceptre won again, defeating the colt by four lengths. Taking

YEAR	AGE	STS	1ST	2ND	3RD	EARNED*
1902	at 2	7	6	0	1	£ 7,574
1903	at 3	7	5	1	1	£20,225
1904	at 4	6	5	0	1	£19,769
Lifetime		20	16	1	3	£47,568
* First-place money only						

into account the age and sex allowances, Sceptre still came out some fourteen pounds the better. What a mare!

The rivalry was not finished. As a four-year-old, Rock Sand reappeared for the Coronation Cup of one and one-half miles at Epsom. There he carried 129 pounds, as did Sceptre, then five. Sceptre beat Rock Sand again, that time by three-quarters of a length, but it was for second place, as both went under to Zinfandel, winner by a length. Zinfandel was a four-year-old, also carrying 129 pounds, and it is a pity that he had not been eligible for the classics as a three-year-old, for it seems possible that he was better than Rock Sand.

The Coronation Cup form between Rock Sand and Sceptre does not quite square with the form of their previous encounters. Sceptre had not wintered well, and her trainer, Alec Taylor, did not have her to his liking. Furthermore, she was nothing like as good over a course with sharp turns, such as Epsom, as she was over a straight galloping course, such as Newmarket.

Two weeks after the Coronation Cup, Rock Sand (136) finally defeated Sceptre (135), leaving her five lengths behind [in third place] in the one and one-half-mile Hardwicke Stakes at Royal Ascot. The victory can hardly be taken as a true bill, however, for it came the very next day after Sceptre had run in the Ascot Gold Cup at two and one-half miles!

At the end of June, Rock Sand won the Princess of Wales's Stakes at Newmarket over one and one-half miles. There were only five starters, and as there was noth-

Mad Hatter, one of Fair Play's $100,000 earners, was out of a Rock Sand mare

ing of much quality in the race besides Rock Sand, the odds on him were 6-100. A similar *nolo contendere* race was won by Rock Sand at Lingfield Park over one and one-quarter miles. There were only three starters, and Rock Sand at 1-3 won easily enough, by three-quarters of a length. Five days later he was a starter for the First Foal Stakes at Newmarket against a solitary opponent, and he won again at odds of 6-100. The race was of such little import that it is difficult to understand why he was entered.

Rock Sand's last race was for the Jockey Club Stakes at Newmarket over one and three-quarters miles. That time, there was no Sceptre in the field, but there was a lot of support for Henry the First, a three-year-old carrying 125 pounds to Rock Sand's 137. Since Henry the First had been good enough to be second in the St. Leger, there was brisk betting on the outcome. Each colt went off at 5-2 in a field of ten. Rock Sand won by one and one-half lengths.

Sir James retired Rock Sand to stud, and after the owner's death the horse was sold to August Belmont of New York, in 1906. The price was reported to be 25,000 pounds.

Nothing very remarkable came from Rock Sand's brief stud career in England, but at Belmont's Nursery Stud near Lexington he sired Tracery, a St. Leger winner and a first-class racer. A good, though not highly fertile stallion, Tracery appears in the pedigrees of Ribot, Princequillo, Alibhai, Dahlia, and many other good horses.

Rock Sand also sired Friar Rock (out of Fairy Gold, dam of Fair Play), a colt declared by trainer Sam Hildreth to be the best he ever saw racing over a distance of ground. Shortly before World War I, Rock Sand was sold again, to a syndicate of French breeders; he died on July 20, 1914, after only one full season at stud in France.

Rock Sand's daughters were not raced extensively, as nearly all of them in the United States were bred by Belmont, who did not believe in much racing for fillies. Each of the $100,000 winners sired by Fair Play (except Display), including the immortal Man o' War, carried the blood of Rock Sand.[3] So, who is to say that the Belmont policy was wrong, especially considering that the years Rock Sand spent at stud in England and France produced little of quality?

End Notes:

1. In 1882 fillies won all the English classic races: St. Marguerite won the One Thousand Guineas; Shotover won the Two Thousand Guineas and the Epsom Derby; Geheimniss won the Epsom Oaks; and Dutch Oven won the St. Leger.

2. Flotsam and Greatorex shared equal weight with Rock Sand. Also in the field were Martinet, Mead, Hammerkop, D'Orsay, and Love Charm.

3. Fair Play's $100,000 winners: the full brothers Chance Play and Chance Shot, whose second dam, Quelle Est Belle, was by Rock Sand; the full brothers Mad Hatter and Mad Play, whose dam, Madcap, was by Rock Sand; Man o' War, whose dam, Mahubah, was by Rock Sand; and Display, who had no Rock Sand blood in his pedigree.

CHAPTER TWO

TRACERY

Some sixty-five years ago, that stalwart puritan Charles Evans Hughes, governor of New York (and later national Secretary of State and Chief Justice), made an effort to suppress the vice of betting through enactment of anti-wagering legislation. As those who remember Prohibition will realize, that was not the only futile attempt on record to legislate mankind toward so-called virtue.

From 1910 to 1913, the racetracks in New York were closed by the Hughes law, so horsemen were forced to go elsewhere to race their stock. Thus, August Belmont II, chairman of The Jockey Club and one of the most successful and prominent American breeders (owner of Hastings, Fair Play, Beldame, Rock Sand, and later breeder of Man o' War) sent his brown yearling colt by Rock Sand—Topiary, by Orme, to be trained in England. The colt, whose second dam was the Cambridge and Cesarewitch winner Plaisanterie, was sent to Palace House, Newmarket. That establishment was presided over by John Watson, as trainer for the genial and much liked Leopold de Rothschild, of the famous banking family. Since the Belmonts for years had represented the Rothschild interests in New York, the connection with the Rothschild stable at Newmarket was altogether natural.

Tracery evidently gave some trouble in his preparation for the races, since he did not start as a two-year-old and did not make his debut until the Derby in 1912. Even then he was not very fit, not much was expected, for his odds were 66-1. There were stories that he had suffered from spavins, and there was some doubt as to his remaining sound. In fact, however, he suffered no further problems from unsoundness.

To the general surprise, Tracery finished a good third to the filly Tagalie and runner-up Jaeger, beaten four lengths and two lengths, with the Two Thousand Guineas winner Sweeper II unplaced at 2-1. Sweeper II was by the American sire Broomstick and along with Whisk Broom II and Borrow helped to establish the firmly held conviction in England that American horses could not stay.

The Derby must have brought Tracery on a good deal as in his next start, for

August Belmont II

the St. James's Palace Stakes at one mile at Royal Ascot, he went off at the short price of 11-10. The field of five included Sweeper II, set to give Tracery seven pounds. Tracery beat Sweeper II by four lengths, establishing that he had good speed and was up to classic standard.

At Goodwood on July 31, he met Sweeper II again, in the one-mile Sussex Stakes, with the same spread in the weights in favor of Tracery. That time, at odds of 1-2, Tracery won by a half-length.

Moving to Doncaster in September for the St. Leger at one mile, six furlongs, and 132 yards, Tracery at 8-1 won by five lengths from Maiden Erlegh and Hector in a field of fourteen. Lomond at 6-4 and Tagalie (winner of the Derby and One Thousand Guineas), joint second favorite at 8-1, were unplaced. Considering Tracery's backwardness at the time of the Derby and the fact that he had met and beaten the best of his age from one mile to the St. Leger distance, the latter race established Tracery beyond doubt as the best of his age.

Early in 1913, there was considerable interest in racing circles as to the relative merits of four-year-old Tracery and five-year-old Prince Palatine, who had won the Ascot Gold Cup of 1912 and was regarded as the best stayer in training. As an opener for his four-year-old season, Tracery came out for the one and one-half-mile Burwell Plate at Newmarket. There were eight starters, among them Lord Derby's high-class Stedfast, who had been second in the Guineas and Derby of 1911. Both carried 132 pounds, and Stedfast went off at odds of 5-4, while Tracery was 2-1. The public still underestimated Tracery, as he won by a length from Jackdaw (132), with Stedfast another half-length away in third.

At Royal Ascot, Tracery was a starter for the Ascot Gold Cup, with 126 pounds up, and so were Prince Palatine (130) and Stedfast (130), the five-year-olds giving the four-year-old Tracery four pounds as weight for age. From a field of eight, the public made Prince Palatine a strong favorite at 4-7, with Tracery second favorite at 6-1.

The race turned out to be a fiasco. With Tracery well in front, and going easily about five furlongs from the finish, a man dashed out onto the track brandishing a revolver and a small flag. Jockey Whalley on Tracery was unable to avoid a collision, and all three fell to the ground—horse, jockey, and revolver brandisher. Fortunately, none of them were seriously injured. With the field racing past the fallen Tracery, Prince Palatine went on to win by one and one-half lengths from Stedfast. Taking a line through Stedfast, a good case can be made that Tracery, in receipt of four pounds, would have been right there at the finish. Of course, both Whalley on Tracery, and Saxby on Prince Palatine each declared with fervor that his own mount would have won, barring the accident.

In the ten-furlong Eclipse Stakes at Sandown Park in July, Tracery was asked to pick up 140 pounds. He gave twelve pounds to the three-year-old Louvois, who had won the Two Thousand Guineas and had been placed second in the Derby upon the sensational disqualification of Craganour. The public was beginning to show some esteem for Tracery, as he was made an odds-on favorite at 1-2, while Louvois was 6-1. The public (or bookmakers) was right beyond a doubt in this case, as Tracery beat Louvois by four lengths, with five others trailing.

On October 2, Tracery came out in a field of seven for the one and three-quar-

			Springfield, 1873	St. Albans, 1857	Stockwell / Bribery
		Sainfoin, 1887		Viridis, 1864	Marsyas / Maid of Palmyra
			Sanda, 1878	Wenlock, 1869	Lord Clifden / Mineral
Rock Sand, 1900				Sandal, 1861	Stockwell / Lady Evelyn
			St. Simon, 1881	Galopin, 1872	Vedette / Flying Duchess
		Roquebrune, 1893		St. Angela, 1865	King Tom / Adeline
			St. Marguerite, 1879	Hermit, 1864	Newminster / Seclusion
TRACERY				Devotion, 1869	Stockwell / Alcestis
			Ormonde, 1883	Bend Or, 1877	Doncaster / Rouge Rose
		Orme, 1889		Lily Agnes, 1871	Macaroni / Polly Agnes
			Angelica, 1879	Galopin, 1872	Vedette / Flying Duchess
Topiary, 1901				St. Angela, 1865	King Tom / Adeline
			Wellingtonia, 1869	Chattanooga, 1862	Orlando / Ayacanora
		Plaisanterie, 1882		Araucaria, 1862	Ambrose / Pocahontas
			Poetess, 1875	Trocadero, 1864	Monarque / Antonia
				La Dorette, 1867	The Ranger / Mon Etoile

THE NATIONAL HORSERACING MUSEUM, NEWMARKET

Tracery

ters-mile Jockey Club Stakes at Newmarket. There is some confusion as to the weights there, as the official *Racing Calendar* reported Tracery as carrying 147 pounds (and so does the *Stallion Register* of 1918), but other accounts state that he was trying to give the three-year-old Cantilever (113) twenty-seven pounds, which would put Tracery at 140 pounds. The second alternative seems the more likely. In any case, Cantilever beat Tracery (odds-on at 4-6) by two lengths. Cantilever was no bad colt, as he had won his two previous races and went on to win the Cambridgeshire carrying a ten-pound penalty.

Tracery's last race was for the one and one-quarter-mile Champion Stakes, run on without a turn, at Newmarket. Long Set was his solitary opponent, but the public was able to obtain the generous odds of 5-6 about Tracery, who won by six lengths. Long Set, a pretty fair racer in his own right, that year had won the Royal Hunt Cup (127), the March Stakes (136) from Cantilever, the Liverpool Cup (130), and the Doncaster Cup (131). For Tracery to give such a horse as Long Set a six-length beating made him at least fifteen pounds the better of the pair.

Taking his racing history as a whole, it seems probable that Tracery was about the same class as his sire, English Triple Crown winner Rock Sand, but did not have the good fortune to come to hand early enough in the two-year-old stakes and early three-year-old classics.

Upon Tracery's retirement to stud, Belmont refused an offer of 40,000 pounds for the horse, and let him remain in England at a stud fee of 400 guineas. By the time Tracery's first foals were of racing age (1917), World War I was in full swing and racing in England was much curtailed. That year, Tracery sired no winners. His stud fee was reduced to 250 guineas and remained there until his sale to Senor S.J. Unzue of Argentina of 53,000 pounds in 1920.

In 1918, Tracery was the sire of only one winner, but that was The Panther, who was to win the Two Thousand Guineas of the next year. Thereafter came a stream of good winners: Monarch, a top two-year-old; Abbots Trace, a high-class handi-capper and fair sire; Flamboyant, a good stayer; Teresina, a very high-class staying filly, and later the dam of Alibhai; Tamar, second in the Derby; and then the Derby winner Papyrus, who appears in the pedigree of both Ribot and Princequillo.

YEAR	AGE	STS	1ST	2ND	3RD	EARNED*
1911	at 2	unraced				
1912	at 3	4	3	0	1	£ 9,647
1913	at 4	5	3	1	0	£10,070
Lifetime		**9**	**6**	**1**	**1**	**£19,717**

* First-place money only

Having used Tracery for three years in Argentina, Señor Unzue accepted a proposal from the late William Allison that Tracery return to England under an arrangement whereby Unzue retained a one-quarter share in the horse and a syndicate acquired the remaining three-quarters at a price of 36,000 pounds. Lloyd's of London agreed to insure the syndicate's share for 36,000 pounds over a three-year period, with the value of the policy declining by one-third each year. As things fell out, Tracery died shortly after the first year of the policy had expired, and the balance of the policy was promptly paid.

Tracery did not have the good fortune to be a very fertile stallion, as during his seven seasons at the Southcourt Stud the average number of covers per mare was 4.9; for his single season at the Cobham Stud, upon his return to England in 1924, he made 165 covers for forty mares. This poor fertility, of course, reduced the number of foals that might have been expected.

The only high-class racer resulting from Tracery's last years at stud was the filly Foliation who was an excellent stayer, bought when barren at the age of fourteen by the great Italian breeder Federico Tesio.

Tesio and the Aga Khan, two of the most successful breeders of the time, each had a very high regard for the blood of Tracery. The Aga Khan did buy the Tracery filly Teresina, who became one of the foundation mares of his stud, and Tesio did breed Nera di Bicci (by Tracery), perhaps as good a filly as he ever bred. Ironically, however, the greatest international influence of Tracery came from another source, and an unlikely one. In 1918, Tracery sired the bay colt Copyright, out of Rectify. In training from two to five years of age, Copyright won only two races, the more important of which was the Gold Vase of two miles at Royal Ascot. His public form suggests that Copyright was more than twenty pounds below the best of his age. Yet, when sent to Argentina as a stallion, Copyright sired Congreve, a very high-class racer, indeed, who became *the* dominant sire in Argentina in the 1930s and 1940s. Among Congreve's stock was Kayak II, who was an inmate of the C.S. Howard stable at the same time as Seabiscuit and was not very far behind him in merit.

In Australia, from the Tracery male line came the good stallions Pantheon, Archery, Psychology, and also a fine racer in Gothic, while in New Zealand appeared Cuddle, the best-staying mare of her time.

No successful line of Tracery was established in the United States, or in France, Italy, or Germany. For a time, it flickered in England with Papyrus, Flamboyant, Obliterate, etc., but today it is very dormant, if not completely dead. When a phenomenon such as this occurs, it has been the history of the *Stud Book* that the blood of a high-class horse like Tracery generally flows down through a few females to re-emerge in very high-class sires again. In Tracery's case, those sires among his daughters' descendants include the aforementioned Ribot, Princequillo, and Alibhai.

CHAPTER THREE

FRIAR ROCK

riar Rock was bred by August Belmont II, who owned both his sire, Rock
Sand, and dam, the grand broodmare Fairy Gold. The latter also was the
dam of the first-class racer and great sire Fair Play (the first stallion to sire
six winners of more than $100,000, these winners including Man o' War).

Friar Rock was put into training with Sam Hildreth, who shared with James
Rowe Sr. the honor of being the most prominent trainer in the United States.
Hildreth brought out Friar Rock as a two-year-old on May 26, 1915, at Belmont
Park, and he proceeded to win his first three starts, in the second of which he
went five furlongs in :58 3/5.

Friar Rock then entered stakes competition and was something less than
invincible, though by no means disgraced. On July 17 at Belmont Park, he won
the Whirl Stakes of five and a half furlongs in 1:03 4/5, a new track record. At
Saratoga, he won the Adirondack Handicap of six furlongs with top weight of 116
pounds. That, however, was a stakes of secondary importance at Saratoga. When
he went for the important Saratoga Special, he was third to Dominant and Puss
in Boots, beaten eight lengths, and when he tried for the important Champagne
Stakes at Belmont Park under 125 pounds, he was fourth in a field of seven
behind Chicle (112), beaten four lengths and giving ground at the finish.

Friar Rock's superior stamina began to tell in his favor when he was three.
On May 25, he was only seventh of twelve starters in the one-mile Metropolitan
Handicap, but on May 30, with 101 pounds up, he won the Suburban Handicap
at one and a quarter miles. In the Suburban, he beat the best older horses then in
training, including Short Grass, Stromboli, and The Finn (127).

Then, on June 10, he won the one and three-eighths-mile Belmont Stakes from
Spur by three lengths, with Chicle fourth. Two weeks later, against older horses,
Friar Rock also won the Brooklyn Handicap of nine furlongs (108) from a field
of seven others, which included Pennant and the great gelding Roamer. The time
was a new track record of 1:50.

L.S. SUTCLIFFE

Friar Rock

After three indifferent races, Friar Rock (113), at weight for age, decisively won the one and three-quarters-mile Saratoga Cup from Roamer (127) and The Finn (126) by margins of two lengths and six lengths.

The three-year-old, then, had won the Belmont Stakes and then beat the best older horses in the Suburban Handicap, the Brooklyn Handicap, and the Saratoga Cup. This was an enormous feat, so he must have been, at his best, at least as good as his half brother, Fair Play. Friar Rock's record as a sire, however, was not in the same class.

There are several possible explanations for this:

(1) Belmont sold Friar Rock. The price reportedly was $50,000 when he sold him to the great breeder and horse trader, John E. Madden, at the end of the Saratoga meeting. The sale was not as surprising as it might appear at first glance, for the Belmont stud already was full of the blood of Rock Sand and was becoming full of the blood of Friar Rock's half brother Fair Play. Thus, there were not too many mares in the Nursery Stud eligible to be bred to Friar Rock. Also,

Belmont had suffered sharp financial reverses in connection with his project to build the Cape Cod Canal, and he undoubtedly needed the money.

(2) Madden, in turn, sold a half-share in Friar Rock to a California breeder, John Rosseter. The arrangement was that Friar Rock should spend alternative stud seasons in Kentucky and California, but this shuttle system did not work out satisfactorily. Friar Rock became the subject of lawsuits between Madden and Rosseter for control and possession of the horse, Rosseter declining to return Friar Rock to Kentucky on schedule.

Since Rosseter's breeding operation was by no means of high quality, Friar Rock's time spent in California was largely wasted. Madden, however, had bred Inchcape in Friar Rock's first season at stud. Inchcape was a colt that appeared to be of the very highest class. He won his first two starts, the second one by seven lengths in the Tremont Stakes, then was sold to the Rancocas Stable, trained by Sam Hildreth, for $165,000.[1] Inchcape broke down and made only one more start as a three-year-old, winning by ten lengths. He sired only a few foals.[2]

(3) The horses trained by Sam Hildreth were generally (according to reports) given Fowler's solution, containing both strychnine and arsenic, as well as other "dopes." Of the numerous high-class horses trained by Sam Hildreth, including

FRIAR ROCK				
Rock Sand, 1900	Sainfoin, 1887	Springfield, 1873	St. Albans, 1857	**Stockwell** / Bribery
			Viridis, 1864	Marsyas / Maid Of Palmyra
		Sanda, 1878	Wenlock, 1869	Lord Clifden / Mineral
			Sandal, 1861	**Stockwell** / Lady Evelyn
	Roquebrune, 1893	St. Simon, 1881	**Galopin**, 1872	Vedette / Flying Duchess
			St. Angela, 1865	King Tom / Adeline
		St Marguerite, 1879	**Hermit**, 1864	Newminster / Seclusion
			Devotion, 1869	**Stockwell** / Alcestis
Fairy Gold, 1896	Bend Or, 1877	Doncaster, 1870	**Stockwell**, 1849	The Baron / Pocahontas
			Marigold, 1860	Teddington / Ratan Mare
		Rouge Rose, 1865	Thormanby, 1857	Melbourne / Alice Hawthorn
			Ellen Horne, 1844	Redshank / Delhi
	Dame Masham, 1889	Galliard, 1880	**Galopin**, 1872	Vedette / Flying Duchess
			Mavis, 1874	Macaroni / Merlette
		Pauline, 1883	**Hermit**, 1864	Newminster / Seclusion
			Lady Masham, 1867	Brother To Strafford / Maid Of Masham

Hourless, Purchase, Grey Lag, Mad Hatter, etc., none made a successful sire, and many of them, such as Grey Lag and Purchase, were almost sterile. Similar insinuations were directed at the late Fred Darling in England; he trained seven Derby winners in twenty years, not one of which was a solid success at stud.

YEAR	AGE	STS	1ST	2ND	3RD	EARNED
1915	at 2	12	5	1	1	$ 5,090
1916	at 3	9	4	0	2	$15,275
Lifetime		21	9	1	3	$20,365

(4) To break up the Madden-Rosseter partnership, Friar Rock, in time, was sold to W.R. Coe's Shoshone Stud in Lexington. He died in January 1928, the year his son Pilate was foaled, Pilate being the subject of a study in this book.

Friar Rock had some success as a sire of broodmares but was never very prominent as a sire of winners. The slings and arrows of outrageous luck—and overall lack of opportunity—may go a long way to account for that.

End Notes:

1. The price was reported as $150,000 in later issues of *The Blood-Horse*.

2. In 1923 Inchcape died in a disastrous barn fire at H.F. Sinclair's Rancocas Farm. The million-dollar fire also killed another young stallion, Cirrus, and many broodmares.

CHAPTER FOUR

PILATE

From time to time, sires without superior racing credentials score surprising successes at stud. Since all of us love bargains, these cases hold a hypnotic fascination for breeders. Cases of this sort include Gallinule (initial stud fee of nine guineas), Bay Ronald (sire of Bayardo, Dark Ronald, Rondeau, etc.), Rabelais (sold for 750 pounds, later the premier sire of his time in France), the leading American sires High Time and Bull Dog—plus Pilate.

After the stud success of such a horse is realized, it nearly always develops that, as Damon Runyon said, "a story goes with it." Of course, a story of some description seems to go with any horse that has failed to become a world-beater—those that never prove any good at stud as well as those that do. If breeders were to believe and act upon all such stories, they would have as many stallions at stud as they have mares. They are on firmer ground to accept the dictum of the famed German chancellor and diplomat, Prince Bismarck, who observed: "No story should be believed until it has been officially denied."

Since the late Colonel Phil T. Chinn was intimately connected with both High Time and Pilate, we had better start with his account of Pilate. The colonel was a good friend of the writer, who found him an unfailing fount of tall stories and entertainment.

Chinn was managing W.R. Coe's Shoshone Stud near Lexington in 1927, when Friar Rock was bred to the gray mare Herodias, she by the "Spotted Wonder," The Tetrarch. Herodias had been one of the yearlings imported in 1917 by Coe when he bought the entire yearling crop from the famous Sledmere Stud in Yorkshire, England. As a race mare in the United States, Herodias had won a race at two, and four races out of ten starts at three, they including a small handicap.

She was out of the Gallinule mare Honora, who bred the high-class colt Lemonora—winner of the Grand Prix de Paris, second in the Two Thousand Guineas, and third in the Derby—and traced back in tail female to Geheimniss (Epsom Oaks, etc.). Geheimniss was pronounced by the famous trainer John Porter to be the fastest filly he had seen. In fact, such was the reputation of Geheimniss for speed that her owner proposed a match, with Geheimniss (then four) to carry equal weights with the great St. Simon (two).

St. Simon's owner, the Duke of Portland, thought that this was asking too much of any two-year-old and declined the challenge, but when St. Simon's trainer, canny old Mat Dawson, heard about it, he put his bristles up and said at once to the Duke of Portland: "I would like your 10,000 pounds and let me stand half of it!" Portland still declined.

Herodias also produced the stakes winners Black Majesty and Bluebeard, so she was a pretty fair broodmare, one from whom a good number of high-class racers since have descended.

Col. Chinn regarded Pilate, the Friar Rock—Herodias colt, as an outstanding individual as a yearling at the time he was sent into training in New York with Bennett Creech. Pilate, however, had the misfortune to crack a stifle in February of his two-year-old year, and the injury proved to be so severe that it was thought for a time that he might have to be destroyed.

Pilate was shipped back to the Shoshone Stud and turned out. Along in August, Col. Chinn noticed with surprise that Pilate was going sound again, moving with apparent freedom in his paddock. So, without saying anything to Coe, Chinn put Pilate back into training at the old Lexington track, where racing had been conducted for about one hundred years.

At that time, the track record for five furlongs, according to Chinn, was 1:00. When in November, Pilate was fit to work five furlongs, Chinn set him down to be tried against the watch at that distance. Waving the exercise boy down to the last part of the gallop, Chinn glanced at his stopwatch and was startled to see that Pilate had worked the distance the first time he was asked in fifty-nine seconds! Chinn was excited "more than somewhat," as Runyon put it, and telephoned Coe in New York that this was beyond doubt the best horse Coe ever had owned.

The next spring, when Pilate was shipped by rail to New York, he had the misfortune to contract pneumonia. When he recovered from that, it was found that the pneumonia had left him "broken winded," so that he made a noise when he galloped. This convinced trainer Creech that Pilate would be useless for racing, or the next thing to it, and he hurried his preparation with a view to getting rid of him in a claiming race as soon as possible.

That hurried preparation resulted in Pilate developing an ankle that became so infected a drain had to be inserted to get rid of the pus. By the time this had healed and Pilate was ready to run, taking with him his cracked stifle, infected stiff ankle, and broken wind, it was August, and racing had moved to Saratoga.

Trainer Creech and stud manager Chinn were on the worst of terms (a very difficult feat to achieve with the ever genial and kindly Col. Chinn), and Creech was determined to prove that Col. Chinn was a fool for advising Coe that Pilate was a high-class colt. Accordingly, he entered Pilate in a six-furlong maiden race to be claimed for $3,000. To Creech's chagrin, Pilate won in a field of sixteen and was duly claimed (by John Whalen). Six days later, Pilate started again in a six-furlong race, this time to be claimed for $2,500 in a field of seventeen, but did not win. Presumably, Creech felt better, but when Pilate proceeded to win seven out of his remaining eight starts as a three-year-old, the trainer must have been looking at Chinn with a stony stare.

From August 25 to November 30, Pilate made ten starts, winning eight races and running second in the other two.[1] He was beaten a neck once and a nose the other time, in the ten-furlong Maryland Handicap, beating the high-class handicappers Mate and Tred Avon. He gradually had climbed the ladder from a $2,000 claiming price to the handicap ranks, his race for the ten-furlong Maryland Handicap being run in 2:02 4/5, with Pilate, despite his wind infirmity, running the first mile in 1:36 3/5 (track record 1:37 3/5). It was obvious that Pilate was

PILATE				
Friar Rock, 1913	Rock Sand, 1900	Sainfoin, 1887	Springfield, 1873	St. Albans / Viridis
			Sanda, 1878	Wenlock / Sandal
		Roquebrune, 1893	St Simon, 1881	Galopin / St. Angela
			St Marguerite, 1879	**Hermit** / Devotion
	Fairy Gold, 1896	**Bend Or**, 1877	Doncaster, 1870	Stockwell / Marigold
			Rouge Rose, 1865	Thormanby / Ellen Horne
		Dame Masham, 1889	Galliard, 1880	Galopin / Mavis
			Pauline, 1883	**Hermit** / Lady Masham
Herodias, 1916	The Tetrarch, 1911	Roi Herode, 1904	Le Samaritain, 1895	Le Sancy / Clementina
			Roxelane, 1894	War Dance / Rose of York
		Vahren, 1897	Bona Vista, 1889	**Bend Or** / Vista
			Castania, 1889	Hagioscope / Rose Garden
	Honora, 1907	Gallinule, 1884	Isonomy, 1875	Sterling / Isola Bella
			Moorhen, 1873	**Hermit** / Skirmisher mare
		Word of Honour, 1892	Saraband, 1883	Muncaster / Highland Fling
			Geheimniss, 1879	Rosicrucian / Nameless

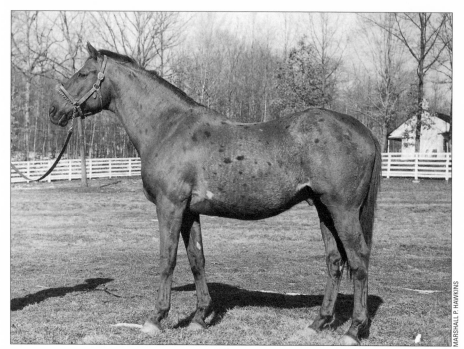

Pilate

becoming a pretty high-class colt.

As a four-year-old, Pilate won twelve races out of twenty-two starts, was second twice and third twice. At five, he won the six-furlong Paumonok Handicap at Jamaica and three other races out of twelve starts.

He set a track record for one mile and seventy yards at Laurel and beat Jack High in an overnight handicap. He was certainly a game, tough campaigner, but on his public form he was something more than fifteen pounds behind the best of his age. Considering his infirmities of broken wind, cracked stifle, and infected ankle (which remained stiff during his racing career), it is impossible to say with any accuracy what Pilate's true racing class was, minus all these physical handicaps.

During his racing career, Pilate had been acquired by Andy Schuttinger, former jockey, who sent him to his stud farm in New Jersey. There Pilate made one stud season that resulted in seven foals, all fillies. One of these was a good, game filly, just short of stakes class. Schuttinger's mares, unfortunately, were not of much class, so these fillies did little more than show that Pilate could sire winners better than their dams. At the end of the season in New Jersey, Schuttinger traded Pilate back to Coe, his original owner, in exchange for two fillies.

When Coe dispersed his stud in the autumn of 1935, Pilate was bought by the late B.B. Jones of Audley Farm, Berryville, Virginia, for $4,600. Thereby hangs the tale—which this time does not have to be denied to be true.

B.B. Jones was a warm friend of the author and was one of the most kindly and charitable men we ever knew. He had put 4,000 boys and girls through college, with loans from a charitable foundation established in memory of his mother. Jones many times told the author that none of these loans ever had defaulted, the repayments being used to put still more boys and girls through college. When he came to this part of the story, Jones invariably burst into tears out of senti-

YEAR	AGE	STS	1ST	2ND	3RD	EARNED
1930	at 2	unraced				
1931	at 3	10	8	1	0	$ 8,985
1932	at 4	22	12	2	2	$10,005
1933	at 5	12	4	2	1	$ 3,930
Lifetime		44	24	5	3	$22,920

ment about how splendid these young people had been. The author also would invariably join in this lachrymose exhibition.

Jones was born in Mississippi about 1860, and his boyhood was passed in considerable poverty. "I had no shoes," he used to say. When he was about nineteen, he contracted tuberculosis and migrated to Oklahoma to have the benefit of the drier climate. He became, in due time, cashier in a bank at Bartlesville. In that capacity, it was part of his duty to drive a buckboard across the various ranches where the bank had loaned money on land and livestock.

During one such inspection drive, Jones said: "I suddenly got a feeling in the pit of my stomach that there was oil in this place." He had no trouble obtaining an oil lease, as none of the oil companies liked the area. He then bought or leased a second-hand drilling rig and put down a hole. About 300 or 400 feet down, Jones struck oil. He sent at once for his brother, Montfort Jones, who then was a banker in Mississippi.

When Montfort Jones descended at a little railroad wayside stop in his immaculate banker's suit, he was greeted by brother B.B., sitting in a worn out buckboard behind a team of mules with the statement: "Montfort, we're rich!"

Montford Jones surveyed B.B. carefully and then replied: "B.B., this heat is getting you!"

What Jones had found turned out to be the Cushing Field, which yielded the brothers about $19,000,000. It was the first major oil strike for any independent in Oklahoma.

B.B. Jones came back from attending the Coe dispersal and telephoned the author. When we called upon him, we could see that there was something he

BERT CLARK THAYER

Phalanx

wanted to say but didn't know quite how to begin. Finally he said almost apologetically: "You know, I have 14 stallions."

The author replied he was well aware of that fact.

"Well," said B.B., "I bought another one!"

"No!" cried the author, who had been trying to get Jones to reduce, at least somewhat, his huge establishment. "Why did you do such a thing?"

"You know," said Jones, "when I looked at that horse, I got exactly the same feeling in the pit of my stomach I had when I drove over that Cushing Field in Oklahoma!"

Before he even knew what the horse was, the author said, "Can I have half?"

"Certainly," said Jones, "I would like to have you as my partner."

The horse was Pilate, who cost Jones $4,600 and who later came to stand at the author's Montana Hall Stud at White Post, Virginia. If the truth must be told (this sometimes happens, even in Turf matters), the author did not really believe too strongly in the prospects of Pilate at that stage. There were good reasons for doubt. None of the Rock Sand-line sires in the United States had been a success, that including Friar Rock. While the Rock Sand mares had been gems almost beyond price, the males of the line simply had failed at stud. Furthermore, Pilate's second dam, Honora, had produced a very high-class racer in Lemonora (Grand Prix de Paris, second in the English Guineas, third in the Derby, etc.) and he had turned out to be one of the worst stallions on record. Furthermore, literally nothing descending in tail female from the first-class mare Geheimniss had been worth the price of its feed as a sire. There were grounds, then, for doubts about Pilate. The author decided to wait until the foals of 1936 showed their form before patronizing his own horse. When Eight Thirty, Lovely Night, and Pontius showed up from a crop of five colts, the author had his doubts dispelled, but it took a long time before the breeding community would accept Pilate as a good sire.

Pilate was not bred to more than seven or eight mares of good credentials in his life, but he got twenty-three stakes winners (9 percent) from 269 named foals. Several of his sons were of exceptional class: Eight Thirty won the Suburban, Metropolitan, Travers, Saratoga, and other stakes and earned $155,475. He sired forty-four stakes winners, including Bolero and Sailor.

Phalanx, also by Pilate, was the champion three-year-old of 1947, when he won the Belmont Stakes, Jockey Club Gold Cup, Wood Memorial, and other stakes and ran second in the Kentucky Derby. Phalanx earned $409,275, and his get included Fisherman and Career Boy.

Other runners by Pilate included Royal Governor, winner of stakes in six seasons (including a Widener Handicap) and earner of $360,920; Pilaster, winner of stakes for five seasons and earner of $259,800; Platter, winner of the Pimlico Futurity, etc.; Miss Doreen, earner of $130,475 and the only stakes winner foaled from the great race mare Princess Doreen; plus Seaward, Dinner Hour, Pirate, and Lovely Night.

(Editor's Note: Phalanx and Royal Governor were bred by the author of this series, who also numbers Pilate horses Quiet and Prefect among his total of twelve stakes winners bred.)

From his lifetime total of 269 named foals, Pilate got an exceptional 80 percent (214) winners.

Physically, Pilate was a horse of medium size, with the pronounced Roman nose of his sire, Friar Rock, and a liberal sprinkling of black spots on his skin and throughout his coat. (The spots could have come from his gray dam and gray maternal grandsire, The Tetrarch.)

The failure of good male lines while the females remain high-class producers—as apparently was true in the case of Rock Sand blood until the appearance of Pilate—is a phenomenon which we never have heard explained adequately.

Hermit led the English sire list for seven successive seasons, but it was found that his daughters were of the highest class as broodmares while his sons, though excellent racers, virtually were useless at stud. Gallinule was an excellent sire, he being from a Hermit mare, but the same pattern was repeated—his daughters excellent, his sons very poor.

Star Shoot, out of a mare by Hermit, led the American sire list five times, but his sons were almost useless at stud while his daughters were among the best. The same pattern had been true of Hamburg and Chaucer.

Many breeders thought the same thing was about to repeat itself, with the Rock Sand line, condemning the sires of that line in advance. The pit of B.B. Jones' stomach, however, proved a better guide than all the knowledge and analysis of the pedigree pundits.

End Notes:

1. As a three-year-old, Pilate finished behind other horses three times. He finished fifth in his second start. On September 10 he finished second at Belmont Park but was awarded the victor's purse upon the disqualification of winner Breezing Thru, who had not been properly entered as to ownership. A nose loss to Clock Tower in the Maryland Handicap accounted for the third.

CHAPTER FIVE

EIGHT THIRTY

The pesky perversity of the way things turn out in breeding seldom has been illustrated better than in the history of Eight Thirty. He was bred and owned by George D. Widener, who had a distinguished career on the Turf for some fifty years. With the vast means at his disposal from the start, it was no surprise that Widener bred and raced a long series of good horses. The perverse thing was that one of the best racers and best sires Widener produced during his long span of years he really bred by accident—one could almost say in spite of himself. This was Eight Thirty.

In the fall of 1935, W.R. Coe dispersed his Shoshone Stud at Lexington. One of the broodmares catalogued was the six-year-old Dinner Time, who had been a high-class filly, placing second in both the Schuylerville Stakes and Spinaway Stakes at Saratoga. In the latter race, she was beaten by five lengths by Top Flight, but no other filly that year did much better against the unbeaten Top Flight.

An unusual aspect of Dinner Time's record was that, while a high-class stakes filly, she never won a single race from her twelve starts. She must have been one of the highest-classed maidens ever.

Dinner Time was sired by High Time, a renowned speed sire who had Domino as a grandsire and Domino again as two of his four great-grandsires. Dinner Time was from Seaplane, a Man o' War mare out of Bathing Girl. (Bathing Girl was the third dam of Man o' War's great son War Admiral, but War Admiral was only a yearling at the time Dinner Time came up for sale.)

Widener wanted Dinner Time, but he probably would have given several thousand dollars more than the $6,000 he paid for her if she had been in foal to a more appealing stallion than Pilate. The latter at the time was held in such low esteem that Coe, his breeder, had been able to reacquire him by exchanging two fillies for the stallion. Few believed in Pilate, but there was nothing Widener could do about it since the Shoshone dispersal was held in the autumn and Dinner Time already was in foal.

BLOOD-HORSE LIBRARY

George D. Widener

Thus, Widener was the breeder of the Pilate foal that Dinner Time produced at his Old Kenney Farm near Lexington during the next spring. The foal, well-named Eight Thirty, was a stylish chestnut with a white stripe and white front pasterns, the white running up above the fetlock on the left fore.

When time came for him to be broken and trained as a yearling, Eight Thirty was sent with the other Widener horses to Erdenheim Farm near Philadelphia, but, being by Pilate, he was not put with the first string of the young horses. Instead, he was turned over to the "chain gang," in the charge of J. Creevey, who was assistant to Widener's head trainer, W.F. Mulholland. The latter, in turn, was under the supervision of Andrew Jackson Joyner, Widener's general racing manager. Creevey remained the trainer of record for Eight Thirty until the 1938 Futurity, when Mulholland took over.

Eight Thirty made his first start at Delaware Park on June 18, 1938, in the usual maiden race with special weights. His private work had been so promising that he was made the favorite at 7-4, and he got off in front and led throughout. Despite swerving in the stretch, he won in 1:00 4/5.

For the Christiana Stakes of five and a half furlongs on July 4, he was only the third favorite, but he won by a short head. Next came Saratoga and the Flash Stakes. The latter was a favorite race of William Woodward Sr., who was fond of pointing out how many high-class horses had won it. Woodward made an effort nearly every year to win the Flash, and in 1938 his Belair Stud entry included Johnstown, his best two-year-old. There were fifteen starters.

Eight Thirty ran much the same sort of race as he had in his two previous efforts, staying a close second in the quickly run race and then getting up to win by a short head. Johnstown was fourth, beaten seven lengths.

The United States Hotel Stakes brought Eight Thirty out against the best two-year-old of the season, the unbeaten El Chico. The race was run in deep mud, which seemed to cause Eight Thirty to lose his action as he was far back in the early running. El Chico skated through the mud and beat him by ten lengths, although Eight Thirty did manage to salvage third place.

In the Saratoga Special, Eight Thirty met El Chico again. The track was better, but the result was another handy triumph for the unbeaten colt. At even weights, El Chico defeated Eight Thirty by three lengths.

Eight Thirty made one more start at Saratoga, coming out for the Albany Handicap under top weight of 122 pounds. With El Chico not in the race and nothing else of much class entered, Eight Thirty was odds-on at 1-2. He won by a length but was disqualified for causing a jam on the far turn.

Following the Albany, Eight Thirty fell lame, having rapped himself at exercise. That caused a suspension in his training schedule for about two weeks and left him some way from his best for the Futurity on October 1. Even so, he ran second, beaten a nose by Porter's Mite. Johnstown finished fourth, beaten two and a half lengths.

There can be little doubt that at that stage Eight Thirty was a better colt than Johnstown, although the latter developed very high form later in the autumn, when he scored in the Breeders' Futurity in Kentucky.

				Sainfoin, 1887	Springfield Sanda
			Rock Sand, 1900		
				Roquebrune, 1893	St. Simon St Marguerite
		Friar Rock, 1913			
				Bend Or, 1877	Doncaster Rouge Rose
			Fairy Gold, 1896		
				Dame Masham, 1889	Galliard Pauline
	Pilate, 1928				
				Roi Herode, 1904	Le Samaritain Roxelane
			The Tetrarch, 1911		
				Vahren, 1897	Bona Vista Castania
		Herodias, 1916			
				Gallinule, 1884	Isonomy Moorhen
			Honora, 1907		
EIGHT THIRTY				Word of Honour, 1892	Saraband Geheimniss
				Commando, 1898	Domino Emma C.
			Ultimus, 1906		
				Running Stream, 1898	Domino Dancing Water
		High Time, 1916			
				Domino, 1891	Himyar Mannie Gray
			Noonday, 1898		
	Dinner Time, 1929			Sundown, 1887	Springfield Sunshine
				Fair Play, 1905	Hastings Fairy Gold
			Man o' War, 1917		
				Mahubah, 1910	Rock Sand Merry Token
		Seaplane, 1922			
				Spearmint, 1903	Carbine Maid of the Hunt
			Bathing Girl, 1915		
				Summer Girl, 1906	Sundridge Permission

BLOOD-HORSE LIBRARY

Eight Thirty

Eight Thirty did not come to hand well at the start of his three-year-old season. His first effort was in the Woodhaven Purse at Jamaica on April 25, when he met Johnstown, plus another good colt in Lovely Night. Eight Thirty chased Johnstown for six furlongs, then tailed off and finished third, a dozen lengths back. He challenged Johnstown again in the important Wood Memorial but gave a dismal display, finishing last after being far back throughout.

Eight Thirty's connections realized that these were not true performances, and he was put aside for five weeks. The son of Pilate re-emerged at Delaware Park and appeared to be a different colt, winning two six-furlong races in romping style. He then re-entered stakes competition in the Kent Handicap at one and one-sixteenth miles. Weighted at 120 pounds, he was receiving six pounds from Challedon and giving three pounds to Sun Lover. The result was Sun Lover first by a neck and Eight Thirty second by two lengths over Challedon. At the weights, Eight Thirty and Challedon appeared about equal.

After adding the Diamond State Stakes at Delaware, Eight Thirty was returned to Saratoga, where he was to win four successive stakes. First was the one-mile

Wilson Stakes, at weight-for-age. The three-year-old was carrying 118 pounds and his older opponents, Pompoon, Main Man, and Fighting Fox, carried 126 each. Fighting Fox recently had beaten Pompoon in

YEAR	AGE	STS	1ST	2ND	3RD	EARNED
1938	at 2	7	3	2	1	$ 19,375
1939	at 3	10	7	1	1	$ 39,125
1940	at 4	8	4	0	3	$ 81,450
1941	at 5	2	2	0	0	$ 15,525
Lifetime		27	16	3	5	$155,475

the $50,000 Massachusetts Handicap, so that pair was known to be in good form. Nevertheless, Eight Thirty started the co-favorite at 2-1 and won by four lengths from Pompoon.

Three days later came the one and a half-mile Saratoga Handicap. All the weights were low for the field of ten, The Chief, a four-year-old, carrying the top impost at 110 pounds. Eight Thirty at 106 was giving weight by the scale, but he won easily by three lengths from Sickle T.

Next came the historic Travers Stakes at one and a quarter miles. Owing to the heavy track conditions, Johnstown, the Kentucky Derby and Belmont winner, was a non-starter, as was the good colt Hash. That left a field of only three runners: Sun Lover in at 122 pounds, Eight Thirty at 117, and Sir Marlboro at 112 under the allowance conditions. At those weights, Eight Thirty was 1-3, and not surprisingly he drew away to beat Sun Lover by five lengths.

Eight Thirty's last race at Saratoga came in the Whitney, which at one and a quarter miles was a weight-for-age race for all ages. Again, only two rivals appeared, and they both were mares, Shangay Lily and Handcuff. Sent off at 1-5, Eight Thirty coasted home by a length in front of Shangay Lily in poor time.

The Whitney left the impression that Eight Thirty was not as good as he had been earlier in the meeting, and there was a good reason for this. He had become very sore in one of his hind legs, and he was taken out of training for the remainder of the season.

Establishing the rankings of the best three-year-olds of a season generally is an interesting puzzle. In 1939 there had been three outstanding colts. Johnstown had beaten Eight Thirty decisively twice in the spring, when Eight Thirty obviously was a long way from being right; Johnstown also had beaten Challedon eight lengths in the Derby and seven lengths in the Dwyer, when Challedon had tried to make a front-running race of it.

Stacked against those results, Challedon (voted the Horse of the Year) had beaten Johnstown badly over a very heavy track in the Preakness and had beaten him again in the Arlington Classic (after Johnstown had gone in his wind and had been overworked badly for the race).

Between Challedon and Eight Thirty, meanwhile, there apparently was not much to choose, with Eight Thirty probably the speedier and Challedon probably the better stayer.

With that in mind, it is to be noted that both Challedon and Johnstown were disappointments at stud, while Eight Thirty became a highly successful sire. He was the quality colt of the three, and was in all probability the best among the trio as a two-year-old. Their results at stud bring to mind something the late Federico Tesio told the author more than thirty-five years ago. He said that he did not like to breed to big, burly, coarse stallions, as he had found out from experience that they seldom transmitted racing class well.

Having seen in his stud records that he had bred to such a horse repeatedly in Sansovino and also had bred to another coarse English Derby winner, Felstead, with equally poor results, we could well understand his beliefs.

When Eight Thirty was a four-year-old, the noted American Turf writer John (Salvator) Hervey described him as being so far from sound that he was "an illustrious cripple." Coming out first for the six-furlong Toboggan Handicap at Belmont Park, he picked up top weight of 127 pounds and quickly proved he was not going through a series of dull races before hitting his best form, as he had at three.

Eight Thirty won the Toboggan by one and a half lengths in 1:09 4/5, time one-fifth of a second slower than Equipoise's record. The reward for that performance was a weight assignment of 128 pounds for the one-mile Metropolitan Handicap. Despite that weight, he was sent right to the front and raced six furlongs in 1:10 1/5. Pace and weight combined to tell, and he gave ground in the stretch, finishing fourth.

The Suburban Handicap carried more prestige than any other handicap in the United States, and Eight Thirty next was sent for that event. Again given top weight, 127 pounds, he was giving three pounds to the Metropolitan winner, Hash.

The first six furlongs were run in 1:09 4/5 and a mile was reeled off in 1:35 1/5. At that point, Eight Thirty had not yet struck the front, but inside the final furlongs of the ten-furlong test he did so and went on to win by one and a half lengths from Can't Wait, to whom he was giving eighteen pounds. The final time of 2:01 3/5 was only one-fifth of a second slower than the Suburban time recorded by Snark, which in some circles was regarded as the probable stakes record. (Whisk Broom II's recorded 2:00 in 1913 was always a subject of much dispute and gnashing of teeth.)

That sterling performance may have taken something out of Eight Thirty, for

SKEETS MEADORS

Royal Coinage, sire of Kentucky Derby winner Venetian Way

four weeks later he failed by one and a half lengths while giving eleven pounds to Isolater in the one and a quarter-mile Brooklyn Handicap. Eight Thirty was burdened with 130 pounds.

The weight dropped off only slightly, to 128 pounds, for the one and three-sixteenths-mile Butler Handicap the next week. Can't Wait, under 111 pounds, took his turn at winning, getting home one and three-quarters lengths in front of War Dog and Eight Thirty, who finished heads apart.

The next target for Eight Thirty was the major event on the New England calendar, the $50,000 Massachusetts Handicap of nine furlongs at Suffolk Downs. For once, Eight Thirty was not the top weight, going into the fray under 126 pounds as compared to 130 on Challedon. In a field of eleven, Eight Thirty went right up with the pace and was in front when a mile was completed in 1:35 3/5, time under the official track record for the distance.

In the final furlong, Eight Thirty continued in front and wound up with a length over Hash (115), with Challedon one and a half lengths farther back. Even considering the pull in weights, the result appeared to put Eight Thirty slightly better than Challedon.

Eight Thirty then was sent once more to Saratoga, where he won the Wilson again, at 1-20, from the fine old mare Esposa. He was saddled next under 129 pounds for the Saratoga Handicap, but his bothersome leg had begun to trouble him again, and he finished third, and in distress. For a time, it was hoped he could be made sound enough for his fall engagements, but the Saratoga Handicap turned out to be his final race of the year.

Mulholland carefully brought Eight Thirty back for one more campaign at five. It was brief, but brilliant. For the Toboggan, Eight Thirty took up 129 pounds, followed in fourth as Roman cut out the early fractions, then strode into command and won by two and a half lengths.

Eight Thirty next tried for the Metropolitan, which he had lost the previous year, and he was assigned 132 pounds, heaviest impost of his career. He was ten lengths behind in the early running as Roman Flag led for the first six furlongs, then shot between horses when asked and drew out to win by two lengths. He was giving from nine pounds (to Hash) to thirty pounds (Bold and Bad) in a field of nine.

Eight Thirty was sore again after the Metropolitan, and three weeks later Widener made the decision to retire him to stud at Old Kenney Farm.

At the time of Eight Thirty's retirement, Hervey wrote of the horse's "fine opportunity to assist in the re-establishment in this country of the male line from Rock Sand, to which he belongs."

There are various ways to judge a sire line. In sheer numbers of stakes winners, the Rock Sand line today is not strong, but in terms of contributing some significant horses, Eight Thirty did indeed revive the line. His sons included Royal Coinage, a high-class two-year-old who, in turn, got 1960 Kentucky Derby winner Venetian Way; Sailor, a brilliant handicapper who sired champion Bowl of Flowers, the high-class Crewman, and other stakes winners; and Bolero, a world-record sprinter who sired thirty-three stakes winners.

Eight Thirty never led the sire list but was among the top twenty for eight years. All told, he sired forty-four stakes winners (15 percent) from 299 named foals. They included Sunday Evening, Door Prize, Big Stretch, Rare Perfume, Head Man, Lights Up, Sungari, and Tellarian. His daughters, as was expected, became valued broodmares. They produced fifty-eight stakes winners, including Evening Out, Rare Treat, Jester, Cornish Prince, Yorkville, and Hold Your Peace.

Eight Thirty died in 1965 at the division of Leslie Combs II's Spendthrift Farm that formerly had been Widener's Old Kenney. He had been a pensioner since 1958.

CHAPTER SIX

BROOMSTICK

In 1892 James R. Keene already was embarking on his policy of importing
English broodmares for his American stud. His agent in England was William
Allison, the special commissioner of *Sporting Life*, who was a great advocator
of Bruce Lowe's figure system of female lines (since largely discredited).

At that time, Keene could not have known with any certainty what an outstanding racehorse and sire Domino was going to be. Since Domino was a yearling in
1892, Keene could have known only that he had an extremely fast yearling.

Keene paid 1,500 guineas for Sylvabelle, a daughter of the great sire Bend Or,
in foal to the Two Thousand Guineas winner Galliard, whose defeat in the Derby
was thought by many to have hastened Lord Falmouth's retirement from the Turf.
Sylvabelle foaled a filly in 1893; then both were imported to Keene's Castleton Stud
in Lexington. The filly was named Elf, and she never started; no reason was reported for this, so lack of merit or unsoundness must remain conjectural. Elf's first foals
were not successful, and in 1900 Keene decided to sell her. His stud manager and
brother-in-law, Major Foxhall Daingerfield was opposed to this, as he believed Elf
was in foal to Ben Brush, whose prospects as a sire Daingerfield esteemed highly.
After two veterinarians examined Elf and pronounced her barren, however, Keene
had his way and for once did not have a good racehorse and top sire forced on him.

The purchaser, for $250, was Colonel Milton Young, then owner of the
McGrathiana Stud in Lexington and a prominent commercial breeder. (Young
stood the great stallion Hanover, who was the leading sire for four years.) In
1901, despite the diagnosis of the veterinarians, Elf foaled a bay colt who was
named Broomstick.

The colt was one of ten yearlings sold by Young in 1902 to Captain Samuel
S. Brown, for a total of $17,100. A wealthy coal magnate from Pittsburgh,
Pennsylvania, and an enterprising character, Brown was the controlling stock-
holder in Churchill Downs at Louisville, Kentucky. He also bought the Kentucky
Association track at Lexington, which had been closed following a mortgage

Broomstick

foreclosure. Brown proceeded to win the Phoenix Stakes at Lexington and then shipped over to Churchill Downs, where he won the 1905 Kentucky Derby with Agile. One is forced to ponder how likely it is to bring off the triple of becoming a millionaire, owning racetracks, and winning a Derby at his own track?

Broomstick was a small yearling, and he remained a small horse, similar in size to his sire Ben Brush, although he was not as long as Ben Brush. He showed, however, considerably more quality than Ben Brush, and he had the sloping rump of his Barb ancestors.

Broomstick was sent South to Brown's winter training quarters near Mobile, Alabama, and like many small horses, he got set early so that when trainer Peter Wimmer brought him North he was thoroughly fit. His first start was in the five-furlong Juvenile Stakes on May 7 at Morris Park, New York, and he won by a head in the excellent time of :59. Three weeks later he won the Expectation Stakes and then went on to win the Great American Stakes. Those three victories meant that Broomstick had to pick up additional weight, and he was unable to carry 129 pounds to victory. Running against the best of his age, however, he was four times second in five starts until, while carrying 127 pounds, he was unplaced to the great filly Hamburg Belle in the Futurity.

As a three-year-old, Broomstick started fifteen times, winning six races and placing in seven, but he was by no means the best of his age. His first start was in an unimportant race on May 12, which he won. He was beaten by good horses in his next three races and won another unimportant race, an overnight at one mile. Encouraged by his colt's performance, Brown left a Pittsburgh hospital to see Broomstick contest the ten-furlong Brighton Handicap. Broomstick was weighted at 104 pounds against top-weighted five-year-old Waterboy, the latter carrying 129 pounds. The race was between the four-year-olds Irish Lad (127 pounds), who later appeared in the distaff family of Tourbillon, and Broomstick. With only twenty yards to go, Irish Lad broke down and failed to keep a straight line, while Broomstick won by a head in 2:02 4/5, thus establishing a new American record.

Broomstick was then beaten twice before being shipped to Saratoga, where he won the important ten-furlong Travers Stakes (129 pounds), but where he had only to beat ordinary horses in Bobadil (116 pounds) and Auditor (111 pounds). Broomstick was beaten in his next start at Saratoga but returned to Sheepshead Bay to win the unimportant Flying Handicap. He won one more overnight race and then kept running second and third.

Broomstick's four-year-old campaign was much less distinguished. He was out fifteen times again and won five races, but although he placed in five stakes, he failed to win one. James R. Keene's three-year-old Sysonby beat him four times without much effort, and Oiseau beat him twice.

BROOMSTICK					
Ben Brush, 1893	Bramble, 1875	Bonnie Scotland, 1853	Iago, 1843	Don John	
				Scandal	
			Queen Mary, 1843	Gladiator	
				Plenipotentiary mare	
		Ivy Leaf, 1864	Australian, 1858	West Australian	
				Emilia	
			Bay Flower, 1859	Lexington	
				Bay Leaf	
	Roseville, 1888	Reform, 1871	Leamington, 1853	Faugh A Ballagh	
				Pantaloon mare	
			Stolen Kisses, 1864	Knight of Kars	
				Defamation	
		Albia, 1881	Alarm, 1869	Eclipse	
				Maud	
			Elastic, 1871	Kentucky	
				Blue Ribbon	
Elf, 1893	Galliard, 1880	Galopin, 1872	Vedette, 1854	Voltigeur	
				Mrs. Ridgway	
			Flying Duchess, 1853	The Flying Dutchman	
				Merope	
		Mavis, 1874	Macaroni, 1860	Sweetmeat	
				Jocose	
			Merlette, 1858	The Baron	
				Cuckoo	
	Sylvabelle, 1887	Bend Or, 1877	Doncaster, 1870	Stockwell	
				Marigold	
			Rouge Rose, 1865	Thormanby	
				Ellen Horne	
		Saint Editha, 1873	Kingley Vale, 1864	Nutbourne	
				Bannerdale	
			Lady Alice, 1855	Chanticleer	
				Agnes	

The chief interest in Broomstick is his stud career. He was first retired to Brown's Senorita Stud in Lexington and bred to a small group of mares in his first season. Seven foals resulted, one of which was a chestnut colt, out of the good race mare Audience, winner of the Kentucky Oaks and Tennessee Oaks; the colt, called Whisk Broom II, was purchased as a yearling by Harry Payne Whitney for $2,500.

Following Brown's death in 1906, his brother, who was his heir, decided to sell the bloodstock on November 23, 1908. At this time Whisk Broom II was a yearling and had been broken and tried by the late A.J. Joyner for Whitney. Joyner was so impressed with Whisk Broom II that he advised Whitney to buy his sire, Broomstick.

Whitney only went to $7,250 to acquire Broomstick, who passed from the Castleton Stud, where he had been conceived, to the H.P. Whitney stud, thus going from the best stud in the United States to the best stud that survived the Castleton dispersal in 1913.

Whisk Broom II was sent to England to be raced in Whitney's name and to be trained by Joyner. He proved to be a high-class racer, but he was about eight to ten pounds below the best of his year there. He was third to Neil Gow and Lemberg in the Two Thousand Guineas but won the Victoria Cup, a good seven-furlong handicap. That victory was very significant because when Whisk

Whisk Broom II

Broom II was returned to the United States for the reopening of racing in New York in 1913, he won the ten-furlong Suburban Handicap, carrying 139 pounds in the official time of 2:00. Generally disbelieved by horsemen, the time was let stand in the record books. Whisk Broom II also won the Metropolitan and Brooklyn handicaps.

Far more important than a dispute on time was Joyner's own estimate of the relative form of English and American horses at that time. Joyner trained for Whitney from 1908 to 1914 in England and was one of the most competent and respected members of the training profession in the United States, both before and after that time. In 1939, Joyner told the author at Saratoga that he thought that English form at that period was about fourteen pounds better than American form. We know of no one half as well qualified to express a professional opinion on this point than was Joyner. In view of the consistent success of American-bred horses in England and France in the last seven or eight years [the late 1960s and early 1970s], British and French breeders might do well to examine the causes for this change.

YEAR	AGE	STS	1ST	2ND	3RD	EARNED
1903	at 2	9	3	4	0	$25,400
1904	at 3	15	6	4	3	$37,970
1905	at 4	15	5	3	2	$11,360
Lifetime		39	14	11	5	$74,730

Broomstick was lightly used in the Whitney stud, where he virtually was a private stallion, as were the Castleton stallions. He had five foals born to him at the age of thirty and had twenty-five crops of foals, which included 280 named foals. Sixty-nine of these, or 25 percent, were stakes winners, compared with a 3 percent average for the breed. Of his two-year-olds, 55 percent were winners, compared with a breed average of 18 percent, and 74 percent of his produce were winners, compared with a breed average of 54 percent.[1]

End Notes:

1. Broomstick led the U.S. general sire list three times, from 1913 to 1915.

CHAPTER SEVEN

SWEEP

Sweep was the last colt of classic stature bred at Castleton Stud. James R. Keene, the owner, and Major Foxhall Daingerfield, his brother-in-law who managed the stud, both were growing old. (They died within two days of each other early in 1913.)

Moreover, ominous shadows were settling over the racing scene in New York. When the Percy-Gray Law[1] was repealed, betting at a racetrack became a criminal offense, and the New York tracks were closed during the whole of 1911 and 1912. They were reopened in 1913, due largely to the efforts of Harry Payne Whitney.

Sweep, like his sire, Ben Brush, was short in height but very lengthy, though he had more quality than did Ben Brush. He represented the favorite Castleton cross, Ben Brush on Domino. That cross worked well both ways; the excellent sire Black Toney was by Peter Pan (a Domino line sire) out of Belgravia (by Ben Brush).

Sweep's racing career was not extensive, but he did very well in the highest class of stakes. As a two-year-old, he ran eight times, won five races, and was second twice and third once. His winning races included the Futurity and the National Stallion Stakes, and his seconds came in the Saratoga Special and the Hopeful.

In the Futurity, his last race of 1909, he broke second and took command in the stretch, thereafter pulling away to win by six lengths from Candleberry. The race then was worth $25,710 to the winner.

As a three-year-old, Sweep came out in an allowance race, which he won, as a prep for the Belmont, then run at one and three-eighths miles. In the Belmont, Sweep was opposed only by Duke of Ormonde, and he led by daylight most of the way, eventually drawing off to win again by six lengths under Jimmy Butwell.

All told, Sweep won four of his five races at three, including the

YEAR	AGE	STS	1ST	2ND	3RD	EARNED
1909	at 2	8	5	2	1	$41,323
1910	at 3	5	4	0	1	$22,625
Lifetime		13	9	2	2	$63,948

Sweep

Lawrence Realization and the Carlton Stakes. He undoubtedly was the best of his year, both at two and three.

Keene's stock was dispersed in 1913 at Madison Square Gardens, and Sweep was purchased for $17,500 by Kentucky horsemen Kinzea Stone, John S. Barbee, and J.C. Carrick. Peter Pan topped the dispersal sale at $38,000.

There is little doubt that Sweep was a higher class racehorse than was Broomstick, also by Ben Brush. His stud life was passed in less favorable circumstances, however, and his record was not nearly so good as the other horse's. Instead of standing at the best stud in the country, with access to a chosen band of mares, such as Broomstick had, Sweep in the main was a public stallion, patronized by breeders with mares of ordinary credentials. The Sweep offspring often had to be raced early and frequently to meet pressing expenses.

Nevertheless, Sweep was a major success. With twenty crops to represent him, Sweep sired 395 named foals. Of these, 66 percent were winners, 44 percent were two-year-old winners, and 12 percent were stakes winners. (Broomstick had an extraordinary 25 percent stakes winners from named foals.)

Sweep led the American sire list twice, in 1918 and 1925, and his forty-eight stakes winners included The Porter, in turn the leading sire of 1937. Sweep's other runners included Untidy, the champion three-year-old filly of 1923, plus the crack two-year-old colts Eternal and Leonardo II. Others included Sweep On, General Thatcher, and Sweep All.

Sweep, son of Ben Brush and sire of The Porter, was the middle link in a line of three generations that led America's sire list, but the line waned. The prospects for revival of the male lines of either Broomstick or Sweep are currently poor, although it often has been said that the only safe time to condemn a sire is at least sixty years after his death.

As a broodmare sire, however, Sweep placed his name in pedigrees of lasting note. His daughters produced Triple Crown winners War Admiral (a leading sire and broodmare sire) and Whirlaway and Kentucky Derby winner Bubbling Over, and Sweep was America's leading sire of broodmares in 1937 and again in 1941.

The stallion died at the age of twenty-four in 1931, at Barbee's Glen-Helen Stud.

End Notes:

1. The Percy-Gray law had criminalized gambling everywhere except at licensed racetracks.

Ben Brush, 1893	Bramble, 1875	Bonnie Scotland, 1853	Iago, 1843	Don John / Scandal
			Queen Mary, 1843	Gladiator / Plenipotentiary mare
		Ivy Leaf, 1867	Australian, 1858	West Australian / Emilia
			Bay Flower, 1859	**Lexington** / Bay Leaf
	Roseville, 1888	Reform, 1871	**Leamington**, 1853	Faugh-a-Ballagh / Pantaloon mare
			Stolen Kisses, 1864	Knight of Kars / Defamation
		Albia, 1881	**Alarm**, 1869	Eclipse / Maud
			Elastic, 1871	Kentucky / Blue Ribbon
Pink Domino, 1897	Domino, 1891	Himyar, 1875	**Alarm**, 1869	Eclipse / Maud
			Hira, 1864	**Lexington** / Hegira
		Mannie Gray, 1874	Enquirer, 1867	**Leamington** / Lida
			Lizzie G, 1867	War Dance / Lecomte mare
	Belle Rose, 1889	Beaudesert, 1877	Sterling, 1868	Oxford / Whisper
			Sea Gull, 1866	Lifeboat / Wild Cherry
		Monte Rosa, 1882	Craig Millar, 1872	Blair Athol / Miss Roland
			Hedge Rose, 1867	Neptunus / Woodbine

SWEEP

CHAPTER EIGHT

THE PORTER

The long, low physical type of the Ben Brush strain reached its apogee with The Porter. Ben Brush looked low but lengthy; his son Sweep looked lower and longer, and the Porter, by Sweep, looked almost like a caricature.

It generally was said that The Porter had to wear a thick set of shoes to measure fifteen hands, while he had the length and body of a big horse. With the handicap of this equipment, it was astonishing that he was a high-class racer and could compete on even terms with such as Exterminator.

The late Captain P.M. Walker told the author that he broke The Porter as a yearling at his Pagebrook Stud near Boyce, Virginia. Capt. Walker said he thought very little of The Porter until the time came for yearling trials. Then The Porter came bounding along so far in front of his competitors that Walker said to himself: "Either this is a very good colt, or the others are not worth a quarter!"

The Porter was bred by New Yorker David Stevenson and was foaled on May 15, 1915, at John S. Barbee's Glen-Helen Stud near Lexington. His dam, Ballet Girl, by St. Leonards, was a winner and dam of three other winners, none of whom showed high class. Ballet Girl was a half sister to the good runner and sire Ballot.

Purchased privately by Samuel Ross of Washington, D.C., The Porter was not brought to the races until October 1 of his two-year-old season. He won half of his six races that year, defeating maidens at Aqueduct in his second race of the year and winning over allowance horses twice in Maryland.

That The Porter was more than ten pounds below the best of his age at two was shown in his only race that year against stakes competition, Pimlico's one-mile Walden Stakes on November 10. The Porter, carrying 117 pounds, finished third behind two high-class colts, War Cloud (125 pounds), who won a division of the Preakness the next year, and Tippity Witchet (127). The Porter was beaten by three lengths by War Cloud and by one and one-half lengths by Tippity Witchet.

Ross could not have entertained too high an opinion of The Porter, because he ran the colt in claiming company in his last race at two (The Porter finished second) and sold him after his third race at three. In the latter, a division of the Preakness, the colt got eight pounds and a two-length beating from Jack Hare Jr.

The Porter was bought by E.B. McLean, publisher of the *Washington Post* and *Cincinnati Enquirer*. The colt first indicated that he was approaching top-class form in the one and one-sixteenth-mile Baltimore Handicap, in which he defeated Cudgel and Omar Khayyam, two four-year-olds considered about the best older colts in training. The Porter received sixteen pounds from them both, instead of the weight-for-age scale of about seven pounds, and he defeated Cudgel by two lengths.

In another one and one-sixteenth-mile handicap, The Porter was asked to give eight pounds to that year's Kentucky Derby winner, Exterminator. The Porter nearly did it, losing by only a head. Later, in the ten-furlong Pimlico Autumn Handicap, The Porter (under 127 pounds) gave Exterminator nine pounds and War Cloud one pound. At those weights, based on previous form, War Cloud was favored. Knowing what we now know about Exterminator's stamina, however, it is not surprising that he won. The Porter was third, six lengths in front of War Cloud.

The Porter faced the best lot of horses he had yet met in the one and one-half-mile Bowie Handicap at Pimlico. The fifteen-horse field included Kentucky Derby winners George Smith (then five), Omar Khayyam, and Exterminator, plus War Cloud and seven-year-old Stromboli. The Porter was assigned 122 pounds, but the distance was too much for him. He finished unplaced, with George Smith (under 130 pounds) the winner, Omar Khayyam (115) second, and Exterminator (120) third.

As a four-year-old, The Porter ran in the colors of his trainer, J.F. Schorr, who did not spare the horse, running him fifteen times. The Porter won seven of those, and he finished unplaced only four times. In his second race of the year, The Porter set a track record at Churchill Downs of 1:41 3/5 for one mile and seventy yards. The time equaled the American record for the distance.

The Porter at four did not quite stay nine furlongs, and he still was about ten pounds below the best in the country. He defeated Exterminator by four lengths going one mile and seventy yards, and he beat Sir Barton, winner that year of what later became the Triple Crown, by five lengths over a mile in heavy going. He gave Sir Barton four pounds in that race, but the result perhaps should not be taken too literally because Sir Barton suffered from very shelly feet and one never knew when the pain would stop him.

The nine-furlong Havre de Grace Handicap that year was probably as revealing as any race as to The Porter's true class. The Porter and Sir Barton were weighted evenly at 124 pounds, five pounds below Cudgel and two pounds below Exterminator. Cudgel won by a half-length from Exterminator, who finished a nose in front of Sir Barton, who was two lengths ahead of The Porter. The chart caller commented that The Porter tired in the stretch.

Racing over a mile at Laurel, The Porter defeated Cudgel by four lengths and set a track record of 1:37 3/5 while in receipt of three pounds from the older horse. In the one-mile Laurel Stakes over a sloppy track, The Porter beat Billy Kelly, Sun Briar, Lucullite, On Watch, and Fairy Wand. In the one-mile Pimlico Fall Serial though, The Porter lost to younger Sir Barton by two lengths. Thus, The Porter appeared about as good as any others of his age group at a mile, but even at his best distance was about six pounds behind the 1916 classic form.

The Porter at five again raced for McLean, who liked running on the Kentucky circuit. In his first race that season, a seven-furlong allowance event at Churchill Downs, The Porter won by two lengths in 1:25, equaling the track record. He then won Latonia's one and one-sixteenth-mile Inaugural Handicap under top weight of 131 pounds.

THE PORTER					
	Sweep, 1907	Ben Brush, 1893	Bramble, 1875	Bonnie Scotland, 1853	Iago / Queen Mary
				Ivy Leaf, 1867	Australian / Bay Flower
			Roseville, 1888	Reform, 1871	Leamington / Stolen Kisses
				Albia, 1881	Alarm / Elastic
		Pink Domino, 1897	Domino, 1891	Himyar, 1875	Alarm / Hira
				Mannie Gray, 1874	Enquirer / Lizzie G
			Belle Rose, 1889	Beaudesert, 1877	Sterling / Sea Gull
				Monte Rosa, 1882	Craig Millar / Hedge Rose
	Ballet Girl, 1906	St. Leonards, 1890	St. Blaise, 1880	Hermit, 1864	Newminster / Seclusion
				Fusee, 1867	Marsyas / Vesuvienne
			Belladonna, 1884	Kingfisher, 1867	Lexington / Eltham Lass
				Bellona, 1878	The Ill-Used / Beatrice
		Cerito, 1888	Lowland Chief, 1878	Lowlander, 1870	Dalesman / Lufra
				Bathilde, 1858	Stockwell / Babette
			Merry Dance, 1879	Doncaster, 1870	Stockwell / Marigold
				Highland Fling,1869	Scottish Chief / Masquerade

Against the class of opposition found at Churchill and Latonia, The Porter seldom had much trouble. When he was brought to New York for the nine-furlong Brooklyn Handicap, however, The Porter finished sixth in a seven-horse field while under top weight of 126 pounds. The Porter did win once in New York that year, easily taking the one-mile Wilton Handicap over inferior rivals.

In Maryland that season, The Porter won the one-mile-and-seventy-yard Harford Handicap, the nine-furlong Havre de Grace Handicap, and the one and three-sixteenths-mile Monumental Handicap, setting a track record of 1:58 2/5 in the last-named. In the one and one-half mile Annapolis Handicap, The Porter failed to concede nine pounds to three-year-old John P. Grier.[1] Neither of those two probably could stay twelve furlongs; in any case, John P. Grier was at least twenty-two pounds behind the year's leading three-year-old, Man o' War.

At six, The Porter won four of his seven races, turning in one of his best efforts in his final start. The race was the one and one-half-mile Annapolis Handicap, in which The Porter carried 120 pounds to Exterminator's 135. The track was sloppy, and Exterminator was unable under those circumstances to give away the weight. The Porter won, beating Exterminator by eight and one-half lengths in

The Porter

the poor time of 2:35.[2]

The Porter was retired to McLean's stud near Leesburg, Virginia. He probably was a high-class stallion with a poor opportunity. This lack of opportunity was not so much in the quality of his mates at the

YEAR	AGE	STS	1ST	2ND	3RD	EARNED
1917	at 2	6	3	1	1	$ 2,541
1918	at 3	13	6	5	1	$10,655
1919	at 4	15	7	2	2	$19,226
1920	at 5	13	6	2	3	$28,044
1921	at 6	7	4	0	1	$13,400
Lifetime		54	26	10	8	$73,866

McLean stud as in the management of the stud itself.

The late Dr. R.L. Humphrey told the author that most of the horses produced at this stud broke down very early in training, and that after some years, McLean consulted him as to the causes for this. Dr. Humphrey had the soil tested and found that it was very deficient in both lime and phosphate.

When these shortages were made good on the pastures and in the hay, McLean rapidly approached the top of the winning owners' list. Not long after breeding such high-class runners as Toro (by The Porter) and Neddie (by Colin), however, McLean decided to disperse his stud.

Among the mares sold at the 1931 dispersal was Garden Rose, a daughter of Colin in foal to The Porter. She was bought for $4,300 by William du Pont Jr. and in 1932 foaled a bay colt named Rosemont. He was the best colt du Pont ever bred in a career spanning forty years and was, in fact, among the last of the high-class horses bred on the lines of the Ben Brush and Domino (Colin's grandsire) cross. Rosemont, The Porter's leading earner with $168,750, was good enough to beat Omaha in the one-mile Withers in 1935, but like most of his tribe, Rosemont did not stay well enough to win beyond that distance in classic company.

The Porter was bought at the McLean dispersal for $27,000 by John Hay Whitney, then owner of Mare's Nest Sud near Lexington. The horse did not make his first season in Kentucky until he was seventeen, a little late in the day to begin all over again. Nevertheless, The Porter led the sire list in 1937, his progeny that year earning $292,262, nearly $30,000 more than was earned by progeny of second-place Man o' War. Rosemont won the Santa Anita and San Antonio handicaps that year as a five-year-old, and The Porter also had out Classic and Withers stakes winner Flying Scot; Suburban and Carter handicaps winner Aneroid; and other stakes winners Pasha, Inhale, and Peggy Porter.

Added-money winners sired by The Porter also included the aforementioned Toro, who won seven stakes, including the American and Latonia derbys and earned $142,530. Others of The Porter's get who demonstrated some class were Haltal, winner of the 1941 Dixie and Saratoga handicaps; Arabs Arrow, a three-

Rosemont

time winner of the Churchill Downs Handicap; Heather Broom, winner of the Blue Grass Stakes and Saranac Handicap in 1939; Porter's Mite, who in 1938 won the Futurity and Champagne stakes and was a stakes winner the following year at three; Porter's Cap, winner of the Washington Park Futurity at two (in 1940) and the Santa Anita Derby at three; Viscounty, winner of eight stakes, including the 1939 Derby Trial; and Stepenfetchit, winner of the 1932 Latonia Derby.

The Porter retired from racing sound and retained his health almost to the time of his death. He was retired from active service after the 1943 breeding season, and he died at Mare's Nest in October 1944 at the age of twenty-nine. He sired thirty-four stakes winners although none of his sons managed to carry on the Ben Brush line as a first-class force in the United States.

The five foal crops against which The Porter raced (1913 through 1917, inclusive) embraced such high-class colts as Friar Rock, George Smith, Hourless, Omar Khayyam, Sun Briar, Sir Barton, John P. Grier, and Man o' War. Of that group, only Man o' War made an exceptionally good sire, and he with a poor opportunity. John P. Grier, with a poor opportunity (standing in New Jersey), made a pretty good one, and Sun Briar, with a very good opportunity (at Court Manor, Virginia), made a pretty good one .

Considering that his early produce were reared on a stud that practically guaranteed unsoundness, The Porter probably was as good or better than all of them except Man o' War.

End Notes:

1. The Porter finished third behind the H.P. Whitney entry of John P. Grier and Damask, beaten almost two lengths.

2. Exterminator finished third, six lengths behind second-placed My Dear.

CHAPTER NINE

JOHN O' GAUNT

La Fleche, the dam of John o' Gaunt, was among the yearlings offered in 1890 at the annual sale of the Royal Stud at Hampton Court. These yearlings generally were held in such low esteem by the racing and breeding fraternity that they widely were referred to as "the Hampton Court Rats." This irreverence for the royal enterprise was somewhat mistaken, since the Hampton Court auction of 1888 had included Sainfoin, who won the Derby, and Memoir, who won the Oaks and St. Leger of 1890.

As a full sister of Memoir, La Fleche attracted the attention of all the owners and trainers present. Among those attending were the Prince of Wales; his racing manager, Lord Marcus Beresford; and his trainer, John Porter. Also accompanying the prince was his new friend, Baron Maurice de Hirsch, who had made a great fortune in Europe through railway construction. Everyone agreed that La Fleche was a beautiful filly and the cream of the bowl.

There was a bid of 5,000 guineas for La Fleche from the Duke of Portland, the owner of Memoir, but the Prince of Wales urged Baron Hirsch to raise it. So, with some reluctance, Lord Marcus Beresford bid 5,500 and became the buyer for the account of Baron Hirsch. This was a world-record price for a yearling up to that time. As La Fleche won 34,703 pounds (the One Thousand Guineas, Oaks, St. Leger, Cambridgeshire, Champion Stakes, and Ascot Gold Cup), one only can observe that it is no bad combination to have good advisers and a lot of money, and to be at the right auction.

That Baron Hirsch was no great horseman was attested by Richard Marsh, who trained La Fleche after her three-year-old season. Marsh was showing the baron through the horses in training at Egerton House (Newmarket) during evening stables. Upon going into La Fleche's box, Marsh asked the baron what horse it was. Hirsch truthfully replied: "I haven't the faintest idea."

Following Baron Hirsch's death, his bloodstock was sold at auction on June 29, 1896. La Fleche was bought for the Sledmere Stud for 12,600 guineas. There is a

La Fleche, dam of John o' Gaunt

WIDENER COLLECTION

tale that actually the buyer was Lady (Tatton) Sykes, and that Sir Tatton was so shocked at the price that he repudiated the purchase. In time, however, (like most husbands) he cooled off and agreed to accept it.

Sledmere sold five yearlings out of La Fleche for an aggregate of 17,900 guineas. In addition to producing John o' Gaunt, she was the dam of Baroness La Fleche, who was a good two-year-old and became a tail-female ancestress of Beau Pere.

When John o' Gaunt appeared at the yearling sale of 1902, he was looked over with keen interest by all the buyers. He had a royal pedigree, being sired by a Triple Crown winner, Isinglass, and out of a triple-classic winner. Charles Morton, then private trainer for J.B. (Jack) Joel, had been commissioned to buy the colt for Joel's uncle Barnato. Morton found that John o' Gaunt had round joints, and he refused to bid. Others thought that John o' Gaunt showed incipient ringbones.

At first, there was no bid at all for John o' Gaunt. Mr. Tattersall, the auctioneer, then said, "If I do not have a bid of 3,000 guineas I shall pass him." (In those days, this was a high price for a yearling.) There still was silence. Sir Tatton Sykes, standing beside Tattersall, then spoke up: "If anyone who buys him is not perfectly satisfied with him after 90 days, he can return the colt to me and his money will be refunded."

There followed the one and only bid: "Three thousand guineas." The buyer was Sir John Thursby.

John o' Gaunt was turned over to the American trainer William Duke, who had gone over to England with Enoch Wishard. They were masters of doping, which had been brought to a high art in the United States but allegedly was unknown in England before they arrived at the turn of the century. Repeatedly they took apparently cheap horses out of selling races, and within a week or two converted them into high-class stakes winners. The British trainers were astounded and could not imagine how it was possible, let alone how it was done.

There is, however, no evidence that Duke ever doped John o' Gaunt. Indeed, the probabilities are that the colt did not need it. In his first start, for a Maiden Plate at Newmarket as a two-year-old, he was favored and finished second, beaten by a head. Next time out, he tried the highest-class company in the Coventry Stakes at Royal Ascot. Something must have been thought of him, as he started second favorite, but he finished unplaced to St Amant, a first-time starter.

For the British Dominion Plate at Sandown Park, he again was favored, but he had the extraordinary bad luck to run up against a first-time starter called Pretty Polly, who turned out to be one of the four or five best fillies ever seen on the British Turf. The official verdict was Pretty Polly over John o' Gaunt [in third] by ten lengths and a neck. British race judges were inclined to be over conservative in those days.

John o' Gaunt's fourth race was for the Hurstbourne Stakes at the Bibury Club meeting. John o' Gaunt won that race, worth 585 pounds, and it was the only race he did win. No more was seen of him as a two-year-old.

As a three-year-old, he made his first start in the one-mile Two Thousand Guineas at Newmarket. Ridden by Mr. George Thursby, an amateur who was a half brother of the colt's owner, Sir John Thursby, John o' Gaunt got away badly

Isinglass, 1890	Isonomy, 1875	Sterling, 1868	Oxford, 1857	Birdcatcher / Honey Dear
			Whisper, 1857	Flatcatcher / Silence
		Isola Bella, 1868	Stockwell, 1849	The Baron / **Pocahontas**
			Isoline, 1860	Ethelbert / Bassishaw
	Dead Lock, 1878	Wenlock, 1869	Lord Clifden, 1860	Newminster / The Slave
			Mineral, 1863	Rataplan / Manganese
		Malpractice, 1864	Chevalier d'Industrie, 1854	Orlando / Indusry
JOHN O' GAUNT			The Dutchman's Daughter, 1854	**The Flying Dutchman** / Red Rose
	St. Simon, 1881	Galopin, 1872	Vedette, 1854	Voltigeur / Mrs. Ridgway
			Flying Duchess, 1853	**The Flying Dutchman** / Merope
		St. Angela, 1865	King Tom, 1851	Harkaway / **Pocahontas**
			Adeline, 1851	Ion / Little Fairy
La Fleche, 1889	Quiver, 1872	Toxophilite, 1855	Longbow, 1849	Ithuriel / Miss Bowe
			Legerdemain, 1846	Pantaloon / Decoy
		Young Melbourne Mare, 1860	Young Melbourne, 1855	Melbourne / Clarissa
			Brown Bess, 1844	Camel / Brutandorf Mare

and finished second to St Amant, beaten four lengths, with Henry the First two lengths behind him.

Two weeks later, all three placed horses in the Guineas came out for the one and a quarter-mile Newmarket Stakes. The placings were reversed, Henry the First winning by a head from John o' Gaunt and St Amant a poor third. The general verdict was that John o' Gaunt should have won easily, his defeat being ascribed to an extremely overconfident ride on the part of his amateur jockey.

For the Derby, John o' Gaunt was second-favorite at 4-1, Henry the First at 17-4, and St Amant at 5-1. The French horse, Gouvernant, was favored at 7-4. The race was run during a terrifying thunderstorm, and but for this, Mr. Thursby—again riding John o' Gaunt as an amateur—declared that he surely would have won. In fact, John o' Gaunt was second to St Amant by three lengths. (This was the closest an amateur ever came to winning the Derby.) Since St Amant had beaten John o' Gaunt in the Coventry Stakes as a two-year-old and again in the Two Thousand Guineas (though John o' Gaunt defeated St Amant in the Newmarket Stakes), the Derby form probably was about right.

It was rumored that St Amant's trainer had put cotton in the horse's ears, so that he would not be frightened by the fearful claps of thunder; John o' Gaunt had no such relief.

John o' Gaunt

John o' Gaunt did not run again after the Derby, but he did not go to stud until he was a five-year-old. His book was full at a fee of 98 pounds, and he was a prominent stallion for his first five seasons. In his first crop, he sired Swynford, who was a first-class staying colt and won the St. Leger of 1910, as well as other high-class races. The next year, John o' Gaunt sired Tootles, who finished second in the Oaks, and a little later came Kennymore, who won the Two Thousand Guineas. After that, nothing of quality came from John o' Gaunt, and he was destroyed in 1924 for lack of patronage.

YEAR	AGE	STS	1ST	2ND	3RD	EARNED*
1903	at 2	4	1	2	0	£585
1904	at 3	3	0	3	0	0
Lifetime		7	1	5	0	£585

* First-placed money only

John o' Gaunt's son Swynford sired the great stallion Blandford, sire of Blenheim II, he sire of Mahmoud and others. In addition, John o' Gaunt sired Mandy Hamilton, the dam of Supremus, who sired the dam of Menow, he the sire of Tom Fool. Since Blenheim II sired the dam of Nasrullah, without John o' Gaunt there would have been no Nasrullah, no Nashua, and no Bold Ruler; and without Tom Fool there would have been no Buckpasser.

John o' Gaunt certainly had unsound legs and was the son of a sore-going horse in Isinglass. Unfortunately, John o' Gaunt passed that unsoundness along to a great many of his produce, and the characteristic reappeared in many of his descendants. Otherwise, he undoubtedly would have made a greater mark at stud.

SWYNFORD

When the Epsom Oaks winner Canterbury Pilgrim was thirteen, she was mated with John o' Gaunt in his first season at stud. The mare's owner, Lord Derby, was taking something of a chance on the soundness of the offspring, for John o' Gaunt, after his comparatively early breakdown, was described as having "bad feet, round joints, and pasterns that were very upright." Swynford fortunately did not inherit these defects, possibly owing to the fact that Canterbury Pilgrim was blessed with the best of legs and feet. Swynford was one of nine living foals from the eighteen mares covered by John o' Gaunt in 1906, and in fact, must have been one of the very first of the sire's get since he was foaled in late January.

At the time Swynford came into the Honorable George Lambton's stable to be broken as a yearling, he was big, thin, somewhat flatsided, and plain. In addition, he had been running outside night and day and had been described as an ugly customer. Lambton wrote that when the breaking tackle first was put on Swynford, he was "strong as a bull and full of courage, though at the same time good-tempered."

When the time came to try Swynford as a two-year-old, Lambton talked things over with his stable jockey, American Danny Maher. Lambton suggested that they ask Well Done, a fair, older sprinter of known form, to concede Swynford ten pounds, but Maher declared that he personally would "eat Swynford," if the latter did not beat Well Done at even weights. Maher had his way, and in the trial, Swynford had beaten everything at the end of three furlongs. So Lambton and Maher at least knew Swynford had good speed. His first race was the Exeter Stakes at Newmarket, and high hopes were held for his success. Swynford, however, came out of the gate like a catapult, completely overpowered Maher, ran himself to a standstill, and finished unplaced.

Shortly afterward, he developed an unsoundness and could not run again until his three-year-old season. That may have been just as well, as Canterbury Pilgrim also was a very hard puller as a two-year-old, but while showing fine speed could not at that age stay more than four furlongs. When she stopped badly in this way at Doncaster, Lambton was greatly discouraged until an old trainer expressed to him the opinion that the filly reminded him very much of Marie Stuart, who also stopped badly as a two-year-old, but who nevertheless became a great filly at three, winning the Oaks and St. Leger.

"Canterbury Pilgrim probably will win the Oaks for you," the trainer told Lambton.

Trained especially for the race, Canterbury Pilgrim did indeed win the next spring's Oaks. Her dam, Pilgrimage, had won both the One Thousand and Two Thousand Guineas and had run second in the Oaks. Pilgrimage also was the basis for successful inbreeding in the Derby stud.

When the spring of his three-year-old season came, Swynford was given a lot of work and really was fitter than anything else in the Lambton stable. Nevertheless, every time the colt was given a serious work, he continued to blow up and stop to nothing. Lambton did not know what to make of Swynford, bred as he was—with a pedigree crammed with the highest class of stayers. It seemed impossible that Swynford simply could not stay.

Finally, a short time before the Derby, Swynford put up a half-way decent gallop, and Lambton told Lord Derby that if he cared to start Swynford for the race, the horse probably would not disgrace them.

Swynford ran very badly in the Derby, but there was an excuse for him—he had been struck into from behind, and the skin was peeled off one of his hind legs from the hock to the fetlock. The injury apparently was not very serious because Swynford was able to run twice at Royal Ascot about two weeks later.

In the one-mile St. James's Palace Stakes, Swynford was third, but he won the one and one-half-mile Hardwicke Stakes.[1] As a maiden, he was in receipt of a lot of weight and only just scraped home. Lambton wrote that, having told Lord Derby that Swynford was a good colt, he by then felt a considerable fool and that everybody except Frank Wootton (then his stable jockey) and himself had given up on the colt.

It so happened that Lambton had won the Ascot Derby with a colt called Decision. After a short rest following the Ascot meeting, Lambton galloped Swynford with Decision, and to his astonishment, Swynford galloped right away from Decision, going through with his work in relentless fashion. Lambton then decided to start Swynford at Liverpool (Lord Derby's home meeting) for the Liverpool Cup. Based on what he had observed, Lambton considered Swynford a good thing for the race. His only doubt was that Wootton, who weighed only about 100 pounds, might not be able to get Swynford around the somewhat sharp turn leading into the home stretch and might instead land in the canal which bordered the turn. These fears proved groundless, as Swynford came around the turn like a polo pony and won in a canter.

Swynford next was trained for the St. Leger—one mile, six furlongs, 132 yards. On the day before the race, Lambton was chatting in the yearling sales paddocks with Danny Maher, who was going to ride Lemberg—that year's Derby winner and Eclipse Stakes dead-heater, who also had been second by a short head in the Two Thousand Guineas. Lambton mentioned that he thought Swynford had a very good chance of beating Lemberg in the St. Leger, but Maher scoffed at the idea: "I dare say that yours is a very nice colt, but simply not the same class as Lemberg."

The American jockey Skeets Martin was there, and said, "Well, I have ridden in several of Swynford's works since Liverpool, and I can tell you I would not like to have to be following him tomorrow."

Since Lambton by then knew that Swynford was a great stayer, he instructed Wootton to go to the front with him at once and to let Swynford stride right out. Wootton followed these instructions and led from the start. When they came into the straight, Maher got Lemberg nicely balanced and moved up to challenge

				Sterling, 1868	Oxford
			Isonomy, 1875		Whisper
		Isinglass, 1890		Isola Bella, 1868	**Stockwell**
					Isoline
			Dead Lock, 1878	Wenlock, 1869	Lord Clifden
					Mineral
				Malpractice, 1864	Chevalier D'Industrie
John o' Gaunt, 1901					The Dutchman's Daughter
			St. Simon, 1881	Galopin, 1872	Vedette
					Flying Duchess
		La Fleche, 1889		St. Angela, 1865	King Tom
					Adeline
			Quiver, 1872	Toxophilite, 1855	Longbow
					Legerdemain
SWYNFORD				Y. Melbourne mare, 1861	Young Melbourne
					Brown Bess
			Hermit, 1864	Newminster, 1848	Touchstone
					Beeswing
		Tristan, 1878		Seclusion, 1857	Tadmor
					Miss Sellon
			Thrift, 1865	**Stockwell**, 1849	The Baron
					Pocahontas
Canterbury Pilgrim, 1893				Braxey, 1849	Moss Trooper
					Queen Mary
			The Palmer, 1864	Beadsman, 1855	Weatherbit
					Mendicant
		Pilgrimage, 1875		Madame Eglentine, 1857	Cowl
					Diversion
			Lady Audley, 1867	Macaroni, 1860	Sweetmeat
					Jocose
				Secret, 1853	Melbourne
					Mystery

THE NATIONAL HORSERACING MUSEUM, NEWMARKET

Swynford

Swynford, but when Lemberg got close, Swynford put in some extra-big strides and again moved away. Maher collected Lemberg and made another challenge, but the same thing happened. By then, the Yorkshire crowd was leaning over the rails of the infield, shouting and waving, so Swynford moved away from the rail, leaving Lemberg ample room to get through. Maher tried, but Lemberg could not get up, and Maher passed the post standing in his stirrups, apparently to make it look as though Swynford had shut off Lemberg. In the last one-hundred yards, Bronzino made a charge on the outside and finished within a head of Swynford. A photograph of the finish shows that little Frank Wootton had become merely a passenger, being far more exhausted than Swynford.

The general opinion at the time was that Maher had ridden a shockingly bad race, needlessly getting shut in, and that Lemberg should have won. On the other hand, Maher told Lambton when they met again at the sales paddocks, "Lemberg will never beat Swynford in a fast-run race over a distance of ground." That proved to be an astute judgment, as events the following year were to prove.

Swynford walked over for the Liverpool St. Leger and retired for the year.

YEAR	AGE	STS	1ST	2ND	3RD	EARNED*
1909	at 2	1	0	0	0	0
1910	at 3	6	4	0	1	£10,694
1911	at 4	5	4	1	0	£14,834
Lifetime		12	8	1	1	£25,528
* First-place money only						

His four-year-old season began with a victory in a minor race—the one and one-half-mile Chippenham Plate at Newmarket. Next time out, Swynford again met Lemberg, in the one and one-half-mile Coronation Cup. The public's estimate of the two colts was shown in the betting—Lemberg, 9-4; Swynford, 5-1. That time, Wootton rode a waiting race on Swynford, and Lemberg, having a little the better speed, won by three-quarters of a length. In the one and one-half-mile Princess of Wales's Stakes at Newmarket, however, Swynford (receiving five pounds) beat Lemberg by one and one-half lengths. Then in the one and one-quarter-mile Eclipse Stakes, at level weights, Swynford beat Lemberg by four lengths.

Following that race, when Swynford was reaching the height of his powers, he smashed one of his fore fetlock joints during exercise, and it was only through patient efforts that he was saved for the stud.

Within a year of the trainer's death, Lambton told the present writer that Swynford in his opinion was the best horse he ever had trained. When questioned about Hyperion, Lambton replied: "I knew to a pound how good Hyperion was, but after he reached his best form, I never knew how good Swynford was."

Swynford began his stud career in 1913 at Newmarket and was an undoubted success. From 1918 through 1926, he was lower than seventh on the list of winning sires only once, in 1920 when he was eighteenth. In 1923 he was first, and in 1924 and 1925 he was second while in 1921 he was third. His best stock were well up to classic standard—he sired six classic winners, and six more were placed in classics.

Strictly on the record, Swynford's fillies were better than his colts, but this may have been due in some measure to bad luck. Only one of his sons, Sansovino, won a classic, and he was by no means a good Derby (1924) winner, later proving a failure as a sire. Swynford's highest-class sons probably were Blandford and Challenger II.

Blandford ran only four times, twice at two and twice at three. He won three times and was second once by a head after stumbling near the finish. Since Blandford will be the subject of a later chapter in this book, it must suffice at this point to note that Blandford was not entered for the classic races but proved to be a far better sire than Swynford.

Challenger II ran only twice in England as a two-year-old and was unbeaten. In the two-year-old Free Handicap, he was rated just about the same as Blenheim II, who won the 1930 Derby and proved to be an influential sire. Challenger II's owner, Lord Dewar, died when the colt was a two-year-old, and all of the colt's future engagements were made void. As a result, Challenger II was sold to Messrs. Brann and Castle for importation into the United States at their stud near Frederick, Maryland.

Shortly after his sale in England, Challenger II got his legs badly lacerated by a mass of barbed wire, and no further attempt was made to train him in England. After his arrival in this country, an attempt was made to train and race him, but this proved to be a failure.

Owing to his location in Maryland, Challenger II's opportunities were limited, and the class of mares to which he was bred generally was by no means the best. Nevertheless, from two mares by Sir Gallahad III, he sired two champions in Challedon, twice voted Horse of the Year, and Gallorette, voted by the American trainers as the best American race mare (wrongly in the opinion of the present writer, as Gallorette could not beat the colts at level weights).

Most of Swynford's stock stayed well but were lacking in quality. One of these was St. Germans, who finished second in Sansovino's Derby and was imported into the United States by Greentree Stud. Unfortunately, St. Germans was a shy foal-getter; nevertheless, he was leading sire one year and sired a champion in Twenty Grand. More unfortunately, Twenty Grand proved to be completely sterile. Swynford also got Derby runner-up (1926) Lancegaye, in turn the sire of 1934 Kentucky Derby winner Cavalcade.

Swynford's fillies included five classic winners: Ferry (1918 One Thousand Guineas); Keysoe (1919 St. Leger); Bettina (1921 One Thousand Guineas); Tranquil (1923 One Thousand Guineas and St. Leger), and Saucy Sue (1925 One Thousand Guineas and Oaks).

End Notes:

1. Swynford raced the mile St. James's Palace Stakes on Thursday and the following day won the Hardwicke Stakes by three-quarters of a length.

CHAPTER ELEVEN

BLANDFORD

Since Blandford was one of the three best stallions that spent his entire stud career in England and Ireland during the first half of the twentieth century (the other two were Hyperion and Nearco), his story merits careful study. Blandford was bred at the British government-owned National Stud, near Kildare, County Kildare, Ireland. He was a very late foal (May 26), but that was not the reason he was not among the National Stud-bred yearlings sold in the July sales at Newmarket in 1920.

When he was a yearling, some work horses broke into Blandford's paddock and gave him such a rough going over that he nearly died of the injuries. Consequently, he was not ready for the auction ring until the December sales of 1920. There he was bought by the Dawson brothers: Sam, of the Cloghran Stud in County Dublin, and R.C., the trainer at Whatcombe who had conditioned Fifinella to win a war-time Derby and Oaks and who afterward won the Derby with Trigo (1929) and Blenheim II (1930). (R.C. Dawson looked more like a college professor than a trainer, being tall and gaunt and wearing a pince-nez with black ribbon attached.)

While the Dawsons gave only 730 guineas for Blandford, it still was a pretty risky enterprise, for he had one of the worst sets of forelegs the present writer ever saw: His pasterns were practically straight up and were short as well. A colt with this particular conformation usually is a pretty good bet to bow his tendons, and Blandford did bow in both forelegs after his second race as a three-year-old. Nevertheless, Blandford was a colt of very high quality and tremendous vitality, and while he could stand training, he undoubtedly was a racer of very high class.

R.C. Dawson made the following statement about Blandford to the editor of *Famous Horses*:

"I tried Blandford very highly in June as a 2-year-old; he gave 23 pounds to a filly called Malva, who subsequently became the dam of the Derby winner Blenheim II (and of King Salmon, winner of the Eclipse Stakes). He won the

Blandford

first time out at Newbury [beating Scamp very easily], and the following week I ran him in the Windsor Castle Stakes at Ascot. He was then suffering from sore shins and stumbled a few yards from the winning post, but ran the winner, Alaric [receiving 10 pounds], to a neck. Blandford did not run again that season, but in May [actual date was April 29] the next year he won the Paradise Stakes at Hurst Park [10 furlongs], beating Spike Island, who afterwards won the Irish Derby. Although successful, Blandford was not yet 'ready,' though coming on every day. As a three-year-old, Blandford was as good as Franklin, then four years old; they were tried at even weights just before the latter won the Coronation Cup [a one and a half-mile stakes for three-year-olds and up of the highest class, often contested by the previous year's classic winners]. How would Blandford have won Captain Cuttle's Derby for which he was not entered! He easily won the [one and a half-mile] Princess of Wales's Stakes at Newmarket in July, but after that a tendon went and closed his racing career."

Blandford was not entered for the Derby because the entries for the classics had closed a few weeks before he was sold at the December sales, and the National Stud had not bothered to enter him.

As a two-year-old, Blandford was assigned 121 pounds on the Free Handicap, five pounds below the top with two other colts having higher weights. He was ranked the same as Scamp, whom he had beaten easily, and ten pounds above

Alaric, to whom he almost had given ten pounds successfully when he had sore shins and stumbled at Ascot. Granted that the handicapper had only two races from which to judge—even handicappers are subject to make mistakes; still, it would seem that the handicapper did rank Blandford several pounds too low. If consideration also is given to the fact that his two-year-old races were run when Blandford was little more than twenty-four months old, the error seems clear.

There was no Free Handicap for three-year-olds at that time, so there is no way of knowing what the handicapper thought about Blandford at that age. Taking R.C. Dawson's statement comparing Blandford's form to Franklin's at face value, however, it might be presumed that Blandford was well up to ordinary classic standard and probably above it. The late Fred Darling, who won seven Epsom Derbys from 1922 to 1941, told the present writer that whenever he had a three-year-old that could hold a four-year-old at even weights over one and a half miles in May, and when the four-year-old had been five to ten pounds behind classic form the previous year, the chances of winning the Derby with his three-year-old were about even money. Clearly, Blandford was that good if not better.

Blandford duly went to stud at Cloghran at a fee of 148 pounds, which was raised to 300 pounds in 1930 and 400 pounds the following year. By that time,

BLANDFORD				
Swynford, 1907	John o' Gaunt, 1901	Isinglass, 1890	**Isonomy**, 1875	Sterling / Isola Bella
			Dead Lock, 1878	Wenlock / Malpractice
		La Fleche, 1889	St. Simon, 1881	**Galopin** / St. Angela
			Quiver, 1872	Toxophilite / Y. Melbourne Mare
	Canterbury Pilgrim, 1893	Tristan, 1878	**Hermit**, 1864	Newminster / Seclusion
			Thrift, 1865	Stockwell / Braxey
		Pilgrimage, 1875	The Palmer, 1864	Beadsman / Madame Eglentine
			Lady Audley, 1867	Macaroni / Secret
Blanche, 1912	White Eagle, 1905	Gallinule, 1884	**Isonomy**, 1875	Sterling / Isola Bella
			Moorhen, 1973	**Hermit** / Skirmisher Mare
		Merry Gal, 1897	**Galopin**, 1872	Vedette / Flying Duchess
			Mary Seaton, 1890	**Isonomy** / Marie Stuart
	Black Cherry, 1892	Bendigo, 1880	Ben Battle, 1871	Rataplan / Young Alice
			Hasty Girl, 1875	Lord Gough / Irritation
		Black Duchess, 1886	Galliard, 1880	**Galopin** / Mavis
			Black Corrie, 1879	Sterling / Wild Dayrell Mare

YEAR	AGE	STS	1ST	2ND	3RD	EARNED*
1921	at 2	2	1	1	0	£ 559
1922	at 3	2	2	0	0	£3,109
Lifetime		4	3	1	0	£3,668

* First-place money only

Blandford had sired Derby winners Trigo and Blenheim II.

Blandford's first yearlings, which went into the sale ring in 1926, were received with something less than high acclaim, averaging only 430 guineas for seven lots. The next year, however, five of Blandford's two-year-olds won 8,631 pounds—a very good showing—and three of his yearlings averaged 1,835 guineas. Afterward, his stock was in strong demand.

In 1934, when his Windsor Lad won the Derby and St. Leger and unbeaten Bahram was a two-year-old, Blandford's stock won a record total of 75,707 pounds, far outdistancing previous progeny-earnings records of Stockwell and St. Simon (the two best sires of the nineteenth century in England and Ireland). When Blandford died on April 24, 1935, at the age of sixteen, he had led the sire list three times[1] (which is more than Nearco did).

This record is all the more remarkable on three grounds: The quality of mares bred to Blandford in his early years at stud was a long way removed from the best, plus Blandford was not the most fertile of stallions. With a full book of mares (generally forty in England and Ireland), he sired only twenty-two living foals in 1934, and only twenty in 1935. It was rumored, in fact, that he needed stimulants to whet his sexual appetite. In addition, a number of French breeders patronized Blandford and raced his produce in France, where their winnings were not included in the British totals. (Baron Edouard de Rothschild bred and raced Brantome, generally regarded as one of the two best colts to race in France between 1900 and 1950, and Edward Esmond bred and raced Mistress Ford, the best two-year-old filly of her year in France.)

With his extraordinary stud performance to consider, we should take a careful look at Blandford's pedigree. On the side of Swynford, his sire, there is a constellation of mares with the highest credentials. Swynford's dam, Canterbury Pilgrim, won the Oaks and produced the great broodmare sire Chaucer; Swynford's two granddams were La Fleche, one of the best race mares on record, and Pilgrimage, winner of both the One Thousand and Two Thousand Guineas and second in the Oaks (where she broke down), and dam of the Derby winner Jeddah, as well as Canterbury Pilgrim.

Yet Swynford sired more than one hundred other sons, which were not in the same street as Blandford as stallions. Indeed, Swynford himself was not as good a sire as Blandford. Hence, we must look at the dam's side to see what it may have contributed.

Blandford's dam was Blanche, bred by Colonel William Hall Walker at the Tully Stud, County Kildare. Col. Hall Walker must have thought something of her as a racer, since he started her in both the Coventry Stakes, the most important two-year-old stakes at Royal Ascot, and the Cheveley Park Stakes, emblematic of the two-year-old filly championship. He also started her in the Oaks as a three-year-old, but in five starts at two and five more at three, Blanche never got in the money. Yet, Col. Hall Walker (afterward made Lord Wavertree when he had presented all his bloodstock to the British government to form the National Stud) remarked that Blanche had run "well up in good company," and there is no denying the "good company."

Blanche was sired by White Eagle (also bred by Col. Hall Walker), who had been a crack two-year-old but who was not quite up to classic form as a three-year-old, though he did run second in the St. Leger. White Eagle was a disappointing sire, but many of his daughters did well at stud (the second dam of Princequillo is by White Eagle). One noteworthy feature of White Eagle's pedigree is that he is inbred with one free generation to Isonomy, an excellent source of stoutness.

The dam of Blanche, Black Cherry, was a good broodmare, but her total winnings were only one hundred pounds. She was sired by a tough, high-class handi-

Brantome

J.A. ESTES

Bahram

capper called Bendigo (winner of the first Eclipse Stakes), whose only importance in the stud book is that he sired Black Cherry. That mare produced thirteen foals—the last one at age twenty-four. Nine of her foals were winners, they including Cherry Lass (One Thousand Guineas and Oaks) and the excellent two-year-olds Black Arrow and Jean's Folly. Blanche was foaled when Black Cherry was twenty.

The next dam, Black Duchess, who won only 195 pounds as a two-year-old, produced eight foals, all winners. One of them was Bay Ronald, a pretty good racer, winner of the City and Suburban Handicap and the Hardwicke Stakes at Ascot. While Bay Ronald must have been at least twelve to fourteen pounds behind classic form, he turned out to be a surprisingly good stallion, siring Dark Ronald (the most influential sire in the *German Stud Book*), Bayardo (a top racer and grandsire of Hyperion), and Macdonald II (a good racer and sire in France). Bay Ronald also was the sire of Rondeau, a good race mare and the dam of Teddy.

Perhaps the vein of gold in Blanche's pedigree started with Black Duchess.

Blandford sired four Derby winners in seven years: Trigo (1929), who also won the St. Leger but was a total failure at stud; Blenheim II (1930), who did not run after the Derby but was a successful stallion; Windsor Lad (1934), who won the St. Leger and the Eclipse Stakes but was not a good sire; and Bahram (1935), who was unbeaten and won the English Triple Crown. As a sire, Bahram was a qualified success in England, where he sired Big Game and Persian Gulf (out of mares with very high credentials), but he was a failure both in the United States and Argentina.

Only two stallions besides Blandford have sired four Epsom Derby winners, Waxy and Cyllene. Blandford's feat is the more remarkable owing to the much greater numbers in the annual foal crops at the time he was at stud.

In addition to Blandford's four Derby winners, he also sired classic winner Pasch, winner of the Two Thousand Guineas (1938) and Eclipse Stakes, plus Brantome, who won the Grand Criterium at two in France and the English Two Thousand Guineas, French St. Leger, and Prix de l'Arc de Triomphe the following year (1934).

Blandford's fillies included classic winners Udaipur, winner of the Oaks (1932), and Campanula, winner of the One Thousand Guineas (1934). In addition, Zelina and Ankaret were classic-placed, finishing second in the Oaks in 1934 and 1935, respectively.

For those interested in dosages, it is to be noted that Blandford's pedigree carried only one cross of St. Simon (with whose blood the *General Stud Book* was saturated at the time Blandford was at stud), but three crosses of Isonomy, the next-highest-ranking strain in the dosage system.

Physically, Blandford was a medium-sized horse of very high quality, splendid constitution and vigor (apart from his defective forelegs), and of a rich mahogany color. Doubtlessly, his comparatively early death prevented him from establishing a still more remarkable record in comparison with some of the other very great sires—St. Simon (who died at the age of 27), Cyllene (30), Hyperion (30), and Nearco (22). Blandford was a pure dominant for bay or brown, as was St. Simon.

End Notes:

1. Blandford led the English sire list twice (1934–35) and the French list in 1935.

CHAPTER TWELVE

BLENHEIM II

While Blenheim II was a good racer, there is some doubt as to just how good he was. Few horses, however, have been the subject of more controversy at different times in their lives. Blenheim II was bred by Lord Carnarvon at his Highclere Stud near Newbury and was sold at the yearling sales to the Aga Khan for 4,100 guineas—a pretty stiff price for a smallish yearling, who never grew higher than 15.3 hands and who was somewhat straight in front.

An unauthenticated story was circulated that a group of practical jokers and merry makers among the yearling vendors had decided that the Aga Khan really had more money than was good for him, and that some of it would be good for them. A resolution was taken that when a representative for the Aga Khan was seen bidding on a yearling—and particularly one they did not fancy—they would help the proceedings along by bidding the price up a couple of thousand guineas.

Blenheim II was selected for that purpose and was bid up about 2,000 guineas above his normal price. After the Aga Khan was known to be the buyer, the champagne corks were popping, and sounds of revelry were heard in the bar.

(The late Colonel Phil Chinn once described to the present writer his own method of getting the "full price" for a yearling at auction: "I had this nice colt at the sales, but as luck would have it there was only one buyer with much ready cash who was interested. I had this gentleman pegged as good for about $15,000, top price for the colt, but I needed some help to get him up there. So, I stationed three men around the ring, and when the colt came in, the bidding went $5,000, $10,000, $14,000. My buyer panicked and bid $15,000, which was the only genuine bid. But after all, it was a nice colt, and the man didn't have to bid.")

With Blenheim II, the Aga Khan had the last laugh, as in seven starts as a two-year-old, Blenheim II won four times and finished second in the other three. His first race was for the five-furlong Manton Plate at Newbury, which he won. In the more important Sandown Park Stud Produce Stakes, Blenheim II was unable to give Bridget Ford nine pounds and finished second. He then won an unimportant

W.A. ROUCH

The Aga Khan leading Blenheim II to the
Derby winner's circle

race at Windsor, a five-furlong plate,
worth only 186 pounds.

Thus, Blenheim II had been out
three times before the Royal Ascot
meeting in June. There, he won the
five-furlong New Stakes, a prestige
race for two-year-olds (won previously by Bayardo, Lemberg, Hyperion,
etc.). Blenheim II was not seen out
again until September, when he was
beaten a short head by Fair Diana in
the six-furlong Champagne Stakes,
the principal two-year-old race of the
St. Leger meeting at Doncaster.

In the autumn at Newmarket,
Blenheim II won the five-furlong
Hopeful Stakes, then was beaten a
half-length by Press Gang at level
weights in the six-furlong Middle
Park Stakes. The two-year-old Free Handicap ranked Blenheim II as the fourth-
best colt, three pounds from the top, with Diolite, Press Gang, and Challenger II
above him.

Blenheim II's first appearance as a three-year-old was in the one-mile Greenham
Plate at Newbury, a race that often served as an introduction to the season for
classic candidates. Blenheim II was prominent for about six furlongs, then
dropped out of it and was not ridden out at the end.

His next start was the one-mile Two Thousand Guineas, which Diolite won
by two lengths from Paradine. Silver Flare finished third, a length away from
Paradine and a head in front of Blenheim II. The key horse was Paradine, who
had been beaten four lengths in the one and one-sixteenth-mile Nonsuch Stakes
by the Aga Khan's Rustom Pasha, who gave Paradine seven pounds as well.
Taking a line through Paradine, it appears that Rustom Pasha was about seven
pounds and five lengths better than Blenheim II. Evidently, the Aga Khan's jockey,
Michael Beary, was of that opinion, since, given his choice, he opted for Rustom
Pasha in the Derby.

That decision left the mount on Blenheim II open for Harry Wragg, who had
won the Derby two years before while riding a waiting race on Felstead. As the

race was run, there were not too many jockeys other than Harry Wragg who likely would have won on Blenheim II. He was drawn on the outside of the field of seventeen, and when the tapes went up, Blenheim II broke away from the field to the right and thus lost several lengths.

Wragg did not hurry his colt but gradually picked up the field and stayed on the outside all the way. Diolite and Rustom Pasha (the latter by the great sire of stayers, Son-in-Law) led past Tattenham Corner into the straight and shortly thereafter Rustom Pasha collapsed. Then in mid-stretch, Iliad challenged and mastered Diolite. Wragg waited until the last 150 yards with Blenheim II. He then ranged up alongside Iliad and went on to win comfortably by a length. Wragg said to the press after the race, "When I came alongside Iliad, I knew I was going to win."

Blenheim II's starting price was 18-1, while his stablemate Rustom Pasha started at 9-2. The time for the race over fast going was 2:38 1/5, compared to Felstead's time of 2:34 2/5 (then a record shared with Call Boy) two years earlier.

The Derby proved to be Blenheim II's last race. His trainer, R.C. Dawson, thought this was a great pity as "Blenheim II stayed so well he might have made a great reputation." Question arises over why, if Blenheim II was known to stay so

				Isonomy
			Isinglass, 1890	Dead Lock
		John o' Gaunt, 1901		**St. Simon**
			La Fleche, 1889	Quiver
	Swynford, 1907			Hermit
			Tristan, 1878	Thrift
		Canterbury Pilgrim, 1893		The Palmer
			Pilgrimage, 1875	Lady Audley
Blandford, 1919				**Isonomy**
			Gallinule, 1884	Moorhen
		White Eagle, 1905		**Galopin**
			Merry Gal, 1897	Mary Seaton
	Blanche, 1912			Ben Battle
			Bendigo, 1880	Hasty Girl
		Black Cherry, 1892		Galliard
BLENHEIM II			Black Duchess, 1886	Black Corrie
			St. Simon, 1881	**Galopin**
		Desmond, 1896		St. Angela
			L'Abbesse de Jouarre, 1886	Trappist
	Charles O'Malley, 1907			Festive
			Isinglass, 1890	**Isonomy**
		Goody Two Shoes, 1899		Dead Lock
			Sandal, 1885	Kisber
Malva, 1919				Shoestring
			Ayrshire, 1885	Hampton
		Robert le Diable, 1899		Atalanta
			Rose Bay, 1891	Melton
	Wild Arum, 1911			Rose of Lancaster
			Martagon, 1887	Bend Or
		Marliacea, 1902		Tiger Lily
			Flitters, 1893	**Galopin**
				Ierne

well before the Derby, Michael Beary chose to ride Rustom Pasha instead.

Blenheim II was sent to stud in France as a four-year old at Marly La Ville. In his second season he sired Mahmoud, who won the Derby of 1936 (his record of 2:33 4/5 still stands[1]) for the Aga Khan, and in his third season, Blenheim II sired Donatello II for Federico Tesio of Italy.

Donatello II won all his races until he contested the Grand Prix de Paris, in which he was second, and some observers thought he was unlucky not to win that one. Tesio afterwards sold Donatello II to Edward Esmond, who sent him to stud in England.

Donatello II was anything but a prepotent stallion, his stock coming in all colors, shapes, and sizes. Nevertheless, he did sire some good racers, notably Alycidon, winner of the triple crown of cup races—the Ascot, Goodwood, and Doncaster Cups—for the first time since Isonomy accomplished the feat in 1879. Another, Crepello, foaled when Donatello II was twenty, won the Two Thousand Guineas and Derby and was a consistently high-class sire (his fillies having been superior to his colts).

While still in Europe, Blenheim II also sired Mumtaz Begum, the dam of Nasrullah.

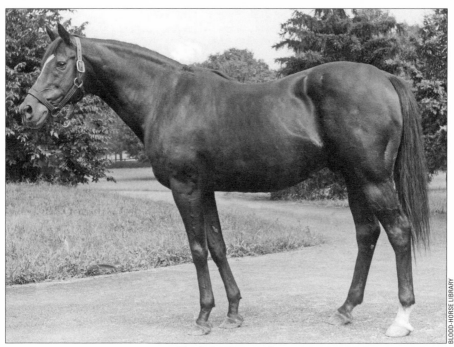

Blenheim II at stud

In 1936 the Aga Khan staggered the breeding community by announcing that he had sold Blenheim II for $250,000 to an American syndicate, headed by A.B.

YEAR	AGE	STS	1ST	2ND	3RD	EARNED*
1929	at 2	7	4	3	0	£ 4,497
1930	at 3	3	1	0	0	£10,036
Lifetime		**10**	**5**	**3**	**0**	**£14,533**
* First-place money only						

Hancock Sr. of Claiborne Farm near Paris, Kentucky. There was considerable ill feeling over this sale on the part of breeders who had signed contracts to breed mares to Blenheim II in future years. The Aga Khan, however, pointed out that a clause in the contracts provided that all such nominations were subject to Blenheim II remaining in his ownership—there can be no doubt that the Aga Khan was within his legal rights in going through with the sale.

There was a canard making the rounds of the rumor circuit in Europe that the Aga Khan had disclosed to a friend that the real reason he had sold Blenheim II was that he had a veterinarian's opinion that Blenheim II could not live six months. This prophecy, if made, deserves to rank with the great boners of all times, since Blenheim II lived to the great age of thirty-one.

After being shipped to the United States, Blenheim II spent the remainder of his life at Claiborne. Among the best of the stakes winners he sired in this country were Whirlaway (1941 Triple Crown and former world-record money winner) and Jet Pilot (1947 Kentucky Derby). Nevertheless, neither of these American-bred sons proved to be a good sire. Blenheim II sired sixty-four stakes winners, and in 1941 he was the leading sire in North America. His other European offspring included Mirza II, Wyndham, Pampeiro, Blue Bear, and Drap d'Or, and his thirty-seven North American stakes winners also included Mar-Kell, Thumbs Up, Miss Keeneland, Free America, Bryan G., Battle Morn, A Gleam, and Saratoga.

Physically, Blenheim II was a horse of refinement, standing 15.3 hands, but he lacked the robust vitality of his sire, Blandford. Blenheim II's somewhat straight pasterns show up from time to time in his descendants. Through Nasrullah and Mahmoud, his name will be carried through many generations of Thoroughbreds in this country, and the same will be true in Europe through those stallions and also through Crepello and Alycidon.

There was nothing on the distaff side of Blenheim II's pedigree to suggest that he likely was to be a high-class racer. His dam, Malva (also the dam of Derby runner-up King Salmon), was a rather low-class sprinter, winning two five-furlong races at two and another five-furlong race at three. She had, however, a staying pedigree, being a daughter of a third-class stallion called Charles O'Malley, who had placed in the Ascot Gold Cup. Wild Arum, the next dam, won 256 pounds

W.A. ROUCH

Donatello II

as a two-year-old and remained in training two seasons more, without winning again. Wild Arum's sire was another poor stallion, Robert le Diable.

Blenheim II's third dam, Marliacea, did not win as a two-year-old but was bought for Lord Carnarvon after winning a selling race as a three-year-old, and she won twice in the next year at one and a half miles. Marliacea bred six foals, of which three were winners, including a fair stayer called Rivoli (by Robert le Diable). Her sire was Martagon, an ordinary stallion.

Not until we come to the fourth dam, Flitters, do we find a decent winner, one who also was sired by a good stallion (Galopin). Thus on the dam's side of Blenheim II's pedigree, it was a pretty long time between drinks—as the governor of one of the Carolinas once remarked to his colleague from the sister state.

End Notes:

1. Mahmoud's Derby record was broken in 1995 by Lammtarra who won in 2:32 1/5.

CHAPTER THIRTEEN

MAHMOUD

The career of Mahmoud included a number of unusual circumstances, as did that of his sire, Blenheim II. Mahmoud was bred in France by the Aga Khan, who owned Blenheim II and who also owned Mahmoud's dam, Mah Mahal. The latter had been a very modest winner of two races, which must have been a great disappointment in light of the excellence of her pedigree. Mahmoud's dam was by a Triple Crown winner and first-class sire, Gainsborough, and she was from the flying Mumtaz Mahal, perhaps the fastest two-year-old filly ever seen in England.

It was rumored in France that Mah Mahal objected so strenuously to the amatory approaches of Blenheim II that, rather than risk a serious accident, those in charge had her inseminated artificially, and she was not covered naturally in 1932. Since all the participants in those events now are dead, there is no way of verifying or refuting the old tale.

In any case, Mahmoud was the first foal of Mah Mahal, being born in the spring of 1933. In due course, he was sent to the yearling sale at Deauville, with a reserve of 5,000 guineas. When that price was not reached, Mahmoud was sent on to trainer Frank Butters, who had charge of the Aga Khan's horses at Newmarket.

Butters later told the author that, on the day after Mahmoud arrived, the Aga Khan telephoned from France:

"What do you think of the gray colt I sent you from France?"

"I think he is all right," Butters replied.

"What do you think he would bring at auction in England?"

"About 8,000 guineas."

"Do you really? In that case, I think I will keep him."

Butters also told the author that Mahmoud developed an acute lameness. Since neither Butters nor the veterinarians could locate exactly where the problem originated, or diagnose the cause of it, the trainer left Mahmoud in his box for about ninety days—until he had cured himself and was going sound again.

The first time Mahmoud appeared in public was the occasion of a fiasco. He

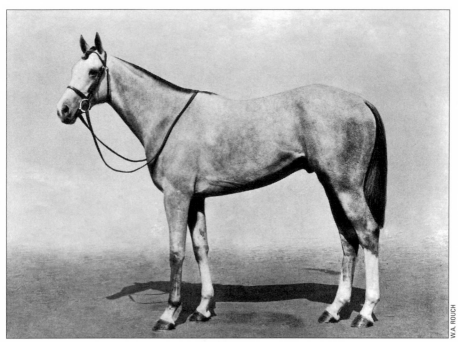

W.A. ROUCH

Mahmoud

was one of sixteen horses entered for the Spring Stakes at Newmarket in the middle of May. There took place something that thirteen riders considered a start, and the thirteen rode their horses to the end. It had been, however, a false start, so the race had to be run over. Only one of the thirteen horses that already had completed the course was sent back to race again, Mahmoud being among those that did not race twice. (The English take this sort of thing without a march on Buckingham Palace, but in France, when a similar event occurred, the author saw the crowd set fire to the stands at Le Tremblay. Are the French somewhat overly emotional, or do they merely hold the sturdy democratic belief that there are circumstances that justify direct action?)

Mahmoud's first official start was made in the New Stakes at Royal Ascot, where he was only sixth-favorite at 10-1 and ran third, beaten by three and a half lengths. Two weeks later, he won the Exeter Stakes at Newmarket in a canter, then at Goodwood, he won the Richmond Stakes by one length, giving weight to all but one of the field.

At Doncaster, during the St. Leger meeting in September, Mahmoud won the traditional Champagne Stakes by three-quarters of a length from Marcel Boussac's Abjer, with Wyndham third. His next race was the Middle Park Plate at Newmarket, and the same three colts met again. That time, Mahmoud was left at the post by about two lengths, and he was beaten two lengths. Abjer won, and Wyndham edged Mahmoud by a head for second.

On the two-year-old Free Handicap, Mahmoud and Abjer each were assigned 132 pounds, one pound below the Aga Khan's Bala Hissar, who had won the seven-furlong Dewhurst Stakes.

There must be considerable doubt about the class of the English two-year-olds of 1935, for of the ten topweights, only one showed any worthwhile form the next season. That one was Mahmoud, and he won only one race—but it was the right one to win, the Derby.

Mahmoud became the first classic candidate to appear in public in 1936, when on April 1 he was one of a party of twenty contesting the Greenham Plate at Newbury. Like his sire, Blenheim II, in the same race in 1930, Mahmoud had to concede weight all around, from three to sixteen pounds. He finished fifth. The going was heavy, which was a considerable disadvantage to a small, light-actioned colt like Mahmoud.

His next race was the one-mile Two Thousand Guineas, run over the straight Rowley Mile course at Newmarket. The weather and going were perfect, and the

				Isinglass
			John o' Gaunt, 1901	La Fleche
		Swynford, 1907		Tristan
			Canterbury Pilgrim, 1893	Pilgrimage
	Blandford, 1919			Gallinule
			White Eagle, 1905	Merry Gal
		Blanche, 1912		Bendigo
			Black Cherry, 1892	**Black Duchess**
Blenheim II, 1927				**St. Simon**
			Desmond, 1896	L'Abbesse de Jouarre
		Charles O'Malley, 1907		Isinglass
			Goody Two Shoes, 1899	Sandal
	Malva, 1919			Ayrshire
			Robert le Diable, 1899	Rose Bay
		Wild Arum, 1911		Martagon
MAHMOUD			Marliacea, 1902	Flitters
				Hampton
			Bay Ronald, 1893	**Black Duchess**
		Bayardo, 1906		Galopin
			Galicia, 1898	Isoletta
	Gainsborough, 1915			**St. Simon**
			St. Frusquin, 1893	Isabel
		Rosedrop, 1907		Trenton
Mah Mahal, 1928			Rosaline, 1901	Rosalys
				Le Samaritain
			Roi Herode, 1904	Roxelane
		The Tetrarch, 1911		Bona Vista
			Vahren, 1897	Castania
	Mumtaz Mahal, 1921			Amphion
			Sundridge, 1898	Sierra
		Lady Josephine, 1912		Americus
			Americus Girl, 1905	Palotta

Cohoes, the sire of Belmont winner Quadrangle

field of nineteen got away to a good start except for Mahmoud, who was left about a length. Cheeky Charlie Smirke had the mount on the Aga Khan's preferred colt, Bala Hissar, who started at 8-1, while Mahmoud, with Steve Donoghue up, was 100-8. By the time the pacemakers reached The Bushes, a quarter-mile from home, Mahmoud was in touch with the leaders. Going down the hill into the dip, he shot ahead, then was challenged by Lord Astor's Pay Up. About thirty yards from the finish, the two colts were level, but Pay Up drew in front by a few inches and won by a very short head.

Since Cheeky Charlie and the Aga Khan's trainer, Butters, were habitually at daggers drawn, Butters was anxious to prevent Smirke from riding the winner of the Derby, for which Butters saddled four runners. Butters himself told the author that he firmly was convinced that the Aga Khan's Taj Akbar (by Fairway) was considerably superior to Mahmoud over one and a half miles. On this account, the trainer put Gordon Richards on Taj Akbar and let his nemesis, Smirke, ride Mahmoud. The Derby was run on May 27, and the going was described as very firm, which in the United States would mean rock hard.

After the Guineas, Mahmoud was quoted at 15-1 for the Derby, while Pay Up was backed down to 5-1. On the day of the race, Pay Up still was 5-1, while

Mahmoud was 100-8 and Taj Akbar was 6-1. At the post, Mahmoud tried to dispose of Thankerton by kicking that rival on the knee.

Coming around Tattenham Corner, Mahmoud was about sixth, at least seven lengths behind the leader, Thankerton. As they came into the stretch, Smirke made his effort with Mahmoud. About halfway down the stretch, a quarter-mile from home, Mahmoud caught and passed Thankerton, and from there to the finish, he was in no danger. Richards made a strong run with Taj Akbar from far back and finished a clear second, three lengths behind Mahmoud. The time was 2:33 4/5, lowering the race record of 2:34, which had been established by Hyperion in 1933 and matched by Windsor Lad in 1934. Mahmoud's Derby record still stands.[1]

A post-Derby photograph shows the Aga Khan smiling genially as he led in the winner, but Frank Butters was looking in the opposite direction from Charlie Smirke. Mahmoud was only the third gray to win the Derby, Gustavus (1821) and the filly Tagalie (1912) having preceded him.

Mahmoud's next race was the one-mile St. James's Palace Stakes at Royal Ascot. Although he was asked to concede seven pounds to Rhodes Scholar, who had been fourth in the Guineas, Mahmoud's odds were 8-11. To general consternation, Rhodes Scholar—from a position just in front of Mahmoud as they entered the straight—pulled away until he had beaten Mahmoud by five lengths. Many observers felt that if Rhodes Scholar had run in the Derby, he would have beaten Mahmoud then, too.

The next race on Mahmoud's program was the St. Leger, run in the early part of September at Doncaster over a distance of one mile, six furlongs, and 132 yards. Unfortunately, Mahmoud suffered an attack of heel bug in mid-August, so that his training was interrupted. He started at odds of 9-2, while Rhodes Scholar (who had won the one and a quarter-mile Eclipse Stakes) was 2-1. Neither was close at the finish. Rhodes Scholar was tenth, and Mahmoud ran third, beaten nearly four lengths by Boswell. Since Boswell was considerably inferior to Precipitation, according to Captain Cecil Boyd-Rochfort (who trained them both), it was a great misfortune that Precipitation could not run.

The St. Leger was Mahmoud's last race, and he went to stud in 1937.

A glance at his pedigree will show how closely Mahmoud was related to Nasrullah. Mahmoud's sire was Blenheim II, and his maternal granddam was Mumtaz Mahal. Nasrullah's maternal grandsire was Blenheim II, and his maternal granddam also was Mumtaz Mahal.

Physically, the two horses were very different. Mahmoud was smaller, standing 15.2 3/4 hands high, and he resembled Blenheim II in general outline, though

YEAR	AGE	STS	1ST	2ND	3RD	EARNED*
1935	at 2	5	3	0	2	£ 5,092
1936	at 3	5	1	2	1	£ 9,934
Lifetime		10	4	2	3	£15,026

* First-place money only

different in color. Many people thought Mahmoud showed a great deal of the Arab in his appearance (though he did not have a level croup). Nasrullah was a big colt, much stronger, but less refined.

Mahmoud was not an outstanding success during his four seasons at stud in Ireland. He did, however, get two notable animals: Irish Guineas and Oaks winner Majideh, who became the dam of English Oaks winner Masaka and of Belmont Stakes winner Gallant Man; and Donatella III, who was the best two-year-old of her year in Italy and who foaled eight stakes winners there and in England.

In 1940 C.V. Whitney bought Mahmoud for about $85,000 and imported him to his farm in Kentucky. The stallion illustrated the point that just as there are horses for courses in racing, there are stallions for countries. Mahmoud was a very good sire for the American racing program, with its fast dirt tracks and emphasis on short to middle-distance racing. He was at best an indifferent sire for Europe, where racing is on the turf, and the emphasis is on middle-distance racing.

Mahmoud sired seventy stakes winners, including eight stakes winners abroad. Moreover, Mahmoud imparted sufficient precocity to his get that he placed sixty-three juveniles on the Experimental Free Handicap for two-year-olds in North America.

His daughters included champion First Flight, plus a pair of the best producers of recent times: Grey Flight, whose nine stakes winners included champion Misty Morn; and Almahmoud, who produced Cosmah and Natalma and thus became an ancestress of Northern Dancer, Tosmah, La Prevoyante, Cannonade, etc.

In the male line, much of Mahmoud's impact today comes through a pair of Greentree Stud-bred stallions, Cohoes (sire of Quadrangle) and The Axe II.[2] Other stakes-winning sons of Mahmoud include Oil Capitol, Vulcan's Forge, Mr. Trouble, Mount Marcy, Mameluke, Olympic Zenith, and General Staff.

Mahmoud died at C.V. Whitney Farm in 1962, at the age of twenty-nine.

End Notes:

1. In 1995 Lammtarra beat Mahmoud's Derby record with a time of 2:32 1/5.

2. In 2006 Mahmoud's sire line was represented in the United States by grade I winner Home at Last, a grandson of Quadrangle.

CHAPTER FOURTEEN

ST. GERMANS

When the late Lord Astor (the second Viscount) embarked on his career in Thoroughbred breeding and racing in England as a young man, his plan was to keep the number of his mares small and their quality high. His first step, however, was more or less accidental. He bought the mare Conjure, an 1895 foal by Juggler, for a hundred pounds for the purpose of breeding hunters. What happened from this modest undertaking was that he bred Winkipop (by William the Third), who proceeded to win ten races for him, including the One Thousand Guineas and the Coronation Stakes at Ascot. (The rich get richer and the poor get children.)

For racing purposes, at least, a more rational step was the purchase of Maid of the Mist (by the great sire Cyllene out of Sceptre, the only filly ever to win four of the five English classics). Maid of the Mist had won the Cheveley Park Stakes— the most important race for two-year-old fillies—and then had won the one and one-half-mile Nassau Stakes at Goodwood as a three-year-old. At the time of purchase, Maid of the Mist had at foot a filly foal called Hamoaze, by Torpoint. This represented an odd mating, as Torpoint was a plodder sired by the Australian Cup horse Trenton. If there was one thing a mare with the pedigree of Maid of the Mist did not seem to need it was the addition of stout, plodding blood as her sire Cyllene had won the Ascot Gold Cup and her dam Sceptre had beaten colts in the St. Leger.

The mating had been made by Sir William Bass, a wealthy and eccentric brewer who was known to have the lowest boiling point among all the testy tempered members of White's Club. There is a story of a practical joke that backfired, using Sir William as the cannon that was supposed to renew the Napoleonic wars. A Frenchman had been put up as a guest for a few weeks at White's. His sponsor, well knowing Sir William's volcanic temper, advised his French friend to go up behind the bald-headed gentleman sitting at the window, slap on his bald head, and then say: "Well, you bloody old fool, how many mistakes have you made today?" The Frenchman, thinking this was one of those peculiar British customs in the strange club life of London, did exactly as directed. When he delivered his slap and repeated the strange sentence beginning, "Well, you bloody old fool ..." the expectant audience of club members, looking forward to at least a renewal of the Battle of Waterloo, was aghast to see Sir William look up and say: "Bless my soul, you're the first man in 25 years who has spoken to me in this club. Come and have dinner!"

Hamoaze, bred by Sir William Bass on all the wrong lines, in fact turned out much better than any of the other daughters of Maid of the Mist at stud. Even as a racing proposition she was not bad. As a two-year-old, she was fourth in the Cheveley Park Stakes (in which Vaila, the granddam of Blue Larkspur, was beaten a neck). As a three-year-old, she won two fair races, was second in the 10,000-pound Jockey Club Stakes of one and three-quarters miles, and was third in the Park Hill Stakes—the "fillies' St. Leger." She was also third, when giving five pounds actual weight to Ambassador, a pretty good racer. So, while Hamoaze was no bad performer on the Turf, she was one of those rare gems at stud—a 100 percent stakes producer.

Her *Stud Book* record read:

1916. BUCHAN, b. c., by Sunstar. Won 16,658 pounds, including Eclipse Stakes twice, Champion Stakes, Doncaster Cup, Chester Vase, Ascot Gold Cup (disqualified); 2nd Two Thousand Guineas and Derby; 3rd St. Leger.

1919. TAMAR, b. c., by Tracery. Stakes winner; 2nd Derby Stakes.

1920. SALTASH, ch. c., by Sunstar. 11,113 pounds. Eclipse Stakes, Gratwicke Stakes.

1921. ST. GERMANS, b. c., by Swynford.

Buchan became a leading sire in England, his fillies being superior to his colts, and one of his daughters became the dam of the good sire Roman, in the United States. Tamar was sold as a stallion to Hungary, and Saltash was sold as a stallion in Australia.

Our concern here, however, is with St. Germans. Physically, he was by no means prepossessing, being small and rather mean looking. Unlike most small horses, which normally come to hand early if they have any racing merit, St. Germans raced according to his late-maturing pedigree, rather than his early-set frame. He was trained at Manton by Alec Taylor, who was the most patient of men and who really did not like racing two-year-olds more than he could help. (Nevertheless, he had two of the best ones in Bayardo and Picaroon.)

Taylor first brought out St. Germans on June 30, 1923, in the British Dominion

Two-Years-Old Plate at Sandown. Something must have been thought of the colt because he started third favorite, but he finished unplaced. He was not out again until October in the Buckenham Stakes at Newmarket, where he was fourth in a field of four. Still at Newmarket, two weeks later, he was a lively favorite at 2-3 for the five-furlong Prendergast Stakes in a field of seven. The winner was Salmon-Trout (who won the following year's St. Leger), and St. Germans was third, beaten a little more than two lengths. At the end of October, he was second in the six-furlong Criterion Stakes to the filly Blue Lake, also trained at Manton. It cannot be argued that St. Germans was any wonderful two-year-old, or even a good one.

The next year, however, following the late-maturing pattern of his sire, Swynford, things were somewhat different. St. Germans began with a victory at Newmarket in the one-mile Craven Stakes. He must have been well tried for it, for he was second favorite. He beat an unreliable customer called Tom Pinch, a full brother to Derby winner Captain Cuttle.

St. Germans then was reserved for the Derby, but luck was all against him. The race was run in a complete quagmire, which was greatly to the advantage of a big, strong, burly colt like Sansovino and to the disadvantage of an undersized colt like St. Germans. Sansovino appeared (for those who could see) to revel in the

			Isonomy, 1875	Sterling
				Isola Bella
		Isinglass, 1890	Dead Lock, 1878	Wenlock
	John o' Gaunt, 1911			Malpractice
			St. Simon, 1881	Galopin
		La Fleche, 1889		St. Angela
Swynford, 1907			Quiver, 1872	Toxophilite
				Y. Melbourne mare
			Hermit, 1864	Newminster
		Tristan, 1878		Seclusion
	Canterbury Pilgrim, 1893		Thrift, 1865	Stockwell
				Braxey
			The Palmer, 1864	Beadsman
		Pilgrimage, 1875		Madame Eglentine
ST. GERMANS			Lady Audley, 1867	Macaroni
				Secret
			Musket, 1867	Toxophilite
		Trenton, 1881		W. Australian mare
	Torpoint, 1900		Frailty, 1877	Goldsbrough
				Flora McIvor
			Sheen, 1885	Hampton
		Doncaster Beauty, 1893		Radiancy
Hamoaze, 1911			Doncaster Belle, 1883	Doncaster
				Belle Agnes
			Bona Vista, 1889	Bend Or
		Cyllene, 1895		Vista
	Maid of the Mist, 1906		Arcadia, 1887	Isonomy
				Distant Shore
			Persimmon, 1893	St. Simon
		Sceptre, 1899		Perdita
			Ornament, 1887	Bend Or
				Lily Agnes

L.S. SUTCLIFFE

St. Germans

horrible conditions, while the rest of the field hated the whole thing. The next year, over the same course, but in civilized conditions, St. Germans was to prove he was better than Sansovino. Nevertheless, he finished second, six lengths back in the Derby.

In the one-mile St. James's Palace Stakes at Ascot, St. Germans failed by two lengths to concede seven pounds to Tom Pinch successfully. It seems somewhat surprising that Taylor would run St. Germans in a mile race, as the course was certainly too short to bring out his best. Even the ten-furlong Eclipse Stakes at Sandown Park was too short for St. Germans, as another three-year-old, Polyphontes, gave him seven pounds and a five-length beating as well.[1] This was not exactly classic form.

In the autumn, however, St. Germans, like his sire before him, began to come to himself. He won the one and three-quarters-mile Lowther Stakes at Newmarket from three others and then won the Royal (Post) Stakes of one and one-quarter miles from three others, one of whom was Diophon, winner of the Two Thousand Guineas. At the Newmarket Houghton meeting, St. Germans took the ten-furlong Limekiln Stakes against his solitary opponent, Obliterate, who was conceding five pounds. Not unnaturally, St. Germans won by eight lengths.

The twelve-furlong Liverpool St. Leger was not much of a problem for St.

Germans, since there was nothing else of much class in the race. The Hampton Court Great Three-Years-Old Stakes of one and three-quarters miles was somewhat more interesting, since the sole opponent of St. Germans was Straitlace, the Oaks winner and generally considered to be a very high-class filly. St. Germans was meeting her strictly at scale weights, and he won by five lengths.

The first outing for St. Germans as a four-year-old was in a four-horse field for the ten-furlong March Stakes, for which the betting was 10-11 on Pharos and 5-4 against St. Germans. The result was enough to make form players jump off a cliff, since Pharos finished third and St. Germans was fourth. These were much the best colts in the race; what is a true believer in form and in the integrity of the Turf to do? To make matters worse, Lord Astor declared to win with St. Germans, but actu-

YEAR	AGE	STS	1ST	2ND	3RD	EARNED*
1923	at 2	4	0	1	1	£ 0
1924	at 3	9	6	2	1	£4,805
1925	at 4	7	3	1	2	£3,160
Lifetime		20	9	4	4	£7,965
* First-place money only						

ally won with Bright Knight (who later went to Audley Farm, Berryville, Virginia, as a stallion).

In the twelve-furlong Burwell Stakes at Newmarket, St. Germans carried 136 pounds to victory against two poor opponents. These races were prep affairs to get St. Germans ready for the Coronation Cup, run at Epsom over the twelve-furlong Derby Course. There St. Germans finally showed that he was a good horse, beyond question. He beat the previous year's Derby winner, Sansovino, by six lengths and beat Plack, the previous year's One Thousand Guineas winner, by ten lengths. Salmon-Trout, the previous year's St. Leger winner, and Twelve Pointer, the Cambridgeshire winner, were farther back. In the Ascot Gold Cup, St. Germans started at even money, but could only run third to Santorb, beaten five lengths. Then, in the twelve-furlong Princess of Wales's Stakes at Newmarket, he was beaten five and one-half lengths at weight for age by Solario, a very good colt; even Obliterate, who was not a very good colt, beat St. Germans four lengths for second place.

St. Germans then carried 137 pounds to victory against an undistinguished field in the two and one-eighth-mile Doncaster Cup. In his last start, St. Germans failed by three lengths to concede twenty-one pounds successfully to the three-year-old filly Tatra in the one and three-quarters-mile Jockey Club Stakes.

What are we to make of all this? St. Germans was certainly no world-beater. By American standards, he would be a plodder, very few of which succeed at stud in the United States. Even the late chargers, like Whirlaway and Phalanx, both of

L.S. SUTCLIFFE

Bold Venture

whom were good two-year-olds, ordinarily do not succeed as sires under the conditions of American racing.

St. Germans was sold as a sire to the United States and ended up at the Greentree Stud. The author asked Major Gerald Deane, the manager of Lord Astor's racing interests, why a horse of the pedigree and racing class of St. Germans had been sold. He replied that the stud already had Buchan, out of the same mare, and had a much higher opinion of Buchan than of St. Germans. The actual racing record of the two colts was not all that different, and the real reason, confessed Deane, was that he financially was strapped at the time and needed the money from his commission on the sale.

In all probability, St. Germans was the best sire bred by Lord Astor in a career as a breeder spanning more than forty years. (Court Martial is the other candidate.) Lord Astor's philosophy in breeding was much like the William Woodward Sr. view of breeding: He tried to make every mating with a view to producing a classic winner. For this purpose, he used almost altogether sires up to classic standard as racehorses. This meant using no pure sprinters. Ironically, Court Martial, one of the two best sires he bred, was by Fair Trial, who really did not stay one and one-quarter miles.

He also based his mares on well-established, very high-class female lines, such as those of Sceptre and Chelandry. (His hunter experiment based on the 100-pound Conjure, was something of an accident, but having turned out well, he kept on with it.)

From 1919 through 1929, Lord Astor was very successful in producing racers of classic standard. He won the Oaks five times and was second in the Derby four times. Similarly, Woodward during the 1930s won the Belmont five times, four of them with colts of his own breeding. Neither Astor nor Woodward, however, compared with the Derby stud in England or the Tesio stud in Italy in breeding influential stallions; the Derby stud bred Swynford, Phalaris, Pharos, Fairway, and Hyperion, as well as Alycidon. (After the deaths of the seventeenth Earl of Derby, Walter Alston, and George Lambton, this remarkable flow of sires ceased.) Tesio bred Nearco, Ribot, and Donatello II. The Derby and Tesio pedigrees were not classic in their structure, as were the Woodward and Astor pedigrees.

Unfortunately, St. Germans was by no means a fertile stallion, and the loss in the number of foals automatically reduced his opportunities. Nevertheless, he sired three colts of very high class in the United States: (1) Twenty Grand, the winner of the Kentucky Derby and Belmont Stakes whose great year in 1931 made St. Germans the leading sire; (2) Bold Venture, winner of the Kentucky Derby and Preakness, and sire of Triple Crown winner Assault who turned out to be completely sterile as did Twenty Grand; and (3) Devil Diver, about the best colt of

J.C. MELLON

Devil Diver

his year, but a bad failure as a sire. The above-mentioned Bold Venture also sired another Derby-Belmont winner in Middleground, but he, too, had misfortune at stud, getting only 130 foals in twenty-one seasons. (The best of Middleground's foals included Resaca and Ground Control.)

St. Germans sired twenty-three stakes winners, and it was a sad fate for any stallion to get three sons of the highest class which were up to classic distance but which were left with scant representation in modern pedigrees.

Another son of St. Germans, however, became a link to important modern runners representing the stallion's male line. The Rhymer, a 1938 foal by St. Germans, won the Widener Handicap and later sired $453,424-earner Vertex. The latter to date has sired a Kentucky Derby winner, Lucky Debonair; a juvenile champion, Top Knight (who also apparently was cursed by poor fertility), plus several other major winners.

End Notes:

1. St. Germans finished third behind Polyphontes and the four-year-old Papyrus.

CHAPTER FIFTEEN

CHALLENGER II

C hallenger II was a product of the National Stud, which had been created by the British government to accept the gift of all the bloodstock of Colonel Hall Walker (later Lord Wavertree) in 1916. The stud was located on the outskirts of the town of Kildare, County Kildare in Ireland. This, together with Hall Walker's training establishment in England, was purchased on an appraisal basis by the British government. So, the astrology-loving Colonel Walker got something for his Turf assets at a time when the war was going very badly for the British and the end was not yet in sight.

Along with the other yearlings from the National Stud, Challenger II was sold at public auction. He was bought by Lord Dewar, a whiskey magnate, for 5,000 guineas. He only ran twice in England, both times as a two-year-old. His first start was in the Richmond Stakes at Goodwood at the end of July. He was balked in the race and had to be switched to the outside, but got up to win in the last stride. There was no other colt of note in the race, so the form did not mean much beyond the fact that Challenger II was resolute when asked for a stiff effort.

His remaining start was in the Clearwell Stakes at Newmarket in the autumn. There he met a pretty good colt in Teacup, and after the two engaged in an eye-to-eye battle, Challenger II got the upper hand and went on to win by three-quarters of a length.

On the Free Handicap for two-year-olds, the Jockey Club handicapper put Challenger II in at 127 pounds and Teacup at 119 pounds. That seems a trifle excessive on the face of it, but more than likely, the handicapper was taking into account that Challenger II was by Swynford and seemed likely to stay well, while Teacup was by Tetratema, whose stock rarely stayed.

It will be noted that Challenger II did not contest any of the prestige races for two-year-olds. His stable companion, Press Gang, on the other hand, won the Middle Park Stakes, beating Blenheim II. Topweight on the Free Handicap was Diolite (129); then came Press Gang (128), Challenger II (127), and Blenheim II

(126). Since the next year, Diolite won the one-mile Two Thousand Guineas, and Blenheim II won the Derby, the handicapper was no fool.

At the end of the colt's two-year-old season, Challenger II's owner, Lord Dewar, died, thereby voiding all engagements made for Challenger II, including the classics. (This rule shortly was abrogated due to the legal efforts of the late Edgar Wallace. Since Wallace thought nothing of writing four mystery novels at the same time, getting a silly rule like this changed must have seemed child's play to him.)

As things stood, there was not much point in keeping Challenger II in training in England. Consequently, he was put on offer by the Dewar Estate. The asking price was 15,000 pounds, but the estate accepted 10,000 pounds offered by C.J. FitzGerald on behalf of William L. Brann and Robert S. Castle, who were founding the Branncastle stud near Frederick, Maryland.

Subsequent to this purchase, Challenger II, coming back from the downs, got in an argument with some barbed wire, which left his hind legs and hocks badly scarred. When he was recovered from this sufficiently, he was shipped to the United States. An attempt was made to train Challenger II on the West Coast, and he made eight starts there as a four-year-old, but was always unplaced.

Installed at Branncastle as premier sire, Challenger II did well from the start and was the leading sire in the United States in 1939, when his son Challedon had his great three-year-old season and was Horse of the Year for the first time.

Challedon was described by the late John Hervey (Salvator) as one of the greatest Thoroughbreds ever seen in the United States. This is a striking illustration of the bias that nearly all students and followers of the Turf develop toward certain individual horses. This bias can be either for or against a specific horse. The author has never known anyone personally who was entirely free of such bias (including the author), the enthusiastic exercise of it is one of those beautiful liberties that harm no one, except in the pocket book. To some extent, we can all be classed with Eric Hoffer's "True Believers," and have completely closed minds about certain horses.

Challedon met Eight Thirty twice, and Eight Thirty beat him both times; the first time was in the Kent Handicap at one and one-sixteenth miles, when Eight Thirty had a weight advantage of six pounds and beat Challedon two lengths, thus coming out about on level terms with Challedon; the second time was in the one and one-eighth-mile Massachusetts Handicap the next year, when Eight Thirty with a four-pound pull in the weights, beat Challedon two and a half lengths, coming out a slightly better colt than Challedon on the handicapping figures. No one ever suggested that Eight Thirty was one of the greatest horses ever seen on the American Turf, though he was a high-class one. Having had it twice proved that Eight Thirty was as good or better than Challedon, how is Challedon entitled to be ranked as one of the greatest colts ever seen on the American Turf? It must be conceded, however, that Hervey was not alone in his suggestion of Challedon's greatness.

The other top performer sired by Challenger II was the splendid filly Gallorette, voted by the American trainers as the best filly seen on the American Turf. There is no doubt that Gallorette was a splendid race mare. She was big, strong, tough, sound, and game. In relation to her own sex, she was a more outstanding performer than Challedon among the colts, but the author, again asserting his constitutional right to express bias, begs to disagree with the conclusion of the trainers. Gallorette started seventy-two times, and won twenty-one races, or slightly less than one third of her races. She failed to win a stakes as a two-year-old and never saw the day when she could beat the best colts on weight-for-sex terms. In her best year, at four, she won six out of eighteen starts.

(Compare this with the record of Regret, who was unbeaten in five starts at two and three, including victories in the Saratoga Special, the Hopeful, and the

Swynford, 1907	John o' Gaunt, 1901	Isinglass, 1890	**Isonomy**, 1875	Sterling Isola Bella
			Dead Lock, 1878	Wenlock Malpractice
		La Fleche, 1889	**St. Simon**, 1881	Galopin St. Angela
			Quiver, 1872	Toxophilite Y. Melbourne Mare
	Canterbury Pilgrim, 1893	Tristan, 1878	**Hermit**, 1864	Newminster Seclusion
			Thrift, 1865	Stockwell Braxey
CHALLENGER II		**Pilgrimage**, 1875	The Palmer, 1864	Beadsman Madame Eglentine
			Lady Audley, 1867	Macaroni Secret
	Great Sport, 1910	Gallinule, 1884	**Isonomy**, 1875	Sterling Isola Bella
			Moorhen, 1873	**Hermit** Skirmisher Mare
		Gondolette, 1902	Loved One, 1883	See Saw **Pilgrimage**
Sword Play, 1921			Dongola, 1883	Doncaster Douranee
	Flash of Steel, 1913	Royal Realm, 1905	Persimmon, 1893	**St. Simon** Perdita
			Sand Blast, 1894	Sheen Sahara
		Flaming Vixen, 1907	Flying Fox, 1896	Orme Vampire
			Amphora, 1893	Amphion Sierra

Challenger II

Kentucky Derby. Over all, Regret started eleven times, for nine victories and one second. Regret could, and repeatedly did, beat the best colts on weight-for-sex terms.)

Challenger II sired a total of thirty-four stakes winners before his death in 1948. In addition to Challedon and Gallorette, they included Bridal Flower, who was the champion three-year-old filly in 1946 (the same year Gallorette was older female champion). Others by Challenger II included Pictor, Bug Juice, Challenge Me, Escadru, Dare Me, and Errard.

The horse, thus, made a very good showing at stud, but it still seems probable that he was an even better sire than his record indicated. His opportunities, both in the quality of his mates and the number of foals sired, were far inferior to the opportunities of a stallion such as Sir Gallahad III. The latter stood at the great Claiborne stud and had the full support of a syndicate of breeders owning choice bands of broodmares. Frederick, Maryland, was out of the way for many breeders and comparatively few of them cared to ship their mares to visit Challenger II.

The author many years ago made an analysis, which covered Challenger II, Sir Gallahad III, and many others on the following basis: Dividing racing class into ten groups, all the way from the highest class, to non-placed starters and nonstarters at the bottom, a checkerboard was constructed, having ten horizontal columns, and ten similar vertical columns crossing them. First was established the racing class of each mare which produced a live foal to a specific stallion, and the mare was assigned to the correct horizontal column; the foal, after its racing class was established, then was assigned to the correct vertical column. In the box where these two columns intersect, a mark was inserted. When this process was completed for all the known foals of a sire, it was easy to observe the pattern of a sire's whole stud record, showing whether the racing merit of his stock was better, the same, or worse than their dams.

This device was one way to illustrate graphically the opportunity enjoyed by each sire, as

YEAR	AGE	STS	1ST	2ND	3RD	EARNED*
1929	at 2 (in Eng)	2	2	0	0	£2,249
1930	at 3	unraced				
1931	at 4 (in N.A.)	8	0	0	0	$ 0
Lifetime		10	2	0	0	£2,249
* First-place money only						

well as the results of such opportunity. For example, the opportunity open to Bull Dog was much inferior to the opportunity open to his full brother, Sir Gallahad III. Yet the results showed that Bull Dog sired 15 percent stakes winners, compared to 11 percent stakes winners for Sir Gallahad III. When to this difference in favor of Bull Dog was added the inferior opportunity he enjoyed, the difference in the merit of the two sires became even more apparent. This was reflected in the fact that Bull Dog sired the very influential stallion Bull Lea and became the maternal grandsire of the very high-class sire Tom Fool. No comparable son or grandson of Sir Gallahad III appeared.

It is somewhat surprising to the author that Challenger II proved to be as good a sire as he did. While he was very much a son of Swynford in color, conformation, and possibly racing capacity (though this was never proved beyond doubt), his pedigree raised certain doubts. His dam, Sword Play, had been a winner of four unimportant races and was sired by a proven stud failure, Great Sport. Apart from producing Challenger II, Sword Play was not a very remarkable broodmare. Her dam, Flash of Steel, was a mere winner and produced five ordinary winners. Furthermore, she was sired by Royal Realm, another proven stud failure.

The third dam, Flaming Vixen, was by Flying Fox (a Triple Crown winner and high-class sire) out of Amphora, a full sister to the high-class sprinter and very good sire Sundridge. This is not exactly a solid pedigree, with no bad holes in it. How could anyone know which way the genes were going to be transmitted by Challenger II? As it turned out, he seemed to transmit more of Swynford than any other ancestor, but how could this be projected in advance?

Challedon

In all probability, American breeders lost a chance to breed many high-class racers through their failure to give Challenger II an opportunity proportionate to his high qualities as a sire.

As a point of lesser interest, it may be pointed out that mares by Challenger II made comparatively little mark on the *American Stud Book*, just as mares by Swynford made comparatively little mark on the *British Stud Book*. The same thing was true of Blandford (by Swynford), who was, considering his relatively poor opportunity in his early years at stud, the best sire to date of the twentieth century in England and Ireland.

Such sex-linked characteristics remain something of a mystery to the author. Most very high-class sires of racers are equally high-class as broodmare sires, but certain other sires that are high-class sires of racers themselves are very high-class broodmare sires, but poor sires of sires. How is this marked difference sorted out, as a matter of inheritance, and how can the bewildered breeder know the answer in advance?

CHAPTER SIXTEEN

POLYMELUS

I
f anyone is foolhardy enough to believe that breeders and owners are good judges of their own racehorses and breeding stock, let him read the tale of Polymelus. Here was a colt that no one wanted to own—for long—and even his last owner bought him largely for the wrong reason (though at the time his reason looked pretty juicy).

Polymelus was sired in the second crop of Cyllene, against which there existed a strong prejudice in the British breeding community. In fact, it was a good many years before any yearling by Cyllene brought more than 1,000 guineas at public auction.

Cyllene's owner, Sir Charles Day Rose, must have regarded him with mixed emotions. He had been a May 28 foal and was so small as a yearling that he had not been nominated for any of the classics. Despite his late foaling date, however, Cyllene was out in March as a two-year-old. He won his debut and three of his four remaining starts that year and also won three of his four starts at three, including the Newmarket Stakes and the Jockey Club Stakes. As a four-year-old, he won both his starts, including the Ascot Gold Cup.

Cyllene became the best sire of his time, getting four winners of the Epsom Derby in eight years (Cicero 1905, Minoru 1909, Lemberg 1910, and Tagalie 1912).[1]

Maid Marian, the dam of Polymelus, had no such immediate credentials. As a two-year-old, she had placed three times in seven outings, some of which were in selling races, and was claimed by the trainer Richard Marsh for 150 pounds. Marsh soon sold Maid Marian to the breeder Francis Luscombe, who had reason to congratulate himself two years later. Maid Marian's half sister, one year younger, was Memoir, who won the Oaks and St. Leger for the fabulously lucky Duke of Portland. Two years younger than Memoir was her full sister La Fleche, winner of the One Thousand Guineas, Oaks, St. Leger, Cambridgeshire, and Ascot Gold Cup.

Cyllene, sire of Polymelus

Those two fillies made their half sister, Maid Marian, valuable as a stud proposition, and Luscombe duly sold Maid Marian to Major J.E. Platt for 3,000 guineas. Some years later, Luscombe was trying to recall the name of this mare he had sold for such a nice profit. A friend chimed in: "It was Maid Marian."

Like a flash, Lord Marcus Beresford, renowned for his quick wit, observed: "Maid Marian be damned! Made Luscombe, you mean."

After producing three winners from her first six foals (including a fair colt in Ercildoune), Maid Marian at the age of sixteen produced Polymelus as her ninth foal. By that time, Maid Marian was owned by Lord Crewe, the son-in-law of Lord Rosebery. Since Rosebery bred Cicero, also sired by Cyllene, the same year as Polymelus was foaled, one may be permitted to wonder if the Rosebery influence had been at work in arranging the mating of Cyllene and Maid Marian.

In any case, Maid Marian already had shown she was capable of breeding a good stallion. Her foal of 1894 was Grafton, by Galopin. Never raced because he went wrong in his wind, Grafton was exported to Australia and proceeded to lead the sire list four times there.

Polymelus went into training at Kingsclere, under the care of John Porter (trainer of seven Epsom Derby winners) and became the last [Derby] winner credited to Porter.[2]

(Cyllene, Cicero, and Polymelus were all very straight in the croup, a characteristic undoubtedly inherited from Arabian ancestors. The stock of this male line through Nearco, Nasrullah, etc., nearly all have drooping quarters.)

Evidently, Porter suspected that Polymelus had some racing merit, for the colt was an even-money favorite in his first start at Ascot. He finished second. Started next in the valuable National Breeders Produce Stakes, Polymelus was unplaced to Cicero (also by Cyllene), who was to win the next year's Epsom Derby.

At Goodwood, Polymelus won the Richmond Stakes, and at Newmarket in the autumn he won the Rous Memorial and Criterion Stakes. In addition, he finished second in the Convivial Stakes at York and was unplaced in the Middle Park Plate (the two-year-old Derby) and in the Imperial Plate.

His was the record of a good two-year-old, some way behind the best of his year.

Until the late autumn, at least, Polymelus' three-year-old record was about the same: unplaced in the Newmarket and Eclipse Stakes (both top-class fixtures); second in the St. James's Palace Stakes at Ascot; winner of the Triennial Stakes at Ascot; third in the six-furlong Stewards' Cup at Goodwood under ninety-nine pounds; winner of two minor events at Yorkshire; second to Challacombe in a

			Doncaster, 1870	Stockwell Marigold
		Bend Or, 1877	Rouge Rose, 1865	Thormanby Ellen Horne
	Bona Vista, 1889	Vista, 1879	Macaroni, 1860	Sweetmeat Jocose
Cyllene, 1895			Verdure, 1867	King Tom May Bloom
		Isonomy, 1875	Sterling, 1868	Oxford Whisper
	Arcadia, 1887		Isola Bella, 1868	Stockwell Isoline
		Distant Shore, 1880	Hermit, 1864	**Newminster** Seclusion
POLYMELUS			Lands End, 1873	Trumpeter Faraway
		Lord Clifden, 1860	**Newminster**, 1848	Touchstone Beeswing
	Hampton, 1872		The Slave, 1852	Melbourne Volley
		Lady Langden, 1868	Kettledrum, 1858	Rataplan Hybla
Maid Marian, 1886			Haricot, 1847	Lanercost Queen Mary
		Toxophilite, 1855	Longbow, 1849	Ithuriel Miss Bowe
	Quiver, 1872		Legerdemain, 1846	Pantaloon Decoy
		Y. Melbourne mare, 1861	Young Melbourne, 1855	Melbourne Clarissa
			Brown Bess, 1844	Camel Brutandorf mare

Polymelus

substandard St. Leger, and also second in the Jockey Club Stakes; and winner of the Gatwick Stakes, a fair race.[3]

At that time, there were changes in the ownership of Kingsclere, and Porter retired. Lord Crewe sold Polymelus to David Faber for a reported 3,000 pounds.

David Faber may have been closely related to the George Faber who was badly trimmed by the great gambler and confidence man Robert Standish Sievier. In 1901, Sievier had two outstanding two-year-olds, Duke of Westminster and Sceptre. Unfortunately, Sievier was pressed for ready cash, a frequently recurring phenomenon. This never bothered him in the least as far as tradesmen were concerned, but it was vital to him to be able to settle his betting accounts or he would be ruled off the Turf.

When Sievier let it be known that he would part with Duke of Westminster, or Sceptre, or both, George Faber commissioned John Porter to inspect them and to buy one of them for him. Porter duly arrived, and after examining the horses, asked Sievier to name a price. Sievier pretended to reflect and then said: "22,000 guineas for Duke of Westminster, and 15,000 guineas for Sceptre. No, I think I'll make it 13,500 guineas for Sceptre." Charles Morton, Sievier's trainer, was present and thought Sievier was mad, since he knew that Sceptre was much the better of the two.

Sievier's trap worked to perfection. Since the clear inference was that there was something wrong with Sceptre, George Faber bought Duke of Westminster, who turned out a complete failure. Sceptre went on to win the One Thousand and Two Thousand Guineas, the Oaks, and the St. Leger, trained by the redoubtable Sievier. At the end of that season, when he was leading owner, Sievier was broke again and had to sell Sceptre to Sir William Bass.

Perhaps David Faber thought he might be getting even for the Fabers by buying Polymelus from John Porter's stable—and he would have got more than even had he only hung on to Polymelus.

As a four-year-old, trained by Baker, Polymelus was unplaced in the City and Suburban Handicap, then finished second twice, and unplaced three times more.

Faber then decided to remove his horses from Baker and send them to Frank Hartigan. As part of this change, Faber ordered Polymelus to

YEAR	AGE	STS	1ST	2ND	3RD	EARNED
1904	at 2	8	3	2	0	£ 2,353
1905	at 3	11	4	3	1	£ 5,685
1906	at 4	10	3	2	0	£ 3,925
1907	at 5	2	1	0	1	£ 4,840
Lifetime		**31**	**11**	**7**	**2**	**£16,803**

be put through the sale ring at Newmarket. There were only two bidders—Frank Hartigan representing Faber and S.B. (Solly) Joel—and they were standing on opposite sides of the ring.

Hartigan bid 3,800 guineas. Instead of raising the bid by the usual 100 guineas, Joel went to 4,000, possibly thinking this figure was the reserve. After some hesitation, Hartigan raised the bid to 4,100. Joel shook his head. The auctioneer, Somerville Tattersall, then began to argue with Joel, pointing out that Polymelus was engaged in the Duke of York Stakes, and had a good chance of winning.

"Yes," replied Joel, "but you can't bet on him there."

Tattersall responded: "He is also in the Cambridgeshire, and you can bet as much as you like there!"

Joel then bid 4,200 guineas and bought Polymelus. Apart from when he joined his uncle, Barney Barnato, in the De Beers diamond syndicate in South Africa, that was probably the luckiest day in Joel's life.

Tattersall proved a good prophet, for Polymelus won both the Duke of York Stakes and the Cambridgeshire; in the latter, he carried 122 pounds, including a ten-pound penalty. He also carried a hefty packet of Joel's money, one bet being struck of 6,000 pounds to 5,000 pounds while the horses were going to the post. It did not take Solly Joel long to retrieve his 4,200-guineas outlay.

Polymelus then won the ten-furlong Champion Stakes at Newmarket. Because

Polymelus' stakes-winning son Polymelian

he was a very long striding colt, it was not surprising that he showed his best form at Newmarket over courses having no turns. (The same thing was true of Sceptre, who never was beaten at Newmarket.)

As a five-year-old, Polymelus finished third in the Coronation Cup, a top-class stakes, and won the Princess of Wales's Stakes, a second-class stakes, concluding his racing career with eleven victories in thirty-one starts and earnings of 16,803 pounds.

There was considerable difference of opinion about the racing class of Polymelus. The Jockey Club's handicapper put him in the Cambridgeshire as a four-year-old with 112 pounds, about fourteen pounds under a normal top. Yet Polymelus carried a ten-pound penalty and won. There can be little doubt that Polymelus was much better in the autumn and at Newmarket than he was elsewhere in other times of the year.

The late Arthur Hancock Sr. told the present writer that he strongly urged Henry Oxnard of the Blue Ridge Stud in Virginia to buy Polymelus when the stallion came up for sale. Instead, Oxnard bought Isinglass' full brother, who proved useless.

Polymelus entered stud at a fee of 98 pounds, then worth less than $500. Somber expectations proved wrong, for during an eight-year period from 1914 to 1921, Polymelus led England's sire list five times, was ranked second twice and third once.

The colts by Polymelus were much superior to the fillies, both on the track and at stud. Despite having been premier sire five times, Polymelus never became leading broodmare sire.

Among the scores of winners sired by Polymelus, his best were:

• Pommern, winner of the 1915 English Triple Crown;

• Humorist, winner of the 1921 Epsom Derby;

• Corcyra, top-class two-year-old, narrowly beaten in the 1914 Two Thousand Guineas;

• Phalaris, winner of sixteen races, champion sprinter, England's leading sire in 1925 and 1928;

• Fifinella, filly winner of the 1916 Epsom Derby and Oaks;

• Cinna, winner of the 1920 One Thousand Guineas.

End Notes:

1. Cyllene led the English sire list in 1909, 1910, and was leading broodmare sire in 1921.

2. Porter's seven Derby winners were Blue Gown (1868), Shotover (1882), St. Blaise (1883), Ormonde (1886), Sainfoin (1890), Common (1891), and Flying Fox (1899). Three of these—Ormonde, Common, and Flying Fox—were winners of the English Triple Crown.

3. This race was John Porter's last win as a trainer as he retired from the Turf in 1905.

CHAPTER SEVENTEEN

PHALARIS

S hortly before J.H. Houldsworth's bloodstock was to be dispersed at auction, the Honorable George Lambton and Walter Alston, respectively trainer and bloodstock adviser to Lord Derby, were seen examining the mare Bromus, one of the lots coming up for sale.

Bromus had won the Seaton Delaval Plate at Newcastle for her only victory in five starts at two, and though she ran five times again at three she did not win again. Furthermore, she was the only winner among the ten foals of her dam, Cheery, who was a non-winner herself. The next dam, Sunrise, also bred ten foals, of which four were winners. Her dam, Sunray, bred eight winners from eight foals, but none of them were of high class.

The next dam, Sunshine, foaled in 1867, had been acquired by Houldsworth from the Scottish iron master James Merry, a considerable power on the Turf. Sunshine had won nine of ten races at two and had won the Coronation Stakes at Ascot at three. Sunshine bred thirteen foals, but only three winners, and only one of them (Bushey Park) was a fair horse.

Houldsworth had a mania for breeding Sunshine and her daughters to Springfield, the best horse he owned in a long career. This policy had not been very successful, but when it could no longer be followed in the case of Sunrise—as she was sired by Springfield—Houldsworth did the next best thing. He bred Cheery, the daughter of Sunrise, to Sainfoin, a son of Springfield. The produce was Bromus, inbred to Springfield with one free generation.

Bromus was an attractive, short-legged mare, with a roomy body. Whether it was her type, her one flash of performance, or her pedigree that was the inducement is not publicly known. In any case she was bought for the Derby stud.

In 1912 Bromus was covered by Polymelus, and in 1913 dropped the bay colt foal called Phalaris. The racing career of Phalaris took place entirely during the years of World War I, when racing in England was much curtailed. Nevertheless, he was in training through four seasons, made twenty-four starts, and won six-

Phalaris

teen races (including two walkovers).

As a two-year-old, Phalaris won two of his three starts, but they did not include any of the traditional great two-year-old stakes. On the Free Handicap, Phalaris was assigned 117 pounds, with top weight going to Fifinella (also by Polymelus) at 126. Making a three-pound allowance for sex, Phalaris would come out twelve pounds from the top. Considering the blazing speed Phalaris was to show later, it is somewhat surprising that he was not a better two-year-old.

When Phalaris was three, Lambton began with a conventional classic program, the one-mile Craven Stakes and then the first classic—the Two Thousand Guineas.

Phalaris finished third in the Craven Stakes and unplaced in the Two Thousand Guineas, and Lambton abandoned the classics for smaller targets. After failing in the Stewards' Handicap with only 99 pounds up, Phalaris scored in the Beaufort Stakes, seven furlongs (119 pounds); the St. George's Handicap, six furlongs (113 pounds); and the Royal Stakes, ten furlongs (124 pounds). In this last race, there were only three starters, and the two others were not much good. Next, in the Limekiln Stakes of ten furlongs, Phalaris carried 120 pounds into second place in a field of eight.

The next year, as a four-year-old, Phalaris was restricted largely to sprinting and won seven out of nine starts, counting a walkover in The Whip. At five and six furlongs, he seemingly was invincible, and he won carrying 142 pounds, 138 pounds, and 136 pounds.

(If you want to score off your friends, or enemies, and lower your popularity ratings, you can bet them that the sprinter Phalaris scored in a traditional race at a distance of more than two miles, carrying 140 pounds. He did. He walked over for The Whip at Newmarket, with 140 pounds, distance two miles, 118 yards.)

In 1918, Phalaris was out five times. Apart from the Challenge Stakes, his last race, in which he walked over, he won the Abingdon Plate, five furlongs (147 pounds); the Lanwades Plate, seven furlongs (141 pounds); the June Stakes (134 pounds); and was unplaced in the Beaufort Handicap, five furlongs (146 pounds).

When it is recalled that even Discovery, the weight-packing champion of the American Turf in the 1930s, was stopped stone cold after his weights passed 139 pounds, these weight-carrying performances by Phalaris are remarkable.

			Bend Or, 1877	Doncaster Rouge Rose
Polymelus, 1902	Cyllene, 1895	Bona Vista, 1889		
			Vista, 1879	Macaroni Verdure
		Arcadia, 1887	Isonomy, 1875	Sterling Isola Bella
			Distant Shore, 1880	Hermit Lands End
	Maid Marian, 1886	Hampton, 1887	**Lord Clifden**, 1860	Newminster The Slave
			Lady Langden, 1868	Kettledrum Haricot
		Quiver, 1872	Toxophilite, 1855	Longbow Legerdemain
PHALARIS			Y. Melbourne mare, 1861	Young Melbourne Brown Bess
	Sainfoin, 1887	Springfield, 1873	St. Albans 1857	Stockwell Bribery
			Viridis, 1864	Marsyas Maid of Palmyra
		Sanda, 1878	Wenlock, 1869	**Lord Clifden** Mineral
			Sandal, 1861	Stockwell Lady Evelyn
Bromus, 1905	Cheery, 1892	St. Simon, 1881	Galopin, 1872	Vedette Flying Duchess
			St. Angela, 1865	King Tom Adeline
		Sunrise, 1883	Springfield, 1873	St. Albans Viridis
			Sunray, 1874	King of the Forest Sunshine

Manna

The limitations of Phalaris, however, were exposed when he failed as a four-year-old to carry 126 pounds into a place in the nine-furlong Cambridgeshire Handicap. The fact is, that Phalaris, having the brilliant speed he so often displayed, could not stay a mile in a fast-run race.

Before Phalaris was put to stud, Lord Derby reportedly offered him for sale at a price of 5,000 pounds. This offer was not accepted, and Phalaris joined Swynford and Chaucer at the Derby stud.

The present writer once asked George Lambton if at the time Phalaris retired to stud he had believed that Phalaris would prove to be a successful sire.

"No," Lambton said. "I cannot say I really believed in him (as the trainer did in Swynford and Hyperion). However, he had absolutely first-class speed, an excellent constitution, and was up to very high weights. Furthermore, he had very good action and was as true as steel for as far as he could go."

Lambton once tried Phalaris with the flying filly Diadem over six furlongs and gave the trial to Diadem by a short head.

In 1925 and again in 1928, Phalaris was the leading sire of winners in England, and he was three times leading broodmare sire.

His best produce were: Fairway (1928 St. Leger, Eclipse Stakes, etc.); Manna (1925 Two Thousand Guineas and Derby); Colorado (1926 Two Thousand Guineas, etc.); Pharos (fourteen races); Sickle (twice leading sire in the United States); Pharamond II (good sire in the United States); Fair Isle (1930 One Thousand Guineas); and Chatelaine (1933 Oaks).

Six of the eight named above were out of daughters of Chaucer. The old definition of good and great for stallions is that a good stallion is a horse that sires a great runner, and a great stallion is a horse that sires a great runner for his owner. Since

YEAR	AGE	STS	1ST	2ND	3RD	EARNED
1915	at 2	3	2	0	0	£ 906
1916	at 3	7	3	1	1	£1,372
1917	at 4	9	7	1	0	£1,966
1918	at 5	5	4	0	0	£1,234
Lifetime		24	16	2	1	£5,478

Lord Derby owned both Phalaris and Chaucer, the above list of horses, by definition, made both of them great stallions.

A variation on the theme is to buy a yearling by a stallion the buyer does not own and have the yearling surpass the fondest hopes of the buyer. In the buyer's opinion, the stallion thereby qualifies as a great sire.

In this way, Phalaris must have been promoted into the ranks of great sires in the mind of H.E. Morriss.

In 1923, Morriss, then a bullion broker residing in Shanghai, cabled Fred Darling, the Beckhampton trainer: "Buy me the best yearling at Doncaster." (Then the great locale for yearling auctions.)

Darling very nearly succeeded, for he bought Manna (Phalaris—Waffles). The best yearling sold at Doncaster probably was Solario, but even Solario was not quite up to Picaroon, who was not offered at the sale.

Manna ran third to Picaroon and Solario in the Middle Park Stakes (the two-year-old Derby) and on the basis of other races could be regarded as the third-best two-year-old. As the spring of 1925 came on, Morriss backed Manna to win a huge stake in the Derby, and he also is reported to have bought the Calcutta Sweepstake (lottery) ticket on Manna for the Derby.

So what happened? Picaroon (the best colt) fell ill and could not start for the Derby. Solario (probably the second-best colt) got his legs entangled with the tapes when they broke at the start of the Derby and was badly left, although he finished fourth.

Manna was off flying and won in a canter by eight lengths.

Morriss was then safe in pronouncing Phalaris to be a great stallion.

While Phalaris was a very good sire, it is only fair to add that his reputation undoubtedly has benefited from the brilliant success of his sons Fairway and Pharos, whose blood has reached every corner of racing throughout the world. He is not to be ranked with Stockwell (sire of the winners of seventeen classic races)[1], St. Simon (sire of the winners of seventeen classic races, and leading sire nine times)[2], Hermit (leading sire seven years in succession), or his own grand-sire, Cyllene (four Derby winners in eight years).[3]

Initially, perhaps, Phalaris blood was regarded as a source of speed. With the intermingling of the stout blood in Lord Derby's stud, however, the Phalaris strain became middle-distance horses capable of classic performances anywhere.

End Notes:

1. Stockwell's winners of the classic races: Blair Athol (Derby, St. Leger), Lord Lyon (Two Thousand Guineas, Derby, St. Leger), Doncaster (Derby), Regalia (Oaks), Lady August (One Thousand Guineas), Repulse (One Thousand Guineas), Achievement (One Thousand Guineas, St. Leger), St. Alban (St. Leger), Call Ou (St. Leger), The Marquis (Two Thousand Guineas, St. Leger), Bothwell (Two Thousand Guineas), Gang Forward (Two Thousand Guineas).

2. St. Simon's winners of the classic races: St. Frusquin (Two Thousand Guineas), Diamond Jubilee (Two Thousand Guineas, Derby, St. Leger), Memoir (Oaks, St. Leger), La Fleche (One Thousand Guineas, Oaks, St. Leger), Persimmon (Derby, St. Leger), Semolina (One Thousand Guineas), Amiable (One Thousand Guineas, Oaks), Winifreda (One Thousand Guineas), Mrs. Butterwick (Oaks), La Roche (Oaks).

3. Cyllene's four Derby winners in eight years: Cicero (1905), Minoru (1909), Lemberg (1910), Tagalie (1912).

CHAPTER EIGHTEEN

PHAROS

haros was a medium-sized colt, sired by a top-class sprinter, Phalaris, in
his first season at stud. He was out of a plodder, Scapa Flow, winner of
three small races, each at one and one-half miles. Scapa Flow nearly was
lost in a selling race at Stockton (a minor track), but a trainer called McGuigan
put in a friendly claim for her and restored her to her owner, Lord Derby.

In conformation, Pharos was no oil painting, being back at the knee (but not
badly), a trait often observed in the get of Phalaris. He also was somewhat sickle-
hocked, but we have all seen good horses with that trait more pronounced than it
was with Pharos.

The late John E. Madden—about as good a judge of racing prospects as there
was around from 1894 to 1929—illustrated what he thought of such minor
defects, when he was challenged to find fault with the conformation of a yearling.
He walked up to the colt, opened his mouth, looked inside, and then delivered
his verdict: "I don't like his back teeth!"

Conformation defects or not, Pharos won fourteen races in four seasons and
never was reported to be unsound. He was a tough, wiry, somewhat compact
racer.

If there is such a thing as a homebred, Pharos fitted the description. Lord Derby
bred him and also bred his sire, his dam, and his maternal grandsire. The writer
once asked the late George Lambton (who trained Lord Derby's horses for nearly
forty years) why Anchora, the granddam of Pharos, had been bought for the
Derby stud. Her racing class was modest and her pedigree was almost shocking.
She was by the plodder Love Wisely, a failure at stud; her dam was by Hazlehatch,
another stud failure; and her female line had produced few winners and no high-
class horses for a long time. About the only redeeming feature we could see
was that Anchora had been owned by George Edwardes, manager of the Gaiety
Theatre and producer of countless musical comedies with all those sparkling
Gaiety Girls. Despite the twinkle in the Lambton eye, this did not seem quite

enough to explain the craving to own Anchora.

"Well," said Lambton, "the explanation is fairly simple. Shortly before 1914, I told Lord Derby that his horses were becoming so delicate I could not train them properly. So I suggested introducing into the stud some fresh blood, to be selected on the basis of demonstrated toughness and soundness.

"I had seen Anchora run at two, three, four, five, six, and seven. She was very robust, and never looked sick or sorry. All courses up to twelve furlongs came alike to her, and all sorts of going from rock hard to fetlock deep seemed equally agreeable. While she had been in training six seasons and had started fifty-one times, she still looked fresh, strong, and well.

"Furthermore, she was a daughter of Love Wisely, who had stood the most severe preparation as a three-year-old for the Ascot Gold Cup (two and one-half miles in June) I ever had heard of. Since we were looking for toughness and soundness (really regardless of fashionable pedigree), here it was. We bought Anchora."

Anchora was the only one of Eryholme's twelve foals to show such remarkable toughness. She was also the only Eryholme foal sired by Love Wisely. Scapa Flow (by Chaucer), Anchora's first foal, was dropped when the dam was nine. She also was the only one of Anchora's five daughters in England to make much mark at stud. While Scapa Flow was no whirlwind on the track, she did win three of her twelve races at three. None of these were of any class and none were at a distance of less than twelve furlongs. Toward autumn, Scapa Flow showed some improvement, making Lambton think there might be more merit in her than the cold race record showed.

At stud, Scapa Flow began well in 1919 with Spithead, a chestnut gelding by John o' Gaunt (not a very remarkable sire of winners). This gelding showed some of the Anchora strain, remaining in training for six seasons and winning 5,641 pounds. He won the Chester Cup at two and one-quarter miles.

Scapa Flow's second foal, produced in 1920, was Pharos. Since the dam and granddam were plodders and the sire was a very high-class sprinter, what was to be expected from this mating? Time showed that Pharos (1) stayed better than did his sire, but was not as speedy; and (2) was speedier than his dam and grand-dam, but did not stay as well.

Lambton gave Pharos a fairly busy two-year-old season by English standards, starting him nine times. He was out first on April 25 in a maiden race at Newmarket, somewhat early for a high-class colt. Pharos won and won again before going to Royal Ascot in June, when he won the Chesham Stakes. Since

Lambton did not start him for the Coventry Stakes or the New Stakes, which carry more prestige and higher stakes than the Chesham, it seems clear that even at that stage he regarded Pharos as being somewhat below top class. Five years later Lambton started Fairway, a full brother to Pharos, in the Coventry Stakes, and he won it.

Pharos won three more races at two, but none of them were of much importance. His stamina limitations were exposed when he failed in a mile race at Newmarket. On the two-year-old Free Handicap, Pharos was put ten pounds below the top, ranking as the fourth-best colt.

When Pharos was three, Lambton wrote in *The Daily Press* that it never occurred to him to think of Pharos as a classic colt until the spring form of the other three-year-olds convinced him that the classic crop was not up to standard.

Lambton set about training Pharos for the Derby (one and one-half miles) with some reservations about his stamina. He nearly brought it off. After being in front a quarter-mile from home, Pharos was beaten by one and one-half lengths in a hard duel with Papyrus. The latter gave to jockey Steve Donoghue his third consecutive Derby.[1] Such was Donoghue's wizardry over the turns and gradients of Epsom that had the jockeys been reversed, the result also might

			Bona Vista, 1889	Bend Or / Vista
		Cyllene, 1895	Arcadia, 1887	Isonomy / Distant Shore
	Polymelus, 1902		Hampton, 1872	Lord Clifden / Lady Langden
		Maid Marian, 1886	Quiver, 1872	Toxophilite / Y. Melbourne mare
Phalaris, 1913			Springfield, 1873	St. Albans / Viridis
		Sainfoin, 1887	Sanda, 1878	Wenlock / Sandal
	Bromus, 1905		**St. Simon**, 1881	Galopin / St. Angela
		Cheery, 1892	Sunrise, 1883	Springfield / Sunray
PHAROS			Galopin, 1872	Vedette / Flying Duchess
		St. Simon, 1881	St. Angela, 1865	King Tom / Adeline
	Chaucer, 1900		Tristan, 1878	Hermit / Thrift
		Canterbury Pilgrim, 1893	Pilgrimage, 1875	The Palmer / Lady Audley
Scapa Flow, 1914			Wisdom, 1873	Blinkhoolie / Aline
		Love Wisely, 1893	Lovelorn, 1888	Philammon / Gone
	Anchora, 1905		Hazlehatch, 1885	Hermit / Hazledean
		Eryholme, 1898	Ayrsmoss, 1894	Ayrshire / Rattlewings

W.W. ROUCH & CO.

Pharos

have been different. On the other hand, Pharos never won over twelve furlongs.

Pharos next tried the Prince of Wales's Stakes at Ascot. He was unplaced, but it says much for the constitution and toughness of Pharos that Lambton was willing to start him again a couple of weeks after his desperate race for the Derby.

Pharos' best win at three was in the Royal Stakes at Newbury over ten furlongs. Perhaps the truest measure of the racing class of Pharos can be obtained, however, from his race as a three-year-old for the Cambridgeshire (a first-class handicap) over nine furlongs at Newmarket. Pharos was set to carry 119 pounds and was fourth, beaten a little over two lengths by the filly Verdict (110 pounds) with Epinard (128) second. This form would make Pharos twelve to fifteen pounds behind Epinard. As Epinard could be reckoned five to seven pounds better than a normal classic colt at that distance, this form makes Pharos about five to seven pounds below the normal classic standard.

As an historical aside, the bookmakers heaved a collective sigh of relief when Epinard barely was beaten. The ring had taken a very nasty jolt when Epinard had trotted home with a record weight for a three-year-old in the six-furlong Stewards' Cup at Goodwood. In fact, the contingent from France, owner Pierre

Wertheimer, trainer Eugene Leigh, and jockey E. Haynes, with their satellites, had begun backing Epinard at 60-1 and went right on backing him down to 3-1. There is a tale that even at that cramped price, Wertheimer backed Epinard on the day of the race with 25,000 pounds more. The British bookies were bloodied but unbowed. They appointed a committee to negotiate terms of payment, which were met in full. Much of this huge Stewards' Cup win was bet back on Epinard for the Cambridgeshire. When Epinard went under by a neck, the bookies (as usual) got their losses back. And from jockey Haynes they may have got more than that, as he was reported to have lost his life's savings. The writer saw that race and is still of the opinion that had Haynes sat still instead of swinging his whip—causing Epinard to swerve and change legs—Epinard would have won.

YEAR	AGE	STS	1ST	2ND	3RD	EARNED
1922	at 2	9	6	2	0	£ 4,960
1923	at 3	9	3	2	3	£ 3,174
1924	at 4	7	4	0	0	£ 5,895
1925	at 5	5	1	1	3	£ 1,665
Lifetime		30	14	5	6	£15,694

Things looked up for Pharos at four. He won the Liverpool Cup, the Duke of York Handicap, and the Champion Stakes, each over ten furlongs. As a result, he came to be regarded as the best horse in training at more then three years old.

The five-year-old season appeared to be unrewarding for Pharos. He won only one race, the Duke of York Handicap again, but this time he carried 128 pounds and gave away lumps of weight to his field.

Three days later, he came out for the Champion Stakes of ten furlongs, weight-for-age at Newmarket. His solitary opponent was Picaroon, a three-year-old receiving seven pounds from Pharos. Odds of 6-4 were laid on—not against—Pharos, but in a fast run race, Pharos was beaten by a half-length. On the face of it, this looked like a tremendous performance for Pharos. Picaroon had been unbeaten the previous season and generally was regarded as much the best colt of his year. His jockey, Frank Bullock, told the writer he thought Picaroon was the best colt he ever had ridden in his long career in the saddle, and that Alec Taylor, the legendary trainer at Manton, put him in the very highest class. As he had beaten both Solario (St. Leger winner) and Manna (Two Thousand Guineas and Derby winner) easily as a two-year-old, Picaroon must have been out of the ordinary.

There was, however, a catch in his form with Pharos. Picaroon had been extremely ill in the spring and had only regained part of his strength when he ran fourth to Solario in the St. Leger in early September. Considering their respective merits at two, this form was clearly wrong.

The question in October, more than a month later, was how far had Picaroon

Pharis

recovered? He looked more muscular than he had at the St. Leger and had won a couple of minor races in the interval, but was he really back at his peak of form? The answer was never known. Pharos was retired to stud and Picaroon died early the next year.

In 1926, Pharos retired to Lord Derby's Woodland Stud at Newmarket to begin a career as a stallion, which in the family pattern—following his sire Phalaris and grandsire Polymelus—proved to be clearly better than his career on the Turf. For those who are guided solely by the racing class of a colt in estimating his probable merit as a stallion, this sire line presents a problem:

Cyllene: Polymelus was much his best son at stud, but Lemberg (Derby), Cicero (Derby), and Minoru (Derby) were considerably better as racers. Perhaps even Cylgad was of higher class, but he broke down early.

Polymelus: Phalaris was much his best son at stud, but Pommern (Two Thousand Guineas, Derby, St. Leger), Humorist (Derby, died in training), and Polyphontes (Eclipse Stakes twice) were better as racers.

Phalaris: Pharos was his best son at stud, but Fairway (St. Leger), Manna (Guineas and Derby), and Colorado (Guineas) were better racers.

Pharos remained in England for three stud seasons, after which he was transferred to Normandy. He remained there until his death in 1937.

During his English stud career, Pharos sired Guineas and Derby winner Cameronian and St. Leger winner Firdaussi. The first proved an ordinary stallion, and the other was shifted around and—if recollections are correct—ended up in Hungary.

Pharos sired his most influential stock after his removal to France. They included fillies En Fraude, winner of the French Oaks; Mary Tudor, winner of the French One Thousand Guineas and the dam of good English sire Owen Tudor; The Nile, winner of the French One Thousand Guineas, and Bernina, winner of the Italian One Thousand Guineas and Oaks.

Pharos' best sons were Pharis, Phideas, and Nearco.

Pharis was unbeaten in three starts, including the Prix du Jockey-Club (French Derby) and Grand Prix de Paris. Pharis left onlookers at these races astonished over his recovery from apparently hopeless positions and the decisive ease of his victories accomplished in storming finishes.

Pharis was to have challenged the English Derby winner, Blue Peter, for the St. Leger, but the race was abandoned owing to the start of World War II.

Pharis was a very strong and somewhat coarse colt. He stood sixteen hands, two inches, and has been described in some quarters as a bull of a horse. His color was given officially as brown, but he was more nearly black.

In his first season at stud, Pharis sired good racers in Ardan and Priam II, both of whom came to the United States and failed to make much mark at stud. When the Germans invaded France in 1940, they promptly seized Pharis and removed him to Germany. When the Americans invaded Germany in 1945, Pharis again was seized, and was restored to Marcel Boussac in France.

During that interval, nearly five stud seasons had been lost, so it is not easy to assess the true merit of Pharis as a stallion. While Pharis sired a good many racers of high class, they did not breed on well, so his name is dropping out of modern pedigrees. Trainers and breeders criticized the Pharis stock (however unfairly) on two grounds: They were not sound, and they frequently "went in the wind."

Phideas won the Irish Two Thousand Guineas and Irish Derby. He ran only in Ireland, so it is difficult to assess his form accurately. He was not patronized very fully at stud, but did fairly well.

For pedigree purposes in male line, a stallion's stud career generally boils down to one colt. For Pharos, that colt was Nearco, whose worldwide fame entitles him to a separate chapter.

Pharos led the English sire list once and the French sire list twice. Since Lord Derby reserved ten seasons each year for British breeders while Pharos was standing in France, Pharos had many runners at the same time in England and France, thereby lessening his chances to lead the list in both countries.

There is no doubt that as a sire, and as a beneficent influence for soundness, constitution, and gameness, Pharos takes a high rank.

End Notes:

1. Donoghue won the Derby with Humorist in 1921, Captain Cuttle in 1922, and Papyrus in 1923. His other Derby victories were on Pommern (1915), Gay Crusader (1917), and Manna (1925).

CHAPTER NINETEEN

NEARCO

I n any ten-year span, there generally are no more than three sires in a country that have great influence on the future stud book. These are, in the French hyperbole, the *chefs-de-race*, the cornerstones on which the breed is built. Owing to their importance in the structure of the breed, a thorough examination of their backgrounds is well worthwhile.

Such a horse was Nearco.

He was bred in Italy by Federico Tesio and Marchese Mario Incisa della Rochetta, the former frequently regarded as the most influential breeder of the twentieth century. Nearco's sire was Pharos, and his dam was Nogara, who could be described as a typical, successful Tesio product. Nogara was a first-class Italian racer, winning the Italian One Thousand and Two Thousand Guineas (each at one mile). In the Tesio stud book, she was said to have had magnificent action and to be at her best between six furlongs and one mile. Physically, she was somewhat small and light.

At stud Nogara bred nine foals, including three classic winners—Nearco, Niccolo Dell'Arca, and Nervesa—plus two colts who placed in the Italian Derby—Nakamuro and Naucide. Niccolo Dell'Arca was unbeaten at three, winning the Italian Derby by twenty lengths and the Gran Premio di Milano in record time, and also winning Berlin's Grosser Preis der Reichshauptstadt. Nervesa won the Italian Oaks.

Nogara's dam, Catnip, could be regarded as an illustration of the Tesio patent on how to breed classic racehorses starting with mares, yearling fillies, or filly foals that cost next to nothing. Tesio bought Catnip at auction in England during the World War I year of 1915 for 75 guineas. She was one of the lots from the Estate of Major Eustace Loder. There was not much competition for her, as in nine starts as a two-year-old she had won 100 pounds in a mile nursery at Newcastle and she had not won at three. In addition, she was in foal to Cock-a-Hoop, who had a stud fee of 18 pounds—and was not worth it. Physically, Catnip was a weedy, unappealing specimen.

BRITISH RACEHORSE

Nearco

Tesio, however, did not mind taking weedy fillies and mares from the over-cast, chilly climate of the British Isles to the warmer climate of Italy, where there was ample sunshine. Experience had taught him that such weedy mares, in the changed environment, generally would breed stock of good frame and general development. There was the additional attraction that these weedy mares and fillies did not bring prices commensurate with their pedigrees.

Catnip was a case in point. She was by Spearmint (Epsom Derby and Grand Prix de Paris) out of Sibola (One Thousand Guineas and second in the Oaks), by The Sailor Prince (Cambridgeshire, etc.). Though Sibola ran in England, she had been bred in the United States. Her female line traced back to the Cub Mare, probably imported to New Jersey as a yearling in 1763 by James DeLancey of King's Bridge, New Jersey.[1] This mare was ranked as No. 1 among the successful American taproot mares in the *Matriarchy of the American Turf* by Miss M.F. Bayliss.

As the decades passed, this line of mares had the advantage of matings with the very best sires in America. For instance, Old Flirtilla was by Sir Archy, the greatest sire of his time (in the early nineteenth century) and, according to Sanders D. Bruce (the compiler of the early volumes of the *American Stud Book*), was mated with her own sire to produce Flirtilla. The latter became an ancestress of, classic winners Masterman (Belmont Stakes), Watervale (Preakness Stakes), and Mad Play (Belmont Stakes), as well as of Mad Hatter (Jockey Club Gold Cup twice) and Sun Beau (world-leading money winner in his time).

Another infusion of top-class blood came when imported Glencoe was mated with Miss Obstinate (a descendant of the Cub Mare) to produce Kitty Clark. The latter in turn was bred to sixteen-time leading sire Lexington and produced Travers Stakes winner Maiden. Matings of Maiden to Leamington produced champion Parole, a major winner on both sides of the Atlantic[2], and also the filly Perfection, winner of the Juvenile Stakes at Morris Park. Bred to the great French-bred stayer Mortemer (Prix de l'Empereur and Ascot Gold Cup), Perfection produced Saluda, dam of Sibola (third dam of Nearco).

How much of this glorious 150-year history of the Cub Mare family in America was known to Tesio in 1915 is uncertain. Reference books on American Thoroughbred history then were virtually unobtainable in Europe. In addition thereto, the attitude of European breeders at that time toward American

				Cyllene, 1895	Bona Vista Arcadia
		Phalaris, 1913	Polymelus, 1902		
				Maid Marian, 1886	Hampton Quiver
			Bromus, 1905	Sainfoin, 1887	Springfield Sanda
Pharos, 1920				Cheery, 1892	**St. Simon** Sunrise
			Chaucer, 1900	**St. Simon**, 1881	Galopin St. Angela
		Scapa Flow, 1914		Canterbury Pilgrim, 1893	Tristan Pilgrimage
			Anchora, 1905	Love Wisely, 1893	Wisdom Lovelorn
NEARCO				Eryholme, 1898	Hazlehatch Ayrsmoss
		Havresac II, 1915	Rabelais, 1900	**St. Simon**, 1881	Galopin St. Angela
				Satirical, 1891	Satiety Chaff
			Hors Concours, 1906	Ajax, 1901	Flying Fox Amie
Nogara, 1928				Simona, 1893	**St. Simon** Flying Footstep
		Catnip, 1910	Spearmint, 1903	Carbine, 1885	Musket Mersey
				Maid of the Mint, 1897	Minting Warble
			Sibola, 1896	The Sailor Prince, 1880	Albert Victor Hermita
				Saluda, 1883	Mortemer Perfection

Dante

Thoroughbreds was much like W.S. Gilbert's description of British peers' attitude toward mere commoners, one of "self-contained dignity combined with airy condescension."

Possibly, Tesio was much more influenced by Catnip's being the daughter of a first-class race mare, Sibola. (Tesio also bought for 210 guineas as a yearling Duccia di Buoninsegna, granddaughter of the extraordinary race mare Pretty Polly, and from her he bred a host of classic winners.)[3]

Tesio left Catnip in England for a time, and there her first foal in his ownership, by Cock-a-Hoop, died, and she then was barren to Lemberg. Her next foal, born in 1918, was the filly Nera di Bicci, by Tracery. According to Tesio's notes, this filly did not come to her full form until the autumn of her three-year-old season, when she seemed unbeatable at any distance: "Her speed was her great forte." Nera di Bicci often has been regarded as the best filly ever produced by Tesio's Dormello operations.

Between 1918 and 1928, when Nogara was foaled, Catnip bred only one useful animal, Nesiotes, by Hurry On, a good winner at three, four, and five who did well as a sire in Italy.

An interesting aspect of Nearco's pedigree is the inbreeding on each side. On the sire's side, one of Pharos' granddams (Bromus) is inbred to Springfield with one free generation; on the other side, the dam's sire, Havresac II, is inbred to St.

Simon with one free generation and has additional inbreeding to St. Simon's sire, Galopin.

The same pattern of crossing inbred strains—but different strains—can be found in the pedigree of Triple Crown winner Bahram. On his sire's side, a great-grandparent, White Eagle, is inbred to Isonomy with one free generation; on Bahram's dam's side, the granddam (Garron Lass) is inbred to St. Simon with one free generation.

This pattern is analogous to the hybrid vigor obtained by crossing separate, inbred strains of corn directly, and in Nearco and Bahram the pattern produced two unbeaten—and really unextended—horses that possibly were the two best racers bred in Europe from 1900 to 1950.

Nearco's racing career calls for comparatively little comment. As a two-year-old, he was out seven times and won all his races, including Italy's principal events for the age—the Criterium Nazionale, Gran Criterium, Premio Tevere, and Premio Chiusura.

As a three-year-old, he won the Premio Parioli (Italian Two Thousand Guineas) and two other races, then in succession won the Gran Premio del Re (one and a half-mile Italian Derby) by a distance, the Gran Premio dell'Impero (one and a half miles) by six lengths, and the Gran Premio di Milano (one and seven-eighths miles) by three lengths.

Tesio must have believed that this last race had not taken much out of Nearco, as he shipped him from Milan to Paris and started him in the fifteen-furlong Grand Prix de Paris only six days later, and this despite Tesio's belief that Nearco was not a true stayer.

The field for the Grand Prix was impressive, to say the least. Among the starters were Bois Roussel (Epsom Derby), Cillas (French Derby), Feerie (French One Thousand Guineas and Oaks), Ad Astra (second French Oaks), Canot (second French Derby), and Nearco. Nearco came right away from his field inside the last furlong to win under a handride by one and a half lengths. Canot was second, and Bois

YEAR	AGE	STS	1ST	2ND	3RD	EARNED
1937	at 2	7	7	0	0	£ 2,477
1938	at 3	7	7	0	0	£15,198
Lifetime		**14**	**14**	**0**	**0**	**£17,675**

Roussel was third, a length farther back. Gordon Richards, rider of Bois Roussel, stated that his mount had been balked and felt that with a clear run he would have won. Richards was, and is, a very fair-minded man, so some weight should attach to his opinion, but having seen an excellent moving picture of the race at the time, the writer was very much impressed with the apparently enormous superiority of

Sayajirao winning the 1947 St. Leger

Nearco over his competitors that day. The Grand Prix completed his record of fourteen victories in fourteen starts.

Photographs of Nearco in training show him to have been somewhat on the leg and give a suggestion that he was a trifle narrow. However, when the writer saw him at stud, after the horse had let down, Nearco was a stallion of very high quality, standing just over 16 hands and really impossible to fault in conformation. The elasticity or fluidity of his movements was remarkable, suggesting the potential for very quick acceleration, very much like the big cats—cheetahs, leopards, etc. (St. Simon was described by his stud groom as having this same fluidity of movement.)

Nearco's success at stud was almost as great as his success on the Turf. Immediately after the Grand Prix, Nearco was sold to English bookmaker Martin Benson (trade name Douglas Stuart; motto "Duggie never owes"), who retired him to the Beech House Stud at Newmarket. The price was 60,000 pounds, then a record.

Nearco was twice champion sire and was among the ten leading sires for fifteen consecutive years. The only stallion in England to compare with him for consistency in the twentieth century to date has been Hyperion, who was champion stallion six times, and among the ten leading sires sixteen times.

Perhaps Blandford (four Derby winners in eight years), though, was as good a stallion as Nearco.

The average distance of the races won by Nearco's offspring was about nine and a half furlongs, which is almost the ideal distance capacity for a sire of classic winners. Nearco must have imparted a high degree of nervous energy to his stock, and some of the highly strung ones, such as Nasrullah and Masaka, were by no means easy to train.

Based on racing class (rather than money won, owing to the small purses during World War II), the best individuals sired by Nearco were—

Colts: Dante (Derby), Nimbus (Two Thousand Guineas and Derby), Nasrullah (Coventry Stakes and Champion Stakes), Sayajirao (St. Leger), and Hafiz II (Champion Stakes).

Fillies: Masaka (English and Irish Oaks), Neasham Belle (Oaks), Noory (Irish Oaks), and Neolight (Coronation Stakes).

Among his sons, Nasrullah, Royal Charger, and Canadian champion Nearctic have accounted for much of Nearco's enormous influence in North American racing and breeding. Nasrullah's sons included eight-time leading American sire Bold Ruler, Royal Charger's included Turn-to (sire of leading sire Hail to Reason), and Nearctic's included leading sire Northern Dancer.

Nearco died at Beech House Stud at the age of twenty-two in June of 1957.

The Tesio stud book at Dormello contains the following note on Nearco: "Beautifully balanced, of perfect size and great quality. Won all his 14 races as soon as he was asked. Not a true stayer, though he won up to 3,000 meters, i.e. 1 7/8 miles (Gran Premio di Milano and Grand Prix de Paris). He won these longer races by his superb class and brilliant speed."

End Notes:

1. In an article on Nearco for *Horse and Horsemen*, noted Turf writer Salvator (John Hervey) states that James DeLancey imported the Cub Mare as a three-year-old in 1765 and after landing in Baltimore, she was sent to New York, where he had established his 230-acre Bouwerie Farm in what is now the very heart of New York City.

2. As a four-year-old, Parole, owned by Pierre Lorillard, upset Tom Ochiltree and Ten Broeck, the leading handicap horses in the country, in the Baltimore Special. As a six-year-old Parole was sent to England, where he won the City and Suburban Handicap, Newmarket Handicap, and Epsom Gold Cup.

3. Duccia di Buoninsegna won the Premio Regina Elena and the Gran Premio d'Italia. As a broodmare, she produced the filly Delleana (Clarissimus), who won

the Premio Regina Elena, Premio Parioli, and the Gran Premio d'Italia, among other races. She, in turn, produced champion Donatello (Blenheim II), who won the 1937 Derby Italiano, Gran Premio d'Italia, etc., as well as his three-parts sister Donatella (Mahmoud), 1941 champion two-year-old filly in Italy.

CHAPTER TWENTY

NASRULLAH

U nlike the short and simple annals of the poor, Nasrullah's racing career was not short and by no means simple. In fact, his true racing ability was extremely difficult to diagnose accurately, for he failed to win a classic and only placed third in one of them. Yet Phil Bull, the best of modern handicappers on the British Turf, wrote of Nasrullah in *Best Horses of 1943* at the end of his three-year-old season: "Last year, I regarded Nasrullah as head and shoulders above the other colts of his age. I gave him a long and rather enthusiastic write up, and I fear that, in spite of his having failed in each of his classic ventures, in spite of his bad temper, his mulish antics, in spite of his exasperating unwillingness to do the job, etc., etc., I fear that I am going to give him another write up. I know he doesn't deserve it, but I can't help it.

"The rumors of Nasrullah's temperamental traits ... proved to have only too painful a basis in fact ... His display on the way down to the post for the Chatteris Stakes was a disgrace. He refused to leave the paddock ... He refused to do anything except behave like a spoilt child ... Could the catcalls and cries of derision which greeted this un-Thoroughbred-like behavior have been heard by Nearco (his sire) at the Beech House Stud, and could their origin have been explained to him, it might have had a serious effect on his fertility."

As a two-year-old, racing during a very dark period of the war, Nasrullah was put through a program mapped out for a very high-class colt. Trainer Frank Butters readied the Aga Khan's homebred colt for a debut on June 12, in the Wilburton Stakes at Newmarket. The colt's reputation preceded him, and he started at odds of 11-8 in a field of eight. He finished third, beaten by one and a half lengths by Nearly, a Nearco filly.

That performance must have been regarded as satisfactory, for on June 30 Nasrullah again was favored, at 7-4, for the important Coventry Stakes at five furlongs. There were seven starters, four of which had won their last previous races and two of which had been placed. Nasrullah won, beating the following year's

Derby winner, Straight Deal, by one and a half lengths.

A month later, on July 28, Nasrullah came out for the six-furlong Great Bradley Stakes at Newmarket and had only one modest opponent in Lord Derby's Feriel. Although Nasrullah was conceding eleven pounds, he was odds-on and won as he liked by four lengths.

On August 26, Nasrullah was in a field of eight for the Middle Park Stakes at six furlongs—the traditional two-year-old Derby. Nasrullah was odds-on again, although he was meeting Lord Rosebery's very high-class and very game filly, Ribbon. Nasrullah went under by a neck to Ribbon but beat his former conqueror Nearly by three-quarters of a length, with Straight Deal unplaced.

The next year, Ribbon was the target of unrelenting fury from all the demons of bad luck. She was placed in the One Thousand Guineas, Oaks, and St. Leger—despite illness, falling on the way to the course, being shut off, and being bumped out of a fair chance. So, in finishing second to Ribbon, Nasrullah had not lowered his colors to any racing weakling.

When Nasrullah was a three-year-old, his temperamental vagaries came into full flower. While he won three of his six races, it is remarkable that he did even that well. In the one-mile Chatteris Stakes, against modest opposition, Nasrullah stopped racing shortly after he struck the front, and champion rider Gordon Richards also stopped riding. Nasrullah won, but coasted past the winning post. In his next race, the Two Thousand Guineas, blinkers were tried on him. This change in equipment made it easier to coax him to the starting gate, but produced no change in the way he ran. When Nasrullah struck the front in the dip, an eighth-mile from home, he stopped racing, and despite the vigorous efforts of Richards, he pulled himself up to finish fourth. Phil Bull complained that Nasrullah must have heard about the place bet of 500 pounds to 400 pounds he had on him and finished fourth just to spite him.

In the Derby, much the same thing happened. Nasrullah went to the front in ample time to go on and win his race, but once in the lead, he again dropped his bit and was outraced by Straight Deal and his stable companion Umiddad in a fairly close finish.

Prior to the St. Leger, Nasrullah was given an easy race in the one and a quarter-mile Cavenham Stakes, which he won at odds of 1-4 in the same sluggish fashion as he had won the Chatteris Stakes. In the St. Leger, however, Nasrullah was ridden very tenderly by Michael Beary, a very fine jockey, but never did strike the front. He probably failed for lack of stamina over the one and three-quarters-mile distance.

Nasrullah's last race was the Champion Stakes, ten furlongs at Newmarket, which has no bend. Here Richards, having learned his lesson the hard way in previous races, held up Nasrullah to the last moment, and when Nasrullah struck the front, there was the winning post. Nasrullah beat Kingsway (winner of the Two Thousand Guineas) by a length, though he again threw up his head at the finish.

The overall merits of Nasrullah as a racehorse can be viewed from the Free Handicaps, framed by the Jockey Club's handicapper, for two- and three-year-olds.

In the two-year-old Free Handicap for 1942, Nasrullah was rated as the best colt at 132 pounds, but Lady Sybil, a filly by Nearco, was assigned 133 pounds, making her four pounds superior to Nasrullah (taking account of the normal sex allowance). V.R. Orchard, summarizing the year's racing in the 1942 *Bloodstock Breeders' Review*, stated that he did not think this high assessment of Nasrullah was justified by his actual racing record. Phil Bull, on the contrary, considered that Nasrullah was underestimated. (Phil Bull has become a cordial friend of the present writer, and in the early days of our acquaintance expressed the vigorous opinion that the present writer did not know enough mathematics to be a passable handicapper—a penetrating observation which prompted a lofty regard for the intellectual acumen of Phil Bull. We feel cowed, therefore, into supporting the

				Cyllene
Nearco, 1935	Pharos, 1920	Phalaris, 1913	Polymelus, 1902	Maid Marian
			Bromus, 1905	Sainfoin
				Cheery
		Scapa Flow, 1914	Chaucer, 1900	St. Simon
				Canterbury Pilgrim
			Anchora, 1905	Love Wisely
				Eryholme
	Nogara, 1928	Havresac II, 1915	Rabelais, 1900	St. Simon
				Satirical
			Hors-Concours, 1906	Ajax
				Simona
		Catnip, 1910	Spearmint, 1903	Carbine
				Maid of the Mint
			Sibola, 1896	The Sailor Prince
				Saluda
Mumtaz Begum, 1932	Blenheim II, 1927	Blandford, 1919	Swynford, 1907	John o' Gaunt
				Canterbury Pilgrim
			Blanche, 1912	White Eagle
				Black Cherry
		Malva, 1919	Charles O'Malley, 1907	Desmond
				Goody Two Shoes
			Wild Arum, 1911	Robert le Diable
				Marliacea
	Mumtaz Mahal, 1921	The Tetrarch, 1911	Roi Herode, 1904	Le Samaritain
				Roxelane
			Vahren, 1897	Bona Vista
				Castania
		Lady Josephine, 1912	Sundridge, 1898	Amphion
				Sierra
			Americus Girl, 1905	Americus
				Palotta

(NASRULLAH is indicated at the left center, as the offspring of Nearco, 1935 and Mumtaz Begum, 1932.)

Nasrullah

enthusiastic views of Mr. Bull as to the racing abilities of Nasrullah.)

A year later on the three-year-old Free Handicap, Nasrullah again received 132 pounds, one pound less than did Straight Deal, and the same as Herringbone (One Thousand and St. Leger) and Ribbon. Again, taking account of the normal sex allowance, Nasrullah was rated three pounds inferior to the two fillies. Once more, waving his red beard in uncompromising defiance, Phil Bull would dissent.

(Bull, of course, was not blind to Nasrullah's faults. Accompanying his biting commentary in *Best Horses of 1943* were photographs of Nasrullah in the pre-Derby post parade, winning the Chatteris Stakes, and scrimmaging with Richards on the way to the post. They were captioned, "Nasrullah pretending to be a gentleman"; "Nasrullah condescends to pass the post in front in the Chatteris Stakes"; and "Nasrullah impersonating a mule.")

Taking into account the mixed reactions to Nasrullah, it seems fairly clear that he was a high-class racehorse but was not absolutely overpowering as was his sire, Nearco, and also Pharis—both sons of Pharos.

The question sometimes has been asked whether the British method of training colts to follow a sedate lead horse, in order to get them to settle down and stop pulling while at work, may not in some cases have been taken too far. These colts may have become so accustomed to following other horses that they become acutely uncomfortable when asked to go to the front on their own, and hence sometimes pull themselves up. Nasrullah is by no means the only British-trained colt that showed this trait. On the other hand, the frequent American method of training purely for speed—as fast as possible and as far as possible—results in making many racers so speed crazy that they can only compete with success in sprints.

YEAR	AGE	STS	1ST	2ND	3RD	EARNED
1942	at 2	4	2	1	1	£1,665
1943	at 3	6	3	0	0	£1,682
Lifetime		10	5	1	1	£3,347

In the case of Nasrullah, his trainer did not even have the consolation of seeing the former jockey for the Aga Khan, (Cheeky) Charley Smirke, humiliated by the colt's operatic displays of temperament. Butters constantly was at daggers drawn with Smirke over the stable trials. Smirke liked to ride in them so that by extending the horses fully he had full information needed for his and Prince Aly Khan's betting programs. Since Butters did not want the horses overdone in their trials, trainer and jockey were at war.

When World War II broke out, Smirke entered the Army and took part in the Italian campaign. At that time, a practical joker came up to Frank Butters on Newmarket Heath and said: "Have you heard that Charley Smirke has been decorated with the Victoria Cross?"

"Really?" said the dignified Butters. "What was he decorated for?"

"Charley stopped a German tank."

"I am not surprised," observed Butters. "When he was riding for me, he could stop anything!"

Physically, Nasrullah was a well-grown (16 hands, 1 1/2 inches), strong, and sound colt. He was, in fact, bigger and more powerful than any of his close-up ancestors. Nasrullah's pedigree was typical of the best operations in the Aga Khan's stud. His sire was Nearco, one of the two best sires in the mid-twentieth century in England—the other being Hyperion. Nasrullah's dam was Mumtaz Begum, a winner of a maiden race and one other small race as a two-year-old in England. Since five furlongs appeared to be her limit, she was put to stud as a three-year-old. She was barren her first season, and then produced a filly by Solario named Sun Princess. Sun Princess failed to demonstrate publicly any racing ability, but became the dam of Royal Charger, a very successful sire. There followed in successive years two fillies from Mumtaz Begum by the Aga Khan's stallion Dastur. The fourth foal, and first colt, was Nasrullah.

Jaipur

Mumtaz Begum was sired by Blenheim II, who had been bought as a yearling by the Aga Khan and who became a top-class two-year-old and then gave the Aga Khan his first Derby victory. The Derby proved to be Blenheim II's last start, as he broke down soon afterwards. His trainer, Dick Dawson, thought that this was a great pity as in his opinion, Blenheim II stayed so well that he might have made a great name for himself. Blenheim II suffered from somewhat upright pasterns, but was not nearly as faulty in this respect as was his sire, Blandford.

Mumtaz Begum's dam was the famous flying gray filly Mumtaz Mahal, generally regarded as the fastest two-year-old seen in England up to that time (with the possible exception of her own sire, The Tetrarch). This line of mares had been a prime source of speed since the days of Americus Girl, the granddam of Mumtaz Mahal. Americus Girl was a daughter of Americus, who was imported into England by Richard (Boss) Croker, the retired chieftain of Tammany Hall whose reputation was better proof against the slings and arrows of outrageous investigation in England than it was in New York. British breeders took a very dim view of Americus, and in a sense they were justified, for he sired only one animal that made any impact on the *General Stud Book*, that being Americus Girl. The line of mares descending from her, however, has become possibly the strongest in the British Isles.

Americus Girl, herself a high-class sprinter, was bred in 1911 to Sundridge, the best sprinter of his time, and the following year she produced a fast filly in Lady Josephine. In addition to Mumtaz Mahal, Lady Josephine, having been bred to Son-in-Law, produced Lady Juror, who could stay fourteen furlongs but did not pass the trait on. Her son, Fair Trial, was a miler, who sired three Guineas winners, and her grandson, Tudor Minstrel, was an outstanding miler.

Nasrullah really stayed as well as anything from that female line. This is somewhat surprising as Blenheim II supplied the only stout blood in the close removes of Nasrullah's pedigree. However, it was not remarkable that Nasrullah should make a good sire. He came from about the best sire line in England, and also from the fastest female line, one as prolific as any for the production of high-class winners. Rustom Mahal, another daughter of Mumtaz Mahal, produced Abernant, possibly the best sprinter since World War II in England and an excellent sire of sprinters.

The main question about Nasrullah as a sire concerned the possible transmission of his own mulish temperament. The fact is that many horses with wayward or very high-strung temperaments have made good sires. Among these are St. Simon, Barcaldine, Bruleur, Ksar, Tourbillon, Hastings, Fair Play. Such stallions frequently prove to be admirable sires if crossed with mares with quiet, sound nervous systems.

Nasrullah first stood at the Barton Grange Stud in Suffolk, and in 1944 was sold to Joseph McGrath and sent to Ireland. He was resold in late 1949 to a syndicate headed by A.B. (Bull) Hancock Jr. and spent the rest of his life at Hancock's Claiborne Farm near Paris, Kentucky. Nasrullah died in 1959 at the age of nineteen.

Nasrullah was one of the few sires to have led the list in two countries. He was the leading sire in England in 1951 and was the leader in the United States five times, in 1955, 1956, 1959, 1960, and 1962. He sired 105 stakes winners from 425 named foals, a percentage of 25. Bold Ruler [who sired eighty-two stakes winners] surpassed Nasrullah in respect to leading the sire list, having topped America's stallions eight times.

The best of Nasrullah's fillies included Belle of All (One Thousand Guineas) and Musidora (Oaks and Guineas), in England, and champion two-year-old fillies Nasrina and Leallah, plus Kentucky Oaks winner Bug Brush, in the United States.

His best sons in Europe included Never Say Die (Derby and St. Leger), Nearula (Two Thousand Guineas), Nathoo (Irish Derby), Grey Sovereign (top sprinter), and Nasram (King George VI and Queen Elizabeth Stakes).

In the United States his most distinguished sons included Noor (champion handicapper), Nashua (Preakness and Belmont, Horse of the Year), Bold Ruler (Preakness, Horse of the Year), Bald Eagle (Washington, D.C., International twice, champion handicapper), Jaipur (Belmont, champion three-year-old), Never Bend (champion two-year-old and sire of Mill Reef). He also sired One-Eyed King, Red God, Fleet Nasrullah, Nadir, and On-and-On.

For those who are interested in family patterns, and particularly the limits to which the nervous systems can be strained, the following observations seem in order:

Two offspring of Nearco that had great racing ability but whose temperaments were so difficult that their racing careers were seriously handicapped were (1) Nasrullah, out of a mare by Blenheim II, whose stock was known to be hot and difficult (i.e., Whirlaway); (2) Masaka, out of a mare by Mahmoud (by Blenheim II).

The contrary influence, a calming nervous system crossed with the over-tense blood of Nasrullah can be seen in the following examples of the two best grandsons of Nasrullah to date: (1) Mill Reef, winner of the English Derby and the Prix de l'Arc de Triomphe, is by Never Bend (a Nasrullah horse who was a champion at two but did not win a classic, although he placed in the Kentucky Derby), and he is from Milan Mill, she by Princequillo; the latter is a good source of stamina and a calm nervous system; (2) Secretariat, winner of the Triple Crown, is by Bold Ruler (a Nasrullah horse who excelled at middle distances) and also from a Princequillo mare, Somethingroyal.

CHAPTER TWENTY-ONE

NASHUA

Wivve the master of Belair Stud in Maryland and long-
time chairman of The Jockey Club in New York, was associated for
many years with A.B. Hancock's Claiborne Stud near Paris, Kentucky.
The Belair mares were boarded at Claiborne and the syndicate-owned stallions in
which Woodward was a shareholder also were quartered there. Woodward's foals,
after weaning, were shipped to Belair, where they remained until going into training as yearlings. Woodward told the present writer he was convinced that the soft
air at Belair, with its proximity to Chesapeake Bay, had a soothing effect on the
nervous systems of growing Thoroughbreds that spent a year there.

The modern history of the Belair Stud began when Woodward bought a number of mares in France during the early part of World War I, when the Germans
were threatening Paris. Good results had followed his purchase of a number of
mares from Edmond Blanc's Haras de Jardy. From one of these families had come
his Omaha (Triple Crown), Flares (Ascot Gold Cup), and Johnstown (Kentucky
Derby and Belmont), plus Jacola (champion filly), Phalanx (Belmont and Jockey
Club Gold Cup), and Gallorette (champion mare).

Woodward was very partial to the French Sardanapale (French Derby and
Grand Prix de Paris) and bought a number of his daughters. Among these
were Sekhmet (1929), who did not win but foaled Segula (1942), she by the
Woodward sire Johnstown. Segula won nine races at three and four, was third in
the Coaching Club American Oaks, and earned $35,015.

While this was not one of the more successful female lines in the Belair Stud,
Segula in 1952 produced Nashua, the best of the brilliant first crop sired by
Nasrullah after his arrival in the United States. With 20-20 hindsight, it can be
seen that this was a judicious mating. Nasrullah needed strains with good nervous
systems and some additional stamina. Segula supplied these needs and also some
additional coarseness and strength to complement Nasrullah's refined pedigree.
Segula's sire, Johnstown, was a very strong, coarse horse, and Nashua inherited a

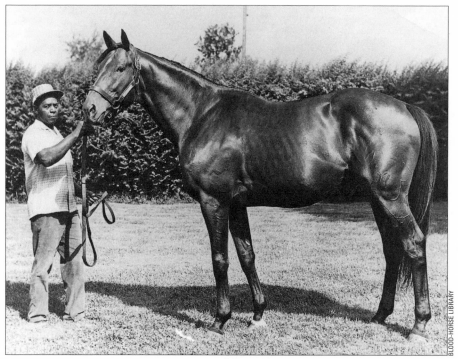

Nashua

fair share of this size and strength. In fact, Nashua may have been the strongest, most powerful three-year-old seen on the American Turf since Man o' War, thirty-five years before. At the time he was retired to stud, Nashua's measurements were taken as height, 16.2 1/4 hands; girth, 73 1/4 inches; weight, 1,090 pounds.

Woodward died in 1953, when Nashua was a yearling, and the colt passed to his son William Woodward Jr., who decided to race only in the United States, instead of shipping some of the homebreds to England as his father had. Nashua had been scheduled to race abroad, but when his breeder died the colt was sent with the other Belair yearlings to trainer Sunny Jim Fitzsimmons in New York.

Nashua won six of his eight starts and was second twice as a two-year-old. Trainer Fitzsimmons declared that Nashua was the best two-year-old he had handled since Dice, some thirty years before. In the Juvenile Stakes in May, Summer Tan conceded five pounds and ran Nashua to a half-length. A week later, Nashua was second by a neck to Royal Note in the Cherry Hill Stakes. Under the encouragement of a tap from the whip, Nashua next scored by about two lengths from moderate opposition in the Grand Union Hotel Stakes, then in the important Hopeful Stakes, at level weights, Nashua beat Summer Tan by a neck. Positions were reversed in the six and a half-furlong Cowdin Stakes, Summer Tan winning by one and a half lengths from Nashua. Nashua then won a Futurity prep in 1:08 1/5, equaling the track record for six furlongs down Belmont Park's Widener Chute. In the Futurity itself, Nashua edged Summer Tan on one side and Royal Coinage on the other.

Sometimes Nashua lugged in, and frequently it was necessary for jockey Eddie Arcaro to resort to the whip to drive him to victory. Taken as a whole and considering his manner of running, Nashua's was the record of a very high-class two-year-old but not a great two-year-old. At any rate, New York handicapper F.E. (Jimmy) Kilroe was of that opinion, for he assigned Summer Tan 128 pounds and Nashua 127 on the Experimental Free Handicap. (Summer Tan had won the Garden State Stakes after Nashua was put by for the year.)

Nashua's three-year-old campaign began in Florida, where the first stakes race was the one and one-eighth-mile Flamingo. Under the whip and bearing out, Nashua won by one and a half lengths from Saratoga, a high-class colt who would chase him through much of the first half of the year. Arcaro said that Nashua "was fooling around." In the one and one-eighth-mile Florida Derby in mud, Nashua scraped home by a neck over longshot Blue Lem.

				Polymelus
			Phalaris, 1913	Bromus
		Pharos, 1920	Scapa Flow, 1914	Chaucer
	Nearco, 1935			Anchora
			Havresac II, 1915	Rabelais
		Nogara, 1928		Hors-Concours
Nasrullah, 1940			Catnip, 1910	Spearmint
				Sibola
			Blandford, 1919	Swynford
		Blenheim II, 1927		Blanche
			Malva, 1919	Charles O'Malley
	Mumtaz Begum, 1932			Wild Arum
			The Tetrarch, 1911	Roi Herode
NASHUA		Mumtaz Mahal, 1921		Vahren
			Lady Josephine, 1912	Sundridge
				Americus Girl
			St. James, 1921	Ambassador IV
		Jamestown, 1928		Bobolink II
			Mlle Dazie, 1917	Fair Play
	Johnstown, 1936			Toggery
			Sir Gallahad III, 1920	Teddy
		La France, 1928		Plucky Liege
Segula, 1942			Flambette, 1918	Durbar II
				La Flambee
			Prestige, 1903	Le Pompon
		Sardanapale, 1911		Orgueilleuse
			Gemma, 1903	Florizel II
	Sekhmet, 1929			Agnostic
			Sans Souci, 1904	Le Roi Soleil
		Prosopopee, 1916		Sanctimony
			Peroraison, 1904	Tarporley
				Conclusion

Back in New York, Nashua met old rival Summer Tan in the Wood Memorial. Summer Tan, who had made a successful three-year-old debut in a prep, led most of the way and appeared to have Nashua measured, until the other colt surged ahead in the final strides. The last furlong of the one and one-eighth-mile race required 14 seconds, so at that stage some observers felt neither colt was particularly impressive.

In the Kentucky Derby on May 7, Nashua met Swaps, a new rival from California, and Nashua knew he had been to the races: Swaps took the lead soon after the start and refused to come back. Nashua got to within a half-length of him, but he could not sustain his challenge and Swaps won by one and a half lengths in 2:01 4/5 for one and a quarter miles.

YEAR	AGE	STS	1ST	2ND	3RD	EARNED
1954	at 2	8	6	2	0	$ 192,865
1955	at 3	12	10	1	1	$ 752,550
1956	at 4	10	6	1	0	$ 343,150
Lifetime		30	22	4	1	$1,288,565

Over a fast track at Pimlico, Nashua took the one and three-sixteenths-mile Preakness by a length from Saratoga in track-record time of 1:54 3/5, and back in New York, he won the one and a half-mile Belmont by nine lengths in 2:29.

After winning the ten-furlong Dwyer Stakes by five lengths from Saratoga, Nashua went to Chicago for the one-mile Arlington Classic. For that race, he worked five furlongs in :56 3/5, which was impressive inasmuch as the world record over a level track was :57 at that time. The Classic, though, was close. Giving Traffic Judge six pounds, Nashua won by a half-length in 1:35 1/5.

A match race with Swaps at one and a quarter miles was arranged for August 31. As things turned out, it was not much of a match. Swaps had a sore spot in the sole of his right front foot which had given trouble earlier in the year and which became inflamed the day before the race. In the race itself, Nashua always was in front and won easily by six and a half lengths. Since Swaps, who had been breaking track records with gay abandon, took nearly 55 seconds to run the last half-mile, Joe Estes remarked in *American Race Horses* that the only thing the race proved was, "Nashua with four good feet was much better than Swaps with three."

Returning to New York, Nashua started for the one and one-eighth-mile Sysonby Stakes on a sloppy track. In a brilliant five-horse field—the others being older horses—High Gun was seven lengths back after a quarter-mile. The first three quarters were run in 1:10 1/5 as Nashua battled Helioscope and Jet Action, with the result that High Gun came on to win. Nashua was worse than second for the first time. He finished third, about two lengths away. How often has this pat-

Diplomat Way winning the 1967 Blue Grass Stakes

tern repeated? A very fast pace aids an early laggard in coming along to take it all. Whatever explanation we give, the fact remains that the first time Nashua faced older horses, he failed.

Three weeks later, under similar track conditions but against less-distinguished company, Nashua won the two-mile Jockey Club Gold Cup by five lengths.

Following the death of William Woodward Jr. soon after the Gold Cup, Nashua was sold by sealed bids for $1,251,200 to a syndicate headed by Leslie Combs II. It made him the highest-priced horse in history to that time.

Nashua remained in training as a four-year-old with Fitzsimmons. His first race was for the one and a quarter-mile Widener Handicap in Florida. Against a crack field, Nashua (127 pounds) won by a head from Social Outcast (121), with Sailor (119) third. Weighted at 129 pounds, Nashua then finished only fifth in the one and a quarter-mile Gulfstream Park Handicap, won by Sailor (119).

Then in succession, Nashua won the Grey Lag (128 pounds) and Camden handicaps (129), but in the one-mile Metropolitan Handicap under 130 pounds he failed by less than a length. He was fourth, giving nineteen pounds to [winner] Midafternoon. Under the same impost, Nashua then was seventh in the seven-furlong Carter Handicap.

The next great handicap was the one and a quarter-mile Suburban; Nashua

Gold Digger

BLOOD-HORSE LIBRARY

(128) bounced back, conceding seventeen pounds to Dedicate and winning by more than a length. The Monmouth Handicap was easy for Nashua (129) in the mud. The result of this was to draw an assignment of 132 pounds for the Brooklyn Handicap, which was refused. For the Atlantic City Handicap, Nashua drew 129 pounds while Swaps and Europe's great Ribot each drew 130 pounds, but Nashua came down with colic and did not start. The two other champions never were intended starters.

In the weight-for-age Woodward Stakes in September, another fast Nasrullah colt, Mister Gus, beat Nashua two and a half lengths on a good track, which Nashua was thought to dislike.

Nashua's last race was for the two-mile Jockey Club Gold Cup. He showed there was nothing wrong with him by winning in 3:20 2/5, lowering the track and American record by two-fifths of a second.

How are we to assess Nashua's racing class? First, he was very sound from start to finish of his career, he stood hard drives very well, and he had an excellent constitution. He recorded some striking times, and he stayed well. Against this, he failed each time he carried 130 pounds, although he ran several of his best races under 128 and 129 pounds. He also failed to give Sailor, a high-class colt, ten pounds, but he had given him eight pounds earlier and defeated him.

Nashua never carried more than 130 pounds in the tradition of Exterminator, Grey Lag, and Discovery, all of whom won with 135 pounds or more. Atlantic City's handicapper put him one pound behind both Swaps and Ribot, and there is some doubt if he was better than Summer Tan when that colt was at his best.

All these factors, taken together, seem to put Nashua well into first class, but not in the super class of very great racers.

As a sire, Nashua was successful but not brilliant. Over a seven-year period from 1964 through 1970, Nashua was in the group of top ten leading sires six times. He was second in 1964 and fourth in 1970.

Unlike most sires, Nashua sent out better fillies than colts. His daughters include Shuvee, the champion distaff earner and 1969 Filly Triple Crown (Acorn, Mother Goose, Coaching Club American Oaks) winner who duplicated her sire's feat of winning back-to-back runnings of the Jockey Club Gold Cup. He also sired two other CCA Oaks winners, Marshua and Bramalea, the latter dam of Epsom Derby winner Roberto.

Nashua stood at Combs' Spendthrift Farm near Lexington from his retirement in the fall of 1956.[1] He died in 1982 at age thirty.

End Notes:

1. Nashua sired seventy-seven stakes winners (12 percent) from 649 named foals. His best racing son was probably 1967 Blue Grass Stakes winner Diplomat Way, who later became a leading broodmare sire through grandson Skip Away.

Nashua's own legacy is as a broodmare sire. Through April 2006, he was represented by 124 stakes winners as a broodmare sire. Thanks to Roberto, in 1972 Nashua was second leading broodmare sire in England. He also is the broodmare sire of Mr. Prospector, through daughter Gold Digger.

CHAPTER TWENTY-TWO

BOLD RULER

Bold Ruler was foaled April 6, 1954, as the fourth produce of Miss Disco. Like all of Mrs. Henry Carnegie Phipps' Wheatley Stable colts, he was trained by James E. Fitzsimmons, and he began his racing career in New York. During April, May, and June, as a two-year-old, he ran five times without defeat.

His first stakes race was the Youthful on May 2, 1956, which he won by three and a half lengths. Then on June 6, he took the Juvenile Stakes by a length in time only one-fifth of a second slower than the track record. In that race, Bold Ruler swerved sharply when the gates opened and strained his back muscles, curtailing any further racing until the autumn.

He had two races leading up to the Futurity. In the first one, Bold Ruler struck his head against the gate at the start, bled from the mouth, and finished second. He won the next race. In the Futurity, Bold Ruler was 5-4 and won by two and a quarter lengths from Greek Game in the third-fastest time recorded for the six and a half-furlong race.

The colt's two remaining races of the year were anticlimactic. In the one and one-sixteenth-mile Garden State Stakes, he ran onto the heels of the pacemaker and dropped right out of it. In the one and one-sixteenth-mile Remsen, he got off to a poor start, was forced to the outside on the first turn, and would not make any further effort.

Bold Ruler had won seven of his ten starts and had been second once, but Garden State winner Barbizon was named champion of the division.

As a three-year-old, Bold Ruler came out on January 30 for the seven-furlong Bahamas Stakes and won by four and a half lengths in 1:22, equaling the track record while conceding Gen. Duke twelve pounds. In the one and one-eighth-mile Everglades Stakes, he again conceded twelve pounds to Gen. Duke and failed by a head, but in the one and one-eighth-mile Flamingo Stakes the weights were level and he beat Gen. Duke a neck in 1:47, a new track record.

In the Florida Derby on March 30, also at one and one-eighth miles, Bold Ruler again carried level weights of 122 pounds with Gen. Duke. Bold Ruler, Gen. Duke, and Iron Liege all were in line at the eighth-pole after a mile in 1:34 3/5, but Gen. Duke went on to win by one and a half lengths from Bold Ruler. The time of 1:46 4/5 equaled the world record.

At that stage, there was not much to choose between Bold Ruler and Gen. Duke, but an accident removed Gen. Duke from competition[1], and a new rival appeared.

Back in New York, Bold Ruler came out for the one and one-eighth-mile Wood Memorial. Gallant Man, who previously had not shown that he was of highest caliber, also was in the field. Jockey Eddie Arcaro set a slow pace on Bold Ruler, getting each of the first three quarters in :24. This should have left Bold Ruler with ample reserves for the stretch run, but when Gallant Man challenged, Bold Ruler could not pull away and under a whipping drive just managed to get his nose in front on the wire. Despite the controlled early pace, the time of 1:48 4/5 set a new track record.

In the Kentucky Derby on May 4, Bold Ruler naturally was the favorite at 6-5, but in the race Arcaro tried to hold him back when Bold Ruler was full of running. On the first turn, Federal Hill bore out, and Bold Ruler was carried out with him and had to be taken back. When straightened out, Bold Ruler would not respond to urging and finished fourth.

The next main objective was the one and three-sixteenths-mile Preakness at Pimlico on May 18. For that event, Bold Ruler was given a tune-up in a one and one-sixteenth-mile race at Pimlico against two inferior animals. He gave a most unimpressive display, having to be whipped to win by a length. The result of this was that Kentucky Derby winner Iron Liege was sent off the favorite for the Preakness at 13-10, with Bold Ruler at 7-5. That time Bold Ruler was allowed to stride along in front and was about two lengths in front throughout the stretch. Iron Liege's challenge failed.

Bold Ruler was favored at 17-20 for the one and a half-mile Belmont on June 15. There was lively curiosity about whether a free-running colt of Bold Ruler's brilliance could stay the distance. John Nerud, trainer of Gallant Man, saw that there was one sure way to find out. He knew that Bold Ruler would not run kindly if restrained off the pace. Therefore, the tactics should be to assure a fast pace for one and a quarter miles, then see how much Bold Ruler had left. With this in mind, he saddled Ralph Lowe's Bold Nero as a pacemaker for Lowe's Gallant Man. To stay with Bold Nero's pace, Bold Ruler had to run each of the first two quarters in :23 2/5, and the third quarter was done in :23 3/5. Just before the quarter-mile pole, Gallant Man went to the front. Bold Ruler had nothing left, for he had run one and a quarter miles in 2:01 2/5, equaling Whirlaway's record for the Kentucky Derby.

Gallant Man went on to win in record time of 2:26 3/5 and Bold Ruler was beaten by twelve lengths in third.

Bold Ruler then was given a good rest. He reappeared in the autumn, and after winning two preliminary races in the Times Square Purse and Jerome Handicap, Bold Ruler came out for the weight-for-age Woodward Stakes at one and a quarter miles. The field for this was a high-society party of four, the others being Gallant Man, Dedicate, and Reneged. After leading at a mile in 1:36, Bold Ruler faded to be beaten three and a half lengths by Dedicate and Gallant Man.

The season was not over, and the best was yet to come. In the Vosburgh Handicap, Bold Ruler carried 130 pounds against older horses and went seven furlongs on a sloppy track in 1:21 2/5, breaking Roseben's record, which had stood for fifty-one years.

He next was asked to shoulder 133 pounds in the one and one-sixteenth-mile Queens County Handicap and won easily. In the one and one-sixteenth-mile

				Polymelus
			Phalaris, 1913	Bromus
		Pharos, 1920		Chaucer
			Scapa Flow, 1914	Anchora
	Nearco, 1935			Rabelais
			Havresac II, 1915	Hors-Concours
		Nogara, 1928		Spearmint
			Catnip, 1910	Sibola
Nasrullah, 1940				Swynford
			Blandford, 1919	Blanche
		Blenheim II, 1927		Charles O'Malley
			Malva, 1919	Wild Arum
	Mumtaz Begum, 1932			Roi Herode
			The Tetrarch, 1911	Vahren
		Mumtaz Mahal, 1921		**Sundridge**
BOLD RULER			Lady Josephine, 1912	Americus Girl
				Hastings
			Fair Play, 1905	Fairy Gold
		Display, 1923		Nassovian
			Cicuta, 1919	Hemlock
	Discovery, 1931			Picton
			Light Brigade, 1910	Bridge of Sighs
		Ariadne, 1926		His Majesty
			Adrienne, 1919	Adriana
Miss Disco, 1944				**Sundridge**
			Sun Briar, 1915	Sweet Briar II
		Pompey, 1923		Corcyra
			Cleopatra, 1917	Gallice
	Outdone, 1936			Sweep
			Sweep On, 1916	Yodler
		Sweep Out, 1926		Under Fire
			Dugout, 1922	Cloak

Bold Ruler

Benjamin Franklin Handicap, his weight was escalated to 136 pounds, but he won by twelve lengths.

It then was decided to tackle the two other outstanding three-year-olds of 1957—Gallant Man and Round Table, in the one and a quarter-mile Trenton Handicap. For this, the weights were Gallant Man, 124; Round Table, 124; and Bold Ruler, 122. The race was run to Bold Ruler's order. He was allowed an early lead of nearly four lengths and then was permitted to increase this to eight. The other runners never got in an effective challenge, and Bold Ruler outraced Gallant Man two and a quarter lengths.

An interesting sequel to this race was Bold Ruler's weight assignments in New York handicaps. F.E. (Jimmy) Kilroe twice rated Bold Ruler at 139 pounds, for the Knickerbocker (one and one-sixteenth miles) and the Roamer (one and three-sixteenths miles)[2]. These were the highest weights ever given a three-year-old in the United States—one pound more than Man o' War's weight when he won the Potomac Handicap in 1920. Bold Ruler was three-year-old champion and Horse of the Year.

As a four-year-old, Bold Ruler suffered from a series of mishaps. He came out for the six-furlong Toboggan Handicap under 133 pounds and, conceding sixteen pounds, he won by a half-length from Clem.

For the seven-furlong Carter Handicap, Bold Ruler's weight rose to 135 pounds, and he won by one and a half lengths, giving away twenty-two pounds to Tick Tock.

Next came the one-mile Metropolitan Handicap and he carried 135 pounds. His old rival, Gallant Man, was in with 130 and defeated Bold Ruler by two lengths. Their score then was four each [of finishing in front of each other].

Bold Ruler had drawn 138 pounds for the seven-furlong Roseben Handicap, but instead he ran in the Stymie Handicap at one and one-eighth miles with 133 pounds and won easily.

The weight inched up to 134 for the one and a quarter-mile Suburban. Only two horses had won it thus burdened—Whisk Broom II with 139 in 1913 and Grey Lag with 135 in 1923. Bold Ruler won by a nose after a dramatic struggle with the high-class Clem (109), running the last furlong in :13 4/5. This may have been the limit of his capacity, but a mighty capacity it was.

The Monmouth Handicap of one and a quarter miles with 134 pounds occasioned a relatively handy victory over Sharpsburg (113).

Back in New York, the weight went up again, to 136, for the one and three-sixteenths-mile Brooklyn Handicap. Bold Ruler finished next to last. Shortly after the race, it was discovered that Bold Ruler's near fore ankle had filled again, and he was retired.

YEAR	AGE	STS	1ST	2ND	3RD	EARNED
1956	at 2	10	7	1	0	$139,050
1957	at 3	16	11	2	2	$415,160
1958	at 4	7	5	1	0	$209,994
Lifetime		33	23	4	2	$764,204

Comparisons between Bold Ruler and Nashua (both sons of Nasrullah) as racers were inevitable: (1) Nashua was sounder; (2) Nashua stayed much better (two-mile Jockey Club Gold Cup, twice); Bold Ruler's limit was about one and a quarter miles; (3) Bold Ruler was better over short courses; (4) Bold Ruler showed much better weight-carrying ability, despite the fact that Nashua was a bigger colt—16.2 1/2 hands to Bold Ruler's 16.1 1/2 hands. Nashua carried 130 pounds twice and failed both times; Bold Ruler won with 136 once, with 135 once, and with 133 and 134 repeatedly; (5) Both colts showed some of the Nasrullah temperament. Bold Ruler was a very free runner and could not be rated off the pace successfully. Nashua gave the impression at times of kidding around so that one did not know if he was running his true race.

With the benefit of hindsight, there are few finer recreations than to occupy the pundit's chair and explain the pedigree of a great sire—especially to an ignoramus (ignoramus: anyone who does not know something you learned yesterday). So, here we go.

Bold Ruler was sired by Nasrullah. The latter was a high-class (if temperamental) racer, who was bred to be a great sire, and he was a great sire, combining early maturity, first-class speed, and stamina up to ten furlongs. Bold Ruler's dam was

Secretariat

Miss Disco, a tough filly who won ten races in fifty-four starts over five seasons and earned $80,250. She won the Test Stakes at Saratoga (seven furlongs) and the New Rochelle, American Legion, and Interborough handicaps. She was tried over longer distances but did not succeed. In addition to Bold Ruler, she was the dam of two other stakes winners and one stakes-placed winner. Besides having merit of her own, Miss Disco was sired by the great handicap horse Discovery, who had a constitution of iron, could win with weights up to 139 pounds, and was well endowed with stamina.

Perhaps it also should be noted that not one of Bold Ruler's first four dams was by a stallion that ever was leading sire or was even very fashionable. (Discovery came to be well regarded when the merits of his daughters as broodmares became clear.) It was the first three dams themselves that showed merit beyond the class to be expected from their sires, but none of these mares showed distance capacity beyond seven furlongs. And this lack of distance capacity has been the most serious limitation in Bold Ruler's stud career.

Any criticism of Bold Ruler, perhaps, is superfluous, for he led the American sire list more often (eight times) than any other sire of this century, sired more stakes winners (eighty-two) than any other stallion except Nasrullah (105) that stood in North America in this century [through 1976][3], and his get includes Triple Crown winner Secretariat, hailed by many as the best racer of this century.

From 366 named foals, he sired 22 percent stakes winners. Bold Ruler, who died in 1971 after a year-long battle with cancer, is the sire of eleven champions— Lamb Chop, Bold Lad, Queen Empress, Bold Bidder, Bold Lad (Ireland), Gamely, Successor, Vitriolic, Queen of the Stage, Secretariat, and Wajima.

He is a sire of sires and a sire of broodmares. His sons prominent in the stud, in addition to the champion colts named above, include Chieftain, Boldnesian, Bold Commander, Bold Bidder, Envoy, and leading sire What a Pleasure.[4] His daughters include Gamely, dam of Cellini, who topped yearlings sold at auction in 1972 and became a stakes winner in Europe at two and three. A yearling by Bold Ruler topped the sales in 1973 when he was sold for $600,000. Named Wajima, he was the three-year-old champion of 1975. Bold Ruler already is the maternal grandsire of thirty-three North American stakes winners, including champions Autobiography and Sensational.[5]

End Notes:

1. Gen. Duke suffered a hoof bruise in the Derby Trial. The bruise later was found to be a fracture of a pedal bone. Gen. Duke was scratched from the Kentucky Derby the morning of the race.

2. Bold Ruler didn't run in either race.

3. The record of number of stakes winners among North American-based stallions has long been surpassed by Danzig (190) and Mr. Prospector (180).

4. In 2006 Bold Ruler's sire line remains extant through several stallions, including Awad (Bold Bidder); Mecke (What a Pleasure); Texas Glitter (Dewan); Is It True, Yes It's True, Delaware Township, and Well Noted (Raja Baba); and Express Tour (Secretariat).

Bold Ruler's most successful line has developed from Boldnesian through his grandson, 1977 Triple Crown winner Seattle Slew (by Bold Reasoning). Seattle Slew's sons at stud include A.P. Indy, Avenue of Flags, Chief Seattle, Doneraile Court, and Vindication. Horse of the Year A.P. Indy is represented by sire sons Pulpit, Aptitude, Malibu Moon, Mineshaft, Stephen Got Even, etc.

Boldnesian also sired Bold Ruckus, who became a top stallion in Canada. Bold Ruckus is represented in the stud by Beau Genius, Bold Executive, and Demaloot Demashoot.

5. Through June 2006 Bold Ruler's daughters had produced 119 stakes winners worldwide, including additional champions Christmas Past, Intrepidity (Europe), Seraphic (Canada), Targowice (France), and Avowal (Canada).

CHAPTER TWENTY-THREE

T. V. LARK

In the chapter on Swaps in this book (*See page 403.*), the question is raised as to the best racer to come out of California breeding—Emperor of Norfolk (1885) or Swaps (1952). There can be little doubt, however, that the best sire produced by California breeding to date has been T. V. Lark, North America's leading sire in 1974.

This book considers various types of sires. Those with first-class racing performance backed by a first-class pedigree, such as Gainsborough, Hyperion, Nearco, Fair Play, and Round Table, present no great amount of trouble to the student of Thoroughbreds. They are expected to be first-class sires, and this generally proves to be the case.

Less easy to understand are successful sires with less than first-class racing performance, but with strong pedigrees (such as Pilate), whose stud careers far outstripped their racing ability. These cases very rarely are predicted at the outset of stud careers. Sires with first-class racing form, but poor pedigree credentials, such as Epinard, Alsab, and Carry Back, generally have stud careers that fall far below the standard of their racing performance.

Perhaps the most difficult of all to understand is the case of a horse with very high racing credentials, coupled with an unappealing pedigree, that has outrun his pedigree and then proceeds to outbreed it at stud. Such a horse was T. V. Lark, and he makes the student of Thoroughbreds reach for the aspirin.

T. V. Lark was sold as an auction yearling in California for $10,000, and it was because he was an attractive youngster that he brought that price. His dam was not a winner, and his sire, imported Indian Hemp, had yet to prove himself in this country. T. V. Lark was in his second crop. Trainer Paul Miller liked the colt's conformation, sensed an intelligence in the horse, and advised owner C.R. McCoy to go as high as $30,000. They did not have to, though, because few others saw what Miller did in T. V. Lark.

He was out fourteen times as a two-year-old, trained at first by Miller, then by

T. V. Lark with Preston Madden

the late Willie Molter, then by a former groom, Paul Parker. T. V. Lark began his career in a three-furlong scamper at Santa Anita on February 20, and he ran second, beaten five and one-half lengths. At the same track, he was well backed to win his next start, on March 4, and he duly obliged by three-quarters of a length.

From that point on, T. V. Lark moved into stakes competition, where he beat some good colts although more of them beat him. The high point of the season was a victory in the Arlington Futurity, in which he raced as a member of the mutuel field and won by a neck from Bally Ache, a leading eastern juvenile and winner of the Preakness Stakes the following year.

T. V. Lark was unplaced in his remaining stakes engagements in Chicago and the East at two. Near the end of December, back at Santa Anita, he won the seven-furlong California Breeders' Trial Stakes from Noble Noor. For the season, T. V. Lark won three races, finished second four times, and was unplaced seven times—nothing very remarkable, but still not bad.

The winter campaign embraced eight races. He won only the first two; the second, in the new year, was a six-furlong allowance race in which he beat Warfare. He ran well in his next four races, all stakes but failed to win any of them. In the nine-furlong Santa Anita Derby, he was unplaced to Tompion and John William.

T. V. Lark then was shipped to Bay Meadows for three races, and he won the first two, a one and one-sixteenth-mile allowance test and the Tropicana Hotel of Las Vegas Stakes at the same distance. His time in the stakes was a shifty 1:42 2/5. On the basis of that, he was odds-on for the nine-furlong California Derby but was unplaced to Noble Noor.

It then was decided to have a shot at the Preakness. At Pimlico, T. V. Lark ran fourth to Bally Ache in a one and one-sixteenth-mile Preakness Prep, and he was sixth to Bally Ache in the classic itself. So far, it was not a glorious record, but when T. V. Lark was returned to California, his prospects began to brighten.

On June 11, he won the one and one-sixteenth-mile Argonaut in 1:41 1/5, defeating an old rival, New Policy. After running third in the Cinema Handicap, he was second to Tempestuous in the ten-furlong Hollywood Derby, run in 2:01 2/5. Then things began to bloom for T. V. Lark.

Taken to Chicago, he won the Arlington Classic at one mile from John William and Kentucky Derby winner Venetian Way. Three weeks later he won a one-mile allowance race from New Policy in 1:34 4/5. On August 27, he won the nine-furlong American Derby in 1:47 1/5, equaling Round Table's track record while conceding New Policy three pounds and beating him by three and one-half lengths. Seeming to have improved about ten pounds, he continued in the winning vein by

			Pharos, 1920	Phalaris
		Nearco, 1935		Scapa Flow
			Nogara, 1928	Havresac II
	Nasrullah, 1940			Catnip
			Blenheim II, 1927	Blandford
		Mumtaz Begum, 1932		Malva
			Mumtaz Mahal, 1921	The Tetrarch
Indian Hemp, 1949				Lady Josephine
			Hyperion, 1930	Gainsborough
		Stardust, 1937		Selene
			Sister Stella, 1923	Friar Marcus
	Sabzy, 1943			Etoile
			Swynford, 1907	John o' Gaunt
		Sarita, 1924		Canterbury Pilgrim
T. V. LARK			Molly Desmond, 1914	Desmond
				Pretty Polly
			Swynford, 1907	John o' Gaunt
		Royal Ford, 1926		Canterbury Pilgrim
			Royal Yoke, 1917	Roi Herode
	Heelfly, 1934			Yokohama
			Campfire, 1914	Olambala
		Canfli, 1928		Nightfall
			Flivver, 1922	Jim Gaffney
Miss Larksfly, 1948				Filante
			Teddy, 1913	Ajax
		Bull Dog, 1927		Rondeau
			Plucky Liege, 1912	Spearmint
	Larksnest, 1943			Concertina
			Blue Larkspur, 1926	Black Servant
		Light Lark, 1937		Blossom Time
			Ruddy Light, 1921	Honeywood
				Washoe Belle

taking the Washington Park Handicap of one mile in 1:34 1/5.

Having been invited to contest the United Nations Handicap, T. V. Lark won his first grass test by one and one-quarter lengths from the previous season's Horse of the Year, Sword Dancer, who gave T. V. Lark seven pounds. T. V. Lark thus had won four $100,000 races. Under the weight-for-age conditions of the Woodward, however, T. V. Lark was no match for the older Sword Dancer, finishing sixth in a field of seven.

YEAR	AGE	STS	1ST	2ND	3RD	EARNED
1959	at 2	14	3	4	0	$181,952
1960	at 3	23	9	3	4	$395,900
1961	at 4	18	5	1	2	$250,627
1962	at 5	17	2	5	0	$ 73,715
Lifetime		72	19	13	6	$902,194

Back in Chicago, T. V. Lark ran second in an overnight handicap, then was unplaced in Kelso's ten-furlong Hawthorne Gold Cup. He was rested until December 26, when he reappeared at Santa Anita and finished fourth, under 123 pounds, in the six-furlong Palos Verdes Handicap. That race, although it came in T. V. Lark's three-year-old season, was in preparation for his four-year-old campaign.

T. V. Lark's three-year-old season had been more rewarding than his two-year-old campaign, he having won six stakes at three. His earnings at three amounted to $395,900. He had proven to be a horse of some speed, yet had not shown that he could get ten furlongs in top company under weight-for-age conditions. (On *The Blood-Horse* Free Handicap for three-year-olds, T. V. Lark was ranked third, at 128 pounds, below Kelso at 134 and Bally Ache at 132.)

If T. V. Lark were pictured as primarily a speed horse at two and three, the picture was changed dramatically at four, although not until well past mid-season. During the California phase of his four-year-old campaign, T. V. Lark won the nine-furlong Santa Catalina Handicap at Santa Anita and the seven-furlong Los Angeles Handicap at Hollywood Park. None of his beaten rivals in the Santa Catalina were very distinguished; in the Los Angeles, he gave New Policy four pounds and beat him by a neck in the cracking time of 1:21 1/5.

T. V. Lark lost eight races in California that year, giving weight to the winners in all but one of them. One of his losses came in the ten-furlong Maturity Stakes, in which he was unplaced to Prove It while trying to concede that rival ten pounds. He was tried twice on turf late in the Santa Anita meeting, finished third in the Washington's Birthday Handicap and fourth (in a dead heat) in the San Juan Capistrano Handicap.

With an inglorious California campaign behind him, T. V. Lark was returned to Chicago, where he had done well at two and three. He began in Chicago by

Indian Hemp, sire of T. V. Lark

running unplaced to John William in the six and one-half-furlong Myrtlewood Handicap, in which the winner equaled the track record of 1:15 1/5. He also was unplaced in the one-mile Washington Park Preview Handicap on August 24, giving five pounds to the winner.

The Washington Park Handicap of one mile, raced on September 4, is of interest chiefly because it gives the handicapper's view at that time of the respective merits of Kelso, who was assigned 132 pounds for the race, and T. V. Lark, weighted at 114. Kelso was fourth and T. V. Lark was last.

On September 9 and September 29, at Hawthorne Park, T. V. Lark ran fifth and then third to Tudorich, both of those races on turf. The second marked the colt's first appearance in the colors of Preston Madden, owner of Hamburg Place near Lexington, who had purchased T. V. Lark privately for a reported $600,000. In his second race in Madden's colors, T. V. Lark won the Hawthorne Gold Cup under 113 pounds, jockey John Longden unable to make the colt's assigned weight of 110. The weights were somewhat in T. V. Lark's favor, since the high-weight, Oink (122), was hardly a top horse.

Two weeks later at Aqueduct, T. V. Lark carried 119 pounds and took the one and five-eighths-mile Knickerbocker Handicap on grass from ten rivals. The weights again may have favored T. V. Lark, but his time, 2:40, was a new American record.

The glorious climax of the season came when T. V. Lark was invited to represent the United States in the Washington, D.C., International at Laurel. The other U.S. representative, naturally, was Kelso, and they carried even weights (126). They were the only horses seriously backed in the race, with Kelso a lop-sided favorite at 2-5 and T. V. Lark held at nearly 4-1.

They were always in front, T. V. Lark sticking right at Kelso, and in the last part of the race getting the better of the argument and winning by three-quarters of a length. Winning under level weight at twelve furlongs against Kelso, the greatest stayer in the country, represented a change of more than twenty pounds in T. V. Lark's favor, compared to his previous form with Kelso.

T. V. Lark was voted the champion grass horse of the year.

At five T. V. Lark was but a shadow of his former self. In seventeen starts, he won two races, including the Philadelphia Turf Handicap, and was second in five good races, including the United Nations and the Laurel Handicap. Perhaps the handicapper was a little too severe with T. V. Lark, or perhaps the horse had lost some of his zest for racing. In any case, he was retired to stud at Hamburg Place with a record of nineteen wins from seventy-two starts. His earnings, $902,194, made him the richest California-bred (since passed by millionaire gelding Native Diver).[1]

Lengthy conversations with Madden, grandson of famed horseman John Madden, revealed a number of things about T. V. Lark and about the current owner of Hamburg Place.

Madden bought T. V. Lark in training and ran him with great success. The purchase was made from a very deep instinct on the part of Madden that T. V. Lark was a top horse and would become a top sire. Quite literally, he fell in love with T. V. Lark in a way far beyond the fondness he had had for other horses.

Owing to this gut feeling, Madden simply disregarded the obvious weak spots in T. V. Lark's pedigree, which when considered in regard to the horse's success as a runner and sire presents a mystery entitled to rank with the Great Train Robbery. The dam, Miss Larksfly (by Heelfly) had placed and earned $550 during a two-year career of eight races. She produced five other foals, three of them moderate winners. The second dam, unplaced Larksnest, produced seven foals to race, one a minor stakes winner.

T. V. Lark's sire, Indian Hemp, had won stakes in England at two but was about twelve to fifteen pounds below the best of his year. In this country Indian Hemp won the one and one-sixteenth-mile Yerba Buena Handicap and four other races from twenty-eight starts. He did become a leading sire in the West, getting twenty-two stakes winners, including T. V. Lark, $297,742-earner Linita, and other $100,000-plus earners Hempen, Ipse, Jungle Savage, Mr. Wag, Old Mose, and Prince Hemp.

When Madden bought T. V. Lark, however, he was pinning his hopes on his instincts and on Indian Hemp's bloodlines, the sire being a son of Nasrullah. Events proved Madden right beyond doubt, because T. V. Lark was a racer of high class, even on an international basis, and became a sire of the first rank as well. Madden explained T. V. Lark's improvement of racing form after the purchase by pointing out that the horse was given longer rests between races. T. V. Lark thus gained added strength and fresh desire to run, Madden said.

No one can deny that Madden hit the bull's eye with T. V. Lark, both on the track and at stud. T. V. Lark sired fifty-three stakes winners, including Buffalo Lark, Quack, Pink Pigeon, T. V. Commercial, and Golden Don. Overall, his runners have earned more than $14 million. He was the second-leading sire in North America in 1972 and 1973, the leader in 1974 (when his runners earned $1,242,000), the third-leading sire in 1975, and fourth in 1976 for racing in North America, England, Ireland, and France. He died early in 1975 at Hamburg Place.

End Notes:
1. As of May 31, 2006, the leading California-bred money winner is two-time Breeders' Cup Classic winner and Horse of the Year Tiznow with $6,427,830. He is followed by Best Pal ($5,668,245), Snow Chief ($3,383,210), Bertrando ($3,185,610), and Free House ($3,178,971). Native Diver resides in forty-second place ($1,026,500). T. V. Lark is no longer in the top fifty.

CHAPTER TWENTY-FOUR

ROYAL CHARGER

It will be found in this collection that virtually all of the most successful sires were high-class two-year-olds; Royal Charger was not. At two, he was unplaced three times and was second twice—not a very promising start. As a three-year-old, however, he soon showed there was something wrong with that picture. In his first start at three, he beat a big field by four lengths in the six-furlong Teversham Handicap, and in his next race he finished second in the one-mile Chatteris Stakes.

This was good enough to justify starting him in the first of the classics, the one-mile Two Thousand Guineas. There he came up against the two best two-year-olds of the previous season—Dante and Court Martial; the latter won from Dante in a controversial race as Dante had the worst possible draw and Court Martial was racing on Dante's blind side (Dante having injured an eye). Royal Charger was third, beaten almost two and one-half lengths.

It was then clear that Royal Charger was a good colt, but there was no support for him in the Derby, in which he started at 50-1 and made no show over the one and one-half-mile course. He was not seen out again until the following September, when he was second in the one-mile Duke of York Stakes in fast time, and then easily won a minor race at Stockton over one mile, plus a better six-furlong race at Newmarket, beating a good sprinter in Golden Cloud. On the three-year-old Free Handicap, Royal Charger was put eleven pounds below Dante and eight pounds below Court Martial, with nine three-year-olds ranked above him.

As a four-year-old, Royal Charger was kept sprinting, with one exception, and he did very well at it.

After finishing second in a six-furlong race at Newmarket and then enjoying a walkover, Royal Charger won the Queen Anne Stakes at Ascot, run over the Royal Hunt Cup course of slightly less than one mile. The time and form figures for this race were not impressive, but the same figures for the five-furlong King's Stand Stakes at Ascot where Royal Charger was third—beaten only two heads—were

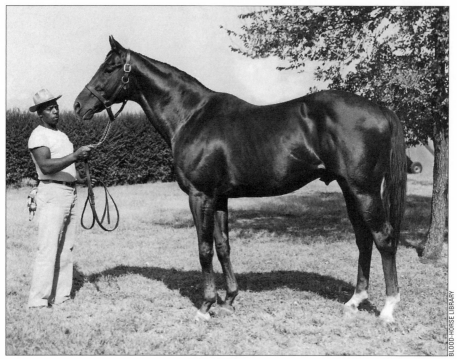

BLOOD-HORSE LIBRARY

Royal Charger

very good indeed. He was conceding twenty-three pounds to Vilmorin and eight pounds to Golden Cloud. The figures were almost up to classic standard and were the best Royal Charger ever recorded, although his victory in the six-furlong Ayr Gold Cup was nearly as impressive.

It was found necessary to keep Royal Charger covered up until the last possible moment, or he would act up and refuse to run his race. This may account for his having been second four times in nine starts at four, as well as first three times (including one walkover).

It cannot be easy for a jockey to uncover his horse at exactly the right moment in a sprint race; a fraction of a second too late and his horse does not have a chance to get there; a fraction of a second too early and his horse has won it and then lost it again. Nasrullah presented the same problem with regard to uncovering him at the last moment, but Nasrullah was not contesting sprint races, and he was a higher-class colt competing in higher-class races.

Royal Charger had a good dosage of Jarvis in his life. His breeder and owner was Sir John Jarvis, and his trainer was Jack Jarvis, also later Sir John Jarvis, the first trainer to be knighted. Jack Jarvis was a very fine man, universally liked and respected, and a very fine trainer. He won the Derby for the sixth Lord Rosebery with Blue Peter and Ocean Swell and also won the Two Thousand Guineas for Lord Rosebery's father with Ellangowan, in 1923. He trained at least one winner of all the classic races except the Oaks, and, as luck would have it, there was a two-year-old filly in his stable the year he died who won the Oaks for Lord Rosebery the next year—Sleeping Partner in 1969.

Royal Charger was sold to the Irish National Stud and took up his stud duties in Kildare as a five-year-old. A good many doubts were expressed concerning Royal Charger's prospects as a stallion. While he was a strong, sound, well-muscled colt of good quality, he was a chestnut by Nearco, and there existed some prejudice against that color when it appeared among Nearco's get. Furthermore, his distance capacity was limited to a mile, and he was not up to classic standard—nor had he been a good two-year-old. Lastly, he showed something of the Nearco kink in temperament that had been displayed so flagrantly by Nasrullah, whose superb merits as a sire yet were not known when Royal Charger went to stud.

In Royal Charger's favor was the demonstrated fact that he had first-class speed and that he was by Nearco out of a half sister to Nasrullah, tracing to perhaps the fastest of all fillies, Mumtaz Mahal. His dam was a non-winner by Solario (St.

Nearco, 1935	Pharos, 1920	Phalaris, 1913	Polymelus, 1902	Cyllene / Maid Marian
			Bromus, 1905	Sainfoin / Cheery
		Scapa Flow, 1914	Chaucer, 1900	St. Simon / Canterbury Pilgrim
			Anchora, 1905	Love Wisely / Eryholme
	Nogara, 1928	Havresac II, 1915	Rabelais, 1900	St. Simon / Satirical
			Hors Concours, 1906	Ajax / Simona
		Catnip, 1910	Spearmint, 1903	Carbine / Maid of the Mint
			Sibola, 1896	The Sailor Prince / Saluda
ROYAL CHARGER				
Sun Princess, 1937	Solario, 1922	Gainsborough, 1915	Bayardo, 1906	Bay Ronald / Galicia
			Rosedrop, 1907	St. Frusquin / Rosaline
		Sun Worship, 1912	Sundridge, 1898	Amphion / Sierra
			Doctrine, 1899	Ayrshire / Axiom
	Mumtaz Begum, 1932	Blenheim II, 1927	Blandford, 1919	Swynford / Blanche
			Malva, 1919	Charles O'Malley / Wild Arum
		Mumtaz Mahal, 1921	The Tetrarch, 1911	Roi Herode / Vahren
			Lady Josephine, 1912	Sundridge / Americus Girl

STACKHOUSE

Royal Orbit

Leger and Ascot Gold Cup), and this factor for stoutness occasionally seemed to appear in Royal Charger's stock.

Royal Charger soon answered the debate strongly in his own favor. From his years in Ireland came Happy Laughter (One Thousand Guineas), Sea Charger (Irish Two Thousand Guineas), Turn-to (crack two-year-old and an excellent sire in the United States), and Royal Serenade (a top sprinter in England and later winner of the one and one-quarter-mile Hollywood Gold Cup).

After Royal Charger's 1951 sale to Neil McCarthy and importation, he sired Royal Orbit (Preakness Stakes), Idun (champion filly as a two-year-old and three-year-old), Royal Native (champion three-year-old filly and champion handicap filly), and Mongo (Washington, D.C., International, Widener Handicap, Monmouth Handicap, and champion grass horse). In fifteen seasons at stud, Royal Charger sired 373 named foals and fifty-nine stakes winners (15.8 percent), and his Average-Earnings Index was 4.08. He died at the age of nineteen in 1961 at Leslie Combs II's Spendthrift Farm near Lexington, where he spent his entire American life.

Royal Charger's was an extraordinary performance at stud for a horse whose credentials were not first class, but the characteristic of breeding better than they ran has been true of various members of his male line for a long time.

Polymelus, only a good handicapper, was champion sire five times;

Phalaris, by Polymelus, was a high-class sprinter and champion sire twice;

Pharos, by Phalaris, was a high-class handicapper and champion sire in England and France;

YEAR	AGE	STS	1ST	2ND	3RD	EARNED*
1944	at 2	5	0	2	0	£ 0
1945	at 3	7	3	2	1	£ 896
1946	at 4	9	3	4	1	£2,035
Lifetime		21	6	8	2	£2,931

* First-place money only

Nearco, by Pharos, was an exception in this line, as he was an unbeaten racehorse as well as a champion sire;

Nasrullah, by Nearco, was only third in one classic but was champion sire in England and five times champion sire in the United States;

Royal Charger, also by Nearco, was about ten pounds below the top as a runner but was author of an extraordinary record at stud.

What is the explanation of this? Other sire lines have struggled to produce sires which can come close to measuring up to their racing class when they go to stud. This line has produced first-class sires without necessarily having to produce first-class racers.[1]

End Notes:

1. Royal Charger's sire line is well represented in modern American pedigrees through his son Turn-to.

TURN-TO

When racing men go in search of high-class stock for their ventures on the Turf, their quests, like those of Ulysses, can take them over the far-reaching seas to distant lands. Claude Tanner was on the watch for a colt that might be good enough to win him the Kentucky Derby, but he had not found anything in the United States that appealed to him sufficiently. So, he wrote abroad to Frank Moore O'Ferrall of the Anglo-Irish Bloodstock Agency, inquiring if he knew of anything that might fill the bill. Moore O'Ferrall replied that he did know of such a colt, one located on the farm next to his own stud at Monasteveran, County Kildare, Eire.

Tanner agreed to buy the yearling colt, which had been bred by E.R. Miville and Mrs. G.L. Hastings and which had been named Source Royal. The yearling was sent from Ireland to the United States in April of 1952. Later in that month, Tanner died, and Mrs. Tanner asked Bull Hancock to sell the colt for her, so Source Royal was offered by Hancock's Claiborne Farm at the Keeneland summer yearling sale.

Hancock decided to bid on him on behalf of one of his clients, and for $20,000 he bought the colt for Captain Harry F. Guggenheim's Cain Hoy Stable. Guggenheim had been a naval officer in World War II and was partial to nautical names for his horses, so he changed Source Royal's name to Turn-to, which in naval parlance suggests "get to work."

Turn-to was fired for osselets as a yearling, foreshadowing the unsoundness that was to plague him and many of his produce. It was not until the following August at Saratoga that he got to the races. The Royal Charger colt had grown into a deep-bodied, well-muscled two-year-old of high quality, and the clockers—those eagle-eyed men of observation—had noted his works with favor. As a result, he was sent off at 9-10 for his first race, a five and one-half-furlong maiden event.

Turn-to won by five lengths. This was satisfactory to the stable, but the odds were not the stuff of which bettors' coups are made on first-time starters.

BERT MORGAN

Turn-to

The Saratoga Special (then the most sporting of all races inasmuch as it was a winner-take-all event) was next on Turn-to's schedule. In it he met Porterhouse, who already had some claim to the two-year-old championship. Turn-to was leading when he swung a little wide entering the stretch. Jockey Eric Guerin seized the chance to drive Porterhouse through the opening between Turn-to and the rail, and when the colts were straightened for the stretch run, Porterhouse held a length advantage. Both were under a drive, and Guerin's whip caused Turn-to to throw up his head. Turn-to, apparently, was struck more than once. He finished second, beaten by a half-length, but Porterhouse was disqualified and Turn-to was declared the winner.

In the six and a half-furlong Hopeful Stakes, the principal two-year-old event at Saratoga, Turn-to was beaten by about five lengths by the odds-on Artismo. That result was not a true bill of the Cain Hoy colt's merits, for he had bucked shins during the race, and he was unable to start again for nearly two months.

As a preparation for the rich Garden State Stakes, Eddie Hayward started Turn-to in a one and one-sixteenth-mile allowance race on October 24. Turn-to was the favorite, but he may have been a little short in his condition, for he was second to Goyamo, beaten by four lengths.

Next came the Garden State, also at one and one-sixteenth miles. Counting nominating and starting fees, the gross value of the race amounted to $269,395. Turn-to started at the surprisingly long odds of 14-1, but jockey Hank Moreno got him off to a fast start and used his early speed to get a position next to the rails. Errard King ranged up beside him and held the lead for a half-mile, but then he dropped back. Full Flight challenged on the last turn, got his head in front, but he also dropped away. Under the whip, Turn-to drew out to a two-length lead, which he still held at the finish.

Three of the top eastern juveniles, Porterhouse, Artismo, and Hasty Road, had been absent from the field, so the rich victory did not earn Turn-to a championship. Hasty Road and Porterhouse shared honors in two-year-old title balloting, but Turn-to was rated at 126 pounds, equal with Porterhouse, atop the Experimental Free Handicap.

After a rest on Long Island, Turn-to was sent to Florida, where he ran three races at Hialeah. He came out on February 2 for a seven-furlong allowance race. He carried 122 pounds, giving away as much as seventeen pounds, and was odds-on at 1-2. Running easily, he went six furlongs in 1:10 and cantered out the remaining distance for a final clocking of 1:23 2/5.

The short-term objective was the Flamingo Stakes at one and one-eighth miles

TURN-TO					
Royal Charger, 1942	Nearco, 1935	**Pharos**, 1920	Phalaris, 1913	Polymelus / Bromus	
			Scapa Flow, 1914	Chaucer / Anchora	
		Nogara, 1928	Havresac II, 1915	Rabelais / Hors Concours	
			Catnip, 1910	**Spearmint** / Sibola	
	Sun Princess, 1937	Solario, 1922	Gainsborough, 1915	Bayardo / Rosedrop	
			Sun Worship, 1912	**Sundridge** / Doctrine	
		Mumtaz Begum, 1932	Blenheim II, 1927	Blandford / Malva	
			Mumtaz Mahal, 1921	The Tetrarch / Lady Josephine	
Source Sucree, 1940	Admiral Drake, 1931	Craig An Eran, 1918	Sunstar, 1908	**Sundridge** / Doris	
			Maid of the Mist, 1906	Cyllene / Sceptre	
		Plucky Liege, 1912	**Spearmint**, 1903	Carbine / Maid of the Mint	
			Concertina, 1896	St. Simon / Comic Song	
	Lavendula, 1930	**Pharos**, 1920	Phalaris, 1913	Polymelus / Bromus	
			Scapa Flow, 1914	Chaucer / Anchora	
		Sweet Lavender, 1923	Swynford, 1907	John o' Gaunt / Canterbury Pilgrim	
			Marchetta, 1907	Marco / Hettie Sorrel	

ALLEN BREWER

Sir Gaylord

(the spring classics, of course, the long-term objectives), and to assure more fitness, Hayward selected a one and one-sixteenth-mile allowance as a final prep race. Aside from Turn-to's stable companion, Giant Cracker, only two other horses appeared to contest the event. They were not much competition. Giant Cracker set the pace until nearing the stretch; then Turn-to went to the front. Again, he won breezing, scoring by three and a half lengths in 1:45 4/5.

For the $100,000-added Flamingo on February 27, the entry of Turn-to and Giant Cracker was an even-money favorite against seven rivals. Turn-to led into the stretch, but wishing to take no chances, Moreno gave him three or four whacks on the left with his whip. Turn-to swerved away from the whip but increased his advantage to three and one-half lengths at the finish.

Turn-to then left Florida for Kentucky as a strong favorite for the Derby. (Guggenheim had won the classic the previous year with a longshot, Dark Star, shocking winner over Native Dancer.) Turn-to never made it to the gate, however, for on March 24 he came out of his stall with a bowed tendon, the origin of which was, and remains, a mystery. His racing career was terminated, and he entered stud the next spring, in 1955.

On *The Blood-Horse* Free Handicap for three-year-olds of 1954, Turn-to was ranked first at 132 pounds, two pounds above the voted champion, High Gun.

Turn-to was a most attractive sire prospect, on pedigree as well as on his high class as a racer. His sire, Royal Charger, a son of Nearco, already was known as a top-class stallion. Turn-to's dam, Source Sucree, had been a minor winner, scoring in a selling race of four and one-half furlongs out of four starts at two. When tried in higher-class company, she had tailed off. She did not race at three, and as she was of the era of the war in France, accurate assessment of her racing class is not possible.

YEAR	AGE	STS	1ST	2ND	3RD	EARNED
1953	at 2	5	3	1	1	$176,807
1954	at 3	3	3	0	0	$103,225
Lifetime		8	6	1	1	$280,032

Source Sucree, however, was a half sister to Ambiorix, the best of his age at two in France and a significant stallion in America. She also was a half sister to Perfume II, the dam of champion My Babu and major winner Sayani. Source Sucree had produced a good-class horse in Cagire II.

Turn-to's female line traced to Marchetta, who gave George Lambton his first experience as a trainer. Although back at the knee, Marchetta stood training well and proved a very game filly, often pulling out a little more to the surprise of her trainer and the handicapper. She was bought for Lord Derby's stud, and she became an ancestress of many high-class horses.

Turn-to was inbred to Pharos (Nearco's sire) with two free generations, inasmuch as Source Sucree was from the Pharos mare, Lavendula.

To say that Turn-to in the stud produced individuals better than himself is tempting, but taking into consideration the brilliant form of his final two major races, the Garden State and Flamingo, it is by no means certain that he actually did. There is no question, however, that he did sire a pair of the most brilliant young colts of the last three decades, First Landing and Hail to Reason, from his first and third crops, respectively.

First Landing lost but once as a champion two-year-old in 1958, earned a career total of $779,577, and sired a distinguished runner in Riva Ridge. Hail to Reason was the champion two-year-old in 1960; although felled by an injury at the start of the autumn money season for juveniles, he subsequently has led the sire list (1970), and his get includes classic winners Proud Clarion, Personality, Hail to All, and Roberto; champions Straight Deal and Regal Gleam, plus Priceless Gem.

Turn-to's twenty-five stakes winners also include Sir Gaylord, Cyane, Waltz, Sally Ship, and Captain's Gig. Sir Gaylord, although not a champion, duplicated his sire's career to a remarkable degree, being among the better two-year-olds of his season (1961), then being brilliant in the winter before breaking down as the

Hail to Reason

pre-race Kentucky Derby favorite, but still being high weight on *The Blood-Horse* Free Handicap. Sir Gaylord's get includes Epsom Derby winner Sir Ivor.

Besides being a successful sire, Turn-to was a fashionable one. He stood at Claiborne from his retirement until 1960, when he and other Cain Hoy horses were moved to Leslie Combs II's Spendthrift Farm near Lexington. Turn-to, syndicated in 1958 on a valuation of $1,400,000, died in 1973 at the age of twenty-two. He sent out 119 auction yearlings, which averaged $25,172, and they included a $140,000 filly, which in 1965 set a record for her sex.

Turn-to was a sire of sires (witness Hail to Reason and Sir Gaylord), and his daughters produced sixty-three stakes winners, including Ack Ack, Horse of the Year in 1971.

CHAPTER TWENTY-SIX

SICKLE & UNBREAKABLE

Sickle was the first foal of the celebrated mare Selene, winner of eight out of eleven starts at two, and again eight of eleven at three. In addition to Sickle, Selene foaled champion racehorse and sire Hyperion, plus successful stallions Pharamond II and Hunter's Moon. Lord Derby bred and owned Sickle's sire and dam, so Sickle was in every sense a Derby stud product.

Trainer George Lambton must have had a pretty good opinion of Sickle, a medium-sized brown colt of good quality, as his first start was in the important New Stakes at Ascot. He was fourth choice in a field of nineteen at 8-1 and finished second by one and one-half lengths to Damon, but beating Adam's Apple (winner of the next year's Two Thousand Guineas) by the same distance. In the important July Stakes at Newmarket, Sickle ran The Satrap (best two-year-old of the year) to three-fourths of a length. The odds were 2-5 The Satrap, 11-4 Sickle. Third was Call Boy, winner of the following year's Derby.

YEAR	AGE	STS	1ST	2ND	3RD	EARNED*
1926	at 2	7	3	3	1	£3,915
1927	at 3	3	0	1	1	£ 0
Lifetime		**10**	**3**	**4**	**2**	**£3,915**
* First-place money only						

At Liverpool, Sickle was given an easier task in the Mersey Stakes, which he won by six lengths from a solitary opponent at odds of 1-3. At Goodwood, his task was not too severe in winning the Prince of Wales's Stakes from six others (none of them of much merit) by five lengths at odds of 6-5.

Stepping up in class in the important Champagne Stakes at Doncaster, Sickle was fourth favorite at 9-2 in a field of eight. He was third behind Damon again, and behind Call Boy, by a neck and a half-length. Stepping down again in class, Sickle at odds of 1-3 won the Boscawen Stakes from three modest rivals by three lengths.

Next, Sickle tried for the Middle Park Stakes (the two-year-old Derby) at Newmarket in October. In a field of twelve, Sickle was joint third favorite at 6-1. There were only two other good horses in the field, Cresta Run (winner of the

Sickle

next year's One Thousand Guineas), who was favored at 3-1, and Call Boy, who was 7-2. Call Boy beat Sickle by a head, and Cresta Run finished unplaced.

Sickle's first three-year-old race was in the one-mile Union Jack Stakes at Liverpool, where Lord Derby loved to run his horses owing to his close ties to Lancashire. Against six other modest opponents, Sickle (130) went under by two lengths to Buckfast (111) at odds of 4-5. For the Two Thousand Guineas, Call Boy was favored at 5-2 in a field of twenty-three, and Sickle was sixth favorite at 10-1. Adam's Apple won it at 20-1 by a short head, with Sickle finishing third, a half-length away.

For the Derby, Sickle was 7-1 in a field of twenty-three but finished unplaced to the favored Call Boy (4-1). That was his last race.

On the two-year-old Free Handicap, Sickle had been weighted at 122 pounds, four pounds from the top, and was considered the third best two-year-old. As a three-year-old, his form seemed about the same, up to one mile.

Sickle was retired to Lord Derby's stud for a year and then was leased to Joseph E. Widener and stood at Elmendorf Farm near Lexington. The deal was for three years with an option to purchase for $100,000, which Widener exercised in 1932.

Sickle headed the U.S. list of winning sires in 1936 and 1938. However, his link in male line with the future was with his son Unbreakable, who was bred in Kentucky but did all his racing in England.

Sickle died at Elmendorf Farm in December of 1943. The best of the forty-five stakes winners sired by Sickle included Stagehand, Reaping Reward, Brevity, Silver Spear, Unbreakable, Cravat, and the filly, Gossip.[1]

			Bona Vista, 1889	Bend Or / Vista
		Cyllene, 1895	Arcadia, 1887	Isonomy / Distant Shore
	Polymelus, 1902		Hampton, 1887	Lord Clifden / Lady Langden
		Maid Marian, 1886	Quiver, 1872	Toxophilite / Y. Melbourne mare
Phalaris, 1913			Springfield, 1873	St. Albans / Viridis
		Sainfoin, 1887	Sanda, 1878	Wenlock / Sandal
	Bromus, 1905		St. Simon, 1881	Galopin / St. Angela
		Cheery, 1892	Sunrise, 1883	Springfield / Sunray
SICKLE			Galopin, 1872	Vedette / Flying Duchess
		St. Simon, 1881	St. Angela, 1865	King Tom / Adeline
	Chaucer, 1900		Tristan, 1878	Hermit / Thrift
		Canterbury Pilgrim, 1893	Pilgrimage, 1875	The Palmer / Lady Audley
Selene, 1919			Cyllene, 1895	Bona Vista / Arcadia
		Minoru, 1906	Mother Siegel, 1897	Friar's Balsam / Galopin mare
	Serenissima, 1913		Loved One, 1883	See Saw / Pilgrimage
		Gondolette, 1902	Dongola, 1883	Doncaster / Douranee

UNBREAKABLE

Following the custom of William Woodward Sr. in sending a few colts every year to be trained by Captain Cecil Boyd-Rochfort at Freemason Lodge in Newmarket, England, Joseph E. Widener sent over his yearling colt by Sickle—Blue Glass in 1936.

Capt. Boyd-Rochfort first sent the colt out for the Zetland Plate at York in May. In a field of nineteen, Unbreakable was not quoted in the betting but ran second, beaten three lengths. In the Windsor Castle Stakes at Ascot, Unbreakable

Unbreakable

was third, beaten a head and a neck, at odds of 8-1. At Newmarket in July, Unbreakable won the Exeter Stakes by two lengths at odds of 4-5, and at the second July meeting he took the Soltykoff Stakes at the same price. He won again, next time out, this time in the Richmond Stakes at Goodwood at 11-10. For the Middle Park Stakes in October, there were only five runners, but they included two good ones, Mirza II, a real flyer (Blenheim II—Mumtaz Mahal), and Scottish Union, who won the St. Leger the next year. Scottish Union beat Mirza II by a head, with Unbreakable two lengths back.

YEAR	AGE	STS	1ST	2ND	3RD	EARNED*
1937	at 2	6	3	1	2	£2,852
1938	at 3	6	1	2	0	£2,520
1939	at 4	2	1	0	0	£1,720
Lifetime		14	5	3	2	£7,092

* First-place money only

It had been a satisfactory season—Unbreakable was ranked sixth on the two-year-old Free Handicap, five pounds from the top.

As a three-year-old, Unbreakable came out in April as favorite for the one-mile Coventry Stakes at Kempton Park. He was 2-1, but finished unplaced to Pasch, who went on to win the Two Thousand Guineas. In that classic, Unbreakable was 20-1 and made no show, and in the Derby he was 40-1 with the same result. Against very modest opposition in the one-mile Waterford Stakes at Ascot, Unbreakable was 3-1 and scored by two lengths. At Liverpool in the Knowsley Dinner Stakes of ten furlongs, Unbreakable was odds-on at 8-11 but went under by a head to Hesperian, who received ten pounds. Brought back to a distance of one mile again in the Sussex Stakes at Goodwood, Unbreakable started at 2-3 in a field of six but was beaten a length by Faroe.

This concluded an unsatisfactory three-year-old campaign. On the three-year-old Free Handicap, Unbreakable was rated sixteen pounds from the top at 117 pounds, with sixteen rivals weighted higher.

Unbreakable was kept in training as a four-year-old and had two races. For the ten-furlong City and Suburban Handicap, he had top weight of 126 pounds and was third favorite at 6-1, but he finished unplaced. Cut back to seven furlongs in the Victoria Cup, he carried second-highest weight of 128 pounds to victory by a length in a field of nineteen as third favorite at 7-1.

In summary, Unbreakable was a good two-year-old but never showed he could get a mile as a three-year-old. The seven furlongs of the Victoria Cup probably was his best distance.

			Cyllene, 1895	Bona Vista / Arcadia
		Polymelus, 1902	Maid Marian, 1886	**Hampton** / Quiver
	Phalaris, 1913	Bromus, 1905	**Sainfoin**, 1887	Springfield / Sanda
			Cheery, 1892	**St. Simon** / Sunrise
Sickle, 1924		Chaucer, 1900	**St. Simon**, 1881	Galopin / St. Angela
			Canterbury Pilgrim, 1893	Tristan / Pilgrimage
	Selene, 1919	Serenissima, 1913	Minoru, 1906	Cyllene / Mother Siegel
			Gondolette, 1902	Loved One / Dongola
UNBREAKABLE		Persimmon, 1893	**St. Simon**, 1881	Galopin / St. Angela
			Pedita, 1881	**Hampton** / Hermione
	Prince Palatine, 1908	Lady Lightfoot, 1900	Isinglass, 1890	Isonomy / Dead Lock
			Glare, 1891	Ayrshire / Footlight
Blue Glass, 1917		Rock Sand, 1900	**Sainfoin**, 1887	Springfield / Sanda
			Roquebrune, 1893	**St. Simon** / St. Marguerite
	Hour Glass, 1909	Hautesse, 1891	Archiduc, 1881	Consul / The Abbess
			Hauteur, 1880	Rosicrucian / Hawthorndale

At stud, back at Elmendorf, Unbreakable sired thirteen stakes winners and the only one of importance was Polynesian, the next link in a chain that led to Native Dancer.

End Notes:

1. Sickle' Star Pilot was champion two-year-old colt in 1945, having won the Hopeful, Futurity, and Pimlico Futurity.

CHAPTER TWENTY-SEVEN

POLYNESIAN

Polynesian was presented as a wedding anniversary gift by P.A.B. Widener II (whose father bred the colt) to his wife in 1943. He was chosen by trainer Morris Dixon from the Elmendorf Farm yearling crop, and he turned out to be the best of the lot. Owing to his having made fifty-eight starts over four seasons, it is possible to assess Polynesian as a racer fairly accurately. He was not as good a two-year-old as was his sire, Unbreakable, or his grandsire, Sickle, but he was a better three-year-old beyond a mile, and he was a sound, game horse through four campaigns.`

Polynesian's dam, Black Polly, died from colic a few weeks after the colt's birth, and Polynesian was reared on a formula of cow's milk fed from a bucket. Black Polly, who won only one race, had produced one previous foal, Black Shot, winner of ten races. She was sired by Polymelian, a speed horse, and was out of Black Queen, who had been second in the Laurel Stakes and Ladies Handicap. The next dam was the good race mare Black Maria. Polynesian was inbred to Polymelus with three free generations. Polymelus was the sire of Phalaris and was the original subject of the male line presently under review.

The two-year-old campaign of Polynesian was not very distinguished, although he won half his ten races. After being third twice in three tries, he bucked his shins and thereafter suffered from azoturia[1], which is a partial paralysis of the muscles. Polynesian was turned out—or dragged out. One day, he was attacked by hornets under a tree in his paddock. In response to that unfortunate circumstance, he raced around in terror until he was covered with sweat, but instead of coming down with pneumonia, he—with the aid of the hornets—more or less worked himself out of the azoturia.

He won his next start; then after finishing third again he won four races in succession, they including the Sagamore Stakes at Pimlico. That stakes was of secondary importance, carrying a value of $6,875 to the winner, and on the Experimental Free Handicap, Polynesian drew a rating below seven other

Joseph Widener (left) and
Mr. and Mrs. P.A.B. Widener II

BLOOD-HORSE LIBRARY

two-year-olds. He was assigned 119 pounds, seven pounds below the co-leaders, Pavot and Free For All.[2]

As a three-year-old, Polynesian began with the Experimental Handicap (which in those days was a race as well as a year-end rating). He finished third under top weight of 119 pounds.[3] A week later, he came out for the Wood Memorial but could not go with Hoop, Jr., and was beaten nine lengths.[4] It was decided to skip the Derby—which Hoop, Jr. won—and to go for the one-mile Withers Stakes. In the latter stakes, he had to meet the hitherto unbeaten Pavot at level weights, but to general surprise, the 1-5 Pavot gave ground in a driving finish and Polynesian won by a half-length.

This brought him up to the one and three-sixteenths-mile Preakness. Polynesian got off well and led into the stretch. Hoop, Jr. challenged but then bowed a tendon and checked himself, and Polynesian beat him by two and a half lengths. Pavot finished fifth.

The Preakness was probably Polynesian's best race, and it may have taken something out of him, for he could finish only fifth in his next race, the Shevlin Stakes. Given a month's rest, he was dropped back to six furlongs for the Saranac Handicap and had trouble winning in 1:10 2/5. He ran up a series of four seconds[5], then back at Pimlico won the Reistertown Handicap. Polynesian next finished sixth in a seven-horse field in the Pimlico Special, but Joe Palmer opined that the Widener colt probably was among the best five in his age group.

Polynesian's four-year-old season showed that he was a top-class sprinter, and at times still a good middle-distance horse. He began by winning the historic Toboggan Handicap at six furlongs under 124 pounds.[6] In the Metropolitan Handicap, he set out at a dizzy pace and eventually collapsed, but he came back under 126 pounds to win the six-furlong Roseben in 1:08 4/5 down Belmont Park's Widener Chute.

In the Suburban Handicap, Polynesian failed to stay the ten furlongs and finished tenth in a field of eleven. Dropped back again to six furlongs, he matched the Delaware Park track record of 1:10 2/5 for six furlongs but then was blocked early in the Fleetwing Handicap and finished third under 132 pounds. Still at six furlongs, Polynesian took up 130 pounds for Monmouth Park's Rumson and won by one and one-quarter lengths from Brookfield (123) in 1:10 3/5.

Stretched out to middle distances again, Polynesian finished fourth in the Wilson Stakes and Whitney Stakes at Saratoga, but the two finishes represented differing efforts. In the first, he was beaten by two necks and a head by champions Pavot and Gallorette and by Larky Day, but in the Whitney, he finished fourteen lengths behind champion Stymie.

Polynesian had been restrained well behind the early pace in the Whitney, with the hope that he could come on later in the race, but the tactic failed. For the Merchants' and Citizens' Handicap, he was put on the front and led for a mile before being worn down by Lucky Draw and losing by a length and a half. In the Saratoga Handicap at ten furlongs, Polynesian again tested Lucky Draw, pushing him to a track record of 2:01 3/5 before failing by less than a length. (Any racehorse is liable to be categorized on the basis of the distances at which he won most

			Polymelus, 1902	Cyllene / Maid Marian
		Phalaris, 1913	Bromus, 1905	Sainfoin / Cheery
	Sickle, 1924	Selene, 1919	Chaucer, 1900	St. Simon / Canterbury Pilgrim
			Serenissima, 1913	Minoru / Gondolette
Unbreakable, 1935		Prince Palatine, 1908	Persimmon, 1893	St. Simon / Perdita
	Blue Glass, 1917		Lady Lightfoot, 1900	Isinglass / Glare
		Hour Glass, 1909	Rock Sand, 1900	Sainfoin / Roquebrune
POLYNESIAN			Hautesse, 1891	Archiduc / Hauteur
		Polymelian, 1914	**Polymelus**, 1902	Cyllene, 1895 — Bona Vista / Arcadia
				Maid Marian, 1886 — Hampton / Quiver
	Polymelian, 1914	Pasquita, 1907	Sundridge, 1898	Amphion / Sierra
			Pasquil, 1890	Plebeian / Pasquinette
Black Polly, 1936		Pompey, 1923	Sun Briar, 1915	Sundridge / Sweet Briar
	Black Queen, 1930		Cleopatra, 1917	Corcyra / Gallice
		Black Maria, 1923	Black Toney, 1911	Peter Pan / Belgravia
			Bird Loose,1916	Sardanapale / Poule Au Pot

CARL KLEIN

Polynesian

often, but this sometimes is not fair. Polynesian's effort against so good a horse as Lucky Draw at ten furlongs should have erased much of the stigma against his middle-distance powers—especially considering that he was a Preakness winner.)

Polynesian again tried ten furlongs in the Washington Handicap at Laurel but could not quite make it, nor could he handle the nine furlongs of the Trenton Handicap at Garden State. As a finale for his four-year-old season, he returned to Pimlico—his track—and won the Riggs Handicap at a mile and three-sixteenths. Between the Saratoga Handicap and Washington Handicap, he had reverted to sprint distances for three races. In the seven-furlong Bay Shore, he carried 130 pounds and was third behind the filly Gallorette (124), but in Atlantic City's Pageant Handicap he carried 126 and matched Clang's world record of 1:09 1/5 for six furlongs around a turn.[7] With the weight back up to 130 pounds and the distance back up to seven furlongs, he was third again, in the Vosburgh Handicap.

After the Riggs, Polynesian was put by until the opening of the New York season of 1947. His first race at five came in the six-furlong Paumonok Handicap, in which he carried 130 pounds and lost by a head to Fighting Frank (125). At one and one-sixteenth miles, he was beaten by five lengths in the Excelsior Handicap, and then for the six-furlong Toboggan he was given the compliment of carrying 134 pounds. It was too much. He finished third.

In the Roseben, 132 pounds stopped him, but from his next nine starts he won eight races—and was badly bumped during the one race he lost. In the main, the races of that streak were at sprint distances and he won with as much as 134 pounds, but twice he won at distances of beyond a mile: Under 129 pounds in the one and one-sixteenth-mile Long Branch Handicap and under the same impost in the one and one-eighth-mile Omnibus Handicap.

In the Monmouth Handicap, Polynesian was slammed into and suffered a shoulder injury, which

YEAR	AGE	STS	1ST	2ND	3RD	EARNED
1944	at 2	10	5	1	3	$ 17,035
1945	at 3	14	5	4	1	$102,190
1946	at 4	20	8	3	5	$113,840
1947	at 5	14	9	2	1	$ 77,345
Lifetime		58	27	10	10	$310,410

forced him to miss all his engagements at Saratoga's August meeting. Coming back at Garden State, he won the Camden Handicap under 129 pounds and set a track record of 1:09 4/5 for six furlongs.

Trainer Dixon then sent the horse to Belmont Park, where he put one over on Ben A. Jones, and nearly everyone else who concerned themselves with matters of the Turf. Polynesian had drawn 140 pounds for the Fall Highweight Handicap, which seemed his obvious target, but on the same Belmont card was a six-furlong race written for Armed, whom Jones was preparing for a match race against Assault. Under the conditions of the latter race, Polynesian would get a break in the weights, so Dixon slipped him into Armed's race, and Polynesian took an early lead and beat the Calumet Farm champion by nearly three lengths.

Polynesian's sights next were set on Pimlico again, and in preparation for the Riggs he was sent out under 134 pounds for the six-furlong Janney Handicap. Giving twelve pounds to The Doge, Polynesian won by a length in what proved his last race. An extremely difficult horse to train, he was withdrawn from the Riggs and sent to Elmendorf to stud.

A medium-sized colt of great quality, he had exhibited great speed, some middle-distance ability, and exceptional soundness.

At stud, Polynesian sired thirty-seven stakes winners, as compared to the thirteen fathered by his sire, Unbreakable. Sickle, sire of Unbreakable, sired forty-five stakes winners. As frequently happens, the importance of Polynesian as a breeding animal boiled down virtually to one horse, and that horse was Native Dancer, three-time champion as a runner and a sire of international influence.

Nevertheless, Polynesian also sired Imbros (a brilliant speed horse who in turn sired the popular California millionaire Native Diver) plus 1956 champion two-year-old Barbizon, also a success at stud, and two-year-old sensation Polly's Jet, sire of a stayer in Turbo Jet II. Polynesian's daughters included the brilliant two-year-old fillies Alanesian, Mommy Dear, and Poly-Hi.

End Notes:

1. Azoturia, also known as "tying up," affects the muscles of horses and ranges from stiffness and mild cramping to an inability to stand.

2. Polynesian shared the 119-pound impost with Air Sailor, Flood Town, and the top weighted filly Busher.

3. In the Experimental Handicap race, Polynesian was co-high weight with Flood Town.

4. Polynesian finished fourth in the Wood Memorial.

5. After the Saranac Handicap, Polynesian finished ninth in the Jerome and won the Valorous Handicap at Belmont before stringing together four second-place finishes.

6. Polynesian began his four-year-old season by finishing third to Buzfuz in the Omaha Handicap at Jamaica. He then won the Toboggan Handicap.

7. This record—which had been originally set by a Broken Tendril gelding in Brighton, England, on August 6, 1929—had also been equaled by Mafosta, at Longacres on July 14, 1946.

CHAPTER TWENTY-EIGHT

NATIVE DANCER

W hen a two-year-old has finished an undefeated season, with nine wins and earnings of $230,495, a recital of his races is a somewhat monotonous undertaking. The real question is: How good was he really? This only can be guessed at by a look at what he did to his rivals.

After winning a five-furlong maiden race on April 19, 1952, Native Dancer was odds-on for the Youthful Stakes, which he won by six lengths in :59 2/5, and in doing so bucked his shins. At Saratoga he took the Flash Stakes (won by many good colts) by two and a quarter lengths, the Saratoga Special by three and a half, and the Grand Union Hotel by three and a half.

The Hopeful is the most important two-year-old stakes at Saratoga and is the first two-year-old stakes at six and a half furlongs. By that time, odds had shortened to 1-4 on Alfred Vanderbilt's homebred. Nevertheless, he had a little competition, and Eric Guerin had to draw his whip to outrace Tiger Skin by two lengths.

As a tune-up for the Futurity (then the most important two-year-old race), Native Dancer took the Anticipation Purse at Belmont Park. His price in the Futurity was 7-20, and there were a few anxious moments for the chalk eaters. Native Dancer was shut in between and behind beaten horses that were slowing up. Finally, he forced a narrow opening and came through to win by two and a quarter lengths from Tahitian King, another son of Polynesian.

This performance was remarkable in that the time, 1:14 2/5 for a straight six and a half furlongs, was a world's record[1], and Native Dancer had not had a clear run.

The East View Stakes at one and one-sixteenth miles was Native Dancer's last race of the year. Sent off with odds of 1-5, Native Dancer ran a somewhat lazy race but won by one and a half lengths.

As a partial answer to the question—how good was he—the two-year-old Experimental Free Handicap ratings were Native Dancer, 130; Tahitian King, 123.[2]

WINANT'S BROS.

Native Dancer

After a light firing of osselets to stop their enlargement, Native Dancer returned to New York from a winter in California. His first races were the standard ones for a classic colt. He took a division of the one and one-sixteenth-mile Gotham[3] and the one and one-eighth-mile Wood Memorial easily, being odds-on in each race.

Then came the most controversial race of the year—the Kentucky Derby. Guerin did not hurry away from the gate, and Native Dancer was behind seven horses as they went into the first turn. Halfway around the turn, Money Broker swerved in and hit Native Dancer. Guerin had to take up slightly but soon moved out from the rail and gained a place just behind the leaders.

To save ground, Guerin moved back to the rail again going around the last turn. Coming into the straight there was a wall of horses in front of Native Dancer, but they began to break their solid formation, so that Native Dancer was free to make his challenge. At the quarter-mile pole he was about two and a half lengths back; at the eighth-mile pole, he was one and a half lengths behind Dark Star, who had led from near the start.

From that point, the evidence becomes a mass of contradictions. The last eighth-mile was run in thirteen seconds—nothing very wonderful for a high-class colt. Some witnesses have said that Native Dancer was charging and was a half-length in front one stride past the winning post; others have said that he was right with Dark Star fifty yards from the finish and then could not pass. In any case, the photograph showed that Native Dancer had lost by a head—his only loss.

Native Dancer was given a two-week rest back in New York and then took the one-mile Withers easily from two other opponents at odds of 1-20.

Native Dancer and Dark Star met again in the one and three-sixteenths-mile Preakness, but Dark Star bowed a tendon, so any question between them never was answered. However, there was a new Richmond in the field in Jamie K., who drove up to Native Dancer. The longshot's bid failed, but Arcaro was beguiled into thinking that with added distance, as in the one and a half-mile Belmont Stakes, he could beat the gray.

The Belmont finish, however, proved a virtual retake of the Preakness finish insofar as finish order and margin were concerned. Again, Native Dancer had the lead and turned back Jamie K. That time, Arcaro came away a believer: "If we go around again, Native Dancer's still not gonna let me get past him." The author saw the race and also came away with the impression that Native Dancer had a good

Polynesian, 1942	Unbreakable, 1935	Sickle, 1924	Phalaris, 1913	Polymelus Bromus
			Selene, 1919	Chaucer Serenissima
		Blue Glass, 1917	Prince Palatine, 1908	Persimmon Lady Lightfoot
			Hour Glass, 1909	Rock Sand Hautesse
	Black Polly, 1936	Polymelian, 1914	Polymelus, 1902	Cyllene Maid Marian
			Pasquita, 1907	Sundridge Pasquil
NATIVE DANCER		Black Queen, 1930	Pompey, 1923	Sun Briar Cleopatra
			Black Maria, 1923	Black Toney Bird Loose
	Discovery, 1931	Display, 1923	Fair Play, 1905	Hastings Fairy Gold
			Cicuta, 1919	Nassovian Hemlock
		Ariadne, 1926	Light Brigade, 1910	Picton Bridge of Sighs
			Adrienne, 1919	His Majesty Adriana
Geisha, 1943	Miyako, 1935	John P. Grier, 1917	Whisk Broom II, 1907	Broomstick Audience
			Wonder, 1910	Disguise Curiosity
		La Chica, 1930	Sweep, 1907	Ben Brush Pink Domino
			La Grisette, 1915	Roi Herode Miss Fiora

P. BERTRAND ET FILS

Dan Cupid

deal in reserve, even though his time had been 2:28 3/5, which in 1953 had been bettered in the Belmont only by Count Fleet (1943) and Citation (1948).[4]

Another three weeks passed, and then another painless victory for Native Dancer was seen in the ten-furlong Dwyer Stakes. Next, trainer Bill Winfrey took Native Dancer on an expedition to Chicago for the one-mile Arlington Classic. Victory there was accomplished by nine lengths at the liberal odds of 7-10.

In the ten-furlong Travers at Saratoga, Native Dancer was 1-20 and won by five and a half lengths. He then went to Chicago again, for the one and one-eighth-mile American Derby. His jockey was Eddie Arcaro, as Guerin had been set down at Saratoga. Native Dancer won, but Arcaro was evasive when asked to classify him with the all-time greats.

At that point, some bruises were cut out of the sole of Native Dancer's left front foot, and he did not run again at three.

The Blood-Horse Free Handicap for three-year-olds ranked Native Dancer eight pounds above Dark Star, his nearest rival. As a two-year-old, his margin had been seven pounds above the second colt.

Native Dancer raced briefly at four. On May 7, he was given a simple six-furlong race at Belmont Park and won it easily by one and one-quarter lengths with 126 pounds up. The one-mile Metropolitan was a more serious matter. Guerin let Native Dancer take his time, and with a quarter-mile to go, he was still seven lengths back of Straight Face (117), who had run the first six furlongs in 1:10 1/5. With only a furlong to go, Native Dancer was still four lengths back. Guerin went to his whip and gave Native Dancer a few whacks. He went into high gear and got up to win by a neck in 1:35 1/5.

Due to an inflammation it was found impossible to run Native Dancer in either the Suburban or Brooklyn hand-icaps. He moved to Saratoga and started in a seven-furlong race, the Oneonta Handicap, which he won by nine lengths (137 pounds).

YEAR	AGE	STS	1ST	2ND	3RD	EARNED
1952	at 2	9	9	0	0	$230,495
1953	at 3	10	9	1	0	$513,425
1954	at 4	3	3	0	0	$ 41,320
Lifetime		22	21	1	0	$785,240

After that, it was impossible to train him, and he was retired to his owner's Sagamore Stud in Maryland.

There were many brisk debates as to whether Native Dancer or Tom Fool (one year his senior) was the better. Factually, Native Dancer had the better record at two and three, and Tom Fool the better record at four.

Native Dancer's pedigree deserves some study, as it is fairly typical of the blend-ing of American, British, and some French strains that have made the American Thoroughbred today as good as (if not better than) any others in the world.

The Honorable Leslie Combs owned a small gray mare (by Sweep, a small horse of the American Ben Brush–Domino cross) called La Chica. She was bred to John P. Grier, another horse (and a good one) of the Ben Brush–Domino strains. This foal, Miyako, and her half sister Planetoid, were stakes winners, and a colt out of La Chica, called El Chico, was the leading two-year-old of 1938.

None of the produce of La Chica had much distance capacity, and when Alfred Vanderbilt bought Miyako in 1940, it was natural for him to breed her to his stout campaigner Discovery. The mating resulted in a roan filly (1943) called Geisha.[5] She did not accomplish much on the track but was not hopeless, having a couple of seconds in three starts at two and winning a maiden race early in the year at three.

Vanderbilt chose the fast Polynesian, full of fast British blood, and apparently that sire restored the speed of Geisha's female line. Native Dancer (how well the Vanderbilt horses are named) was foaled on March 27, 1950, at Dan W. Scott's farm near Lexington.

Native Dancer was a big, vigorous, very strong horse, going back in these

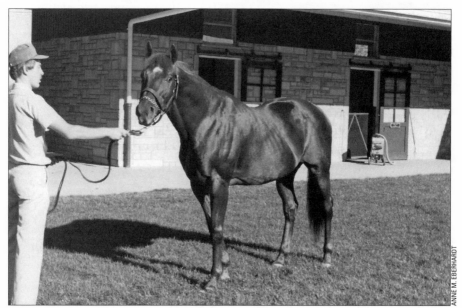

ANNE M. EBERHARDT

Raise a Native

respects to his maternal grandsire Discovery. His color had come through four generations from the French-bred Roi Herode.

Often in the male line of Phalaris (four generations up the top line in Native Dancer's pedigree) have there been instances of horses of less than highest racing class becoming important links in the sire chain. Native Dancer was both an extraordinary racer and a major sire, one who authored international influence in the best races. Three years a champion, he stood out in proven racing ability over his male-line ancestors, and he sired forty-four stakes winners before his death in 1967.[6]

Whereas often a stallion's ability to preserve his sire line as a viable force in breeding depends upon his getting one outstanding son, Native Dancer sired several sons who in turn passed on classic ability. These included Dan Cupid, a good but not great colt who was raced in France and who sired Sea-Bird, acclaimed in 1965 as one of the great European horses of the century.

Contrasting to Dan Cupid, a French classicist, was Raise a Native, a Native Dancer colt so brilliant that he won all his four races before an injury negated his chance to prove whether he had his sire's stamina. Raise a Native, however, already has sired Majestic Prince, winner of the 1969 Kentucky Derby and Preakness.

Native Dancer, whose only loss came in the Derby, has haunted the race ever since. In addition to his grandson Majestic Prince winning the classic, Native Dancer sired the 1966 Derby winner, Kauai King, while another son, Dancer's Image, was first past the post in the controversial 1968 running. Also, Northern Dancer, from a Native Dancer mare, won the race in 1964.

Native Dancer also sired Native Charger, a Flamingo–Florida Derby winner whose get has ranged from a filly (Forward Gal) brilliant and precocious enough to be a two-year-old champion (but no sprinter) to the later-maturing High Echelon, who, like his grandsire, won the Belmont.

Others among Native Dancer's foals included Hula Dancer, winner of the English One Thousand Guineas in 1963 after being a champion at two in France; plus Good Move, Secret Step, Native Street, and Protanto.[7]

End Notes:

1. Native Dancer's time of 1:14 2/5 tied the world's record. The record had been set by Porter's Mite at Belmont on September 17, 1938.

2. Laffango was also assigned 123 pounds.

3. In 1953 the Gotham was run in two divisions. Laffango took the second division.

4. Middleground, the 1950 Belmont winner, also ran the distance in 2:28 3/5.

5. Miyako only produced three registered foals. The 1940 mating between Miyako and Discovery resulted in a grey colt named Great Beyond; the 1942 mating produced Geisha. A third mating produced the roan colt Columbus, who was a stakes winner over jumps.

6. There is a discrepancy in the number of stakes winners. Hewitt has forty-five; The Jockey Club Information Systems has forty-three; *Sires and Dams of Stakes Winners* credits him with forty-four, the additional being Carnival Dancer who won the Granville Stakes at Ascot in England.

7. The Raise a Native branch of the Native Dancer sire line speaks for itself. Native Dancer also established a European branch that has since been repatriated to the United States. Native Dancer's son Atan established a line that includes Sharpen Up and his sons Kris, Diesis, and Selkirk. The Dan Cupid branch thrives in Europe through Sea-Bird's son Arctic Tern, the sire of Bering.

CHAPTER TWENTY-NINE

FAIRWAY

When Fairway first appeared on the racing scene, he was greeted as a younger brother of Pharos—five years younger in fact. However, it was not long before he staked out his own claim as a racer of the first class, doubtless a higher class than had been attained by Pharos.

The history of Fairway's sire, Phalaris, has been set out in a previous chapter in this book and the history of his dam, Scapa Flow, and her family is given in the chapter on Pharos.

After producing Pharos in 1920, Scapa Flow was barren for two seasons. Then, in 1923, she produced Pentland, a colt without much racing merit, sired by an obscure stallion called Torloisk. Probably the reason for breeding her to such a poor sire was that Scapa Flow previously had been barren, and it did not seem worth risking a season to a high-class sire until Scapa Flow seemed likely to breed again. In 1924, Scapa Flow was barren again, but by that time Pharos was known to be a high-class colt, so Scapa Flow was sent to Phalaris again. The result, on April 15, 1925, was Fairway.

In appearance, Fairway differed from his brother Pharos. Fairway was taller and longer than Pharos, and much darker in color—while Pharos was clearly a bay, Fairway was so dark he easily could be called brown. Fairway had as good a set of legs and feet as you could want to see and two grand ends, with a very light middle, giving him something of a greyhound aspect.

Like many of the progeny of Phalaris, Fairway was nervous and sometimes would break into a sweat. Frequently this meant little, and the Phalaris stock generally ran well after sweating freely before a race.

Fairway had a most beautiful, long, light action—the extra length of his stride undoubtedly inherited from his grandsire, Polymelus. When horses of this type become unbalanced, it often is very difficult to get them rebalanced in a race.

Lord Derby's manager at that time, the Honorable George Lambton, was convinced early that Fairway was a first-class colt, and he was determined to win the

George Lambton (center) with stable lads

first important two-year-old race with him—the Coventry Stakes at Royal Ascot. To give Fairway a preliminary eye-opener, Lambton sent him to York in May to run in the Eglinton Stakes. Though starting favorite, Fairway ran greenly and finished only sixth.

In the Coventry Stakes at Royal Ascot in June, Fairway won as he liked, starting at the generous price of 7-1, due no doubt to his indifferent display in the Eglinton Stakes.

At Newmarket the next month, Fairway came out for the important July Stakes. There he came up against a high-class colt in Hakim (half brother to the Grand Prix de Paris winner Lemonora) and got up to beat Hakim a head on the post.

In the Champagne Stakes at Doncaster (one of the constellations in the diadem of the traditional English two-year-old stakes, together with the Coventry, the Gimcrack, the Middle Park, and the Dewhurst), Fairway was odds-on and won easily. This finished his two-year-old season, as he was slightly lame after the race.

As a three-year-old, Fairway was to have had his first race in the Two Thousand Guineas, but the day before the race it was discovered that an abscess had developed in his mouth, so he did not start. The important race between the Two Thousand Guineas and the Derby in those days was the Newmarket Stakes—ten furlongs across the flat. Fairway won it easily.

Next came the Derby. There Fairway's nervous system betrayed him. In the paddock he was cool enough, but as soon as he went onto the course he literally was mobbed, with enthusiasts even trying to pluck hairs from his tail. Fairway broke into a profuse lather, and by the time he reached the starting post he was soaking wet. In the race itself he did nothing, finishing a long way back of Felstead.

Fairway then was given a good rest before reappearing for the ten-furlong Eclipse Stakes at Sandown Park in July. The public had become distrustful of Fairway, and at one time his odds were 7-1. Two bettor favorites were the filly Book Law (winner of the previous year's St. Leger) and Royal Minstrel, who narrowly had been beaten in the Two Thousand Guineas. In the Eclipse, Fairway won as he liked by eight lengths from Royal Minstrel.

In the St. Leger in September, Fairway was a short-priced favorite and won easily from Palais Royal II and Cyclonic. The present writer witnessed that race and carried away the impression that Fairway had action unsurpassed in its lightness and beauty.

The Champion Stakes in October completed Fairway's season. In that ten-furlong race across the flat at Newmarket, Fairway won fairly easily by a neck from Foliation, a good mare bred on Northern Hemisphere time in Argentina.

It was decided to keep Fairway in training as a four-year-old, and all began well.

	Polymelus, 1902	Cyllene, 1895	Bona Vista, 1889	Bend Or / Vista
			Arcadia, 1887	Isonomy / Distant Shore
		Maid Marian, 1886	Hampton, 1872	Lord Clifden / Lady Langden
			Quiver, 1872	Toxophilite / Y. Melbourne Mare
Phalaris, 1913	Bromus, 1905	Sainfoin, 1887	Springfield, 1873	St. Albans / Viridis
			Sanda, 1878	Wenlock / Sandal
		Cheery, 1892	St. Simon, 1881	Galopin / St. Angela
			Sunrise, 1883	Springfield / Sunray
FAIRWAY	Chaucer, 1900	St. Simon, 1881	Galopin, 1872	Vedette / Flying Duchess
			St. Angela, 1865	King Tom / Adeline
		Canterbury Pilgrim, 1893	Tristan, 1878	Hermit / Thrift
			Pilgrimage, 1875	The Palmer / Lady Audley
Scapa Flow, 1914	Anchora, 1905	Love Wisely, 1893	Wisdom, 1873	Blinkhoolie / Aline
			Lovelorn, 1888	Philammon / Gone
		Eryholme, 1898	Hazlehatch, 1885	Hermit / Hazledean
			Ayrsmoss, 1894	Ayrshire / Rattlewings

Fairway

He easily won the one and a half-mile Burwell Stakes at Newmarket, then won the Rous Memorial Stakes at Ascot, run over the Hunt Cup Course, just short of a mile. Pointing for the valuable Eclipse Stakes again, Fairway was given an outing in the one and a half-mile Princess of Wales's Stakes at Newmarket and won easily enough.

Next came the great surprise. In the field for the Eclipse Stakes there was only one other runner with the slightest chance of beating Fairway. This was Royal Minstrel, who had gone under by eight lengths to Fairway in the same race the year before. This time, Royal Minstrel challenged in resolute style and went on to win by four lengths. At the time, it was claimed that Fairway had run many pounds below his real form, as Royal Minstrel showed a net improvement of twelve lengths over his previous year's form with Fairway. It is not absolutely certain that this form was wrong.

Captain Cecil Boyd-Rochfort (now Sir Cecil) trained Royal Minstrel, who had been a highly nervous colt. Boyd-Rochfort's head lad, Barnett, spent many hours with Royal Minstrel on the Limekilns and other Newmarket gallops, letting the colt stroll about and pick at the grass until he became happy and relaxed. Hence Royal Minstrel was a vastly improved colt over his three-year-old form. It was a remarkable training exploit to get any son of Tetratema (who sired sprinters) to win a first-class race at ten furlongs, especially when the last part of the course is uphill.

In the autumn, Fairway again won the Champion Stakes and then he won the two and a quarter-mile Jockey Club Cup, both at Newmarket. So much for the myth that the speed-horse Phalaris could not sire a stayer.

Fairway was kept in training as a five-year-old with the Ascot Gold Cup as his main objective, but he was unable to start.

Lambton reported that Fairway was tried over two and a quarter miles with Bosworth (an Ascot Gold Cup winner) at weight-for-age. Two good handicappers were put in to make pace for the first mile and two more added for the last one and a quarter miles. With the horses ridden right out, Fairway beat Bosworth about a length. Lambton considered this the finest Cup trial he ever had heard of.

YEAR	AGE	STS	1ST	2ND	3RD	EARNED*
1927	at 2	4	3	0	0	£ 6,390
1928	at 3	5	4	0	0	£29,707
1929	at 4	6	5	1	0	£ 6,625
Lifetime		15	12	1	0	£42,722

* First-place money only

As a sire, Fairway was extremely consistent: He led the sire list in 1936, 1939, 1943, 1944, was second in 1935, 1937, 1942, and third in 1946.

In a sense, Fairway was not a fortunate sire in that only one of his sons—Fair Trial—was a real success at stud. Since Fair Trial, coming from the Americus Girl family, was lacking in the transmission of stamina, the Fairway male line has begun to drop out of the classic picture here, though it remained very successful in Argentina. It has been maintained by a succession of milers and scored a resounding success in England with Brigadier Gerard (by Queen's Hussar, a miler, he by March Past, whose sire, Petition, was a champion sire by Fair Trial).

Fairway's own progeny had a stamina index of just over nine furlongs. Like most sires, Fairway sired better colts than fillies, which generally trained into the lean greyhound type and carried insufficient flesh and muscle to be at full strength.

Fairway's best colts were Blue Peter (Derby, Two Thousand Guineas in 1939), Pay Up (Two Thousand Guineas in 1936), Watling Street (Derby in 1942), Kingsway (Two Thousand Guineas in 1943), Honeyway (Champion Stakes in 1946), plus Fair Trial, Full Sail, and Fair Copy.

His best fillies were Tide-way (One Thousand Guineas in 1936), Garden Path (Two Thousand Guineas in 1944), and Ribbon (Middle Park Stakes in 1942).

Fairway spent his whole stud life at Lord Derby's Woodland Stud at Newmarket.

Blue Peter

He painlessly was put down in November of 1948.

Most sire lines depend for their continuation on one horse; in this case the horse was Fair Trial. Unfortunately for Fairway, his best racing son, Blue Peter, was somewhat disappointing at stud.

CHAPTER THIRTY

FAIR TRIAL

E very racing man should have a benevolent uncle to leave him several million dollars in cash, plus a fine stud of Thoroughbreds. This happens to very few of us mortals, but it did happen to J.A. Dewar, whose uncle Thomas Dewar, the distiller, left him one million pounds sterling, as well as all his bloodstock. One of the animals included in this bequest was Cameronian, who won the Epsom Derby of 1931. (Cameronian never could have started for the Derby if the longstanding rule avoiding all engagements upon the death of the nominator had not been repealed through the legal efforts of Edgar Wallace, author of mysteries and other popular works.)

One of the mares in the Thomas Dewar stud was Lady Juror, a 1919 foal by Son-in-Law, he being a great sire of stayers. Lady Juror's dam was Lady Josephine, she by Sundridge and from the great foundation mare Americus Girl. Lady Juror had been a good race mare, winning over five and six furlongs as well as winning the Jockey Club Stakes at one and three-quarters miles. Before foaling Fair Trial, Lady Juror bred The Black Abbot (Gimcrack Stakes), Jurisdiction, The Recorder, and Riot, winners of a total of 16,648 pounds.

It is of considerable interest to note that, while Lady Juror (like a true Son-in-Law) could stay one and three-quarters miles, all of her produce bred back to the short-distance capacities of her dam, Lady Josephine, and granddam, Americus Girl. (Lady Josephine was the dam of the brilliant speedster Mumtaz Mahal, second dam of Nasrullah.)

Fair Trial was a good-sized, lengthy colt sired in Fairway's first crop. As he was by a St. Leger winner and out of a Jockey Club Stakes winner, there was some reason to think that Fair Trial might stay well. This hope proved unfounded. Fair Trial bred back, both in his chestnut color and in his distance capacity, to the Lady Josephine–Americus Girl strain in his pedigree.

When he was sent to trainer Fred Darling at Beckhampton, Fair Trial was found to be so immature as a two-year-old that he was not trained at all at that age. Even

209

Fred Darling (left) and John A. Dewar

at three, his training was delayed by the handicaps of shelly feet and bad knees. Hence, his first appearance in public was put off until May 24, in a small race of one mile at the provincial course of Salisbury. Fair Trial started at even money, and with Gordon Richards in the saddle won easily enough.

Fair Trial went next to Royal Ascot in the middle of June and won the Queen Anne Stakes at about one mile, giving ten pounds and a three-length beating to a useful filly in Solerina. In July, Fair Trial came out for the one and a quarter-mile Eclipse Stakes at Sandown Park and encountered high-class competition for the first time. Also in the field were four-year-old Windsor Lad, the previous year's Derby and St. Leger winner, carrying 136 pounds, and three-year-old Theft, carrying 121 pounds. Fair Trial carried 118 pounds, meaning that Windsor Lad was conceding four pounds more than weight-for-age.

Fair Trial had the lead early in the homestretch in the Eclipse, but he could not hold it. Windsor Lad came on to beat Theft by three-quarters of a length, Theft in turn gaining a like margin over Fair Trial. On the face of it, that race made Fair Trial about nine pounds below classic form. Theft, who beat him while giving Fair Trial three pounds, had been runner-up to unbeaten Bahram in the Two Thousand Guineas and fourth in the Derby.

Fair Trial had only two more outings as a three-year-old, both in October (possibly because the more yielding ground of autumn was less trying on his doubted knees). In the Select Stakes of one mile at Newmarket, Fair Trial went off at 1-2 and won by six lengths, but there was nothing much behind him. In the Ormonde Plate, also at one mile, at Newbury, Fair Trial went off at 1-4 and won by five lengths.

The Jockey Club handicapper evidently accepted the Eclipse Stakes form as correct, for on the Free Handicap for three-year-olds he gave Fair Trial 125 pounds, with Theft three pounds above him. The Triple Crown winner, Bahram, topped the list at 136 pounds.

As a four-year-old, Fair Trial was out four times and won three races. In the Spring Plate of nine furlongs at Newmarket, he was 3-10 to beat Bobsleigh (who had been a good colt) at level weights, and he duly obliged, by two lengths. In the March Stakes over ten furlongs on the flat at Newmarket, Fair Trial carried 132 pounds and was odds-on again, at 4-9. Fair Trial's stamina limitations became apparent, as he was beaten by two lengths by Lord Derby's Plassy, although he was in receipt of four pounds.

At Ascot, Fair Trial was 3-10 for the Rous Memorial Stakes at seven furlongs, 155 yards, and he won by a length from modest opposition. In July at Lingfield Park, Fair Trial came out against Boswell in a two-horse race over a straight mile. Fair Trial continued to be an odds-on favorite, going off at 1-10 against his three-year-old rival (who later won the St. Leger). The distance was too short for Boswell and just about right for Fair Trial. Giving Boswell twelve pounds, Fair Trial won by six lengths. The race was designed as a preparation for another attempt at the Eclipse Stakes, but Fair Trial strained a tendon, which later gave

Fairway, 1925	Phalaris, 1913	Polymelus, 1902	Cyllene, 1895	Bona Vista / Arcadia
			Maid Marian, 1886	**Hampton** / Quiver
		Bromus, 1905	Sainfoin, 1887	**Springfield** / **Sanda**
			Cheery, 1892	St. Simon / Sunrise
	Scapa Flow, 1914	Chaucer, 1900	St. Simon, 1881	Galopin / St. Angela
			Canterbury Pilgrim, 1893	Tristan / Pilgrimage
		Anchora, 1905	Love Wisely, 1893	Wisdom / Lovelorn
FAIR TRIAL			Eryholme, 1898	Hazlehatch / Ayrsmoss
	Son-in-Law, 1911	Dark Ronald, 1905	Bay Ronald, 1893	**Hampton** / Black Duchess
			Darkie, 1889	Thurio / Insignia
		Mother-in-Law, 1906	Matchmaker, 1892	Donovan / Match Girl
Lady Juror, 1919			Be Cannie, 1891	Jock of Oran / Reticence
	Lady Josephine, 1912	Sundridge, 1898	Amphion, 1886	Rosebery / Suicide
			Sierra, 1889	**Springfield** / **Sanda**
		Americus Girl, 1905	Americus, 1892	Emperor of Norfolk / Clara D.
			Palotta, 1893	Gallinule / Maid of Kilcreene

Fair Trial

way and forced his retirement.

In summation, Fair Trial was a very good miler but was about eight to ten pounds behind classic form. As mentioned earlier in this book, the entire line of Phalaris was marked by various instances of horses well below greatness as runners, succeeding at stud to a far greater degree than on the race track. Phalaris, himself, fit that pattern, as did Pharos and Royal Charger, and, to a lesser degree, Nasrullah.

To some extent, Fair Trial duplicated the pattern admirably, for he himself became a leading sire, and two of his sons, Petition and Court Martial, led the sire lists in England. Whereas others of the Phalaris line contributed at least one son capable of carrying on the excellence of the direct male line, Fair Trial sired good horses (generally limited in stamina) but as a fount of classic ability, his branch of the male line dwindled, even though Court Martial was a prolific sire of stakes winners.

The line, however, is not dead, having received a resuscitation in England in the emergence of the brilliant Brigadier Gerard, whose first foals arrived in 1974. He was represented in 1976 by two stakes winners: General and Etienne Gerard. Brigadier Gerard is by Queen's Hussar, he by March Past, a son of Petition. Recent additional winners representing the line in England and in France are Highclere, Polygamy, and English Prince. Representatives of the Fair Trial line in North America include sprint champion Impressive, by Court Martial.[1]

YEAR	AGE	STS	1ST	2ND	3RD	EARNED*
1934	at 2	unraced				
1935	at 3	5	4	0	1	£2,735
1936	at 4	4	3	1	0	£2,365
Lifetime		**9**	**7**	**1**	**1**	**£5,100**
*First-place money only						

Fair Trial at stud quickly proved a consistent success, but one of a different type than his sire, Fairway. The latter's produce had an average winning distance of more than nine furlongs whereas the average winning distance of Fair Trial's get was 6.92 furlongs. Fair Trial apparently transmitted the speed of Lady Josephine and Americus Girl but not the stamina of Son-in-Law, and very little of Fairway.

Beginning with his first crop's two-year-old season, 1940, and continuing through 1950, Fair Trial was among the top six stallions on the British sire list annually except for one year. He topped the list in 1950, and from that pinnacle he plunged to twenty-sixth the next year and never again was in the top ten. He died in 1958 after twenty-two seasons at stud.

In his first crop, Fair Trial got Lambert Simnel, who won the 1941 Two Thousand Guineas, becoming the first of three colts by the sire to win that mile classic. Lambert Simnel was followed by Court Martial in 1945 and then by Palestine in 1950. Moreover, Fair Trial sired a winner of the filly counterpart in Festoon, 1954 One Thousand Guineas winner. Palestine was a champion miler as well as being a classic winner. In North America, Fair Trial had seven stakes winners, including King Bruce II, Bandit, and Mafosta.

At the time of the horse's death, the *Bloodstock Breeders' Review* commented that as a sire of mares, "Fair Trial compares most favourably with all the best contemporary broodmare sires ... and there also is no cause for complaint about their quality." One of his daughters, Daily Double, produced Meld, the remarkable filly who in 1955 won the One Thousand Guineas and Oaks and then defeated colts in the St. Leger. Meld, who, in turn, produced a Derby winner in Charlottown, was by Alycidon, a premier stayer.

Court Martial, who won the Guineas and ten-furlong Champion Stakes and was third in the Derby, had a remarkable record at stud, being six times England's leading juvenile sire as well as leading the general sire list in England twice in succes-

Court Martial

sion, in 1956 and 1957. Court Martial in England was known as a sire of sprinters and milers, but after his importation to this country he sired Goofed, a filly that excelled at longer distances and won the one and a half-mile Ladies Handicap in 1963.[2] Court Martial sired a total of seventy-two stakes winners. He sent out nine North American stakes winners, including Fashion Verdict, Face the Facts, and Desert Law, in addition to Impressive and Goofed.

Fair Trial's son Petition confounded pedigree analysts by winning the 1948 Eclipse Stakes at ten furlongs, which generally was beyond the abilities of the Fair Trials against major competition. Petition won it, but it was a near thing, as he held on to win by a head over a top-class field of Sayajirao, Noor, and Migoli.

Petition's progeny included the great filly Petite Etoile, who stayed one and a half miles against classic company, and his four North American stakes winners included Day Court, who set a track record for one and a quarter miles in the Hawthorne Gold Cup.

Sons of Fair Trial fared well as sires of classic-distance horses in Australia, New Zealand, and Argentina, a circumstance which the *Bloodstock Breeders' Review* accepted as a matter of British birthright: "There is nothing surprising in the fact that the progeny of Fair Trial's sons abroad can win big races over the Derby or St. Leger distance. For many years now, we have become accustomed to seeing horses that descend even from pure sprinting lines which have proved capable of staying a distance of ground on overseas or Continental race courses."

It is worth noting that the nervous systems of Fair Trial and his produce were far more stable than were those of Fairway, Nearco, and Nasrullah, but Fair Trial lacked the others' very high racing class. As the nervous energy dropped, the racing class declined, as also was true of milers descending from Fair Trial—until the appearance of Brigadier Gerard. The latter not only showed brilliant speed but also won the one and a half-mile King George VI and Queen Elizabeth Stakes. The dam of Brigadier Gerard was by Prince Chevalier, a French Derby winner whose stock stayed well.

End Notes:

1. Impressive died in 1988. He sired twenty-three stakes winners, including Argentinean champion sprinter Arg High Command. A current representative of the Fair Trial line in North America is Patton, a grade III stakes winner by Lord At War (a son of General and a grandson of Brigadier Gerard). Argentinean-bred Lord At War, who sired forty-seven stakes winners, died in 1998.

Other modern representatives of the Fair Trial line include the New Zealand-bred and -based Shannon, who descends from Petition's son Petingo, and European champion Snurge, a son of the pensioned Ela-Mana-Mou who also descends from Petition through Petingo. Snurge stands in Ireland.

2. Goofed became the dam of French stakes winner Lyphard (by Northern Dancer), who sired 112 stakes winners and was a leading sire in France and the United States. Goofed also produced group I winner Nobiliary and grade II winner Barcas.

CHAPTER THIRTY-ONE

PHARAMOND II & MENOW

Pharamond II was a full brother to Sickle and one year his junior. In his two-year-old season, Pharamond II was not up to the standard of his brother. Pharamond II was out six times and won only his last race, for which he earlier had not even been an intended starter.

His first race was the Zetland Plate at York in May. In a field of fourteen his price was 6-1, but he was back in the pack. However, in his next race, the Windsor Castle Stakes at Ascot, Pharamond II was sent off the 9-2 second choice and in a field of eighteen finished third, beaten by one and one-half lengths. This was a better showing, so for the valuable National Breeders' Produce Stakes, Pharamond II was made a 2-1 favorite. He finished unplaced in a field of twenty-one.

YEAR	AGE	STS	1ST	2ND	3RD	EARNED*
1927	at 2	6	1	2	1	£3,320
1928	at 3	5	1	0	0	£ 375
Lifetime		**11**	**2**	**2**	**1**	**£3,695**
* First-place money only						

At Liverpool in the Lancashire Breeders' Produce Stakes, Pharamond II was well liked at odds of 5-6, but in a field of five he failed by a neck to give Dark Doll fifteen pounds. The Buckenham (Post) Produce Stakes at Newmarket attracted only three runners—Pharamond II, 3-2; The Wheedler, 2-1; and Scatter, 5-2. Again Pharamond II went under, but only by a short head.

Next came the Middle Park Stakes at Newmarket, which had drawn a field of eight, but not another good horse was in it. Pharamond II was the third choice at 6-1, but he won by a head from Parwiz, who afterward became a fair handicapper. It had been intended to start Fairway in the Lord Derby colors for the Middle Park, but since Fairway showed some lameness after winning the Champagne Stakes at Doncaster, it was decided to let Pharamond II deputize for him.

Trainer George Lambton told the writer that Fairway was so much better than Pharamond II that it was very difficult to bring them together with a weight difference.

Pharamond II

In the two-year-old Free Handicap, Pharamond II was assigned 110 pounds, sixteen pounds from the top, with twenty-two others ranked above him.

As a three-year-old, Pharamond II began in the Nonsuch Stakes at Epsom in April. He made no show in that race, or in the Two Thousand Guineas. Thereafter, he was dropped in class to the Kempton Park Great Jubilee Handicap, where he carried only 98 pounds. Still he made no show. In the one-mile St. James's Palace Stakes at Ascot, Pharamond II was 6-1 in a field of eight and again was unplaced. Finally, in a field of three in the one and three-eighths-mile Ellesmere Stakes and carrying only 103 pounds, Pharamond II won—by a neck at odds of 8-13.

This not-very-glorious racing career eventuated the sale of Pharamond II. The price asked was 10,000 pounds ($50,000).

One of the visitors who came to look at Pharamond II was Hal Price Headley of Lexington. Headley told the writer that it was practically dark when he arrived on a gloomy evening in the late autumn or early winter and that Pharamond II barely was discernible where he stood in straw nearly up to his knees and in a barn covered with black tar paint. Headley did not ask to have Pharamond II brought out, because as he put it, "I did not want Lord Derby's men to learn how interested I was."

Instead, Headley beat a retreat through the gloom and wrote from Lexington: "If Lord Derby would not be insulted, I would like to offer 4,000 pounds (not 10,000) for Pharamond II." Headley got the horse at his price.

At stud, Pharamond II was a solid success, but for the purpose of this book, his interest lies in one son—Menow. However, his thirty-five stakes winners also included Cosmic Bomb, By Jimminy, and the fillies Creole Maid, Athenia, and Apogee. Pharamond II died in 1935.

PHARAMOND II				
Phalaris, 1913	Polymelus, 1902	Cyllene, 1895	Bona Vista, 1889	Bend Or / Vista
			Arcadia, 1887	Isonomy / Distant Shore
		Maid Marian, 1886	Hampton, 1872	Lord Clifden / Lady Langden
			Quiver, 1872	Toxopholite / Young Melbourne mare
	Bromus, 1905	Sainfoin, 1887	Springfield, 1873	St. Albans / Viridis
			Sanda, 1878	Wenlock / Sandal
		Cheery, 1892	St. Simon, 1881	Galopin / St. Angela
			Sunrise, 1883	Springfield / Sunray
Selene, 1919	Chaucer, 1900	St. Simon, 1881	Galopin, 1872	Vedette / Flying Duchess
			St. Angela, 1865	King Tom / Adeline
		Canterbury Pilgrim, 1893	Tristan, 1878	Hermit / Thrift
			Pilgrimage, 1875	The Palmer / Lady Audley
	Serenissima, 1913	Minoru, 1906	Cyllene, 1895	Bona Vista / Arcadia
			Mother Siegel, 1897	Friars Balsam / Galopin mare
		Gondolette, 1902	Loved One, 1883	See Saw / Pilgrimage
			Dongola, 1883	Doncaster / Douranee

MENOW

The success of Menow typified the swing away from the traditional American strains of Domino, Ben Brush, and Fair Play on the part of the down-to-earth, professional horsemen of Kentucky.

Sir Gallahad III, Bull Dog, and Sickle were having their impact. Headley had been a traditional American breeder at his large Beaumont Farm in Lexington, and had used the inbred Domino-line sire Ultimus (by a son of Domino, out of a daughter of Domino) until the horse died in 1921. For Headley, Ultimus had sired a good horse

MORGAN PHOTO SERVICE

Hal Price Headley with Menow

in Supremus, from the imported mare Mandy Hamilton. Headley tried an imported cross again, breeding Supremus to Regal Roman, by Roi Herode (bred in France, and coming from French strains). This cross produced the fine filly Alcibiades, winner of the Kentucky Oaks and the Clipsetta and Debutante stakes.

With Alcibiades, Headley turned to imported blood once more, and using Pharamond II as the sire, bred Menow. It seemed as though the very channels of his success forced Headley, at successive steps, away from the customary American blood and into using more and more foreign strains. By the time Menow arrived, only one out of his eight great-grandparents represented American blood—six of them were English, one was French.

Being a May 19 foal, Menow was not hurried unduly as a two-year-old. His first start was at Washington Park (Chicago) in an allowance race over a sloppy track. Running rather greenly, Menow finished second, beaten by two lengths. Nine days later, he came out for a maiden race over a very heavy track. There was a ding-dong struggle with another Pharamond II colt, Calumet Farm's Pharacase, and after they bumped each other repeatedly in the stretch Menow won his race by a nose.

Moving up in class for the Washington Park Futurity on June 26, 1937, Menow ran coupled in the betting with his stable companion Bourbon King (at that time thought to be the better of the pair). Tiger, from the Milky Way Farm of Mrs. Ethel V. Mars, led all the way and ran the six furlongs in 1:11, with Menow finishing second, two lengths back.

Five weeks later, Menow came out for the Arlington Futurity. He

YEAR	AGE	STS	1ST	2ND	3RD	EARNED
1937	at 2	6	3	2	0	$ 68,825
1938	at 3	11	4	1	3	$ 71,275
Lifetime		17	7	3	3	$140,100

presented a dull and stale appearance in the paddock and ran a very dull race, finishing unplaced. As a consequence, Menow was not seen out again until September 18 in the Champagne Stakes at Belmont Park. At that time, the Champagne was regarded as a curtain raiser for the Futurity, and both were run down the straight Widener Chute. For the Champagne, Menow was 12-1, while Sky Larking was an even-money favorite.

At the place where the Widener course intersected the main track, Menow was leading slightly from Sky Larking, when Sky Larking stumbled and snapped one of his forelegs. Menow went on to win easily by four lengths from Calumet's Bull Lea (later a greater sire than Menow, or any other horse of his time). Bull Lea was

MENOW				
Pharamond II, 1925	Phalaris, 1913	Polymelus, 1902	Cyllene, 1895	Bona Vista / Arcadia
			Maid Marian, 1886	Hampton / Quiver
		Bromus, 1905	Sainfoin, 1887	Springfield / Sanda
			Cheery, 1892	St. Simon / Sunrise
	Selene, 1919	Chaucer, 1900	St. Simon, 1881	Galopin / St. Angela
			Canterbury Pilgrim, 1893	Tristan / Pilgrimage
		Serenissima, 1913	Minoru, 1906	Cyllene / Mother Siegel
			Gondolette, 1902	Loved One / Dongola
Alcibiades, 1927	Supremus, 1922	Ultimus, 1906	Commando, 1898	Domino / Emma C.
			Running Stream, 1898	Domino / Dancing Water
		Mandy Hamilton, 1913	John o' Gaunt, 1901	Isinglass / La Fleche
			My Sweetheart, 1904	Galeazzo / Lady Chancellor
	Regal Roman, 1921	Roi Herode, 1904	Le Samaritain, 1895	Le Sancy / Clementina
			Roxelane, 1894	War-Dance / Rose Of York
		Lady Cicero, 1913	Cicero, 1902	Cyllene / Gas
			Ste Claire II, 1904	Isinglass / Santa Brigida

conceding Menow three pounds.

In the Futurity, Menow was coupled with both Bourbon King and Dah He as second favorites at 9-5, behind the 7-5 Milky Way pair of Tiger and Mountain Ridge. Menow drew out from the field, until at the finish he was four lengths clear of Tiger, who had headed Fighting Fox in the last stride. The main subject of conversation about the race was the time, 1:15 1/5 for the six and a half furlongs—a new world record. The best previous time down the Widener had been 1:16 2/5, credited to Pompoon in the 1936 Futurity.

This type of event casts some doubt about the overall importance of time. Both Tiger and Fighting Fox (second and third, respectively) must also have broken the previous time record yet neither of them turned out to be exceptional.

Due to striking his right foreleg in training, Menow was not able to run again as a two-year-old. On the Experimental Free Handicap, Menow was given top weight of 126 pounds, with Tiger second at 124. This meant that in the view of the handicapper the foals of 1935 were an ordinary crop, with no Alsab, Count Fleet, Tom Fool, or Native Dancer among them. John Hervey, the dean of Turf historians, observed that Menow was a little on the strong and heavy side to be expected to stay the classic distances at three. Hervey perhaps was too tactful to point out that neither Menow's sire nor either of his two grandsires could do so.

After a training spell during the winter in Florida, Menow started his three-year-old campaign at Keeneland in a six-furlong Trial Handicap with 122 pounds up on April 15, 1938. In a four-horse field, Menow was 1-10. He won all right, in 1:11 2/5, but he did not show the early speed that had been his trademark as a two-year-old. On April 21, things were a little more exciting, as Menow and Bull Lea were to hook up at one and one-sixteenth miles. No doubt because of the form of the two colts in the previous year's Champagne Stakes, Menow was made favorite at 3-10, while Bull Lea was 3-1. Menow had to concede Bull Lea six pounds, but the way the race was run, this did not make much difference. Bull Lea got off winging, and Menow was left flat-footed. Menow never was able to get in a challenge, and Bull Lea won easily in 1:44, lowering the track record by four-fifths of a second.

A week later, the two colts met again in the Blue Grass Stakes of one and one-eighth miles. That time, Menow had to concede only two pounds. The betting public had been influenced by the form of the previous race: Bull Lea now was 3-5, and Menow (coupled with Dah He) was 17-10. Menow got off well and showed his old early speed, going to the front at once. Bull Lea, however, stayed with him and in a hard drive got up in time to beat Menow by a neck. Menow ran the last furlong in 13 seconds, which is not quite up to classic standard. Again, however, a new track record had been established, the 1:49 3/5 breaking the previous mark by nearly three seconds.

In the Kentucky Derby, Menow led for the first mile, but when he was challenged by Lawrin and Dauber, he gave in and was beaten a half-dozen lengths in fourth. However, Bull Lea finished considerably farther back.

Menow was shipped to Pimlico for the Preakness, in which his performance was almost a duplication of his race for the Kentucky Derby. He led for the first mile and then folded up to finish third to Dauber and Cravat, beaten seven lengths.

A week later, the one-mile Withers was run at Belmont Park. Since there was nothing much in the field, Menow was allowed to take his chance, and the chance was not so bad. He won as he liked from Thanksgiving, but the time of 1:37 2/5 was nothing remarkable.

Although Headley did not care to admit it for publication, he now realized that Menow was not a good candidate for the one and a half-mile Belmont Stakes, so Menow was pointed for the one and one-eighth-mile Massachusetts Handicap at Suffolk Downs. His weight assignment for this race was only 107 pounds, while the brilliant four-year-old War Admiral had to carry 130 pounds, the same weight that was drawn by Seabiscuit.

The conditions of the race suited Menow perfectly. The track was very muddy from heavy rains, and there was considerable hesitation in letting War Admiral run, as he was known to dislike heavy going. Seabiscuit did not start. Despite the weight concession of twenty-three pounds by War Admiral to Menow, the public would not look beyond War Admiral, who started at 2-5. Menow was 10-1.

Menow galloped through the mud as if he loved it, with what John Hervey called his trip hammer stroke, which is typical of speed horses in the mud. Menow led all the way and won by eight lengths, while Busy K., War Minstrel, and War Admiral were necks apart in that order.

Having seen Menow score in a big stakes at nine furlongs, Headley thought he would try another one at ten furlongs. He shipped Menow to Chicago for the Arlington Classic. Again the track was muddy, but that time Menow carried 123 pounds instead of 107. His old rival Bull Lea was in the field, as was Nedayr. Menow was sent to the front at once, using the same tactics that had won the Massachusetts Handicap. However, he could not really shake off Bull Lea, and at the end of six furlongs, Bull Lea went on his way. Menow more or less collapsed, finishing fifth, while Bull Lea was beaten at the finish by Nedayr.

Back at Belmont Park, on September 17, Menow drew 126 pounds for the one-

BLOOD-HORSE LIBRARY

Capot

mile Jerome Handicap. Although favored at 6-5, he ran only fourth to Cravat, Can't Wait, and The Chief and was observed to be slowing down at the end of the race. However, he redeemed himself in the one and one-sixteenth-mile Potomac Handicap at Havre de Grace, where he won with 122 pounds up, beating Bull Lea (118) by a length in 1:44.

Menow's last race was the Havre de Grace Handicap, an all-age event. Seabiscuit was top-weighted at 128 pounds, and Menow carried 120. Seabiscuit naturally was a heavy favorite at 1-2, and Menow was second choice at 5-1. Again, Menow was sent to the front from the break, and Seabiscuit did not peg him back until they had gone a mile. At the finish, Menow was seen to waver, and he finished third. It was found that he had broken down in both forelegs, so that there was no hope of racing him again. Headley announced at once that Menow would be retired to Beaumont Farm and begin his stud duties in 1939, alongside his sire Pharamond II.

Menow repeatedly had shown first-class speed, both at two and three, but never showed that he could stay more than nine furlongs, and could get that distance only on muddy tracks, where his stride placed him at a great advantage.

Menow was a successful stallion, siring thirty-two stakes winners before his death at the advanced age of twenty-nine at Beaumont in 1964. (Bull Lea died the same year.) He sired three champions: Askmenow, best two-year-old filly of 1942; Capot, winner of the Preakness and Belmont and co-Horse of the Year in 1949; and Tom Fool, unbeaten in ten races in his four-year-old campaign as 1953's Horse of the Year. Capot was almost sterile and sired only thirteen foals, but Tom Fool has enhanced the sire line. Tom Fool is the sire of Buckpasser, Tim Tam, Jester, and Tompion.

CHAPTER THIRTY-TWO

TOM FOOL

Major Louie Beard and the present writer were having a drink together at Saratoga one August day in 1951, when the Major remarked, "You are going to see a great two-year-old come out tomorrow." Having heard similar remarks hundreds of times—and having a well-founded dislike for backing two-year-olds the first time out—we did nothing. Nothing but look foolish the next day, when Tom Fool easily broke his maiden in his first start.

Tom Fool had been bred by Duval Headley at his Manchester Farm, which neighbors Keeneland. John Gaver had purchased the colt privately as a yearling for John Hay Whitney's and Mrs. Charles S. Payson's Greentree Stud, which Maj. Beard managed.

The purchase appeared to be a bargain even before Tom Fool got to the races. The first foal of his dam, Gaga, was Aunt Jinny, a year older than Tom Fool, and as a juvenile Aunt Jinny was champion of her sex. This, of course, was not apparent at the time John Gaver bought Tom Fool for Greentree.

Gaga had won seven races in three seasons of campaigning, but her best effort had been a third-place finish in a minor stakes. She came, however, from an attractive line of mares. Her dam was Alpoise, who foaled one of the last of Sir Gallahad III's stakes winners in Algasir, but who—Joe Palmer remarked—never looked so good as when she was sold for $106,000 while in training.

Tom Fool's third dam, Laughing Queen, won the Selima Stakes and was a full sister to Futurity winner Pompey, a notable sire. The next dam was Cleopatra, considered the best race mare of her time.

After his successful debut, Tom Fool was moved up in class for the Sanford Stakes, which he won by two and one-quarter lengths. Trainer John Gaver then sent him out against the leading colt of the year to that time—Cousin, who had won five straight for Alfred Vanderbilt. Tom Fool won by a length in the Grand Union Hotel Stakes, but Cousin reversed the decision in the Hopeful, winning by one and one-quarter lengths.

Tom Fool

Gaver then prepared Tom Fool for the Futurity, and the colt met Cousin again in a prep, the Anticipation Purse. Neither fared exceptionally well. Tom Fool had some traffic problems but escaped to run second behind Calumet Farm's rapid Hill Gail.

As a result of two losses, Tom Fool's odds lengthened to 5-1 for the Futurity, which then was run down the straight Widener Chute at Belmont Park. Jockey Ted Atkinson guided Tom Fool over to the far side, where the going was supposed to be best, and he got to the lead, holding off Primate to win by one and three-quarters lengths. Hill Gail was fourth. (The time of 1:17 1/5 does not compare very favorably with Native Dancer's six and one-half-furlong world record of 1:14 2/5, accomplished in the next year's Futurity, but Tom Fool partisans point out that there was a stiff wind blowing against him.)

Tom Fool then had his only middle-distance test of his first season, being sent out for the one and one-sixteenth-mile East View Stakes at Jamaica. The field was weak, and Tom Fool was under pressure to beat Put Out by a neck over the sloppy track.

In his first race as a three-year-old, a six-furlong event at Jamaica on April 7, Tom Fool won by a neck from his Futurity runner-up, Primate. His next race was the one and one-eighth-mile Wood Memorial, curtain-raiser for the Kentucky Derby. After being in front at the eighth-mile pole, Tom Fool succumbed to a magnificent charge by Master Fiddle and went under by a neck.

At first it might have seemed that Tom Fool had recognized his pedigree, neither his sire, Menow, nor his maternal grandsire, Bull Dog, having been famous for the stamina of their produce. Two days later, however, Tom Fool came down with a fever and severe cough. The classics passed, and it was June 26 before Tom Fool was seen under colors again. He was second in his first outing since the interruption, but then was fourth in a preliminary for the Arlington Classic. Gaver skipped the Classic.

Back at Saratoga, Tom Fool got in with 106 pounds for a race over the Wilson Mile course. The track was sloppy, and Tom Fool was climbing in the early part, but he came from seven lengths off the pace to win by four and one-half lengths. In his next race, however, he was beaten in the last stride by Count Flame, going nine furlongs in a prep for the Travers Stakes. The track again was sloppy.

For the Travers, slop once again prevailed. Tom Fool shared the bottom weight,

				Cyllene
			Polymelus, 1902	Maid Marian
		Phalaris, 1913		Sainfoin
			Bromus, 1905	Cheery
	Pharamond II, 1925			**St. Simon**
			Chaucer, 1900	Canterbury Pilgrim
		Selene, 1919		Minoru
			Serenissima, 1913	Gondolette
Menow, 1935				Commando
			Ultimus, 1906	Running Stream
		Supremus, 1922		John o' Gaunt
			Mandy Hamilton, 1913	My Sweetheart
	Alcibiades, 1927			Le Samaritain
			Roi Herode, 1904	Roxelane
		Regal Roman, 1921		Cicero
			Lady Cicero, 1913	Ste. Claire
TOM FOOL				Flying Fox
			Ajax, 1901	Amie
		Teddy, 1913		Bay Ronald
			Rondeau, 1900	Doremi
	Bull Dog, 1927			Carbine
			Spearmint, 1903	Maid of the Mint
		Plucky Liege, 1912		**St. Simon**
			Concertina, 1896	Comic Song
Gaga, 1942				Peter Pan
			Pennant, 1911	Royal Rose
		Equipoise, 1928		Broomstick
			Swinging, 1922	Balancoire
	Alpoise, 1937			Sundridge
			Sun Briar, 1915	Sweet Briar
		Laughing Queen, 1929		Corcyra
			Cleopatra, 1917	Gallice

Buckpasser

at 114 pounds, and he made the pace and still was in front by one and one-half lengths with a mile behind him and two furlongs to run. The last furlongs were too much, and One Count (126) swept past to win by three lengths. Tom Fool dropped to third.

Rested a month and brought back to one mile, Tom Fool carried 120 pounds in the Jerome Handicap. He won by seven lengths over Mark-Ye-Well, from whom he received ten pounds. Again at a mile, Tom Fool carried 126 pounds, gave weight to good older horses, and won the Sysonby Handicap by a length and a quarter.

Gaver stretched him out again, to one and three-sixteenths miles, for the Roamer Handicap for three-year-olds. Under 126 pounds, he was giving fifteen to Quiet Step (bred by the writer) and fell back after getting to within a length of the leader. Quiet Step won by two lengths.

In the nine-furlong Grey Lag Handicap, Tom Fool (119) was sent against the brilliant four-year-old Battlefield (118). All through the last quarter-mile the two were locked, stride for stride; the photograph showed Tom Fool had won by a nose.

The next time out, the horses were much the same group, but Battlefield got one additional pound and that time he won the photo finish with Tom Fool. Tom Fool's last race of the year was Jamaica's Empire City Handicap at one and three-sixteenths miles. Facing only three-year-olds, and none of them top-class, Tom Fool carried 128 pounds. He got a good challenge from Marcador (109) and just held on to win by a head.

Tom Fool's claim to greatness rests on his four-year-old campaign.

As a two-year-old, he probably had been the best of his year, but not by very much. As a three-year-old, he had not been able to run in the classics, had won only once at as far as one and three-sixteenths miles, and

YEAR	AGE	STS	1ST	2ND	3RD	EARNED
1951	at 2	7	5	2	0	$155,960
1952	at 3	13	6	5	1	$157,850
1953	at 4	10	10	0	0	$256,355
Lifetime		30	21	7	1	$570,165

had been beaten badly at ten furlongs while receiving twelve pounds in the Travers. At four, though, he got ten furlongs, carried extraordinary weights, and never was beaten.

He began by taking the five and one-half-furlong Sation Handicap by two and one-half lengths under top weight of 128 pounds. For the six-furlong Joe H. Palmer Handicap, Tom Fool drew 130 pounds and won by one and one-half lengths. Although in each he had beaten the crack sprinter Tea-Maker, these were overnights, preps, and after them Gaver had Tom Fool ready for tougher competition. Ahead were the three handicaps comprising New York's grueling triple for older horses, a series won only once before (by Whisk Broom II) and only once afterward (by Kelso).[1]

In the one-mile Metropolitan Handicap, Tom Fool carried 130 pounds, and Royal Vale, coming off three successive wins, carried 127. Both made their moves at the same time, but Tom Fool started the move with a length's advantage. Royal Vale cut into the margin, but by only a half-length.

A week later, the pair met in the ten-furlong Suburban Handicap. It was a crossroads for Tom Fool. A colt then still unproven at ten furlongs, he went into one of America's greatest handicaps carrying 128 pounds and giving four pounds to his runner-up in the Metropolitan. The Suburban transformed Tom Fool's image.

Atkinson took him to a three-length lead on the backstretch, but then Royal Vale began cutting into the margin. Through the stretch, Royal Vale ran at him, but Tom Fool held him off, winning by a nose in 2:00 3/5, then the second-fastest clocking ever at Belmont. After the race, Royal Vale's jockey, Jackie Westrope, remarked: "A gamer horse beat us." One Count was well beaten.

The triple series was interrupted by the seven-furlong Carter Handicap, which

Tom Fool won, equaling the stakes-record 1:22, under 135 pounds. The final race of the handicap triple was the Brooklyn. Again going one and one-quarter miles, Tom Fool that time was burdened with 136 pounds, eight more than he had carried in the Suburban. There was not a good competitor in the field, so the main question was whether Tom Fool could handle the weight, which he did, winning easily.

Tom Fool ran in no more handicaps. In his final four races, he carried the weight-for-age maximum of 126 pounds. The races virtually were walkovers, and for none of them were the pari-mutuel windows open. He won the Wilson Mile, the ten-furlong Whitney, and the mile Sysonby, then was sent to Maryland for his second race outside New York, the Pimlico Special. He won in 1:55 4/5, a track record for one and three-sixteenths miles.

Tom Fool, who was assigned 148 pounds for the Fall Highweight Handicap but did not start, was retired after the Pimlico Special.

When he first went to stud, he apparently was not interested in the activities of the breeding shed, but in time that disinclination subsided. Once his first runners went to the races, he was shown to be an immediate success. The first crop included Futurity winner Jester and Kentucky Derby-Preakness winner Tim Tam.

The Greentree stallion sired thirty-six stakes winners, led by millionaire Buckpasser, Horse of the Year in 1966. Tom Fool's others included Silly Season, Tompion, Dunce, and Cyrano.

In several instances, the best offspring of his sons to date appear to be fillies, the young Buckpasser having sired La Prevoyante and Numbered Account, Tim Tam having sired Tosmah, and Jester having sired Steeple Jill.[2] Tompion's best runners, however, were colts, among them Blue Tom, Chompion, and Timmy My Boy.

End Notes:

1. In 1984 Rokeby Stable's Fit to Fight won all three and became the fourth and, to this date, last to win the handicap triple crown.

2. Tom Fool was the leading broodmare sire in England in 1965.

CHAPTER THIRTY-THREE

PETER PAN

The first high-class colt by champion Commando to appear was Peter Pan, one of eleven foals sired in Commando's second stud season and out of a sixteen-year-old Hermit mare, Cinderella. (This was not the same Cinderella, by Tomahawk, who was the dam of the savage-tempered Hastings, he the sire of Fair Play.)

While Peter Pan won some of the most important races and some of his performances were close to track-record time, one is left with the impression that he was not quite in the same class as his sire, Commando, or grandsire, Domino.

Peter Pan won half of his eight starts as a two-year-old. The colt scored in his first start, a maiden race, and three days later took the Surf Stakes. In the more important Double Event Stakes, Peter Pan, after establishing a six-length lead, failed to stay, and was beaten two and a half lengths. In the still more important Brighton Junior Stakes, Peter Pan could only finish fifth behind the best two-year-old at the time, Salvidere.

Moving to Saratoga, Peter Pan came out for the Flash Stakes, which had been won by a great many colts of importance in American Turf history. There Peter Pan established his usual early break, then was headed briefly in the stretch, but he came again to win by a short head.

Peter Pan next tried for the Saratoga Special, but Salvidere again beat him, by four and a half lengths.[1] Fortunately for Peter Pan, Salvidere was not nominated for the Hopeful Stakes, the most important of Saratoga's two-year-old fixtures. In that race, Peter Pan was given time to settle down a little, and he came from behind to win in time that was only one-fifth of a second slower than the track record.

Two weeks later in the Futurity, the most important two-year-old race of the year, Salvidere again was ineligible, and James R. Keene named three starters—Peter Pan, Pope Joan, and Ballot. Pope Joan drew off into a four-length lead but faltered badly near home. Behind her were seven horses, about level. From that cavalry charge, jockey W. Shaw got Electioneer home a neck in front of Pope

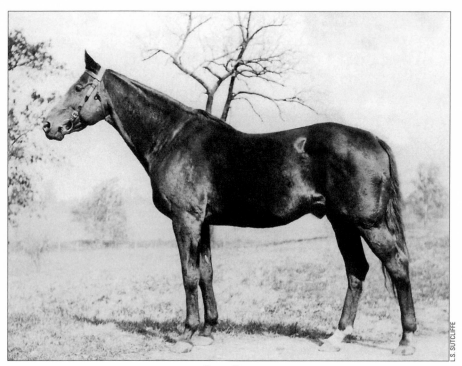

Peter Pan

Joan, with Peter Pan only fifth.

Since Electioneer was by Voter, a Keene stallion—in whom Keene had given a complimentary season—the breeder and owner of Peter Pan was furious. All stallions at his Castleton Stud were reserved as private sires for Keene's exclusive use. To lose the most important two-year-old race of the year as the result of his own generosity was too much for Keene's fiery temperament, and so far as is known, he never again allowed an outside mare to be bred at Castleton.

As a three-year-old, Peter Pan began his campaign in the one-mile Withers Stakes. After going the first five furlongs in 1:00 1/5, Peter Pan failed to last home, going under by a neck to Frank Gill. A week later in the one-mile Carlton Stakes, Peter Pan failed by a half-length while giving eleven pounds to Dinna Ken.

In the eleven-furlong Belmont Stakes, the Keene entry of Peter Pan and Superman was 7-10, and they ran first and second in that order. Peter Pan then took the ten-furlong Standard Stakes, and four days later added the twelve-furlong Brooklyn Derby, leading all the way. The very next week he won the ten-furlong Tidal Stakes by four lengths. That schedule shows how hard American horses were raced in those days (and many horses still are).

Carrying 129 pounds in the twelve-furlong Coney Island Jockey Club Stakes was too much for Peter Pan, and he and jockey Walter Miller went under to Frank Gill by four lengths.[2] Trainer James Rowe Sr. changed jockeys, and five days later Peter Pan, with Joe Notter up, led through the eleven-furlong Advance Stakes against older horses and beat Salvidere, the nemesis of his two-year-old days.

Next came the ten-furlong Brighton Handicap, in which Peter Pan took on older horses, giving up to ten pounds by the weight-for-age scale to champion handicapper Dandelion. Peter Pan got away badly and worked his way slowly through the field of fourteen. Notter went to the whip in the stretch, and Peter Pan got up to beat McCarter (to whom he gave fourteen pounds) by a nose, for his sixth victory in his last seven starts. That was his last race, and his best performance.

Taking his racing career as a whole, it can be seen that Peter Pan was a good colt but not of the same overwhelming class as Commando and Domino. At stud, Peter Pan never ranked higher than fifth on the sire list. Since he stood at the H.P. Whitney stud (about the best in the United States), his record is not very remarkable.

Given his choice of all the sires in the Keene dispersal of 1913, Rowe picked Peter Pan for his new employer, Whitney. (He must have known that Colin

PETER PAN				
Commando, 1898	Domino, 1891	Himyar, 1875	Alarm, 1869	Eclipse / Maud
			Hira, 1864	Lexington / Hegira
		Mannie Gray, 1874	Enquirer, 1867	Leamington / Lida
			Lizzie G, 1867	War Dance / Lecomte mare
	Emma C., 1892	Darebin, 1878	The Peer, 1855	Melbourne / Cinizelli
			Lurline, 1869	Traducer / Mermaid
		Guenn, 1873	Flood, 1877	Norfolk / Hennie Farrow
			Glendew, 1876	Glengarry / Glenrose
Cinderella, 1888	Hermit, 1864	Newminster, 1848	Touchstone, 1831	Camel / Banter
			Beeswing, 1833	Dr Syntax / Ardrossan mare
		Seclusion, 1857	Tadmor, 1846	Ion / Palmyra
			Miss Selon, 1851	Cowl / Belle Dame
	Mazurka, 1878	See Saw, 1865	Buccaneer, 1857	Wild Dayrell / Little Red Rover mare
			Margery Daw, 1856	Brocket / Protection
		Mabille, 1868	Parmesan, 1857	Sweetmeat / Gruyere
			Rigolboche, 1861	Rataplan / Gardham mare

was a poor foal getter and that his English-bred stock had not succeeded.) Among the sons of Commando, Peter Pan was the best sire, but then he had by far the best opportunity.

Two of Peter Pan's sons made some mark in the *American Stud Book*:

Pennant won the Futurity of 1913 but was not a racer of great importance. His claim to fame was that he sired Equipoise, who was a crack two-year-old and, after missing virtually the whole of his three-year-old career due to foot trouble, went on to become the handicap champion of his time, winning ten out of his fourteen starts at four. At a time of falling purses, Equipoise won twenty-nine races and earned $338,610 in fifty-one starts. Unfortunately, Equipoise died after only four stud seasons and did not leave a worthy successor; one son, Shut Out, won the Kentucky Derby and Belmont Stakes, but did not prove a very good sire.

YEAR	AGE	STS	1ST	2ND	3RD	EARNED
1906	at 2	8	4	1	1	$ 29,660
1907	at 3	9	6	2	0	$ 85,790
Lifetime		17	10	3	1	$115,450

Black Toney, by Peter Pan, was third in Pennant's Futurity and was a minor stakes winner. He had been bought as a yearling by Colonel E.R. Bradley, the famous gambler, and raced with such modest success that Bradley did not use him very much in his early years at stud. It was not until Black Servant (who should have won the Kentucky Derby from Bradley's other entry, Behave Yourself), showed his form, along with Miss Jemima[3], Black Gold (who did win the Kentucky Derby), and others, that Bradley realized that Black Toney was a sire out of the ordinary. Black Toney never was used extensively but performed the remarkable feat of siring his best son, Bimelech, at the age of twenty-six. Bimelech was the best two-year-old of his year and won the Preakness and Belmont Stakes at three, but was not a great sire.[4] Black Toney was also the sire of Bridal Colors, dam of Relic, a good sire in the United States and Europe. Black Toney's son Black Servant sired a very good racer in Blue Larkspur, who probably was the best of his year. He was the winner of ten races from sixteen starts at two, three, and four, including the Belmont Stakes. Blue Larkspur became a good broodmare sire, but his best son at stud was Revoked, who was no better than a second-rate sire. Another of Black Toney's sons, however, was Balladier who, in Double Jay and Spy Song, got two high-class racers and influential sires. Double Jay and Spy Song, both deceased, still are represented by sons at stud, so Peter Pan's line continues.[5]

End Notes:

1. Peter Pan finished third behind Salvidere and McCarter.

2. Peter Pan finished fifth behind Frank Gill, Montgomery, Salvidere, and Philander. Frank Gill won by four lengths, and three heads separated the next four finishers.

3. Miss Jemima is designated as the champion two-year-old filly of 1919.

4. Bimelech sired thirty stakes winners from 362 foals (8 percent).

5. In 2006 no tail-male descendants of Peter Pan are active as sires in the United States, but the Commando–Domino line is kept viable through the sons of Broad Brush.

CHAPTER THIRTY-FOUR

BLACK TONEY

lack Toney was one of those unusual horses that, despite being a long way
behind the best of their age on the Turf, turn out to be the best sires of
their crops. Such horses hold a particular fascination for the smaller breeders who cannot afford to pay for the sires of the highest initial and most obvious
credentials. Sometimes the age of miracles seems not past.

The foals of 1911 were the next-to-last crop bred by James R. Keene's Castleton
Stud, under the management of his brother-in-law, Major Foxhall Daingerfield.
(Castleton itself had been sold to David M. Look in 1910.) Black Toney was bred
on the familiar Castleton pattern of crossing the strain of Domino with the strain
of Ben Brush, in this case the sire being Peter Pan, a grandson of Domino, and the
dam was Belgravia, a daughter of Ben Brush. The entire Castleton yearling crop
was sold, and Black Toney ended up in the ownership of Colonel E.R. Bradley of
the Idle Hour Stud, Lexington. Pennant, also by Peter Pan, became the property
of H.P. Whitney of New York.

Black Toney's female line is full of interest to those who have a taste for
unlikely romance in Turf affairs. His fourth dam was the celebrated Queen Mary,
a Gladiator mare owned by the trainer, William l'Anson of Malton, Yorkshire.
l'Anson bred Queen Mary when she was only a three-year-old, and the following
spring she produced a filly, Haricot. l'Anson assumed that Haricot would be useless for racing, and he sold Queen Mary. One day on the downs, l'Anson, having
used Haricot as a hack to ride to the post office, etc., found to his astonishment
when he was riding her himself that she was far from useless for racing.

Realizing his mistake in selling the dam, Queen Mary, he set off in search of her.
After considerable effort and detective work, he traced her to a farm in Scotland
and duly approached the farmer with a view to repurchase. After various oblique
discussions, l'Anson asked if Queen Mary was for sale.

"Yes," replied the thrifty Scot, "but I will have to have 100 pounds for her."

"Why 100 pounds?" inquired l'Anson, since this was a stiff price for a farm mare.

"Because," replied the farmer, "she is in foal to a gay bonny Clydesdale stallion."

l'Anson swallowed his mortification and paid the price demanded. That, anyway, is the legend of how l'Anson came to breed Blink Bonny, Queen Mary's daughter who in 1857 won the Epsom Derby and came right back to win the Oaks two days later.

Including an 1851 foal designated as a half-bred, Queen Mary produced sixteen foals for l'Anson. They included Blink Bonny, who after her own classic success produced Derby and St. Leger winner Blair Athol.

H.C. ASHBY

E.R. Bradley with Matt Winn (left) in the Derby winner's circle

Queen Mary's foals also included Bonnie Scotland, who is of more import to the story of Black Toney. Bonnie Scotland sired Bramble, who, in turn, sired Ben Brush, founder of a strong sire line in the United States. Queen Mary also became an ancestress of the great English sire Hampton, major racer and sire Bayardo, and St. Leger winner Caller Ou.

After producing sixteen foals for l'Anson, Queen Mary was acquired by H. Chaplin, for whom she produced two foals before her death at twenty-nine in 1872. The last of Queen Mary's foals was Bonnie Doon, produced when the mare was twenty-seven, and Bonnie Doon became the third dam of Black Toney. Thus, Black Toney's dam, Belgravia, was inbred to Queen Mary with three free generations.

Belgravia won two races at three and later became a good mare, producing three stakes winners. The next dam, Bonnie Gal, was a winner in England and produced the dam of Watercress, who was a high-class racer and a fair stallion in the United States. All in all, Black Toney's close-up female line was a good one but not an outstanding one.

Black Toney was raced extensively at two—perhaps too extensively. He started nineteen times and won seven races, finished second five times, and ran third five times. On the face of it, this is the record of a very good two-year-old, but when we look at the actual races it is less impressive. Several of Black Toney's victories were scored against inferior opposition, and his races against the best of his age showed that he was not close to them when judged by any handicapping standard.

Black Toney was beaten by eleven lengths and ten lengths in one race by Little Nephew and Old Rosebud, respectively, and later Old Rosebud beat him by nine lengths. At Saratoga, Little Nephew gave Black Toney eight pounds and beat him by four and a half lengths, and twice Roamer beat him by three and a half lengths.

Nevertheless, Black Toney did on occasion show relatively well against high-grade horses. Pennant, from the same Castleton crop as was Black Toney, beat him by three lengths in the Futurity, with Black Toney third. Even so, getting two pounds from Pennant, Black Toney figured out at about twelve to fifteen pounds below the winner.

The Bradley colt did win one stakes, the Valuation.

At three, Black Toney was out eight times and won three races. Probably his best performance was in the Independence Handicap at Latonia on July 4, when he won at one and three-sixteenths miles under 115 pounds. There were no first-class horses in the field.

When Black Toney went to Canada, he could finish only fourth of seven in the Canadian Derby, and when he went to New York he was beaten by about twenty lengths by the older Borrow in the Yonkers Handicap, despite receiving twelve pounds in actual weight. The most kindly critic would have had to say that Black

				Himyar, 1875	**Alarm** Hira
		Commando, 1898	Domino, 1891	Mannie Gray, 1874	Enquirer Lizzie G.
			Emma C., 1892	Darebin, 1878	The Peer Lurline
Peter Pan, 1904				Guenn, 1883	Flood Glendew
		Cinderella, 1888	Hermit, 1864	Newminster, 1848	Touchstone Beeswing
				Seclusion, 1857	Tadmor Miss Sellon
			Mazurka, 1878	See Saw, 1865	Buccaneer Margery Daw
BLACK TONEY				Mabille, 1868	Parmesan Rigolboche
		Ben Brush, 1893	Bramble, 1875	Bonnie Scotland, 1853	Iago Queen Mary
				Ivy Leaf, 1864	Australian Bay Flower
			Roseville, 1888	Reform, 1871	Leamington Stolen Kisses
Belgravia, 1903				Albia, 1881	**Alarm** Elastic
		Bonnie Gal, 1889	Galopin, 1872	Vedette, 1854	Voltigeur Mrs. Ridgway
				Flying Duchess, 1853	The Flying Dutchman Merope
			Bonnie Doon, 1870	Rapid Rhone, 1860	Young Melbourne Lanercost Mare
				Queen Mary, 1843	Gladiator Plenipotentiary Mare

Black Toney

Toney was a long way from being a top three-year-old.

Col. Bradley did not think it worthwhile to send Black Toney back to New York at four. The colt's ten starts at that age were confined to the Kentucky circuit, where he won two races and placed in five others. Neither of his victories came in stakes.

Black Toney stood one season at stud, 1916, then was returned to the races at six, when he made three starts. The horse was beaten a head in an allowance race at Latonia, then was sent to Windsor, Ontario, when he led all the way to win a one-mile allowance race. In his final start, Black Toney was fifth in a field of six in a handicap at Kenilworth Park.

In summation, Black Toney had raced enough to give a pretty accurate picture of his class as a runner. He had been a useful two-year-old (third in the Futurity), but every time he came up against a high-class racer he failed to make the result close. As he got older, Black Toney's class did not improve; if anything, there was some deterioration. It is difficult to make out a case for Black Toney closer than twenty pounds to the best of his age.

How was it, then, that Black Toney became such an outstanding sire?

Does the explanation of his success rest on opportunity? In terms of number of foals, this is clearly not the answer, for in twenty-one years at stud he sired only

221 foals. As he was a stallion of good fertility, those numbers might indicate that Col. Bradley was not too anxious that the horse have a full book of mares. (Black Toney stood for $2,000 at a time when Pennant, a far superior racehorse, was standing for $1,000.)

One suspects, too, that Col. Bradley himself did not believe very strongly in Black Toney during the early years he was at stud; not until Miss Jemima and Black Gold came along did he realize that Black Toney was a much better sire than was North Star III, who had been the premier stud at Idle Hour.

In terms of quality of the mares Black Toney had in his early years, opportunity again would seem insufficient in explanation of the horse's success. In one sense, though, he had a very good selection of mares, one denied many other sires: Col. Bradley was a strong adherent (i.e., one who has not yet obtained all he expects to get) of the Keene–Daingerfield pattern of breeding imported mares to the fast Domino-line American sires. Over the years, Col. Bradley followed that system, and he scored his best successes on that basis.

The master of Idle Hour seldom gave large prices for his imported mares, and thus he bought many that had not shown much merit on

YEAR	AGE	STS	1ST	2ND	3RD	EARNED
1913	at 2	19	7	5	5	$ 6,618
1914	at 3	8	3	2	0	$ 4,290
1915	at 4	10	2	3	2	$ 1,907
1916	at 5	unraced				
1917	at 6	3	1	1	0	$ 750
Lifetime		40	13	11	7	$13,565

the racecourse. Nearly all of the Bradley imports carried some of the best English blood, though, and Col. Bradley emphasized to the author that he insisted on good conformation.

In the great days of Castleton Stud, too, the imported mares that had produced a long string of great racers generally had been individuals that had not done much on the racecourse. Col. Bradley, hence, was inclined to de-emphasize racing class as a criterion in the selection of his broodmares.

Black Toney, then, in one sense had a very good opportunity, the opportunity of being crossed with mates of very good blood. He also had the advantage of hybrid vigor in his foals, since Bradley's imported mares presented an outcross for the Domino–Ben Brush blood.

Whatever the explanation, Black Toney was, indeed, an extraordinary sire. He got forty stakes winners (18 percent), and a number of them were brilliant racers. He never led the sire list but ranked among the top twenty on ten occasions.

In his initial season at stud, between his four-year-old and six-year-old campaigns, he sired four foals, and one of them was Miss Jemima, one of the two

Bimelech

best two-year-old fillies of her year. The next year, before he made his brief reappearance at the races, Black Toney sired three foals, and one of them was Black Servant, runner-up in the Kentucky Derby and winner of the Blue Grass Stakes. (Black Servant later sired Blue Larkspur.)

Thereafter, Black Toney's best runners included Black Gold, winner of the Kentucky Derby, Louisiana Derby, etc.; Brokers Tip, winner of the Kentucky Derby; Bimelech (the last colt he sired), unbeaten two-year-old champion in 1939 and a champion again at three; Balladier, the champion two-year-old of 1934 and later the sire of Double Jay; Black Helen, champion three-year-old filly of 1935, when she won over colts in the Florida Derby and also won the Coaching Club American Oaks; Black Maria, champion handicap female of 1927 and 1928; and Big Hurry, winner of the Selima and dam of five stakes winners, including Searching. Black Toney also sired Broadway Jones, Beanie M., and Beau Butler.

If by the strictest standards Black Toney came up short as a racehorse, by the strictest standards he was a major success as a sire.

CHAPTER THIRTY-FIVE

BLACK SERVANT

B lack Servant and the brilliant filly Miss Jemima provided the first intima-
tions to Colonel E.R. Bradley that he had a good sire in Black Toney. Black
Servant was no world beater, but his sire had been about twenty pounds
below the best of his year; so for Black Toney to sire Miss Jemima in his first crop
of four foals and Black Servant in his second crop of three foals (in 1918) was
bound to give his owner pause for thought.

Miss Jemima was co-champion two-year-old filly of 1919, and Black Servant
was a stakes winner and a Derby runner-up. Their breeding followed the pattern
of crossing Domino-line sires with imported mares. Miss Jemima was from Vaila
and Black Servant from Padula, the mares having been purchased in England during World War I, when bloodstock prices were very depressed. Although their
pedigrees were nothing to brag about by British standards, Col. Bradley's results
certainly were highly satisfactory.

Black Servant began his racing career in Kentucky, where he scored his only
victories at two, winning at Churchill Downs in the spring and at Latonia in June.
Col. Bradley raced him three times in stakes at Saratoga, his best performance
there being a third-place finish behind Nancy Lee in the United States Hotel
Stakes.

(Reminiscing on his young days, Col. Bradley once told the author that there
was quite a difference between the Kentucky circuit and Saratoga; in fact, he said,
it had taken him about fifteen years
to breed a horse good enough to
win a decent race at Saratoga. In his
kindly way, he was saying not to be
discouraged by early failures.)

After a juvenile campaign of seven

YEAR	AGE	STS	1ST	2ND	3RD	EARNED
1920	at 2	7	2	1	1	$ 3,750
1921	at 3	12	4	5	1	$27,475
1922	at 4	3	1	1	0	$ 1,225
Lifetime		22	7	7	2	$32,450

starts, Black Servant was prepped for the following spring's Kentucky Derby.
Considering his form at Saratoga the previous August, it must have been hard

BLOOD-HORSE LIBRARY

Black Servant

to justify much optimism. Nevertheless, Black Servant won his first two races at three, taking a one and one-sixteenth-mile allowance race at Lexington and then winning the nine-furlong Blue Grass Stakes. In the latter, he beat stablemate Behave Yourself by a length.

In the Derby, the Harry Payne Whitney pair of Tryster and Prudery (which had beaten Black Servant at two in the Saratoga Special) was favored at 11-10, after Grey Lag was scratched. Col. Bradley's entry of Black Servant and Behave Yourself was the third choice at nearly 9-1. Jockey Lawrence Lyke and Black Servant set a scorching pace, running six furlongs in 1:11 3/5. At that point, Charles Thompson, on Behave Yourself, set sail from sixth position, and he caught Black Servant in the stretch. Although the stable had wanted to win with Black Servant, Thompson drove Behave Yourself on and won by a head.

There was in the Bradley camp much indignation with Thompson for having won with the wrong horse. The party to blame more, though, if blame had to be apportioned, was Lyke, who had ridden Black Servant as if the race had been a six-furlong sprint. The colt was left without reserve for the final quarter-mile, which was run in :25 3/5.

Black Servant's good race in the Derby leaves one wondering how sound he was after that effort. He lost his first time out after the Derby but then won the May 30 Proctor Knott Handicap, at one and a quarter miles, by six lengths. He made seven more starts that year, winning one. He did not race at four, then at five made a victorious reappearance in a six-furlong handicap with top weight of 119 pounds. He lost in his only two other races that year.

Col. Bradley never wavered in his belief in Black Servant, retiring him to stud while giving Derby winner Behave Yourself to the Remount Service. Although he did not become the sire Black Toney did, Black Servant established a place for himself in history by siring two-time champion and Horse of the Year Blue Larkspur, possibly the best colt Col. Bradley bred in a career spanning forty years.

Black Servant was bred to only one mare in his first season at stud, and from her got a winner. His first full crop included steeplechase stakes winner Beelzebub, a foal of 1925, and he sired Blue Larkspur the following year. He also sired one of the best fillies of the 1930 crop, in Barn Swallow, who won the Matron, Alabama Stakes, and Kentucky Oaks, and finished second in the Coaching Club American

			Domino, 1891	Himyar Mannie Gray
		Commando, 1898	Emma C., 1892	Darebin Guenn
	Peter Pan, 1904		Hermit, 1864	Newminster Seclusion
		Cinderella, 1888	Mazurka, 1878	See Saw Mabille
Black Toney, 1911			Bramble, 1875	Bonnie Scotland Ivy Leaf
		Ben Brush, 1893	Roseville, 1888	Reform Albia
	Belgravia, 1903		Galopin, 1872	Vedette Flying Duchess
		Bonnie Gal, 1889	Bonnie Doon, 1870	Rapid Rhone Queen Mary
BLACK SERVANT			Doncaster, 1870	Stockwell Marigold
		Bend Or, 1877	Rouge Rose, 1865	Thormanby Ellen Horne
	Laveno, 1892		Macaroni, 1860	Sweetmeat Jocose
		Napoli, 1878	Sunshine, 1867	Thormanby Sunbeam
Padula, 1906			Cremorne, 1869	Parmesan Rigolboche
		Thurio, 1875	Verona, 1854	Orlando Iodine
	Padua, 1886		Paul Jones, 1865	Buccaneer Queen Of The Gipsies
		Immortelle, 1879	Mulberry, 1861	Beadsman Strawberry

Oaks while giving seven pounds to the winner.

Other added-money winners sired by Black Servant included Matron and Acorn Stakes winner Baba Kenny (dam of Hopeful and Spinaway Stakes winner Bee Mac), Baltimore Handicap winner B'ar Hunter, Aqueduct Handicap winner Black Mammy, plus Espinoza, Jillion, Sweet Chariot, Be Mine, and Big Pebble.

CHAPTER THIRTY-SIX

BLUE LARKSPUR

C olonel E.R. Bradley bred two horses that were elected to the Hall of Fame at the Saratoga National Museum of Racing.[1] One was the filly Busher, and the other was Blue Larkspur, champion three-year-old of 1929.[2]

As has been pointed out earlier in this book, Col. Bradley followed one of the patterns of breeding pursued by James R. Keene's earlier Castleton Stud. This involved mating stallions of the fast Domino male line with imported English mares. The pattern was the same, but the quality of the mares imported was not quite so high in the case of Col. Bradley's Idle Hour Stock Farm.

In the case of Blue Larkspur, the breeding patterns that produced a champion included some of the above and also involved a pattern similar to that used by the 17th Earl of Derby. The stud of Lord Derby, whose brain trust included Walter Alston, produced the wonderful mare Selene through inbreeding to the classic-winning mare Pilgrimage with three free generations. Selene produced the great runner and sire Hyperion, plus Sickle, Pharamond II, and Hunter's Moon.

Col. Bradley turned up with a similar pattern of inbreeding to a particular mare in the case of Padua, who became the fourth dam of Blue Larkspur as well as being the second dam of Blue Larkspur's sire, Black Servant.

Padua was not in the same exalted class as a racer or producer as was Pilgrimage (ancestress of Selene), but there still was a good deal to be said for her. She was by no means fashionable in pedigree, being by Thurio, a failure as a sire, and out of Immortelle, a moderate earner; neither Immortelle's sire nor her dam was distinguished as breeding stock. Padua raced forty times in four seasons and won six races ranging in distance from five furlongs to one and a half miles. This performance could be regarded as racing merit unexpected on the basis of pedigree. Furthermore, Padua produced eleven winners among thirteen foals.

As it happened, the two mares who became channels for the inbreeding pattern that produced Blue Larkspur were the worst of Padua's daughters. These were Padula (by Laveno, a failure at stud), and Padilla (by Macheath, also a failure).

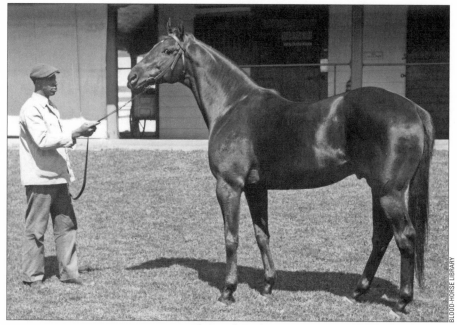

BLOOD-HORSE LIBRARY

Blue Larkspur

Padilla (who was not owned by Col. Bradley) bred a filly of considerable class in Vaila, who was by the non-distinguished Fariman. Vaila won the Moulton Stakes at two in England and was beaten only a neck in the Cheveley Park Stakes, generally the two-year-old filly championship race. Vaila did not win at three, but that year was second in the Atalanta Stakes and third in the Falmouth Stakes. Thus, there was a filly of nearly first-class speed coming from a line of mares all of which had been sired by stud failures.

Col. Bradley bought Vaila in 1915 and imported her to Idle Hour. She was mated with his imported North Star III, who had shown first-class speed in winning the Middle Park Stakes, then England's championship event for two-year-old colts. The result of that mating was Blossom Time, who won a division of the Pimlico Futurity in 1922. Blossom Time was only a moderate winner at three, but, with earnings of $45,955, was the second-highest earner among fillies in her foal crop. (Vaila produced four other stakes winners, including Miss Jemima and Broadway Jones.)

Once he had Blossom Time and Black Servant in the stud, Col. Bradley had on hand the vehicles to inbreed to Padua with three free generations. In breeding Black Servant to Blossom Time, he also was following the pattern of crossing a Domino-line stallion with an imported English family.

The result of the first cross of Black Servant and Blossom Time was Blue Larkspur. Blossom Time had three later foals by Black Servant, and two were stakes-placed; the mare's four other foals were by Black Toney, sire of Black Servant, and included three winners.

Blue Larkspur first came out in an allowance race, against fifteen others on May 17, 1928, sprinting four and a half furlongs down the old Widener Chute at Belmont Park. At odds of 10-1, he finished third, beaten by about two lengths. A week later, he was even-money in a similar race and won by a nose.

He then was deemed ready for stakes competition and was started next in the Juvenile Stakes, which drew a field of seventeen. He was sent off at 12-1, but gave the good colt Jack High five and a half pounds and beat him one and a half lengths. The author well remembers his impression of Blue Larkspur as the colt walked onto the track, combining power, quality, and a calm temperament.

In the National Stallion Stakes, his fourth race, Blue Larkspur (117) had the best of the weights against Jack High (122), but after some scrimmaging at the start and crossing over later in the running, he was just up to win by a nose over Jean Valjean. Jack High was third in a three-horse photo.

Probably more accurate form was that shown in the six-furlong Saratoga Special

			Commando, 1898	Domino / Emma C.
		Peter Pan, 1904	Cinderella, 1888	Hermit / Mazurka
	Black Toney, 1911		Ben Brush, 1893	Bramble / Roseville
		Belgravia, 1903	Bonnie Gal, 1889	**Galopin** / Bonnie Doon
Black Servant, 1918			Bend Or, 1877	Doncaster / Rouge Rose
		Laveno, 1892	Napoli, 1878	**Macaroni** / Sunshine
	Padula, 1906		Thurio, 1875	Cremorne / Verona
		Padua, 1886	Immortelle, 1879	Paul Jones / Mulberry
BLUE LARKSPUR			Sundridge, 1898	Amphion / Sierra
		Sunstar, 1908	Doris, 1898	Loved One / Lauretta
	North Star III, 1914		St. Angelo, 1889	**Galopin** / Agneta
		Angelic, 1901	Fota, 1890	Hampton / Photinia
Blossom Time, 1920			Gallinule, 1884	Isonomy / Moorhen
		Fariman, 1900	Bellinzona, 1889	Necromancer / Hasty Girl
	Vaila, 1911		Macheath, 1880	**Macaroni** / Heather Bell
		Padilla, 1900	**Padua**, 1886	Thurio / Immortelle

Blossom Time, dam of Blue Larkspur

in August, when Blue Larkspur beat Jack High a length at level weights. For the six and a half-furlong Hopeful, Blue Larkspur carried 130 pounds and conceded three pounds to Jack High. Blue Larkspur did not have a clear run and failed by one and a half lengths to beat the other colt, who had escaped interference.

Blue Larkspur could have gone into winter quarters regarded as the champion colt of his age if he had won the Futurity, but in a field of twenty-four he was kicked at the post, was away poorly, and never had much chance. High Strung won the climactic juvenile test, as Jack High was third and Blue Larkspur was eighth.

At two Blue Larkspur thus had proven to be among the best of his year and certainly better at two than both his sire, Black Servant, and his paternal grandsire, Black Toney. The question left to answer was how well he could cope with the classic distances at three.

Blue Larkspur's three-year-old campaign was begun in late April, in a race of one mile and seventy yards at Lexington. He met the Man o' War gelding Clyde Van Dusen and had to be shaken up to beat him by a neck. By the date of the Kentucky Derby, though, two misfortunes had overtaken Blue Larkspur. One was that his trainer, Derby Dick Thompson, had been confined to a hospital, and there really was nobody in the stable taking responsibility of Blue Larkspur. This might have been overcome if the weather had not worked against him, but rain turned the Derby track to mud, and no one took it upon himself to have Blue Larkspur re-shod with caulks.

The colt lost his action in the going and finished only fourth in a field of twenty-one. The winner was none other than Clyde Van Dusen.

The Bradley colt then was sent to New York, where he started for the one-mile Withers Stakes. In a field of nine, he showed he still had his best form of the previous year, beating his old rival Jack High (who finished third) by a half-length in 1:36.

For the Belmont Stakes at one and a half miles, the track again was wet. On the surface, this might have seemed to be to Blue Larkspur's disadvantage, but that time he was shod properly and showed that he was not, after all, a poor mudder.

The author had a good look at him in the saddling enclosure and was shocked to see that his ankles were so enlarged that they suggested midget-sized bowling balls. One wondered if he could get the twelve furlongs, not so much because of his pedigree, but because of his apparent physical condition. Blue Larkspur had no such doubts, though, and won by three-quarters of a length from African, with Jack High beaten about five lengths in third position.

YEAR	AGE	STS	1ST	2ND	3RD	EARNED
1928	at 2	7	4	1	1	$ 66,970
1929	at 3	6	4	1	0	$153,450
1930	at 4	3	2	1	0	$ 51,650
Lifetime		16	10	3	1	$272,070

For the twelve-furlong Dwyer, Blue Larkspur was 4-5 and evidently could have given Grey Coat seven pounds successfully had jockey Mack Garner stayed alert. Garner on Blue Larkspur thought he had the race won in the stretch, but Grey Coat came along to beat him.

Blue Larkspur had lost twice at three, and each time an obvious excuse suggested itself. Fortune allowed him only one more race that year, in the Arlington Classic in Chicago. He again caught a wet track, which perhaps provided a welcomed cushion for his ankles. Racing one and a quarter miles, he beat Clyde Van Dusen by seven and a half lengths as the Derby winner finished third.

Returned to New York, Blue Larkspur was being pointed for the Miller Stakes, then an important event, but he bowed a tendon while in training.

Despite the bow, Blue Larkspur came back brilliantly at four, but he got in only three races before permanent retirement. He returned at Arlington Park in a nine-furlong purse race, giving eleven pounds to a Fair Play four-year-old, Fair Ball. Blue Larkspur was not pressed and finished second, beaten five lengths.

Myrtlewood

Next came the Stars and Stripes Handicap, also at nine furlongs. In a field of sixteen, Blue Larkspur (121 pounds) defeated Misstep (124) with the leading money earner of the time, Sun Beau (125), finishing third. The time of 1:49 2/5 was a new track record.

In the final race of his career, Blue Larkspur went out for the weight-for-age Arlington Cup at one and a quarter miles. He won easily, by three and a half lengths, from Petee-Wrack, Toro, and Sun Beau, all high-class horses. The time of 2:03 4/5 was only one-fifth of a second away from the track mark.

One of the drawbacks to American racing is that when a colt shows both pre-cocity and speed there is an overwhelming temptation to exploit his ability early, often to the detriment of his later racing possibilities. The result can be that unsoundness is developed early, and we are left wondering about the true merit of a horse. This experience was particularly noticeable in connection with the fast Domino line: Commando made only three starts at three and none thereafter, Colin raced but once after the Belmont, and Pennant raced once at three but broke down afterwards.

In the case of Blue Larkspur, he had his problems and yet was able to contest enough major races that a fair idea of his worth was attainable. The author recalls an evening spent with horsemen some years ago, during which those assembled were asked to write on a slip of paper the names of the three best horses they had seen run. We were surprised when racing columnist Charles Hatton put down Blue Larkspur as the best horse he ever had seen perform. While we would not go that far, there is little doubt that Blue Larkspur was a very high-class colt, one who could carry his speed over a distance.

As has been pointed out in other chapters of this book, the farm that bred him often is one of the worst possible places for a high-class racer to stand after retirement. Blue Larkspur combined the blood of each of the three best strains of the Idle Hour stock, and as is usual in such cases, his best stock came from mares sent to him by outside owners. Blue Larkspur's produce from such mares included Myrtlewood, Revoked, and Blue Swords.

Blue Larkspur sired forty-four stakes winners, and while his male line today is not strong, his daughters were highly valued and bred on exceptionally. A stallion's claim to importance could stand on having sired the foundation mare Myrtlewood alone, but Blue Larkspur's stakes-winning daughters also included But Why Not, Blue Delight, Our Page, Alablue, Elpis, and Bee Ann Mac. His stakes-winning sons included Hawley, Oedipus, and Sky Larking.

End Notes:

1. After 1976 two more champions bred by Bradley were inducted into the Racing Hall of Fame. In 1978, champion steeplechaser Oedipus was inducted, and in 1990, two-time champion Bimelech was inducted.

2. Blue Larkspur is considered by most racing historians to be Horse of the Year for 1929 as well as champion handicap horse of 1930.

CHAPTER THIRTY-SEVEN

BALLADIER

L ike the annals of the poor, Balladier's racing history was short, but it was long enough to show that he was among the best of his age. He did not start until August, at Saratoga. Colonel E.R. Bradley, his breeder and owner, did not trouble to put him in the usual maiden race, but chose a five and a half-furlong allowance affair called the Idle Hour Purse. Balladier's works must have been pleasing, as he was backed down from 4-1 to 5-2 in a field of six. At the half-mile mark he was only fourth, but he came through his field in good style to score by one and a half lengths with Don Meade aboard.

From that race, he moved straight into stakes competition in the United States Hotel Stakes of six furlongs. Among Balladier's nine rivals was Omaha, who also already had won a race and who was destined to win the following year's Triple Crown. Balladier was favored at 16-5, with Omaha at 8-1. Balladier broke on top and led all the way to win drawing out. Omaha was fourth, beaten nearly six lengths.

In the Hopeful, also at Saratoga, two-year-olds run six and a half furlongs for the first time. There was a field of sixteen in Balladier's year, and the Bradley colt was again favored at 5-2. He stumbled leaving the gate and lost all chance, finishing down the track. The race was won by Psychic Bid, with Rosemont second, Esposa third, and Omaha fourth.

At Belmont Park, in the Champagne Stakes at the same distance, Balladier showed that the form of the Hopeful was wrong, giving Omaha seven pounds and beating him a nose in 1:16 3/5, a new track record.

Balladier's last race was in the Futurity, again at six and a half furlongs. There was a field of fourteen, with Psychic Bid (130 pounds) the favorite, based on the form in the Hopeful. Balladier (122) was second favorite. Balladier got away slowly, then finished with a rush. He did not have time to get on terms with Chance Sun, who won by four lengths. Omaha (122) was again fourth, beaten a length by Balladier.

Balladier

Balladier was injured in the Futurity and did not race again.

There can be very little doubt that Balladier was considerably better than Omaha as a two-year-old. How they would have compared as three-year-olds we will never know.

What we do know is that, despite his great showing at three, Omaha was a failure as a sire. Of the others that Balladier raced against, only Rosemont made a fair showing as a sire, granted the very restrictive opportunity that his owner William du Pont Jr. chose to give him. It was not exactly a vintage year for the production of great sires.

Taking his five starts as a whole (in one he stumbled at the start and had no chance), in which he won three and was second once, together with the fact that when he had to come from behind Balladier showed a good capacity for charging, he was a colt of very high class. This record was about level with the two-year-old form of Blue Larkspur, who had the good fortune to go on at three and four and indicate that he probably was the best of his age. The two colts were closely related; Balladier was by Black Toney, while Blue Larkspur was by a son of Black Toney; both were out of daughters of North Star III.

Blue Warbler, the dam of Balladier, was a very high-class filly as a two-year-old, being unplaced only once in eight starts, when she lost her rider in the Pimlico Futurity. She came out at Latonia in June, as favorite in an allowance race. The winner was Flyatit, who had won her previous start, and who later was to become the dam of the great filly Top Flight. The next time out, Blue Warbler was a winner, beating Flyatit six lengths, and her next start was in the Schuylerville Stakes at Saratoga. She was second, but beat Mother Goose, who later won the Futurity. Blue Warbler then won the Spinaway, the principal stakes

YEAR	AGE	STS	1ST	2ND	3RD	EARNED
1934	at 2	5	3	1	0	$18,320
Lifetime		5	3	1	0	$18,320

for juvenile fillies at Saratoga, with Mother Goose fourth. This was followed by a second in the Tomboy Handicap, where Blue Warbler (126) failed by two lengths to give nine pounds to the good filly Nedana (117). In the Matron Stakes, Blue Warbler (127) gave Swinging thirteen pounds and beat her a neck; Swinging achieved immortality by producing Equipoise as her first foal. Blue Warbler next finished second in the Fort Thomas Handicap versus males.

Her last start of the year was in the Pimlico Futurity.

As a three-year-old, Blue Warbler made only four starts, and the suggestion of

BALLADIER				
Black Toney, 1911	Peter Pan, 1904	Commando, 1898	Domino, 1891	Himyar / Mannie Gray
			Emma C., 1892	Darebin / Guenn
		Cinderella, 1888	Hermit, 1864	Newminster / Seclusion
			Mazurka, 1878	See Saw / Mabille
	Belgravia, 1903	Ben Brush, 1893	Bramble, 1875	Bonnie Scotland / Ivy Leaf
			Roseville, 1888	Reform / Albia
		Bonnie Gal, 1889	Galopin, 1872	Vedette / Flying Duchess
			Bonnie Doon, 1870	Rapid Rhone / Queen Mary
Blue Warbler, 1922	North Star III, 1914	Sunstar, 1908	Sundridge, 1898	Amphion / Sierra
			Doris, 1898	Loved One / Lauretta
		Angelic, 1901	St. Angelo, 1889	Galopin / Agneta
			Fota, 1890	Hampton / Photinia
	May Bird, 1913	Thrush, 1902	Missel Thrush, 1897	Orme / Throstle
			Chemistry, 1888	Charibert / Retort
		May Bruce, 1896	May Duke, 1889	Muncaster / Maibaum
			Lady Bruce, 1888	Bruce / Stella

Spy Song

the charts is that she was overtaken by unsoundness. She won her first outing at Lexington over a mile easily enough and also her second at Churchill Downs, giving stablemate Buckwheat Cake fourteen pounds. Buckwheat Cake the next time out was second, beaten a length for the Kentucky Oaks, while Blue Warbler was pulled up to finish last in the same race. That something was beginning to go wrong was confirmed when in an allowance race of six furlongs at Latonia, Blue Warbler was beaten ten lengths in fourth.

There can be little doubt that Blue Warbler was about as high-class a filly as there was foaled in 1922. Her dam was May Bird, who only made one start in England and was left at the post. May Bird must have shown something in her work, as her odds on this occasion were 5-1. Col. Bradley imported her at the end of her two-year-old career, in 1915. He tried racing her in the United States in 1916; she made nine starts, without winning, though she was twice placed. May Bird was a daughter of a very speedy stallion called Thrush (he twice won at a mile), who was a failure as a sire. May Bird's dam, May Bruce, was sired by another stud failure, May Duke, but nevertheless showed some racing merit. She was in training for six seasons and started thirty-six times, winning seven races of small value up to distances of one and three-quarters miles. The next dam, Lady Bruce, by Bruce (another stud failure) never ran.

This female line compared poorly with Blue Larkspur's female line. Blue Larkspur's second dam was the good race mare and broodmare Vaila, and his fourth dam (to whom he was inbred [3x4]) was Padua, who was good both on the turf and at stud.

As might have been expected from this background, Balladier did not prove to be as good a sire as was Blue Larkspur. When both stallions were offered for sale by Col. Bradley, however, Balladier was ten and Blue Larkspur was already sixteen, so the buyer, Joe A. Goodwin, chose Balladier.

Bradley had stood both stallions previously, but decided to sell one because of the similarity in their pedigrees. Undoubtedly, Balladier as a sire was handicapped by the unsoundness so frequently seen in the stock of North Star III as well as in many of the Domino line of sires. (When Col. Bradley introduced sound strains into his stud, in the form of La Troienne and War Admiral blood, he produced horses that could stand racing without breaking down, among them Bimelech and Busher.)

Balladier sired only sixteen stakes winners, but in Spy Song and juvenile champion Double Jay he got two sons that not only displayed high class at the races, but also proved significant stallions. Double Jay sired forty-five stakes winners; many of his better ones were fillies, but among his major-winning sons are Bagdad, Bupers, and Spring Double. Spy Song sired twenty-eight stakes winners, and his top sons include juvenile champion Crimson Satan. Other sons of Balladier that were successful stallions included Papa Redbird and Ky. Colonel. Balladier died in 1950 and was buried at Goodwin's Patchen Wilkes Farm near Lexington.

CHAPTER THIRTY-EIGHT

DOUBLE JAY

In the previous chapter in this book, the author lamented that Balladier's racing career ended after only five starts as a two-year-old. Balladier had time to prove only that he was among the best of his crop. He defeated Omaha in three of their four meetings, so perhaps he could have been the best of the crop, but, like so many horses possessing the blood of Black Toney and North Star III, Balladier had fragile legs, and he could not stand training for long.

It seemed that Balladier would need some tough, sound mares among his mates, and this prescription certainly was filled in the case of Broomshot. The latter had raced through her eighth year, had started 126 times, and had won seventeen races. Furthermore, Broomshot's dam, Centre Shot, had been a stakes winner, had won a total of twenty-five races, and had produced stakes winners Oswego, Little Sister, and Pongee.

Double Jay, Broomshot's 1944 Balladier foal, was bred by John W. Stanley, who paid Ed Janss a $100 profit for Broomshot on the same night Janss had purchased the mare from E.D. Axton at a Lexington sale conducted by Fasig-Tipton Company in 1941. Janss had paid $700 for the mare—in a sale in which some mares sold for as little as $10—and Stanley then got her for $800.

The mare was in foal to Balladier at the time, and later she was returned to the same sire and produced Double Jay, her only stakes winner. (It will be noted that Broomshot was eighteen when she produced Double Jay. The author often has heard old-time horsemen call attention to the probability that a mare that has been raced severely for a long time will foal her best ones in her old age. We know of no research to support this proposition, but one usually can think of examples to support whatever might be wished: Kizil Kourgan was nineteen when she foaled Ksar; Pearl Cap was sixteen when she foaled Pearl Diver, and Alice Hawthorn was nineteen when she foaled Thormanby.)

Stanley sold Double Jay privately for a reported $10,000 as a yearling to James V. Tigani and James E. Boines, who raced the colt under the name of Ridgewood

Double Jay with trainer Duke McCue

Stable. The year after Double Jay was sold, his full brother went for $26,000 to Maine Chance Farm[1], quickly giving Stanley a $36,000 gross on an investment of $800—a return such as would cause even Jay Gould and Jim Fiske to raise inquisitive eyebrows.

Double Jay was brought out at Hialeah in February of 1946, and from three races during the winter he got two seconds and a third, the third coming in the Hialeah Juvenile Stakes. Shipped to the North, he won a four-furlong maiden race at Narragansett in April, then narrowly won an allowance race. On May 25, Double Jay tried for a stakes again, but went under to Fleet West, a filly who never won another stakes.

Having had three races close together, Double Jay was given a rest until September, when he came back to win four consecutive races, all of them stakes. The first was the Newport Stakes at six furlongs, which he won by a nose in 1:11 from C.V. Whitney's Bastogne. There he showed some gameness, coming on again in the final sixteenth after being challenged in the stretch. Next, Double Jay was out for the James H. Connors, in which he carried 117 pounds and defeated Miss Kimo (119) by one and a quarter lengths. Donor (122) was third, three-quarters of a length away, a result that at the weights made Double Jay about equal to Donor.

The next two races were against stronger competition. Double Jay won the Garden State Stakes by one and a half lengths from World Trade, with Faultless in the beaten field. He then took the one-mile Kentucky Jockey Club Stakes at Churchill Downs by three lengths from the non-staying Education.

Double Jay's fall streak earned him a split with Education on polls for the two-year-old colt championship. Considering the quality of Double Jay's opposition, the evidence that he was the best of the year was pretty flimsy, but on the Experimental Free Handicap he was rated equal with Cosmic Bomb atop the colt's list. (The filly First Flight was rated with them in actual weight, thus topping the list when her sex allowance is taken into account.)

In 1947 Double Jay was sent to Kentucky to be pointed for the Kentucky Derby, and his first race was a six-furlong sprint on April 26. He was third, beaten by nearly four lengths. Three days later, he was beaten at a mile by Faultless and Cosmic Bomb, and by Derby Day he was a longshot. Double Jay was next-to-last in the classic and pulled up sore.

The colt did not get back to the races until the Saratoga-at-Jamaica meeting, in which he was beaten three lengths by Hornbeam in the six-furlong Gideon Putnam Hotel Handicap. He next tried the one and one-sixteenth-mile Mars

Balladier, 1932	Black Toney, 1911	Peter Pan, 1904	Commando, 1898	Domino / Emma C.
			Cinderella, 1888	Hermit / Mazurka
		Belgravia, 1903	**Ben Brush**, 1893	Bramble / Roseville
			Bonnie Gal, 1889	Galopin / Bonnie Doon
	Blue Warbler, 1922	North Star III, 1914	Sunstar, 1908	Sundridge / Doris
			Angelic, 1901	St. Angelo / Fota
		May Bird, 1913	Thrush, 1902	Missel Thrush / Chemistry
			May Bruce, 1896	May Duke / Lady Bruce
DOUBLE JAY	Whisk Broom II, 1907	Broomstick, 1901	**Ben Brush**, 1893	Bramble / Roseville
			Elf, 1893	Galliard / Sylva Belle
		Audience, 1901	Sir Dixon, 1885	Billet / Jaconet
			Sallie McClelland, 1888	Hindoo / Red and Blue
Broomshot, 1926	Centre Shot, 1905	Sain, 1894	St. Serf, 1887	St. Simon / Feronia
			The Task, 1889	Barcaldine / Satchel
		Grand Shot, 1900	Foul Shot, 1882	Musket / Slander
			Grand Lady, 1892	Grandmaster / Fine Lady

Handicap but was beaten badly and thereafter was dropped down to a six-furlong allowance race, which he won.

Again at six furlongs, in the Camden Handicap at Garden State, Double Jay (115) tried the older Polynesian (129) and was no match for the latter, who set a track record of 1:09 4/5. Back in New York, Double Jay got eleven pounds from Cosmic Bomb and thirteen pounds from Phalanx in the nine-furlong Discovery Handicap, and he split that pair at the wire, finishing second. The latter result gave a pretty accurate measure of Double Jay's form—about eleven to twelve pounds below the best of his year.

Against lesser horses, Double Jay scored comfortably in a nine-furlong purse race and then won the $36,000 Jersey Handicap from Fervent, who gave him eleven pounds. Dropping back to six furlongs, and running against opposition less than the best, the Ridgewood Stable colt carried 126 pounds to an easy victory in the Benjamin Franklin Handicap in 1:10 3/5.

Next, Double Jay once more tried higher-class opposition, getting two pounds from Cosmic Bomb in the nine-furlong Trenton Handicap and going under by five lengths. That result placed Double Jay still about ten pounds below top class, a figure that was verified when he lost by a neck to Cosmic Bomb while getting eight pounds in the one and three-sixteenths-mile Roamer Handicap.

YEAR	AGE	STS	1ST	2ND	3RD	EARNED
1946	at 2	10	6	3	1	$ 77,550
1947	at 3	17	6	4	3	$ 95,075
1948	at 4	13	2	2	5	$ 76,555
1949	at 5	6	3	0	0	$ 49,175
1950	at 6	2	0	0	0	$ 650
Lifetime		48	17	9	9	$299,005

The Scarsdale Handicap at one and one-sixteenth miles found Double Jay running true to form again, as he was third to the older With Pleasure (129) and the filly Gallorette (119), beaten two and a half lengths while carrying 118 pounds.

When placed against lesser opposition again, Double Jay won handily in the Riggs Handicap and took the Prince George Autumn Handicap by a nose.

Double Jay's three-year-old season found him running consistently enough to give a good picture of his form compared to that of the leaders. He was tough, durable, and reliable, up to one and three-sixteenths miles, and was something like ten pounds below the classic colts of his age.

Double Jay's four-year-old handicap career began with the Pimlico handicap-per rating him at 124 pounds for the Dixie Handicap[2], but he finished nowhere, behind winner Fervent (121) and runner-up Stymie (127). He faced Stymie (130) again in the one and one-sixteenth-mile Aqueduct Handicap and was beaten by

Bagdad

some four lengths to finish third under 126 pounds. In the nine-furlong Omnibus Handicap, Double Jay carried level weights with Lucky Draw (runner-up) and lost by nine and a quarter lengths to finish fourth, then under top weight of 123 pounds for the ten-furlong Massachusetts Handicap, Double Jay ran third, beaten two lengths by Beauchef (115) and the filly Harmonica (110).

These races again underlined that Double Jay could not match the best of his time, but at four he did win two of thirteen races, his lone stakes triumph coming in the Trenton Handicap.

During the colt's four-year-old season, Tigani bought out Boines' interest in Double Jay for a reported $100,000, and he continued to race Double Jay at five and six. At five, Double Jay was sent to California, where he matched Santa Anita's track record of 1:48 3/5 for nine furlongs in the American Handicap. Double Jay won two other races that year, then was retired after failing to place in a pair of races at six.

Double Jay had demonstrated that he was below the best, but he was a horse-man's horse, one who could take a lot of racing and win more than his share. He obviously had inherited the sound, tough qualities of his dam, as well as some of

Doubledogdare

the speed of his sire.

Young Bull Hancock, who would succeed his father as master of Claiborne Farm, had seen Double Jay against Education in the Kentucky Jockey Club Stakes at two, and the race had left a lasting impression.

"Double Jay was trained by Duke McCue," Hancock once recalled, "and Duke was a wild man if ever there was one ... I happened to be in the secretary's office when Duke came in to make his entry for Double Jay. Everybody was kidding him, and he couldn't take kidding. Somebody said, 'Duke, what the hell are you putting that damned horse in there for? You should have left him in New Jersey. Education will top him out of the gate and open up so far you'll never catch him, not even if they go around twice.'

"Well, Duke just went crazy. He reached into his pocket and pulled out eight $100 bills. 'My horse will be in front of Education at every pole,' he said. 'Any pole he's not, you win a hundred; any pole he is, I win the hundred.'

"So, they covered him, and I went back to the races the next day. I thought no horse in the world could top Education, and if it did, I didn't think it possibly then could stay a mile. That sucker Double Jay topped him and won it. So, I made up my mind right then and there that I wanted to stand that horse."

That he had left such an impression that day was a fortuitous thing for Double Jay, for even Hancock described him as having "lost his glamour" by the time he was retired:

"Mr. Tigani ran him a little too much ... He wanted to syndicate him, but I told him the timing was bad and suggested we just stand him. Tigani was a little skeptical, but we started the horse off at $500 and he hit right off the bat. Pretty soon, we had him up to $5,000, and the old man was having so much fun that he didn't want to syndicate him. Finally, he sold a quarter to Mr. (John) Hertz and a quarter to me."

With the advantage of standing at Claiborne, Double Jay had a great variety of mares available for his book, unlike Blue Larkspur and some others of the Domino male line that were retired to virtually private studs whose best mares were full of the same blood as the stallions.

Double Jay stood at Claiborne for twenty-two seasons and sired 453 named foals. A total of forty-five (10 percent) of his foals won stakes. Double Jay got good fillies, and he became the leading broodmare sire of 1971 and of 1975.[3]

Among the stakes-winning fillies sired by Double Jay were champion Doubledogdare plus Manotick, Splendored, Plotter, Shirley Jones, Irish Jay, Ole Liz, and Queen's Double. His stakes-winning sons included Besomer, Tick Tock, Bagdad, Clandestine, Jay Fox, Sunrise Flight, Noble Jay, Choker, Bupers, Repeating, Spring Double, and Jay Ray.

For a racehorse well below the top as a runner, this was quite a success story at stud.

End Notes:

1. The colt was bought by Lester Manor Stable for the account of Mrs. Elizabeth Graham's Maine Chance Farm.

2. Double Jay's four-year-old season began on January 15, 1948, at Santa Anita. He made five starts at the Arcadia, California, track, with placings in the Maturity, San Antonio, and Santa Anita handicaps. He returned to Jamaica racetrack in early April to win an overnight handicap, then finished second under 125 pounds in the Excelsior Handicap. He added a score in the Trenton Handicap at Garden State prior to the Dixie.

3. He also was leading broodmare sire in 1977 and 1981.

CHAPTER THIRTY-NINE

PENNANT

Pennant was foaled in 1911, near the end of the glorious era of James R. Keene's Castleton Stud. He was born in the same crop as Black Toney, both being sons of the Keene stallion Peter Pan. The entire Keene crop was sold, as there was no racing in New York in 1912, and Colonel E.R. Bradley purchased the 1912 yearlings on behalf of W.A. Prime. A slump in the market, in which he was heavily involved, precluded Prime from taking them, so Col. Bradley paid for the lot and then offered the yearlings at auction.

James Rowe had trained Pennant's stakes-winning half brothers Iron Mask and Transvaal for Keene, and he took Pennant for $1,700 on behalf of Harry Payne Whitney. (Rowe trained for Keene during the time of his greatest triumphs, and thus conditioned such as Commando, Sysonby, Colin, Peter Pan, and Sweep.)

Like so many of the other high-class horses bred by Keene, Pennant was by a sire of an American line and out of an imported English mare. His sire, Peter Pan, was by Commando, he by Domino, son of Himyar. The dam, Royal Rose, was by Royal Hampton. Neither Peter Pan nor Commando was refined and bloodlike, and the same was true of Royal Hampton, so it was not surprising that Pennant was not a very refined specimen.

Royal Rose was only a minor winner at two and three, but she was a half sister to Pink Domino, the dam of Sweep. In addition to Pennant, Iron Mask, and Transvaal, Royal Rose foaled stakes winner Lancastrian.

Racing was resumed in New York in 1913, and Rowe that spring won the three great handicaps—the Metropolitan, Brooklyn, and Suburban—with Whisk Broom II, an American-bred who had been racing in England. Rowe did not bring the two-year-old Pennant out until August 12 at Saratoga. He must have known that he had something out of the ordinary, for he did not bother to run the colt first in a maiden race. He gave him his first start in an allowance race, in which all but one of the eight other starters had raced before.

Pennant did not disappoint him. He won by two lengths from the high-class

271

Pennant

L.S. SUTCLIFFE

Stromboli (one of the first sons of Fair Play) and equaled the track record of 1:05 4/5 for five and a half furlongs. In his next race Pennant pulled right away from his opponents in the stretch and won at odds of 1-4 by six lengths.

The Futurity was the colt's third and last race of the year. It was run that year at Saratoga, instead of at Belmont Park, and was contested over a slow track at six furlongs. Pennant, favored at 8-5, came from fourth, about five lengths off the pace, to take command in the stretch, and he won by a length from the good filly Southern Maid. Fifth, at 15-1, was Col. Bradley's Black Toney, who later became a great sire, indeed a better one than Pennant.

The Pennant program of three races within nineteen days as the entire juvenile campaign was fairly typical of the training methods Rowe employed whenever he had a two-year-old that he liked. He later used the same schedule with the great filly Regret, and earlier in his career he actually had resigned his position as trainer for the Dwyer Brothers in opposition to what he considered the over-racing of Miss Woodford.

In the case of Pennant, the light campaign may have been by necessity rather than design, for a contemporary report indicated that he was sore on the way to the post for his first race. At any rate, he broke down while winning his first start at three, in June at Belmont Park.

The Whitney stud had no urgent need of Pennant as a sire, as Whitney had purchased the colt's sire, Peter Pan, from the Keene dispersal in 1913. So, Pennant was returned to training, and he was able to race again as a five-year-old. Although he had not raced in more than two years, his first race upon his reappearance was in a major handicap, the Brooklyn, a nine-furlong event in which he was carrying 123 pounds. Pennant received eight pounds from Roamer, who was favored at 11-5. Pennant, at 7-1, beat the favorite by about four and a half lengths, but he in turn was beaten two lengths by the three-year-old Friar Rock (108). Having the horse ready to run so well after such a long layoff was a noteworthy feat on the part of trainer Rowe.

Pennant then was dropped to a six-furlong overnight race, and with nothing much sent against him was favored at 2-5. He won as he pleased, by three lengths. On August 7, Pennant came out again, for the one-mile Delaware Handicap at Saratoga. There were some good horses in the field of six, among them The Finn (119) (who had been the best three-year-old of the previous season), old rival Stromboli (125), and Ed Crump (120). Pennant was favored at 1-2, despite his impost of 127 pounds, and he won by two lengths from Stromboli.

Next trying a distance of nine furlongs again, Pennant took up 130 pounds for the Champlain Handicap. Stromboli was in with 123 pounds, The Finn with 117. The

				Alarm
			Himyar, 1875	Hira
		Domino, 1891	Mannie Gray, 1874	Enquirer
				Lizzie G
	Commando, 1898		Darebin, 1878	The Peer
		Emma C., 1892		Lurline
			Guenn, 1883	Flood
Peter Pan, 1904				Glendew
			Newminster, 1848	Touchstone
		Hermit, 1864		Beeswing
			Seclusion, 1857	Tadmor
	Cinderella, 1888			Miss Sellon
			See Saw, 1865	Buccaneer
		Mazurka, 1878		Margery Daw
PENNANT			Mabille, 1868	Parmesan
				Rigolboche
			Lord Clifden, 1860	Newminster
		Hampton, 1872		The Slave
			Lady Langden, 1868	Kettledrum
	Royal Hampton, 1882			Haricot
			King Tom, 1851	Harkaway
		Princess, 1872		Pocahontas
			Mrs. Lincoln, 1866	North Lincoln
Royal Rose, 1894				Bay Middleton Mare
			Sterling, 1868	Oxford
		Beaudesert, 1877		Whisper
			Sea Gull, 1866	Lifeboat
	Belle Rose, 1889			Wild Cherry
			Craig Millar, 1872	Blair Athol
		Monte Rosa, 1882		Miss Roland
			Hedge Rose, 1867	Neptunus
				Woodbine

shift of weight in The Finn's favor, plus the added furlong, enabled that horse to draw away to win by two and a half lengths, while the weight shift put Pennant and Stromboli virtually even; Stromboli edged the other horse by a nose for second.

Pennant was brought back again at six, but he did not get beyond the spring meetings on the Maryland circuit. In the five and one-half-furlong Harford Handicap at Havre de Grace, he was not quite up to dealing with 132 pounds successfully and ran third, beaten five lengths by Sand Marsh (123). Still in Maryland, he got four pounds off for the six-furlong Philadelphia Handicap and under 128 pounds at 4-5 defeated Leochares (130) by a half-length.

YEAR	AGE	STS	1ST	2ND	3RD	EARNED
1913	at 2	3	3	0	0	$15,880
1914	at 3	1	1	0	0	$ 545
1915	at 4	unraced				
1916	at 5	4	2	1	1	$ 3,400
1917	at 6	4	3	0	1	$ 5,490
Lifetime		12	9	1	2	$25,315

At the same meeting, Pennant then came out for the Susquehanna Handicap at one mile and seventy yards, again carrying 128 pounds. That time he gave two pounds to Leochares, but the weight shift did not reverse the previous finish. The Susquehanna proved his penultimate race.[1]

While the H.P. Whitney stud probably was the best breeding establishment in America at the time, it by no means was the best place for Pennant to go to stud. The Whitney stock largely was composed of produce of Peter Pan and Broomstick, and because Pennant was a son of Peter Pan, a large number of the mares were unavailable to him. The Broomstick stock was available, provided the individuals did not have crosses of Peter Pan.

Pennant needed a little stoutness in the blood of his mates to overcome his own apparent distance limitations. His racing record suggested that he was the best two-year-old of his year and at five and six belonged to the best of the handicap division, but twice he showed that he did not really care to go nine furlongs. The conclusion is that Pennant was a good miler and was somewhat lacking in stoutness.

Broomstick was not famous for the stamina of his stock, so his blood alone in Pennant's mares could not be expected to supply Pennant with any help in regard to stoutness. The Whitney stud was oriented strongly toward the production of early maturing two-year-olds and sheer speed; Whitney, in fact, virtually had abandoned Keene's policy of reinforcing the American speed strains of his stallions with the stoutness of imported English blood in his mares.

It is not surprising then, that Pennant was not an overwhelming success at stud. He did get a fine percentage of stakes winners, 16 percent (thirty-nine) from 248 foals, and was among the leading twenty sires on eight occasions, but the only truly first-class colt he got was the great Equipoise. The latter was out of a Broomstick mare, Swinging, whose dam was imported and had a non-sprinting pedigree.

Other high-class horses sired by Pennant included Preakness winner Dauber, Futurity winner Bunting, steeplechase champion Jolly Roger, Brooklyn and Dwyer winner The Chief, Kentucky Oaks winner Mary Jane, Champagne Stakes winner Valorous, and Hopeful Stakes winner Red Rain.

It seems a paradox, but Pennant stood at probably the best farm in America and yet did not have a very good opportunity at stud. Considering this, his record is a fine one although Black Toney, a much inferior horse to Pennant as a racer,

Jolly Roger

had a superior record in terms of producing high-class horses. Black Toney had a better opportunity, standing at the Idle Hour Farm of Col. Bradley, who believed in the pattern of reinforcing American speed with English mares.

Pennant lived until the age of twenty-seven and was totally blind when he died at the Whitney farm in 1938.[2]

End Notes:

1. Pennant's final race was the Pimlico Spring Handicap on May 8, in which he faced nine others, including Leochares. Carrying 132 pounds, he won by a head from Crimper. Leochares finished fourth.

2. According to a note dated January 3, 1934, and found in *The Blood-Horse* archives, Major Louie A. Beard—bloodstock adviser to both Mrs. Payne Whitney of Greentree Stud and her brother-in-law Harry Payne Whitney, stated that Pennant bred bad feet and bad-shaped feet, "duck-bill" feet as well as bad hind legs.

CHAPTER FORTY

EQUIPOISE

S ome colts arouse a degree of loyalty and enthusiasm among their supporters that defies understanding. When they win, it is time to celebrate, and when they lose, it is a sorrowful occasion. Whatever happens, there is a river of loyal emotion surrounding them, and the devotion of their followers remains unshaken.

The identity of the owner usually does not matter, but the trainer and jockey can come in for criticism at times (almost never praise). The colt belongs to the racing public, and such details as legal ownership are matters of indifference. The horse becomes a folk hero and survives triumph and disaster alike better than can any statesman or general.

Achieving such a status requires a high order of ability, but it depends also upon the presence of the risk of defeat. Generally, the folk hero kind of horse does not have the overwhelming and consistent superiority of a Man o' War. Everybody knew what was going to happen when Man o' War ran and racegoers freely acknowledged his greatness, but the spine-chilling excitement was not there, except perhaps when he was to face John P. Grier while giving away eighteen pounds—an assignment that raised a question even in Man o' War's case.

In the case of Exterminator, the feeling was different. There was not the presumption of victory, and in fact, he lost half of his one-hundred starts. Still, he would go anywhere and race over any distance, and while he might be beaten, he was game to the core, always facing the battle with unflinching courage. That, and his longevity as a racer, brought him his unswerving band of devotees.

Such a colt, too, was Equipoise. He went everywhere and met all the best horses of his time over all track conditions and over all distances. The author recalls him as not a particularly impressive colt in the matter of size or muscular development, but to some he was a picture colt in terms of refinement and symmetry. His dark chestnut coat earned him the nickname "The Chocolate Soldier," from his public, and as was true of his great-great-grandsire Domino, he appeared

C.V. Whitney

BLOOD-HORSE LIBRARY

to change colors in different lights. There were times when Equipoise looked like a dark, liver chestnut, and there were times when he looked almost brown.

More remarkable was the Equipoise personality. He was a quiet colt, but there was a magnetic field of courage emanating from him that was very moving. In the end, it was his unfailing courage even more than his high physical abilities that stamped him as a great—and greatly loved—racehorse.

Equipoise was sired by Pennant, who was a good sire (getting 16 percent stakes winners) despite having the limitation of being a son of Peter Pan in a stud largely dominated by Peter Pan mares.

H.P. Whitney, who raced Pennant, bred Equipoise, who became the first major horse raced by Whitney's son, C.V. Whitney, when the breeder died. Equipoise was bred from Swinging, who won ten of eighteen races at two and placed in several stakes. Swinging was not as good as were her stablemates, Mother Goose and Maud Muller, and she was not, in fact, in the first string of the Whitney stable. Trainer James Rowe did not race a two-year-old eighteen times if he thought he had a good one.

Swinging, who won two races at three, had an attractive pedigree, being by Broomstick and out of Balancoire II, who had run in France at two and three and was a stakes winner. Balancoire II was by Meddler, a very high-class racer and a prominent sire of broodmares. The next dam was Ballantrae, a high-class mare in England, where she won the Cambridgeshire. In addition to being the third dam of Equipoise, Ballantrae became the third dam of Djebel, who won the Middle Park Stakes, Two Thousand Guineas, and Prix de l'Arc de Triomphe and was the leading sire in France multiple times.

Equipoise began his racing life in the chain gang of the H.P. Whitney stable, in Maryland rather than with the first team in New York. This possibly was because he was somewhat small, having been a May foal. The second division was trained by Freddy Hopkins, who sent Equipoise out for his first start at Bowie on April 7, 1930, before the colt was fully two years old. The youngster won that day and eight days later won another overnight race at Havre de Grace.

Equipoise then was asked to take on unbeaten Vander Pool in the Aberdeen Stakes, and the Whitney colt finished third. Equipoise was left in stakes competition, however, and was a starter for the Nursery Stakes at Pimlico. Start was all he did, as he stumbled and tossed Raymond "Sonny" Workman, who was riding him for the first time.

A week later, Equipoise appeared in New York for the first time, and, with Workman aboard, overcame traffic problems to come away from Vander Pool by four lengths in the Youthful Stakes. The race indicated that Equipoise was improving, but the rider of Vander Pool claimed foul against him and Equipoise was disqualified and set back to last.[1] It was the first of three disqualifications suffered by Equipoise (who never was disqualified into a win).

In the Keene Memorial, Equipoise again had traffic problems early, but he drew away to defeat Happy Scot by two lengths over a slow track for his first official stakes triumph. Ten days later, he got up to beat Happy Scot in the final twenty yards of the Juvenile Stakes. He then took the National Stallion by six lengths and

Pennant, 1911	Peter Pan, 1904	Commando, 1898	Domino, 1891	Himyar Mannie Gray
			Emma C., 1892	Darebin Guenn
		Cinderella, 1888	Hermit, 1864	Newminster Seclusion
			Mazurka, 1878	See Saw Mabille
	Royal Rose, 1894	Royal Hampton, 1882	**Hampton**, 1872	Lord Clifden Lady Langden
			Princess, 1872	King Tom Mrs. Lincoln
		Belle Rose, 1889	Beaudesert, 1877	Sterling Sea Gull
			Monte Rosa, 1882	Craig Millar Hedge Rose
EQUIPOISE				
Swinging, 1922	Broomstick, 1901	Ben Brush, 1893	Bramble, 1875	Bonnie Scotland Ivy Leaf
			Roseville, 1888	Reform Albia
		Elf, 1893	Galliard, 1880	Galopin Mavis
			Sylva Belle, 1887	Bend Or Saint Editha
	Balancoire II, 1911	Meddler, 1890	St Gatien, 1881	The Rover Saint Editha
			Busybody, 1881	Petrarch Spinaway
		Ballantrae, 1899	Ayrshire, 1885	**Hampton** Atalanta
			Abeyance, 1885	Touchet Minnie Hauk

Equipoise

the Great American by two.

After seven stakes races in eight weeks, it was evident that Equipoise was about as good a two-year-old as had been seen out in 1930, and he was given a rest before Saratoga.

On August 9, he came out for the Saratoga Special. There were four in the field, but it was a two-horse race. Equipoise was quoted at 7-10 and Jamestown at 8-5, but the oddsmakers were wrong. The Whitney colt never could get to Jamestown, who won by two and a half lengths.

A month later, Equipoise took on the Herculean task of carrying 132 pounds for the Champagne Stakes, then run at seven furlongs. He was giving A.C. Bostwick's Mate thirteen pounds and nearly managed it successfully, going under only by a head in the sensational time of 1:21 4/5.

A week later, Equipoise met Jamestown again, in the Futurity. Both carried 130 pounds and, in a field of fifteen, Jamestown was at 5-2 and Equipoise about 7-2. The favorites were first and second all the way, and although Equipoise was charging on Jamestown at the finish, the Whitney colt went under by a head. The author was fortunate enough to see that breathtaker of a race, and it left no doubt that Equipoise would be the better of the pair the next year.

Mate was third, beaten three lengths, in the Futurity, in which there was a shift of five pounds in Equipoise's favor, demonstrating to the doubters that weight shifts do make a difference, even to two-year-olds.

Equipoise was sent back to Maryland for the six-furlong Eastern Shore Handicap at Havre de Grace. He was carrying 126 pounds and was asked to concede up to nineteen pounds to his opponents, but there was not a worthy rival in the field. Off at 3-5, Equipoise won as he pleased, by five lengths.

Jamestown, Equipoise, Mate, etc., made up an extraordinary band of juveniles, as was recognized at the time. Remarkably, there was still one more crack two-year-old in 1930 yet to be tested by Equipoise, and he was Greentree Stable's late-developing Twenty Grand. Back in New York, Equipoise encountered that colt in the Junior Champion Stakes and had to give him eleven pounds. With that much in his favor, Twenty Grand ran over Equipoise in the stretch and won by a length.

Next came two never-to-be-forgotten meetings between Equipoise and Twenty Grand.

Both colts were sent out to Churchill Downs for the one-mile Kentucky Jockey Club Stakes, in which each of seven starters carried 122 pounds. Five of the runners might better have been kept in

YEAR	AGE	STS	1ST	2ND	3RD	EARNED
1930	at 2	16	8	5	1	$156,835
1931	at 3	3	1	0	0	$ 3,000
1932	at 4	14	10	2	1	$107,375
1933	at 5	9	7	1	1	$ 55,760
1934	at 6	6	3	1	1	$ 15,490
1935	at 7	3	0	1	0	$ 150
Lifetime		51	29	10	4	$338,610

the barn. For the last quarter-mile, Equipoise and Twenty Grand drew away from the others in a do-or-die duel. First Twenty Grand made up two lengths and had a shade the better of it, and then Equipoise came at him again. The pair passed the post locked together, with the verdict going to Twenty Grand by a nose. The time was 1:36, fastest for a mile by two-year-olds to that time.

The same pair of colts met Mate in the one and one-sixteenth-mile Pimlico Futurity, with the track conditions very muddy. All three had 119 pounds aboard. When the start was made, Equipoise was standing sideways, and was badly left, with the whole field crossing over in front of him. He did not pick up his first horse until there was only a half-mile left to run. Equipoise had to circle his field on the outside, rounding the far turn, while Twenty Grand was able to save ground. Closing with splendid gameness under punishment, Equipoise got up in the last twenty yards between Mate and Twenty Grand and beat Twenty Grand a half-length, with Mate a neck further back.

When jockey Workman was asked if this had been his greatest race, he replied with understandable enthusiasm: "Hell, it may have been the greatest race any-

H.C. ASHBY

Shut Out winning the 1942 Kentucky Derby

body ever saw!" To make it even more dramatic, it was found that Equipoise had shed both front shoes during the running.

Equipoise had won half his sixteen races, fourteen of them stakes. He was not incontestably the best of his age by a wide margin, as Man o' War had been, but then, it was an extraordinary crop and Equipoise was generally considered the best of the lot, though not by much.

The three-year-old campaign for Equipoise was a tragedy. After starting out with an easy win at Havre de Grace, he was pointed for the Chesapeake Stakes, for which his odds were 3-20. He finished last and "pulled up distressed." Nevertheless, he was sent after the Preakness (then run prior to the Kentucky Derby), but after challenging gamely could do no better than fourth behind Mate, who won by one and a half lengths from Twenty Grand and Ladder.

Equipoise had developed a quarter crack, and he was never wholly sound again. The injury put an end to his racing at three, often the most productive year for colts. (Pennant, the sire of Equipoise, had been unable to run at either three or four years of age[2]; soundness was not the hallmark of the family.)

Equipoise, however, came back as a four-year-old to win ten of fourteen starts and clinch a reputation as one of the greatest horses of his time. He began by giving the good sprinter Hygro fourteen pounds and a beating at five furlongs and then took the Harford Handicap under 128 pounds. In the more important

Toboggan Handicap of six furlongs in New York, he picked up 129 pounds and won by a length.

For the one-mile Metropolitan, John B. Campbell made the mistake of accepting the form of the previous year's Preakness at face value and asked Mate (128) to give Equipoise (127) weight. It did not take Equipoise long to prove how wrong this was, as he drew away with speed to spare, beating Sun Meadow, with Mate third.

Then followed a triumphant trip to Chicago. On June 30, in the unimportant Delavan Handicap, Equipoise with 128 pounds up, met his former conqueror Jamestown and, with something to spare, raced the mile in 1:34 2/5, a new world record. Four days later, he gave the high-class filly Tred Avon twenty-two pounds, and, with 129 pounds up, was pulling up at the wire. Five days later, he took the Arlington Gold Cup from Gusto and Mate.

By then the weight began to be piled on. In the Arlington Handicap, Equipoise was assigned 134 pounds and just failed by a neck to concede twenty-three pounds to Plucky Play, a good horse. Back at Saratoga, neither the Wilson nor the Whitney Stakes gave Equipoise any trouble under the feather of 126 pounds. From there he went to Havre de Grace, where he ran his worst race, finishing last in a six-furlong handicap, but he next won the Havre de Grace Cup Handicap from Gallant Sir.

In the one-mile Laurel Stakes, he was badly bumped and ran third to Jack High, and in the Washington Handicap, he failed by a head to give Tred Avon seventeen pounds.

Trainer Tom Healey had Equipoise at five in the first string of the Whitney stable in 1933, and he was rewarded by a string of seven stakes victories in a row. First came the Philadelphia at Havre de Grace, then the Metropolitan, in which Equipoise (128) gave Okapi twenty-six pounds. The ten-furlong Suburban was a more serious task, but with 132 pounds up—conceding from eleven to twenty-five pounds—he won by two lengths. In Chicago, he carried 135 pounds to win the Arlington Handicap, and he later beat Gallant Sir again in the Hawthorne Gold Cup.

There was now a question as to how far Equipoise could go, even granted his wonderful form from six to ten furlongs. He answered this by winning the traditional Saratoga Cup of one and three-quarters miles, beating Gusto one and a half lengths. When he tried the two-mile Jockey Club Gold Cup, going such a route for the only time in his career, Equipoise was beaten and was eased a furlong from home. Although his feet were hurting, he was started in the Havre de Grace Handicap under 132 pounds and failed by only a length to beat Osculator (104).

Equipoise was kept in training as a six-year-old and won three of his six starts.

Carry Back, a classic-winning descendant of Equipoise

He won the Philadelphia and Dixie handicaps under 130 pounds, and also the Whitney Gold Trophy at the United Hunts meet at Belmont. Trying for the Metropolitan for the third time, with 132 pounds up, he actually won but swerved and was disqualified again. (This incident was dramatized in very amusing fashion in the successful play "Four Men on a Horse.") For the Suburban, Equipoise had to take up 134 pounds and lost by a nose to Ladysman (114), whose trainer solemnly assured the author that "weight didn't make any difference." There was one more effort at Narragansett in an allowance race of six furlongs, where Equipoise actually went under [finishing third] to Okapi.

Still, this was not enough. Equipoise was in training again as a seven-year-old. First, he was second to Sweeping Light, while conceding nineteen pounds. Then he gave nine pounds and a beating to the sterile Twenty Grand (who was trying a comeback) and was promptly disqualified again, for bearing in. His last start was in the $100,000 Santa Anita Handicap, with 130 pounds up, and he was conceding weight to everything. Mate finished sixth, Equipoise seventh, and Twenty Grand tenth.

When Equipoise finally was retired, the C.V. Whitney stud was based on Peter

Pan, Broomstick, and their descendants. Equipoise himself was by Pennant (a son of Peter Pan) out of Swinging (a daughter of Broomstick). Thus, there was a minimum of free blood in the Whitney stud open to Equipoise. As would be expected, his best stock came from outside mares: Classic winner Shut Out, from a mare by Chicle; Coaching Club American Oaks winner Level Best, from a mare by Man o' War; the Saratoga Cup horse Bolingbroke, from a mare by Fair Play; and Metropolitan winner Attention, from a mare by Bubbling Over.

Equipoise topped the sire list in 1942, the year his Shut Out won the Kentucky Derby, Belmont, etc., for Greentree, but that was four years after his early death. Equipoise stood only four seasons before his dying as a result of an intestinal infection.

He sired nine stakes winners, those mentioned above plus Lotopoise, Equifox, Gramps, Swing and Sway, and Equipet.

Equipoise was the last but one among the champion horses resulting from the cross of the Domino and Ben Brush strains, a cross that had been established with great results during the era of James R. Keene's Castleton Stud in the years 1900–10. The last one was Alsab, a great racer with a subnormal pedigree.

Representatives of Equipoise's sire line included classic winner Carry Back, whose sire was Saggy. The latter was by Equipoise's son Swing and Sway, who won the Diamond State Stakes and Whitney Stakes and Empire City Handicap. Alsab's line exists through Ack Ack, son of Battle Joined, he by Armageddon, by Alsab.

End Notes:
1. *The Blood-Horse* of May 17, 1930, reports it was a steward's inquiry.
2. Pennant made just one start at three, which he won.

CHAPTER FORTY-ONE

CELT

Among the battalion of first-class racers that James R. Keene bred at his Castleton Stud, near Lexington, under the management of his brother-in-law, Major Foxhall Daingerfield, was Celt, foaled in 1905. The pattern of breeding was the familiar one of Domino, or his son Commando (very fast American-line sires), mated with an imported English mare. Had anyone else bred Celt, it would have been a matter of jubilation, but in the Keene stable, Celt was not even the best colt of his year. Celt, it seems, had the misfortune to be foaled in the same year and same stable as unbeaten Colin.

Although he only made two starts as a two-year-old and only two more as a three-year-old, we have a fairly good measure of Celt's racing class, which was very high. He first came out on September 7, 1907, as part of the Keene entry for the seven-furlong Flatbush Stakes at Coney Island, New York. The other part of the entry was Colin (120), who already had been out eight times, without defeat, and was giving Celt fifteen pounds. The entry was held at the prohibitive odds of 2-5 and duly ran first and second, Colin beating Celt three lengths. Taken literally, this would mean that Colin was at least twenty-five pounds better than Celt. Since they were running as an entry, and it was the first race for Celt, though, it seems likely that Joe Notter did not press Celt too hard, giving him the advantage of an easy introduction to racing.

On September 21, Celt came out for the Junior Champion of about six furlongs at Brooklyn. While there was only a field of four, and Celt was odds-on at 7-10, he had a pretty good opponent in Uncle, one of the first good colts sired by Star Shoot. Both Celt and Uncle had 107 pounds up, so it was a fair test. The chart reported that Celt won easily by one and a half lengths from Uncle. How much to allow for the "easily," in addition to the one and a half lengths, is anybody's guess, but it is safe to hazard the guess that Celt was something more than ten pounds better than Uncle on this showing.

Since Uncle was a multiple stakes winner that year and had run Colin to a

287

length at level weights in the Saratoga Special, this made Celt a first-class two-year-old, by ordinary standards, but neither he nor any other juvenile looked it when Colin was around.

As a three-year-old, Celt did not come out until May 28 at Belmont Park, in a weight-for-age race that attracted only a party of three. One of the others was four-year-old Jack Atkin (126), who made a considerable reputation for himself. Under the conditions, Celt (109) was receiving seventeen pounds, at nine furlongs. With Notter up again, Celt beat Jack Atkin handily by a length. He had loafed in the stretch, so that Notter felt called upon to shake his whip.

KEENELAND-COOK

Celt

The next race was the last for Celt and the most important and revealing in his life. This was the one and a quarter-mile Brooklyn Handicap at Gravesend on June 1. The handicapper asked Celt (106) to give seven pounds to Fair Play (99) and eight pounds to King James, another very high-class colt. All were three-year-olds. Celt was expected to be capable of this, as his odds were 4-5, while Fair Play was 6-1 and King James was 15-1. Celt beat Fair Play by one and a half lengths. The *Daily Racing Form* comment read: "Won easily ... Celt was much the best ... Second driving." The time was 2:04 1/5, a new track record.

This form makes Celt something more than ten pounds better than Fair Play. In fact, it was not until both Celt and Colin had stopped racing, in June of 1908, that Fair Play began to look like a first-class colt. At stud, however, it was a different story.

Fair Play went on to become one of the great sires in American breeding history, while neither Celt nor Colin did so. In all fairness, it must be recalled that Fair Play had the advantage of being mated with the great band of Rock Sand mares, and some of their daughters, in August Belmont's Nursery Stud, while neither Celt nor Colin had a comparable opportunity.

Celt was retired to stud. He was included in the Keene dispersal sale of 1913 and bought by the late A.B. Hancock Sr., father of Bull Hancock and grandfather of A.B. Hancock III and Seth Hancock. A.B. Hancock Sr. told the author more than once that he was influenced in buying Celt for $20,000 by the colt's outstanding form with Fair Play and King James in the Brooklyn Handicap.

At that time, Hancock's operations were conducted at the Ellerslie Stud, Charlottesville, Virginia. Turf affairs were at a low ebb in 1913, as racing had been closed in New York in 1910 and was only resumed in 1913. Hancock told the author that the depression for breeders became so acute, that at one point he was taking mares off to county fairs and selling them for what they would bring as saddle horses. Hence, it can well be supposed that as a professional "market breeder," the financial conditions did not permit Hancock to collect a very choice band of broodmares as mates for Celt.

As an illustration of how grim the situation was for market breeders, Hancock told the author the following story: On the train from Washington to New York, to attend the sale of his yearlings, Hancock met a friend of his who was a Wall Street financier. When asked where he was going, Hancock replied that he was on the way to attend the sale of his yearlings at public auction.

"By the way," said Hancock, "would you consider doing me a favor?"

"Certainly," replied his friend. "What is it?"

"May I instruct the auctioneer to put in a complimentary bid on your behalf

				Eclipse
			Alarm, 1869	Maud
		Himyar, 1875		Lexington
	Domino, 1891		Hira, 1864	Hegira
			Enquirer, 1867	Leamington
		Mannie Gray, 1874		Lida
			Lizzie G., 1867	War Dance
Commando, 1898				Lecompte Mare
			The Peer, 1855	Melbourne
		Darebin, 1878		Cinizelli
	Emma C., 1892		Lurline, 1869	Traducer
				Mermaid
			Flood, 1877	Norfolk
		Guenn, 1883		Hennie Farrow
CELT			Glendew, 1876	Glengarry
				Glenrose
			Speculum, 1865	Vedette
		Rosebery, 1872		Doralice
	Amphion, 1886		Ladylike, 1858	Newminster
				Zuleika
			Hermit, 1864	Newminster
		Suicide, 1876		Seclusion
Maid Of Erin, 1895			Ratcatcher's Daughter, 1862	Rataplan
				Lady Alicia
			Solon, 1861	West Australian
		Barcaldine, 1878		Mrs. Ridgway
	Mavourneen, 1888		Ballyroe, 1872	Belladrum
				Bon Accord
			Albert Victor, 1868	Marsyas
		Gaydene, 1879		Princess Of Wales
			Flora Macdonald, 1871	The Scottish Chief
				Mayflower

Celt winning the Brooklyn

of $400 on each of my yearlings, just to get the bidding started?"

"Yes, indeed," countered his friend. "I hope it will help you."

Following the sale, Hancock had to wire his friend: "You bought eleven yearlings!"

Presumably by this time, Hancock was out of reach, on his way back to Charlottesville. The author never heard what happened to a hitherto beautiful friendship.

The upward surge in financial matters did not really begin until Hancock organized the syndicate to purchase Sir Gallahad III in 1926. This gave Hancock the support of important owners-breeders such as William Woodward Sr., Marshall Field, Robert Fairbairn, and the Phipps family, but by that time, Celt had been dead a long time.

The golden opportunity open to Sir Gallahad III was never open to Celt, but there was a connection between the two. Woodward had purchased from Hancock as a yearling the filly Marguerite, by Celt out of Fairy Ray, she by the Cup horse Radium. Marguerite made only one start and was unplaced, but as Woodward told us a number of times, "showed good speed in training." Since, according to their owners, most unplaced fillies "showed good speed in training," this was not an overwhelmingly convincing recommendation. Nevertheless, Marguerite is the principal channel for the descent of Celt's blood. Mated with Sir Gallahad III, Marguerite foaled the Triple Crown winner Gallant Fox, the very fast handicapper Fighting Fox, and the best two-year-old in England in 1938, Foxbrough. In addition, a number of stakes winners have descended from Marguerite's daughters.

As a pointer to the way Woodward's thoughts were running, Marguerite's female line is revealing. Marguerite's dam was by a Cup horse, Radium, and the next dam was by a true classic horse in St. Frusquin. Woodward won the Belmont Stakes five times in ten years and often advised the author: "Breed to stoutness; when you get one bred this way that can run, you have a very high-class colt or filly."

As an additional pointer of some historical interest, when during the 1940s, Woodward embarked upon a program of inbreeding to Sir Gallahad III (frequently, with one free generation), it turned out to be a marked failure, quite as clear as the 1930s had found him successful when no such inbreeding had been attempted.

That is not to assert that such inbreeding is never successful. When it has succeeded, as in the cases of Flying Fox, Havresac II, and Ksar—all inbred with one free

YEAR	AGE	STS	1ST	2ND	3RD	EARNED
1907	at 2	2	1	1	0	$ 6,425
1908	at 3	2	2	0	0	$22,540
1909	at 4	2	1	0	1	$ 4,105
Lifetime		6	4	1	1	$31,645

generation—the results have gone beyond the most optimistic expectations, but the choice of the animal used as the focus of inbreeding was in each case of the highest class both as to stoutness and soundness.

In the case of Celt, there can be little doubt as to his high racing class. There remained some doubt as to his soundness, and there is also some doubt as to the stoutness of his pedigree. Celt himself was never asked to go beyond ten furlongs, and his class was evidently so much higher than his opponents' that we do not know much about his stoutness.

In any case, his male line, Commando–Domino–Himyar, was noted for its speed; and Celt's dam, Maid of Erin, was by the English horse Amphion, who was a first-class speed horse, not up to classic distances, and who sired speed horses, the most notable of which was the first-class sprinter and sire, Sundridge. At stud, Celt generally was a highly successful sire of two-year-olds and sprinters, but not of classic contenders.

Celt died young, in 1919, and two years later became America's leading sire, posthumously. He sired a total of thirty stakes winners, including Futurity Stakes winner Dunboyne, Clover Stakes winner Coquette, Demoiselle Stakes winner Celandria, plus Cinderella, Green Gold, and Edwina. One of his get that stayed particularly well was Embroidery, winner of the Louisville Cup and St. Leger Handicap.

Marguerite with Gallant Fox as a foal

L.S. SUTCLIFFE

Celt sired nine stakes winners in a single crop, in 1917, and the year he led the sire list he had six stakes winners at the races.

His career is that of a very good racer that had a somewhat limited opportunity at stud. His pedigree to achieve the best results called for supplementary stoutness in the pedigrees of his mates. This he received in the case of Marguerite's dam, and through Marguerite his blood continued.

CHAPTER FORTY-TWO

COLIN

S ire lines are tenuous bits of business, the flourishing strength of today subject to decline, and disappearance, within a single generation. Usually, a sire line lives on because of a single individual within each generation rather than because of a number of great stallions, all contributing successful sons in their turn. Generally, however, large numbers of sons are available, from which one may emerge as the significant link.

That Colin's line has survived and as recently as 1971 turned up a Horse of the Year (Ack Ack) is particularly remarkable, for the line was founded on a decidedly shaky flooring. Colin in twenty-three crops got but eighty-one foals. Among these was Neddie, sire of Good Goods, he in turn sire of the brilliant Alsab. A $700 bargain yearling, Alsab was great on the track but moderate at stud. Still, he got a son, Armageddon, who kept the thread going, being the sire of Battle Joined, who, in turn, sired the young stallion Ack Ack. Thus, while the line was never strong in numbers, it has trickled through the generations, one saver at a time.[1]

Colin's fame, though, now as always rests primarily in his own ability as a racer. He not only pulled off the nearly-unique trick of going unbeaten throughout his career, but he so implanted his name in the minds of American horsemen that he remains one of the four or so generally reckoned the best of the twentieth century. (The others are Sysonby, Man o' War, and Citation, with Secretariat apparently a candidate, but too close in memory to be placed in history.)

Colin's dam, Pastorella, was purchased by James R. Keene for $10,000 as the highest-priced mare in the 1901 dispersal of Marcus Daly's Bitter Root Stud. Winner of the Zetland Stakes and Ascot Biennial Stakes at two in England, Pastorella was to produce eleven foals, of which Colin was the only good one. (Incidentally, Keene purchased Optime, by Orme, for $6,600 at the Daly sale. Optime was in foal to Melton and the following year produced Sysonby, who like Colin made fifteen starts. Colin won all of his races; Sysonby, all but one.)

Colin, foaled three years after Sysonby, was sired by Commando, a champion

James Keene (left) and James Rowe Sr.

son of the great nineteenth-century horse Domino. When Keene first saw the Commando—Pastorella foal, his attention was riveted to his unsightly hocks. From a photograph, one would judge that Colin had a generous bog spavin on one and a thoroughpin on the other!

When it came to running, though, not much fault could be found with Colin. When James Rowe Sr. put the Keene youngsters through their first speed trials, Colin stood out at once, and he won his first start, against twenty-two other maidens, by an easy two lengths. Three days after his debut, Colin came back to set a track record of :58 in winning the National Stallion Stakes down the old straight course at Belmont Park.

Next came the Eclipse Stakes, in which he stood off a prolonged challenge from Beaucoup, emerging with bucked shins. That proved his only narrow escape at two.

Away from the races for twenty-four days after the Eclipse, Colin came back to trounce the field in the $25,000-added Great Trial Stakes, and then he rattled off victories in the Brighton Junior, Saratoga Special, Grand Union Hotel Stakes, Futurity, Flatbush Stakes, Produce Stakes, Matron (then open to males), and Champagne Stakes. In the Matron, he carried 129 pounds, gave seven pounds to Fair Play (later to sire Man o' War), and beat him by three lengths. He had beaten the same colt by five, eased up, in the Produce.

Colin thus had made twelve starts at two and won them all, but at three he was out only three times. Rowe saddled him for the Withers Stakes, and Colin won easily, but he came out of the race lame. Early reports had him out of the Belmont Stakes, coming up only a week later, but that proved groundless. Estimates of his condition varied from his being just sore, to having a bowed tendon, or having two bowed tendons. Whatever the real situation, it seems certain that he was not 100 percent for the Belmont.

The race, then one and three-eighths miles, was run in heavy fog and rain, the field of four virtually invisible from the stands until entering the final two furlongs. Joe Notter by that time had Colin going along five lengths in front and began easing his mount, at which point Fair Play came charging up and just missed by a head. Many concluded that Notter had misjudged the finish line and thought the race was over. The Hall of Fame rider always maintained that he saw Fair Play coming and tried to rouse Colin but that after the long race in the mud Colin had not the response Notter asked for.

Having gone unbeaten through fourteen races, including the barely saved Belmont Stakes while not at his best, Colin would seem to have played cat and mouse with fate quite sufficiently. Crescendos, as a rule, are followed by something less grand, and we have seen Nijinsky II lose the Arc after going unbeaten through the English Triple Crown, Secretariat lose two races after his incomparable American Triple Crown, and Brigadier Gerard lose one only near the very end of three seasons.

Colin, though, was not through after the Belmont, for Keene had a notion of proving something. The Percy-Gray law[2] was repealed around that time, and that meant betting on a race was a crime. Keene claimed Colin could fill the stands even though no betting was allowed, and so the colt was sent out for the Tidal

				Eclipse
			Alarm, 1869	Maud
		Himyar, 1875		Lexington
			Hira, 1864	Hegira
	Domino, 1891			Leamington
			Enquirer, 1867	Lida
		Mannie Gray, 1874		War Dance
			Lizzie G., 1867	Lecompte Mare
Commando, 1898				Melbourne
			The Peer, 1855	Cinizelli
		Darebin, 1878		Traducer
			Lurline, 1869	Mermaid
	Emma C., 1892			Norfolk
			Flood, 1877	Hennie Farrow
		Guenn, 1883		Glengarry
COLIN			Glendew, 1876	Glenrose
				The Baron
			Stockwell, 1849	Pocahontas
		St. Albans, 1857		The Libel
			Bribery, 1851	Splitvote
	Springfield, 1873			Orlando
			Marsyas, 1851	Malibran
		Viridis, 1864		Pyrrhus The First
			Maid Of Palmyra, 1855	Palmyra
Pastorella, 1892				Touchstone
			Newminster, 1848	Beeswing
		Strathconan, 1863		Chanticleer
			Souvenir, 1856	Birthday
	Griselda, 1878			Voltaire
			Voltigeur, 1847	Martha Lynn
		Perseverance, 1865		Flatcatcher
			Spinster, 1853	Nan Darrell

Colin

Stakes at Sheepshead Bay some three weeks after the Belmont Stakes.

The ironic forces that work against unbeaten careers scarcely could have found a neater spot, but Colin—like Ribot of another place and another time—got through it. While he failed by a half-crowd to fulfill his owner's boast, he did win the race, scoring easily by two lengths.

The Tidal was not a prearranged farewell to competition, for Keene had plans to run Colin again at four. The changing law diminished the appeal of racing in this country, however, so Keene sent Colin to England, where he was trained by Sam Darling at Beckhampton. Colin won the only trial Darling put him through, but he broke down before he could run in public. He was kept in England, going to stud at Heath Stud, Newmarket, with a fee of 98 guineas, one to the groom.

Colin met with a poor response from British breeders. The latter may have been influenced by the stud failure of the noted American racer Foxhall, who had won the Grand Prix de Paris and Cesarewitch, and had carried nine stone (126 pounds) to victory in the Cambridgeshire as a three-year-old.

Colin was returned to America and was included in the Keene estate dispersal in New York in 1913, being purchased for $30,000 by James Corrigan and

Price McKinney. Five years later, the buyers dispersed their Wickliffe Stud, and E.B. McLean bought Colin then for $5,100. The horse lived through the age of twenty-seven, during which year he got his last three foals, and he died in 1932 at Captain Raymond Belmont's Belray Farm near Middleburg, Virginia.

Colin was a shy breeder, but of his eighty-one foals came eleven stakes winners, an extraordinary 14 percent. His best runners, in addition to Neddie, were On Watch and Jock.

YEAR	AGE	STS	1ST	2ND	3RD	EARNED
1907	at 2	12	12	0	0	$129,205
1908	at 3	3	3	0	0	$ 48,905
Lifetime		15	15	0	0	$178,110

He also sired Slow and Easy, the second dam of Coaltown, who at his best perhaps stirred memories of an unbeaten ancestor.

End Notes:

1. This sire line remains extant in 2006 through Ack Ack's son Broad Brush, winner of the 1987 Santa Anita and Suburban handicaps and 1986 Wood Memorial, etc. Broad Brush sired eighty-nine stakes winners and was leading sire in 1994. Pensioned in 2004, Broad Brush is represented by several sons at stud, including Breeders' Cup Classic winner Concern, Peter Pan Stakes winner Best of Luck, Pimlico Special winner Include, and Jerome Handicap winner Schlossberg (at stud in Chile).

2. The Percy-Gray law had criminalized gambling everywhere except at licensed racetracks.

CHAPTER FORTY-THREE

HIGH TIME

Igh Time probably was as intensely inbred as any Thoroughbred since the early nineteenth century, when it was fashionable to breed the great sire Sir Archy to his own daughters. High Time's sire was Ultimus, who was by a son of Domino and out of a mare by Domino, and High Time's dam was Noonday, also a Domino mare. Thus, of the seven males in the first three generations of High Time's ancestry, Domino was three of them.

High Time, a foal of 1916, was bred by the Wickliffe Stud of steel magnates Price McKinney and James W. Corrigan, but the mating that produced him was arranged by Miss Elizabeth Daingerfield, whose enthusiasm for the blood of Domino was unbounded.

When High Time went to racing, it soon was found that he had phenomenal speed, but he could not carry it very far. The only race he won was the Hudson Stakes for two-year-olds, and he also had a third in the Great American Stakes for two-year-olds. [He set a track record in the Hudson, five furlongs in :58 2/5 at Aqueduct.]

At three, High Time was trained for a time by that prince of tall-story tellers, Colonel Phil T. Chinn, for Sam Ross and Admiral Cary T. Grayson, both of Washington, D.C. (Grayson, who had been physician to presidents Taft and Wilson, was well up there with Col. Chinn as a teller of stories, although he was a trifle hampered by having some regard for the facts.)

Col. Chinn is the focal point and hero of the tale of High Time, and he often recounted the story to the author. Naturally, the jaunty and fun-loving colonel never told it exactly the same way twice, varying the episodes to suit his moods and the susceptibilities of his audience. The basics, though, were pretty constant.

Col. Chinn said that High Time could outwork any other horse that ever drew breath—for three furlongs. His blazing time trials did not go unnoticed by Sam Hildreth, one of the great trainers in the country and a friend of Chinn. Hildreth went to the colonel, asking only to be told on which day Chinn was "going to

KEENELAND-COOK

Phocion Howard (left) and Col. Phil Chinn

murder the bookmakers." When the great day came, Hildreth and Chinn both "sent it in" to the bookies for all they would take.

High Time ran his phenomenal three furlongs, as per schedule, but then collapsed to a walk. Looking back on it, Chinn's sense of fun was greater than his regret over the disaster.

"High Time," he said solemnly, "was the only horse I ever saw that could come into the home stretch on top by 15 lengths, and get beat by 80." He said there was some kind of obstruction in High Time's head that shut off his breathing, so that when that first breath was gone, he was finished. (High Time was also a bleeder.)

At the time of the race, Chinn was so outraged with High Time that when Grayson came around to the stables after the race, Chinn took a gallant and haughty stand.

"If," he stated, "you will get this horse out of my barn by sundown, there will be no training bill. Otherwise, the charges will be doubled."

High Time, thus, was retired from the track in what might be described as disgrace. He went to stud in Kentucky, after a stopover at Captain P.M. Walker's Pagebrook Stud at Boyce, Virginia. After Col. Chinn recovered from the shock of the High Time financial disaster—but one of many in the man's long life—he forgot all about the horse and his act of treachery against the Chinn fortunes.

Three years later, however, High Time sneaked back into the colonel's life, and began to do the square thing by Chinn's bank account. Col. Chinn was made to listen to a tale about two outstanding yearling colts at the farm of Dr. Marius Johnston. The man who kept after Col. Chinn about the colts was Hiram Steele, a good friend and a very fine judge of yearlings. ("There never was a better judge of yearlings!" summarized the colonel.) Still, Chinn was not too anxious to inspect these marvels that Steele had found, as he knew that Dr. Johnston, though a wealthy man, never would pay to breed to a high-class stallion.

According to the colonel, Dr. Johnston had a great deal of money invested in stocks and bonds and was so nervous about the market that "every time the Dow-Jones average went down two points, they had to take him to the hospital!" Since any investment except Thoroughbred horses, land to breed them on, and a good supply of bourbon whiskey was unthinkable to Col. Chinn, Dr. Johnston's worries about the stock market seemed to him simply uproarious.

One day, early in the morning, Chinn was driving along the narrow road bordering the Johnston farm, and he saw Hiram Steele driving in the other direction. Steele got out and said, "Now, Colonel, these two colts are in the barn right over the fence, and I am not going to let you pass until you go and have a look at them."

So Chinn, facing a roadblock, gave in, climbed the fence, and inspected the two yearlings.

"My Lord!" he said. "They were standouts! You never saw two finer colts!"

Chinn and Steele then went up the hill to Dr. Johnston's house and roused the good doctor by throwing pebbles at his bedroom window. When he came downstairs, Dr. Johnston inquired what he could do for them. Chinn, after a few ameni-

High Time pedigree chart

				Gen 6
Ultimus, 1906	Commando, 1898	**Domino**, 1891	Himyar, 1875	Alarm / Hira
			Mannie Gray, 1874	Enquirer / Lizzie G.
		Emma C., 1892	Darebin, 1878	The Peer / Lurline
			Guenn, 1883	Flood / Glendew
	Running Stream, 1898	**Domino**, 1891	Himyar, 1875	Alarm / Hira
			Mannie Gray, 1874	Enquirer / Lizzie G.
		Dancing Water, 1887	Isonomy, 1875	Sterling / Isola Bella
			Pretty Dance, 1878	Doncaster / Highland Fling
Noonday, 1898	**Domino**, 1891	Himyar, 1875	Alarm, 1869	Eclipse / Maud
			Hira, 1864	Lexington / Hegira
		Mannie Gray, 1874	Enquirer, 1867	Leamington / Lida
			Lizzie G., 1867	War Dance / Lecompte Mare
	Sundown, 1887	Springfield, 1873	St. Albans, 1857	Stockwell / Bribery
			Viridis, 1864	Marsyas / Maid Of Palmyra
		Sunshine, 1867	Thormanby, 1857	Melbourne / Alice Hawthorn
			Sunbeam, 1855	Chanticleer / Sunflower

HIGH TIME

High Time

ties, asked how much the doctor wanted for the two colts down in the barn.

"Twenty-five hundred dollars!" said the doctor.

"They are my colts!" said Chinn. "Let us now cement the occasion with a sip of bourbon."

After this rite had been performed, Chinn casually said. "By the way, doctor, how are these colts bred?" (As if that mattered to Chinn.)

"They are both by High Time!" replied the doctor, who doubtless had obtained the stud services for nothing.

"Doctor!" said Chinn in some alarm, "if I had known that, I would gladly have paid you $2,500 not to come here!"

"Why, colonel," said the doctor, "you don't have to buy those two colts."

"No! No!" protested Chinn. "My word is my bond. I have bought them, so I will keep them."

The gist of this story is that one of the colts was the great gelding Sarazen, the best horse of his year, and the other one was Time Exposure, who was, said Chinn, only about five pounds behind Sarazen. Time Exposure was a stakes winner of twenty-two races.

After winning seven straight races with Sarazen, Chinn sold him at Saratoga to Mrs. Graham Fair Vanderbilt for $35,000.[1] The author asked Chinn why he sold such a champion for such a paltry sum. His answer was: "I had a date with a certain party (very attractive) in New York, and I didn't have the cash to get there!"

Despite Col. Chinn's oft-repeated testimony to the physical marvels of Sarazen as a yearling, the horse while in racing was a light-fleshed, scrawny gelding of no more than medium size. Where the needed power came from to produce his flashing speed was a mystery to the author.

YEAR	AGE	STS	1ST	2ND	3RD	EARNED
1918	at 2	6	1	0	1	$3,950
1919	at 3	1	0	0	0	$ 0
Lifetime		7	1	0	1	$3,950

Sarazen's greatest day came when he won the last of the International Series in 1924, a series arranged to test the best American horses against French champion Epinard. The distance of the final race was one and a quarter miles, which Sarazen never had attempted before. With his short-running High Time background, there was some doubt if he could go that far, but go it he did, and in the spectacular time of 2:00 4/5. Chinn once claimed, when Sarazen ran past a colt belonging to a friend; "Why, Sarazen ran that eighth of a mile in ten seconds flat, with his mouth open!"

Sarazen's female ancestry was as offbeat as everything else about him. His dam was Rush Box (unknown to fame) by a sire called Box, whom no one had ever heard of; next dam by Singleton (ditto); and next dam by Faraday (ditto). Rush Box reportedly had been used to plow the garden at the Johnston residence. This circumstance elicited from John E. Madden, the wholesale breeder and trader of Thoroughbreds, the protest: "When you can breed a quarter-horse to a plow mare and get a colt that beats everything in America, it is time for me to sell out!"

As soon as Chinn knew that Sarazen and Time Exposure were very high-class racers, he realized he had to buy High Time. There was a question, however, as to how this financial feat was to be accomplished. The price was $50,000, a sum that was absent from the Chinn exchequer. Since Col. Chinn and the banks were not exactly on terms of instant credit when sums such as $50,000 were mentioned, the matter required deep thought. Inspiration, after much reflection, duly came.

Chinn had a good friend in W.T. (Fatty) Anderson, a professional horseman and gambler. The colonel's mind went back to a glorious score they once had made together in Havana. Anderson was renowned as a trencherman of almost unlimited capacity, and the idea had occurred to Chinn of staging an eating contest between Fatty and the local Cuban champion. The challenge was made and accepted, rules were drawn up, and the stakes posted. Chinn arranged with Fatty

Sarazen, with Earl Sande up

a system of signals, so that in case Anderson was nearing the exhaustion point, Chinn would have a chance to hedge the bets.

After about twenty-two courses, half a large apple pie was put down in front of each contestant. Anderson had reached about the end of what he could do, but was game to the finish. He asked the waiter if he could not put two helpings of ice cream on top of the pie. Whereupon, the Cuban champion hastily pushed back his chair from the table and surrendered.

At the time when Chinn needed the $50,000, Anderson was in California, and Chinn knew that Anderson would be either broke or rolling in cash. (Anderson did not believe in banks!) Chinn sent off a wire: "Could you spare $25,000?" The answer came back: "Any man that needs $25,000 can use $50,000. Anderson." Crisis solved!

High Time became the mainstay of the Chinn breeding operations, his yearlings selling well year after year. When the financial crash came following 1929, the colonel's fortunes crashed with it, and he went through bankruptcy. High Time had to be sold and went to Charles Fisher's (General Motors) Dixiana Stud.

Year after year, High Time sired a high proportion of two-year-old winners, and he was one of the two great speed sires of his time. The other was Wise Counsellor, who had an almost equally offbeat pedigree, being by an obscure sire called Mentor, tracing in tail male to Hanover, whose line was assumed generally to be dead when Wise Counsellor appeared.

Unfortunately, the male lines of both High Time and Wise Counsellor failed to breed on, though a good many stakes winners came from their daughters.

High Time was America's leading sire in progeny earnings in 1928, and he ranked among the top twenty on twelve occasions. In three years, he led all other sires in number of two-year-old winners, and he tied for the lead in another year. In seventeen crops, he sired 289 named foals, of which thirty-seven (13 percent) were stakes winners. In addition to Sarazen and Time Exposure, they included High Strung, winner of the Futurity and the champion two-year-old colt of 1928.

Of High Time's 289 foals, 164 were winners at two, a percentage of 57, which placed High Time first when measured against other leading sires of a twenty-five-year period (1916–1940).

High Time on two occasions sired six stakes winners in a single year, the second year that occurred being 1929, when he was thirteen years old. He died at Dixiana in 1937, and with him died the last good chance of prolonging his branch of the Domino line. Also with High Time died efforts to intensify the blood of Domino through close inbreeding.

End Notes:

1. Reported as $30,000 in an article by Kent Hollingsworth in the September 11, 1965, issue of *The Blood-Horse*.

CHAPTER FORTY-FOUR

FAIR PLAY

The breeder of Fair Play, August Belmont II, had been chairman of The Jockey Club for about thirty years at the time of his death in 1924. He came by his love of the Turf naturally, as his father, August Belmont I, had been a leading owner and breeder in his day and had imported the Epsom Derby winner of 1884, St. Blaise, from England for his stud.

August Belmont I had a somewhat curious history. He was born in Germany under the name of Schonberg. He was trained in the famous Rothschild banking house in Europe and was sent to the United States while still young to look after the Rothschild interests here. There were persistent rumors that he was, in fact, an illegitimate Rothschild. Whether the rumor was true or false, nobody seemed to care very much in those free-wheeling days. After marrying a daughter of Commodore Perry, Belmont used his wealth to achieve—and retain—great social prominence.

There were three Belmont sons, among whom August Belmont II was the one who elected to continue his father's Turf career. He leased the Nursery Stud near Lexington for his breeding operations but never owned any land of his own in Kentucky.

Fair Play came from the mating of two animals that had been bought by Belmont. The sire, Hastings, was bought as a two-year-old in training, and when he finished unplaced in the Futurity of 1895, hot words were exchanged between Belmont and his trainer, Andrew Jackson Joyner. Hastings went on to win the Belmont Stakes of 1896 and became the leading sire of 1902 and 1908.

Hastings developed a savage temper, and much of what became known as the high courage of the Fair Play descent is attributed to him.

Fair Play's dam, Fairy Gold, had won the Woodcote Stakes for two-year-olds, at the Epsom Derby meeting, in 1898, the year Jeddah staggered humanity by winning the Derby at odds of 100-1. (Lord Rosebery remarked to Jeddah's trainer, Richard Marsh, that "he was laughing out of one side of his face, and crying out of the other.")

In the United States, Fairy Gold bred five stakes winners, including the 1916 three-year-old champion, Friar Rock, whom the late trainer Sam Hildreth declared was the best colt he ever saw over a distance of ground.

Belmont could not have been too impressed with the dogmas of Bruce Lowe's figure system, or with William Allison, Bruce Lowe's high priest in England, since Bruce Lowe seemed positive that the No. 9 family of mares could never produce a good sire. Within a few years, there appeared from the No. 9 family Cyllene (sire of four Derby winners in eight years in England), Star Shoot (five-time leading sire in America), Dark Ronald (the most influential sire in the history of the German Turf), and Fair Play in the United States. (*The Devil's Dictionary* refers to "positive" as "Mistaken at the top of one's voice.")

There possibly is even more luck in racing than elsewhere, though it is in ample supply in every section of life. It was Fair Play's bad luck to be born in 1905, when two better colts were foaled at James R. Keene's nearby Castleton Stud. These were Colin (unbeaten) and Celt (unbeaten except by Colin). On the other hand, it was Fair Play's good luck that by the end of June in his three-year-old season Colin and Celt had become unsound and were forced to retire. This made Fair Play look pretty good—and he was more than pretty good.

As a two-year-old, Fair Play was out ten times and won three races, including two stakes. He was second three times and was third twice. Such is the record of a good colt but by no means an overpowering one. After being fourth in his first start, Fair Play won his second race, and he then won the Montauk Stakes and Saratoga's Flash Stakes.

In the Hopeful, the most important two-year-old race at Saratoga, Fair Play failed by two lengths to give ten pounds to Jim Gaffney successfully. He was out again at Saratoga but could only finish third to James R. Keene's Restigouche in the United States Hotel Stakes.

Belmont then made an error of judgment. He ran Fair Play against Colin, in fact ran him three times against Colin, who won each time. The last time, Colin gave Fair Play seven pounds and won by three lengths.

As a three-year-old, Fair Play was much improved, being first or second fifteen times in sixteen starts. He could stay and he was sound, but the beginning of the campaign was not auspicious as Fair Play lost his first five starts.

His first start was in a five and a half-furlong race, which was too short for him, in addition to which he practically was left at the post. His next start was in a six-furlong sprint, which still was too short for him, though he ran second.

In the one-mile Withers, Fair Play faced Colin, with the inevitable result: Colin won, by two lengths.

Next came the one and three-eighths-mile Belmont Stakes, run in a torrent of rain and on a sea of mud. Fair Play went under to Colin again, but only by a head. Colin was said to have either one or two bowed tendons, and his jockey, Joe Notter, was said to have mistaken the finishing post (placed beyond the usual one, as in some of the races at Longchamp today) and to have eased Colin. Notter, however, denied that story.

Only two days later, Fair Play came out again in the Brooklyn Handicap of ten furlongs. He faced Keene's other top colt, Celt, and went under by one and a half lengths. The winner's time, 2:04 1/5, bettered the track record by one-fifth of a second.

The twelve-furlong Brooklyn Derby (now the Dwyer) had no Keene colt in it, and Fair Play won. Pulled back to ten furlongs again in the Suburban Handicap, Fair Play (114 pounds) went under to Keene's champion handicapper, the four-year-old Ballot (127), by more than five lengths.

In his nine remaining races at three, Fair Play won six and was second three times, and twice track-record-breaking times were necessary to beat him.

				West Australian, 1850	**Melbourne** Mowerina
			Australian, 1858	Emilia, 1840	Young Emilius Persian
		Spendthrift, 1876		Lexington, 1850	Boston Alice Carneal
			Aerolite, 1861	Florine, 1854	Glencoe Melody
	Hastings, 1893			King Tom, 1851	Harkaway **Pocahontas**
			Tomahawk, 1863	Mincemeat, 1851	Sweetmeat Hybla
		Cinderella, 1885		Brown Bread, 1862	Weatherbit Brown Agnes
			Manna, 1874	Tartlet, 1858	Birdcatcher Don John Mare
FAIR PLAY				Stockwell, 1849	The Baron **Pocahontas**
			Doncaster, 1870	Marigold, 1860	Teddington Ratan Mare
		Bend Or, 1877		Thormanby, 1857	**Melbourne** Alice Hawthorn
			Rouge Rose, 1865	Ellen Horne, 1844	Redshank Delhi
	Fairy Gold, 1896			Galopin, 1872	Vedette Flying Duchess
			Galliard, 1880	Mavis, 1874	Macaroni Merlette
		Dame Masham, 1889		Hermit, 1864	Newminster Seclusion
			Pauline, 1883	Lady Masham, 1867	Brother To Strafford Maid Of Masham

Fair Play

Possibly his best race was the ten-furlong First Special at Gravesend. Fair Play (122), giving away from four to seventeen pounds, won in 2:03 2/5, breaking the track record by four-fifths of a second.

In the Jerome, Fair Play set another track record, going one and five-sixteenths miles at Belmont Park.

Such performances made Fair Play look like a very good colt, indeed. In assessing his merit, however, it is safer to rely on his form with the Keene trio of Colin, Celt, and Ballot, all of whom could beat him, and it is doubtful if he was within ten pounds of Colin (when sound).

There is far more to interest the student in Fair Play as a sire than in Fair Play as a racehorse. Fair Play was retired to stud as a five-year-old, after an abortive trip to England as a four-year-old. He became mulish and difficult there and finally refused to start at all.

When Fair Play reached Nursery Stud, Belmont already had six stallions of his own there and only about thirty mares. One of those sires was Rock Sand, the English Triple Crown winner of 1903 whom Belmont had bought from the estate of Sir James Miller in 1906.

The coincidence that Fair Play followed Rock Sand as a stallion was to have momentous consequences for the *American Stud Book*.

James R. Keene at Castleton had achieved extraordinary success with the Domino–Commando line and imported English mares and to a lesser extent with Ben Brush and imported mares, and the H.P. Whitney stud exploited the Peter Pan–Broomstick cross with good if less spectacular results (Equipoise was the only first-class horse produced in the Whitney stud by the Peter Pan–Broomstick cross), so, too, did the Fair Play cross on Rock Sand mares produce a string of good horses.

Fair Play was the first stallion in America to sire six winners of more than $100,000 each: Man o' War, Display, Mad Hatter, Chance Shot, Chance Play, and Mad Play. Everyone of them except Display carried the blood of Rock Sand on the dam's side; and Display was a plodder who never won in New York.

YEAR	AGE	STS	1ST	2ND	3RD	EARNED
1907	at 2	10	3	3	2	$16,735
1908	at 3	16	7	8	1	$70,215
1909	at 4	6	0	0	0	$ 0
Lifetime		32	10	11	3	$86,950

Keene and Whitney bred for early maturity and speed, but the Keene pedigrees had some stoutness on the dam's side, and they swept the boards in three-year-old racing in a way the Whitney horses never could match.

The late William Woodward Sr. told the author that, when he was forming his Belair Stud, before 1920, August Belmont advised him: "Billy, breed to stoutness, because when you get one that can run, you have a very good horse." Woodward followed his advice, and won the one and a half-mile Belmont Stakes five times in ten years.

With no quick-maturing, sprinting blood in his pedigree and virtually none in the pedigrees of the Belmont mares, it was not to be expected that Fair Play would sire quick-maturing, sprinting stock. Nor did he. His percentage of stakes winners (18 percent) was lower than that of Broomstick (25 percent) and also lower than that of Domino (42 percent) and Commando (37 percent). Furthermore, his percentage of winners was only 51 percent as against a breed average of 54 percent. This last figure, however, is somewhat misleading, since Belmont chose not to train a substantial number of his fillies.

As with other late-maturing, staying strains, the wastage was considerable, but the good ones were very, very good.

Physically, Fair Play strongly resembled his maternal grandsire, Bend Or, also a chestnut with a white face and also an excellent sire. Bend Or, though, was a horse of placid disposition, while Fair Play was full of fire. Fair Play led the sire list three times, in 1920, 1924, and 1927, and he was probably the best colt bred and raced by Belmont in the United States.

Man o' War, his great son, was certainly a better racehorse than was Fair Play, but Belmont had the misfortune to sell him, and Tracery was also probably a better colt (he won the St. Leger, etc.) but Belmont raced him in England and sold him as a stallion to Argentina.

Display

Even in recent years, some 60 percent of American stakes winners have carried the blood of Fair Play, and there is no better source for soundness and stoutness among the American strains than he.

His grandsire, Bend Or, sired the mighty Ormonde (unbeaten English Triple Crown winner) and Fair Play did as well: He sired the great Man o' War.

Fair Play died in December of 1929, and there is a bronze statue of him at E. Barry Ryan's Normandy Farm in Lexington.[1]

End Notes:

1. E. Barry Ryan bought Normandy Farm, part of Joseph Widener's Elmendorf Farm, in the 1950s. It is now owned by Nancy Polk. Ryan died in 1993.

CHAPTER FORTY-FIVE

MAN O' WAR

At irregular intervals, sometimes spaced many years apart, horses appear on the Turf that have an electrifying effect on racing men. The blood surges, and the pulses quicken at the very sight of such Olympians on the track, and this reaction is not strictly related to racing performances.

In France, Ksar (1918) had it, so that it was a national disaster when he was beaten, which happened a few times. Native Dancer had it, and in recent times, Secretariat had it.

Going back farther, Colin (1905) had it, and the writer listened to old-time horsemen talk about him with an otherworld expression on their faces. Man o' War was the first great horse the author ever saw perform. We can still remember vividly the first time we ever saw him. It was Futurity Day at Belmont Park. In order to be sure to get a good look at Man o' War, we left the stands early. In those days there were some large trees in the Belmont paddock, as well as clumps of laurel. Rounding some of the laurel bushes, one was flanked by tall trees whose branches nearly met overhead, like a gothic arch. Underneath this arch, framed by the dark shadows behind, stood a chestnut colt, with ears pricked. He radiated majesty, energy, and power—a veritable Alexander—awaiting the moment for new worlds to conquer. It was fifty-five years ago, and we never saw such a sight again.

Man o' War was foaled on March 29, 1917, at August Belmont's Nursery Stud near Lexington, the result of a mating between the home sire Fair Play, with Mahubah, a daughter of another home sire, Rock Sand (winner of the Triple Crown of 1903 in England). Mahubah, who had won only one race, was described by her trainer as having very good speed but being excessively nervous (like the dam of Lexington). Belmont, who did not approve of strenuous racing of fillies in any case (especially after the disappointing stud career of champion Beldame), did not persist and sent Mahubah to stud after very few starts.

Mahubah bred five foals, all by Fair Play, and three were stakes winners. First came a filly, Masda, born when Mahubah was a five-year-old; Masda won a stakes and also bred three stakes winners.

With a barren year intervening, Mahubah next foaled Man o' War.

When Belmont decided to sell his 1918 crop of yearlings, the United States was in World War I, and Belmont had been commissioned as a major in the army. He wanted to give his entire time and effort to the war, and he had no way of knowing that the war would be over in November of 1918. Allegedly, his first inclination was to hold out Man o' War, which he regarded as the best of his crop, but on second thought, he decided to sell everything.

There may have been something to this tale, as Louis Feustel—who afterward trained Man o' War—later said that when he inspected the Nursery Stud yearlings at the farm, he had not been shown Man o' War. After fruitless efforts to sell the entire yearling crop, for prices reported as from $42,000 to $30,000, the yearlings were put up for sale at Saratoga. Man o' War was among them.

Sam Riddle

The author once asked the late Max Hirsch and the late Colonel Phil Chinn, who each enjoyed exalted reputations as judges of yearlings, why each one had not bought Man o' War for his own account. The answers were revealing:

Max Hirsch said (seriously), "He was too nervous. He had pawed a deep trench in the dirt underneath the webbing of his stall door."

Col. Chinn, who really neither knew nor cared about pedigrees and thought they were a prime subject for jesting, remarked, "His third dam was by Macgregor. That Macgregor cross stopped me." This comment was followed by a joyful chuckle.

The second dam of Man o' War was by Merry Hampton, who was a very poor sire, and the fourth dam was by Underhand, another very poor sire. None of these mares made a worthwhile mark on the track or at stud. Furthermore, Man o' War's only American strain was his sire line, back to Australian. So, three-quarters of Man o' War's pedigree was very good and one-quarter was very bad.

What are the odds against breeding a colt like Man o' War in any case? From a line of mares like he came from, one would need a computer to calculate the odds.

Many tales were circulated as to who was the underbidder for Man o' War. The most likely candidate seems to have been Robert L. Gerry, who was looking for a hunter prospect and was attracted by Man o' War's size. This circumstance was not unlike the advice the late Edward Kennedy received from many quarters—to castrate his big gray colt and put him by as a steeplechaser. The colt was The Tetrarch.

By such slender threads are fame, fortune, and stud book history woven together.

The Saratoga sale average that year was $1,038, and Man o' War brought $5,000, so there must have been at least two bidders who were keen to have him. Praise for him at that stage was not universal, as Louis Feustel said of his first sight of the colt: "Very tall and gangling, he was thin and so on the leg as to give the same ungainly impression one gets in seeing a week-old foal."

Feustel, to his honor, confessed that he thought some of the other Belmont colts might be better. Man o' War was somewhat Roman-nosed and short in the neck.

The most expensive yearling at the sale was Golden Broom, bought by Mrs. Walter M. Jeffords Sr. at $15,600. She was the niece of Mrs. Samuel D. Riddle, whose husband bought Man o' War. Riddle had been a good amateur rider in his younger days and was increasing his stable at the time he bought Man o' War.

Fair Play, 1905	Hastings, 1893	Spendthrift, 1876	Australian, 1858	West Australian / Emilia
			Aerolite, 1861	Lexington / Florine
		Cinderella, 1885	Tomahawk, 1863	King Tom / Mincemeat
			Manna, 1874	Brown Bread / Tartlet
	Fairy Gold, 1896	Bend Or, 1877	Doncaster, 1870	Stockwell / Marigold
			Rouge Rose, 1865	Thormanby / Ellen Horne
		Dame Masham, 1889	Galliard, 1880	**Galopin** / Mavis
MAN O' WAR			Pauline, 1883	**Hermit** / Lady Masham
	Rock Sand, 1900	Sainfoin, 1887	Springfield, 1873	St. Albans / Viridis
			Sanda, 1878	Wenlock / Sandal
		Roquebrune, 1893	St. Simon, 1881	**Galopin** / St. Angela
			St Marguerite, 1879	**Hermit** / Devotion
Mahubah, 1910	Merry Token, 1891	Merry Hampton, 1884	Hampton, 1872	Lord Clifden / Lady Langden
			Doll Tearsheet, 1877	Broomielaw / Mrs. Quickly
		Mizpah, 1880	Macgregor, 1867	Macaroni / Necklace
			Underhand Mare, 1863	Underhand / The Slayers Daughter

KEENELAND-MCCLURE

Man o' War

(After Man o' War's prowess on the Turf had become a legend, Riddle at times assumed airs of pomposity in reminiscence. One day in the presence of his wife, who supplied most of the ready cash, he announced: "The greatest day in my life was the day I bought Man o' War." Mrs. Riddle cut him down to size: "Sam, the greatest day in your life was the day you married me.")

Both Man o' War and Golden Broom were sent to training quarters at Berlin, Maryland. It was then customary in this country to try yearlings in the autumn over a quarter-mile. When these two colts were pitted against each other, Golden Broom won by a half-length, which led to the erroneous conclusion, lasting into their two-year-old season, that Golden Broom was the better of the pair.

This subject of yearling trials should be of extreme interest to racing men. The late A.J. Joyner, who trained many high-class horses (including Fair Play and Whisk Broom II), and the late William Woodward Sr., who bred and owned a galaxy of good ones (Triple Crown winners Gallant Fox and Omaha, for instance), assured the author that yearling trials were "never wrong." By this they meant that the best yearling would prove eventually to be the best racehorse in any group of yearlings. It is a fact that West Australian (foaled in 1850), first winner of the English Triple Crown, was backed by owner John Bowes for the Derby on the strength of his yearling trial, while Lord Lyon (Triple Crown), Hermit (Derby), and Bend Or (Derby) all were tried as yearlings and known then to be high-class colts. Why has the practice dropped out in England and Ireland?

One of the remarkable things about Man o' War was his constitution. When he was shipped out of Berlin to the old Havre de Grace track (now gone), he caught cold and ran a temperature of 106 degrees—but he was back at work within a week.

By the time the stable reached New York, the clockers had had ample opportunity to assess the merits of Man o' War. So sensational were his works that he was odds-on at 3-5 his first time out, in a field of maidens on June 6.

Man o' War came down a straight five furlongs in :59, winning by six lengths. Three days later, he was out again in the five and a half-furlong Keene Memorial Stakes. An old rivalry was renewed there, as Man o' War met On Watch, sired by Fair Play's old conqueror Colin. Man o' War came away at the finish to win by three lengths. In the

YEAR	AGE	STS	1ST	2ND	3RD	EARNED
1919	at 2	10	9	1	0	$ 83,325
1920	at 3	11	11	0	0	$166,140
Lifetime		**21**	**20**	**1**	**0**	**$249,465**

Youthful Stakes on June 21, Man o' War gave On Watch twelve pounds and still won by two and a half lengths. Two days later, he was out again for the Hudson Stakes with an impost of 130 pounds. His odds were 1-10, and he won eased. Eleven days later, he won the six-furlong Tremont Stakes easily, carrying 130 again and giving fifteen pounds to Upset.

Thus, Man o' War had won five races in a one-month period, and he had made sport of 130 pounds, conceding lumps of weight with it.

After racing shifted to Saratoga, Mrs. Jeffords' Golden Broom won the Saratoga Special, and another informal trial with Man o' War was arranged. After a few strides, it was clear that Man o' War by then was the better of the pair, and he went his three furlongs in 11 seconds each.

After an easy win in the United States Hotel Stakes came a race that has caused endless discussion—the Sanford Memorial, on August 13, at six furlongs. Again Man o' War carried 130 pounds to Upset's 115. Many legends have it that jockey Johnny Loftus had Man o' War facing the wrong way when the start was made. Nevertheless, two horses, The Swimmer and Captain Alcock came away after him.

Golden Broom broke on top, followed by Upset. Loftus headed for the rails on the turn, and when Golden Broom began to tire, Willie Knapp on Upset took a slight lead on the outside. Lapped on the outside of Man o' War was Donnacona.

As Man o' War was pocketed with only a furlong to go, Loftus decided there was going to be no opening and pulled to the outside, to begin his charge. It was too late, and Upset lasted to win by a half-length.

Man o' War met Upset five times again and beat him every time, and what the racing public thought of Man o' War's defeat in the Sanford was reflected in the betting in the Grand Union Hotel Stakes ten days later: Man o' War again had 130 pounds up, to Upset's 125, and bettors made Man o' War 1-2. He won easily by a length.

In the six-furlong Hopeful, still at Saratoga, Man o' War again had 130 up, and he won by four lengths from the good filly Cleopatra, with Upset fifth. Man o' War was becoming fractious in his eagerness to run, and he held up the start of this race for twelve minutes by his unruliness.

Man o' War's next race was the Futurity at Belmont Park, then regarded as the most important two-year-old fixture of the year. Man o' War's weight was 127 pounds, after he had carried 130 in six successive races. His best opponent was John P. Grier (117), owned by H.P. Whitney and trained by James Rowe Sr. Man o' War was not in front for the first half-mile, but after that, he surged past John P. Grier and Dominique to win easily by two and a half lengths.

The *Daily Racing Form* handicapper, C.C. Ridley, gave his assessment of the 1919 two-year-olds: Man o' War, 136 pounds; Blazes, 120; and Upset, 116. This spread of sixteen pounds between top-weighted Man o' War and Blazes, second top-weight, was six pounds more than the spread assigned on the English Free Handicap of 1913 between The Tetrarch (perhaps the most sensational two-year-old of the twentieth century in England) and the second colt on the list [Corcyra].

As a two-year-old, Man o' War could demolish his fields with authority, yet his times recorded at that age were not truly extraordinary. He never ran six furlongs in better than 1:11. That particular phenomenon we often have observed: Where one horse demonstrates a great superiority over his competitors, his winning time often is quite ordinary, and if the superior horse had been absent, several of his competitors probably could have recorded a better time.

The best explanation we have heard of this apparent anomaly is that at some point in the race the superior horse pushes his competitors past their exhaustion points, and their speed dwindles away. This exhaustion phenomenon could occur within a hundred yards, whereas, had this exhaustion not occurred, their speed and action possibly could have been maintained to result in a very good time.

An example of this in modern times was the three-length victory of Brigadier

Gerard over Mill Reef in England's one-mile Two Thousand Guineas. The going was fast, but the time for the race was exactly the average over many years. Yet, Mill Reef went on to set new time records for the Eclipse Stakes and the Prix de l'Arc de Triomphe. The same colt, however, in competition with Brigadier Gerard at one mile, could not even record average time for the Two Thousand Guineas.

In the autumn, as a two-year-old, Man o' War began to fill out to his generous frame. At Saratoga in August, he weighed 970 pounds, at Belmont Park he weighed 1,020 pounds, and over the winter his weight increased to 1,150 pounds and his height to 16 hands, 2 inches. As a three-year-old, he girthed 72 inches, which is not exceptional for a colt of that size. In appearance, however, he was wide in the fork between his front legs and deep through the heart.

Riddle thought the ten furlongs of the Kentucky Derby was asking too much of a three-year-old at the beginning of May with 126 pounds up. (How Man o' War would have laughed had he known of his owner's solicitude for him.) So, Man o' War opened his three-year-old campaign in the nine-furlong Preakness Stakes, run ten days after the Derby. He dashed off into an early four-length lead and cantered home by one and a half lengths from Upset and Wildair, each representing the H.P. Whitney stable, then the most powerful in the United States.

Man o' War next went to New York for the one-mile Withers Stakes—the nearest American equivalent to the English Two Thousand Guineas. Again, Man o' War broke fast and was under restraint all the way, winning under a stout pull by two lengths in 1:35 4/5 from Wildair. His time was two-fifths of a second faster than the American record (run around a turn), then held by the filly Fairy Wand. If one interprets this time literally, it means that Wildair equaled the old American record and therefore was as good as any horse previously seen in America over a mile. Wildair simply was not that good, so the time test has its limitations as a measure of class.

In the Belmont, then run over eleven furlongs, Man o' War had only one opponent, Donnacona, who did not have much merit. Man o' War won by twenty lengths in the time of 2:14 1/5, another American record. Man o' War next carried 135 pounds to an easy victory in the one-mile Stuyvesant Handicap, over a solitary rival in receipt of thirty-two pounds.

Man o' War's next race, the nine-furlong Dwyer Stakes, was the most famous in his career. James Rowe Sr., trainer for H.P. Whitney, had trained more horses of the highest class, going back to Hindoo (1878), than anyone else then active (or perhaps even since then) in America. He had tried Man o' War seven times and beaten him once through a fluke with Upset, and he had been second three times with Upset, once with Wildair, and once with John P. Grier.

Rowe had trained Sysonby and unbeaten Colin, both enshrined among the four or five best horses seen in America in the twentieth century. After all, Wildair had been within two lengths of Man o' War in the Withers, and John P.

War Admiral

Grier had been within two and a half lengths of him in the Futurity. So, when Rowe declared that no horse in the world could give John P. Grier eighteen pounds, as the conditions of the Dwyer required, the racing world listened with respect.

The author saw that race fifty-four years ago, and it is still vivid in memory. There were only two starters, both chestnut colts. John P. Grier was small, like so many of the Ben Brush strain; Man o' War looked like a muscular giant. The air was filled with rumors: Feustel did not want to run Man o' War and had given him a full feed at lunch time; Man o' War had his shoes removed; Riddle, confronted by these obstacles, insisted that Man o' War run anyway. We now regret that we never asked either Riddle or Feustel about the truth of such tales.

As the colts broke, John P. Grier was completely hidden by the larger Man o' War. We could not see Grier at all, until the colts had gone about a half-mile, which was covered in :46, two-fifths of a second faster than the track record; six furlongs took 1:09 3/5, one and two-fifths seconds faster than the track record, and the two colts were still locked together. Into the stretch they came, and jockey Eddie Ambrose called for a great effort from John P. Grier, who got past Man o' War for a few strides. A shout went up from the crowd: "He's beat!"

Then we saw Clarence Kummer draw his whip and use it on Man o' War, who seemed to lengthen stride. The mile was reached in 1:36, two-fifths of a second faster than the track [Aqueduct] record. There gallant little John P. Grier faltered, and Man o' War came on to win by one and a half lengths in 1:49 1/5, a new American record. Note that it required :13 1/5 to run the last furlong. Man o' War had not quickened; he, too, was faltering, but not as badly as John P. Grier. Two very good colts had given literally their full reserves of speed and stamina and Man o' War had a little more left at the end. To Rowe's surprise, Man o' War had proven at least twenty-one pounds better than John P. Grier, who probably was the next best three-year-old of the year and who later proved to be a good sire.

The rest of Man o' War's Turf career was an uninterrupted series of triumphs during which he never was brought to a drive. At Saratoga, he took the Miller Stakes and the historic ten-furlong Travers. Back at Belmont Park, he won the thirteen-furlong Lawrence Realization by about a hundred lengths, lowering the previous record for the distance by four and one-fifth seconds. In the Jockey Club Gold Cup, then run at one and a half miles, he set another record, 2:28 4/5.

In Maryland, he shouldered 138 pounds for the Potomac Handicap, and over a heavy track set another track record, 1:44 4/5 for one and one-sixteenth miles. That time Man o' War was giving Wildair thirty pounds.

A match race then was made with Sir Barton, the best of the 1916 U.S. crop, who had won the Kentucky Derby, Preakness, Withers, and Belmont Stakes. This was over ten furlongs, to be run at Windsor, Ontario, Canada, for a $75,000 purse [and $5,000 gold cup] to the winner. It was not much of a race, as Sir Barton was suffering from sore feet at the time. Man o' War won by seven lengths in 2:03, lowering the track record by six and two-fifths seconds.

The famous gambler Chicago O'Brien was present at this contest and was told he was a fool when he wagered $100,000 on Man o' War at odds of 1-20. After Man o' War romped home, O'Brien asked: "Can you tell me any other way I could make $5,000 in two minutes?"

Man o' War's earnings of $249,465 set a new American record, surpassing those of Domino, made in 1893.

Handicapper Walter S. Vosburgh told Riddle that if Man o' War remained in training as a four-year-old he would be set to carry more weight than any other horse ever had shouldered in America. Since Roseben had carried 150 pounds and 148 pounds more than once, Riddle sensibly decided to retire Man o' War.

In his new sphere at stud there were both triumph and tragedy. There were 90 named foals in his first five crops, and 26 (29 percent) of these won stakes, compared to a national average of 3 percent. Overall, he sired 64 stakes winners from

ANNE M. EBERHARDT

Tiznow, a modern representative of the Man o' War sire line

379 named foals, for a percentage of 16.9 percent. The tragedy is that he virtually was a private stallion, and the records show that his mates by and large were rubbish. Both their racing records and their produce records were badly subnormal, and it is hard to say what Riddle was thinking, if anything.

Despite his mares, Man o' War was the leading sire of 1926, and he was among the top ten leading broodmare sires for twenty-two years. His best son, War Admiral, led the sire list in 1945, but it is through another son, War Relic, that the strength of Man o' War's sire line lies today, War Relic being the sire of Relic and Intent. In Reality, grandson of Intent and sire of Desert Vixen, is among the present Man o' War-line stallions.[1]

In addition to 1937 Triple Crown winner War Admiral, Man o' War sired 1929 Kentucky Derby winner Clyde Van Dusen, and his other distinguished sons and daughters included Bateau, American Flag, Florence Nightingale, Crusader, Edith Cavell, Mars, Annapolis, Battleship, and Scapa Flow.

Man o' War lived to be thirty years old, and a large statue was erected at the site of his grave at Faraway Farm.

Before his death, he was visited annually by thousands, including Mr. Dionne, the father of the quintuplets in Canada. When he thanked the groom, Will

Harbut, for letting him see Man o' War, that worthy replied: "Don't care too much about you seeing Man o' War, but I sure want him to see you."

The question remains: How good was Man o' War on an international standard? While there, of course, is no clear answer to this question, we can at least place it in a frame of reference.

First we might accept the judgment of trainer A.J. Joyner, who trained from 1908 to 1914 in England and sent Whisk Broom II back to the United States in 1913, where he won all three of the major handicaps in New York—the Metropolitan, Brooklyn, and Suburban—with top weights going up to 139 pounds. Whisk Broom II certainly was a standout in the United States, but he was about ten pounds behind the classic colts, Lemberg (Derby) and Neil Gow (Two Thousand Guineas), in England. Joyner believed that at that stage English form was about fourteen pounds better than American form.

Now let us look at Man o' War's handicap ratings. As a two-year-old, he was ranked sixteen pounds better than the next-best colt; as a three-year-old, he was at least twenty-one pounds better than the next-best colt. If we subtract Joyner's figure of fourteen pounds, Man o' War still would be seven pounds better than the average English classic form of that era. Speculation? Yes. Certainly wrong? No.

End Notes:

1. In 2006, active U.S. stallions tracing in tail-male line to Man o' War include Tiznow, Honour and Glory, Bertrando, Successful Appeal, Valid Expectations, Binalong, and Officer.

CHAPTER FORTY-SIX

WAR ADMIRAL

Typical of Samuel D. Riddle's management of Man o' War at stud, the horse's three best sons on the track, American Flag (1922, dam by Roi Herode), Crusader (1923, dam by Star Shoot), and War Admiral (1934, dam by Sweep), each were out of mares with poor credentials although each mare was sired by a good stallion.

After all, this was the pattern on which Man o' War himself had been bred, and for all one knows Riddle may have been trying to repeat it. When it turned up a Triple Crown winner, such as War Admiral, who can say the program was a complete failure? Well, for one thing, the five full sisters of War Admiral that accomplished nothing might indicate its general failure.

The Blood-Horse has commented before: "What Man o' War would have sired had he been bred to mares of the quality bred to Bold Ruler or Nasrullah is conjecture, of course, but it is suspected that his record as a sire would have been more illustrious than his record as a race horse." The present author agrees.

As it is, we are left to deal with the background and career of War Admiral. For American purposes, the story starts when Walter M. Jeffords Sr. imported at a cost of $4,000 an unraced daughter of the Derby and Grand Prix de Paris winner Spearmint. The mare, called Bathing Girl, was in foal to Harry of Hereford, a poor sire but a full brother of Swynford. The resulting foal was a filly, named Annette K. after the famous Australian swimmer Annette Kellerman.

Annette K. grew to be not quite 15 hands, 1 inch; her career on the Turf consisted of one race, in which she was unplaced. Riddle, who had purchased her from Jeffords, compounded the lack of size by breeding her to Sweep (then aged twenty-one), a small horse that sired small stock. The result of this mating was Brushup, a filly that stood less than fifteen hands high. Brushup started three times and could not win, so, here we have three successive generations of mares, not one of which won a race.

Harrie B. Scott was then manager of Faraway Farm, and he suggested mating the tiny Brushup to Man o' War. Such a cross at least had the advantage of combining the blood of Fair Play, Ben Brush (sire of Sweep), and Domino (sire of Sweep's dam). Whatever the reasoning, War Admiral was the result. He was foaled on May 2, 1934.

Scott told the author that when War Admiral was a yearling Jeffords admired him greatly, but that Riddle did not care for him and offered to sell him to Jeffords. The latter, however, declined.

When Scott asked Jeffords his reason (since he had expressed his liking for War Admiral), the reply was: "Don't you see, if this colt turned out as well as I think, it would lead to an almighty family row (Mrs. Jeffords was Mrs. Riddle's niece), and I probably couldn't even breed to Man o' War anymore." Still, whenever Jeffords saw War Admiral he would stand and sigh.

Brushup, dam of War Admiral

In the autumn of 1935, the small, brown yearling colt (he took his color from his maternal grandsire, Sweep) passed into the care of George Conway to start training at Berlin, Maryland, where Man o' War had been trained before him. Conway had become head trainer for Riddle in 1926 and thus had more of the Man o' War stock under his supervision than any other man. Conway trained all three of Man o' War's best sons—American Flag, Crusader, and War Admiral.

Although War Admiral was a May foal, like many small horses, he came to hand early. He made his first start on April 25 at Havre de Grace and his second at Belmont Park a month later, winning both. On June 6 he went for the five-furlong National Stallion Stakes, but was third, two and one-half lengths behind Pompoon, who turned out to be the best two-year-old of the year.

(As an illustration of the part played by luck in racing, a friend told us that in 1936 he had a nice two-year-old that would justify some financial support in a maiden race. He tried this twice in Maryland, with signal lack of success. In these two races, his colt ran into War Admiral first, and then Pompoon. Wiser? Perhaps. Richer? No.)

In the Great American Stakes, War Admiral again was beaten, that time by one and one-half lengths by Fairy Hill (later a winner of the Santa Anita Derby).

Back in Maryland in September, War Admiral won the Eastern Shore Handicap by five lengths, and that was the only stakes he won as a two-year-old. On October 10 he was second in the Richard Johnson Handicap at Laurel.

On the Experimental Free Handicap, compiled by John B. Campbell, War Admiral was ranked seventh from the top at 121 pounds. As a two-year-old, War Admiral clearly was inferior to his sire, Man o' War, at that age, but he also clearly was superior to Man o' War's other best sons, American Flag and Crusader, as two-year-olds.

The sire line's pattern of marked improvement from two to three, which had characterized Fair Play, American Flag, and Crusader, held true as well in the case of War Admiral, although he only grew to 15 hands, 2 inches.

War Admiral's three-year-old campaign began on April 14, with a six-furlong race at Havre de Grace, which he won. (When Fair Play tried this, it proved too short for him.) Ten days later he took the one and one-sixteenth-mile Chesapeake Stakes by six lengths, going to the front from the start.

War Admiral's spring form caused Riddle to alter his long-held views about 126 pounds being too much to ask a three-year-old to carry at the beginning of May,

	Man o' War, 1917	Fair Play, 1905	Hastings, 1893	Spendthrift, 1876	Australian / Aerolite
				Cinderella, 1885	Tomahawk / Manna
			Fairy Gold, 1896	Bend Or, 1877	Doncaster / Rouge Rose
				Dame Masham, 1889	Galliard / Pauline
		Mahubah, 1910	Rock Sand, 1900	Sainfoin, 1887	Springfield / Sanda
				Roquebrune, 1893	St. Simon / St. Marguerite
WAR ADMIRAL			Merry Token, 1891	Merry Hampton, 1884	Hampton / Doll Tearsheet
				Mizpah, 1880	Macgregor / Underhand mare
	Brushup, 1929	Sweep, 1907	Ben Brush, 1893	Bramble, 1875	Bonnie Scotland / Ivy Leaf
				Roseville, 1888	Reform / Albia
			Pink Domino, 1897	Domino, 1891	Himyar / Mannie Gray
				Belle Rose, 1889	Beaudesert / Monte Rosa
		Annette K., 1921	Harry of Hereford, 1910	John o' Gaunt, 1901	Isinglass / La Fleche
				Canterbury Pilgrim, 1893	Tristan / Pilgrimage
			Bathing Girl, 1915	Spearmint, 1903	Carbine / Maid of the Mint
				Summer Girl, 1906	Sundridge / Permission

War Admiral

and War Admiral was sent to Louisville for the Kentucky Derby. There he was made an 8-5 favorite in a field of twenty. He drew the No. 1 post position, under which circumstance it is essential that a colt get off in the first flight. Otherwise, he is bound to be shut off at the first turn, and he may be blocked beyond hope of recovery. Fortunately, jockey Charley Kurtsinger was able to send War Admiral to the front at once, and he gradually improved his position. He won by one and three-quarters lengths from Pompoon, and the time of 2:03 1/5 was the second-best in the history of the race to that year.

War Admiral and Pompoon met again in the Preakness, a week later. War Admiral was odds-on at 3-10, and Pompoon was 4-1. Again War Admiral drew the No. 1 post position, and again he got off in front. Kurtsinger kept War Admiral well off the rail to obtain the best going, and on the last turn, jockey Wayne Wright on Pompoon took advantage of this, cutting to the inside of War Admiral and thereby gaining more than a length. Suddenly, the two colts were almost head and head. Down the stretch they came, eight lengths clear of the field. Wright plied the whip strenuously to Pompoon, but Kurtsinger never touched War Admiral, who won by a head in time two-fifths of a second slower than the track record. Doubtlessly, the shorter distance of the Preakness (one and three-sixteenths miles) was somewhat to Pompoon's advantage.

In the one and one-half-mile Belmont Stakes, run three weeks later, there was only a field of seven, and War Admiral's odds were 9-10. War Admiral stumbled as the field got away, and sheared away an inch-square portion of his right forefoot. Unmindful of this, though the blood was squirting up against his belly as he ran, War Admiral again went to the front, and after the first quarter-mile, under rating, ran into a three-length lead. He held the same margin at the finish, winning in the time of 2:28 3/5, which was one-fifth of a second better than Man o' War's time over the same track.[1] Sceneshifter was second, while Pompoon was beaten by eighteen lengths.

It took about four and one-half months for War Admiral to grow a new hoof, and by that time it was late October. The best of his season, consequently, was something of an anti-climax. On October 26, War Admiral won a one and one-sixteenth-mile overnight race at Laurel, beating a good older horse in Aneroid. In the ten-furlong Washington Handicap, he defeated the best older horses then

YEAR	AGE	STS	1ST	2ND	3RD	EARNED
1936	at 2	6	3	2	1	$ 14,800
1937	at 3	8	8	0	0	$166,500
1938	at 4	11	9	1	0	$ 90,840
1939	at 5	1	1	0	0	$ 1,100
Lifetime		26	21	3	1	$273,240

in training, barring Seabiscuit, and four days later won the one and three-sixteenths-mile Pimlico Special under 128 pounds, conceding up to twenty-eight pounds to the field.

Riddle decided to keep War Admiral in training as a four-year-old (unlike Man o' War), and the colt was out early on February 19 for a seven-furlong overnight race in Florida. He won without difficulty, and two weeks later he took up 130 pounds in the ten-furlong Widener Handicap. There was nothing else approaching War Admiral's class in the race, and he won easily by one and one-half lengths, giving away from thirteen to twenty-nine pounds.

Back in New York on June 6, he picked up 132 pounds and won the one-mile Queens County Handicap, conceding six pounds to the Suburban Handicap winner, Snark, and twenty pounds to the Metropolitan winner, Danger Point.

Three weeks later came the one and one-eighth-mile Massachusetts Handicap, the most important race in New England. War Admiral was assigned 130 pounds for it, and Hal Price Headley's three-year-old Menow (who had been the top two-year-old of the previous year) had 107 pounds. Considerable rain had made the footing slippery, a type of going strongly favorable to Menow, with his short, piston-like stride and lightweight. Menow reveled in the going and won decisively, with War Admiral a bad fourth.

War Admiral won four races at Saratoga, the Wilson mile (over Fighting Fox and Esposa) in the mud, the ten-furlong Saratoga Handicap, the ten-furlong Whitney, and the one and three-quarters-mile Saratoga Cup.

He then showed he could stay two miles, easily winning the Jockey Club Gold Cup.

Finally came a long-awaited meeting between War Admiral and Seabiscuit, which took place in the one and three-sixteenths-mile Pimlico Special on November 1. War Admiral had made it a rule to break like a shot, and Seabiscuit was not known for early speed. Great was the surprise, therefore, when George (Ice Man) Woolf went to the whip leaving the gate and shot Seabiscuit into a two-length lead. Going down the backstretch, Kurtsinger got War Admiral on even terms with Seabiscuit, and some observers thought that War Admiral had a slight lead with a half-mile to go.

Seabiscuit, however, gradually drew away again and won by three lengths in new-track-record time of 1:56 3/5.

It should be remembered that it also was at Pimlico over the same distance that Pompoon had run War Admiral to a head in the Preakness. These two races suggested that at Pimlico War Admiral's form was at least ten pounds inferior to his form over tracks elsewhere. (The old saying, "horses for courses," often holds true.)

Two weeks later War Admiral won the Rhode Island Handicap and then was sent to Florida again. At five, he won an overnight race on February 19 in preparation for another assault on the Widener Handicap, but he never started again. The horse came down with a temperature; then in May he wrenched an ankle, and he was retired to stud.

How are we to assess War Admiral's class as a racehorse? He was a good but not top-class two-year-old; he was a top-class three-year-old, the best of his year and well up to normal classic standard; as a four-year-old, he again was the best of his age, stayed two miles well, and carried 132 pounds with success. He had excellent early speed, a great advantage on American oval tracks, racing around two 180-degree turns. Still, he simply was not overpowering, as Man o' War had been.

All things considered, War Admiral was Man o' War's best son, both on the track and at stud. He was the leading sire of 1945, the year his daughter Busher was Horse of the Year at three, and he sired a total of forty stakes winners (10.8 percent) from 371 named foals, and the best of them, in addition to Busher, included Blue Peter, Busanda, Bee Mac, Striking, Searching, and Admiral Vee.

War Admiral did not sire a son that carried on the Man o' War male line successfully, that role being left to War Relic, a Man o' War stallion who was not as good as War Admiral but who had the advantage (rare among a Riddle-bred) of having a good pedigree on the bottom as well as on the top.

While not a sire of sires, War Admiral, however, was an outstanding sire of broodmares, and he led the broodmare sire list in 1962 and 1964. His daughters have produced 112 stakes winners, including Buckpasser, Hoist the Flag, Priceless Gem, Affectionately, Gun Bow, Crafty Admiral, and Iron Liege. War Admiral was not kept as a private stallion (as Man o' War had been), having the advantage of being sent a great many more non-Riddle-owned mares than was his sire. It is significant that his best daughter, Busher, and his champion juvenile son, Blue Peter, both were from outside mares.

War Admiral stood at Riddle's Faraway Farm in Kentucky until 1958, after which Riddle's estate moved him to Preston Madden's Hamburg Place. War Admiral died the next year and was buried at Faraway, beneath the statue of Man o' War.[2]

End Notes:

1. Man o' War's Belmont was run over one and three-eighths miles rather than one and one-half miles, but Man o' War did win the Jockey Club Gold Cup at Belmont over a mile and a half in 2:28 4/5.

2. War Admiral's remains were later moved to the Kentucky Horse Park, the same location to which his sire's remains and statue were moved.

CHAPTER FORTY-SEVEN

WAR RELIC

The late John Hervey (Salvator) possibly was the most learned and graceful
Turf writer the author can recall. His articles abounded with classical allu-
sions and vivid descriptions. He put the feel of racing into words, and that
is, after all, the chief object in writing about it. One thing he was reluctant to do,
however, was to grapple with the most important of all questions for breeders—just
where, within as narrow a range as possible, should a given horse be rated among
those of the same age?

Reading Hervey's article on War Relic in *American Race Horses of 1941*, however, one is somewhat confused by the atmosphere that Hervey created; War
Relic, after winning his maiden race as a three-year-old, lost his next six starts
in succession, and yet was to be regarded as a great horse. He did not actually
say he was a great horse, but he set out to leave that impression and he succeeded. It was a little like watching Houdini; the author wishes he could do the
same thing.

How did Hervey do it? War Relic was never a great horse and was not, in
fact, even a first-class colt, as the following record will show.

War Relic did not start as a two-year-old, because of a strained back. His
first outing in public was on April 21, 1941, in a six-furlong maiden affair at
Narragansett Park, which he won in the ordinary time of 1:12 4/5. In his next
start, he was beaten by more than a length by an ordinary animal called Homeward
Bound in 1:13. In his next start, Hervey reported that the colt was startled by the
noise of the crowd, and shied into the inner rail, losing his jockey.

Moving to New York, Samuel D. Riddle's homebred was put into a Class C Graded
Allowance race at one and one-sixteenth miles. There, he did run the first six
furlongs in 1:11, but had nothing left when the challenge came, and pulled up,
finishing last. Despite lack of credentials, he was a starter in the one-mile Withers,
which was won by King Cole, the favorite, himself not a high-class colt. The chart on
War Relic read: "… had speed for a half, then faltered steadily."

War Relic

In an allowance race of seven furlongs, after pressing the pace to the stretch, War Relic again collapsed, finishing eighth. After a change of trainers, from R.C. Utz to W.A. Carter, War Relic again was started in a six-furlong allowance race. That time he was second, beaten one and one-half lengths in 1:12 4/5.

Back in Boston at Suffolk Downs, War Relic went after a six-furlong allowance race, run in a sea of mud. Apparently, the mud, or inferior opposition, suited him, as he won in 1:13 2/5. His next effort was at a mile against five others. Hervey made the excuse that War Relic was blocked entering the far turn and then was carried very wide entering the home stretch. At any rate, he lost again in the rather poor time of 1:38 2/5. There may have been some truth in Hervey's explanation, as War Relic won his next race at a mile in 1:37 3/5.

All that indifferent form had put him into the Massachusetts Handicap with the feather of 102 pounds. Two days before the race he was put into an all-aged affair, which had some fair horses in it, including Widener Handicap winner Many Stings (115 pounds), plus Alaking and Tragic Ending. War Relic (107) got the lead near the mile post and went on the extra seventy yards in 1:42 2/5.

His rating at that stage is clear from the Massachusetts weights: Fenelon

(130), Foxbrough (122), Your Chance (120), Market Wise (111), and War Relic (102). Under these conditions, Foxbrough was conceding twenty pounds in actual weight and ten pounds by the weight-for-age scale. The mile was run in 1:35 4/5, and in the last eighth-mile War Relic pulled away from Foxbrough to win by three-quarters of a length. That result would make Foxbrough about eight pounds the better of the pair at weight-for-age. The time for the race was very good, 1:48 3/5.

After the unexpected triumph, War Relic was shipped to Saratoga, where he was to meet Whirlaway in the Saranac Handicap, of one mile. Whirlaway, who was coming from Chicago, where Attention had defeated him in the Classic, was carrying 130 pounds; War Relic was assigned 117 pounds. The pair came into the home stretch with Whirlaway not too far back, but he was up to his old trick of drifting out, which carried him nearly to the outside rail before he got to racing straight again. Whirlaway produced one of his dramatic charges, and he and War Relic crossed the finish line together, on opposite sides of the course. When the photograph was developed, after examination with a microscope, the race was awarded to Whirlaway. It would take a good geometrician to figure out how much extra distance Whirlaway covered, in addition to conceding the thirteen pounds. Still, it

				Spendthrift, 1876	Australian Aerolite
		Fair Play, 1905	Hastings, 1893		
				Cinderella, 1885	Tomahawk Manna
			Fairy Gold, 1896	**Bend Or**, 1877	Doncaster Rouge Rose
	Man o' War, 1917			Dame Masham, 1889	Galliard Pauline
			Rock Sand, 1900	Sainfoin, 1887	Springfield Sanda
		Mahubah, 1910		Roquebrune, 1893	St. Simon St. Marguerite
			Merry Token, 1891	Merry Hampton, 1884	Hampton Doll Tearsheet
WAR RELIC				Mizpah, 1880	Macgregor Underhand mare
			Rock Sand, 1900	Sainfoin, 1887	Springfield Sanda
		Friar Rock, 1913		Roquebrune, 1893	St. Simon St. Marguerite
			Fairy Gold, 1896	**Bend Or**, 1877	Doncaster Rouge Rose
	Friar's Carse, 1923			Dame Masham, 1889	Galliard Pauline
			Superman, 1904	Commando, 1898	Domino Emma C.
		Problem, 1914		Anomaly, 1896	**Bend Or** Blue Rose
			Query, 1906	Voter, 1894	Friar's Balsam Mavourneen
				Quesal, 1886	Himyar Queen Ban

was a creditable effort for War Relic.

Next came another trip to Narragansett, to prepare for the Narragansett Special, renewing the rivalry with Whirlaway.[1] As a tune-up, War Relic started in an all-aged event of one mile and seventy yards, which he won by a neck, with something in hand. The weights for the Narragansett Special were Whirlaway, 118, and War Relic, 107, a shift of two pounds in Whirlaway's favor from their encounter in the Saranac. Perhaps the most interesting feature of the race is the slow pace at which the early stages were run—:25 3/5, :50 1/5, 1:14 3/5. What Whirlaway needed was a fast early pace, so that he could have a bunch of exhausted horses, all slowing down, when he began one of his famous come-from-behind charges. In the Special, the pace was picked up, the fourth quarter being covered in :24 2/5, but it only produced a mile in 1:39. This was not enough to leave a good horse exhausted. At that point, Ted Atkinson, in front on War Relic, asked for a burst of speed, and War Relic soon opened a lead of four lengths.

Whirlaway was unable to match him, and the farther they went down the stretch, the greater grew War Relic's margin, until he passed the post a winner by four and one-half lengths from Whirlaway. Taking this form literally, War Relic came out about as good a colt as Whirlaway, something no one in his right mind would accept. The honors of the race belonged to Atkinson, for setting such a slow pace that he would have a fresh horse at the time Whirlaway could be expected to make his challenge.

YEAR	AGE	STS	1ST	2ND	3RD	EARNED
1940	at 2	unraced				
1941	at 3	17	9	4	0	$89,195
1942	at 4	3	0	0	0	$ 350
Lifetime		20	9	4	0	$89,545

There was considerable agitation in the press for a return engagement, but nothing came of it. Whirlaway went on to New York to win the Lawrence Realization and force Market Wise to put up a new American record to beat him in the Jockey Club Gold Cup. Meanwhile, War Relic (117) started for the nine-furlong Governor's Handicap at Narragansett. He won it, but only by three-quarters of a length from Equifox (108), in 1:51 (track record, 1:49 2/5).

War Relic started three times as a four-year-old, but did not win again.

His one claim to racing fame was that he beat Whirlaway four and one-half lengths, when receiving only eleven pounds. The internal evidence of the time fractions of that race shows beyond doubt that it was falsely run.

A glance at War Relic's pedigree shows that he is inbred to two of the pillars of the Belmont Stud, namely both Fairy Gold and Rock Sand, with two free generations each. He was by the great Man o' War, and his dam, Friar's Carse, won the Keene

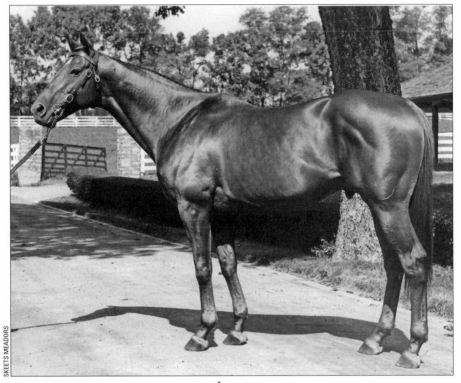

SKEETS MEADORS

Intent

Memorial, Fashion, and Clover Stakes.[2] Back of this were two mares that were stakes winners, and the line traces eventually to Dixie, one of the most noted pre-Civil War matrons in Kentucky.

War Relic had a full sister, Speed Boat, who became the dam of Level Best, the best filly sired by Equipoise and the best filly of her year.[3]

War Relic was the last important stakes winner sired by Man o' War, who was twenty-one years older than War Relic. Hervey indulged in a long panegyric on Man o' War's record as a sire, which was not in fact justified, as he only led the sire list once. What was remarkable about Man o' War's record was that his record was as good as it was in the face of the miserable opportunity afforded him by owner Riddle, whose mares were of markedly subnormal quality, and who kept Man o' War virtually as a private stallion and limited his book to twenty-five mares a year. If Lexington could handle a book of more than seventy mares a year, without apparent impairment in the quality of his produce, it is almost certain that Man o' War, with his herculean constitution, could have done the same. A book of fifty mares would have doubled his opportunity, but such is fate sometimes, even among the greatest of heroes.

War Relic was not a great success as a sire, ranking sixth on the general list once and thirteenth twice and siring fourteen stakes winners. They included champion Battlefield, plus Intent, Relic, and Missile.

Intent and Relic became the strongest links in what remained of the Fair Play–Man o' War sire line. Intent sired the brilliantly fast Intentionally, whose sons include In Reality, a major winner and a prominent sire.[4]

Relic was sent to Europe, but his best son, Olden Times, raced in this country and also has become a high-ranking sire. Relic also sired the remarkable broodmare Relance, dam of three top-class European winners, Relko, Reliance, and Match II.

End Notes:

1. As a tuneup for Narragansett, War Relic won the Kenner Stakes at Saratoga on August 12, defeating two others. He ran the mile and three-sixteenths in 1:58 2/5.

2. Friar's Carse was regarded as the champion two-year-old filly of 1925.

3. Speed Boat was named best two-year-old filly of 1940. Since 1936, champions have been officially recognized.

4. The Fair Play line today is extant through War Relic's son Intent, the main conduit being In Reality, whose sons Relaunch and Valid Appeal have established flourishing lines. War Relic died in 1963 and was originally buried alongside his sire at Faraway Farm. His remains, among with those of Man o' War and War Admiral, were later moved to the Kentucky Horse Park.

CHAPTER FORTY-EIGHT

CHANCE PLAY

August Belmont II did not live to see Chance Play run, as the breeder died in 1924, when Chance Play was a yearling. His Nursery Stud was dispersed, and Chance Play was among the group acquired by the Log Cabin Stud (W. Averill Harriman and George Walker). His full brother, Chance Shot (1924), went to Joseph E. Widener. These were the last two high-class horses bred by Belmont, as well as the last two high-class racers sired by the great stallion Fair Play. Belmont had also bred both their sire and their dam.

In the autumn of 1924, it was well known around Belmont Park that Chance Play was the best yearling that had been tried there. As a two-year-old, his works were no secret from the clockers, so when he first came out in a maiden race on May 12, at Jamaica, it is not surprising that he was even-money in a field of thirteen. Over a slow track, he won by five lengths in :59 4/5. Four days later, he took the Youthful Stakes, at odds of 1-4 in 1:05 1/5, only two-fifths of a second slower than the track record, but in the Flash Stakes at Saratoga, he was only fourth, beaten about two lengths. About three weeks later, he won an allowance race at Saratoga against ordinary competition.

In the six and a half-furlong Hopeful Stakes, also at Saratoga, Chance Play ran third in a field of fifteen, against the best of his age. The winner was Pompey, who conceded five pounds to Chance Play and beat him nine lengths. In the Futurity, Pompey won again, conceding eight pounds, but he only beat Chance Play a length. The chart said: "Chance Play was racing fast at the end." In the one-mile Junior Champion Stakes, Chance Play, conceding six and a half pounds, went under to the Man o' War colt Mars by a half-length, giving ground at the end of it.

His was the record of a good two-year-old, but by no means an outstanding one. The fact was that Chance Play was somewhat delicate and did not have the constitution to stand up to a strenuous campaign, with races close together. He was a pale chestnut in color, which many horsemen associate with delicacy.

Chance Play began his three-year-old campaign with an easy victory over six

Chance Play

furlongs in a minor handicap on June 7.[1] A week later, he won a similar handicap with equal ease, at odds of 1-2, but in the one-mile Shevlin Stakes against better colts, he was only fourth to Macaw. Chance Play then took another minor handicap at one and one-sixteenth miles.

He was not started in the Kentucky Derby, the Preakness, or the Belmont. His first start against classic colts over a classic distance was in the one and a half-mile Dwyer Stakes. There, Crusader, probably the best three-year-old colt of the year, gave Chance Play three pounds and beat him a nose in 2:29 3/5, a new track record. Third was Espino, a really stout colt, two lengths back of Chance Play and conceding him twelve pounds. As Crusader had won the Belmont, beating Espino only a length at level weights, this race showed that Chance Play was not too far from classic form.

Chance Play was then put by until September, when he was one of a party of five for the one and five-eighths-mile Lawrence Realization. This was possibly Chance Play's worst race, as he finished absolutely last. The chart read: "Quit and was not persevered with."

His next effort was in the one-mile President's Plate. There were only three starters, each with 126 pounds up. Macaw won by a length from Chance Play, who beat his old rival Pompey by a head.

The next stage of the campaign was in Maryland, where Chance Play (123) was asked to give Pompey two pounds, and he beat him by about a length over one and one-sixteenth miles in the Potomac Handicap. For the one-mile Laurel Stakes, there was really a high-class field of eleven. Croyden, Sarazen, Mars, and Crusader all beat Chance Play, but he did finish in front of the great race mare Princess Doreen. His last start of the year, in the ten-furlong Maryland Handicap, probably gave a good assessment of where Chance Play belonged at that stage of his career. Crusader (126) gave Chance Play seven pounds and beat him three lengths. This must be taken to mean that Chance Play was at least twelve pounds in back of Crusader, but that form does not quite square with the form in the twelve-furlong Dwyer Stakes.

There was quite an improvement in Chance Play's form from three to four years of age. He was, at four, in the hands of J.I. Smith, who had not trained him in his early days. Chance Play (128) began by taking the Toboggan Handicap of six furlongs (perhaps America's most prestigious sprint race) by one and a half lengths. Pompey (120) was third. It will be recalled that at two Pompey was much the better of the pair.

CHANCE PLAY					
Fair Play, 1905	Hastings, 1893	Spendthrift, 1876	Australian, 1858	West Australian / Emilia
			Aerolite, 1861	Lexington / Florine
		Cinderella, 1885	Tomahawk, 1863	**King Tom** / Mincemeat
			Manna, 1874	Brown Bread / Tartlet
	Fairy Gold, 1896	Bend Or, 1877	Doncaster, 1870	Stockwell / Marigold
			Rouge Rose, 1865	Thormanby / Ellen Horne
		Dame Masham, 1889	Galliard, 1880	Galopin / Mavis
			Pauline, 1883	Hermit / Lady Masham
Quelle Chance, 1917	Ethelbert, 1896	Eothen, 1883	Hampton, 1872	Lord Clifden / Lady Langden
			Sultana, 1869	Oxford / Besika
		Moari, 1885	Poulet, 1877	Peut Etre / Printaniere
			Queen Of Cyprus, 1873	**King Tom** / Cypriana
	Qu'elle Est Belle II, 1909	Rock Sand, 1900	Sainfoin, 1887	Springfield / Sanda
			Roquebrune, 1893	St. Simon / St Marguerite
		Queen's Bower, 1899	St. Florian, 1891	St. Simon / Palmflower
			Gipsy Queen, 1886	Kingcraft / Paradise

In the ten-furlong Suburban Handicap, Crusader (127) was asked to concede only two pounds to Chance Play (125). Crusader showed that at this time he was much the best handicap horse in America, as he ran off with the race by seven lengths from Black Maria (120) with Chance Play nowhere.

Chance Play next failed by only a neck to concede twenty pounds to Light Carbine in the Queens County Handicap of one mile, again beating Pompey, and in the nine-furlong Brooklyn Handicap, Chance Play (121) ran a very creditable race, going under by only a head in the last stride to Peanuts (112). There, Crusader was asked to shoulder 132 pounds and was beaten badly. As the time for this race was only one-fifth of a second away from the track record, it showed that Chance Play had become a pretty good colt, especially as he had Display, Pompey, Black Maria, and Espino behind him.

This race evidently took something out of Chance Play, for he turned in a poor effort in the unimportant nine-furlong Brookdale Handicap.

Given a two-week rest, Chance Play was shipped out to Lincoln Fields for the ten-furlong Lincoln Handicap. Carrying top weight of 122 pounds, he won, setting a new track record of 2:04 1/5. Princess Doreen was third, sharing equal top weight. Back at Saratoga, Chance Play took the Merchants' and Citizens' Handicap of one and three-sixteenths miles from Black Maria and Pompey, conceding weight to both.

Then came the more instructive part of the season. Chance Play had beaten the best sprinters in the Toboggan and repeatedly had shown that he was about the best at middle distances, barring Crusader. Now he was tried over the longer Cup courses. He first won the Saratoga Cup from Forever and Ever, and Espino, who had beaten him easily in the Lawrence Realization the year before. Next, he came out for the two-mile Jockey Club Gold Cup. He led all the way until the final yards, when Brown Bud (receiving eleven pounds) got up to him and crossed over, slamming Chance Play into the fence. Brown Bud was disqualified, and Chance Play was declared the winner. (It is a curious fact that Display, who was third, won more than $250,000 but never did win a stakes in New York.)

It was by then October, and Maryland racing was starting its autumn program.

YEAR	AGE	STS	1ST	2ND	3RD	EARNED
1925	at 2	7	3	1	2	$ 12,666
1926	at 3	10	4	3	0	$ 22,080
1927	at 4	12	6	3	0	$ 86,800
1928	at 5	10	3	2	0	$ 16,400
Lifetime		39	16	9	2	$137,946

In the nine-furlong Havre de Grace Cup Handicap, Chance Play (124) and Crusader (129) met again. At those weights, Crusader was a top-heavy favorite at 3-4 and Chance Play was 8-1. The public was decid-

342

Some Chance

edly wrong, as Crusader never saw the way Chance Play went; the winning margin was about four lengths better than Crusader, who finished fourth.

The next meeting of the handicap stars was in the ten-furlong Washington Handicap at Laurel. Crusader (128) was the co-topweight, Chance Play (127) was next, but Display had been dropped down to 112 pounds. Chance Play led until well into the stretch but simply could not concede Display fifteen pounds and was beaten about three lengths, as was Crusader. Since the time was within two-fifths of the track record, it was asking a bit much.

The next meeting between Chance Play and Display was in the one and one-sixteenth-mile Gadsden D. Bryan Memorial Handicap at Bowie. Chance Play (128) was only asked to concede Display four pounds, and with this eleven-pound shift in the weights in his favor, Chance Play beat Display three lengths. One would have to estimate that Chance Play was ten pounds better than Display, but not fifteen pounds better.[2]

As a five-year-old, Chance Play ran ten times more, for three wins and two seconds, but only won $16,400, against $86,800 in his four-year-old season, when he reached the peak of his form. At four, he probably had been one of the two best

Quelle Chance, dam of Chance Play

horses in training, Crusader being the other.

When they went to stud, there was no comparison, as Crusader was a dismal failure while Chance Play became leading sire in 1935 and again in 1944, and was in the first twenty six times more. This is all the more remarkable, since he spent quite a few years at the Aknusti Stud near Delhi, New York, where his opportunities were severely limited. He was bought by Calumet Farm, and his opportunities expanded. He sired a string of good horses, including Futurity winner Some Chance, Jockey Club Gold Cup and Champagne Stakes winner Pot o' Luck, Hopeful winner Psychic Bid, plus Grand Slam, Good Gamble, Now What, Alex Barth, Harford, etc. He got a total of twenty-three stakes winners, but he never sired one that was quite as good as he was himself at his best. Today, his male line is very dormant, if not moribund.

Chance Play had a pedigree with much to recommend it. His dam, Quelle Chance, also produced Chance Shot, winner of the Belmont Stakes, Withers, etc., and Pari Mutuel, a stakes winner and sire. His granddam, Qu'elle Est Belle II, won the Prix de Diane (French Oaks) and was third in the French One Thousand Guineas. Since she was by Rock Sand, the Fair Play–Rock Sand cross made famous by Belmont's Nursery Stud, by such horses as Man o' War, Mad Hatter, and Mad Play, was existent in Chance Play.

Any horse that becomes leading sire twice must be a good sire, and especially when much of the best part of his life has been spent in Siberia (i.e., Delhi, New York). There was always a suggestion of softness about Chance Play, though, that left a lingering doubt in the mind as to his worth in the *Stud Book*.

A horse of at least equal racing merit, foaled in the same year as Chance Play, was Coronach in England (Derby and St. Leger), who was of an even lighter chestnut coat, with a flaxen mane and tail. His trainer, Fred Darling, once told the author that despite Coronach's great racing class, he always regarded him as soft. At stud, Coronach generally was pronounced a failure, though he sired two animals of exceptional merit in Corrida (Arc de Triomphe twice) and Niccolo Dell'Arca (Italian Derby by twenty lengths) in Italy.

The author does not know why coat color should have anything to do with either racing or breeding class, but he does know that a great many experienced racing men think it does.

End Notes:

1. Harriman bought out George Walker's interest when Chance Play was three, and the colt raced for Harriman's Arden Farms Stable.

2. The winner of the race was Cloudland (106) with Chance Play second and Display three lengths back in third.

CHAPTER FORTY-NINE

BAYARDO

T he breeder of Bayardo was A.W. Cox, an individual about whom many
unsubstantiated tales circulated. One of these was that as a young man
Cox had been in Australia, and on the eve of his departure for his return
voyage to England, he had become involved in a poker game during which he
enjoyed a run of luck. Having won all the chips at the table, Cox was preparing to
leave when one of the players said: "The only thing I have left is a quarter-share
in a mine that probably is valueless, but I will play you for that, if you like." Cox
agreed, and runs of luck being what they are, he won the quarter-share in the
mine, as well as all the ready cash in the game.

The share was in the Broken Hill mine, and on the voyage home, Cox received
a cable at Colombo (long before the days of radio on ships) that there had been a
fresh strike of ore at Broken Hill and that the shares had risen dramatically. Cox
decided to ignore the recommendation that he sell. At Suez, another cable was
awaiting him, announcing a further upward spiral in Broken Hill shares. Again
Cox refused to sell. By the time he reached England, the Broken Hill shares had
reached a level that made Cox a man of substance—well able to afford a life of
leisure, a breeding farm, and a racing stable.

Cox bought a house at Newmarket and leased the Jockey Club's forty-five acres
of paddocks there. His horses, however, were trained by Alec Taylor at Manton in
Wiltshire. Cox had a breeding philosophy that was simple in the extreme, and,
judging by the results, also was profitable in the extreme. His dictum was: "Pile
Galopin on Galopin, and damn the rest." In the interests of accuracy, it should be
pointed out that when he piled Isonomy on Isonomy, the results (in the case of
Lemberg) were almost as good. (Cox so neglected the Jockey Club paddocks that
his tenancy was about to be terminated, when Bayardo and Lemberg appeared
and silenced his critics.)

Bayardo was out of Galicia (1898), who was by Cox's favorite stallion, Galopin.
The fact that Galopin (1872) was twenty-six years old when Galicia was foaled

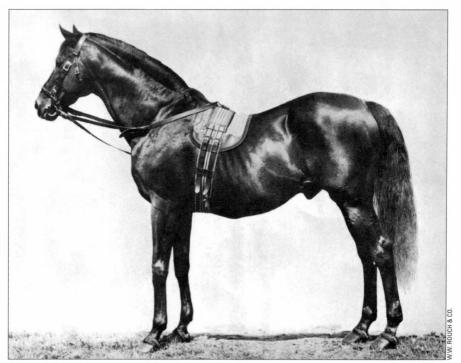

Galopin

did not seem to worry Cox. Galopin indeed had been a superlative racer, being defeated only once, in a bumping match in the Middle Park Plate. He was considered by trainer John Dawson to be a long way in front of Petrarch (one year younger), who had won the Middle Park Plate, the Two Thousand Guineas, the St. Leger, and the Ascot Gold Cup. In addition, Galopin had been leading sire three times and was the sire of perhaps the greatest of all racers and sires in St. Simon, as well as Derby and St. Leger winner Donovan.

In three starts as a two-year-old, Galicia won the Ascot Biennial Stakes and then split a pastern. Although she started five times as a three-year-old without winning, it is difficult, owing to her accident, to assess her racing class fairly.

Galicia was out of Isoletta, by Isonomy, sire of two English Triple Crown winners—Isinglass and Common—and himself winner of the Cambridgeshire, plus the Ascot, Goodwood, and Doncaster Cups. Isoletta never ran but produced five winners from her first six foals. The next dam, Lady Muncaster, bred three ordinary winners out of nine foals. She had been, however, a pretty good racer, winning six of her nine starts as a two-year-old, and two of her four starts as a three-year-old.

Lady Muncaster was out of Blue Light, a minor winner, and dam of only two winners. The next dam, Borealis, was a fair winner, and was out of Blink Bonny, winner of the Derby and Oaks as well as being dam of Blair Athol (Derby and St. Leger). The next dam was Queen Mary, one of the best taproot mares in the *General Stud Book*.

When Galicia went to stud, her first live foal was sired by Eager, the champion speed horse of his time. Named Eastern, this colt was a pretty fair winner at two and three, and won up to one and a half miles. The next colt, Carpathian, was by Isinglass, and had an inbreeding to Isonomy. Since this colt did not start, presumably he suffered from the unsoundness frequently found among the Isinglass stock.

The next foal was Bayardo (1906). Galicia's mate in 1905 was Bay Ronald, who had been only a fair racer, if that. Bay Ronald's best races were in the ten-furlong City and Suburban Handicap, which he won as a five-year-old with only 110 pounds up, and the one and a half-mile Hardwicke Stakes at Ascot, as a four-year-old. Nevertheless, Bay Ronald had made a surprisingly good start at stud, having sired Macdonald II in France, he a colt up to classic standard, and a very good filly in Rondeau, later the dam of the major sire Teddy. Although Cox could not have

BAYARDO	Bay Ronald, 1893	Hampton, 1872	Lord Clifden, 1860	Newminster, 1848 — Touchstone / Beeswing
				The Slave, 1852 — Melbourne / Volley
			Lady Langden, 1868	Kettledrum, 1858 — **Rataplan** / Hybla
				Haricot, 1847 — Lanercost / Queen Mary
		Black Duchess, 1886	Galliard, 1880	**Galopin**, 1872 — Vedette / Flying Duchess
				Mavis, 1874 — Macaroni / Merlette
			Black Corrie, 1879	**Sterling**, 1868 — Oxford / Whisper
				Wild Dayrell Mare, 1861 — Wild Dayrell / Lady Lurewell
	Galicia, 1898	**Galopin**, 1872	Vedette, 1854	Voltigeur, 1847 — Voltaire / Martha Lynn
				Mrs. Ridgway, 1849 — Birdcatcher / Nan Darrell
			Flying Duchess, 1853	The Flying Dutchman, 1846 — Bay Middleton / Barbelle
				Merope, 1841 — Voltaire / Juniper Mare
		Isoletta, 1891	Isonomy, 1875	**Sterling**, 1868 — Oxford / Whisper
				Isola Bella, 1868 — Stockwell / Isoline
			Lady Muncaster, 1884	Muncaster, 1877 — Doncaster / Windermere
				Blue Light, 1870 — **Rataplan** / Borealis

Bayardo

known it at the time, Bay Ronald also had sired Dark Ronald (1904), who became the most influential sire in Germany.

Doubtless the factor that influenced Cox the most was that this mating with Bay Ronald would give an inbreeding to Galopin with two free generations.

When Bayardo as a yearling was sent to Alec Taylor at Manton, he was a medium- to small-sized colt, somewhat over at the knees—a characteristic that had marked both Bay Ronald and Galopin. Many unusually sound racers have this trait, and Bayardo was able to stand a very strenuous campaign both at two and three without leg trouble. From his pedigree, one would not have marked Bayardo down as likely to be the best two-year-old of his year. However, that is exactly what he was, beyond any doubt.

In the British style of preparing two-year-olds for their first starts, Bayardo was tried with three-year-old Seedcake at even weights, 120 pounds each, and three other two-year-olds. Bayardo won easily, by six lengths. Exactly what Taylor learned from this trial is hard to say, except that Bayardo was better than his other two-year-olds. Seedcake had run eight times, always unplaced, and in the first race of the Ascot meeting, he finished last.

The first race chosen for Bayardo was the five-furlong New Stakes at Ascot. In a field of thirteen, Bayardo was only fourth favorite, at 7-1, but he won easily by one and a half lengths from Perdiccas and Perola (winner of the next year's Oaks). In his next outing, the National Breeders' Produce Stakes, then the most valuable two-year-old race in England, Bayardo had to carry 128 pounds, that including the great jockey Danny Maher, and he won by a length from 13 others, at odds of 7-4.

The Richmond Stakes at Goodwood carried a lot of tradition, since it had been won in the past by such noted racers as Wheel of Fortune, Bend Or, Friar's Balsam, Orme, and Persimmon. For its renewal in 1908, Bayardo took up 134 pounds and won by three lengths from Vivid (119 pounds) at odds of 1-3.

Bayardo now rested until the Newmarket First October Meeting, when he took the about five-furlong Buckenham Stakes from two opponents at odds of 1-25. On Friday of the same meeting, Bayardo won the Rous Memorial Stakes from a single rival by one and a half lengths at odds of 1-20.

Next came the two most important two-year-old races of the autumn. In the six-furlong Middle

YEAR	AGE	STS	1ST	2ND	3RD	EARNED*
1908	at 2	7	7	0	0	£13,039
1909	at 3	13	11	0	0	£24,797
1910	at 4	5	4	1	0	£ 6,698
Lifetime		**25**	**22**	**1**	**0**	**£44,534**
* First-place money only						

Park Plate (the two-year-old Derby), Bayardo was 1-6 in a field of four, with 129 pounds up and again beat Vivid, this time by a length. The next leg of the two-year-old crown was the seven-furlong Dewhurst Stakes, still at Newmarket. Here Bayardo had to carry 131 pounds, and in a field of six again defeated Perola at odds of 1-3. That concluded Bayardo's campaign for 1908.

The next year began inauspiciously for Bayardo. The spring at Manton was cold and windy, and Bayardo did not come to hand well. Taylor knew his colt was not fit to do himself justice and advised Mr. Fairie (the name under which Cox raced) not to start Bayardo for the Two Thousand Guineas. Cox, however, mapped out the engagements for his horses himself, and short of a complete breakdown, they ran where they had been engaged to run.

In the meantime, there was in training a colt called Minoru, who had been leased by Lord Marcus Beresford from Colonel Hall Walker to run in the colors of King Edward VII. As a two-year-old, Minoru had been placed twenty-two pounds below Bayardo on the Free Handicap. Lord Marcus, therefore, was somewhat skeptical when the royal trainer, Richard Marsh, told him that Minoru had improved over the winter and might have a good chance in the Two Thousand Guineas. As a tune-up for this race, Marsh suggested running Minoru in the one-mile Greenham Stakes at Newbury. When Lord Marcus arrived on the course to inspect Minoru before the race, he grumbled: "Looks more like 100 pounds in the Stewards' Cup (a six-furlong handicap) than the Two Thousand Guineas." Just the same, Minoru won, giving five pounds to the odds-on choice, Valens.

It now became clear that with Bayardo far from his best, Minoru might have a chance in the Two Thousand Guineas. In the race itself, Bayardo was quoted at 8-13 and Minoru at 4-1. Minoru won by two lengths, with Bayardo only fourth, beaten five lengths. The result was that Bayardo lost his favoritism for the Derby. The betting on Derby Day was 3-1 Sir Martin, 7-2 Minoru, and 9-2 Bayardo.

Sir Martin, the new candidate, was an American colt, by Ogden—Lady Sterling, by Hanover, bred by John E. Madden at Hamburg Place, Lexington, and sold to an American, Mr. L. Winans, with a view to winning the Derby. Sir Martin had only started once in England but had made a very favorable impression.

(At this point, a very tall tale needs to be told, and as Joe Palmer used to remark, "anyone can believe that who wants to." It was widely known that Col. Hall Walker, the well-known proprietor of the Tully Stud in Ireland and breeder of Minoru, was a strong believer in astrology. He attached great importance to knowing the exact time and place where each of his foals was born. He explained to Lord Marcus Beresford in 1907, that he had a yearling colt that was bound to win the Derby of 1909. The astrological charts indicated that this was a certainty. Hall Walker pointed out what a wonderful thing it would be if King Edward VII could win the Derby with a colt in the royal colors, since no reigning monarch ever had won the race. The subject of the horoscope was Minoru, and Lord Marcus Beresford did lease him, along with four other yearlings.)

Accounts of the Derby of 1909 are conflicting. However, it seems that Sir Martin was leading in the straight, when with no interference from any other runner, he fell (some said that he crossed his legs). Naturally, this caused the jockeys behind him to pull up their horses and to swing to the right to avoid injuring the fallen horse and jockey. One of those who had to pull up and swerve was Danny Maher on Bayardo. In a statement after the race, Maher calculated that this incident had cost Bayardo about sixteen lengths. Minoru, on the other hand, dashed through the opening on the inside near the rail, and saving a lot of ground and not having to be checked, made for the winning post at top speed. There was a hair-raising finish between Minoru and Louviers, with the judge giving the verdict to Minoru by a short head. There was pandemonium on the course. King Edward VII was mobbed by well-wishers, and finally was rescued from the crowd by policemen. At this point, an enthusiastic wag called out: "Don't worry, Teddy, we'll come and bail you out."

The Derby had not hurt Bayardo, and he went to Ascot to win the one-mile, five-furlong Prince of Wales's Stakes by three-quarters of a length, at odds of 2-3. In the ten-furlong Sandringham Foal Stakes at Sandown Park, Louviers, the Derby second, was a 2-1 favorite to beat Bayardo, who started at 4-1. Each colt carried 136 pounds. Evidently, few people believed Maher's tale about the loss of sixteen lengths in the Derby, but Bayardo took up the winning thread again, by one and a half lengths with Louviers unplaced.

Next came the important ten-furlong Eclipse Stakes. Bayardo again was odds-on at 8-17 against three four-year-olds and won easily by two lengths. In the Duchess of York Plate of ten furlongs, Bayardo was 2-11 and again beat Valens by two lengths.

Bayardo now had a rest of about six weeks before the St. Leger in September. Marsh fully expected to win with Minoru, who had never been better. However, when it came to racing, none of the six others could live with Bayardo, who settled his field in about three strides. Bayardo's odds were 10-11, while Minoru's were 7-4. Minoru only won one more race after this, while Bayardo went from strength to strength. Bayardo had such an easy time in the St. Leger that he was pulled out only two days later for the one and a half-mile Doncaster Stakes. Starting at odds of 1-7, Bayardo won as he liked by a length.

At the Newmarket Second October Meeting, Bayardo came out for the Champion Stakes of ten furlongs across the flat, with no turns. His odds were 4-9, and he beat a gallant old battler, Dean Swift, by only a neck. At the same meeting, Bayardo started for the one and three-quarters-mile Lowther Stakes. At odds of 9-100 and with 133 pounds up, he beat White Eagle by one and a half lengths.

Toward the end of a busy season, Bayardo, at odds of 7-100, won the ten-furlong Sandown Foal Stakes easily by a length. At Newmarket again, he won the one and a quarter-mile Limekiln Stakes at odds of 1-33, and in the one and a half-mile Liverpool St. Leger, he beat a solitary opponent at odds of 1-66.

Bayardo had started thirteen times as a three-year-old, something very unusual for a high-class colt in England, then or now. Yet the next year he appeared to be better than ever.

In 1910, as a four-year-old, Bayardo's objective was the Ascot Gold Cup. However, having done well over the winter and being fit early, he was sent after the one and a half-mile Newmarket Biennial Stakes, where he had to carry 140 pounds. As usual, Bayardo was odds on, this time 9-100, and he won by three-quarters of a length. Next he went after the one and a half-mile Chester Vase, where his burden was only 135 pounds. While he was odds-on again, at 1-5, Maher cut it pretty finely over the saucer-shaped Chester track with its very short straight, and Bayardo won by only a head from William the Fourth.

Perhaps for this reason, there was a large field for the Ascot Gold Cup—thirteen runners against a usual field of about six. Sir Martin, who had fallen in the previous year's Derby, had good support for the Gold Cup as he had won the Coronation Cup, beating Louviers and Bachelor's Double. W.K. Vanderbilt's Sea Sick II, a very high-class stayer from France, also was in the field. Ordinarily, Maher kept Bayardo covered up until very late in his races and left him with a tremendous amount of ground to make up very late. This time, however, he let Bayardo loose much earlier, and Bayardo came right away from his horses in a most electrifying way to win easily by four lengths from Sea Sick II. [Sir Martin finished unplaced.]

Bayardo's next engagement was in the one and a half-mile Dullingham Plate, again at the Newmarket Second July Meeting. There he had to carry 148 pounds but won just the same by a length at odds of 1-8. Then a needless disaster was in the offing.

In the Goodwood Cup of two and a half miles, Bayardo, with 136 pounds up, was odds-on at 1-20 in a field of three. One of the others was Magic, a three-year-old, who had only 100 pounds up, and whose price was 20-1. Weight-for-age at this distance and time of year was twenty pounds, so Bayardo's task did not seem to be very serious, considering the modest credentials of Magic. In the race, Fred Rickaby Jr. let Magic stride along and gave something of a breather whenever they met rising ground. Bayardo was kept well back, but every time Rickaby looked back from the top of an up-grade, he found that Maher had gained while going uphill. When Maher finally decided to close seriously, though, it was too late, and Bayardo failed to get up by a neck. This was his last race.

A number of excellent judges of racing in England have told the present writer that they thought Bayardo was the best racehorse seen in England during the twentieth century.

Bayardo was a marked success at stud, but he died early, at eleven. He was stricken by thrombosis. (His skin covers the jockeys' weighing scales at Manton.) He sired three classic winners, including consecutive winners of England's Triple Crown—Gay Crusader (1917) and Gainsborough (1918). Gainsborough, in turn, sired Hyperion.

Bayardo's remaining classic winner was Bayuda, who won the Oaks in 1919, giving the sire his seventh victory in a classic race within three years.

CHAPTER FIFTY

GAINSBOROUGH

L ady James Douglas, the breeder of Gainsborough, picked his name out of a railway guide instead of an art museum, which the name might suggest. She evidently subscribed to the idea that good horses need to have good names, a doctrine that was carried out with further success in the case of Gainsborough's best son, Hyperion (out of Selene).

She was said to have been a lady of strong views, which in the case of Gainsborough at least, served her well. One can afford to have strong views when backed by the Hennessy Brandy fortune. She had bought Rosedrop (by St. Frusquin), the Epsom Oaks winner of 1910, from Sir William Bass, the owner of the great race mare Sceptre.

Doubtless, Lady Douglas was influenced by Alec Taylor, the famous Manton trainer, who had had Bayardo under his care, and who had charge of Bayardo's stud career as well. Rosedrop's first foal was the filly La Tosca, by Bayardo, foaled in 1914, and her next, also by Bayardo, was the bay colt Gainsborough, foaled January 24, 1915. In 1916, when Gainsborough was a yearling, World War I showed no signs of coming to an end in the near future, and racing was much restricted in England. Lady Douglas, therefore, decided to submit her yearling colt to Tattersalls' sale at Newmarket. She placed a reserve of 2,000 guineas on him, and he passed through the ring unsold.

It so happened that the late Joseph E. Widener had sent a representative to buy the colt, but his train from London had been delayed by the fog. He was too late to bid at the auction but offered to meet the reserve price upon his arrival. Lady Douglas then sought the advice of Taylor, who was generally pretty brief in his recommendations. He said: "They have had their chance to buy your colt. Keep him." (Though extremely dignified and reserved, Alec Taylor was not without a grim vein of humor. He once observed to Mr. Tattersall, of the auctioneering firm: "You are in the only good end of the Thoroughbred industry; you are the only people who get something out of a bad horse ..." Pointing to one of the owners training with him, Taylor said: "He is my most patient owner. He has had horses with me for 22 years, and we have never won a race yet.")

The usually lucky Duke of Portland was, for once, unlucky in the case of Gainsborough. He was prepared to buy the colt but received a notice from the Exchequer requesting citizens to use all available funds to buy war loan bonds. This ended any chance that he would buy Gainsborough—or anything else.

With his unquestioned patriotism, especially in that time, the Duke may have been sensitive to Lloyd George's observation about dukes in general: "The cost of maintaining a duke is about the same as the cost of maintaining a battleship."

Rosedrop, the dam of Gainsborough, had been a good racer, as in addition to the Oaks she won the Great Yorkshire Stakes of twelve furlongs. She won another race at three and had won a very minor race at two. Her dam, Rosaline, who never ran, had bred one other winner out of five foals in England. Rosaline was sired by Trenton, a first class Cup horse in Australia, and a good source of stamina. The next dam, Rosalys (by Bend Or) ran at two and three without winning and bred only one winner, a very minor one, out of seven foals. Her dam, Rosa May, did not run, and bred two small winners out of four foals before being exported to France.

The chief feature of Rosedrop's pedigree was stoutness in all its sires, but there was nothing in the line of mares to suggest that anything of the class of Rosedrop was likely to appear. Yet Rosedrop not only appeared, but she bred one better than herself in Gainsborough.

In 1917, when Gainsborough was a two-year-old, the regular racing calendar had been abandoned, but a number of extra meetings were scheduled, to enable breeders and owners to identify the best colts and fillies of the year for future breeding purposes. Thus, the substitute race for the Derby, generally run the first week in June, was run at Newmarket on July 31. On the same day, Gainsborough made his first start, in a division of the five-furlong Thurlow Plate. Unquoted in the betting, he finished fourth in a field of twenty-one. His next start was at the Newmarket Third Extra Meeting on August 28. In the Ramsey Plate of five furlongs and 140 yards, Gainsborough (119 pounds) finished third to Violinist (119), beaten three lengths by the winner and two lengths by Scatwell (129). Rowland Leigh must have used this form as his basis in framing the two-year-old Free Handicap. Scatwell was assigned 126 pounds, with Gainsborough in second place at 122.

In the Ramsey Plate, Gainsborough must have run considerably better than expected as his starting price was 100-14. In his last start of the year, at

Newmarket's Fourth Extra Meeting on September 11, Gainsborough won the Autumn Stakes of six furlongs in a field of twelve. This form was promising as five of the two-year-olds that finished behind Gainsborough had each won its last previous start. Gainsborough won by two lengths, although he was only third favorite, at 5-1.

As a three-year-old, Gainsborough first appeared for the five-furlong Severals Stakes. He was not much expected to win, as his odds were 10-1, and he finished unplaced. Two weeks later, Gainsborough was third favorite for the Two Thousand Guineas at one mile, and he won by one and a half lengths from Somme Kiss. In the New Derby, run that year at Newmarket on June 4, Gainsborough was odds-on, at 8-13, and won by one and a half lengths from Blink, who had been third in the Two Thousand Guineas.

Alec Taylor then showed what he thought of Gainsborough's stamina by starting him against two four-year-olds for the Newmarket Gold Cup of two miles and twenty-four yards. (This was a wartime substitute for the Ascot Gold Cup.) Joe Childs had to declare three pounds overweight, as he could not do less than 113. This did not stop Gainsborough from winning by a half-length from Planet at odds of 2-5.

GAINSBOROUGH	Bayardo, 1906	Bay Ronald, 1893	Hampton, 1872	Lord Clifden, 1860	Newminster / The Slave
				Lady Langden, 1868	Kettledrum / Haricot
			Black Duchess, 1886	Galliard, 1880	**Galopin** / Mavis
				Black Corrie, 1879	Sterling / Wild Dayrell Mare
		Galicia, 1898	**Galopin**, 1872	Vedette, 1854	Voltigeur / Mrs. Ridgway
				Flying Duchess, 1853	The Flying Dutchman / Merope
			Isoletta, 1891	Isonomy, 1875	Sterling / Isola Bella
				Lady Muncaster, 1884	Muncaster / Blue Light
	Rosedrop, 1907	St. Frusquin, 1893	St. Simon, 1881	**Galopin**, 1872	Vedette / Flying Duchess
				St. Angela, 1865	King Tom / Adeline
			Isabel, 1879	Plebeian, 1872	Joskin / Queen Elizabeth
				Parma, 1864	Parmesan / Archeress
		Rosaline, 1901	Trenton, 1881	Musket, 1867	Toxophilite / W. Australian Mare
				Frailty, 1877	Goldsbrough / Flora McIvor
			Rosalys, 1894	Bend Or, 1877	Doncaster / Rouge Rose
				Rosa May, 1887	Rosicrucian / May Queen

THE NATIONAL HORSERACING MUSEUM, NEWMARKET

Gainsborough

stitute for the St. Leger) at Newmarket, Gainsborough was 4-11 in a field of five, which contained three fillies. He won by three lengths from the Oaks winner, My Dear. In the one and three-quarters-mile Jockey Club Stakes, however, with a purse of 5,000 pounds-added, he met his Waterloo. Prince Chimay, whom Gainsborough had beaten easily by seven lengths in the September Stakes, now had a three-pound pull in the weights, but this did not seem sufficient to give him much chance to defeat Gainsborough. Yet, Prince Chimay beat Gainsborough by a length. Since both colts were trained by Taylor at Manton, he was in a position to have a pretty good idea as to their respective merits. Apparently, it never occurred to him that Prince Chimay could, or would, beat Gainsborough, and certainly the odds of 2-11 on Gainsborough showed that many supported his view.

There are three separate possible explanations of this strange upset: (1) Some of the Manton horses were coughing at the time, and it is possible Gainsborough was coming down with the cough. (2) Gainsborough was used to making his own pace, but that time he had been startled by a whip cracking in back of him at the start, and it took Childs some time to get him relaxed and well settled in the race. (3) Jockey Otto Madden, on Prince Chimay, shot his colt out at The

Bushes, a quarter-mile from the winning post and poached several lengths lead on Gainsborough before Childs could set his colt in high gear.

Prince Chimay was exported as a stallion to France, from where his grandson Bois Roussel returned to England to re-establish the sire line of St. Simon, after it had become practically extinct in its country of origin.

The defeat in the Jockey Club ended Gainsborough's racing career in 1918, but he did not begin his stud duties until 1920. The present writer does not know the reason for this lapse of a year but calls attention to the fact that the same lapse occurred in the cases of St. Simon and Hurry On. All three became great stallions, and are entitled to rank as keystones in the structure of the British Thoroughbred.

Gainsborough soon became established as a solid success at stud. From the time his third crop was running in 1925, he never stood lower than eighth on the sire list until 1935. He was leading sire in 1932 and 1933, was once second, twice third, and three times fourth. The average distance of the races won by his produce was 10.29 furlongs, which might have been expected from the stoutness of his own pedigree.

Lady Douglas died before her champion Gainsborough, who lived until he was thirty. She permitted

YEAR	AGE	STS	1ST	2ND	3RD	EARNED*
1917	at 2	3	1	0	1	£ 670
1918	at 3	6	4	1	0	£13,410
Lifetime		9	5	1	1	£14,080
* First-place money only						

him to be used rather freely as a stallion, sometimes putting as many as fifty-six mares to him in one season. It never has been demonstrated to the present writer's knowledge that this practice injures a stallion or the quality of his produce. Indeed, even more strenuous seasons were given to Lexington. For a seven-year period beginning at age nine (1859), he covered an average of seventy-two mares per season to average forty-one reported foals a year. In the midst of this program, Lexington sired the cracks Kentucky, Asteroid, and Norfolk, all in the same crop. John E. Madden bred Star Shoot to ninety mares in one season when the horse was fifteen, to produce fifty-two named foals, of which thirty-six were winners and twelve were stakes winners. Hambletonian, the foundation sire of the trotting breed, was credited with 105 foals in one year, but it has been reported that he was bred pretty much throughout the year.

On the other hand, Major Foxhall Daingerfield, at the time he was breeding so many great racers at Castleton (Commando, Sysonby, Colin, Celt, Peter Pan, Sweep, etc.) permitted very few mares to be bred to any one stallion. Domino left only sixteen foals in two seasons, and Commando only twenty-seven in three seasons and a fraction.

There does not seem to be any correlation between the reproductive inclination of stallions and the quality of their stock. Both The Tetrarch and Blandford were reluctant dragons in the breeding shed, but both were excellent sires.

A photo of Gainsborough as a yearling shows him to have been a heavy-bodied colt with long pasterns. A photo of him as a two-year-old shows a medium-sized colt of good quality and constitution but somewhat immature for his age. A photo of him as a three-year-old, taken with Joe Childs in the saddle and a decisive-looking Lady James Douglas at his head, shows a well-developed, muscular colt of medium size but somewhat ewe-necked. This peculiarity of the neck frequently goes with a high carriage of the head, and those characteristics were even more marked in Gainsborough's son, Hyperion. By the time Gainsborough was photographed as a mature stallion he had developed a crest, but the high carriage of the head remained.

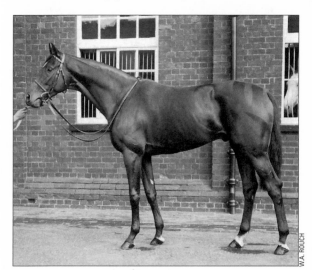

Singapore

Though he won the wartime Triple Crown and Gold Cup, Gainsborough lacked the devastating speed of his sire, Bayardo, and was ranked below Bayardo as a racer by Taylor, who trained both of them. He also was ranked by Taylor as being below Gay Crusader, a Bayardo colt who won the English Triple Crown the year before Gainsborough won it. (Gay Crusader was not a major success at stud, but his name lives today, through daughters, in the pedigrees of Princequillo and Djebel.)

Gainsborough's best son, Hyperion, won the Derby and St. Leger in 1933 and became a great stallion. Gainsborough's other classic winners were Solario (St. Leger of 1925 and Ascot Gold Cup of 1926), Singapore (St. Leger of 1930), and Orwell (Two Thousand Guineas of 1932).

CHAPTER FIFTY-ONE

SOLARIO

Solario was the first high-class horse sired by Gainsborough and was a result of his second season at stud. He was bred by Lord Dunraven at his Fort Union Stud, Adare, County Limerick, in Ireland. As a yearling, Solario was sold at Doncaster to Sir John Rutherford for 3,500 guineas and was the fourth-highest priced yearling in the sale. The second-highest priced yearling was Manna (Phalaris—Waffles, by Buckwheat) at 6,000 guineas; two years later Manna defeated Solario in the Derby.

Solario's dam was Sun Worship (1912) by the very good sprinter Sundridge. Sun Worship ran three times as a two-year-old without winning. Her first foal, however, was the gelding, Broken Faith, who at nine won the Goodwood Stakes of two and three-eighths miles. The second foal, Voleuse, was bought by the Aga Khan, and won three of her five races as a two-year-old. After being barren a year, Sun Worship foaled Solario in 1922.

Sun Worship was out of Doctrine (by Ayrshire), who had been a good racer, winning more than 5,000 pounds. Her winning races included the Coronation Stakes at Ascot, but she bred only one minor winner. The next dam, Axiom, did not win in nine starts at two and three but was one of Electric Light's twelve foals, of which nine were winners.

This was a branch of the No. 26 family in Bruce Lowe's figures, and at that time there was a strong prejudice against that family in England. In buying Solario, Sir John Rutherford either did not know this or chose to ignore it in favor of a fine individual.

As a two-year-old, Solario made his first appearance at Ascot, in the Chesham Stakes, one of the less-important juvenile fixtures there. In a field of four, Solario was 3-1 but could only finish third, beaten eight lengths. Two weeks later, in a field of nine for the Exeter Stakes at Newmarket, Solario turned one up for the bookmakers when he won by a head at odds of 100-8. The second horse, Chang-chia, was nothing wonderful, so the form indicated Solario was some way below

W.A. ROUCH

Solario

first class at that stage.

Then came a more revealing test. In October at Newmarket, Solario came out for the Middle Park Stakes, called the two-year-old Derby. The favorite in a field of eight was Picaroon at 1-2, with Manna second favorite at 9-2. Solario was unquoted in the betting. After losing a little ground at the start, Solario came on to beat Manna by a neck for second place and finished one and one-half lengths behind Picaroon. These undoubtedly were the best two-year-old colts of 1924. In the Free Handicap they were weighted: Picaroon 127 pounds, Solario 120, and Manna 118.[1]

In the spring, as a three-year-old, Solario's first race was the one-mile Craven Stakes at Newmarket. He met his Middle Park rival, Picaroon, who was odds-on at 2-5. Solario was 8-1 in a field of six and finished third to Picaroon, beaten by three and one-half lengths.

Soon after that race something happened that greatly benefited Solario—Picaroon fell ill and could not run until the autumn.

Solario's next race was the Two Thousand Guineas over one mile at Newmarket. Owing to the absence of Picaroon, Solario was a 7-1 second favorite in a field of thirteen. Manna had not been out as a three-year-old and started at 100-8. However, he was good and fit and was allowed to stride along with the pace all the way. Manna won easily by two lengths, and Solario was fourth, beaten by more than ten lengths.

Neither Manna nor Solario ran again before the Derby on May 27. Manna was only third favorite at 9-1 while Solario was 10-1. Steve Donoghue let Manna go with the pace again, and he came home alone by eight lengths. The day was wet (the present writer was there); the British refer to such weather as "unsettled." One of the starting tapes, which were wet, broke when the start was given and became entangled in Solario's legs. Jockey Michael Beary expected a recall, but there was none, so Solario was left by a good many lengths. He made up a lot of ground to finish fourth. Judged by subsequent form, Solario must have had a good chance in the Derby but for this accident.

We must now go back to the yearling sales at Doncaster. Before the sales, Fred Darling, the Beckhampton trainer, had received a cable from H.E. Morriss, a bullion broker in Shanghai. It simply read: "Buy me the best yearling at Doncaster."

Darling must have been torn between Manna and Solario, for George Lambton had been a bidder on Solario (for the Aga Khan) up to 3,000 guineas. As the Aga

		Bay Ronald, 1893	**Hampton**, 1872	Lord Clifden Lady Langden
	Bayardo, 1906		Black Duchess, 1886	Galliard Black Corrie
		Galicia, 1898	**Galopin**, 1872	Vedette Flying Duchess
Gainsborough, 1915			Isoletta, 1891	Isonomy Lady Muncaster
		St. Frusquin, 1893	St. Simon, 1881	**Galopin** St. Angela
	Rosedrop, 1907		Isabel, 1879	Plebeian Parma
		Rosaline, 1901	*Trenton, 1881	Musket Frailty
SOLARIO			Rosalys, 1894	Bend Or Rosa May
		Amphion, 1886	Rosebery, 1872	Speculum Ladylike
	Sundridge, 1898		Suicide, 1876	Hermit The Ratcatcher's daughter
		Sierra, 1889	Springfield, 1873	St. Albans Viridis
Sun Worship, 1912			Sanda, 1878	Wenlock Sandal
		Ayrshire, 1885	**Hampton**, 1872	Lord Clifden Lady Langden
	Doctrine, 1899		Atalanta, 1878	**Galopin** Feronia
		Axiom, 1888	Peter, 1876	Hermit Lady Masham
			Electric Light, 1876	Sterling Beachy Head

Khan was interested mainly in fillies, Solario must have been a very tempting colt for a good judge like Darling—in any case, his choice fell on Manna.

When Morriss realized that Manna was a very live proposition for the Derby, he backed Manna for very large sums, and he also was reported to have bought the Calcutta Sweepstakes ticket on Manna from the ticket holder. With luck really running for Morriss, nothing seemingly could go wrong. First, the best colt, Picaroon was shelved due to illness; then, the second-best colt, Solario, got tangled up in the tapes and took no real part in the Derby. It has been observed by many a bore: "It's better to be born lucky, than ..." Manna never won another race.

Solario's next race after the Derby was the one and one-half-mile Ascot Derby, in which he carried 122 pounds to Manna's 132. The betting was Manna at 8-13 and Solario 11-4. That time Solario won, defeating Manna by two lengths. Strictly on form, that made Manna somewhat the better colt.[2]

YEAR	AGE	STS	1ST	2ND	3RD	EARNED*
1924	at 2	3	1	1	1	£ 1,105
1925	at 3	6	3	0	1	£14,585
1926	at 4	3	2	0	0	£ 5,245
Lifetime		12	6	1	2	£20,935

* First-place money only

At the Newmarket First July Meeting, Solario came out for the one and one-half mile Princess of Wales's Stakes. Ridden that time by Joe Childs instead of Beary, Solario won again, by one and one-half lengths at odds of 11-4. (Third in the race was St. Germans, later the sire of Twenty Grand.)

In the St. Leger in September, over a distance of one mile, six furlongs, and 132 yards, Solario and Manna were joint favorites at 9-2. Manna had come through a searching test of his stamina successfully at Beckhampton and seemed very fit and well. Solario, according to Reg Day, had made abnormal improvement. A good many years ago, Day told the writer that he had some doubts concerning Solario's speed but not his stamina. To resolve these doubts, he put the best five-furlong sprinters he had in the last part of Solario's gallop before the St. Leger. To his astonishment, Solario went right away from his sprinters. By St. Leger time, according to Day, Solario was a great horse.

The St. Leger itself was anticlimactic. Solario won easily enough, and Manna pulled up lame after the race, never to run again. Picaroon finished fourth, but he later won the Champion Stakes of ten furlongs, beating Pharos.

As a four-year-old, Solario came to his full powers. He first won the one and one-half-mile Coronation Cup at Epsom by fifteen lengths and then carried off the Ascot Gold Cup easily by three lengths. At the time of his victory in the

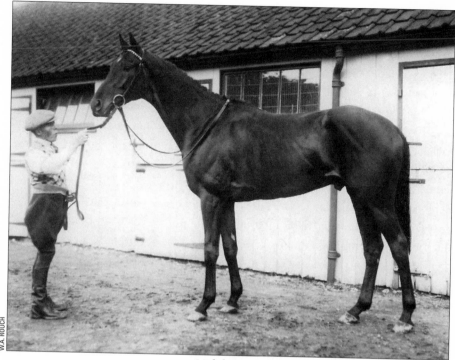

W.A. ROUCH

Mid-day Sun

Coronation Cup, J.B. Joel offered 75,000 pounds for Solario, and the Aga Khan topped this with an offer of 100,000 pounds. Sir John kept his horse.

In the autumn at Newmarket, Solario contested the one and three-quarters-mile Jockey Club Stakes. Carrying 136 pounds, he went under by a neck to Foxlaw (130), then was disqualified for bumping, and placed last. On that minor note of disappointment, Solario's Turf career was closed.

Solario went to stud at a fee of 500 guineas, which remained unchanged until his death in 1945. In 1932 Sir John Rutherford died, and Solario was sold at public auction. His arrival in the sale ring was much anticipated, and the thought that he would fetch a record price for a stallion at public sale soon was realized. Lord Glanely had put together a syndicate to buy the horse for as much as 40,000 guineas, but when that figure was reached, he and the syndicate chairman, Lord Rosebery, determined to keep going to avoid losing the horse to America. Eventually, they defeated American Frank Hills and won the prize—for 47,000 guineas.

As a sire, Solario was consistent, ranking in the top ten on the leading sire list on twelve occasions. He led the list in 1937 and was second twice and third twice. He also was the leading broodmare sire in 1943.[3] He died at the age of twenty-three, on March 15, 1945, three months before the death of his sire, Gainsborough.

The average distance of races won by Solario's get was 10.90 furlongs, somewhat too long to suit the American racing program. Though he sired many good colts, Solario did not have the luck to sire one that bred on with first-class success. Hence his male line did not come close to that of his paternal half brother, Hyperion. Solario's name, however, is found in many pedigrees (Royal Charger's, for instance) through his daughters.

Solario sired two Derby winners and one Oaks winner. Mid-day Sun won the Derby in 1937, and Straight Deal took it in 1943. The same year Mid-day Sun won at Epsom, a Solario filly, Exhibitionist, won both the One Thousand Guineas and the Oaks, giving the sire three classics in the year he led the sire list. In addition, Mid-day Sun placed in the Two Thousand Guineas and St. Leger, Straight Deal placed in the St. Leger, and two other Solario colts, Orpen and Dastur, were placed in all three of the colt classics in their years.

Physically, Solario was an exceptionally handsome colt, bigger than his sire, and he had very high quality. He was strong and sound and had the long shoulder and high withers that characterize most stayers.

End Notes:

1. All the colts were weighted behind the filly Saucy Sue, who was assigned the top weight of 128 pounds.

2. Manna finished third, second going to Sparus.

3. One source shows that Solario also led the broodmare sire list in 1949 and 1950.

CHAPTER FIFTY-TWO

HYPERION

When Gondolette was bought in 1912 by Lord Derby's stud from Colonel Hall Walker, the main objective undoubtedly was to secure a means of inbreeding to Pilgrimage, who had won the One Thousand and Two Thousand Guineas and apparently was winning the Oaks when she broke down. Pilgrimage's performance at stud had been equally distinguished, for she had been the dam of Jeddah (Derby at odds of 100-1) and Canterbury Pilgrim, the latter winner of the Oaks for Lord Derby. Canterbury Pilgrim also was the dam of Swynford and Chaucer, who in 1912 were the two leading sires in the Derby stud.

The scheme of inbreeding to a mare, instead of the more usual pattern of inbreeding to a stallion, was successful beyond reasonable expectations. Gondolette herself had been a modest performer on the Turf, winning three very small races as a two-year-old and a total of 395 pounds, and nothing thereafter from fifteen starts at three and four.

Hall Walker might not have sold her in 1912 had he suspected her merits as a broodmare. She became the dam of Great Sport (1910), a fair two-year-old who was beaten narrowly in the bumping of the disqualification Derby in 1913. She also produced Let Fly (1912), who was a very good two-year-old in 1914, when he won the New Stakes, Exeter Stakes, and Dewhurst Plate; Let Fly later was second in the Derby and won the Champion Stakes.

The desired cross of Pilgrimage was provided by Gondolette's sire, Loved One, a son of Pilgrimage who had won only 1,847 pounds. When this cross was tried in the Derby stud, the results were Ferry (by Swynford, winner of the One Thousand Guineas) and Sansovino (by Swynford, winner of the Derby). These each gave an inbreeding of two free generations to Pilgrimage. That the best results of this inbreeding to Pilgrimage came through a channel that the Derby stud presumably did not want is something ironic. When she was purchased in 1912, Gondolette was in foal to Minoru, a Hall Walker-owned stallion that the Derby stud never patronized before or afterward.

In 1913 Gondolette foaled a Minoru filly named Serenissima. By the time she was a two-year-old, World War I was in progress and racing opportunities were restricted, but the filly ran six times in 1915—without winning. In 1916 Serenissima won two of nine races, one of these over one and a half miles at Lingfield.

When Serenissima went to stud, the program of inbreeding to Pilgrimage was started. Serenissima's second foal was Selene (1919), by Chaucer (grandson of Pilgrimage). This mating gave an inbreeding to Pilgrimage with three free generations. Selene was deemed too small to be kept in the classics. This was a very costly exercise in judgment, for she was a first-class racer, winning eight out of eleven races as a two-year-old, including the championship race for juvenile fillies, the Cheveley Park Stakes. At three, she again won eight of eleven races, including the Park Hill Stakes, run over the St. Leger course at Doncaster, one mile, six furlongs, 132 yards. Some handicappers gave it as their opinion that Selene was good enough to have won the Derby of 1922 had she been entered.

In the next year after foaling Selene, Serenissima produced Tranquil (by Swynford, like Chaucer a grandson of Pilgrimage). Tranquil was a big, strong, coarse filly that was kept engaged in the classics. She duly obliged by winning the One Thousand Guineas and the St. Leger, as well as the Jockey Club Cup of two and a quarter miles. It is something of a commentary on British training methods that when the going grew hard at Newmarket in June of 1923, George Lambton asked his friend, Charles Morton—who trained at Wantage in Berkshire, where the going was good—if he would take Tranquil to prepare her for the St. Leger. Morton agreed, and a considerable time went by without any word as to a preliminary race for Tranquil before the St. Leger. Lambton naturally grew uneasy, and called Morton:

"Are you going to give Tranquil a race before the St. Leger?"

"No."

"Are you planning to try her before the St. Leger?"

"No."

"Do you believe she will be fit for the race?"

"Yes."

"Good-bye."

Tranquil duly won the St. Leger handily from Papyrus, the Derby winner. In 1926, Serenissima produced Bosworth, by Son-in-Law (without the aid of inbreeding to Pilgrimage), and this colt won the Ascot Gold Cup and was beaten narrowly for the St. Leger.

When Serenissima's Selene went to stud, her record was almost as remarkable as it had been on the Turf. Her foaling record:

1. Sickle (1924), by Phalaris. He was one of the best two-year-olds of his year, winning three of his seven races. As a three-year-old, he was third in the Two Thousand Guineas. Sickle was sold to the United States where he twice became leading sire, as well as becoming the great-grandsire of Native Dancer.

2. Pharamond II (1925), by Phalaris. He was a good two-year-old, winning the Middle Park Stakes, and also winning at one and three-eighths miles as a three-year-old. He also was sold to the United States, where he sired Menow and became the grandsire of Tom Fool.

3. Hunter's Moon (1926), by Hurry On. A good winner, he was just short of classic form (fourth in the Derby). He was exported to Argentina, where he became a very good sire.

4. Salamis (1927), by Phalaris. No good. Placed at three.

5. Guiscard (1928), by Gay Crusader. Fair winner at four.

Then came Hyperion. Selene's 1930 colt by Gainsborough.

Hyperion had a very interesting pedigree. His sire, Gainsborough, was a Triple Crown and Gold Cup winner who already was established as a sire of the first

				Lord Clifden
			Hampton, 1872	Lady Langden
		Bay Ronald, 1893		Galliard
			Black Duchess, 1886	Black Corrie
	Bayardo, 1906			Vedette
			Galopin, 1872	Flying Duchess
		Galicia, 1898		Isonomy
Gainsborough, 1915			Isoletta, 1891	Lady Muncaster
			St. Simon, 1881	**Galopin**
		St. Frusquin, 1893		St. Angela
			Isabel, 1879	Plebeian
	Rosedrop, 1907			Parma
			Trenton, 1881	Musket
		Rosaline, 1901		Frailty
HYPERION			Rosalys, 1894	Bend Or
				Rosa May
			Galopin, 1872	Vedette
		St. Simon, 1881		Flying Duchess
			St. Angela, 1865	King Tom
	Chaucer, 1900			Adeline
			Tristan, 1878	Hermit
		Canterbury Pilgrim, 1893		Thrift
Selene, 1919			Pilgrimage, 1875	The Palmer
				Lady Audley
			Cyllene, 1895	Bona Vista
		Minoru, 1906		Arcadia
			Mother Siegel, 1897	Friar's Balsam
	Serenissima, 1913			Galopin Mare
			Loved One, 1883	See Saw
		Gondolette, 1902		Pilgrimage
			Dongola, 1883	Doncaster
				Douranee

W.W. ROUCH & CO.

Hyperion

rank. The dam, Selene, was the best female racer of her year, out of a mare who had produced another classic-winning filly, but beyond this the paternal grand-sire, Bayardo, was inbred with two free generations to Galopin, while Selene was inbred with three free generations to Pilgrimage (crossing inbred strains).

(It will be noticed that Hyperion's pedigree gives an inbreeding to St. Simon with three free generations, but it also should be noticed that Hyperion bore no resemblance to St. Simon, who was a leggy, short-bodied horse, bay or brown in color, with almost no white on him, and who also was a pure dominant for bay or brown in his produce. Hyperion was a very short-legged horse with a long body, chestnut in color, with four white feet. St. Simon was a very highly strung colt who was a profuse sweater in training; Hyperion was as calm as possible, and it was very difficult to get him to sweat at all.

Of Hyperion's fourteen nearest ancestors, only two were chestnut—Canterbury Pilgrim [great-granddam] and Rosedrop [granddam]. It seems possible that Hyperion's markings were inherited from Rosedrop, whose photograph shows three white feet and just a suspicion—owing to the faulty lighting that may have prevailed—of white on the fourth foot.)

Flawless as this pattern may appear on paper, it very nearly failed in fact. To begin with, Selene failed to come in season in the spring of 1929, and she nearly was sent home without being covered by Gainsborough. Finally, she was covered in May; Hyperion was foaled on April 18, 1930.

Selene was a small mare, sired by a small horse in Chaucer, who had to wear a set of thick shoes to stand 15 hands in his early days in training. Gainsborough was only medium-sized, and his sire, Bayardo, often was described as less than medium-sized. All this lack of size close up in his pedigree caught up with Hyperion, who was very small as a foal and yearling; in fact, a special feed trough was constructed for him since he could not eat out of the standard-height troughs. (Lord Derby was reported to have been so discouraged with Hyperion's failure to grow as a yearling, that he suggested that it would be best to castrate him!)

Whatever Hyperion lacked in height he made up in strength of body. A photograph of him as a two-year-old shows a short-legged, light-boned colt, with the muscling of a wrestler, but also very high-headed and ewe-necked.

YEAR	AGE	STS	1ST	2ND	3RD	EARNED*
1932	at 2	5	3	0	1	£ 5,105
1933	at 3	4	4	0	0	£23,179
1934	at 4	4	2	1	1	£ 1,225
Lifetime		13	9	1	2	£29,509
* First-place money only						

Knowing that Hyperion required a tremendous lot of work to get him fit, George Lambton sent him to Doncaster in May for experience, and as a pipe-opener before Ascot in June. Hyperion was not expected, and he was unquoted in the betting. He finished fourth in a field of nineteen; he was only beaten once more until he was a four-year-old.

At Ascot in the important New Stakes of five furlongs, Hyperion was second favorite at 6-1 in a field of twenty-two. The only one very seriously backed to beat him was the filly Nun's Veil, at 6-4. Hyperion broke the time record for the course in beating Nun's Veil three lengths. For a colt with a staying pedigree to do such gave good warning that he was something out of the ordinary.

Then Hyperion went to Goodwood to dead-heat with Marshall Field's filly Stairway in the Prince of Wales's Stakes, a result that must have been disappointing since Hyperion was at odds-on at 4-6.

At the Newmarket First October Meeting, Hyperion was only third in a four-horse field for the Boscawen Stakes, won by Manitoba at 4-6. Hyperion's price was 5-2. In the seven-furlong Dewhurst Stakes at the Second October Meeting in heavy going, however, Hyperion in a six-horse field was 100-7 and won convincingly by two lengths. The best of his rivals—as subsequent events were to reveal—

was Felicitation, who finished last.

The Jockey Club handicapper could not have been too impressed with the two-year-old colts that year, for he put three fillies at the top of the handicap before listing Manitoba at 127 pounds, Hyperion at 126, and Felicitation at 123. Generally, when a group of fillies appears at the top of the two-year-old handicap, the colts are believed to be a poor lot, but in this case, both Hyperion and Felicitation turned out to be first-class racers.

When spring came in 1933, Hyperion was still not very big—15 hands, 1 1/2 inches, and he looked even smaller owing to the size and length of his body. He had not been entered in the Two Thousand Guineas, so the first race selected for him was the one and a half-mile Chester Vase in May. George Lambton complained that he did not know what to make of Hyperion, who was so lazy that he showed nothing at home.

After Hyperion had won the Chester Vase by two lengths against opposition that was not very formidable, his supporters naturally felt encouraged. Still, Lambton kept inquiring from his jockey, Tommy Weston, how in the world he expected Hyperion to win the Derby when every time they worked together, Scarlet Tiger (123 pounds on the Free Handicap) would beat him ten lengths and give him ten pounds as well.

"Just the same," Weston would reply, "Hyperion will win the Derby. You'll see!"

Starting favorite at 6-1 in a field of twenty-four, Hyperion won by four lengths, and most observers thought the judge was looking at something else, for Hyperion was the easiest winner in some time. King Salmon was second and Statesman third. Perhaps the most surprising thing about the race was that Hyperion made a new record for the race, winning in 2:34.

Two weeks after his frolic in the Derby, Hyperion was at Ascot for the one and five-eighths-mile Prince of Wales's Stakes. There were only six starters, and Hyperion was set to carry 131 pounds. Despite the weight, he was favored at 1-2. Second favorite was the Aga Khan's Shamsuddin (115) at 6-1. Hyperion beat Shamsuddin easily by two lengths.

Hyperion was not out again until the St. Leger, which he won easily enough by three lengths from Felicitation, with Scarlet Tiger third and King Salmon fourth. It had been the plan to give Hyperion a race before the St. Leger, but this had not been possible, owing to his having slipped his patella bone twice in training. (This corresponds to the knee cap in human beings.)

The present writer asked Lambton how it was possible to present a colt like Hyperion fit to run for a classic race like the St. Leger over a distance of nearly fif-

Pensive in the Kentucky Derby winner's circle

teen furlongs without giving him a tune-up race in public first. After all, Hyperion had not had a race in public for almost three months.

The reply was: "When I am unable, or for any reason find it inadvisable, to give a colt a preliminary race, I try to time the colt's preparation so that he will be fit about ten days before the important race. After that, provided he is fit, I do no serious work with him beyond keeping his wind clear. This can be done with short, sharp bursts, for not more than three to five furlongs. In that way, the colt comes up to the race feeling fresh and well."

The present writer is not a trainer, but records this observation from one who was a very great trainer.

The famous John Porter of Kingsclere made a practice not to run a colt between Ascot in June, and the St. Leger in September. He expressed the view that it was impossible to keep a colt at concert pitch over this length of time and that it was better to let a colt have a slack time after Ascot and then bring him up to his best again.

The St. Leger was Hyperion's last race as a three-year-old, and at the end of 1933 George Lambton ended his connection as trainer for the Derby family, which had lasted nearly forty years. This was done because Lord Derby feared that the strain of training such a big stable was becoming too much for a man of Lambton's age

(73), and offered to settle 100,000 pounds on him for life. Lambton simply said: "I don't want your money," and walked out of the room. Lambton continued as a public trainer until his death in 1945, and his breach with Lord Derby was fully healed.

He was succeeded as trainer for the Derby stable by Colledge Leader, a member of a well-known family of Newmarket trainers. Lambton told Leader that with his robust constitution and lazy ways, Hyperion would "fill up" much more quickly than most horses and required more frequent work than nearly anything else Lambton had trained.

When Hyperion began his four-year-old campaign in the ten-furlong March Stakes, he had 138 pounds up but still was odds-on at 4-10. He won, but only by a neck from Angelico (118) with Felicitation third, three lengths back, while in receipt of six pounds.

Next, Hyperion won the one and a half-mile Burwell Stakes at Newmarket by three-quarters of a length from King Salmon at level weights of 136 each. This represented a decline in form, compared with Hyperion's Derby and St. Leger victories over King Salmon, which had each been achieved by an easy margin of four lengths or more. Taking the three-length margin over Felicitation in the St. Leger at face value, this more than three-length change in form with King Salmon seemed to put Hyperion in danger of defeat by Felicitation in the two and a half-mile Ascot Gold Cup. On the basis of their form in the one and a quarter-mile March Stakes, Hyperion was still three lengths and six pounds the better, but over twice the distance this might not hold true.

By the day of the Gold Cup, this danger seemed increased because Felicitation won the Churchill Stakes of two miles the day before in a canter by ten lengths. Furthermore, it was known that Frank Butters, his trainer, considered Felicitation the best colt, over a long distance, he had ever trained. The betting on the race was Hyperion 8-11, Felicitation 9-2, Mate (an American colt) 8-1, and Thor II, the French Derby winner of the previous year, 100-7.

Heavy rain had fallen from noon until after one o'clock and the going was very soft. The royal procession up the course had to be canceled.

This soft going put an additional premium on stamina, which Gordon Richards, on Felicitation, was not slow to exploit. He let his mount stride along, so that by the time the Swinley Bottom had been reached, Felicitation was ten lengths in front of the field. As they came into the stretch, Hyperion made an effort to challenge Felicitation, but when Weston, on Hyperion, saw there was no chance of getting on terms with Felicitation, he dropped his hands, and Thor II passed

Hyperion near the finish to take second place. Felicitation won by eight lengths from Thor II, with Hyperion another one and a half lengths back, in third.

What was the explanation? Was it the soft going? Was it the superior stamina of Felicitation? Was it the superior riding tactics of Richards, which put the burden on the others of making up the lengths in soft going over the last half-mile of Ascot, which is uphill? Trainer Leader and jockey Weston each blamed the other. Recriminations were heated, and it later ended with the termination of Weston's contract as stable jockey.

Whatever it was, the defeat was stunning, and left Lord Derby in a quandary as to the best program for Hyperion—retire him now, or give him one more race and try to leave the Turf with a victory? The latter course was decided on, and the race chosen for Hyperion's farewell was the one and a half-mile Dullingham Stakes at Newmarket. Hyperion (142 pounds) had only one opponent, Lord Rosebery's three-year-old Caithness (113 pounds). The betting was 2-11 Hyperion. Weston, on Hyperion, allowed that master judge of pace, Harry Wragg, to make the running on Caithness. Weston delivered his challenge so that Hyperion was leading by about a length in The Dip, an eighth-mile from home, and most observers expected Hyperion to come right away from Caithness up the hill. Wragg, famous for his late efforts as the "head waiter," kept pace with Hyperion and delayed his effort until the last fifty yards. Wragg sat down to ride in earnest, and Caithness first drew level and then got his head in front in the last stride.

On the three-year-old Free Handicap, Caithness was ranked sixteen pounds below the topweight, Windsor Lad. Since Hyperion was giving sixteen pounds more than weight for age and was beaten a short head, his performance was just about up to full classic standard. Incidentally, Windsor Lad—worked out through this handicap to be at about the same rating as Hyperion—recorded a time in the Derby at Epsom identical with that made by Hyperion the year before, 2:34.

Trainer Lambton, however, did not rank Hyperion as a racehorse as highly as Swynford, whom he also had trained. He said to the present writer and to others: "I knew to a pound how good Hyperion was. I never knew how good Swynford was." There is also some question if Lambton regarded Hyperion as being quite up to the class of Fairway.

When Hyperion went to stud, he carried with him credentials unequaled by any other British-bred horse in the twentieth century. In performance, he had won the Derby easily in record time, also had won the St. Leger easily, and as a two-year-old he had set a new record for the New Stakes at Ascot over five furlongs.

In pedigree: (1) His dam was the best racing filly of her time and was already

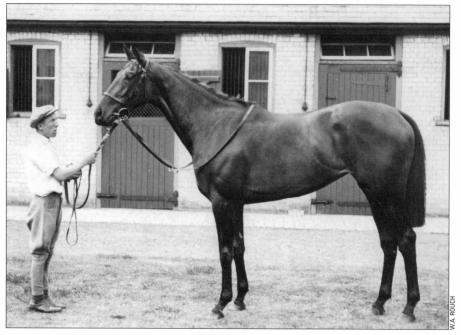

W.A. ROUCH

Sun Chariot

proved to be a first-class broodmare. The next two dams also were first-class broodmares.

(2) His sire was a Triple Crown winner, a Gold Cup winner, and a first-class sire. His grandsire was an even better racer and the sire of two Triple Crown winners in successive years. (Not even St. Simon could accomplish that.)

The only thing really against him was his lack of height and the absurd prejudice against horses with four white feet.

Hyperion made the best stud record of any other stallion of the twentieth century in England, Ireland, or France.[1] He was the leading sire in England six times—1940–42, 1945, 1946, and 1954. For purposes of comparison, Nearco was leading sire twice, Blandford three times, Fairway four times, and Pharos three times (twice in France). Hyperion was among the top ten leading sires sixteen times, a record surpassed only by St. Simon. Hyperion also was the leading broodmare sire four times.

At the conclusion of this book, some comparisons will be made on the overall records of the greatest sires. Suffice it to say that these comparisons show that Hyperion was a distinctly better sire than was Nearco, whose blood currently is at the crest of fashion.

Hyperion's best sons included:

Heliopolis, third in the 1939 Epsom Derby and twice the leading sire in the United States; Alibhai, unraced sire of fifty-four stakes winners; Khaled, unbeaten two-year-old leader and sire of sixty-one stakes winners; Owen Tudor, winner of the 1941 Epsom Derby; Pensive, winner of the 1944 Kentucky Derby; Gulf Stream, leading two-year-old, runner-up in the 1946 Epsom Derby, and a major sire in Argentina; Aureole, winner of the 1954 King George VI and Queen Elizabeth Stakes and a leading sire in England; Aldis Lamp, fourteen times the leading sire in Belgium; and Sun Castle, winner of the 1941 St. Leger.

Heliopolis, Khaled, and Alibhai were major influences on American breeding.

Hyperion's fillies included the brilliant Sun Chariot, who in 1942 won the One Thousand Guineas and Oaks and then beat colts in the St. Leger; Godiva, winner of the 1940 One Thousand Guineas and Oaks; Sun Stream, winner of the same double in 1945; Hycilla, winner of the 1944 Oaks; Hypericum, winner of the 1946 One Thousand Guineas, and Opaline II, topweight on the two-year-old Free Handicap in 1960.

Hyperion thus had seven English classic winners, which won eleven classic races.

Hyperion lived to the age of thirty, as his sire (Gainsborough) had before him, and as did another male-line ancestor, Touchstone, a century before. Hyperion was put down on December 9, 1960, at Lord Derby's Woodland Stud, Newmarket.

End Notes:

1. In the 1990s Sadler's Wells led the English/Irish sire list every year except 1991. Sadler's Wells continued to dominate into the twenty-first century.

CHAPTER FIFTY-THREE

HELIOPOLIS

Heliopolis was foaled in 1936 and was in the first crop of foals sired by Derby and St. Leger winner Hyperion, and he was the best of the crop both as a two-year-old and three-year-old. Nevertheless, on the Free Handicaps, he was rated ten pounds from the top as a two-year-old, with ten horses ranked above him, and eleven pounds from the top as a three-year-old, with three ranked above him.

Still, Heliopolis was typical of the sort of racers that were exported from England before World War II to become very successful sires in other countries, particularly when they were endowed with good, solid pedigrees of high credentials.

Heliopolis' sire, Hyperion, had about as good a pedigree as could be found, and he also had been a double-classic winner. Heliopolis' dam, Drift, had been a winner at two and won three races as a three-year-old, they including the Caledonian Hunt Cup at a distance of one and five-eighths miles. At stud, Drift already had produced the Fairway filly Tide-way, who won the One Thousand Guineas.

The next dam, Santa Cruz, had won four times as a three-year-old and was a half sister to the sires Bridge of Canny and Bridge of Earn. Her dam, Santa Brigida (by St. Simon) was a high-class race mare (Yorkshire Oaks, etc.), and the fourth dam, Bridget, was a full sister to Derby and St. Leger winner Melton.

Thus, Heliopolis had for his first three dams mares each of which had been high-class winners as well as producers of high-class winners. In addition, his pedigree showed inbreeding with three free generations to Oaks winner Canterbury Pilgrim, she the dam of Swynford and Chaucer. This pattern of inbreeding to outstanding mares, rather than the usual inbreeding to stallions, occurred repeatedly in the pedigrees of Lord Derby's stud.

Offsetting these regal credentials to some extent was the fact that Heliopolis was not a very attractive animal. Like many of the offspring of Hyperion, he had a plain head. The racing columnist for *The Sporting and Dramatic News* observed in the paddock before the Derby: "Heliopolis looks dipped in the back, and although

SKEETS MEADORS

Heliopolis

better ribbed up than Dhoti (afterward a successful sire in Australia), seems made in two pieces. He is not a bad sort, though. The two-piece effect is accentuated by his big quarters and may be due to the fact that he has not yet muscled over his loins." (The writer's impression of Heliopolis was that he also was straight shouldered, as was Hyperion.)

Heliopolis first came out as a two-year-old on July 14 in the five-furlong Chesterfield Stakes at the second July meeting at Newmarket. He was among the 20-1 field, so could have occasioned little disappointment when he finished unplaced. At the York meeting in August, he ran better than expected, finishing second to Panorama by a half-length in the five-furlong Prince of Wales's Plate. Panorama was odds-on at 1-8, while winning his sixth successive race, and he gave 20-1 Heliopolis thirteen pounds. (Panorama, incidentally, became a renowned sire of sprinters.)

At the Doncaster St. Leger meeting in September, Heliopolis came out for the traditional Champagne Stakes of six furlongs, in which all the runners carried level weights (with sex allowance). Unfortunately for Heliopolis, Panorama again was in the field, and with a thirteen-pound shift in the weights in favor of

Panorama, Heliopolis obviously did not have much chance. Panorama again was odds-on, at 8-13, while Heliopolis was 7-1. Heliopolis swerved badly at the start, and Panorama won again.

The important Imperial Produce Stakes on October 1 at Kempton Park drew a field of nineteen, and the first three at the finish were sons of Hyperion, each with 113 pounds up. Heliopolis (7-2) won by a head from Casanova (13-8), with Admiral's Walk two lengths back. Among the unplaced was Blue Peter, making his first start, and relatively unfancied at 100-7. In his next start, Blue Peter was second in the Middle Park Stakes, and trainer Jack Jarvis telegraphed his owner, Lord Rosebery: "We will win the Derby." Oh, for a few more tips like that one! Blue Peter not only won the Derby the next year, but the Two Thousand Guineas as well.

The Jockey Club handicapper should go to the head of the school for handicappers for ranking Blue Peter as the second-best colt on the Free Handicap—one of the very few times, if not the only time, that a colt that did not win a race as a two-year-old has been so rated.

At three, Heliopolis assumed the normal schedule of a colt whose main target was the Derby. He came out first at Newmarket in the one-mile Craven Stakes

Hyperion, 1930	Gainsborough, 1915	Bayardo, 1906	Bay Ronald, 1893	Hampton / Black Duchess
			Galicia, 1898	**Galopin** / Isoletta
		Rosedrop, 1907	St. Frusquin, 1893	**St. Simon** / Isabel
			Rosaline, 1901	Trenton / Rosalys
	Selene, 1919	Chaucer, 1900	**St. Simon**, 1881	**Galopin** / St. Angela
			Canterbury Pilgrim, 1893	Tristan / Pilgrimage
		Serenissima, 1913	Minoru, 1906	Cyllene / Mother Siegel
			Gondolette, 1902	Loved One / Dongola
HELIOPOLIS				
Drift, 1926	Swynford, 1907	John o' Gaunt, 1901	Isinglass, 1890	Isonomy / Dead Lock
			La Fleche, 1889	**St. Simon** / Quiver
		Canterbury Pilgrim, 1893	Tristan, 1878	Hermit / Thrift
			Pilgrimage, 1875	The Palmer / Lady Audley
	Santa Cruz, 1916	Neil Gow, 1907	Marco, 1892	Barcaldine / Novitiate
			Chelandry, 1894	Gold Finch / Illuminata
		Santa Brigida, 1898	**St. Simon**, 1881	**Galopin** / St. Angela
			Bridget, 1888	Master Kildare / Violet Melrose

on April 14. Heliopolis evidently was not quite fit, for he was only sixth-favorite at 10-1 and finished unplaced to Signal Light. His next appearance was in the Chester Vase of one and a half miles plus fifty-three yards, at the beginning of May. He started favorite at 7-2 in a somewhat undistinguished field of ten and won by three lengths. Hyperion (1933) and Windsor Lad (1934) each had won the Chester Vase instead of contesting the one-mile Two Thousand Guineas.

Heliopolis had every chance in the Derby, lying second until after rounding Tattenham Corner, then going to the front. He was being tracked closely by Blue Peter, who ranged alongside of him about three furlongs from home. The two colts raced neck and neck for a few strides, and then Eph Smith on Blue Peter drew his whip. Blue Peter responded at once, leaving Heliopolis astern. As he struck the rising ground in the final furlong, Heliopolis lost further ground, giving the impression that he did not stay. In the meantime, Gordon Richards on Fox Cub had been making up a lot of ground, and he passed Heliopolis to be second. On the basis of this form, Heliopolis was ranked eleven pounds behind Blue Peter.

YEAR	AGE	STS	1ST	2ND	3RD	EARNED*
1938	at 2	4	1	1	2	£ 5,122
1939	at 3	7	4	0	2	£ 9,670
1940	at 4	3	0	1	0	£ 0
1941	at 5 (in U.S.)	1	0	0	0	$ 0
Lifetime		15	5	2	4	£14,792

* First-place money only

Following his defeat in the Derby, Heliopolis appeared only in second-class races. At Royal Ascot, he took the one and five-eighths-mile Prince of Wales's Stakes by one and a half lengths, at odds of 6-1. The returns for this race read much as though Prince Aly Khan and his favorite jockey at the time, (Cheeky) Charlie Smirke, were having one of their plunges with Pointis, who was a hot favorite at 7-4 but finished third. Three days later, however, at odds of 100-8, and burdened with only 105 pounds (far too light for Smirke), including the crack lightweight jockey Doug Smith, Pointis easily won the one and a half-mile Hardwicke Stakes by three lengths. (It would be interesting to know whether Prince Aly Khan won or lost on those two races.)

Back at Newmarket, Heliopolis also won the one and a half-mile Princess of Wales's Stakes at odds of 2-3 by three lengths from a poor lot of horses. At Goodwood, starting at odds-on of 1-4 for the one and a half-mile Gratwicke Produce Stakes, Heliopolis, carrying 131 pounds, won from a poor field by a neck.

For his last start of the year, at Hurst Park in August, Heliopolis again was odds-on at 8-11 in the Hyperion Stakes at a distance of one and five-eighths miles plus forty yards, but he finished unplaced to four-year-old Portmarnock (125

TURF PIX

Olympia with owner Fred Hooper (far left)

pounds) and the Ascot Gold Cup winner, Flyon (128 pounds), also a four-year-old. Since Heliopolis carried 118 pounds in that race, using the weight-for-age scale for four-year-olds, he comes out somewhat below classic standard, which indeed he was.

Heliopolis was kept in training at four, but his campaign netted only one placing from three starts. He came out on May 1 at Newmarket and finished fifth at 8-1 behind Quick Ray in the one and a half-mile Chippenham Stakes while giving four pounds to the winner. In the Burwell Stakes over one and a half miles at Newmarket three weeks later, he again finished fifth, trailing Casanova at 100-8 while giving the winner eight pounds.

In his last race in England, Hyperion ran in the Stonehenge Plate at Newmarket on June 12 and finished second to Casanova at 8-1 and at level weights.

Heliopolis was sold to C.B. Shaffer for a reported $20,000 and was brought to the United States. At five, he was last in a field of five in an allowance race at Hialeah before being sent to stud at his new owner's Coldstream Stud near Lexington. He was characteristic of the sires that had been imported prior to the war—not up to classic form but endowed with excellent pedigrees. Many of these proved very successful sires, among them Sir Gallahad III[1], Sickle, and Pharamond II.

Heliopolis was a pronounced success at stud. He led America's sire list in 1950 and again in 1954, and he sired fifty-three stakes winners. His runners included champion fillies Parlo, Aunt Jinny, Grecian Queen, and Berlo. He also sired a number of brilliant colts, but of them only Olympia proved a major and consistent success at stud.

In addition to the brilliant Olympia, Heliopolis got High Gun (winner of the 1954 Belmont and champion at three and four), Summer Tan (Experimental Free Handicap highweight in 1954 and later a distinguished handicapper), plus Helioscope, Globemaster, Greek Ship, Greek Song, and Ace Admiral.

Heliopolis stood at Coldstream until 1951, when Henry Knight bought that farm from Shaffer, syndicated Heliopolis, and moved the stallion to his Almahurst Farm near Nicholasville, Kentucky. The horse died at Almahurst in 1959 at the age of twenty-three.

End Notes:

1. Sir Gallahad III was a classic winner; he won the Poule d'Essai des Poulains.

CHAPTER FIFTY-FOUR

ALIBHAI

Alibhai was bred by the late Aga Khan, who sold him as a yearling to L.B. Mayer following the outbreak of World War II. Mayer was getting into racing on a big scale in California. Unfortunately, Alibhai bowed in both front legs before he was able to start, and when the present writer saw the colt in the spring of 1941, it was fairly clear that Alibhai never would be able to stand training. Nevertheless, we offered Mayer $5,000 for the colt as a prospective stallion but were courteously refused. Then in 1948, the present writer with Leslie Combs II returned to California and bought Alibhai from Mayer for $500,000[1] on behalf of a group of Kentucky breeders.

Although Alibhai had no racing record, his highly successful stud career makes his pedigree of some interest. His sire, Hyperion, already has been the subject of a previous article in this book. The dam, Teresina, was bred by the famous Sledmere Stud in Yorkshire and bought by George Lambton for 7,700 guineas on behalf of the Aga Khan.

This purchase required a certain amount of fortitude, as the two previous yearlings out of Blue Tit, Teresina's dam, had been Westward Ho (by Swynford), who sold for 11,500 guineas, and Blue Ensign (by The Tetrarch), who sold for 14,500 guineas. Both of these colts had been purchased by shipping magnate Lord Glanely, and neither of them had been of much use. However, the late Aga Khan was very partial to the blood of Tracery, Teresina's sire, and in fact, had instructed Lambton to buy (at the same sale) the colt by Tracery out of Miss Matty; Lambton thought the colt was too small, and he was bought instead by a farmer named Ben Irish. Two years later, under the name of Papyrus, the same colt won the Derby, and the Aga Khan had reason to grumble: "And so I missed my first Derby." (At the best of times, judging yearlings is a risky affair, and it is some consolation to know that even the Homer of yearling judges, George Lambton, could cease to nod to the auctioneer at the wrong time.)

Teresina was a late-maturing filly, taking after her sire Tracery, who did not

Alibhai

make his first start until the Derby. Teresina ran twice as a two-year-old in 1922 and was third in her second race, the Linton Stakes (maiden), run in the autumn at Newmarket. As a three-year-old, the filly won one race out of eight starts, but she constantly was competing against the best of her age. She began by running second against colts in the one and a quarter-mile Newmarket Stakes, then was third in the Oaks, beaten by a neck and a head.

In the one-mile Coronation Stakes at Royal Ascot, Teresina was second by one and a half lengths, and she again was second in the one and a quarter-mile Eclipse Stakes against colts. She then scored her only victory of the year in the Great Yorkshire Stakes at one and a half miles and went on to be third in the St. Leger, beaten by three and a half lengths. (It is to be noted, however, that Teresina beat Tranquil, the St. Leger winner, on two occasions.) Perhaps her best performance at three was in the two and a quarter-mile Cesarewitch, where (carrying 106 pounds) she ran the four-year-old Rose Prince (115 pounds) to a short head.

As a four-year-old, Teresina was out seven times and won three races, including the Goodwood Cup at two and five-eighths miles and the Jockey Club Stakes at one and three-quarters miles. The previous year's Derby winner, Papyrus (giving nine pounds), was second and the Arc de Triomphe winner, Parth, was third in the Jockey Club.

The Aga Khan bred Teresina to the best speed sire of the time, Tetratema, and from these matings came Gino and Alishah, two good colts but below the classic standard. He also mated Teresina with his own horse, Diophon (Two Thousand Guineas), and from this mating he obtained the filly Theresina, who won the Irish Oaks and later became a good broodmare.[2]

Teresina's dam, Blue Tit, had been a very minor winner, but in addition to Teresina, she had foaled a very high-class filly called Blue Dun. Tracing back the female line, the winners are frequent but not of very high class. The next dam, Petit Bleu (by the speed sire Eager) was a fair winner of more than 2,000 pounds.

On the basis of such a pedigree, it is surprising that Alibhai should have passed on enough speed and early maturity for American racing.

Alibhai became the archetype of what breeders often hope their unraced or lightly raced young stallions will become. He was, in fact, the needle in the haystack, the unraced horse that proved able to transmit extraordinary ability in an

				Bay Ronald, 1893	Hampton Black Duchess
			Bayardo, 1906		
				Galicia, 1898	Galopin Isoletta
		Gainsborough, 1915			
				St. Frusquin, 1893	**St. Simon** Isabel
			Rosedrop, 1907		
				Rosaline, 1901	Trenton Rosalys
Hyperion, 1930					
				St. Simon, 1881	Galopin St. Angela
			Chaucer, 1900		
				Canterbury Pilgrim, 1893	Tristan Pilgrimage
		Selene, 1919			
				Minoru, 1906	Cyllene Mother Siegel
			Serenissima, 1913		
ALIBHAI				Gondolette, 1902	Loved One Dongola
				Sainfoin, 1887	Springfield Sanda
			Rock Sand, 1900		
				Roquebrune, 1893	**St. Simon** St Marguerite
		Tracery, 1909			
				Orme, 1889	Ormonde Angelica
			Topiary, 1901		
Teresina, 1920				Plaisanterie, 1882	Wellingtonia Poetess
				Gallinule, 1884	Isonomy Moorhen
			Wildfowler, 1895		
				Tragedy, 1886	Ben Battle The White Witch
		Blue Tit, 1908			
				Eager, 1894	Enthusiast Greeba
			Petit Bleu, 1902		
				Letterewe, 1891	Barcaldine Royal Letter

Traffic Judge

activity in which he never had engaged.

Alibhai sired fifty-four stakes winners. The leading money-earner by Alibhai was the gelding Bardstown ($628,752), twice winner of the Widener Handicap; and second was 1954 Kentucky Derby winner Determine ($573,360), who sired a Derby winner in Decidedly and a juvenile champion in Warfare (he, in turn, sired champion Assagai). Other sons of Alibhai included Metropolitan and Suburban handicaps winner Traffic Judge ($432,450), sire of twenty-two stakes winners; On Trust ($554,145); Your Host ($384,795), sire of five-time Horse of the Year Kelso; plus stakes winners Solidarity, Alidon, Cover Up, Trusting, Chevation, Sharpsburg, Oligarchy, and Mr. Consistency.

Alibhai's daughters included Bornastar, champion handicap female in 1958; Flower Bowl, dam of Graustark and champion Bowl of Flowers; plus stakes winners Lurline B. and Secret Meeting. He is the maternal grandsire of eighty-four North American stakes winners, including Eddie Schmidt, Shirley Jones, Roman Line, and T. V. Commercial.

Alibhai died at the age of twenty-two in 1960. Autopsy revealed that his heart weighed thirteen pounds and two ounces, compared to a norm of eight to ten pounds for a racehorse.

End Notes:

1. At the time, the price ($500,000) was the highest price ever paid for a Thoroughbred.

2. A second mating of Teresina to Diophon produced the stakes-winning colt Tereson.

CHAPTER FIFTY-FIVE

OWEN TUDOR

O wen Tudor won World War II Derby and Ascot Gold Cup substitutes, and he was one of only two colts by Hyperion to win an English classic. (The other was Sun Castle, in the same crop, winner of the St. Leger.) Nevertheless, Owen Tudor was somewhat below Hyperion—both on the Turf and at stud.

Owen Tudor was bred by Mrs. R. Macdonald-Buchanan, whose father, Lord Woolavington, was the owner of Derby winners Captain Cuttle and Coronach. Owen Tudor was a good-sized, brown Hyperion colt out of Mary Tudor II, she a Pharos mare out of Anna Bolena, a daughter of Teddy.

Mary Tudor II won the Poule d'Essai des Pouliches (French One Thousand Guineas), Prix Vermeille, and Prix Chloe, and she was second in the Prix de Diane (French Oaks). The mare was bought by Lord Woolavington shortly before his death in 1935. Her sire, Pharos, was considered to be about the best stallion of his time, and her dam was also a French classic winner (Poule d'Essai des Pouliches), so there was every reason to think that Mary Tudor II might breed a first-class horse.

Owen Tudor raced three times as a two-year-old. For his debut, he won the Salisbury Stakes at Salisbury from Orthodox and Sugar Palm. Then followed a poor performance in the Criterion Stakes at Newmarket. In his next start, also at Newmarket, he was beaten a short head by City of Flint in the Boscawen Stakes.

The Free Handicap for two-year-olds put him at 122 pounds (eleven pounds below Poise) with eight two-year-olds ranked above him.

YEAR	AGE	STS	1ST	2ND	3RD	EARNED
1940	at 2	3	1	1	0	£ 339
1941	at 3	7	3	1	0	£5,621
1942	at 4	3	2	0	0	£1,710
Lifetime		13	6	2	0	£7,670

As a three-year-old, Owen Tudor won three of seven races. First time out he took the one-mile Column Stakes at Newmarket by three lengths at odds of

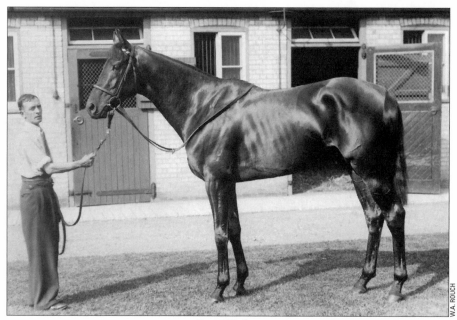

Owen Tudor

6-4. His next race was the one-mile Two Thousand Guineas, for which he was favored at 11-4, but he finished unplaced behind Lambert Simnel and Morogoro. At Salisbury, over ten furlongs, he failed by two lengths to give Fairy Prince ten pounds, although starting favorite at 7-4. For the New Derby Stakes, run on June 18 at Newmarket, Owen Tudor, ridden by William Nevett was 25-1, but he won in good style from Morogoro by one and a half lengths.

For the twelve-furlong St. Simon Stakes at Newbury, Owen Tudor was second favorite at 9-4 in a field of seven but was unplaced behind Sun Castle. For the New St. Leger Stakes of one and three-quarters miles, Owen Tudor again was second favorite, but again the race was won by Sun Castle, with Owen Tudor unplaced. With Sun Castle out of the way, Owen Tudor came back to win the Newmarket St. Leger by two lengths from eight others.

Owen Tudor was not exactly a model of consistency as a three-year-old, but his best form was undeniably good. A. Fawcett, the official handicapper, ranked Owen Tudor at 133 pounds and Sun Castle at 129 pounds in the three-year-old Free Handicap.

As a four-year-old, Owen Tudor won two of three races. At Salisbury, he won the one and one-half-mile Trial Plate by eight lengths at odds of 1-2.

Again at Salisbury, and again odds-on, at 4-7, he was unplaced for the one and three-quarters-mile Quidhampton Plate.

For the Gold Cup, run that year at Newmarket, Owen Tudor was favored at 5-2 in a field of nine, and he won by three lengths. Looking back at the records of the other runners, it seems clear that Owen Tudor did have a lot to beat. In any case, his trainer, Fred Darling, told the present writer that Owen Tudor was not a prime favorite of his, and Darling did not speak too highly of his charge when Owen Tudor was at stud.

Though Owen Tudor's stud career was a disappointment— he never stood higher than seventh (twice) on England's list of winning sires, and was only in the first ten three times in the course of a long life—he was a link in some fairly important chains, so his career deserves some study.

The most striking feature of his stud career was its uneven character. The average distance of races won by Owen Tudor's produce was 10.22 furlongs, which almost is the figure one would expect of a sire of plodders. Yet, when mated with mares of the Lady Josephine (Mumtaz Mahal) line, he sired Tudor Minstrel (1944) and Abernant (1946)—two of the very fastest horses seen in England in the last thirty years.[1] Abernant has left no son likely to carry on the line, but Tudor Minstrel sired Tudor Melody, who has been a highly successful sire of speedy

Hyperion, 1930	Gainsborough, 1915	Bayardo, 1906	**Bay Ronald**, 1893	Hampton / Black Duchess
			Galicia, 1898	Galopin / Isoletta
		Rosedrop, 1907	St. Frusquin, 1893	**St. Simon** / Isabel
			Rosaline, 1901	Trenton / Rosalys
	Selene, 1919	**Chaucer**, 1900	**St. Simon**, 1881	Galopin / St. Angela
			Canterbury Pilgrim, 1893	Tristan / Pilgrimage
OWEN TUDOR		Serenissima, 1913	Minoru, 1906	**Cyllene** / Mother Siegel
			Gondolette, 1902	Loved One / Dongola
	Pharos, 1920	Phalaris, 1913	Polymelus, 1902	**Cyllene** / Maid Marian
			Bromus, 1905	Sainfoin / Cheery
		Scapa Flow, 1914	**Chaucer**, 1900	St. Simon / Canterbury Pilgrim
			Anchora, 1905	Love Wisely / Eryholme
Mary Tudor II, 1931	Anna Bolena, 1920	Teddy, 1913	Ajax, 1901	Flying Fox / Amie
			Rondeau, 1900	**Bay Ronald** / Doremi
		Queen Elizabeth, 1908	Wargrave, 1898	Carbine / Warble
			New Guinea, 1890	Minting / Newhaven

W.A. ROUCH

Tudor Minstrel

stock. Tudor Minstrel's sons also included Tomy Lee, who won the 1959 Kentucky Derby but who was virtually sterile.

Owen Tudor was represented in France by the brilliant runner and successful stallion Right Royal V, winner of the Poule d'Essai des Poulains (French Two Thousand Guineas), Prix du Jockey-Club (French Derby), etc., and also winner of England's King George VI and Queen Elizabeth Stakes. When Right Royal V was a three-year-old, in 1961, Owen Tudor stood second on the French sire list.

His other classic winners were Tudor Minstrel (1947 English Two Thousand Guineas) and Theodorica (1955 Italian Oaks), and he also was represented by stayer Elpenor (Prix du Cadran and Ascot Gold Cup). In this country, his Tudor Era won the 1958 Washington, D.C., International at one and a half miles only to be disqualified, but he came back the next year to win the Man o' War Stakes.

Thus, Owen Tudor sired a brilliant sprinter in Abernant and a brilliant miler in Tudor Minstrel, and he also could sire Cup horses.

The male line of Owen Tudor received a boost in France, when Kashmir II (son of Tudor Melody, he by Tudor Minstrel), sired both the French One Thousand and Two Thousand guineas winners.[2] Right Royal V, who died in 1973, left Irish Sweeps Derby winner Prince Regent and Prix de l'Arc de Triomphe runner-up Salvo among his sons.[3]

End Notes:

1. Abernant, champion two-year-old colt of 1948 and champion sprinter in 1949–50, was a son of Rustom Mahal, a daughter of Mumtaz Mahal. Tudor Minstrel, champion two-year-old colt in 1946, was a son of Sansonnet, a daughter of Lady Juror. Both Mumtaz Mahal (The Tetrarch) and Lady Juror (Son-in-Law) were daughters of Lady Josephine, winner of the Coventry Stakes.

2. In 1974 Dumka (Kashmir II—Faizebad, by Prince Taj) captured the Poule d'Essai des Pouliches and Moulines (Kashmir II—Golden Glory II, by Never Say Die), the Poule d'Essai des Poulains.

3. Owen Tudor's male line is still viable in England, where his descendants include champion European sprinter Cadeaux Genereux, who won the Diadem Stakes (Eng-III) and Criterion Stakes (Eng-III) at three and the July Cup (Eng-I) and William Hill Sprint Championship (Eng-I) at four, and his group I-winning son Bahamian Bounty, sire of group I winners Pastoral Pursuit and Goodricke. The line of descent: Owen Tudor, Tudor Minstrel, Will Somers, Balidar, Young Generation, Cadeaux Genereux. Representatives of this line can also be found in South Africa (Safawan, Winter Romance, etc.) and Europe (Touch of the Blues, Cajun Cadet, etc.).

KHALED

There was a strong group of breeders and racing men in England and Ireland who resented the late Aga Khan's policy of selling the best stallions and stallion prospects developed by his vast breeding program. His sales deprived British breeders of access to some of their highest-class sires, including Blenheim II, Mahmoud, Bahram, and Nasrullah. There was no economic pressure which forced such sales, and undoubtedly they had some effect in lowering the standard of the British Thoroughbred, just as the sales of Rock Sand (maternal grandsire of Man o' War) and Cyllene earlier in the century were a serious forfeiture to the development of the British Thoroughbred.

Perhaps most significant among these British breeders was the late Lord Derby, who had bred the best sires in the British Isles preceding World War II—Phalaris, Pharos, Fairway, and Hyperion. Despite being offered very large sums for each at a time when his resources greatly were being reduced through taxation, Lord Derby had sold none of them. In fact, the present writer heard that out of a 400 guinea stud fee to Hyperion, Lord Derby was able to keep only 10 guineas for himself. This sort of bulldog tenacity is what had carried the British through the Napoleonic wars and World War I, and the British did not like it when their Thoroughbred supremacy was being threatened by a man who was not under similar economic pressure.

Lord Derby made plain his feelings by excluding the Aga Khan from access to Hyperion and Fairway. Thus, the Aga Khan could acquire their blood only through private purchase or at public auction. In this way, the late Aga Khan and the late Prince Aly Khan acquired Stardust (by Hyperion) at the yearling sales and Khaled (in utero) by the purchase of his dam, Eclair, at the 1942 December sales.

Eclair had been a very good filly on the Turf, winning five of her last six races as a three-year-old, they including the one-mile Falmouth Stakes and the one and a quarter-mile Leicestershire Oaks and Atalanta Stakes. Handicapper Phil Bull reported: "She was a very good filly indeed, probably the best of her year." Prior to Khaled's appearance, Eclair had produced six foals in England, all of which had been winners. Eclair was sired by the gray Ethnarch, a son of The Tetrarch and a useful handicapper who could get about a mile. Ethnarch was not a remarkable sire and was by no means a fashionable one.

The dam of Eclair was Black Ray, a little mare who had been bought by Captain Cecil Boyd-Rochfort for the late Marshall Field from J.B. (Jack) Joel. Although not considered good enough to retain in the Joel stud, Black Ray proved one of the most prolific and successful matrons of her time: She foaled in nineteen successive years without a miss, and among her produce were Jacopo and Foray, each of whom headed the two-year-old Free Handicap; as well as Eclair and her sister Infra Red, who became the fourth dam of Mill Reef (Derby, Arc de Triomphe, etc.).

Black Ray won one of two races as a two-year-old, the only year she raced, and her dam, Lady Brilliant (by Sundridge), also was a minor winner. The next dam, Our Lassie, won the Oaks and was a half sister to Your Majesty, who won the St. Leger and became a distinguished sire in Argentina.

While the sires of the first two dams (Ethnarch and Black Jester) were failures at stud, the sire of the third dam (Sundridge) was a good stallion, introducing the factor for speed into the pedigree, and the sire of the fourth dam (Ayrshire) was only a qualified success. Thus, although the distaff side of this pedigree was not as solid with racing class as were the pedigrees frequently found in the stud of the late Lord Derby, the producing record of the first two dams was of a high order, so the pedigree as a whole was appealing enough.

As a two-year-old, Khaled ran three times and won three times. He first appeared on Derby Day, when that classic still was contested at Newmarket (World War II in Europe having just ended). Although Khaled won, as Phil Bull put it, "There was little to enthuse about over his first outing ... He had little to do, and it took him an unconscionable time to get the upper hand of the game little Pandemonium and the not very genuine Seingalt. They led him most of the way, and though he beat them comfortably enough in the end, he was being vigorously ridden some distance from home and did not strike the front until well on the rise (out of the dip at Newmarket) to the winning post."

For Khaled, the race on Derby Day was in preparation for the traditional Coventry Stakes at Ascot. Before the latter, it became obvious that the public had not been much impressed with Khaled's first race, as Lord Derby's Sky High was odds-on at 2-7 while Khaled drifted out to 9-1. Halfway through the race, Sky High was leading and going smoothly. Below the distance, as the English say, Gordon Richards put Khaled under pressure, and the latter ran on too strongly for Sky High and won by one and a half lengths. Since Khaled had been described as backward and half-fit for the race, the result was impressive, more so because the last part of the Ascot course is uphill.

Khaled was not seen out again until the Middle Park Stakes in October. He won again, but his performance was by no means sparkling. After a half-mile he caught the leader, Hypericum (also by Hyperion and winner of the One Thousand Guineas the following year), and went to the lead as they went into the dip. Gordon Richards had to keep driving Khaled, all the way up the hill to the winning post, and he won by only three-quarters of a length from the filly.

Ordinarily, a two-year-old that is undefeated and has won the two most important two-year-old races of the year would be an automatic choice to top the two-year-old Free Handicap. Khaled, however, was ranked sixth—four pounds below the top. The reason was that the best colts of the season kept sidestepping each other, and there were four unbeaten colts in the top seven places. In any case, Khaled stood a good candidate for the three-year-old classics.

Khaled began his three-year-old campaign in the one-mile Column Produce Stakes at Newmarket. He was set to give seven pounds to Lord Derby's Downrush, who had won five of his seven races as a two-year-old and had been second in the

			Bay Ronald, 1893	Hampton Black Duchess
		Bayardo, 1906	Galicia, 1898	Galopin Isoletta
	Gainsborough, 1915	Rosedrop, 1907	St. Frusquin, 1893	St. Simon Isabel
			Rosaline, 1901	Trenton Rosalys
Hyperion, 1930		Chaucer, 1900	St. Simon, 1881	Galopin St. Angela
			Canterbury Pilgrim, 1893	Tristan Pilgrimage
	Selene, 1919	Serenissima, 1913	Minoru, 1906	Cyllene Mother Siegel
			Gondolette, 1902	Loved One Dongola
KHALED		The Tetrarch, 1911	Roi Herode, 1904	Le Samaritain Roxelane
			Vahren, 1897	Bona Vista Castania
	Ethnarch, 1922	Karenza, 1910	William the Third, 1898	St. Simon Gravity
			Cassinia, 1905	Carbine Scene
Eclair, 1930		Black Jester, 1911	Polymelus, 1902	Cyllene Maid Marian
			Absurdity, 1903	Melton Paradoxical
	Black Ray, 1919	Lady Brilliant, 1912	Sundridge, 1898	Amphion Sierra
			Our Lassie, 1900	Ayrshire Yours

BOB HOPPER

Khaled

other two, and who also had recorded the second-best *Timeform* figure of any two-year-old in 1945. In the Free Handicap, Downrush was ranked six pounds below Khaled, so it was no certainty that Khaled, giving away the seven pounds, would be able to beat him.

The strategy of Lord Derby's stable was to jump Downrush right off from the gate and see if Khaled could catch him. Their purpose apparently was to get as close a line as possible on Khaled in order to assess the chances of their own colt, Gulf Stream (later a leading sire in Argentina), in the classics. Jockey Harry Wragg came along at a crackling pace on Downrush, and after a half-mile, Downrush led Khaled by at least five lengths, but Gordon Richards came along with Khaled and beat Downrush up the hill. The *Timeform* figure of 1:28 was well up to classic standard.

There was one fly in the ointment—Harry Wragg reported after the race that he had heard Khaled making a noise before he came alongside Downrush, so it seemed likely that Khaled was "gone in the wind." Unfortunately, that analysis proved all too true. As it was, Khaled ran second in the Two Thousand Guineas, four lengths behind Happy Knight, after being boxed in and well behind the leaders halfway through the race. Jockey Bobby Jones had to take him around the outside of a group of horses, while Happy Knight was setting up a commanding lead, and Khaled never found a position to put in a challenge. He finished second, beaten by four lengths, but still was in front of Gulf Stream, who had been considered his superior at two.

Khaled's race for the Derby was run in a different fashion. From the start he was in a forward position and at the mile post was sent into the lead. He kept this position well into the straight and then collapsed in a few strides to finish unplaced. The race was won in poor time by the plodder Airborne, with Gulf Stream second. The probabilities are that Airborne was the only colt in the race who could stay twelve furlongs at that stage of development.

At Ascot, Khaled was brought back to a distance of one mile, and

YEAR	AGE	STS	1ST	2ND	3RD	EARNED
1945	at 2	3	3	0	0	£3,456*
1946	at 3	5	2	1	1	£3,920*
In Eng/Ire		8	5	1	1	£6,376*
1948	at 5	4	1	0	0	$3,100
In U.S.		4	1	0	0	$3,100
* First-place money only						

he won the St. James's Palace Stakes fairly easily from Aldis Lamp (later an outstanding stallion in Belgium) and Radiotherapy. His last race was the ten-furlong Eclipse Stakes at Ascot (instead of Sandown Park), where in a lifeless performance he was beaten six lengths by Gulf Stream with Edward Tudor second.

Both Khaled's trainer, Frank Butters, and handicapper Phil Bull earlier had been very confident that Khaled would be able to stay one and a half miles, and without his wind infirmity, this may well have been the case.

Khaled was sent to stud in Ireland, and after one stud season there he was sold to Rex Ellsworth, the well-known California breeder. When Ellsworth inquired of Prince Aly Khan concerning Khaled's wind affliction, he received the reply: "I'm afraid that goes with him."

(Editor's Note: The writer of this book met Rex Ellsworth in California prior to the latter's trip abroad in search of a stallion for his California stud. Ellsworth asked his preference among the stallions which might be available. Abram Hewitt replied, first, Nasrullah, and second, Khaled, to which his later comment, "It would be gratifying to do as well for oneself as one can do with one's advice to others," certainly applies.)

Ellsworth went to Europe with $100,000, which was not enough to buy a proven stallion and was, in fact, not enough to buy the young Khaled, either. The Mormon horseman used the $100,000 as a down payment and returned to the United States to "rustle up the other $60,000" of the purchase price. Khaled

stood one season in Ireland before Ellsworth imported him.

Arriving in California after the 1947 breeding season, Khaled was put back in training and won once from three races at Santa Anita in January of 1948. Khaled stood that season at stud (and got thirty-seven foals from the year), then once again was put back on the track. He finished last in a race on December 28, his final outing.

Correspondent, with Eddie Arcaro up

Khaled quickly proved a success, both in class and fecundity. From his second California-sired crop came forty-five foals, of which twenty-six won at two, a number of juvenile winners surpassed only by Star Shoot's twenty-seven from a 1914 crop of fifty-two foals.

The first outstanding son of Khaled was Correspondent, who earned $207,292 and won the Hollywood Gold Cup. Two years later emerged a horse of overwhelming class in Swaps, Khaled's leading earner ($848,900), winner of the 1955 Kentucky Derby, Horse of the Year in 1956. Ellsworth's gamble in buying Khaled would have paid off handsomely without Swaps, but with the advent of that homebred champion, Ellsworth gained national prestige. He eventually sold Swaps for $2,000,000.

Khaled's other outstanding runners included $599,285-earner Terrang, Coaching Club American Oaks winner A Glitter, plus El Drag, Hillary (sire of Hill Rise, etc.), Candy Dish (dam of Candy Spots), Khalita, Linmold, New Policy, Physician, Divine Comedy, Going Abroad, Take Over, and Corn Off the Cob. He sired a total of sixty-one stakes winners before his death in 1968.

CHAPTER FIFTY-SEVEN

SWAPS

Whatever argument there may be about the greatest horse to come out of California breeding to take on the Easterners—Emperor of Norfolk (1885) or Swaps (1952)—there can be no dispute about the contrasting life styles of their owners. E.J. (Lucky) Baldwin (Emperor of Norfolk) was an exponent of the rugged, individualistic, blatant life of the Old West. He loved to gamble and put on a show. One of his favorite pastimes was driving a four-in-hand onto the old Santa Anita racecourse, hitched to a glittering conveyance whose roof was inhabited densely by females in gaudy array. Men of this stamp inevitably have their ups and downs, and when Baldwin had a down he started off for the Klondyke at the age of seventy-two to recoup his fortune.

Rex Ellsworth, Swaps' breeder and owner, in contrast, was a quiet-spoken, deeply religious Mormon, who did not drink, smoke, or cuss, and was a steady family man with the background of a cowboy in Arizona. When you think that he bought his first Thoroughbreds for a few hundred dollars apiece, at the Lexington fall sales, drove them back to Arizona in an open truck, and built up his breeding empire from that modest base until he was twice leading breeder in the United States, it has been an extraordinary achievement. The life of a breeder who races his own stock is rarely "roses, roses, all the way," without interruption. Ellsworth had some bumps over the years. Although the author has not seen him for the past twenty-five years, he would back Ellsworth's pluck and courage to pull him through. In that sense, both Lucky Baldwin and Ellsworth are similar—as part of the American tradition that took the risks and built the country.

Swaps was the best horse Ellsworth bred. His first start, on May 20, 1954, brought a winning effort. He then ran third in the Westchester Stakes but redeemed himself by winning the Juvenile Stakes in :58 2/5 on June 10. In the Haggin Stakes, he was again third, and then he was unplaced in the Charles S. Howard Stakes.

This was a series of five races in seven weeks, and justified a lay-off until

Swaps

December 30, in preparation for his three-year-old campaign. His successful comeback was in a minor affair called the Amarillo Ranch Purse, of six furlongs. This meant that technically he had won half of his starts as a two-year-old and had been unplaced but once. There was nothing very startling about this, but the next year witnessed a change.

In his first race in 1955, Swaps won the San Vicente by three and a half lengths and then he took the Santa Anita Derby, but only by a half-length from Jean's Joe.

Trainer Mesh Tenney shipped Swaps east for the Kentucky Derby, and the colt came out in public there on April 30. He won the Jefferson Purse in such brilliant style that he was second favorite for the Kentucky Derby, after Nashua, who was a strong first favorite at 1.30-1. Nashua's main rival was supposed to have been Summer Tan, who had been ranked a pound above him in the previous year's Experimental Free Handicap. Swaps was generally regarded as "just one more of those California horses," that will learn to respect their betters when they encounter the cream of the New York colts, but in the Jefferson Purse he was so exciting that he made Summer Tan third choice.

Swaps led nearly all the way in the Derby and turned back Nashua's effort to head him on the turn into the stretch. Swaps won from Nashua by one and one-half lengths with Summer Tan six and a half lengths farther back. The time, 2:01 4/5 was excellent and was matched eight years later by Chateaugay, a son of Swaps. Horses simply do not run that fast at that time in their three-year-old careers unless they are very good ones.

Ellsworth chose to go on back to California, rather than to contest the Preakness and Belmont, both of which Nashua took in good style. Swaps reappeared in California on May 30 in the one-mile Will Rogers Stakes. He took that one by twelve lengths in the startling time of 1:35. Next, Swaps took on older horses in the one and one-sixteenth-mile Californian. Among his opponents were Mister Gus, who once beat Nashua over ten furlongs at weight-for-age, and Determine, the winner of the previous year's Kentucky Derby. Not only did Swaps defeat a good field of older horses, but he did it in world-record time of 1:40 2/5.

A month later Swaps came out for the Westerner (now the Hollywood Derby) and at odds of 1-20 covered the ten furlongs in 2:00 3/5. The ease with which he did it surpassed even the time figures. Swaps then came partway east again, as far as Chicago. The American Derby of one and three-sixteenths miles was his tar-

				Bayardo, 1906	**Bay Ronald**
Khaled, 1943	Hyperion, 1930	Gainsborough, 1915			Galicia
				Rosedrop, 1907	St. Frusquin
					Rosaline
			Selene, 1919	Chaucer, 1900	St. Simon
					Canterbury Pilgrim
				Serenissima, 1913	Minoru
					Gondolette
	Eclair, 1930	Ethnarch, 1922		The Tetrarch, 1911	Roi Herode
					Vahren
				Karenza, 1910	William the Third
					Cassinia
		Black Ray, 1919		Black Jester, 1911	**Polymelus**
					Absurdity
SWAPS				Lady Brilliant, 1912	Sundridge
					Our Lassie
	Beau Pere, 1927	Son-in-Law, 1911		Dark Ronald, 1905	**Bay Ronald**
					Darkie
				Mother-in-Law, 1906	Matchmaker
					Be Cannie
		Cinna, 1917		**Polymelus**, 1902	Cyllene
					Maid Marian
Iron Reward, 1946				Baroness La Fleche, 1900	Ladas
					La Fleche
	Iron Maiden, 1941	War Admiral, 1934		Man o' War, 1917	Fair Play
					Mahubah
				Brushup, 1929	Sweep
					Annette K.
		Betty Derr, 1928		Sir Gallahad III, 1920	Teddy
					Plucky Liege
				Uncle's Lassie, 1916	Uncle
					Planutess

get. He never had run on grass before, but gave the good colt Traffic Judge seven pounds and beat him a length in 1:54 3/5, to equal the American record for the distance on turf.

There was insistent drumming in racing circles for a match between Swaps and Nashua. Eventually it was arranged—126 pounds each at ten furlongs, purse $100,000, winner take all, at Washington Park. Just as the Kentucky Derby may not have been a truly run race, the match turned out to be certainly not truly run. For some time, Swaps had been troubled by soreness in the sole of his right front foot. In fact, his trainer knew this, and there were rumors that he tried to get out of the race. Swaps came out of the race sore in this foot, and that may help to explain his six and one-half length defeat by Nashua. Arcaro came out of the gate, putting the whip to Nashua, and carried Swaps wide on the first turn. In any case, Swaps never really came to grips with Nashua, and on public form, at least, was soundly beaten. It was the only time that year he was beaten, in nine starts. He raced no more at three.

Tenney got Swaps ready for his four-year-old racing in California and gave him

YEAR	AGE	STS	1ST	2ND	3RD	EARNED
1954	at 2	6	3	0	2	$ 20,950
1955	at 3	9	8	1	0	$418,550
1956	at 4	10	8	1	0	$409,400
Lifetime		25	19	2	2	$848,900

his first race there on February 17, 1956, in the Los Angeles County Fair Handicap. He scored an easy victory over the good handicapper Bobby Brocato. Fearing the effect of the sloppy tracks at that time of year on Swaps' delicate foot, Ellsworth shipped him to Florida, where there were hopes of a fresh encounter with Nashua. This did not materialize, but Swaps did have one race there. It was the unimportant Broward Handicap, which he won under 130 pounds in the world-record time of 1:39 3/5 for a mile and seventy yards.

Nashua and Swaps were out the same day at Gulfstream Park, but not in the same race. Nashua was unplaced in the Gulfstream Park Handicap on a day that Swaps merely had a workout between races.

Back Swaps went to California to have a go at the Californian again. Swaps had the race won when Bill Shoemaker eased up on him, through overconfidence, and Porterhouse made a late charge and nipped him right at the wire. Swaps then began a series of five victories that from a time and weight standpoint were extraordinary. For the last four of these he had 130 pounds each time, and he always won under a strong hold. To start with, he won the Argonaut Handicap of one mile in 1:33 1/5, breaking Citation's world record. Then he actually ran a mile faster on the way

Chateaugay

to another world record, 1:39 for one and one-sixteenth miles. In the American Handicap, he equaled the world record of 1:46 4/5 for nine furlongs, conceding fifteen pounds to Bobby Brocato and nineteen pounds to Mister Gus.

His next target was the Hollywood Gold Cup, even though his sore foot had been bleeding again after the American. He won this one too, eased up in the astonishing time of 1:58 3/5, missing the world record by two-fifths of a second. Had he been ridden out, he undoubtedly could have bettered it. Swaps then dispelled any doubts as to how far he could go in the one and five-eighths-mile Sunset Handicap. Again, he shattered a world record, with a time of 2:38 1/5.

Next came another foray to Chicago. In the Arch Ward Memorial, Swaps could not handle the soft turf, and finished only seventh to Mahan, but on the dirt again, Swaps (130) won the Washington Park Handicap of one mile for a new track record of 1:33 2/5, smothering Summer Tan in the process.

This turned out to be the last race for Swaps. He was to have gone for the United Nations Handicap, but trouble recurred in his ailing foot. Then on October 9, he fractured a cannon bone, and as soon as possible he was returned to California.

In 1956 Ellsworth sold a half share in Swaps to John W. Galbreath for $1 mil-

MIKE SIRICO/NYRA

Affectionately

lion, and he later sold the remaining half to Mrs. Galbreath for a similar amount. Swaps went to stand at Galbreath's Darby Dan Farm near Lexington and remained there until he was syndicated in 1967 and moved to Leslie Combs II's Spendthrift Farm. He died in 1972.

From a racer as brilliant as Swaps at his best, what was to be expected at stud? The first drawback was that he had not been a particularly good two-year-old; secondly, his dam had not been a winner, though two full brothers of Swaps had been stakes winners in the $100,000 range and two full sisters had become dams of stakes winners; thirdly, his maternal grandsire, Beau Pere, though a good sire, had been a poor performer. Swaps' own sire, Khaled, though a good sire, had been a little short of classic form. As against this, his second [Iron Maiden], third [Betty Derr], and fourth [Uncle's Lassie] dams had all been stakes winners, and dams of stakes winners.[1]

The result at stud, in fact, was very uneven. In his early years at stud, Swaps sired three very high-class racers: Chateaugay (Kentucky Derby and Belmont Stakes), his full sister Primonetta (Alabama Stakes, etc., and voted best handicap mare of 1962), and Affectionately (best two-year-old filly of 1962 and best handicap mare of 1965). After these, the quality of his stock declined rather sharply. Swaps was in the first ten list of leading sires of winners only three times.

Swaps sired a total of thirty-five stakes winners. In addition to the three champions named above, they included No Robbery, Main Swap, Fathers Image, Eurasian, and Green Gambados. His opportunity to establish a strong branch of the Hyperion line in this country was lessened by the exportation of several of his better sons, including Chateaugay and Fathers Image. No Robbery sired several stakes winners, however, and Chateaugay's leading son, $739,673-earner True Knight, entered stud here.

Physically, Swaps was a horse of commanding presence and scope. He went back in his color to Hyperion, his grandsire, who was the only chestnut among the horse's four grandparents. In conformation, Swaps was of a different type, however, Hyperion having been very short in stature, heavily barreled, and long for his height.

End Notes:

1. Three of Swaps' first four dams were also the dams of Kentucky Derby winners: Iron Reward (Swaps, 1955), Iron Maiden (Iron Liege, 1957) and Uncle's Lassie (Clyde Van Dusen, 1929).

CHAPTER FIFTY-EIGHT

BRULEUR

Frenchmen are world famous as sturdy individualists, each one devoted to his own tastes in Wine and (beautiful) Women, with Song a poor third. Each Frenchman also has his own convictions about art, politics, the three juicy eighteenth- and nineteenth-century revolutions in his country, and its numerous Republics. Some Frenchmen also like horses.

Bruleur was French of the French, both in performance and pedigree, and his breeder, Evremond de Saint-Alary, was the quintessence of the French point of view about racing and breeding. Saint-Alary admired the Dollar strain of sires above all others, that strain renowned over the decades for its qualities of stamina, gameness, and resistance.

Saint-Alary had bred the great Cup horse Omnium II[1], a grandson of Dollar who won the French Derby (Prix du Jockey-Club). Omnium II, in turn, had sired for Saint-Alary the grand race mare Kizil Kourgan, winner of the country's two filly classics, plus the Prix Lupin and the Grand Prix de Paris against colts. In the Grand Prix of nearly two miles, Kizil Kourgan not only defeated French Derby winner Retz, but also beat the brilliant English filly Sceptre. (Kizil Kourgan's jockey, Willie Pratt, used to cross himself whenever the filly's name was mentioned.)

Basse Terre, dam of Bruleur, also was bred by Saint-Alary and was foaled in the same year as Kizil Kourgan (1899). She, too, was by Omnium II, but was far from being in the same class as the other filly. Basse Terre did win three races at three and placed seven times, and she proved to be a fine broodmare. In addition to Bruleur, she produced Basse Pointe, who earned the equivalent of some $100,000 and won the Prix Vermeille and other important races.

In 1909 Saint-Alary bred Basse Terre to his own stallion, Chouberski. This required considerable fortitude, as well as faith, for Chouberski had made but one start in his life, winning the minor Prix Reiset. The stallion had not sired a single horse of any class—but he did sire Bruleur, so Saint-Alary was not wrong. (The coming of the war hampered Chouberski's later stud career, and he did not

Bruleur

BLOOD-HORSE LIBRARY

sire another high-class runner although a number of his daughters became good producers.)

Like many of Saint-Alary's horses, Bruleur was unraced as a two-year-old. In the tradition of many high-class horses on the French Turf, he made his debut in the ten-furlong Prix Juigne, a race specifically for three-year-olds making their first starts. In a field of seventeen, Bruleur finished fourth, beaten three and three-quarters lengths. A week later, on April 20, he was sent out in a field of fifteen for the important Prix Hocquart and was beaten only a neck by Pere Marquette.

Given a rest of three weeks, Bruleur won the Prix des Lilas, a relatively minor race at one and a half miles. He was odds-on at 3-5 and won by three lengths under George Stern, the leading jockey in France at the time.

Ten days later, again with Stern aboard, he was sent off at 7-10 for the one and three-eighths-mile Prix La Rochette, a more important event, and he won as expected.

These races all were leading to the most important French classics. The Prix du Jockey-Club of twelve furlongs was run on June 15 and attracted a field of seventeen. The winner turned up in Dagor, the last high-class colt sired by Flying Fox. Dagor won by two lengths from Baldaquin, with Bruleur another length back at odds of 12-1.

Two weeks later came the Grand Prix de Paris, run over one and seven-eighths miles with 128 pounds aboard. This was the sort of race made to order for Bruleur, and he duly won from nineteen others by a length. His victory was not a great surprise, as his odds were only 7-2. The race probably took something out of him, as a week later he was only sixth in a field of nine for the Prix du President over one and five-eighths miles.

Bruleur then was given a rest for two months and re-emerged in a small handicap of ten furlongs at Chantilly. He was given plenty of weight, about 137 pounds, and failed by three-quarters of a length to concede about twenty pounds successfully to Nil Bleu II. The race was evidently a pipe-opener for the Prix Royal-Oak

(French St. Leger) run over the same course as the Grand Prix, one and seven-eighths miles. Bruleur won again, by two lengths, beating good colts in Isard II, Nimbus, and Dagor.

Again, the race may have taken something out of Bruleur, as he ran a poor race to be unplaced, at odds of 9-2, in the Conseil Municipal. Nimbus, whom he had beaten easily in the Royal-Oak, was the winner. Bruleur's last race of the year was at Le Tremblay in the one and five-eighths-mile Prix Edgard Gillois, in which he failed by four lengths in heavy going while conceding about twenty pounds to Coraline.

Taking his three-year-old campaign as a whole, it is fair to say that Bruleur was far from invincible but was undoubtedly a very high-class stayer when fresh and well over one and seven-eighths miles at Longchamp, where he twice beat the best colts of his year.

As a four-year-old, Bruleur made only three starts, all over very long distances. In the second leg of the Prix Edgard Gillois, at two and three-eighths miles, he went under by a neck to Ecouen, with each carrying 132 pounds. On June 11, he beat Dagor two lengths in the Prix La Rochette, over two and three-quarters miles.

Only five days later, Bruleur appeared at Royal Ascot to contest the Ascot Gold

			Androcles, 1870	**Dollar** Alabama
		Cambyse, 1884	Cambuse, 1877	Plutus Campeche
	Gardefeu, 1895		Bruce, 1879	See Saw Carine
		Bougie, 1887	La Lumiere, 1871	Heir Of Linne Grand Mademoiselle
Chouberski, 1902		The Bard, 1883	Petrarch, 1873	Lord Clifden Laura
	Campanule, 1891		Magdalene, 1877	Syrian My Mary
		St. Lucia, 1880	Rosicrucian, 1865	Beadsman Madame Eglentine
BRULEUR			Rose Of Tralee, 1869	Knowsley Vimeira
		Upas, 1883	**Dollar**, 1860	The Flying Dutchman Payment
	Omnium II, 1892		Rosemary, 1870	Skirmisher Vertumna
		Bluette, 1886	Wellingtonia, 1869	Chattanooga Araucaria
Basse Terre, 1899			Blue Serge, 1876	Hermit Blue Sleeves
		St Gatien, 1881	The Rover, 1856	The Flying Dutchman Meeanee
	Bijou, 1890		Saint Editha, 1873	Kingley Vale Lady Alice
		Thora, 1878	Doncaster, 1870	Stockwell Marigold
			Freia, 1873	Hermit Thor's Day

Cup of two and a half miles. While he was a natural favorite at 3-2 in a field of ten, the decision to run Bruleur scarcely was judicious. He had shown as a three-year-old that he did not tolerate two races close together. In addition, Bruleur had to make the journey across to Ascot by rail and boat. In those circumstances, it is not surprising that Bruleur only ran fourth, beaten more than four lengths by Aleppo, Willbrook, and Junior, none of whom was in the same class as he was, taking their form as a whole.

The Ascot Gold Cup turned out to be Bruleur's last race, and the horse was retired to Saint-Alary's Haras de Saint-Pair-du-Mont in Calvados. Bruleur developed a savage temper, and the only person who could handle him safely was a woman.

Bruleur became the premier sire of high-class stayers in France. He sired four winners of the French Derby—Ksar (1921), Pot au Feu (1924), Madrigal (1926), and Hotweed (1929). The last-named also won the Grand Prix de Paris.

Bruleur also was represented four times by winners of the Prix de l'Arc de Triomphe—by Ksar (1921 and 1922), Priori (1925), and the filly Samos (1935). In addition to his French stayers, he sired the classic filly Brulette, who in England won the 1931 Epsom Oaks plus the Goodwood Cup. (Brulette produced Desert Sun, who foaled two mares represented by North American stakes winners. Desert Sun foaled Creme Brulee, the dam of Hedevar and Cloudy Dawn, and also produced Desert Vision, the dam of Desert Love, Desert Law, and Astray.) Also in England, Bruleur was represented by Palais Royal, who won the Cambridgeshire and was second in the St. Leger.

Bruleur was the leading sire in France in three seasons—1921, 1924, and 1929. He was runner-up in 1931 to his son Ksar, who, in turn, begot three-time leading French sire Tourbillon.

YEAR	AGE	STS	1ST	2ND	3RD	EARNED
1912	at 2	unraced				
1913	at 3	11	4	3	1	524,870 Fr
1914	at 4	2	1	1	0	44,000 Fr
1914	at 4 (in Eng)	1	0	0	0	0
Lifetime		14	5	4	1	568,870 Fr

There was a scandalous, but amusing, story surrounding one of Bruleur's noted sons, Pot au Feu. That colt came up for sale as a yearling at Deauville at a time when the Aga Khan was embarking on his Turf career in France. When Pot au Feu entered the ring, the Aga Khan opened the bidding with a complimentary bid of the equivalent of $1,000. Silence followed. His Highness looked around in surprise, as he was accustomed to paying top prices for any yearlings he liked.

Pot au Feu was knocked down quickly to the Aga Khan, and immediately rumors began to circulate. The story bandied about was that on the last day of the breeding season two years before, there were three mares still in season booked to

BLOOD-HORSE LIBRARY

Pot au Feu

Bruleur. The stud groom, thinking of the usual tip that was forthcoming whenever a visiting mare was declared in foal, took counsel with himself and bred two of the three mares to Bruleur and the third to the farm teaser. The third mare got in foal and produced Pot au Feu. If the story were true, the Aga Khan surely was entitled to the last laugh when Pot au Feu won the French Derby.

As soon as Pot au Feu's racing days were over, the Aga Khan disposed of him.[2] The author once had occasion to go through the Aga Khan's breeding records with Mme. Vullier, who managed His Highness' stud at La Marly, and we noted that she had crossed out the name of Bruleur in ink and had written in the name of another horse as the true sire of Pot au Feu.

The author does not vouch for the truth of the tale that Pot au Feu was sired by a teaser, but we can say that the story was believed by many French breeders.

End Notes:

1. The *French Stud Book* shows Monsieur Th. Dousdebes as breeder of Omnium II.

2. The Aga Khan sold Pot au Feu to C.B. Shaffer who stood him at his Coldstream Farm. According a 1929 article by Neil Newman, the Aga Khan regretted the sale and periodically tried to buy the stallion back. Newman describes Pot au Feu as "a grand looking horse with the sweetest disposition and a purposeful way of walking that endears him to all who see him."

CHAPTER FIFTY-NINE

KSAR

B y 1918, when World War I was drawing to a close, Evremond de Saint-Alary had been breeding Thoroughbreds for about thirty years, and he had settled down with deeply rooted convictions. Above all, he liked stayers that, in the true French tradition, were game and also sound. This led him to concentrate on the blood of Dollar. Using Dollar's son Upas (French Derby, etc.) as a sire, Saint-Alary bred the high-class Omnium II,[1] who also won the French Derby, plus the Conseil Municipal (twice).

Looking about for mates for Omnium II, Saint-Alary bought the high-class race mare Kasbah, winner of the French Oaks (Prix de Diane), at a reported price of $30,000, a very high figure in those days. His judgment was vindicated when Kasbah in 1899 foaled the chestnut filly Kizil Kourgan, who certainly was one of the greatest fillies ever seen in France, or perhaps anywhere else.

As a three-year-old, Kizil Kourgan won the French One Thousand Guineas (Poule d'Essai des Pouliches), then the Prix Lupin (a very important stakes), beating colts. She then took the French Oaks and the Grand Prix de Paris (one and seven-eighths miles in June) again beating colts, among them French Derby winner Retz, plus the great English filly Sceptre as well. Kizil Kourgan also added the Prix Royal-Oak (French St. Leger) run over the same course as the Grand Prix. Kizil Kourgan had won three classics without a defeat, when she finally ran a poor race in the autumn against inferior opposition. (The only fillies to win four classics were Formosa and Sceptre, both in England. Formosa won all the classics except the Derby in 1868, but she only dead-heated in the Two Thousand Guineas. Sceptre in 1902 won all the classics, except the Derby, in which she was beaten, being then in season; however, she was beaten by Kizil Kourgan in the Grand Prix de Paris.)

When Kizil Kourgan was retired, Saint-Alary bred some minor winners from her, and then twice bred her to his own stallion, Chouberski, the winner of his only start over one and seven-eighths miles. The matings with Chouberski produced indifferent results, and he next bred her to Chouberski's son, Bruleur, to whom she produced a bay colt, Kwang Su, in 1916. The colt bred back to the heavy, coarse Bruleur side of his pedigree and apparently was useless or unsound.

Kizil Kourgan was barren in 1917, and then in 1918, at the age of nineteen produced another foal by Bruleur. This was the chestnut colt Ksar. The Bruleur—Kizil Kourgan foals were inbred with one free generation to Omnium II, to whom Ksar bore a marked resemblance.

Saint-Alary decided to sell Ksar as a yearling, and the colt was bought for the then-record French yearling price of 151,000 francs by Edmond Blanc, who also had paid the English record price of 37,500 guineas for Flying Fox in 1900 at the Duke of Westminster's dispersal. Both horses carried the same degree of inbreeding (to which many breeders object), and in both cases Blanc turned out to be right. His comment, after having bought Ksar was: "Yes, he is ugly, but he is ugly in exactly the same way as Omnium II. Besides, he is a beautiful walker!"

Actually, Ksar was about the most refined and bloodlike horse the author ever saw, and had the finest set of forelegs, bar none. He suffered, however, from large flat feet, which hampered him on hard going. Also, despite having forelegs of unsurpassed structure and quality, Ksar was markedly sickle hocked—a characteristic that he passed on to Tourbillon—but his hocks never caused him the least trouble in training.

Unlike most of the late-maturing Bruleur stock, Ksar raced at two, but he only started twice. His first appearance was in the seven-furlong Prix de la Salamandre, the most important race for juveniles between the six-furlong Prix Morny at Deauville and the championship stakes, the one-mile Grand Criterium in October. There was only a field of four, and Ksar was joint second favorite at 7-5, with Petsik a strong odds-on choice at 3-10. Ksar, ridden by the great old jockey George Stern, who was the stable jockey in the glory days of the Blanc stable, starting in 1904, won by a short head from Petsik.

Ksar's next and last start as a two-year-old was in the nine-furlong Prix Saint Roman, run immediately after the Prix de l'Arc de Triomphe won by Comrade (purchased for 25 pounds as a yearling during the war). Ksar started at the short price of 11-10 in a field of seven, but went under by a half-length to Soldat II.

Ksar's three-year-old campaign was one long succession of triumphs in the most important French stakes, interrupted only by a failure in the Grand Prix de Paris, for which there may have been a valid explanation. His first start was in the important Prix Hocquart (one and a half miles) for which, surprisingly, he started only second favorite to Baron Edouard de Rothschild's Tacite. The betting was close, Tacite at 6-5 and Ksar at 7-5. The race itself was not close, as Ksar beat Tacite by three lengths. After dismounting, jockey Stern—who habitually carried around with him a pugnacious and somewhat sour expression—said, "This is an exceptional horse."

The Prix Lupin was the next important race for three-year-olds on May 29, run over a course of one and three-eighths miles. It attracted a field of seven, but this time Ksar was odds-on at 3-5, while Tacite was 5-1. The result was the same as in the Hocquart, but Ksar only won by three-quarters of a length from Tacite.

The French Derby (Prix du Jockey-Club) was run at Chantilly on June 12 over the traditional Derby distance of one and a half miles. For some reason, Frank Bullock was sent over from England to ride Ksar, while George Stern had the mount on Marcel Boussac's Grazing. They finished first and second, with Ksar an easy victor by one and a half lengths in a field of nineteen. He started at the short price of 11-10.

On June 26, the Grand Prix de Paris was run at Longchamp over its usual distance of one and seven-eighths miles. Ksar was made a hot favorite at 6-5 in a field of seventeen, but ran a very bad race behind the English colt Lemonora, Flechois, and Harpocrate. Since Ksar habitually defeated both Flechois and Harpocrate with

KSAR					
KSAR	Bruleur, 1910	Chouberski, 1902	Gardefeu, 1895	Cambyse, 1884	Androcles / Cambuse
				Bougie, 1887	Bruce / La Lumiere
			Campanule, 1891	The Bard, 1883	Petrarch / Magdalene
				St. Lucia, 1880	Rosicrucian / Rose Of Tralee
		Basse Terre, 1899	**Omnium II**, 1892	Upas, 1883	Dollar / Rosemary
				Bluette, 1886	Wellingtonia / Blue Serge
			Bijou, 1890	St Gatien, 1881	The Rover / Saint Editha
				Thora, 1878	Doncaster / Freia
	Kizil Kourgan, 1899	**Omnium II**, 1892	Upas, 1883	Dollar, 1860	The Flying Dutchman / Payment
				Rosemary, 1870	Skirmisher / Vertumna
			Bluette, 1886	Wellingtonia, 1869	Chattanooga / Araucaria
				Blue Serge, 1876	Hermit / Blue Sleeves
		Kasbah, 1892	Vigilant, 1879	Vermouth, 1861	The Nabob / Vermeille
				Virgule, 1865	Saunterer / Violet
			Katia, 1883	Guy Dayrell, 1867	Wild Dayrell / Reginella
				Keapsake, 1873	Gladiateur / Humming Bird

Ksar

considerable ease, there was evidently something wrong with the form.

Various explanations were forthcoming. One was that the ground was very firm, and Ksar's flat feet could not cope with it without stinging him; this may possibly have been so. Secondly, he had been through three races over a distance of ground against the best colts in France, and this was too much for his rather delicate constitution; in other words, there were those who thought that Ksar had gone over the hill and was stale. There were also those who thought that Ksar could not stay one and seven-eighths miles. His breeder told the author that he did not think that Ksar was a true stayer. Since the horse later won the Prix du Cadran at two and a half miles, you can see that Saint-Alary's standards were a trifle high.

Ksar was rested and did not reappear until the Prix Royal-Oak (run over the same course as the Grand Prix) in September. He seemed to be a giant refreshed and had new strength and development beyond the way he looked in his spring campaign. Ridden by Bullock again, he slammed Flechois and Harpocrate, which had beaten him in the Grand Prix, as well as Grazing and Tacite. After a rest of three weeks, Ksar came out for the Arc de Triomphe as about the hottest favorite on record at 11-10 in a field of twelve. He again won as he liked, by two lengths, with Stern back in the saddle again.

His last race of the season was somewhat of an anti-climax. After a rest of only ten days (not enough for Ksar), he only managed to dead heat with Vatel in the Prix Edgard Gillois at one and five-eighths miles. He was giving sixteen pounds to Vatel, whom he had beaten easily before.

As a four-year-old, Ksar was out early, on April 2, in the one and a quarter-mile Prix des Sablons, traditionally the most important spring stakes in France for older colts. He must have been training well, as his odds were only 3-5 in a field of nine. With Bullock up again, he won as he liked.

Next, Ksar came out for the two and a half-mile Prix du Cadran, the French equivalent of the Ascot Gold Cup. The public did not exactly share Saint-Alary's views as to Ksar's ability to stay and made him an odds-on favorite at 3-10. Again, he beat Flechois and Harpocrate, this time by a length.

Ksar's next race was the one and nine-sixteenths-mile Prix du

YEAR	AGE	STS	1ST	2ND	3RD	EARNED
1920	at 2	2	1	1	0	24,500 Fr
1921	at 3	7	6	0	0	1,041,900 Fr
1922	at 4	6	4	2	0	595,375 Fr
Lifetime		**15**	**11**	**3**	**0**	**1,634,775 Fr**

President de la Republique at Saint-Cloud. This time, his jockey was Joe Childs who had not ridden him before. Childs was an extremely good jockey, especially in distance races, where he loved to wait and come from behind. The consensus was that Childs in fact waited a little too long, and Ksar just failed by a head to peg back the Irish colt Kircubbin. This was quite a shock for the chalk players who had backed Ksar at 3-10.

It evidently was felt that Ksar needed another public appearance before trying for his second Arc de Triomphe, so he was sent out on September 24 for the one and a half-mile Prix du Prince d'Orange, a stakes of no great importance. He won it all right at odds of 2-5, by four lengths against ordinary stakes horses.

Ksar duly appeared again for the Arc de Triomphe on October 8 and won it again from Flechois, by two and a half lengths. The interesting feature of the race was that among the three-year-old starters, both Ramus, the French Derby winner, and Kefalin, the Grand Prix winner, were down the course.

The last start of the season and the last race of Ksar's life was the Prix Gladiateur of about three and seven-eighths miles. The going was heavy and at odds of 1-10, Ksar went under to Flechois by two lengths.

Ksar was retired from the Turf as the only $100,000 winner whose sire and dam also had each won more than $100,000. There is no doubt that by French standards of the time Ksar was an outstanding racer, but there is some question as to where French form stood in relation to English form. It must be remembered that in that era French races were closed to English horses, except for the Grand Prix and the Arc de Triomphe. (There was also a *semaine International* in the autumn, when certain races were open to non-French horses, and horses bred on the European continent—excluding England and Ireland—received weight concessions of eleven pounds.) Many racing men in France at the time told the author that they were of the opinion that the French form was somewhere about fourteen pounds behind the English. This was, of course, pure conjecture, as there was not much crossing of the Channel to test out the matter. Ksar undoubtedly was a higher-class racer than was his sire Bruleur, but hardly as good a stallion. He led the sire list in France in 1931 and sired the classic winners Tourbillon (French Derby), Thor (French Derby and second in the Ascot Gold Cup, defeating Hyperion), Ukrania (French Oaks), and Le Ksar (English Two Thousand Guineas). He got a number of other high-class winners.

Ksar did one thing that Bruleur did not do—he sired a great stallion (Tourbillon).

Edmond Blanc died in 1920, and his world-famous Jardy stud began to go downhill from that moment. Hence, Ksar's opportunities were not what they would have been if Blanc had been in charge of his stud career. Like Bruleur's, Ksar's stock matured late and were long on stamina, but short on first-class speed.

In his old age, Ksar was bought by the author and was imported to the United States, in the hope that by crossing his stout blood with the speed of native American strains something beneficial might result. Unfortunately, Ksar nearly died on the voyage over, and only made two stud seasons in the United States, from which a good many winners of ordinary quality emerged, but nothing of importance.

End Notes:

1. The *French Stud Book* shows Monsieur Th. Dousdebes as breeder of Omnium II.

CHAPTER SIXTY

TOURBILLON

I t is a pleasant, though generally useless, occupation to explain successes in breeding ventures and on the Turf, after the events. In the case of Tourbillon, it all seems so clear in retrospect that one is left wondering why a dozen other breeders did not think of the same thing. When George Bernard Shaw was reviewing Oscar Wilde's sparkling comedy, *The Importance of Being Earnest*, he wrote that on going into the theatre lobby during the intermission and listening to the conversation, it seemed clear to him that everyone in London could have written a better and wittier comedy—except George Bernard Shaw.

Our story begins when the American Herman Duryea took his American stock to France before World War I to escape the collapse of racing in New York from 1910 to 1913. In 1910, he bred in France a filly named Banshee, by Irish Lad, out of the good American stakes winner Frizette (by Hamburg). Banshee was a high-class filly, running second in the Prix Morny at Deauville and winning the Poule d'Essai des Pouliches (French One Thousand Guineas) as a three-year-old. When Banshee was retired, Duryea bred her to his own stallion, Durbar II, with whom he had won the Epsom Derby. While a Derby winner, Durbar II was considerably inferior to Sardanapale and La Farina in France.

The result of this mating was Durban, who was purchased by Marcel Boussac, along with a good many other horses from the Duryea estate. Durban also turned out to be a high-class filly on the Turf, winning as a two-year-old the Grand Criterium d'Ostende in Belgium and the Grand Criterium over one mile at Longchamp, the latter race emblematic of the two-year-old championship of France. As a three-year-old, she was beaten in the English One Thousand Guineas and French Oaks (Prix de Diane), but she did win the important Prix Vermeille at a distance of one and a half miles.

It must have been obvious to Boussac that with this first-class accumulation of speed (and some stamina) in three straight generations of mares, he should cast about for a source of high-class distance capacity, well up to classic standard, in order to meet the requirements of the French racing program. What better than the great classic winner Ksar, winner of the French Derby, Prix Royal-Oak, and twice winner of the Prix de l'Arc de Triomphe? The concentrated French strains of Omnium II and Dollar would give a complete outcross to the American strains in Durban, in whom Hanover appeared twice.

Acting on this logic (and perhaps other thoughts as well), Boussac twice sent Durban to Ksar, and from these matings he obtained the high-class filly Diademe—plus Tourbillon. It is doubtful that Tourbillon was quite as good a racer as Ksar had been, but he was a horse of a different style of racing.

Marcel Boussac

As a two-year-old, Tourbillon was slightly more precocious than was Ksar, coming out on July 23 instead of in September as Ksar had done. For his debut, at Chantilly in a race of five and one-half furlongs, he could not have been too much "expected," as he started at odds of 6-1 in a field of fifteen. Nevertheless, he won by a half-length, and there were three previous winners in the field. Six days later, he came out for the Prix d'Aumale, an important event of six furlongs, with 50,000 francs added. Tourbillon had created a sufficiently good impression to start favorite against thirteen others, but went under by two lengths to Taraskoia.

A month later, he was sent to Germany to contest the Prix de l'Avenir (Futurity) over six furlongs at Baden-Baden, with 120,000 francs added. Tourbillon duly won the race, giving about thirteen pounds to the second horse, Filmenau. His last race of the year was for the Grand Criterium at Longchamp, a race that had been won by his dam. The warm favorite, Indus, won at odds of 19-10, while Tourbillon was only sixth, at 9-1. His was the record of a good two-year-old, but by no means a smasher.

As a three-year-old Tourbillon, true to his Ksar–Bruleur blood, showed marked improvement over his two-year-old form. He first appeared in the one and five-sixteenths-mile Prix Greffulhe, one of the successive Prix des Produits leading up to the two principal spring classics for three-year-old colts, the Prix du Jockey-Club (French Derby) and the Grand Prix de Paris. The public accepted the form of the previous autumn, when Indus had been a decisive winner over Tourbillon in the Grand Criterium. In fact, Tourbillon hardly could have been thought to be very fit, as he was only sixth favorite at 17-1 in a field of fifteen, while Indus went off at 5-2. Nevertheless, Tourbillon won by a length, with Indus third, beaten one and one-half lengths.

Next came the Prix Hocquart, at one and one-half miles on May 10. The public's eyes had been opened about Tourbillon, and his odds were only 13-10 in a field of eight. He won again, beating a Bruleur colt, Bruledur, by three lengths. The still-more important Prix Lupin of one and five-sixteenths miles was contested on May 31. In it Tourbillon was odds-on at 3-5 against eight others, including Indus. He won again, by a length, with Indus unplaced.

Then came his first true classic, the Prix du Jockey-Club at one and one-half miles. In a field of sixteen, Tourbillon was a strong favorite at 2-1, and he won again, beating Bruledur by two lengths. A neck farther back was Barneveldt.

Two weeks later, on June 28, the same group of colts contested the one and seven-eighths-mile Grand Prix de Paris. Like his sire Ksar, Tourbillon was a hot

		Chouberski, 1902	Gardefeu, 1895	Cambyse / Bougie
	Bruleur, 1910		Campanule, 1891	The Bard / Saint Lucia
		Basse Terre, 1899	Omnium II, 1892	Upas / Bluette
Ksar, 1918			Bijou, 1890	**St. Gatien** / Thora
	Kizil Kourgan, 1899	Omnium II, 1892	Upas, 1883	Dollar / Rosemary
			Bluette, 1886	Wellingtonia / Blue Serge
		Kasbah, 1892	Vigilant, 1879	Vermouth / Virgule
TOURBILLON			Katia, 1883	Guy Dayrell / Keepsake
	Durbar, 1911	Rabelais, 1900	St. Simon, 1881	Galopin / St. Angela
			Satirical, 1891	Satiety / Chaff
		Armenia, 1901	Meddler, 1890	**St. Gatien** / Busybody
Durban, 1918			Urania, 1892	Hanover / Wanda
	Banshee, 1910	Irish Lad, 1900	Candlemas, 1883	Hermit / Fusee
			Arrowgrass, 1889	Enquirer / Sparrowgrass
		Frizette, 1905	Hamburg, 1895	Hanover / Lady Reel
			Ondulee, 1898	St. Simon / Ornis

Tourbillon

favorite for the race. He went under to Barneveldt and Taxodium by a neck and one and one-half lengths. Only a week later, the same colts came out for the Prix du President de la Republique of one and five-eighths miles at Saint-Cloud. Tourbillon again was the favorite, at 9-5, over Barneveldt at 5-2, but that time Barneveldt won decisively by six lengths.

Tourbillon then was rested until mid-September, when he was one of a party of seven in the Prix Royal-Oak (French St. Leger), run over the Grand Prix course of one and seven-eighths miles. Naturally, Barneveldt was favorite, at 7-10, having defeated Tourbillon twice, but there was in the field a new, very late maturing colt in Deiri, who was well-backed. While Tourbillon was 44-10, Deiri was 48-10. Deiri came home a comfortable winner by two lengths from Tourbillon, with Bruledur third by a neck. Barneveldt was fourth.

When the ex-jockey Willie Pratt had inspected Deiri as a two-year-old, his comment had been, "He might make a backend ten-year-old."

(Deiri was half-owned by the trainer, W. Claude Halsey, whose stable in France was some way from the front rank at the time. One day, Halsey was going to Longchamp with Frank Carter, the leading trainer in France. Carter was moaning and complaining about the bad run of luck he was having:

"I haven't won a race for three weeks!"

"I don't know why you are complaining," said Halsey. "I haven't won a race either!"

"I know that," said Carter, gloomily, "but you're used to it!")

The great race of the autumn in France is the Arc de Triomphe, for three-year-olds and up at one and one-half miles, weight-for-age. Tourbillon again started favorite, at 2-1, against nine others. The result was something of an upset, with the great filly Pearl Cap (later the dam of the Epsom Derby winner Pearl Diver) the winner by a length from the four-year-old Amfortas (also by Ksar). The crack Belgian colt (and later great sire) Prince Rose was third.

The Arc was Tourbillon's last race, and some comparison of his form with that of his sire Ksar is in order. Tourbillon's spring form as a three-year-old was much the same as Ksar's, but whereas Ksar came out in the autumn and proved that he was a great horse, against all ages and all comers, Tourbillon's form tailed off into a distinct decline. In fact, he never won another race after the French Derby.

YEAR	AGE	STS	1ST	2ND	3RD	EARNED
1930	at 2 (in Ger)	1	1	0	0	26,550 DM
In Germany		1	1	0	0	26,550 DM
1930	at 2 (in Fr)	3	1	1	0	33,000 Fr
1931	at 3 (in Fr)	8	4	2	1	1,490,655 Fr
In France		11	5	3	1	1,523,655 Fr

Tourbillon's jockey, Charlie Elliott, told the author that Tourbillon was not a natural stayer, but that if he could hold him up to about the last 150 yards of a race, he could produce a tremendous burst of speed. This meant, of course, that in races where the pace was moderate, Tourbillon had a great advantage, while in races such as the Arc de Triomphe, which is invariably run at a hot pace from end to end, Tourbillon no longer had his reserves left at the critical moment for his habitual burst of speed.

Historically, colts capable of devastating bursts of speed have made very good sires. This was true of St. Simon, Nearco, and many others.

Tourbillon's pedigree represented the kind of model that appealed greatly to the late William Woodward Sr., who told the author several times that he tried to have his pedigrees as "solid" as possible. By that, Woodward meant a pedigree with as few names as possible representing neither racing nor breeding class. According to the author's recollection, Woodward never succeeded in producing a pedigree as "solid" as Tourbillon's. The colt's first two dams were classic winners, and his third dam (Frizette) was a good stakes winner and a splendid broodmare and taproot. His sire's first two dams were classic winners of the highest class. One had to go back to the third generation to find an animal without first-class credentials (Chouberski).

Is it any wonder that Tourbillon became a first-class sire? He became, in fact, the best French sire to date in the twentieth century, leading the sire list three times (he was also three times second and twice third). Had he not been virtually a private stallion, reserved for the mares owned by Marcel Boussac, he undoubtedly would have made a still better record. In this connection, it is interesting to observe that the late Lord Derby (the seventeenth Earl), whose stud developed all the successful sire lines in England, except the Hurry On line, never kept any of his stallions as private sires. His included such as Swynford, Pharos, Fairway, Hyperion, and Alycidon.

The chart below indicates the wisdom of his policy.

DERBY STUD	MAJOR OFFSPRING FROM OUTSIDE MARES	MAJOR OFFSPRING FROM HOME MARES
Swynford	Blandford, Challenger II, St. Germans	Sansovino
Pharos	Nearso, Pharis, Cameronian	
Fairway	Blue Peter, Meadow	Fair Copy
Hyperion	Owen Tudor, Alibhai, Aldis Lamp	Gulf Stream

Furthermore, Lord Derby did not reserve the right to approve outside mares, feeling that the mares' owners knew far more about them than he did. How different is this policy than the many cases of "approved mares only" which so frequently are seen in stallion advertisements.

Tourbillon was a highly nervous horse, as were his sire and grandsire, and developed something of a temper, which also went with his male line. He had the splendid forelegs and sickle hocks of his sire, Ksar, but was not quite as bloodlike and majestic in personality and appearance.

Among the great races of the French Turf won by Tourbillon's stock were: Prix du Jockey-Club—Cillas and Coaraze; Grand Prix de Paris—Caracalla; Prix de l'Arc de Triomphe—Djebel and Caracalla; Prix Royal-Oak—Caracalla and Tourment; Poule d'Essai des Poulains—Gaspillage, Djebel, and Tourment; Poule d'Essai des Pouliches—Esmeralda; Prix Lupin—Tornado and Ambiorix; Prix du Cadran—Turmoil; Grand Prix de Saint-Cloud—Djebel, Coaraze, and Magnific; Grand Criterium—Ambiorix; Prix Morny—Esmeralda, Coaraze, and Cadir.

In England, Tourbillon's son Djebel won the Middle Park Plate and Two Thousand Guineas, and Caracalla won the Ascot Gold Cup. Another son, Goya II, won the Gimcrack Stakes.

Although Caracalla was unbeaten, Djebel probably was the highest-class colt sired by Tourbillon. Djebel also led the French sire list three times, but his branch of the male line has not bred on very well.[1] One of Boussac's remarkable experiments was to breed Djebel (by Tourbillon) to a daughter of Tourbillon, and from this mating he obtained the outstanding filly Coronation (Arc de Triomphe, etc.). Coronation, however, never produced a live foal.

Tourbillon's influence in the United States has come chiefly through Ambiorix, winner of the two-year-old champion-

Adaris	U.S.A.		Le Volcan	Colombie
Amasis	Chili		Magnific	Uruguay
Ambiorix	U.S.A.		Marcius	Afrique du Sud
Cadir	Brésil		Méridien	France
Cagire	Angleterre		Micipsa	France
Caracalla	France		Olmedo	France
Charleval	Australie		Ringo	France
Cillas	Irlande		Tarpan	Hollande
Coaraze	Brésil		Timor	Argentine
Djask	Afrique du Sud		Tornado	France
Djebel	France		Tourment	France
Goya	U.S.A.		Tournoi	Canada
Hylas	France	Tourbillon	Turmoil	France
Last Post	France	1928-1954	Whirlebwind	Allemagne
		et ses fils étalons		

A.P.R.H. PHOTO

Tourbillon with a list of his sons at stud

ship race, the Grand Criterium, of one mile. Ambiorix's stamina was not quite up to the French classic standards. He won two of the Poule des Produits in the spring, the ten and one-half-furlong Prix Greffulhe, and the Prix Lupin of the same distance, but he was second in the twelve-furlong Prix Hocquart and also in the twelve-furlong French Derby. He was not started in the one and seven-eighths-mile Grand Prix de Paris.

As a two-year-old, Ambiorix was ranked seven pounds above the filly Coronation, but as a three-year-old, he was ranked thirteen pounds below her and was only eighth in the ratings of the French official handicapper.

Ambiorix was imported and stood at Claiborne Farm. He sired fifty-two stakes winners and led the sire list in 1961.

End Notes:

1. A resurgence of the Djebel branch of the Tourbillon line in Europe marked the end of the twentieth century through his tail-male descendant Ahonoora and his sons, including Indian Ridge, Inchinor, and Dr Devious.

CHAPTER SIXTY-ONE

DJEBEL

During the late 1930s Marcel Boussac was becoming the foremost breeder in France and the owner of the country's most powerful racing stable. The chief reasons for this emergence were his ownership of Tourbillon, probably the best French sire to date in the twentieth century, and his extensive patronage of Pharos, standing in France as the property of Lord Derby. By breeding to Pharos, Boussac obtained Pharis, who started only three times but is thought by many French racing men to have been the best racer ever seen in France (possibly excluding Ribot, and with a side glance at Sea-Bird). Sons of Tourbillon included Djebel, who was the first of many high-class racers by the sire that were bred and raced by Boussac. It was a close thing, the matter of Boussac being the breeder of Djebel. He had entered his dam, Loika, in the December sales, but decided at the last moment to withdraw her. She had not been a winner and had not proven to be an easy mare to get in foal. Her second dam was Cambridgeshire winner Ballantrae, an ancestress of Equipoise. Loika's dam, Coeur a Coeur, by Teddy, was foaled when her dam was twenty-two years of age.

Since Djebel was foaled in 1937, his racing career was to some extent interrupted by World War II. Nevertheless, we have a pretty good line on him and his capabilities. His first start was on June 11, 1939, at Chantilly, in a five-furlong affair for two-year-olds that had not started previously. Lord Derby's Lighthouse (by Pharos) was a hot favorite in a field of six at 9-10 and justified the odds, beating Djebel a length. Djebel's next race was in another five-furlong contest, at Longchamp, where he was 11-10 in a field of seven and won by three lengths.

In the relatively important Prix d'Aumale on August 1 at Chantilly, Lighthouse again beat Djebel a length. Probably this form for Djebel was pretty high, as Lighthouse was second the next year in the English Derby. Djebel next tried one of the major races for two-year-olds in France, the Prix Morny at Deauville, run over a straight six furlongs. Djebel that time beat Lighthouse, but in turn went under to Furane by three-quarters of a length. On the strength of this result,

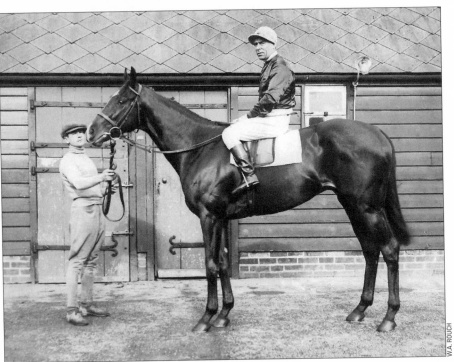

W.A. ROUCH

Djebel

Djebel was sent over to Newmarket to run for the Middle Park Stakes, the so-called two-year-old Derby. He duly won it, by two lengths, from Tant Mieux, about the best of the English two-year-olds, and Godiva, who won the One Thousand Guineas in England the next year.

In 1940, of course, the war was on, but Djebel at three raced until the German invasion of France made things too hot. He began by winning the ten-furlong Prix Lagrange by two lengths at the cramped odds of 2-5. He then went over to Newmarket again and won the one-mile Two Thousand Guineas by two lengths from Stardust and Tant Mieux.

With racing suspended by the German invasion of France, Djebel was not out again until October, when he won the one-mile Prix d'Essai at Auteuil. In his last start of the year, in the one and five-eighths-mile Prix de Chantilly, also run at Auteuil, Djebel was odds-on at 1-2, but only ran third to Quicko and Raffaello, beaten one and a half lengths.

The Germans permitted racing to resume at Longchamp in 1941. The author has been told that the usual method of transportation in those days was to ride bicycles, so that the parking areas were a forest of bikes, with practically no automobiles. Presumably, the horses rode in luxury in vans from Chantilly and Maisons-Laffitte, while the humans provided their own motive power.

Djebel began the season on April 12 by taking the fairly important Prix Boiard of ten furlongs at Longchamp. His odds were 2-5 in a field of five, which included Horatius, also in the Boussac stable. His next outing was at the same place on May 24, when he won the Prix d'Harcourt, a traditional stakes of one and a half miles. There he took his revenge on Quicko, who had beaten him in his last start the previous year. The result was well anticipated, for Djebel was 3-10 and Quicko, who finished third, was 6-1. Djebel conceded five pounds and won by a neck. On June 8, there was another success for Djebel in the ten-furlong Prix d'Hedouville, a race of less importance that did not have another horse of class in the field of six.

In the Grand Prix de Saint-Cloud (run that year at Longchamp) at one and five-eighths miles, Djebel (134) went under by a length to Maurepas. This defeat, coupled with the closeness of Djebel's earlier win at one and a half miles, raised a question as to Djebel's stoutness. Maurepas, however, beat him again by a length at level weight in the shorter Prix de Chantilly (one and three-sixteenths miles), suggesting that at that stage Maurepas simply was the better of the two.

The Prix de l'Arc de Triomphe, for three-year-olds and up at weight for age

DJEBEL					
Tourbillon, 1928	Ksar, 1918	Bruleur, 1910	Chouberski, 1902	Gardefeu Campanule	
			Basse Terre, 1899	Omnium II Bijou	
		Kizil Kourgan, 1899	Omnium II, 1892	Upas Bluette	
			Kasbah, 1892	Vigilant Katia	
	Durban, 1918	Durbar II, 1911	Rabelais, 1900	St. Simon Satirical	
			Armenia, 1901	Meddler Urania	
		Banshee, 1910	Irish Lad, 1900	Candlemas Arrowgrass	
			Frizette, 1905	Hamburg Ondulee	
Loika, 1926	Gay Crusader, 1914	Bayardo, 1906	Bay Ronald, 1893	Hampton Black Duchess	
			Galicia, 1898	Galopin Isoletta	
		Gay Laura, 1909	Beppo, 1903	Marco Pitti	
			Galeottia, 1892	Galopin Agave	
	Coeur a Coeur, 1921	Teddy, 1913	Ajax, 1901	Flying Fox Amie	
			Rondeau, 1900	Bay Ronald Doremi	
		Ballantrae, 1899	Ayrshire, 1885	Hampton Atalanta	
			Abeyance, 1885	Touchet Minnie Hauk	

over one and a half miles, is invariably the most important race in France. In it, Djebel was only third to the three-year-old Le Pacha, beaten a short head and two lengths. Le Pacha was the best of the 1938 generation but had the reputation of being a one-paced plodder. Hence, the race again raised question as to Djebel's distance capacity in a fast-run race such as the Arc de Triomphe, which is nearly always run at a cracking pace.

Again in 1942, the Germans permitted racing at Longchamp. On April 6, Djebel won the ten-furlong Prix des Sablons, then France's most important race for horses older than three. Second was Adaris, his stablemate, and the entry was 9-10 in a field of sixteen. Djebel then took the Prix Boiard, also at ten furlongs, to the surprise of practically no one. His odds were 1-10. About the only remarkable thing here was the weight scale, ranging from 140 pounds on Djebel down to a bottom weight of 133 pounds.

Djebel then took the Prix d'Harcourt of one and a half miles at odds of 1-5, but as there was not another horse of class in the race, this may not have meant too much. Another victory followed in the unimportant Prix d'Hedouville at ten furlongs. This was almost money for nothing.

YEAR	AGE	STS	1ST	2ND	3RD	EARNED
1939	at 2 (in Eng)	1	1	0	0	£ 775
1940	at 3 (in Eng)	1	1	0	0	£5,340
In England		2	2	0	0	£6,115
1939	at 2 (in Fr)	4	1	3	0	48,100 Fr
1940	at 3 (in Fr)	3	2	0	1	22,500 Fr
1941	at 4 (in Fr)	6	3	2	1	370,000 Fr
1942	at 5 (in Fr)	7	7	0	0	2,913,660 Fr
In France		20	13	5	2	3,354,260 Fr

The next race, however, probably did mean something. It was the one and nine-sixteenths-mile Grand Prix de Saint-Cloud, run at Longchamp. Djebel won again, but only by a head from Le Pacha (receiving two pounds). This seemed to show that Djebel had improved from four to five years of age, as Le Pacha had beaten him in the Arc de Triomphe the year before.

An easy race came Djebel's way in the one and five-sixteenths-mile Prix de Chantilly. The last race of the year and the last race of Djebel's career was the Arc de Triomphe. For it, Le Pacha and his stablemate started at 4-5, with Djebel priced at 18-10. Djebel won handily, by two lengths, and Le Pacha was unplaced. The time, however, was a very poor 2:37 over off going.

Djebel had gone through his five-year-old season unbeaten in seven races.

Any colt that can win the Middle Park in England, the Two Thousand Guineas in England, and the Arc de Triomphe in France at the end of an unbeaten season as a five-year-old must be accounted a very high-class racer.

SKEETS MEADORS

My Babu

There is just one shadow overhanging the record as a whole. Immediately after the end of World War II, there naturally was considerable bitterness on the part of those French breeders, owners, and trainers who had been unable to secure adequate feeding rations for their animals due to the controls imposed by the German occupying authorities. Some establishments, it was maintained, were able to obtain adequate rations, and this gave them an unfair advantage over their less-fortunate competitors. The Boussac establishment generally was supposed to have been among the more fortunate. Even if this charge could have been proven, however, it certainly did nothing to account for Djebel's victories in the Middle Park in 1939 and the Guineas in 1940—which occurred before the German invasion of France.

Djebel's victories in England occurred near the beginning of a period lasting from 1938 (Bois Roussel's Derby) until 1950 (Galcador's Derby), when the French horses were superior to the British in the English classics. This superiority could be laid at the door of the French sires Tourbillon, Djebel, Pharis, and Vatellor. The two best sires in England at the time, Hyperion and Nearco, could not seem

Luthier

to match them, but the long-term carrying power of the blood of Hyperion and Nearco proved superior to that of the four French sires mentioned above.

Physically, Djebel was a small horse of the quick type and of high quality. He was a remarkable sire, leading the French sire list in three consecutive years, 1947–49. He was second on the list in 1950 and again was among the top ten in four of the next five years.[1] He died at Boussac's stud in 1958.

Among the best offspring of Djebel were Coronation, winner of the Arc de Triomphe; Galcador, winner of the Epsom Derby; Appolonia, winner of the French Oaks and French One Thousand Guineas; Cordova, winner of the Prix Morny; Djeddah, winner of the Champion Stakes; Argur, winner of the Eclipse Stakes; Djelfa, winner of the French One Thousand Guineas; Djebellica, winner of the Irish Oaks; Janiari, winner of the Prix Vermeille; Clarion, winner of the Grand Criterium; Montenica, winner of the French Oaks; Hugh Lupus, winner of the Irish Two Thousand Guineas, and My Babu, winner of the English Two Thousand Guineas.

My Babu, who was imported to this country, sired forty-one stakes winners, including Our Babu, Gambetta (dam of Gamely), Milesian, Primera, Garwol,

Crozier, and Bronze Babu. He is also the broodmare sire of champion Damascus, a leading stallion.

Djeddah, by Djebel, likewise sired fillies that later produced major runners in this country. His daughters included stakes winner Lalun, dam of Never Bend and Bold Reason, plus Breath O'Morn, dam of Proud Clarion and Knightly Dawn.

In terms of tail-male line, Djebel's strong branches through My Babu included that of Primera, sire of Aunt Edith and other major winners. In recent years, a strong classic link in England has traced to Djebel through his son Hugh Lupus. The latter sired English St. Leger winner Hethersett, who in turn sired Epsom Derby winner Blakeney. The last-named is the sire of the 1975 English Oaks and Irish Guinness Oaks winner, Juliette Marny.

Another present line is that of Le Lavandou, he a son of Djebel and the sire of Le Levanstell. The last-named is the sire of Levmoss, winner of the Arc de Triomphe and the Ascot Gold Cup.

Another branch prominent in recent years is that of Klairon, a son of Clarion, he by Djebel. Klairon's get includes Lorenzaccio, winner of the Champion Stakes in England, and also Luthier, a major winner in France who ranked first on the general sire list in France in 1976 and second on the juvenile sire list in 1974.[2]

End Notes:

1. ThoroughbredHeritage.com lists Djebel as leading French sire in 1956 as well.

2. Luthier also ranked first on France's leading sire list in 1982–84. He was France's leading broodmare sire from 1987 to 1990 and in 1992–93 and 1995. Lorenzaccio sired Ahonoora, who is the source of this sire line in Europe today, mainly through Indian Ridge and his sons.

CHAPTER SIXTY-TWO

AMBIORIX

F rom the standpoint of a series on sire lines, the chief interest in Ambiorix
lies in how the character and capacities of his particular sire line changed
in the course of four generations. The great-grandsire of Ambiorix,
Bruleur, was a late-maturing colt, even by French standards, and did not reach
his best form until the distances were at least one and seven-eighths miles, as in
the Grand Prix de Paris; Bruleur's son Ksar was a pretty fair two-year-old and was
supreme among French colts from ten furlongs to two and a half miles; Ksar's
son Tourbillon, having some speedier blood introduced through his dam, was a
still better two-year-old and was the best of his age up to the Derby distance of
twelve furlongs, but not beyond that; Ambiorix, son of Tourbillon, again having
more speed introduced into his pedigree through his dam, was a still better two-
year-old than Tourbillon but was not quite up to the twelve-furlong French Derby
(Prix du Jockey-Club) test.

Clearly, here was a pattern extending over four generations, where each succeeding generation was faster than the preceding one, and also had less distance
capacity. The careers of the four horses illustrate the vast differences in racing
qualities demanded by the French and American racing programs. In France, the
two most important races are the Prix du Jockey-Club and the Prix de l'Arc de
Triomphe, each at one and a half miles. In those two races, the sons of Bruleur
(the late-maturing stayer) were successful a total of eight times; the stock of his
contemporary, Teddy, were successful only once. It seems that for French classic
racing, Bruleur was a considerably better sire than was Teddy, whose stock were
faster but did not get the trip in the longer classics. Transferred to American racing programs, the blood of Teddy was highly successful, chiefly through his sons
Sir Gallahad III, Bull Dog, and Sun Teddy, and the mare La Troienne, whereas the
blood of Bruleur was a failure.

When we discuss the relative merits of different bloodlines, we must take into
consideration the relative differences of the racing programs. The late Professor

BLOOD-HORSE LIBRARY

Ambiorix

Einstein would have been much pleased with these lines of observation, although he never applied his mathematical abilities to Turf speculation. (Just think of the havoc Einstein could have created as a handicapper.)

Foaled in 1946, Ambiorix was bred by Marcel Boussac, whose stud was by far the best in France at the time. Among the reasons for Boussac's standing was his ownership of Tourbillon. Boussac also bred many mares to Lord Derby's Pharos, who introduced the much-needed factor for greater speed into French breeding. (Boussac bred the unbeaten Pharis, who was sired by Pharos.)

By breeding Lavendula (by Pharos), a three-time winner as a two-year-old to Tourbillon, Boussac produced Ambiorix, the last of the very high-class colts sired by Tourbillon. The sire was eighteen years old and the dam sixteen years old when Ambiorix was foaled. Following the general French custom of very light racing of two-year-olds, Ambiorix made only three starts at that age. When he first appeared, on June 24 at Longchamp, he must have taken something of a reputation with him, as his odds were only 8-5 in a field of nine. Ambiorix evidently was given a fairly easy race, as he finished only sixth to Le Texas, who started at 11-10.

A month later, Ambiorix was sent over to Goodwood in England to contest the

Selsey Maiden Stakes. This was a race of no importance, and why Ambiorix was sent over for such a race is unknown to the author. One is tempted to suspect an old-fashioned betting coup, as Ambiorix started at 10-1 in a field of twenty-two and won by six lengths. This was certainly a good thing, but the author does not know who tasted the betting sweets of victory or the extent of punishment inflicted on the English bookmakers.

The only remaining race of the year for Ambiorix was the one-mile Grand Criterium at Longchamp, run in October. That race generally establishes the championship among French two-year-olds. Since the cat had been let well out of the bag by the six-length victory in the Selsey Stakes at Goodwood, Ambiorix was a very warm favorite at 21-10 in a field of twelve. He won easily enough, by two lengths, turning the tables on his former conqueror Le Texas, who was third.

On the Handicap Optional (Free Handicap), Ambiorix headed the list at sixty kilograms, with Amour Drake second at fifty-nine. Since Amour Drake the next year won the French Two Thousand Guineas and was second, most unluckily beaten, in the Epsom Derby, that weighting indicated Ambiorix was a very high-class colt by French standards at least.

As a three-year-old, Ambiorix was out only four times and had two wins and

				Gardefeu
			Chouberski, 1902	Campanule
		Bruleur, 1910		Omnium II
			Basse Terre, 1899	Bijou
	Ksar, 1918			Upas
			Omnium II, 1892	Bluette
		Kizil Kourgan, 1899		Vigilant
			Kasbah, 1892	Katia
Tourbillon, 1928				**St. Simon**
			Rabelais, 1900	Satirical
		Durbar II, 1911		Meddler
			Armenia, 1901	Urania
	Durban, 1918			Candlemas
			Irish Lad, 1900	Arrowgrass
		Banshee, 1910		Hamburg
AMBIORIX			Frizette, 1905	Ondulee
				Cyllene
			Polymelus, 1902	Maid Marian
		Phalaris, 1913		Sainfoin
			Bromus, 1905	Cheery
	Pharos, 1920			**St. Simon**
			Chaucer, 1900	Canterbury Pilgrim
		Scapa Flow, 1914		Love Wisely
Lavendula, 1930			Anchora, 1905	Eryholme
				Isinglass
			John o' Gaunt, 1901	La Fleche
		Swynford, 1907		Tristan
			Canterbury Pilgrim, 1893	Pilgrimage
	Sweet Lavender, 1923			Barcaldine
			Marco, 1892	Novitiate
		Marchetta, 1907		Peter
			Hettie Sorrel, 1891	Venus' Looking Glass

two seconds. His first appearance was in the Prix Greffulhe at one and five-six-teenths miles, one of the traditional Poules des Produits, run every spring to help sort out the classic three-year-olds. Ambiorix was odds-on at 1-5 and won by a length. His next race was the more important Prix Hocquart, at one and a half miles. Ambiorix was again at odds-on, 3-10, in a field of twelve, but could only

A.B. Hancock Jr.

run second to Val Drake, beaten a length. That race cast the first suspicion on the stamina of Ambiorix.

For the Prix Lupin, back again to the distance of one and five-sixteenths miles, Ambiorix still was odds-on at 2-5, and had little trouble winning from an undistin-guished field of seven. The next race for Ambiorix was the Prix du Jockey-Club, run at Chantilly over twelve furlongs. Ambiorix went under, at odds of 4-5, to Good Luck in a small field of seven. The margin of defeat was a half-length.

It is to be noted that both times Ambiorix attempted to go one and a half miles he was beaten and both times he raced one and five-sixteenths miles he won. There can be very little doubt that Ambiorix simply did not stay at one and a half miles.

Ambiorix was imported by the late A.B. (Bull) Hancock Jr. and became a lead-ing sire while standing at Hancock's Claiborne Farm. Speaking of the acquisition of Ambiorix, Hancock once recalled:

"I tried to buy My Babu, but they wanted too much money for him. Ambiorix, a three-parts brother to My Babu, was a three-year-old that year and had been the best two-year-old the year before. He was the favorite for the French Derby. Well, Boussac gave some orders to the jockey that more or less indicated he didn't think the horse would stay. Ambiorix finished second, and the papers panned Boussac pretty badly—said it was his orders that had beaten the colt.

"Boussac felt the colt was not really his type of horse and agreed to sell him. That was just right for me. I paid $250,000 for him." The colt then was syndi-cated by Hancock.

Ambiorix, with his make-up tilting toward speed and away from the stout blood of his male line, could be expected to be much more suitable for American racing conditions than were other representatives of the male line. In tail female, he descended from one of the good families in Lord Derby's stud in England, that of Marchetta, a family that had produced many high-class sires.

Onto the Marchetta influence had been grafted Swynford, which brought in the great broodmare and Oaks winner Canterbury Pilgrim. The next cross was to Pharos, whose dam was Scapa Flow, she also dam of classic winners Fairway and Fair Isle. Pharos also brought in another line of Canterbury Pilgrim.

Ambiorix and his close rel-ative, My Babu, who later also was imported, were proba-bly about the same in racing class as Nasrullah, but they were nothing like so success-ful at stud. Nasrullah came

YEAR	AGE	STS	1ST	2ND	3RD	EARNED
1948	at 2 (in Eng)	1	1	0	0	£832
In England		1	1	0	0	£832
1948	at 2 (in Fr)	2	1	0	0	1,583,750 Fr
1949	at 3 (in Fr)	4	2	2	0	3,054,850 Fr
In France		6	3	2	0	4,638,600 Fr

from the fastest line of sires in England (aside from pure sprinters) and also from the fastest female line in Europe. This comparison of bloodlines coupled with rac-ing class of about equal merit showed once again the importance of speed in the build-up of successful American bloodlines.

This, however, can be taken too far, even for American racing conditions. No successful line of The Tetrarch ever was established in the United States. Several horses in that line were flyers in Europe, but in the main could not get beyond six furlongs. Also, High Time and Wise Counsellor, who were very successful American sires of sheer speed horses and nothing more, have suffered a virtual black out of their blood over the last twenty-five years.

Perhaps the line is very fine, in this country, between the essential speed and the degree of stoutness required for the classic races and most important handi-caps. The great Italian horseman Federico Tesio (breeder of Nearco, Ribot, etc.) despised sprinters as such and never used them for mating to his own mares, but he observed that in the pedigrees of nearly all first-class racers could be found the name of one or more animals possessing outstanding speed. This mixture of first-class speed with classic stoutness was a good part of Tesio's great art as a breeder.

Ambiorix led the American sire list in 1961, and he sired fifty-one stakes win-ners and had an Average-Earnings Index of 2.42 to rank in the top three per cent of sires. Much of his influence came through his daughters, which included the champion runner High Voltage, plus Polamby, Levelix, Make Sail, Rash Statement, Sarcastic, and Fortunate Isle. Ambiorix mares produced seventy-eight stakes winners, including Ragusa, a classic winner and major sire in Europe;

High Voltage

Bold Commander, sire of classic winner Dust Commander; plus Stupendous, Impressive, Selari, Captain's Gig, Vitriolic, and Poleax.

Ambiorix's male line could not be described as strong. Nevertheless, one of his stakes-winning sons, Count Amber, got Amberoid, who in winning the 1966 Belmont Stakes did what the grandsire failed to do—stay one and a half miles in classic company. Ambiorix's sons also include Amber Morn (sire of two Queen's Plate winners), Gray Phantom, Ambehaving, Ambiopoise, Hitting Away, Prego, Rehabilitate, Pinjara, and Pleasure Seeker.

Ambiorix died in 1975 at twenty-nine as a pensioner at Claiborne.

CHAPTER SIXTY-THREE

THE TETRARCH

From time to time, sometimes at intervals as long as twenty-five or thirty years, a meteor streaks across the firmament of the Turf so brilliant in its blazing course that racing devotees are left breathless and spellbound in their admiration. Such a colt was The Tetrarch, who as a two-year-old in 1913 made such a record as has been unsurpassed in its brilliance on the English Turf. In fact, he still is spoken of as probably the fastest two-year-old ever seen in England.

A more unlikely origin than The Tetrarch's would be difficult to find for a colt of such standing. He was sired by Roi Herode, who was imported from France to Ireland by Edward Kennedy of Bishopscourt, Straffan Station, County Kildare. The reason given for this importation was that Kennedy was determined to restore what he called the lost line of Herod to the British Isles. Kennedy had tried one such experiment before, importing from Australia a horse of that male line, but the horse accomplished nothing and had died about the same time of the purchase of Roi Herode.

Another reason for buying Roi Herode may have been his showing in the Doncaster Cup of 1909. Roi Herode, then a five-year-old, carried 136 pounds into second place in that two and one-eighth-mile race, which was won by Amadis, a three-year-old carrying 123 pounds. Third was Dark Ronald, who was bred by Kennedy and who became the most important stallion in Germany.

In all, Roi Herode started twenty-four times in four seasons and won only three races, but he finished second in six, including the French St. Leger. It is worth noting that Roi Herode was unplaced in both his races at two and thereafter was raced in long-distance events without much success. He generally was well up near the pace and then faded in the last stages of his races. His most important victory was in the Provinces in France, where he won the Grand Prix de la Ville de Vichy as a four-year-old.

Roi Herode's sire, Le Samaritain, did not shine as a two-year-old, either. In five starts, he was second once and third once, but at three and four he showed some form in winning the Prix Daru, Grand Prix de Deauville, and the Grand St. Leger de France (at Caen).

Not until we go back to Le Sancy, the sire of Le Samaritain, do we strike a really good racehorse. Le Sancy did win a race at two and was second that year (1886) in the Grand Criterium. He improved with age, until at five and six he carried nearly everything before him. The late Charles Morton (who trained Sceptre and won all the English classics for J.B. Joel) was much impressed by Le Sancy in the horse's final campaigns. He once took a colt from England to Deauville for the Grand Prix there, knowing that there was not a racer back home that could defeat the colt while giving him as much weight as Le Sancy would. After Le Sancy had beaten his candidate in the Grand Prix de Deauville, Morton retired to England licking his financial wounds, as he was very free with his betting money whenever convinced that a horse of his held a good chance.

The main point of the above survey of three generations of sires leading to The Tetrarch is that they all were late-maturing racers and all were deemed much better at medium and long distances than at short distances. Yet, when H.S. (Atty) Persse was preparing Roi Herode for the Chester Cup as a six-year-old in 1910, he told the present writer that he was greatly surprised to find that the horse really had good speed but did not stay exceptionally well. The inference was that, in the opinion of Persse, Roi Herode had been trained for four seasons in France under a mistaken view of his true capabilities.

Roi Herode broke down during his preparation for the Chester Cup and was sent to Kennedy's Straffan Stud when the 1910 breeding season already was well advanced. By that time, Kennedy had only about three mares that had not been covered, but one of those was Vahren. That mare was mated with Roi Herode in May, and in April 1911 produced what looked like a chestnut colt liberally sprinkled with black spots.

Because The Tetrarch was inbred to Thormanby, Kennedy must have been pleased with what he saw. (Black spots under a chestnut coat can be traced at least to Pantaloon, who was foaled in 1824 and was unbeaten at three. Thormanby, a grandson of Pantaloon, also had the spots, and Thormanby appears three times in The Tetrarch's pedigree. Bend Or, an 1877 foal out of a Thormanby mare, carried the black spots, and from him they spread widely through the Thoroughbred population and commonly are called Bend Or spots.)

In time, The Tetrarch's coat turned to gray and developed white spots in addition to the black ones. Inevitably, he came to be nicknamed The Rocking Horse.

Vahren, The Tetrarch's dam, had been picked up by Kennedy for about 200 pounds for stud purposes following her racing career. She had not won as a two-year-old but did win twice at three and once at four. She never won a race of less than nine furlongs, winning at distances up to eleven furlongs. Vahren was sired by Bona Vista, the 1892 Two Thousand Guineas winner, who also sired Cyllene before being sent to Hungary. Vahren was out of Castania, who bred four minor winners among twelve foals, none of whom won more than 480 pounds. Castania did not race, nor did her dam, Rose Garden, the latter of whom produced only one winner from six foals. The next dam, Eglentyne, ran six times at two and three without winning, but she produced seven winners from fourteen foals, including One Thousand Guineas winner Briar-Root.

Thus, we are back to 1874 before finding a racer with much form produced by this female line. What Kennedy saw in Vahren is anyone's guess, and for some time it looked as if his guess had been wrong. In her first six seasons at stud, Vahren failed to produce a foal that lived. Kennedy, though, despite his receding chin, was a man of strong determination, and he persevered with Vahren.

In 1908, when she was eleven, Vahren produced Nicola, a Symington filly who proved a good two-year-old under the training of Atty Persse, who specialized

Roi Herode, 1904	Le Samaritain, 1895	Le Sancy, 1884	Atlantic, 1871	**Thormanby** / Hurricane
			Gem of Gems, 1873	Strathconan / Poinsettia
		Clementina, 1880	**Doncaster, 1870**	Stockwell / Marigold
			Clemence, 1865	Newminster / Eulogy
	Roxelane, 1894	War Dance, 1887	Galliard, 1880	Galopin / Mavis
			War Paint, 1878	Uncas / Piracy
		Rose of York, 1880	**Speculum, 1865**	Vedette / Doralice
			Rouge Rose, 1865	**Thormanby** / Ellen Horne
Vahren, 1897	Bona Vista, 1889	Bend Or, 1877	**Doncaster, 1870**	Stockwell / Marigold
			Rouge Rose, 1865	**Thormanby** / Ellen Horne
		Vista, 1879	Macaroni, 1860	Sweetmeat / Jocose
			Verdure, 1867	King Tom / May Bloom
	Castania, 1889	Hagioscope, 1878	**Speculum, 1865**	Vedette / Doralice
			Sophia, 1871	Macaroni / Zelle
		Rose Garden, 1878	Kingcraft, 1867	King Tom / Woodcraft
			Eglentyne, 1874	Hermit / Mabille

THE TETRARCH

The Tetrarch

in two-year-olds. The next year, Vahren foaled a John o' Gaunt filly that ran five times at two without winning. That filly was sent to Russia, and she was reported to have won the Russian Oaks. In 1910, Vahren produced another John o' Gaunt foal, a colt, who won one minor race at one and one-half miles.

The next year came The Tetrarch.

Kennedy was much impressed by the strength and vigor of The Tetrarch as a foal, and he showed him with great pride to visitors at Straffan Station Stud. More than one Irish breeder advised Kennedy to have the colt gelded and put by to become a steeplechaser, but Kennedy stuck to his opinion that The Tetrarch was destined to be a high-class colt.

When Persse, who had trained Roi Herode briefly, visited Straffan Station before the Doncaster yearling sale of 1912, he found the Roi Herode—Vahren youngster to be an extremely well-developed colt with an air of being lord of all he surveyed. Kennedy strongly advised Persse to buy him at the forthcoming sale, largely on the basis of what he had observed in the paddocks.

Straffan Station had a field of about five furlongs in length, where Kennedy liked to turn out yearlings. Mounted on a hack, Kennedy would take a lengthy bull whip, or something very similar, and crack it behind his yearlings to see them go.

"Every time I have done this," he told Persse, "that gray Vahren colt simply gallops right away from the others."

Persse went to Doncaster determined to buy the gray colt, and he got him on a bid of 1,300 pounds. Regrettably, Persse had a slight case of financial cramp at the moment and was unable to pay the entire purchase price himself. He was sharing a house at Doncaster with four or five other trainers, and he implored each of them to take a share in the spotted gray; he was met not only with refusal but also considerable derision from all parties.

Persse thus took the colt back to his training quarters still unpaid for.

Shortly thereafter, Persse's cousin, Dermot McCalmont, turned up, having been serving as a major in the Indian Army. McCalmont had inherited a great fortune in Ireland and was planning to take up residence there and embark on a career as a racehorse owner. After the usual family greetings, McCalmont asked Persse how many yearlings he had bought for him, pursuant to the authorizing letter McCalmont had sent from India.

Persse, perhaps thinking sluggishly for a moment, first said that he had not received the letter and therefore had purchased nothing for McCalmont. Remembering his financial stress, Persse than mentioned that he had bought a gray colt for himself and that McCalmont could have a half-interest if he liked. After inspecting the Roi Herode yearling, McCalmont

YEAR	AGE	STS	1ST	2ND	3RD	EARNED
1913	at 2	7	7	0	0	£11,336
Lifetime		7	7	0	0	£11,336

agreed to take a half-share, then while walking back to Persse's house, he said, "Look, Atty, I know you don't have any money, and I just inherited this fortune. Why don't I take all the colt and relieve you of the financial burden."

Unfortunately for himself, Persse agreed—and so missed owning The Tetrarch.

When the next spring came, Persse had a few two-year-olds about fit to run, whereas The Tetrarch had done virtually no serious work. Putting The Tetrarch into a serious work for the first time with his other two-year-olds, Persse told the rider: "This colt has done very little and will tire after about three-eights of a mile. When he begins to tire, let him drop out of it."

As the work unfolded, Persse nearly fell off his hack in astonishment. His two-year-olds nearly ready for a race were all being pushed along vigorously, while there came The Tetrarch at least ten lengths in front and only cantering. Persse retired to his house to think things over. He certainly had a colt out of the ordinary. The question was, how far out of the ordinary?

Persse determined to answer the question by putting The Tetrarch to a pretty stiff test. He told the present writer that he tried The Tetrarch three times against Captain Symons, an older colt capable of winning a 1,000-pound handicap with a good weight. The first time, he asked Captain Symons to give The Tetrarch fourteen pounds (the weight arrangement British trainers usually make when they think they have a two-year-old that might be a classic prospect). The Tetrarch won off by himself, in a canter.

A week or so later, Persse decided to ask The Tetrarch a tremendous question. He tried him with Captain Symons at level weights, but the result was the same as that of the previous trial; The Tetrarch won as he liked. Persse realized then that he might have a two-year-old of extreme ability, so he asked The Tetrarch to give twenty-one pounds to the older Captain Symons. The result was exactly the same as before.

Persse entered The Tetrarch in a maiden plate at Newmarket on April 17. In a field of twenty-two, The Tetrarch was only the third choice, at 5-1. Persse had backed him with every penny he had in the world, and he took the precaution of arriving at the course late so that he neither would have to mislead any of his friends nor shorten the starting-price odds by owning up about the colt. With Steve Donoghue up, The Tetrarch trotted home by four lengths, doubtlessly starting Persse on the road to the comfortable fortune he left when he died at ninety-plus years.

The Tetrarch was out next for the six-furlong Woodcote Stakes at Epsom on June 3, the day before the famous bumping Derby in which the hot favorite, Craganour, was disqualified in favor of the 100-1 Aboyeur. (That also was the Derby in which a suffragette rushed onto the course and felled the King's horse at Tattenham Corner, being fatally injured in the process.) At even money, The Tetrarch cantered home again, this time by three lengths.

On June 17, McCalmont's colt, at 1-3, came out for the five-furlong Coventry Stakes, the most important two-year-old race at Royal Ascot. He simply cantered home, ten lengths in front of a field of seven others.

His next race was the National Breeders' Produce Stakes, then the most valuable two-year-old race in England, and The Tetrarch barely escaped defeat. The start has been described in various ways, some saying it merely was "ragged," others contending that The Tetrarch was facing the wrong way when the field was sent away. At any rate, it took the 1-9 choice a while to catch his field, and after he got the lead he began to lose ground to the filly Calandria. The Tetrarch held her off to win by a neck.

L.S. SUTCLIFFE

Stefan the Great

The result of that narrow escape was that The Tetrarch was sent off at the comparatively generous price of 1-3 for his next race, the six-furlong Rous Memorial at Goodwood. He gave thirteen pounds to Princess Dorrie (who won the Oaks the following year) and beat her by six lengths, with four others trailing. In the Champion Breeders' Foal Stakes at Derby, The Tetrarch was 1-20 and strolled home by four lengths.

A week later there were only three starters for the important Champagne Stakes at Doncaster. One of The Tetrarch's rivals, Stornoway, was owned by tycoon publisher Edward Hulton, who had expressed himself as more than anxious to test The Tetrarch. The bookmakers evidently anticipated that it would not be much test, and The Tetrarch was favored at 1-5, the other colt going off at 5-1. The Tetrarch won by three lengths, untroubled by Stornoway.

The Tetrarch then became the hottest winter-book favorite for the Derby within living memory, but the Champagne Stakes unfortunately turned out to be the final race of his career. Something is known of the kind of three-year-old he was, however, for Persse told us that a week before his scheduled run in the Two Thousand Guineas The Tetrarch was tried against Land of Song. Giving the other twenty-one pounds, The Tetrarch won the trial by seven lengths; Land of Song later finished a good third in the Two Thousand Guineas.

BRITISH RACEHORSE

Mumtaz Mahal and her 1929 colt, Furrokh Siyar

Persse was asked the inevitable question: Did he think The Tetrarch could have stayed the twelve furlongs of the Derby? He replied that he simply did not know, but that The Tetrarch never had shown any signs of being a non-stayer in his works and races at up to a mile.

The Tetrarch struck his off foreleg at exercise during the week before the Guineas. For a time, he seemed to be coming around well enough to contest the Derby, and he was given a twelve-furlong gallop in the middle of May. Three days later, however, he reinjured the foreleg, and he was declared from the Derby and retired.

Persse once described The Tetrarch: "His development in every respect was abnormal. He was a very strong-shouldered horse, possessed of a tremendously long rein, with a wonderful hind leg that gave him that remarkable leverage. Indeed, his development behind the saddle was phenomenal. He had that almost straight, powerful hind leg which all good horses have, pronounced second thighs, was very high and truly molded over the loins, and had a beautiful, intelligent head. He was slightly dipped in his back, and this dip became very pronounced in his old age.

"His action was remarkable. When he galloped, his back seemed to get shorter and his legs longer. That was due to extraordinary hind leverage; his hind legs seemed to project right out in front of his forelegs."

At stud, The Tetrarch had a mixed record. In the first place, the life was not immediately interesting to him, and he frequently would stop to gaze at a bird on the roof while being led to the breeding shed. He sired but 130 foals in his career, and after 1923 was for all practical purposes sterile. He originally stood at Thomastown Stud, Kilkenny, but had been moved to Ballylinch Stud some time before his death at the age of twenty-four in 1935.

The Tetrarch's first crops made a start for him as a stallion that matched the brilliance of his own one year of racing, as he equaled St. Simon's feat of becoming England's leading sire when his oldest horses were only three years old (1919).

The horse that never had an opportunity to prove his own stamina sired three winners of the longest classic, the St. Leger—Caligula (1920), Polemarch (1921), and Salmon-Trout (1924). His other classic winner was Tetratema, who won the Two Thousand Guineas in 1920 and became the leading sire in 1929. The Tetrarch's sons also included The Satrap, a champion at two, and Stefan the Great, another good two-year-old. The spotted wonder's major influence in succeeding generations, however, was authored in his siring Mumtaz Mahal, still known as one of the fastest two-year-old fillies in the annals of the Turf. Mumtaz Mahal became an ancestress of several of the twentieth century's most influential stallions, including Nasrullah, Royal Charger, Tudor Minstrel, and Mahmoud.

CHAPTER SIXTY-FOUR

TETRATEMA

When that blazing speed phenomenon, The Tetrarch, had to be retired as a three-year-old, following his breakdown in training, it was natural for his owner, Major Dermot McCalmont, to mate him with any mares that he happened to own. One of these was the Symington mare Scotch Gift (1907) who, like The Tetrarch, had been bred by Edward Kennedy and raced by McCalmont.

Scotch Gift had been a precocious two-year-old, winning four of her first five starts, but she won nothing thereafter. Her total earnings came to 1,033 pounds, or a little more than $5,000. Still, her racing record was better than that of her dam Maund, who had won only four races in twenty-two starts over three seasons for a total of 746 pounds; at that point, Maund was picked up by Kennedy for 80 pounds for stud purposes, but what he saw in her beyond her cheap purchase price is a mystery to the present writer.

Maund was by Tarporley, an unsuccessful son of St. Simon, out of Ianthe, a minor winner and moderate producer. Ianthe was the only winner from Devonshire Lass, a non-starter. The next dam, Hippodrome, after winning one race in fifteen starts, had bred two winners from thirteen foals. That takes us back five generations, to 1868, without either a good broodmare or a good race mare in this female line.

Scotch Gift, however, the dam of Tetratema, was an improvement on any of her first three dams, both as a racer and as a broodmare. Two of her first four foals had been fair winners prior to her series of matings with The Tetrarch. Scotch Gift bred four foals by The Tetrarch over a seven-year period, and all were colts. The two bays, Arch-Gift (1916) and Corban (1918), were winners but of not much caliber; Arch-Gift, in fact, did not win until he was a four-year-old, which for the offspring of two speedy parents is remarkable in itself. Taking their color from The Tetrarch, the two grays—Tetratema (1917) and The Satrap (1924)—each was champion two-year-old of his year, as their sire had been. Since genetic factors

Tetratema

such as coat color are supposed to be inherited independently of all other genetic factors, one is free to make what he wants of this correlation of coat color and racing ability.

Tetratema did not see a racecourse until July 21, as a two-year-old, when he was one of a field of thirteen for the valuable National Breeders' Produce Stakes at Sandown Park. Trainer H.S. (Atty) Persse was famous for his raids on the bookmakers with two-year-olds their first time out, and something must have leaked out concerning the merits of Tetratema (much to the disgust of Persse, who used to lock his stable lads in their quarters after a trial to prevent their getting in touch with the local touts at pubs, etc.). While Lady Phoebe, a fast filly by Orby, was favorite at 2-1, Tetratema was only 9-4. Ridden by Australian Brownie Carslake, Tetratema won easily by four lengths.

The colt's next appearance was on August 1 in the six-furlong Molecomb Stakes at Goodwood. While the race was worth only 847 pounds and drew only five runners, the field included Orpheus, who turned out to be about the second best two-year-old. Tetratema was odds-on at 1-2, while Orpheus was 2-1. Both colts carried 131 pounds, a pretty stiff assignment for that time of year, and again Tetratema won by a margin of four.

For the prestigious six-furlong Champagne Stakes at Doncaster on September 9, there were only five starters, each carrying 126 pounds. Tetratema again was odds-on, at 8-15, while Orpheus was 25-2, and again Tetratema beat Orpheus by four lengths, confirming the Goodwood form to a pound.

On October 10, Tetratema picked up the valuable Imperial Produce Plate at Kempton Park, in which, with 132 pounds up, he was conceding ten pounds to Vivaldi and thirteen pounds to Nespola, both first-time starters and the only other competitors. Tetratema's price was a prohibitive 7-100, and he won by a length.

For the October 17 Middle Park Plate at Newmarket, it was decided to allow Tetratema a chance to see what he could do, because that event had evolved as the traditional two-year-old Derby. Tetratema carried 129 pounds, and starting at odds of 1-4 in a field of five, he won by six lengths.

At that point, considerable debate was started as to whether as a two-year-old Tetratema was as good as, or better than his sire, The Tetrarch, and whether Tetratema could be expected to stay the twelve-furlong distance of the Derby the next year.

The Tetrarch, 1911	Roi Herode, 1904	Le Samaritain, 1895	Le Sancy, 1884	Atlantic / Gem of Gems
			Clementia, 1880	Doncaster / Clemence
		Roxelane, 1894	War Dance, 1887	Galliard / War Paint
			Rose of York, 1880	Speculum / Rouge Rose
	Vahren, 1897	Bona Vista, 1889	Bend Or, 1877	Doncaster / Rouge Rose
			Vista, 1879	Macaroni / Verdure
		Castania, 1889	Hagioscope, 1878	Speculum / Sophia
			Rose Garden, 1878	Kingcraft / Eglentyne
TETRATEMA	Symington, 1893	Ayrshire, 1885	Hampton, 1872	Lord Clifden / Lady Langden
			Atalanta, 1878	Galopin / Feronia
		Siphonia, 1888	St. Simon, 1881	Galopin / St. Angela
			Palmflower, 1874	The Palmer / Jenny Diver
Scotch Gift, 1907	Maund, 1898	Tarporley, 1892	St. Simon, 1881	Galopin / St. Angela
			Ruth, 1883	Scottish Chief / Hilda
		Ianthe, 1887	The Miser, 1877	Hermit / La Belle Helene
			Devonshire Lass, 1883	Hampton / Hippodrome

In the two-year-old Free Handicap, Tetratema was placed twelve pounds higher than the second-highest weighted colt, Orpheus. The Tetrarch had been placed only ten pounds above his nearest rival, Corcyra. Furthermore, Tetratema's style of racing was deemed to be in his favor. He was content to race along with his field without pulling until he was asked for his effort close to home. Then he would come right away from his rivals with authority. The Tetrarch, on the other hand, used to devastate his field in the first quarter-mile or even eighth-mile and would simply canter along to the winning post.

The chief protagonists in the debate were William Allison, then one of the most widely read racing journalists on racing and breeding matters, and Edward Moorhouse, founder and chief writer for the *Bloodstock Breeders' Review*. Allison took the view that Scotch Gift was poorly bred to produce a racer with adequate stamina. Moorhouse, on the contrary, took the view that since Scotch Gift was inbred to St. Simon with two free generations

YEAR	AGE	STS	1ST	2ND	3RD	EARNED
1919	at 2	5	5	0	0	£10,951
1920	at 3	7	4	1	0	£ 8,045
1921	at 4	4	4	0	0	£ 2,782
Lifetime		16	13	1	0	£21,778

and to Hampton with three free generations (both were prime sources of stamina) Scotch Gift could, and probably would, transmit good stamina.

The course of events proved Allison's negative view to be the right one.

Persse himself had no doubts concerning the realities of the situation. He wanted to have Tetratema fighting fit for the one-mile Two Thousand Guineas, and to assure the colt's fitness, the trainer sent Tetratema out for the one-mile Greenham Stakes at Newbury on April 9. To the vast surprise of the racing world, Tetratema (130 pounds) went under by a half-length to the 7-1 second-choice, Silvern (127) in heavy going.

For the first time since his initial start, Tetratema's odds were longer than even money when he appeared for the Two Thousand Guineas. He was 2-1, and Silvern was 20-3 in a field of seventeen. Persse told the present writer that, in view of Tetratema's doubtful stamina, Carslake wanted to hold up the colt for a late run. Persse, however, gave Carslake the opposite instructions—to send Tetratema right along from the start. The trainer believed that with Tetratema's great speed, there was a good chance that he would kill off the other colts, which in trying to stay in touch with Tetratema would have nothing left for a late challenge. Persse proved to be right, as Tetratema just lasted to beat Allenby by a half-length.

Tetratema remained favorite for the Derby, starting at 3-1 in a field of nineteen, but his lack of stamina caught up with him and he was unplaced for the first time

Royal Minstrel

in his life. An old rival, Orpheus, was third to the plodder Spion Kop.

What Persse thought of the colt is clear from the program he then followed with Tetratema. Tetratema's next race was the five-furlong Fern Hill Stakes at Ascot, where at odds-on again, the colt won by six lengths. Tempted by the rich purse of the one and one-quarter-mile Eclipse Stakes, Persse started Tetratema, and the colt was joint favorite with Buchan and Allenby at 5-2. The distance, however, proved again beyond Tetratema's compass, and again he was unplaced, while Buchan won the stakes for the second time.

Tetratema's next race, the six-furlong King George Stakes at Goodwood, must have been quite a thriller. The two fastest horses in training met, three-year-old Tetratema (129 pounds) challenging the great six-year-old mare Diadem (137 pounds). There were no other starters. Tetratema won by three-quarters of a length, but Carslake said after the race that Tetratema did not have another ounce left when he just got the better of the mare. (When it is recalled that Diadem was a slim, small-to-medium-sized mare, her feat of picking up 137 pounds and putting the fastest colt in training to his utmost is a wonderful tribute to her ability and to her gameness.)

Bazaar

After the King George, Tetratema's last race at three was anticlimactic. In the five-furlong Kennett Stakes on October 13 at Newmarket, Tetratema, at odds of 1-20, beat a solitary opponent by two lengths.

Tetratema was kept in training as a four-year-old and won all four of his races. At Ascot, with 143 pounds up, he won the five-furlong King's Stand Stakes by a length, giving thirteen pounds to the runner-up. At Newmarket, again toting 143 pounds, he won the six-furlong July Cup, by one and one-half lengths from two others. At Goodwood, Tetratema again won the King George Stakes by a length from his old competitor, Orpheus, each carrying 141 pounds. Then at the Newmarket First October meeting (run, in perverse British style, in September), Tetratema won the five-furlong Snailwell Stakes by one and one-half lengths, with only 136 pounds up.

There then remained no doubt that Tetratema had been the fastest horse in training at two, three, and four, although he never had won beyond a mile.

Comparing Tetratema with his sire, The Tetrarch, Persse expressed to the present writer a very strong preference for the latter. Naturally, he refused to put this difference in terms of pounds, but he thought that it would have taken a large weight difference to bring them together.

Physically, Tetratema was a medium-sized, neat-looking colt of good constitution. He also was sound, although he did have short pasterns, a characteristic seen in many speedy horses of limited-distance capacity. The Tetrarch, on the other hand, was a colt of abnormal strength and development, having as a two-year-old the size and strength of a four-year-old. Persse told the present writer that when in heavy training, The Tetrarch ate twenty-two quarts of oats a day.

True to his performances on the Turf, Tetratema became a very high-class sire of sprinters, and today his blood is associated with precocity and speed. (So much for the inbreeding of his dam to prime stamina sources, St. Simon and Hampton.) The average distance of races won by Tetratema's stock was 6.35 furlongs.

Tetratema did not suffer from the partial infertility of The Tetrarch, and he was very consistent as a sire of winners. Beginning when his oldest runners were three, Tetratema was among the top ten leading sires for twelve years with one exception. He was leading sire in 1929 and three times was second.

Tetratema sired two classic winners, 1929 Two Thousand Guineas winner Mr. Jinks and 1931 One Thousand Guineas winner Four Course (who was second in the Oaks). He also sired 1929 Eclipse Stakes winner Royal Minstrel, runner-up in the 1928 Two Thousand Guineas, plus juvenile champion Foray II, unbeaten filly Tiffin, and classic-placed Theft. In this country, he was represented by Bazaar, a co-champion filly at two and three in 1933 and 1934, and by other stakes winners Pumpkin and Rolls Royce.

Tetratema died at the age of twenty-two, in 1939, at Maj. McCalmont's Ballylinch Stud, County Kilkenny, where he had been foaled.

CHAPTER SIXTY-FIVE

TEDDY

Following the death of Hugh Lupus, the first Duke of Westminster, in 1899, his breeding stock was sold at public auction in March 1900. The Duke had been the foremost breeder in England and had been the only man to breed and own two Triple Crown winners—Ormonde and Flying Fox—and the latter, then a four-year-old, was the prime attraction of the sale.

After spirited bidding, the buyer proved to be Edmond Blanc, a leading breeder and owner in France whose Jardy stud was located at Saint-Cloud, near Paris. The price was a world-record 37,500 guineas (about $190,000) and provoked a round of well-worn clichés, such as "a fool and his money are soon parted." Blanc had plenty of money, which was derived from the catering business at Monte Carlo, Baden-Baden, and similar resorts for wealthy pleasure seekers. He was a man of strong opinions, and he told the Duke of Portland during a visit to France that he was never mistaken about the merits of any of his horses.

In the case of Flying Fox, at least, he was correct. The horse turned out to be a first-class sire, and it has been calculated that Blanc made about 200,000 guineas from him. In Flying Fox's first crop was Ajax, who was unbeaten, running only five times in all.

Ajax's only race at two was in the six-furlong Prix St. Firmin in the autumn, for which he was favored at 7-4 in a field of fourteen. He won easily, by a length.

His three-year-old career began in the one and a half-mile Prix Noailles, restricted to animals one of whose parents had been imported into France. Macdonald II was favorite, but Ajax again won easily by a length. The more important Prix Lupin of one and five-sixteenths miles saw Ajax win again easily, by two and a half lengths, this time at odds of 4-5 in a field of eight.

For the Prix du Jockey-Club (French Derby) of one and a half miles, Ajax was at a still shorter price, 1-2 in a field of eleven. Ajax won again, by a half-length from Macdonald II, but only after a struggle. The Grand Prix de Paris at one and seven-eighths miles in June (for three-year-olds carrying 128 pounds) was the last

Teddy

race for Ajax. In a field of thirteen, he was 5-4 and won from W.K. Vanderbilt's Turenne by a half-length, with Macdonald II third.

In all his races, Ajax was ridden by George Stern, then the leading rider in France. Stern looked much like a bantamweight prize fighter, having a very pugnacious expression, and he frequently rode in a very pugnacious style, forcing openings which were really too narrow to get through and shutting off others in equally determined fashion. The late Charles Morton engaged Stern to ride Sunstar in the Two Thousand Guineas and Epsom Derby of 1911. Before the Derby, the air was thick with rumors of a jockey ring to "put George Stern over the rails." When he heard this, Morton had the first good laugh he enjoyed for weeks: "If there was anybody who had no need of a nurse in a rough race, it was George Stern."

Ajax was trained by an Englishman, Robert Denman, who told the author he considered that Ajax was the best horse he had trained in the course of a long career. Denman looked very much like the drawings of John Bull, having a ruddy complexion, square face, and bluff and hearty manner.

Ajax is found in the pedigree of Nearco, whose maternal grandsire, Havresac II, was out of an Ajax mare, and also twice in the pedigrees of Omaha, Flares, Granville, and other products of William Woodward Sr.'s Belair Stud. For the purposes of this series, however, the importance of Ajax comes through one channel.

Ajax sired Teddy, foaled in 1913.

In 1906 Blanc imported the six-year-old mare Rondeau from England into France as a prospective mate in future years for Flying Fox and his son Ajax. Rondeau had been owned by Sir James Miller and was sold the same year as Rock Sand (the maternal grandsire of Man o' War), following Miller's death. Rondeau had been the first racer of much merit sired by Bay Ronald, who was himself an ordinary handicapper but who sired Macdonald II, Dark Ronald, and Bayardo.

At the start of her two-year-old career, Rondeau ran in the colors of Charles Archer, brother of the famous jockey Fred Archer, and was ridden by Charles Archer Jr. They exploited her in selling races, and after winning her second seller in a row she was bought at the ensuing auction by Sir James Miller for 500 guineas. For her new owner, she won three two-year-old races, including the one-mile Prince of Wales's Nursery.

As a three-year-old, she kept better company and won the twelve-furlong Dullingham Plate and the fourteen-furlong Lowther Stakes at Newmarket. For the ten-furlong Free Handicap, she was assigned 126 pounds, but was unplaced. At four, Rondeau again won the Dullingham Plate, with 136 pounds up, and was second in the two and a quarter-mile Cesarewitch, beaten one and a half lengths.

Ajax, 1901	Flying Fox, 1896	Orme, 1889	Ormonde, 1883	**Bend Or** / Lily Agnes
			Angelica, 1879	**Galopin** / St. Angela
		Vampire, 1889	**Galopin**, 1872	Vedette / Flying Duchess
			Irony, 1881	Rosebery / Sarcasm
	Amie, 1893	Clamart, 1888	Saumur, 1878	Dollar / Finlande
			Princess Catherine, 1876	Prince Charlie / Catherine
		Alice, 1887	Wellingtonia, 1869	Chattanooga / Araucaria
			Asta, 1877	Cambuslang / Lady Superior
TEDDY				
Rondeau, 1900	Bay Ronald, 1893	Hampton, 1872	Lord Clifden, 1860	Newminster / The Slave
			Lady Langden, 1868	Kettledrum / Haricot
		Black Duchess, 1886	Galliard, 1880	**Galopin** / Mavis
			Black Corrie, 1879	Sterling / Wild Dayrell mare
	Doremi, 1894	**Bend Or**, 1877	Doncaster, 1870	Stockwell / Marigold
			Rouge Rose, 1865	Thormanby / Ellen Horne
		Lady Emily, 1879	Macaroni, 1860	Sweetmeat / Jocose
			May Queen, 1868	Claret / Lady Blanche

Blanc had experienced good fortune in buying a still better race mare in Airs and Graces (Epsom Oaks), who bred the high-class Jardy, he from Flying Fox's second crop. Jardy had won the Middle Park Plate and run second in the Derby to Cicero when he had a temperature. Blanc's luck with Rondeau, however, for a long time was consistently bad. For seven breeding seasons from 1906 to 1912, Rondeau produced only two live foals, a colt and a filly, both by Flying Fox, neither of which started.

When the German army was marching on Paris in 1914, Blanc decided to sell all his yearlings. Since Rondeau was thirteen at the time Teddy was foaled and had not bred a winner, there was no overwhelming demand for Teddy. He was bought by Jefferson Davis Cohn, for 5,400 francs (about $1,000). Cohn had been secretary to Lord Michelham, the breeder of Plucky Liege. Cohn acquired Plucky Liege and by mating her to Teddy bred Sir Gallahad III, Bull Dog, Quatre Bras II, and others. This was all far in the future at the time of Blanc's sale.

YEAR	AGE	STS	1ST	2ND	3RD	EARNED
1915	at 2	unraced				
1916	at 3	7	5	0	2	137,000 Fr
1917	at 4	1	1	0	0	8,000 Fr
Lifetime		8	6	0	2	145,000 Fr

There was no racing at all in France in 1915, so it never can be known what sort of two-year-old Teddy was. Racing on the continent was resumed on a very restricted scale in 1916, beginning at San Sebastian in Spain. Teddy made his first start in the Grand Prix of San Sebastian, for three-year-olds and up at one and a half miles. In a field of twenty-six, Cohn was represented by four starters and W.K. Vanderbilt by three. The Vanderbilt entry was 7-4, and the Cohn entry stood at 3-1. From this it can be inferred that Teddy was not regarded as a world beater before he first appeared in public.

Cohn had taken over Blanc's trainer (Denman) and his jockey (Stern). Teddy was set to carry 110 pounds, and Stern could not make the weight, so Teddy was ridden by R. Stokes while Stern rode Cohn's five-year-old Spirit (136 pounds). The pair ran first and second, Teddy winning by three lengths. This was probably the most important race run during the war years for French horses, as it carried a purse of 100,000 francs, and it established Teddy at once among the best of his generation.

Teddy's next start was in the St. Leger de San Sebastian at one and three-fifths miles. He won with George Stern aboard, but the victory may not have meant too much, since there were only four starters and three of them belonged to Cohn. The outsider of the party finished fourth. Still at San Sebastian, Teddy next

Sun Again

appeared in the King of Spain's Gold Cup, a twelve-furlong race with a purse of 50,000 francs. Teddy could only finish third to his stable companion Rabanito.

In the autumn, racing was resumed in France, at Moulins, well to the rear of the battle lines. On October 3, Teddy won a small race there at one and three-eighths miles, and next he won a little better class affair over the same distance two days later. Six days later, he won still another race of a little better class, that time over one and a half miles. At the end of October, Teddy contested one more one and a half-mile event, finishing third to two good colts in Antivari and Sans-le-Sou while beaten four and a half lengths.

The most interesting feature of Teddy's racing career came to light with his sole race as a four-year-old. Back at Chantilly, headquarters for racing in France, Teddy came out for the ten-furlong Prix des Sablonnieres. While the purse was only 8,000 francs, the field included the six-year-old La Farina, who along with Sardanapale was one of the best horses seen on the French Turf since the time of Gladiateur (1865). Both La Farina and Sardanapale could and did "lose" to Durbar II, who easily won the Epsom Derby of 1914.

So, when Teddy beat La Farina a neck at level weights it meant that he was in all probability the best colt to have run in France during the war years. This reading of Teddy's class was confirmed when La Farina went on to win his next two starts.

Teddy went to stud in 1918 and was a sustained success from the outset. His stud career in France, however, was a good illustration of the circumstance of sires for countries. Good as he was in France, it is probable that he would have been even more successful in either England or the United States.

Teddy was by Ajax, who won at all distances up to one and seven-eighths miles, and was out of a mare who won at one and three-quarters miles and was just beaten in the two and a quarter-mile Cesarewitch; Teddy himself won up to one and five-eighths miles. Nevertheless his stock lacked just that touch of stamina required by the highest class of races in the French racing program, and Teddy in France never sired a colt or filly capable of winning a classic race beyond one mile. On the other hand, Bruleur and his son Ksar sired six winners of the twelve-furlong French Derby from 1921 to 1933, but the Bruleur–Ksar strain was a failure in the American racing program, having an excess of stamina and insufficient speed for American conditions.

Undoubtedly, the best colt sired by Teddy was the Italian-bred Ortello, who was outstanding in Italian racing and won the Prix de l'Arc de Triomphe in France as well. Ortello bore no resemblance to Teddy in color (chestnut, with some white, in contrast to Teddy's solid bay), which is probably unimportant, and neither were they similar in make and shape; Ortello was a giant in size and very angular, in contrast to Teddy's medium size and well-rounded barrel and quarters.

Neither of Teddy's next-best sons, Sir Gallahad III (French Two Thousand Guineas and Lincolnshire Handicap) and Asterus (Hunt Cup at Ascot, Champion Stakes, and French Two Thousand Guineas) could stay beyond ten furlongs in a rapidly run race. A fair idea of their class may be obtained from the fact that Asterus was set to carry 113 pounds as a three-year-old in the Cambridgeshire and finished third; this form was at least ten pounds below the form of a true classic colt in England at the time.

Sir Gallahad III won the one-mile Lincolnshire Handicap as a four-year-old carrying 117 pounds; top weight in the handicapping was Epinard, with 140, but he did not start.

In the years closely following the end of World War I, racing men in both France and England generally believed that the French form was somewhere between fourteen and twenty-one pounds below that of the English. Thirty years later, the results of the classic races in England showed that the French form had become superior to English form. The late Andrew Jackson Joyner, who trained

MORGAN PHOTO SERVICE

Case Ace

in England for H.P. Whitney from 1908 to 1914, told the author that he thought that during that time the English form was about fourteen pounds superior to that of the Americans.

Currently, the American form is demonstrably superior to the English (Epsom Derbys of 1968, 1970, 1971, 1972, won by Sir Ivor, Nijinsky II, Mill Reef, Roberto) while the French form has again fallen behind the English.

Cohn lost his fortune during the market crash of 1929, being heavily committed in shares of the Wagon Lits Company. So, he sold Teddy in 1931 to F. Wallis Armstrong of New Jersey and Kenneth N. Gilpin of Virginia. Teddy lived until 1936 but did not make a great impression on the American Turf with his American-bred stock. His best produce in the United States were Case Ace and Sun Teddy. Case Ace showed good speed, but not much stamina and did not last very long in training. Case Ace was only a qualified success at stud but did sire an unbeaten two-year-old and Belmont Stakes winner in Pavot; the latter was not a success at stud. Sun Teddy sired a fast, unsound colt in Sun Again. Neither of these branches of the Teddy line has a good prospect of surviving.[1]

It was the importation of two of his European-sired sons that authored Teddy's major influence in this country. Sir Gallahad III led the American sire list four times, the first being 1930, a year before his sire's importation. Bull Dog, a full brother to Sir Gallahad III, led the list in 1943 and sired Bull Lea, a five-time leader of the list. Bull Lea, however, sired no son that became a comparable success at stud.

Another branch of Teddy's male line has survived in Europe, with varying fortunes and characteristics. Teddy sired a large and coarse colt called Aethelstan, who was a good racer, but not a first-class one. Aethelstan sired a huge and very backward colt called Deiri. When the late William Pratt, a noted jockey and trainer in France, as well as being the nephew of Fred Archer, saw him, he observed: "He might make a back-end 10-year-old."

Nevertheless, Deiri defeated the great Tourbillon in the Prix Royal-Oak (French St. Leger). Deiri was not a success at stud but did sire the plodder Deux Pour Cent, who sired the crack Tantieme, twice winner of the Arc de Triomphe. Tantieme sired Tanerko (Prix du President de la Republique), who sired Relko (Epsom Derby, French Two Thousand Guineas, and Coronation Cup). Relko made his stud career in England, siring fifty-five stakes winners.

In France, Teddy was first on the sire's list in 1923, second in 1926, 1928, and 1932, and third in 1925. He was also second on the Italian sire list in 1929, owing to the exploits of Ortello.

Teddy and Sir Gallahad III each sired more than sixty stakes winners. Teddy's sixty-seven stakes winners came from a total of 356 named foals, giving him 18.8 percent stakes winners from foals, whereas Sir Gallahad III sired 567 named foals, giving him 11.3 percent stakes winners from foals.

End Notes:

1. Ironically, it is the Sun Again branch of the Teddy sire line that has survived. Damascus, a great-grandson of Sun Again, is the source of this line, whose modern representatives include Skip Away, Swiss Yodeler, Gilded Time, Afternoon Deelites, Say Florida Sandy, and Old Topper.

CHAPTER SIXTY-SIX

SIR GALLAHAD III

S ir Gallahad III was in the vintage French crop of 1920, which also included the brilliant Epinard, plus Prix de l'Arc de Triomphe and Ascot Gold Cup winner Massine, French Derby winner Le Capucin, and Grand Prix de Paris winner Filibert de Savoie. Sir Gallahad III was not a standout among that group of stars, but he was a high-class colt and one that served as the medium of at least two successful betting coups.

He first appeared at Deauville in August 1922 among a field of six for the five-furlong Prix de Villers. His reputation had preceded him, and he went off at odds of 7-10, but he finished fifth, beaten about nine lengths. The irony of this race was that the sixth and last was Massine, who was the best of the generation, at least at ten furlongs and beyond. The next start for Sir Gallahad III also was at Deauville in the unimportant, five-furlong Prix de St. Gatien. In a field of five, Sir Gallahad III was 26-10 and finished last.

The scene then was set for what evidently was a betting coup. At the end of September, in the four and one-half furlong Prix de la Mediterranee, a race of no importance, there was a field of twenty-seven, and Sir Gallahad III was backed down to 42-10. With the American jockey Frank O'Neill up, he won easily by two lengths. In all probability, owner J.D. Cohn landed a big bet at the expense of the Greek betting syndicate that operated outside the legal pari-mutuel system at the tracks.

On October 26, Sir Gallahad III won a race of slightly higher class over five furlongs at Longchamp, scoring by three lengths in a field of nine. This was no occasion for a betting coup, as his price was only even money. Four days later, at Saint-Cloud, in deep going, Sir Gallahad III beat a field of eight over six and one-half furlongs by a length at the cramped odds of 3-10.

The following April, Sir Gallahad III began establishing his reputation as a springtime horse. On April 9 in the ten-furlong Prix Edgard de la Charme, at the price of 6-10, he beat three others by two lengths. Almost three weeks later, he took the one-mile Prix Daphnis from two others at odds of 1-10. Those races were curtain raisers for the first of the classics, the one-mile Poule d'Essai des Poulains (French Two Thousand Guineas). Sir Gallahad III was odds-on at 1-4 in a field of six and won by three-quarters of a length from the Aga Khan's Niceas, the only other horse of any class in the field.

Things were not so easy the next time. In the important one and five-sixteenths-mile Prix Lupin, there was only a field of five, but Sir Gallahad III ran into a first-class colt, Massine. Sir Gallahad III was the betting favorite of 9-10, and Massine was 2-1. When Massine tied into Sir Gallahad III, matters were settled quickly. Massine, a colt of beautiful action and a true stayer, strode to the front, and Sir Gallahad III collapsed to finish last.

There were eighteen runners that year for the Prix du Jockey-Club (French Derby) at one and one-half miles. Massine was not among them, and Le Capucin was a hot favorite at 18-10. The choice won by a neck from Niceas, who beat Sir Gallahad III another neck.

On June 24, the Grand Prix de Paris was run at Longchamp over one and seven-eighths miles. Sir Gallahad III displayed marked intelligence on that occasion; as if he knew that the task was beyond his powers, he threw his jockey and jumped into the lake in the infield.

Despite that dramatic performance, Sir Gallahad III was favored for the one and five-eighths-mile Prix du President de la Republique at Saint-Cloud at odds of 28-10 in a field of ten. Again showing that the distance was beyond his powers, Sir Gallahad III finished last.

At Deauville in August, Sir Gallahad III was brought back to a distance of six furlongs in the Prix des Marettes. The public made him the odds-on favorite at 1-2 in a field of six, but Niceas beat him three lengths at level weights. There was just a suggestion of chicanery, as three days later Niceas and Sir Gallahad III met again, in a three-horse field for the most important mile race at Deauville, the Prix Jacques-Le-Marois. The public swallowed the form of the previous race and made Niceas an odds-on favorite at 1-2, while Sir Gallahad III was 5-2. Strange to say, Sir Gallahad III beat Niceas by two lengths.

A month later, Sir Gallahad III was one of a party of four in the Prix Royal-Oak (French St. Leger) at one and seven-eighths miles. The odds-on favorite at 8-10 was the Grand Prix winner, Filibert de Savoie. Because the latter was the only colt in the field with any pretensions to stay the course, it was not surprising that he won by four lengths. Sir Gallahad III was second, beating two inferior colts.

On September 26, Sir Gallahad III was in a field of eight for the La Coupe d'Or of ten furlongs over the straight course at Maisons-Laffitte. The conditions of the race provided that any colt foaled on the European continent (excluding England and Ireland) outside of France was entitled to a reduction of eleven pounds from the weights carried by French horses of the same age. Federico Tesio had brought in his four-year-old Italian champion, Scopas, who got into the race with 127 pounds against 123 pounds on the younger Sir Gallahad III. The writer, after ascertaining that Scopas had traveled well from Italy, made the biggest bet of his student life on Scopas and had the gratification of seeing him win easily at odds of 53-10, while Sir Gallahad III, the hot favorite at 14-10, finished last. (The proceeds of said bet bought an automobile, and the writer became a great swell among students.)

In the race for the sprinters' championship, the Prix de la Foret of seven furlongs, Sir Gallahad III was the second favorite, but he finished fourth in a field of five. He ended the season with one more sprinting effort, in the Prix du Petit-Couvert of five furlongs. Carrying 136 pounds, he was third to the two-year-old filly Heldifann (113), who beat him a little more than a length. (Heldifann was owned by Miss Fannie Heldy, the future Mme. Marcel Boussac.)

The second betting coup apparently engineered with Sir Gallahad III was in

			Orme, 1889	Ormonde / Angelica
		Flying Fox, 1896	Vampire, 1889	**Galopin** / Irony
	Ajax, 1901	Amie, 1893	Clamart, 1888	Saumur / Princess Catherine
			Alice, 1887	Wellingtonia / Asta
Teddy, 1913			Hampton, 1872	**Lord Clifden** / Lady Langden
		Bay Ronald, 1893	Black Duchess, 1886	Galliard / Black Corrie
	Rondeau, 1900	Doremi, 1894	Bend Or, 1877	Doncaster / Rouge Rose
			Lady Emily, 1879	**Macaroni** / May Queen
SIR GALLAHAD III			Musket, 1867	Toxophilite / W. Australian mare
		Carbine, 1885	Mersey, 1874	Knowsley / Clemence
	Spearmint, 1903	Maid of the Mint, 1897	Minting, 1883	Lord Lyon / Mint Sauce
			Warble, 1884	Skylark / Coturnix
Plucky Liege, 1912		St. Simon, 1881	**Galopin**, 1872	Vedette / Flying Duchess
			St. Angela, 1865	King Tom / Adeline
	Concertina, 1896	Comic Song, 1884	Petrarch, 1873	**Lord Clifden** / Laura
			Frivolity, 1867	**Macaroni** / Miss Agnes

JACK WILKES/LIFE

Sir Gallahad III

his four-year-old debut, in the 1924 Lincolnshire Handicap of one mile, the first important race of the flat racing season in England. The French contingent may have been a little devious in preparing for this race. Along with Sir Gallahad III, the crack French colt Epinard was entered. The previous October, Epinard had nearly carried a then-record 128 pounds on his three-year-old back to victory in the nine-furlong Cambridgeshire, so it was certain that Epinard would be assigned a staggering top weight, while Sir Gallahad III, on the basis of French form, would be entitled to a very substantial pull in the weights. As things turned out, Epinard was assigned 140 pounds and Sir Gallahad III only 117. Sir Gallahad III was made fighting fit for the race, and with only 117 pounds up appeared a handicapping certainty.

In a field of twenty-seven, Sir Gallahad III was a hot favorite at 9-2 and won as he liked by three lengths. While this resulted in a nasty shock for the British bookmakers, it was nothing like the sum they had paid out the year before over Epinard, when he carried a record weight for a three-year-old to victory in the six-furlong Stewards' Cup at Goodwood.

Sir Gallahad III was sent back to France for the ten-furlong Prix des Sablons at Longchamp. The event was then the most important stakes for four-year-olds in the French spring racing program. In a field of five, Sir Gallahad III was 2-1, but Massine beat him easily, again. At the end of April, again at ten furlongs, Sir Gallahad III won a good stakes, the Prix Boiard, with 136 pounds up, beating the previous year's French Derby winner, Le Capucin, by nearly a length at level weights. The going was heavy and on the face of it, this may have been Sir Gallahad III's best performance.

There was a well-worn path, on the course, near the rails, used by the track staff in walking back to town. It provided firm going while the rest of the track was very holding. Sir Gallahad III was fast away from the gate, so his jockey, O'Neill, had no trouble getting him onto that firm path, while the rest of the field was floundering in soggy turf.

YEAR	AGE	STS	1ST	2ND	3RD	EARNED
1922	at 2 (in Fr)	5	3	0	0	49,400 Fr
1923	at 3 (in Fr)	13	4	2	2	328,575 Fr
1924	at 4 (in Fr)	5	3	1	1	173,225 Fr
In France		**23**	**10**	**3**	**3**	**551,220 Fr**
1924	at 4 (in Eng)	1	1	0	0	£2,075
In England		**1**	**1**	**0**	**0**	**£2,075**

Again carrying 136 pounds in the nine-furlong Prix Daphnis, Sir Gallahad III beat three ordinary horses five lengths at odds of 1-4.

At that point, a match race was arranged, pitting Sir Gallahad III against Epinard over six and one-half furlongs. The conditions required Epinard to concede eleven pounds, but the public made him a 1-4 favorite, while Sir Gallahad III was 18-10. The writer saw that match and his heart went out to Epinard, whose feet were so sore that his handlers had to whack him with a board to induce him to walk out onto the track. Epinard's trainer, Eugene Leigh, told us that Epinard always had suffered from thrush and at that time it was clear his feet were very sore indeed. Sir Gallahad III won the match by a short neck. On the face of it, the form made Epinard about ten pounds better than Sir Gallahad III, but, when sound and well, Epinard was probably substantially better even than that.

At the end of July, Sir Gallahad III came out for his last start, in the five-furlong Prix du Gros-Chene at Chantilly. Sir Gallahad III was odds-on at 2-5 in a field of four, but was beaten a length by an old rival, Niceas, at level weights of 132 pounds.

Sir Gallahad III made one season at stud in France, and it resulted in nothing of particular merit. He then was sold for $125,000 by J.D. Cohn to A.B. Hancock Sr., who was acting on behalf of a syndicate composed of himself, William Woodward Sr., Marshall Field, and R.A. Fairbairn. The horse arrived at Hancock's Claiborne

Gallant Fox

Farm near Paris, Kentucky, to make his first American stud season in 1926, and in his very first American crop he got Gallant Fox, who won the Triple Crown for Woodward in 1930.

Sir Gallahad III led the general sire list in Gallant Fox's Triple Crown year, and he also led it three more times, in 1933, 1934, and 1940. In addition to Gallant Fox, his sixty-four stakes winners included two other Kentucky Derby winners, Gallahadion (1940) and Hoop, Jr. (1945). His major runners also included Escutcheon, Gallant Sir, High Quest, Hadagal, Tintagel, Fighting Fox, Foxbrough, Fenelon, Roman, Vagrancy, Good Morning, and Algasir.

The line of Sir Gallahad III was not so strong as might be expected of a successful horse given the opportunities he had. With his ownership and location, he had the advantage of being bred to good mares, and while he produced a large number of good broodmares, his sons did not author a sire line that has great strength at present.

One son, Roman, however, twice was the leading juvenile sire and got a Preakness winner in Hasty Road. Another branch of the Sir Gallahad III male line was that of the Canadian Victoria Park, sire of the young stallion Kennedy Road.

Another line led to Crafty Admiral, who got a high number of winners.

A high fertility and a long life assisted Sir Gallahad III's record as a broodmare sire. He lived to the age of twenty-nine and sired a total of 567 foals. His daughters produced a total of 180 stakes winners, including Challedon, Beaugay, Gallorette, Revoked, Jet Pilot, Judy-Rae, Iron Maiden, Alablue, Rare Perfume, Atalanta, Battle Morn, County Delight, Armageddon, Nothirdchance, Victory Morn, and Royal Native.

He was the leading broodmare sire for ten consecutive years (1943–52) and led the list a total of twelve times.

Plucky Liege (dam of Sir Gallahad III), in the present writer's opinion, ranks with Selene (dam of Hyperion, Sickle, Pharamond II, and Hunter's Moon) and possibly Nogara (dam of Nearco and Niccolo Dell'Arca) among the most influential broodmares of the twentieth century, insofar as producing stallions is concerned. In addition to Sir Gallahad III, Plucky Liege foaled Bull Dog, also a leading North American sire, plus two other European classic winners.

Plucky Liege was foaled in 1912, and as a two-year-old she ran six times in England, winning her last four races in succession. None of her juvenile races were of importance, and each was at the minimum distance of five furlongs. Nevertheless, the Jockey Club handicapper took a very favorable view of the form of Plucky Liege and assigned her 117 pounds on the Free Handicap. That rating was nine pounds below the top and made her the third-ranked filly, one pound under Lady Josephine (another extraordinary mare, afterward the dam of Mumtaz Mahal and Lady Juror).

As a three-year-old, Plucky Liege was out seven times without winning! After running unplaced in the mile One Thousand Guineas, she was reserved for five-furlong races. Even so, she was unplaced in all her subsequent starts except one, in which she was third, a length behind Friar Marcus. If the latter performance be taken as true form, it made her about fifteen pounds from the top fillies of her year, as Friar Marcus, who gave her fifteen pounds, had been the champion two-year-old and was probably the best sprinter among the year's three-year-olds.

Considering her pedigree, Plucky Liege's good speed, early maturity, limited distance capacity, and relative deterioration from two to three were not to be expected.

Her sire, Spearmint, was an ordinary two-year-old, but was a very high-class three-year-old, winning the Epsom Derby in record time from a good field and also winning the Grand Prix de Paris at one and seven-eighths miles. Nearly all the stock by Spearmint were slow to mature and stayed very well.

The dam of Plucky Liege was Concertina, a non-starter. Concertina bred fourteen foals, of which Plucky Liege was the twelth born and ninth and last among the winners (all unimportant). Concertina was sired by the mighty St. Simon, who stayed brilliantly enough to win both the Ascot Gold Cup and Goodwood Cup as a three-year-old.

Concertina's dam, Comic Song, was sired by the stayer Petrarch, a winner of the St. Leger and Ascot Gold Cup. Comic Song, who never ran, produced ten foals before being exported from England to Russia at the age of fourteen, and while five of the foals were winners, even the best two failed to win more than 110 pounds.

The next dam, Frivolity, was good as a two-year-old, winning the important Middle Park Plate, but she failed to win at three and at four. She produced twelve foals, of which four were very minor winners and a fifth was a moderate winner. Frivolity, who was sired by English Guineas and Derby winner Macaroni, was from Miss Agnes, an 1850 foal who won once in thirteen starts over three seasons. Miss Agnes, a daughter of St. Leger winner Birdcatcher, produced sixteen foals, of which eleven were winners. Apart from Frivolity, her best were Bismarck and Couronne de Fer, each of whom was moderate.

Taking the records of the first four dams of Plucky Liege, one finds an aggregate record of fifty-two foals, of which thirty were winners, but the only winner of quality was Frivolity, the third dam. The sires of each of the mares were of high quality, and each stayed well. With that genetic background, it is indeed a puzzle to account for Plucky Liege's speed, early maturity, and non-staying character.

Plucky Liege herself produced twelve foals, five fillies and seven colts. The first four fillies, all by Teddy, were winners Marguerite de Valois, Noor Jahan, Noble Lady, and Elsa de Brabant, and the last filly was Diane de Poitiers (by Aethelstan II), who made one start and failed to win.

It was her sons that created Plucky Liege's place of distinction, as six of the seven became stakes winners. Let us consider them in chronological order.

1) Sir Gallahad III, 1920, by Teddy. Winner of the French Two Thousand Guineas, etc., four-time leading U.S. sire, twelve-time leading broodmare sire.

2) Chivalry, 1922, by Good Luck. A winner at three, he made no mark as a sire.

3) Bull Dog, 1927, by Teddy. Although only a minor stakes winner, he became the leading sire in America (his sons included Bull Lea), and he led the broodmare sire list three times.

4) Quatre Bras II, 1928, by Teddy. A stakes winner at two in France and at six in the United States, he sired nine stakes winners.

5) Admiral Drake, 1931, by Craig an Eran. Winner of the Grand Prix de Paris,

BERT MORGAN

Gallorette

he placed in the French Guineas and Derby and became a leading sire in Europe. Admiral Drake's get included Phil Drake, who became the third colt to win the English Derby and the Grand Prix de Paris, and Amour Drake, who won the French Two Thousand Guineas and was a close second in the English Derby.

6) Bel Aethel, 1933, by Aethelstan II. Winner of the important Prix Daru and other stakes in France, he was imported to stand in the United States. He died young, but he sired five stakes winners and in 1943 led juvenile sires in number of winners, with fifteen.

7) Bois Roussel, 1935, by Vatout. He had only three starts, winning the English Derby and the Prix Juigne and running third to Nearco in the Grand Prix de Paris. He led the English sire list once and the broodmare sire list twice. Bois Roussel's best sons included English St. Leger winner Tehran (in turn the sire of champion Tulyar), Prix de l'Arc de Triomphe winner Migoli (sire of Gallant Man), St. Leger winner Ridge Wood, and Irish Derby winners Fraise du Bois and Hindostan.

(Despite his good record, Bois Roussel lacked a burst of speed. Charles Elliott, who rode him in the Derby, said that after going six furlongs or so he asked Bois Roussel to move up to obtain a reasonably good place for the run down to

479

Tattenham Corner. He was unable to do so, and it was not until the field was into the straight that horses began to come back to Bois Roussel. Even then, he did not display a burst of speed, but the field was made up of a group of non-stayers that stopped. The late Fred Darling, who trained Bois Roussel for the Derby, told the writer that he did not think the colt had a chance in the race, as he knew he lacked speed, while another colt in his stable, Guineas winner Pasch, did have speed. Pasch failed to stay and finished third, much to the chagrin of Sir Gordon Richards, who had chosen him instead of Bois Roussel as his mount.)

While Sir Gallahad III and Bull Dog became leading American sires, their half brothers Admiral Drake and Bois Roussel had little appeal to the American breeding community, with its preoccupation with sheer speed. Yet, it should be noted that when a daughter of Admiral Drake (Source Sucree) was mated with the speedy Royal Charger, the result was Turn-to, a first-class horse on the track and in the stud in this country.

Overall, four sons of Plucky Liege each became leading sires (an aggregate of seven times) and each became a leading broodmare sire (an aggregate of nineteen times). This record was achieved in England, France, and North America.

The writer knows of no other mare in the history of the Thoroughbred that can match that record. The point could be made that Plucky Liege never produced a single sire of the quality of a Lexington, St. Simon, Blandford, Hyperion, or Nearco, but what other mare can boast of a record of six stakes-winning sons, of which three were classic winners and four became leading sires?

CHAPTER SIXTY-SEVEN

ROMAN

R oman was one of those rare horses, who—like Black Toney, High Time, Bull Dog, Pilate, and Bull Lea—was considerably better at stud than he had been on the racecourse. As a racer, he had considerable merit as a sprinter but still was substantially below the best of his age, even at his best distance of six furlongs. He was a rather heavy-barreled, strong-quartered colt of good size, and he retired perfectly sound after three campaigns.

In his two-year-old year, Roman began racing very early, on February 15, running second in the three-furlong Seminole Stakes and again on March 4, running second in the Juvenile Championship, at the same distance.[1] Moving north, he won the Lafayette Stakes, on April 26, over the Headley Course at Keeneland, and at the Churchill Downs meeting in May, he won the Bashford Manor Stakes.[2]

Two months later Roman won the five and one-half-furlong Hyde Park Stakes at Arlington Park. Roman won one more two-year-old race before being fourth in the Breeders' Futurity in October—the only time he was unplaced that year. It should be noted that Roman did not contest any of the principal two-year-old stakes, and he was not included in the list of the best two-year-olds of the year in the *American Race Horses* series, though the author, John Hervey, wrote that he "narrowly escaped" that distinction. On the Experimental Free Handicap, he was placed at 117 pounds, thirteen pounds below leader Bimelech and below a dozen other colts.[3]

As a three-year-old, Roman was at first trained for the classics, but it soon was found that their distances were beyond his powers. He again was very consistent, however, being in the first three fourteen times out of eighteen starts. He twice managed to win stakes races of a mile, the Jerome Handicap at Belmont Park at the end of September in 1:37 1/5, and the Laurel Stakes at Laurel, in 1:38 4/5, beating a pretty good colt in Pictor.

His best course, however, appeared to be six furlongs, at which distance he won the Chicago Handicap in 1:10 1/5, a new track record. Three times he tried

Roman

matching strides with Bimelech, the best colt of his age, first in the Blue Grass Stakes at Keeneland and then in the Kentucky Derby.

In the latter race, Roman carried Bimelech so fast for the first mile that Bimelech did not have enough left to withstand the late challenge of Gallahadion, and went down to a surprising defeat.

Roman skipped both the Preakness and the Belmont, but in the one-mile Withers, he again carried Bimelech so fast that when Corydon came along Bimelech again went under.

Those races and others showed that, while Roman had first-class speed, he lacked the stamina of a classic colt, and he was not invincible even at six furlongs.

As a four-year-old, Roman showed considerable improvement as a sprinter, but only after a series of defeats. He came out first for the six-furlong Toboggan Handicap at Belmont Park. The late J.B. Campbell, the New York handicapper, was not given to making many serious mistakes, but he seemed to have made one there, putting Roman in at 122 and Eight Thirty, a first-class colt, at 129. The race was not close, Eight Thirty winning in a canter, with Roman down the track. In the one-mile Metropolitan Handicap (one of the three big handicaps in the New York spring-summer season) Campbell readjusted his sights and made the spread between Eight Thirty and Roman fourteen pounds, putting Eight Thirty in at 132 and Roman at 118. Still, the result was just the same as the Toboggan, with Eight Thirty the winner again. At that stage, Roman must have been at least twenty to twenty-five pounds below Eight Thirty.

Dropping back to six furlongs in a race of lower class, Roman was assigned 114 pounds in the Roseben Handicap. He still showed no form, finished fifth in a field of seven. Dropping still further in class, Roman contested the six-furlong Hastings Handicap of only $2,500. Burdened with only 115 pounds, he finished last of six, beaten a dozen lengths.

The program of dropping Roman in class was continued when he came out for a Class C Handicap of six furlongs. Finally, he showed some return to form, winning with 120 pounds up in 1:12. Thus encouraged, Roman's connections brought him out for the five and three-quarters-furlong Fleetwing Handicap, with $5,000 added. Roman carried co-top weight in a field of ten proven speed horses. Jockey Don Meade sent Roman straight to the front, and he stayed there, his fractions being :22 3/5, :46, 1:08 1/5. The track record as well as the record for the race was

Sir Gallahad III, 1920	Teddy, 1913	Ajax, 1901	Flying Fox, 1896	Orme / Vampire
			Amie, 1893	Clamart / Alice
		Rondeau, 1900	Bay Ronald, 1893	Hampton / Black Duchess
			Doremi, 1894	Bend Or / Lady Emily
	Plucky Liege, 1912	Spearmint, 1903	Carbine, 1885	Musket / Mersey
			Maid of the Mint, 1897	Minting / Warble
		Concertina, 1896	St. Simon, 1881	Galopin / St. Angela
ROMAN			Comic Song, 1884	Petrarch / Frivolity
	Buchan, 1916	Sunstar, 1908	Sundridge, 1898	Amphion / Sierra
			Doris, 1898	Loved One / Lauretta
		Hamoaze, 1911	Torpoint, 1900	Trenton / Doncaster Beauty
			Maid of the Mist, 1906	Cyllene / Sceptre
Buckup, 1928	Look Up, 1922	Ultimus, 1906	Commando, 1898	Domino / Emma C.
			Running Stream, 1898	Domino / Dancing Water
		Sweeping Glance, 1916	Sweep, 1907	Ben Brush / Pink Domino
			Reginella, 1895	Melton / Regina

1:07 2/5, set by Fighting Fox, with 126 pounds. While this was not a wonderful performance, it showed that Roman was returning to form.

Going to Saratoga, Roman came out for the seven-furlong American Legion Handicap with top weight of 126 pounds. The track was sloppy, so Roman's times of :22 4/5, :46 2/5, 1:11 2/5, and 1:25 were creditable. Roman made one more appearance at Saratoga, in an overnight handicap of six furlongs. The track was so heavy that there were only three starters: Roman (126), Parasang (120), and Dini (112). The conditions, with this weight up, were too testing for Roman, who was used up racing Dini, with the result that Parasang came along to beat them both easily. Dini finally beat Roman by three lengths.

Back in New York, Roman was one of the field of fifteen for the $7,500 Bay Shore Handicap. With 126 pounds up again, Roman ran into heavy traffic problems and was knocked back to finish fourteenth, after being as good as third at five furlongs.

Next came the great effort of Roman's life, which set the seal on his fame as a sprinter. This was in the Fall Highweight Handicap, where all the weights are adjusted upward about fifteen pounds. After being run for years over a straight course at Belmont Park, either the old course or the Widener Chute, it was transferred to the main course. This made it necessary to start the race on the backstretch, near the far turn, giving a great advantage to the early speed horses. Jockey Meade got Roman (140 pounds) off flying, but eased him back to fourth, staying handy to the pace, for which the quarter was in :22 4/5, and the half :45 4/5. By that time, Roman was lapped on Speed to Spare (124). There was a stern battle between them, and Roman finally drew away to win by a length. The time, 1:10, equaled the track record. This was a notable achievement; Roman's exceptional strength, early speed, and soundness gave him considerable advantages in a race of that sort, where all the weights were raised.

YEAR	AGE	STS	1ST	2ND	3RD	EARNED
1939	at 2	9	6	2	0	$13,155
1940	at 3	18	8	3	3	$27,705
1941	at 4	13	4	0	3	$15,200
Lifetime		40	18	5	6	$56,060

Roman next tried for the seven-furlong Vosburgh Handicap of $5,000 under 132. He tried to give Joe Schenck twenty-three pounds and The Chief eighteen, and he could not quite manage this. He was beaten a head and one and a quarter lengths. That was Roman's farewell to New York racing, and he moved to Maryland.

First, he tried to win the one-mile Laurel Stakes again, but after he had been

Romanita (center) winning the Monmouth Oaks

trained and raced as a sprinter all season, the distance proved too far for him. He only finished fifth to Pictor, who won by six lengths in the slow time of 1:40 1/5. Since Pictor was giving Roman eight pounds as well, it was clear that Roman was no longer a force to be reckoned with at a mile.

Prior to being retired to stud, Roman was given one more race, at Keeneland, in a $1,200 handicap of six furlongs. Roman (134) tried to give Three Percent twenty-seven pounds and Smacked sixteen pounds and failed by two and a half lengths to do it; the time was 1:11 2/5 over a muddy track.

What Roman's breeder and owner, J.E. Widener, thought of Roman's prospects as a sire may be judged by the report that he was leasing out Roman as a stallion. After all, the American Turf was overcrowded with sprinters, and what reason was there to believe that Roman would prove to be an exceptional sire, even in that category.

This presents a very interesting problem to breeders who have to assess the prospects every year of the young sires retiring to stud. Since the stallion registers going back for one-hundred years or more bear depressing testimony to the fact that less than one in twenty such sires "make good," and failures are very expensive propositions in the long run, the credentials of young sires require careful

Hasty Road

study with a penetrating eye.

What were Roman's credentials? First, he was retired absolutely sound after three strenuous campaigns. This in itself is very rare in the United States and was a big plus in his favor. Second, he was a colt of great early speed, which, when conditions were in his favor, he could carry for six furlongs. Still, he was no Roseben, and ran too many unconvincing races at six furlongs to be considered a great sprinter, or even quite a first-class sprinter. His stamina limitations had to be considered as a minus, off-set to some extent by his strength, constitution, and weight-carrying ability.

A peculiar factor in Roman's case was that he was not typical of the closest removes in his pedigree. His sire, Sir Gallahad III, got middle distance performers in profusion, and a fair proportion of them stayed very well—such as Gallant Fox, Fenelon, and Black Devil. Sir Gallahad III sired very few out-and-out sprinters, such as Roman. The dam, Buckup, was a stakes winner, sired by the English Cup horse Buchan, who won and was disqualified in the two and one-half-mile Ascot Gold Cup. Buchan did not sire sprinters. Roman's second dam, Look Up, was by the intensely inbred Ultimus, who was noted for the speed of his stock. (In fact, Ultimus probably could be considered a pure dominant for speed. Off hand, the author can only think of one colt by Ultimus, Luke McLuke, who showed any distance capacity, and in that case the first three dams were sired by great Cup horses.)

Look Up's dam, Sweeping Glance, was by Sweep, who also got fast stock that did not care to go too far.

From this background, it would appear that Roman bypassed the Sir Gallahad III and Buchan three-quarters of his pedigree and went straight back to the Ultimus and Sweep inheritance. To some extent, the factor of pure speed dominated the sire record of Roman, too, although he did not sire only sprinters.

Roman sired nineteen foal crops before his death at L.P. Doherty's The Stallion Station in 1960. An extraordinary percentage of his foals—47 percent—won at two, and Roman led the juvenile sire lists as to earnings and as to number of winners on two occasions each.

As the above resume would indicate, the Romans had a great deal of speed, but they included Hasty Road, winner of the Preakness and Widener as well as being a co-champion two-year-old, and Romanita, winner of the Monmouth Oaks as well as being a co-champion two-year-old filly. Other high-class Romans not restricted to sprint distances included Queen Hopeful, I Will, Roman Patrol, Cosmic Missile, Times Roman, Chief of Chiefs, and Kentucky Derby runner-up Roman Line. Roman sired a total of fifty-four stakes winners, and at the time of this book's publication was the strongest line descending from the once-powerful Sir Gallahad III sire line.

Roman's primary contribution as a breeding animal may be his daughters. He was the leading broodmare sire in earnings in 1965; his daughters include stakes winners Roman Zephyr and Pocahontas, dams, respectively, of Roman Brother and Tom Rolfe, both champions in 1965. Roman is the maternal grandsire of a total of eighty-six North American stakes winners, the others including Sweet Patootie, I'm For More, Savaii, Chieftain, Iron Peg, Desert Love, Swinging Mood, Desert Law, Proudest Roman, and Astray.

End Notes:

1. Roman's first start was on January 31, 1939, at Hialeah. He won by two lengths.

2. Roman won an allowance race at Keeneland on April 15 as a tuneup for his victory in the Lafayette Stakes.

3. Roman was indeed placed below a dozen other colts, but one filly could be added to the list of those above him: Alfred G. Vanderbilt's Now What, the top-weighted filly at 119 pounds.

BULL DOG

S ince Bull Dog was a full brother of Sir Gallahad III, his appearance on the Turf was awaited with considerable interest. His first race was over four and a half furlongs on July 21, 1929, in the Prix Tristan et Yseult, a small affair at Le Touquet (a minor course at a seaside resort on the English Channel). In a field of eight, J.D. Cohn's homebred finished sixth, beaten about six lengths. The race evidently was in preparation for the first important two-year-old race of the year, the Prix Robert Papin over six furlongs at Maisons-Laffitte on July 28. In a field of fourteen, Bull Dog was quoted at 9-1 and finished second, beaten four lengths by Chateau Bouscaut, the next year's French Derby winner.

The next important stakes for two-year-olds was the Prix Morny (Deauville) on August 18, also at a distance of six furlongs. There were eleven runners in the field, and the odds against Bull Dog were 11-1. That time, Bull Dog finished seventh, again four lengths behind Chateau Bouscaut, who was a hot favorite at 13-10. The Morny

YEAR	AGE	STS	1ST	2ND	3RD	EARNED
1929	at 2	3	0	1	0	24,000 Fr
1930	at 3	5	2	0	0	175,100 Fr
Lifetime		**8**	**2**	**1**	**0**	**199,100 Fr**

concluded Bull Dog's two-year-old campaign, which, it is of particular interest to note, did not show Bull Dog to be a colt of early maturity or of much speed, the two characteristics most marked in his produce as a sire in the United States.

Bull Dog's three-year-old campaign started in a more promising fashion. His first race was a pretty fair stakes called the Prix Daphnis of one mile, run at Le Tremblay. In a field of fourteen, Bull Dog was an outsider at 30-1, but managed to win by a length. His next start was in the Poule d'Essai des Poulains (French Two Thousand Guineas), a race that had been won by Bull Dog's brother, Sir Gallahad III. Bull Dog started third favorite at 7-2 in a field of seven, but he could finish only fourth, beaten nine lengths by Xandover and Chateau Bouscaut.

An easier race, but still one of stakes class, was selected next for Bull Dog, the Prix Rollepot at Saint-Cloud, over seven and a half furlongs. Bull Dog was even

J.A. ESTES

Bull Dog

money in a field of seven but finished last. On June 18, Bull Dog came out for the one-mile Prix Citronelle, a minor stakes at Le Tremblay. In a field of ten, he went off at 5-1 but finished fourth, beaten six lengths. Recognizing that he was not up to classic form, his connections did not start Bull Dog in the French Derby or Grand Prix de Paris.

On July 13, Bull Dog went back to Le Touquet for the one-mile Prix Fleche d'Or, a pretty good stakes; and he won by two lengths (at unreported odds). Since there was no horse of any reputation in the field, the merit of his victory is uncertain.

The Fleche d'Or was Bull Dog's last race. Owing to the brilliant start Sir Gallahad III had made (as the sire of Gallant Fox) in the United States in 1930, Bull Dog was purchased at a reported price of $80,000 for stud duty by C.B. Shaffer's Coldstream Stud of Lexington. There he spent the remainder of his life, and he died in 1954.

Taking his racing career as a whole, it is safe to say that on public form Bull Dog's form was at least fifteen pounds (and possibly more than twenty pounds) behind the form of his full brother, Sir Gallahad III. Yet there can be very little doubt that Bull Dog was a better sire than Sir Gallahad III. Bull Dog sired 345 named foals, of which fifty-two were stakes winners (15 percent). Sir Gallahad III sired 567 named foals, of which sixty-four were stakes winners (11 percent).

Bull Dog's get were noted for early maturity and speed. His sons Occupation, Occupy, and Our Boots were all Futurity winners, but Bull Dog's major mark on the *American Stud Book* was made through another son, Bull Lea, who was the leading sire five times and was chiefly responsible for the monumental success of Calumet Farm during the 1940s.

Bull Dog ranked among America's leading sires with amazing consistency. He led the sire list in 1943, and from 1936 through 1946 he never ranked lower than sixth, while being twice second and three times third during that period.

As a broodmare sire, he led the list three times—in 1953, 1954, and 1956, and he was in the top ten almost annually from 1945 through 1961 [with the exception of 1959].

How anyone could have known in advance that Bull Dog (given his indifferent racing record) would prove to be such a high-class sire of early maturity, high speed, and limited distance capacity passes the understanding of this writer. None of the six other sons of Plucky Liege showed that genetic character: Sir Gallahad III sired middle-distance stock, and Admiral Drake and Bois Roussel each sired,

Teddy, 1913	Ajax, 1901	Flying Fox, 1896	Orme, 1889	Ormonde Angelica
			Vampire, 1889	**Galopin** Irony
		Amie, 1893	Clamart, 1888	Soukaras Princess Catherine
			Alice, 1887	Wellingtonia Asta
	Rondeau, 1900	Bay Ronald, 1893	Hampton, 1872	**Lord Clifden** Lady Langden
			Black Duchess, 1886	Galliard Black Corrie
		Doremi, 1894	Bend Or, 1877	Doncaster Rouge Rose
			Lady Emily, 1879	**Macaroni** May Queen
Plucky Liege, 1912	Spearmint, 1903	Carbine, 1885	Musket, 1867	Toxophilite W. Australian Mare
			Mersey, 1874	Knowsley Clemence
		Maid of the Mint, 1897	Minting, 1883	Lord Lyon Mint Sauce
			Warble, 1884	Skylark Coturnix
	Concertina, 1896	St. Simon, 1881	**Galopin**, 1872	Vedette Flying Duchess
			St. Angela, 1865	King Tom Adeline
		Comic Song, 1884	Petrarch, 1873	**Lord Clifden** Laura
			Frivolity, 1867	**Macaroni** Miss Agnes

(Row label: BULL DOG)

Miss Dogwood

on the whole, horses that matured late and were plodders.

Physically, Bull Dog was a stallion of high quality, even superior in that respect to his sire, Teddy, and to Sir Gallahad III. He was a dark bay, with black points, and had good size and constitution. In addition to Widener Handicap winner Bull Lea (sire of Citation, Coaltown, etc.), and the Futurity specialists (Occupation, Occupy, and Our Boots), Bull Dog's stakes winners included major sires The Doge and Johns Joy, plus Miss Dogwood, Boss, Canina, Evening Tide, Miss Mommy, Buster, War Dog, Cassis, Miss Ferdinand, Bull Reigh, Coldstream, Eternal Bull, Tiger, and Nectarine.

Daughters of Bull Dog produced eighty-nine stakes winners, of which the best included Tom Fool, Dark Star, Aunt Jinny, Royal Coinage, and Rough'n Tumble, plus Sea Snack, Star Pilot, Hampden, Three Rings, Spartan Valor, Pet Bully, Imbros, Decathlon, Count of Honor, Mommy Dear, Talent Show, and Donut King.

CHAPTER SIXTY-NINE

BULL LEA

C.B. Shaffer decided in 1936 to become a market breeder, and among the yearlings that thus were sent from his Coldstream Stud near Lexington, Kentucky, to undergo the scrutiny of the marketplace was a son of Bull Dog—Rose Leaves, by Ballot. The youngster's sire, Bull Dog, had been imported to Coldstream in 1930. The dam, Rose Leaves, had been unplaced at two, but by 1936 she already had sent out four stakes winners—Espino, Nectarine, Ruddy, and Bois de Rose. She was nineteen when the Bull Dog colt was foaled.

The Coldstream youngster was sold at Saratoga and elicited a bid of $14,000, fourth-highest paid for an auction yearling that year. The buyer was Warren Wright Sr., who thusly secured the most important cog in the Calumet Farm wheel that was to roll through fourteen seasons as the nation's leading breeder and twelve as leading owner.

The Bull Dog youngster was named Bull Lea and was turned over to trainer Frank Kearns, who brought him out in June of his two-year-old season in Chicago. He was fifth in his first start but broke his maiden in his second outing. Thereafter, he won one race in seven tries, and he was second in two of the major juvenile races, the Hopeful and the Champagne Stakes, and third in the Saratoga Special. A minor injury forced him to miss the Belmont Futurity, but he still was ranked as the fifth-best of the year behind champion Menow (126 pounds to 121) on the Experimental Free Handicap.

Like numerous carriers of the Calumet red-and-blue silks would in later years, Bull Lea at three turned in an impressive performance in the spring at Keeneland. In his first start of the year, he led from wire to wire to defeat champion Menow (third) in the one and one-sixteenth-mile Mereworth Purse, setting a track record of 1:44. Menow had given him five and a half pounds in that race and a week later in the nine-furlong Blue Grass Stakes was giving the Calumet colt two pounds. Bull Lea allowed the Hal Price Headley champion to set the pace, but he came on in the stretch to win by a neck, again setting a track record, 1:49 3/5, which was

Warren and Lucille Wright

MORGAN PHOTO SERVICE

nearly three seconds faster than the old mark.

Bull Lea was among the front rank of contenders for the Kentucky Derby ten days later, and he eventually went off as the second choice to the Wood Memorial winner, Fighting Fox. The brilliance of his first two spring outings had vanished, however, and Bull Lea never was closer than seventh, eventually finishing eighth behind winner Lawrin. In the Preakness, the story was much the same, as Bull Lea straggled home sixth behind winner Dauber. Menow, who had run fourth in the Derby, ran third at Pimlico.

Kearns gave Bull Lea a rest of two months, bringing him back in July at Arlington Park, where he won a one-mile allowance event. He next tried the Classic and had the lead at the head of the stretch, but Nedayr caught him in the final strides. At Saratoga, Bull Lea won the one and three-sixteenths-mile Kenner Stakes by a nose over Fighting Fox but finished a tiring sixth behind the same colt (who finished third) in the Travers Stakes.

Sent to Narragansett, Bull Lea at the third track won a race leading to his main target and then let the big prize get away. In the James C. Thornton Memorial at one and one-eighth miles, he won by a neck over Purple King, with Travers fourth Stagehand third. In the one and three-sixteenths-mile Narragansett Special, he had the lead again in the stretch, but Stagehand, a three-year-old who early in the year had defeated older Seabiscuit in the Santa Anita Handicap, came along to edge him.

The win-one-lose-a-big-one pattern nevertheless was preferable to Bull Lea's next performance, as he went back to New York and ran last in the Jerome Handicap at Belmont. Only a week later, he was in Maryland and ran a strong second to old rival Menow in the Potomac Handicap.

Still traveling, he appeared next in New York for the Continental Handicap, in which he was second to Roguish Girl. At Narragansett, he beat a weak field in the Autumn Stakes but was third to older Mucho Gusto under top weight of 124 in the Aquidneck Handicap.

Bull Lea's final start at three was in the Pimlico Handicap. Carrying top weight of 122 pounds, Bull Lea ended his campaign as he had begun it, leading from wire to wire, this time at one mile and seventy yards.

Bull Lea had started sixteen times at three and, while no one could claim greatness in his three-year-old form, the late John Hervey regarded the colt's performance in a trying campaign commendable: "He must be reckoned a hardy and rugged young Thoroughbred whose ability to withstand the exigencies of severe racing, frequent shipments, and all sorts of conditions is truly exceptional."

Bull Lea at four succeeded in winning a major race at one and a quarter miles, and so impressive was his Widener Handicap triumph at that distance that he seemed temporarily in a strong position for championship honors of 1939. The winter began with hopes of a Seabiscuit–War Admiral clash in Hialeah's Widener, but both were withdrawn, leaving the previous year's three-year-old champion, Stagehand, the favorite for the climactic winter handicap.

Bull Lea met Stagehand in that colt's four-year-old debut, in the nine-furlong

Bull Dog, 1927	Teddy, 1913	Ajax, 1901	Flying Fox, 1896	Orme / Vampire
			Amie, 1893	Clamart / Alice
		Rondeau, 1900	Bay Ronald, 1893	Hampton / Black Duchess
			Doremi, 1894	Bend Or / Lady Emily
	Plucky Liege, 1912	Spearmint, 1903	Carbine, 1885	**Musket** / Mersey
			Maid of the Mint, 1897	Minting / Warble
		Concertina, 1896	St. Simon, 1881	Galopin / St. Angela
BULL LEA			Comic Song, 1884	Petrarch / Frivolity
	Ballot, 1904	Voter, 1894	Friar's Balsam, 1885	Hermit / Flower of Dorset
			Mavourneen, 1888	Barcaldine / Gaydene
		Cerito, 1888	Lowland Chief, 1878	Lowlander / Bathilde
Rose Leaves, 1916			Merry Dance, 1879	Doncaster / Highland Fling
	Colonial, 1897	Trenton, 1881	**Musket**, 1867	Toxophilite / W. Australian Mare
			Frailty, 1877	Goldsbrough / Flora McIvor
		Thankful Blossom, 1891	Paradox, 1882	Sterling / Casuistry
			The Apple, 1886	Hermit / Black Star

Bull Lea

McLennan Handicap, and succumbed to the favorite only in the closing strides. The Calumet colt received four pounds in the McLennan and got seven from Stagehand in the Widener.

Irving Anderson guided Bull Lea into the lead early in the stretch in the Widener, and under 119 pounds the colt drew away easily, defeating Sir Damion by two and a half lengths, with Stagehand coming on for third.

After being shipped north to prepare for the spring campaign, Bull Lea developed leg trouble. He was sent to Calumet near Lexington, where it was planned he would be put back in training later for a return at five. He failed to stand training, and early in 1940 his retirement to stud was announced.

Wright's seeming misfortune was, in fact, a lucky stroke, for in his first crop Bull Lea sired Calumet's champions Twilight Tear and Armed. Twilight Tear was Horse of the Year at three whereas Armed matured later, gaining that honor at six. Also in his first crop, Bull Lea sired Brownell Combs' champion Durazna. Thus began the siege on racing that was Calumet in the 1940s and early 1950s.

Bull Lea sired a total of 377 named foals, of which fifty-seven (15 percent) were stakes winners and nine were U.S. champions—Citation, Armed, Twilight Tear, Bewitch, Coaltown, Next Move, Two Lea, Real Delight, and Durazna.[1]

Calumet's Citation won the Triple Crown in 1948 and later became racing's first millionaire; Calumet's Iron Liege and Hill Gail (both by Bull Lea) won Kentucky Derbys; in addition to those named, Calumet raced such major winners (by Bull Lea) as Faultless, Mark-Ye-Well, Miz Clementine, Bubbley, Yorky, and Gen. Duke. Bull Lea's stakes winners also included Degage, Bull Page, Alerted, and Level Lea.

Bull Lea led the sire list five times, in 1947–49 and in 1952 and 1953, and he was among the top ten sires for twelve consecutive years. He sired a total of thirteen horses that earned $300,000 or more, sharing that distinction with Bold Ruler, the eight-time leading sire of a later era, when many stakes were more lucrative.

Bull Lea, as would be expected, also was a great broodmare sire, leading that category four consecutive years, 1958–61. His daughters produced 105 stakes winners, including A Gleam, Lea Lane, Barbizon, Bardstown, Leallah, Pucker Up, Idun, Restless Wind, Lady Golconda (dam of

YEAR	AGE	STS	1ST	2ND	3RD	EARNED
1937	at 2	9	2	2	2	$ 7,300
1938	at 3	16	7	4	1	$39,575
1939	at 4	2	1	1	0	$47,950
Lifetime		27	10	7	3	$94,825

Forego), Tim Tam, On-and-On, Ambiopoise, Bramalea, Quadrangle, Advocator, and Eastern Fleet.[2]

Bull Lea, thus remains prominent in pedigrees of major stakes winners, but in terms of a sire line, Bull Lea's descendants are not strong today. In 1973, for instance, only seven stakes winners traced to Bull Lea in the male line. Considering the momentous talents of several of his sons—most notably Citation—their performances at stud taken as a whole could be regarded as disappointing, especially in regard to any one of them taking up the baton of the male line and sending it into the next generations with strength.

With respect to the line from whence came Bull Lea (he a son of Bull Dog, who like Sir Gallahad III was by Teddy—Plucky Liege), which this book's chapters have addressed, note should be made of the recent success of Damascus, who ranked second on the 1975 general sire list.

Although we mistakenly suggested in an earlier chapter that the line of Sun Teddy appeared to have little chance of survival, that son of Teddy did sire Sun Again, who, in turn, sired Sunglow, he the sire of champion Sword Dancer, who sired champion Damascus. Thus, while Teddy sired the redoubtable brothers Sir Gallahad III and Bull Dog, prominent strength of the Teddy line at the moment rests with the line of the less-renowned Sun Teddy.[3]

End Notes:

1. Bull Page was named 1951 Canadian Horse of the Year.

Damascus, a descendant of Teddy through Sun Again

2. Gate Dancer, out of the Bull Lea mare Sun Gate, won the 1984 Preakness and Super Derby and earned $2.5 million to become Bull Lea's chief earner as broodmare sire.

3. The line remains extant in 2006 through several of Damascus' sons: Bailjumper (sire of Skip Trial, in turn sire of Skip Away), Cutlass (sire of Friendly Lover), Eastern Echo (sire of Swiss Yodeler), Marsayas (sire of Rod and Staff), Private Account (sire of Expense Account, Private Terms, Top Account, plus grandsire of Say Florida Sandy, Afternoon Deelites, Soul of the Matter, Accounted For), Time for a Change (sire of Time Bandit), and Timeless Moment (sire of Gilded Time, in turn sire of Old Topper and Early Flyer).

CHAPTER SEVENTY

QUESTIONNAIRE

J ames Butler was a grocery tycoon with an extensive chain of stores in the greater New York area. When he became interested in racing, he built and operated the Empire City track north of New York City. This first resulted in a battle with the solons of The Jockey Club, who saw no reason to grant Butler any dates free of competition with the other New York tracks. After a somewhat spirited and acrimonious dispute, Butler won out, and Empire City became a recognized track on the New York circuit.

Along with his track, Butler decided to breed his own horses, so he set up a breeding farm near White Plains, New York, in Westchester County. This was highly unconventional, although good horses had been bred on Long Island and Staten Island. The soils of Westchester County are not very fertile and have a granite base; the limestone and phosphorus looked on with favor by nearly all breeders are notably lacking at White Plains. Doubtless, Butler thought that these elements could be added to his pastures, so that his horses could compete successfully with the Kentucky-breds. In fact, he proved his point, as he brought out a number of good horses. (Butler may have heard the famous remark attributed to the great French breeder, Edmond Blanc: "I will breed a Derby or Grand Prix winner in the Boulevard Haussmann, if you will let me feed him what I want!")

The best colt Butler bred was Questionnaire, but it did not look that way during the colt's two-year-old season. Questionnaire made fourteen starts, and had two wins and four seconds. One of the placings came in the one-mile-and-seventy-yard Ardsley Handicap at the end of the season. As there was not much of class in the field, this was not especially promising. More revealing was what happened when he met H.P. Whitney's Boojum, one of the two best colts of that year. In a maiden race at Belmont Park, Boojum as a first-time starter went off at odds of 7-10 and beat Questionnaire by eight lengths.

From two to three years of age, Questionnaire made abnormal improvement. He was out twenty-one times at three and won eleven races. He was unplaced

Questionnaire

only three times, when he made a disastrous invasion of Maryland in October following five hard races in September in New York. He was almost certainly the third-best colt of his year, and on the basis of one race, may have been the second-best.

As a three-year-old, he began about where he had left off at two, running second in a six-furlong allowance race on May 13. On May 22, he was third in the seven-furlong Swift Stakes, beaten two lengths. Two days later he was third against older horses in the Metropolitan Handicap, with 103 pounds up. This race was famous for one of the very few bad mistakes ever made by Walter Vosburgh, the handicapper for The Jockey Club. He put the crack four-year-old Jack High in the race with only 110 pounds. Most racing men thought that in his old age, Vosburgh had confused Jack High with Hi Jack, a much inferior racer. In any case, Jack High ran off with the race in 1:35, a new record for the course[1], and beat Questionnaire three and one-half lengths. Even so, it was a very good performance for the three-year-old.

Questionnaire next took a nine-furlong allowance race as a prep for the one and one-half mile Belmont Stakes. In the Belmont he met Gallant Fox, who already had won the Kentucky Derby and the Preakness, and Whichone, who had been one of the two best two-year-olds of the previous year. Partisanship in the backers of Gallant Fox and Whichone was so intense that many lifelong friends ceased speaking to each other. No one gave Questionnaire much chance, and indeed at this stage of his development, he did not have much chance.

There were only four starters; Gallant Fox beat Whichone three lengths, with Questionnaire another three lengths away.

Questionnaire then took an ordinary handicap easily with top weight of 118 pounds, and on July 7 won a similar handicap. Five days later he won still another. The interesting thing here was that Flying Heels (118) was set to give Questionnaire six pounds. This showed Vosburgh's opinion at this stage, and he was wrong. On July 19 and July 23, Questionnaire won a handicap and the Mount Kisco Stakes, and on the 26th, Questionnaire (119) took the Empire City Derby, at ten furlongs, beating Spinach (112) by six and one-half lengths. In the autumn, in Maryland, Spinach took his revenge.

During August, Questionnaire was given a well-deserved rest. He came out again at Belmont Park in a nine-furlong allowance race and won it. The next race, on September 6, was the most revealing, and possibly the best, of Questionnaire's

QUESTIONNAIRE				
Sting, 1921	Spur, 1913	King James, 1905	Plaudit, 1895	**Himyar** / Cinderella
			Unsightly, 1897	Pursebearer / Hira Villa
		Auntie Mum, 1898	Melton, 1882	Master Kildare / Violet Melrose
			Adderly, 1892	Ayrshire / Sandiway
	Gnat, 1912	Voter, 1894	Friar's Balsam, 1885	Hermit / Flower of Dorset
			Mavourneen, 1888	Barcaldine / Gaydene
		Mosquito, 1903	Commando, 1898	**Domino** / Emma C.
			Sandfly, 1889	Isonomy / Sandiway
Miss Puzzle, 1913	Disguise, 1897	**Domino**, 1891	**Himyar**, 1875	Alarm / Hira
			Mannie Gray, 1874	Enquirer / Lizzie G.
		Bonnie Gal, 1889	Galopin, 1872	Vedette / Flying Duchess
			Bonnie Doon, 1870	Rapid Rhone / Queen Mary
	Ruby Nethersole, 1907	Star Ruby, 1892	Hampton, 1872	Lord Clifden / Lady Langden
			Ornament, 1887	Bend Or / Lily Agnes
		Nethersole, 1898	Tournament, 1887	Sir Modred / Play Thing
			Fairy Slipper, 1894	St. Serf / Cinderella

career. This was in the one and five-eighths-mile Lawrence Realization, where Gallant Fox (126) had to concede to Questionnaire (123) only three pounds. On their running in the Belmont, this should have been easy, but in fact it was not; it was a desperate race. The pair went one and one-half miles in 2:28 2/5, compared with Gallant Fox's time of 2:31 4/5 in the Belmont, and then ran the extra furlong in :12 3/5, with Gallant Fox just managing to get his head in front. This race made Questionnaire only about three and a half pounds behind Gallant Fox. Had anyone maintained this in the spring months he would have been laughed to scorn.

Questionnaire was out only five days later to take a ten-furlong handicap under 118 pounds in 2:02 4/5. This series of races evidently had taken something out of Questionnaire, as his form began to deteriorate. He could not quite give Mr. Sponge nine pounds in the one-mile Jerome Handicap, and then he was second in another handicap. He next invaded Maryland and contested the chief races there, but was unplaced in all three of them in October. At the beginning of November, he went back to Empire City and won his last start of the year in an ordinary handicap. It had been a pretty grueling campaign, and Questionnaire had not flinched so long as he had anything to give.

YEAR	AGE	STS	1ST	2ND	3RD	EARNED
1929	at 2	14	2	4	0	$ 3,950
1930	at 3	21	11	3	4	$44,801
1931	at 4	5	4	1	0	$30,185
1932	at 5	2	2	0	0	$10,550
1933	at 6	3	0	0	0	$ 125
Lifetime		45	19	8	4	$89,611

Questionnaire's four-year-old campaign was limited, at least in comparison with his previous two, but it was glorious. He was out five times and won four races, competing in the most important handicaps in New York. He began on May 18 in the unimportant Fair Play Handicap of seven furlongs at Belmont Park. Naturally, he had top weight, and he won. Next came the one-mile Metropolitan, where Questionnaire was joint top weight (122) with Mokatam, and Questionnaire won by four lengths. For this victory, Questionnaire was penalized five pounds in the Suburban, where he had to take up 128 pounds and Mokatam 123 pounds. This was not a bad assessment, as Mokatam won, but only by a neck.

On June 20, Questionnaire (127) went after the Brooklyn Handicap, then run at nine furlongs, and won it with top weight in 1:49. To win two of the three big handicaps in New York and be beaten only a neck in the third was no small feat. Only Whisk Broom II had done better, taking all three in 1913, and since then only Tom Fool and Kelso have won all three.[2]

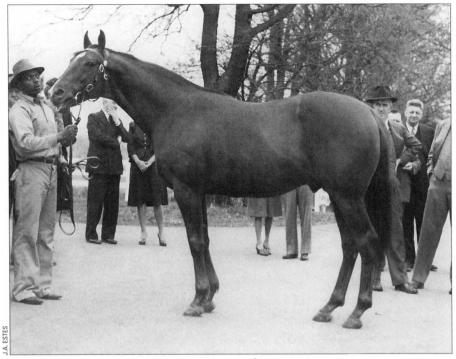

Requested

Questionnaire's last race as a four-year-old brought a five-length victory in the Empire City Handicap, with nothing of much class among his rivals. At that point, Questionnaire went wrong, but was brought back at five.

Grand as his four-year-old record was, we must bear in mind that Gallant Fox, Whichone, and Boojum were all out of training when he made it. Beyond doubt, Questionnaire was the best handicap horse in the country, but this still did not make him the best colt of his generation.

Questionnaire's comeback as a five-year-old was a great success as far as it went, but it only went for two races. The first outing was in the Paumonok Handicap of six furlongs at Jamaica. Questionnaire (130) won by one and one-half lengths with top weight. He then won the one and one-sixteenth-mile Kings County Handicap, again carrying 130 pounds. That was all for the year.

Still another attempt was made to bring Questionnaire back to the races, as a six-year-old. He made three starts and finished unplaced each time.

Questionnaire had something of an off-beat pedigree for such a high-class performer. In tail male, he descended from Himyar (the sire of Domino), but not through the outstanding line of Domino. He came through the branch of Plaudit

(Kentucky Derby) and King James (a good handicapper, but some way behind Celt and Fair Play, to say nothing of Colin, in the same crop). King James sired Spur, who was a good three-year-old, being unplaced only once in twenty-one starts and winning the Withers and Travers. Spur passed into the ownership of James Butler, who bred his son Sting. For Butler, Sting proved to be a pretty good handicapper, winning the one-mile Metropolitan with 114 pounds up and the Suburban with 122 pounds. For the Brooklyn he was assigned 127 pounds, but broke down in the race. One would have to say that Questionnaire probably was better than any other of this line of sires back to Plaudit.

Questionnaire's dam, Miss Puzzle, was a pretty tough filly, if not a very high-class one. She ran sixteen times at two, winning three. At three, she started eighteen times and won a selling race at Empire City. Miss Puzzle was by Disguise, who was not a great success as a sire and whose stock did not stay particularly well.

Standing at White Plains, New York, Sting naturally had had a very restricted opportunity as a sire, and he made no great impression upon the *Stud Book*. His son Questionnaire, however, passed into the ownership of Greentree Stud at Lexington. He was a quite consistent sire, ranking in the first ten on the sire list five times and in the first twenty a total of nine times. He never rose above seventh on the list, though.

Questionnaire's good sons included Free For All, who headed the Free Handicap at two and who later sired Rough'n Tumble. Another of Questionnaire's twenty-four stakes winners was the high-class Requested, winner of the Flamingo, Wood Memorial, etc., and sire of several major winners, including My Request, Miss Request, Cerise Reine, and Lord Putnam.

Questionnaire's stakes winners also included Stefanita, the 1943 champion three-year-old filly; Hash, winner of the Lawrence Realization; plus Carolyn A., Bold Gallant, Wine List, Alquest, and Third Degree.

End Notes:
   1. The time was also a new American record.
   2. Rokeby Stable's Fit to Fight won all three in 1984.

CHAPTER SEVENTY-ONE

ROUGH'N TUMBLE

When a colt runs seven times, wins his first six races, and then breaks down early in his three-year-old campaign, there is not enough hard evidence to classify him with much satisfaction. Could he go on? Was he a colt of classic stature, or a mere flash of undoubted speed? In the case of Free For All, there is no way of telling.

He was bought by John Marsch at the 1943 Keeneland summer yearling sale for $11,000, the top price of Walter J. Salmon's Mereworth Farm consignment. The colt's background resembled a game of musical chairs among the large breeding farms in Kentucky. The second dam, Panasette, was a stakes winner, with the familiar C.V. Whitney farm cross of Whisk Broom II with a mare by Peter Pan (Panasine). Panasette was mated with another Whitney stallion, imported Chicle, whose dam, Lady Hamburg II, was sired by Hamburg. Panasette's Chicle foal must not have been too promising, because she was culled off to Mose Goldblatt as a yearling in 1935. (Goldblatt trained a number of rejects from Whitney's first string over the years, and, on the whole, did very well with them.)

The Chicle—Panasette filly that Goldblatt took in 1935 was named Panay. He did fairly well with her at two, when in four starts she won once, was twice second and once third. In December 1936, she was sold to Calumet Farm, which at that time was building its broodmare band. Panay apparently did not suit Calumet very well. Her first two foals were culled out at auction; the first, a colt by Chance Play, brought $400, and the second, by Hard Tack, $550. At that point, Calumet had had enough of Panay, and the mare was put in the Lexington fall sales, in foal to the Greentree stallion Questionnaire. Mereworth bought her for $1,400.

On March 3, 1942, Panay foaled a promising-looking colt that resembled Questionnaire. The $11,000 Free For All brought as a yearling was a neat return on the purchase price of the dam; this further was improved upon by the $15,000 received for her next yearling, by Hairan. It was a trifle surprising that Free For All topped the Mereworth consignment. He was a small colt (standing only

ALLEN F. BREWER

Free For All

15 hands at two), rather lengthy like his sire, and slightly dipped in the back.

Marsch's luck with two-year-olds was becoming legend. The Chicago contractor had won the Belmont Futurity and Washington Park Futurity two years in succession, with Occupation in 1942 and Occupation's full brother, Occupy, in 1943. Occupation also won the Arlington Futurity and Breeders' Futurity; Occupy finished second in both of those races the following year, being beaten by Marsch's Jezrahel in the Arlington Futurity.

Occupation, Occupy, and Jezrahel were bred by Marsch in partnership with Thomas C. Piatt.[1] Their dams foaled fillies in 1942, and Marsch and Piatt sold the foals as yearlings at Keeneland. Marsch then entered the market as a buyer, and coming up with Free For All made him look all the more like a man with the Midas touch insofar as two-year-olds were concerned.

On June 17 of his juvenile year, Free For All came out at Hawthorne in a field of eight, none of the others of especially high caliber. He smothered his rivals, winning by eight lengths and missing the track record by only three-fifths of a second. Shifting to Washington Park four days later, Free For All ran off with the Hyde Park Stakes, winning by five lengths from Sir Bim. He set a track record of 1:04 3/5 for the five and one-half furlongs and at once was acknowledged to be the best two-year-old on the Chicago circuit.

Before the Arlington Futurity on July 15, Free For All was given a prep race. Flood Town, then regarded as the best juvenile seen out that year in New York, had shipped in and also was in the prep. The other included Marsch's Errard, who had been considered a better prospect than Free For All during the spring. Free For All could not smother that type of opposition, but he did win, scoring over his stablemate by three-quarters of a length. Errard earlier in the race had put away Flood Town.

Rumors circulated that Errard could have won had the Marsch stable so wished, and both Marsch colts were run back in the Futurity only four days later. Flood

Town, Sir Bim, Spartan Noble, and Darien were their opposition. Flood Town elected to make a front-running race of it, and he led Errard by a half-length at the far turn. Moving into the stretch, Flood Town still had the better of Errard, as Free For All easily moved forward. At the quarter pole, Free For All nailed Flood Town and thereafter moved away to win in hand, by two and one-half lengths, as Sir Bim came along for second.

By that time, Free For All's dominance was such that only three cared to take on him and Errard in the Washington Park Futurity. Errard led most of the way; then Free For All came along on the outside and took charge inside the final furlong, drawing out to win by one and one-quarter lengths. Icangetit closed to be second.

That was Free For All's last race at two, and at year's end he was given equal top weight with Pavot on the Experimental Free Handicap.

Free For All made his three-year-old debut on May 17, 1945, at the Keeneland-at-Churchill Downs meeting, easily winning the six-furlong Forest Retreat Purse over a muddy track. He was 1-10 for the race, and he carried top weight of 122 pounds. The victory brought his unbeaten skein to six and made him the pre-race favorite in some quarters for the Kentucky Derby (run that year on June 9). Added prestige was gained a week later when trainer Burley Parke received word

ROUGH'N TUMBLE				
Free For All, 1942	Questionnaire, 1927	Sting, 1921	Spur, 1913	King James / Auntie Mum
			Gnat, 1912	**Voter** / Mosquito
		Miss Puzzle, 1913	Disguise, 1897	Domino / Bonnie Gal
			Ruby Nethersole, 1907	Star Ruby / Nethersole
	Panay, 1934	Chicle, 1913	**Spearmint**, 1903	Carbine / Maid of the Mint
			Lady Hamburg, 1908	Hamburg / Lady Frivoles
		Panasette, 1928	**Whisk Broom II**, 1907	Broomstick / Audience
			Panasine, 1910	Peter Pan / Ladasine
Roused, 1943	Bull Dog, 1927	Teddy, 1913	Ajax, 1901	Flying Fox / Amie
			Rondeau, 1900	Bay Ronald / Doremi
		Plucky Liege, 1912	**Spearmint**, 1903	Carbine / Maid of the Mint
			Concertina, 1896	St. Simon / Comic Song
	Rude Awakening, 1936	Upset, 1917	**Whisk Broom II**, 1907	Broomstick / Audience
			Pankhurst, 1910	**Voter** / Runaway Girl
		Cushion, 1917	Nonpareil, 1909	Yankee / Fancywood
			Hassock, 1912	Martinet / Agnes Brennan

Rough'n Tumble

that Eddie Arcaro had accepted Free For All as his Derby mount.

Marsch's colt never got a chance against the best of his generation at three, though, because he broke down while finishing fourth in the May 26 Derby Trial Stakes at one mile. That ended Free For All's racing career, moving any speculation of his future class or ability at distance racing into the realm of pure conjecture.

Free For All did not prove to be as good a stallion as did his sire, Questionnaire. Free For All entered stud at the Lexington nursery of Dr. Charles E. Hagyard, who later purchased a two-thirds interest from Marsch. The stallion escaped with only slight injuries when lightning struck a fence in his paddock in 1947. Dr. Hagyard sold Free For All at the 1957 Keeneland fall mixed sale for $5,700 to W.D. Rorick of Kansas. The horse died in Colorado in 1964.

Free For All sired nine stakes winners, including Rough'n Tumble, who represented his chief contribution to American breeding.

Bred by Dr. Hagyard, Rough'n Tumble was sold privately as a yearling to Mrs. Frances Genter. He began his racing life as a claimer. His first race at two was against maidens on June 20, 1950, at Arlington Park, and he was under a claiming tag of $7,000. There was a field of twelve going five furlongs, and the result was something of a surprise to the public and perhaps to Rough'n Tumble's connections, too. The colt led all the way and won by four and a half lengths.

He then made quite a step up in class, being sent for the five and a half-furlong Primer Stakes. The public thought this a bit too much of a step and sent him away at 25-1 in a field of thirteen, but Rough'n Tumble won again, coming from behind to score by a half-length in the good time of 1:04 4/5. There was not another colt of class in the race, but such could not be known at so early a stage in the career of the runners.

Dropping back from stakes company to an allowance race should have proven easy for Rough'n Tumble, and the public sent him away at 9-5 in a field of eleven in a five and a half-furlong event, but he found in Longleat a horse good enough to

YEAR	AGE	STS	1ST	2ND	3RD	EARNED
1950	at 2	7	2	3	2	$ 25,230
1951	at 3	9	2	2	2	$101,750
Lifetime		16	4	5	4	$126,980

beat him by three lengths. The track was slow, which might have had something to do with the result.

Rough'n Tumble then was taken to Belmont Park, and right away he ran into Battlefield, who subsequently was to win the Futurity and the year's two-year-old championship. When they met in an allowance race, Battlefield was 11-10 and Rough'n Tumble 32-1. The choice won it, with Rough'n Tumble third, beaten only one and one-quarter lengths. That was not too bad a showing for the Genter colt, confirming that he was of stakes caliber. He then ran third, beaten about three lengths, in the Futurity, and later he placed in the Garden State and Remsen stakes.

The net of his two-year-old racing was to rank Rough'n Tumble as a good, but not outstanding, two-year-old. Taking his form against Battlefield as correct, he was about seven pounds below the best of the year.

Rough'n Tumble was taken to Santa Anita for winter racing and made his first start at three on January 19 in a six-furlong allowance race. He closed well to be third behind Phil D., beaten by two and one-half lengths. The pair met again in the San Felipe Stakes of seven furlongs, and Phil D. won again. His margin was a half-length, with Rough'n Tumble third, about a length back. This improvement on the part of Rough'n Tumble was confirmed in a one and one-sixteenth-mile prep for the Santa Anita Derby, the colt winning by two lengths with Phil D. third.

Ten days later, on February 24, Rough'n Tumble won the Santa Anita Derby of nine furlongs, beating ten rivals while racing as the 9-5 favorite. Because he for the second time won going away, with Phil D. fourth, Rough'n Tumble appeared to be a high-class colt. He was sent to Kentucky, but developed a splint and had to be fired.

ARLINGTON PARK

Minnesota Mac winning the 1967 Chicagoan at Arlington Park

He then was sent to Chicago and did not start again until July 4, when he put in a bad race and finished sixth in a field of eight in the one-mile Jamestown Handicap.

Perhaps on the theory that he had not been quite fit, Rough'n Tumble was dropped back to allowance company. Going nine furlongs, he did show improvement, running a close second to Bernwood. On July 21, he came out for the ten-furlong Arlington Classic, along with twelve others. He finished only sixth, but the result was somewhat instructive. He was three lengths behind Battlefield, who, in turn, was beaten a neck by winner Hall of Fame.

On August 4, Rough'n Tumble carried 123 pounds in the Sheridan Handicap of one mile and was defeated by three-quarters of a length by Bernwood (116) in track-record time of 1:33 4/5. To Market (124) was unplaced. That probably was Rough'n Tumble's best performance, taking the weights into account.

Next for Rough'n Tumble was the ten-furlong American Derby. He was unplaced behind Hall of Fame.

Rough'n Tumble had been injured and never raced again, but repeated attempts were made to return him to competition. Thus, he did not go to stud until he was six in 1954, when he was taken to Joe and Tom O'Farrell's Windy Hills Farm in Maryland to stand for a $250 fee. After Joe O'Farrell moved to Florida to become manager of Ocala Stud, Rough'n Tumble was moved to stand there. Following a practice then common at Ocala Stud, Rough'n Tumble was returned to Maryland for one later season, 1959, after which he was sent back to Florida.

From an initial $250 stud fee, the stallion's fee rose to $10,000, and he eventually was syndicated.

The success of Rough'n Tumble's runners went hand-in-glove with the rapid development of the Florida breeding industry. The stallion sired a total of twenty-four stakes winners, the most distinguished being millionaire Dr. Fager, who was Horse of the Year in 1968. The stallion's stakes winners also included champion My Dear Girl (later dam of major winner and sire In Reality); other $200,000-plus-earners Conestoga, Flag Raiser, No No Billy, Ruffled Feathers, and Yes You Will, plus Alley Fighter, Gunflint, Minnesota Mac, Treasure Chest, and Wedlock.[2]

His performance at stud was superior to his ranking as a racehorse and also to the quality of his pedigree. Rough'n Tumble's dam, Roused, by Bull Dog, was not a winner and produced only minor winners other than the Free For All colt. The granddam, Rude Awakening, was placed in stakes but produced only one winner. Rude Awakening was by Upset, a poor sire, and was from unraced Cushion, who produced two minor stakes winners.

Genetic superiority could not have been expected from such a pedigree, and when it did appear, its source remained a mystery.

End Notes:

1. J. Marsch is listed as the breeder of Occupation, Occupy, and Jezrahel; however, the 1942 foals from the dams of these horses are listed as bred by Marsch and Piatt.

2. The sire line of Rough'n Tumble is mainly kept viable today through Minnesota Mac, grandsire of champion Holy Bull, the sire of 2005 Kentucky Derby winner Giacomo.

CHAPTER SEVENTY-TWO

PRINCE ROSE

In the study of sire lines, there are few aspects more fascinating than the history of the decline and resurgence of lines and the circumstances under which they occur.

In England, St. Simon (1881) led the sire list nine times and had been the best sire of the nineteenth century (sire of the winners of seventeen classic races). His best son at stud was Persimmon (1893), winner of the Derby, St. Leger, and Ascot Gold Cup, and leading sire four times. Persimmon's best son as a racer was Prince Palatine, foaled in 1908 out of Lady Lightfoot.

Prince Palatine had been bred by Colonel Hall Walker at his Tully Stud, Kildare, Ireland. The colonel was much addicted to astrology, but in the study of Prince Palatine's horoscope, his astrology consultant must have been studying at the wrong phase of the moon; for when the famous Irish veterinarian J.H.H. Peard approached Hall Walker in England to put a price on the Persimmon—Lady Lightfoot yearling, a sale was made for 2,000 pounds, for the real buyer, Mr. Pilkington.

Hall Walker afterwards explained the price away by saying that, at the time, he was making some alterations to his house and needed the money to keep from going into debt. Since he left an estate of more than 800,000 pounds twenty-five years later, this explanation is on the feeble side.

As a two-year-old, Prince Palatine was out six times and won three races, including the important Imperial Produce Plate at Kempton Park. At three, he won at Goodwood and also won the St. Leger, and at four, he won the Ascot Gold Cup, the Doncaster Cup, the Jockey Club Stakes, and the Eclipse Stakes. At five, he won the Ascot Gold Cup again, as well as winning the Coronation Cup. There can be no doubt that he was a very high-class stayer, who also had been a good two-year-old. In fact, Frank O'Neill, an American jockey then riding chiefly in France, told the author he thought Prince Palatine was the highest-class stayer he ever rode.

Rose Prince, sire of Prince Rose

J.B. (Jack) Joel, who had the sprinter Sundridge at stud, offered Pilkington 45,000 pounds for Prince Palatine, subject to a 5,000-pound reduction in price if the horse were to be beaten in the Goodwood Cup. Prince Palatine was beaten, and Joel and his trainer were much upset.

Prince Palatine spent a few years at Childwickbury Stud and convinced Joel that he was a shy foal getter; what he did sire was not very good, anyway. So, Joel sold the horse to the Duc Decazes in France, where his fertility again was poor. After World War I, Prince Palatine was brought to the United States by Preston Burch, who passed him on to the Xalapa Farm of E.F. Simms, where a few years later the stallion was destroyed in a fire.

During his stay in the United States, Prince Palatine sired a colt called Prince Pal, who got a very high-class racer in Mate. Prince Palatine also sired Blue Glass, the dam of Unbreakable, he the sire of Polynesian and grandsire of Native Dancer.

During his stay in France, Prince Palatine sired Rose Prince (1919), who was in training for four seasons and was a winner each season. Rose Prince's most notable achievement was to win the great long distance handicap in England, the Cesarewitch (two and one-quarter miles), as a four-year-old with 115 pounds up, beating the Aga Khan's good filly Teresina (afterward the dam of Alibhai) by a short head. Rose Prince's owner, the American A.K. Macomber, reportedly gave the English bookmakers a nasty jolt, winning a packet. A few years later the same owner won the Autumn Double, the Cesarewitch and the Cambridgeshire, with Forseti and Masked Marvel. The author saw a canceled check from the bookmakers Ladbroke & Co. of 50,000 pounds for this achievement. How many more checks there were the author does not know.

Rose Prince was by no means a successful stallion, but he did have an intriguing pedigree, his granddam Rose de Mai having won the Poule d'Essai des Pouliches (French One Thousand Guineas) and the Prix de Diane (French Oaks). The next dam [May Pole] had won the Grand Criterium and the Poule d'Essai des Pouliches.

Rose Prince was mated with the mare Indolence, she by Gay Crusader, a Triple Crown winner, but a disappointing sire. Indolence was a winner of one minor race at three. The result of the mating was the bay colt Prince Rose, the fourth foal of the dam. Owing to the death of his breeder, Lord Durham, Prince Rose was sold as a foal at the Newmarket December sale. He brought 260 guineas and was sent to Belgium.

On the face of it, there was little reason to expect Prince Rose to be anything

			St. Simon, 1881	**Galopin** St. Angela
		Persimmon, 1893		
			Perdita, 1881	**Hampton** Hermione
	Prince Palatine, 1908			
			Isinglass, 1890	Isonomy Dead Lock
		Lady Lightfoot, 1900		
Rose Prince, 1919			Glare, 1891	Ayrshire Footlight
			War Dance, 1887	Galliard War Paint
		Perth, 1896		
			Primrose Dame, 1885	**Barcaldine** Lady Rosebery
	Eglantine, 1906			
			Callistrate, 1890	Cambyse Citronelle
		Rose De Mai, 1900		
PRINCE ROSE			May Pole, 1886	Silvio Merry May
			Bay Ronald, 1893	**Hampton** Black Duchess
		Bayardo, 1906		
			Galicia, 1898	**Galopin** Isoletta
	Gay Crusader, 1914			
			Beppo, 1903	Marco Pitti
		Gay Laura, 1909		
Indolence, 1920			Galeottia, 1892	Galopin Agave
			Pepper and Salt, 1882	The Rake Oxford Mixture
		Grey Leg, 1891		
			Quetta, 1885	Bend Or Douranee
	Barrier, 1910			
			Right-Away, 1887	Wisdom Vanish
		Bar the Way, 1901		
			Barrisdale, 1891	**Barcaldine** Wharfedale

out of the ordinary as a racer, or as a sire. Yet, he proved to be one of the best Thoroughbreds in Europe during the first half of the twentieth century.

Normally, racing men do not pay too much attention to the form of two-year-olds in Belgium, where the number of horses in training is limited and the breeding stock does not have the very highest credentials. Hence, when Prince Rose won four of his seven starts as a juvenile in Belgium and was hailed as the champion of his age in that country, it excited no great interest or comment elsewhere.

Prince Rose

The next year, however, things were different.

Prince Rose won seven stakes in succession in Belgium, including the Grand Prix de Bruxelles, the Grand Prix d'Ostende, and the Grand International d'Ostende. Even these achievements might not have attracted much notice outside Belgium, except for the circumstance that in the last of them, Prince Rose defeated two French cracks, the filly Pearl Cap (French One Thousand Guineas and Oaks) and Amfortas.

In October, Prince Rose was sent to Paris for the Prix de l'Arc de Triomphe. The same three horses again filled the first three places, but that time Pearl Cap was the winner, Amfortas was second, and Prince Rose was third after being seriously bothered. The French jockeys in those days were not always the soul of hospitality to foreign runners. From an international point of view, the race was very informative in that behind the first three were Brulette (English Oaks) and Tourbillon (French Derby).

As a four-year-old, Prince Rose resumed his winning ways in Belgium, taking four successive stakes, and then he went to Paris again to win the important Prix du President de la Republique (now the Grand Prix de Saint-Cloud) of one and nine-sixteenths miles. Prince Rose broke down thereafter and did not race again. He had won sixteen of his twenty starts and had shown himself to be first class at two, three, and four.

His importance to Belgian breeding was such that he was nationalized, i.e., his sale to go outside of Belgium was prohibited. The threat of German invasion was becoming more and more menacing, however, and L.L. Lawrence (resident in Paris in charge of Metro-Goldwyn-Mayer motion picture interests) was able to lease Prince Rose for stud duty in France.

There Prince Rose accomplished something in a few years that very few sires have achieved. He sired three colts that became first-class sires in three different countries—Prince Bio (1941) in France, sire of Sicambre (French Derby and Grand Prix de Paris); Prince Chevalier (1943) in

YEAR	AGE	STS	1ST	2ND	3RD	EARNED
1930	at 2	7	4	0	0	--
1931	at 3	8	7	0	1	--
1932	at 4	5	5	0	0	--
Lifetime		20	16	0	1	2,139,000 Fr

England, sire of Arctic Prince (Epsom Derby and maternal grandsire of Brigadier Gerard); Princequillo (1940) in the United States, sire of Round Table, Prince John, and many others.

Prince Rose was killed by artillery fire in France at the age of sixteen.

In 1933, the St. Simon male line—after having been almost all conquering in England until 1913—had become practically extinct there. Also, it was on a serious decline in France, never had prospered in the United States, and was only strong in Italy through Havresac II. Taking all of that into account, its resurgence—through Prince Rose and later Ribot—is extraordinary.

The late Colonel Vuillier, originator of the doctrine of "dosage" and pedigree adviser to the late Aga Khan, remarked in his book *Les Croisements Rationnels* that when the male lines of Stockwell (1849) and Newminster (1848) threatened to swamp all other male lines in England, and then declined badly, "for one who knew the history of the *Stud Book*, this moment was bound to come."

Could one say also, though, when the St. Simon line had declined so severely that its resurgence was "bound to come"?

CHAPTER SEVENTY-THREE

PRINCEQUILLO

I f an international background is what you are looking for in Thoroughbreds, then Princequillo is your horse. His connections run back through Ireland, England, Belgium, France, and Argentina, to the United States, where he achieved his fame both on the track and at stud.

Princequillo ran in all manner of races, from a $1,500 claiming race to stakes competition of the highest class, and at stud, after beginning with a fee of $250 with no great rush of patronage, he made his way to the top. He twice was America's leading sire, and his sons and daughters have bred on with notable success.

In all probability, Princequillo would not have been conceived were it not for the threat of World War II, and, once born, he probably would not have come to this country except for the war. The chain of events leading to his birth and importation was somewhat unlikely.

In 1923 American A.K. Macomber sent Rose Prince from France to run in England's Cesarewitch at two and one-quarter miles. Rose Prince was weighted at 115 pounds as a four-year-old, meaning that he was regarded as being some fourteen to eighteen pounds away from being a top-class colt. He won the handicap by a head from Teresina (later the dam of Alibhai) and landed a packet in bets for Macomber and his friends.

Although he was a long way below classic form, Rose Prince was left in England for stud duty. He was not really a success, but among the breeders who patronized him was Lord Durham, who sent to him, the poor race mare Indolence. The latter was by Gay Crusader, another indifferent stallion. The result of the mating was Prince Rose, a 1928 foal that was sold as a weanling that December at Newmarket after Lord Durham had died. Prince Rose fetched only 260 guineas from the Belgian owner Dr. H. Coppez, who sent him to his native country.

Prince Rose was called the best racehorse ever seen in Belgium. He also was a stakes winner in France and finished third in the Prix de l'Arc de Triomphe.

Prince Rose for a time was nationalized in Belgium, which meant his exportation was prohibited by the government, but with the probability of a German invasion growing stronger, L.L. Lawrence was able to arrange for his transfer to France.

Lawrence, who was head of the Metro-Goldwyn-Mayer affairs in Europe, sent to Prince Rose the mare Cosquilla in the spring of 1939, before the actual outbreak of war.

Cosquilla traced to a line of mares in the Tully Stud of Hall Walker (later Lord Wavertree). In 1913, three years before Hall Walker gave his stud to the British government to become a National Stud, he bred a filly called Mindful. She was a daughter of Minoru, who had won the Two Thousand Guineas and Derby while under lease to King Edward VII, but who had little impact at stud aside from producing Serenissima (the second dam of Hyperion).

Mindful, who did not race, was mated to White Eagle, who was a pretty fair broodmare sire although his stud record as a whole was disappointing. The result of the mating was the filly Quick Thought, who ran almost entirely in selling races and whose best effort in two seasons was to run third in a seller valued at 198 pounds.

Quick Thought later was bred to Papyrus, yet another sire with an indifferent stud record. That mating, however, produced a pretty good filly in Cosquilla. The latter was unraced at two, then at three and four won a total of seven races in France. Cosquilla's best effort probably came when she finished second in the one and five-eighths-mile Grand Prix de Deauville, beaten by only a neck in a large field. She actually was not very far below classic standard, and she was sound and tough and stayed well.

Cosquilla carried the colors of the well-known Argentine owner S.J. Unzue, and she was ridden by Argentine jockey D. Torterolo. After racing, Cosquilla became the property of Lawrence, who in 1939 bred her to Prince Rose. Owing to the prospect of a German invasion of France, Lawrence shipped Cosquilla to Ireland, where in the spring of 1940 she produced her Prince Rose foal, a bay colt named Princequillo.

Lawrence decided to ship a portion of his bloodstock to the United States in the autumn of 1940, and Princequillo was in the draft thus imported. He arrived as an underfed and scrawny-looking weanling.

At the start of his racing days, Princequillo was under the care of New Orleans horseman Anthony Pelleteri. The latter's name appeared on the race programs as trainer and owner, although, as we presently will see, there is some doubt as to who the real owner was at that point.

In any case, Princequillo, somewhat on the small side, did not appear at the outset to possess any overwhelming credentials. He was sired by an unproven stallion of Belgian background, and the first three sires on his bottom side were indifferent at best. The only bright spot on the female side was the racing class of his dam, but little was known of that at the time in the United States. Moreover, there had not been a good colt produced from the first three generations of the female line.

Thus, it was not surprising that Princequillo's first appearance came in a maiden claiming race, he eligible to be claimed for $1,500. Princequillo had shown enough in his morning work to be made an 8-5 choice in such company, but he was beaten by one and one-half lengths over five and three-quarters furlongs at Empire City. He next appeared at Saratoga, stepped up to $2,500, and he again was second. In his third start, he broke his maiden, scoring by three lengths in another $2,500 claimer.

Soon afterward, Princequillo's career came under the influence of Horatio Luro of Argentina. The latter has had a distinguished career on the American Turf, but it was not pure horsemanship which created his interest in Princequillo.

Luro told the author, for whom he trained a good number of horses a few years later, that he had begun some business discussions with L.L. Lawrence, breeder of Princequillo. Lawrence had asked Luro to telephone his office to arrange an

Prince Rose, 1928	Rose Prince, 1919	Prince Palatine, 1908	Persimmon, 1893	St. Simon / Perdita
			Lady Lightfoot, 1900	Isinglass / Glare
		Eglantine, 1906	Perth, 1896	War Dance / Primrose Dame
			Rose de Mai, 1900	Callistrate / May Pole
	Indolence, 1920	Gay Crusader, 1914	Bayardo, 1906	Bay Ronald / Galicia
			Gay Laura, 1909	Beppo / Galeottia
PRINCEQUILLO		Barrier, 1910	Grey Leg, 1891	Pepper and Salt / Quetta
			Bar the Way, 1901	Right-Away / The Barrisdale
Cosquilla, 1933	Papyrus, 1920	Tracery, 1909	Rock Sand, 1900	Sainfoin / Roquebrune
			Topiary, 1901	Orme / Plaisanterie
		Miss Matty, 1914	Marcovil, 1903	Marco / Lady Villikins
			Simonath, 1905	St. Simon / Philomath
	Quick Thought, 1918	White Eagle, 1905	Gallinule, 1884	Isonomy / Moorhen
			Merry Gal, 1897	Galopin / Mary Seaton
		Mindful, 1913	Minoru, 1906	Cyllene / Mother Siegel
			Noble Martha, 1895	Noble Chieftain / Lady Martha

appointment for further discussion, but when Luro phoned and gave his name to Lawrence's secretary, he was told that Lawrence never had heard of him and would not take the call.

"Is that so?" Luro thundered to himself. "We'll see who will speak when the time comes."

Luro knew that Lawrence was the breeder of Princequillo, and he thought that he still owned the colt, as well. When Luro saw that Princequillo could be claimed for $2,500—and looked a good prospect at the price—he stepped in and claimed him on behalf of the Boone Hall Stable, in which he had an interest himself. As the Señor later told the author, the reason for the claim was his belief that Lawrence was the real owner of Princequillo. Lawrence said that he had leased Princequillo and had "willingly accepted the clause permitting Pelleteri to run him in claiming races, as I should again,

YEAR	AGE	STS	1ST	2ND	3RD	EARNED
1942	at 2	10	3	2	3	$ 3,575
1943	at 3	15	7	2	2	$68,990
1944	at 4	8	2	1	2	$23,985
Lifetime		33	12	5	7	$96,550

for I would not have anyone subjected to onerous charges for training and racing if an animal showed he did not warrant the continued expense."

Having acquired the horse in his personal vendetta, Luro stepped Princequillo up to $5,000, and the colt ran third. Perhaps thinking he was overreaching, Luro dropped him back to $2,500, at which level he again was third, and he was third yet again for $4,000.

Running next for $3,500 at six furlongs, Princequillo won but was disqualified for bearing into another horse. He did come back to win again in November, but at that stage Luro's $2,500 claim still did not seem likely to become one of the all-time best bargains.

Having been shipped to New Orleans, Princequillo, for once out of the claiming ranks, won an $800 allowance race of six furlongs, then was rested for two months. In March, the three-year-old was fourth and second in additional six-furlong allowances.

Granted Luro's intimate knowledge of French racing and European pedigrees, one may hazard a guess that he was trying to fool somebody by exploiting Princequillo as a sprinter. When Princequillo was returned to New York, Luro sent him out at one and one-sixteenth miles in an allowance race, and the horse was 9-1. Princequillo won by a half-length from Towser.

By then, Luro believed his cheap sprinter of the year before had developed into a potential stakes colt, and Princequillo after a rest of six weeks was given his first

SKEETS MEADORS

Princequillo

test in an added-money event. For the nine-furlong Peter Pan Handicap, he got in with only 107 pounds, but still ran only fourth to Slide Rule (120). Dropping back to allowance company, Princequillo won by seven lengths over one and one-sixteenth miles on June 1.

Then came the great unveiling for which Luro must have been waiting—Princequillo as a stayer. He was entered at one and five-eighths miles in a $5,000 handicap for classes B and C, and he got in with only 107 pounds, compared to 126 on the distinguished stayer Bolingbroke. Princequillo was the outsider in the field, but he won the race easily, leading Bolingbroke home by two and one-half lengths. The one-time $1,500 claimer with the exotic pedigree had arrived.

Next up was the Dwyer at ten furlongs, and Princequillo could not quite handle Vincentive at nearly even weights. He ran third. Dropping back into allow-ance company, Princequillo finished fourth after jockey Conn McCreary held him too far out of it in the early running. The traditional long-distance races of the Saratoga-at-Belmont meeting still were some weeks away, so Luro tried Princequillo again in a middle-distance stakes, the one and three-sixteenths-mile Empire City Handicap, and he was third behind Chop Chop.

After a five-week respite, Princequillo appeared for the Saratoga-at-Belmont meeting, and his transformation into one of America's leading handicappers by then was completed. His first two races each were at ten furlongs instead of Cup distances. In the first of them, the Whitney, the field included Shut Out and Bolingbroke, each older than Princequillo. As a three-year-old, Princequillo got in at 103 pounds to the others' 117 each. McCreary brought him up along in the stretch, but the six-year-old Bolingbroke beat him a nose. The time of 2:02 was exceptional in the deep, slushy going.

For the Saratoga Handicap, the weights were slightly more in Princequillo's favor, as he carried 108 pounds to Shut Out's 126 and Bolingbroke's 122. The good pace at which the race was run suited Princequillo's stamina, and he was running second to Shut Out after a mile. In the final quarter-mile, Princequillo swept into the lead and won by five lengths, matching Sir Barton's 1920 stakes record of 2:01 4/5.

Next came the traditional Saratoga Cup, a weight-for-age stamina test of one and three-quarters miles. Only three started: Bolingbroke at 126 pounds, Princequillo at 116, and the mare Dark Discovery at 121. Steve Brooks, instead of McCreary, rode Princequillo, and his tactics were not the same as the other rider's had been. Brooks sent Princequillo to the front after a mile. Rounding the final turn, Bolingbroke made up ground, and the pair turned for home on almost level terms. There followed a stirring duel, and close to home it appeared as though Bolingbroke would take it, repeating his victory of 1942. With a final supreme effort, however, Brooks lifted Princequillo just past Bolingbroke and won by a short head. The time of 2:56 3/5 lowered the thirty-seven-year-old track record by a second.

After that titanic effort, sending Princequillo to Chicago to start in the Washington Park Handicap only a week later really was asking too much. Although he carried only 113 pounds in the $50,000 stakes, he could finish only fourth behind Royal Nap, Thumbs Up, and Marriage. It then was decided, sensibly, to give Princequillo a rest.

When he re-emerged in the fall, his objective was the two-mile Jockey Club Gold Cup at Belmont Park. Chief interest in the race centered on the renewed rivalry between Princequillo and Bolingbroke, meeting for the fifth time. At varying weight spreads, the three-year-old had beaten the older horse three times in four meetings, and in the Gold Cup they were at weight-for-age, which put 117 pounds on Princequillo to 124 on Bolingbroke. The race did not turn out to be between the pair, however, as there was a new Richmond in the field in the form of Fairy Manhurst.

Fairy Manhurst, who represented William du Pont's frequent and largely unsuccessful practice of inbreeding closely to Man o' War, had won the Lawrence Realization the week before. In the Gold Cup, he set the pace, with Princequillo tracking him, into the stretch. When Princequillo made his challenge, Fairy Manhurst had something left and the two raced as a team for some way. As he had done in the Saratoga Handicap, McCreary rather abruptly swung Princequillo over to the rails, and although the mud was deepest there, the colt came on with renewed strength and drew out to win by two and one-half lengths. Brooks had kept Bolingbroke far behind, and he was not able to catch Fairy Manhurst for second, although running the fastest of any at the finish.

Princequillo struck himself during the running of the Cup and his leg was filled the next day. Accordingly, he was declared from his next engagement, the New York Handicap, and put aside for the season.

As Princequillo had become famous, a lively duel developed between Luro and Prince Djordjadze, co-owner of Boone Hill Stable with his wife, the former Audrey Emory of Cincinnati (who put up the money). The Prince found fault with Luro for not knowing how to train Princequillo (wrong) and for the fact that Luro did not go to the stable on Sunday (right). Luro's complaint was that Prince Djordjadze never had paid a training bill (right). At any rate, when Princequillo next won a stakes, at four, the trainer was not Luro, but Dave Englander.

The chief interest in Princequillo's four-year-old campaign lies in the evaluation by the prince of handicappers, John B. Campbell, of Princequillo compared to other handicap horses of the time. For his first race, Princequillo was ranked by Campbell as three pounds above Bolingbroke for the nine-furlong Stromboli Handicap on May 18. Princequillo finished last of four, at 6-1.

Campbell then asked First Fiddle, regarded as the best handicapper in training, to carry 126 pounds and give twelve to Princequillo in the nine-furlong Tenny Handicap. Four Freedoms, another four-year-old getting twelve pounds from First Fiddle, won the race, with Princequillo last in a three-horse field. In his next race, again in a nine-furlong handicap, the Longstreet, Princequillo once more was last, in a three-horse field, giving four pounds to winner Wait A Bit.

Thus, in his first three races at four, Princequillo had failed to beat a single horse to the wire. Nevertheless, Campbell hiked the horse's weight to 120 and made him second below First Fiddle (126) for the Brooklyn Handicap.

MIKE SIRICO

Princequillo in winner's circle with Prince Djordjadze

The Brooklyn was at ten furlongs, one furlong longer than Princequillo's previous races, and perhaps Campbell thought the horse was scheduled to sprout wings at the eighth pole. Princequillo did not. He finished sixth in a field of nine, while Four Freedoms (116) won from Wait A Bit (116) and First Fiddle. If it was easy to second-guess Campbell before the Brooklyn, it must have seemed impossible not to afterward, and yet his assessment that Princequillo was still, indeed, a high-class racehorse soon was to be vindicated.

In his next race, Princequillo took up top weight of 120 pounds for the Questionnaire Handicap on the basis of one sixth and three last-place finishes, and he won it. Going one and five-eighths miles, more like his distance, he won handily and equaled the track record of 2:43 at Jamaica.

At Belmont Park, Princequillo carried top weight of 121 pounds against seven second- and third-class handicappers, to which he conceded from four to sixteen pounds, in the one and three-sixteenths-mile Merchants' and Citizens' Handicap. Again he proved the assessment correct, winning in the good time of 1:56 1/5.

Conditions of the Whitney Stakes sent Princequillo to the post at level weight (117) with Devil Diver as well as Bolingbroke. He was not quite up to that task of ten furlongs, although he was beaten only a half-length by Devil Diver. His old rival Bolingbroke was three and one-half lengths behind Princequillo at the wire.

The closest thing to a definitive assessment available is Campbell's weights for the ten-furlong Saratoga Handicap: Devil Diver 135, First Fiddle 128, and Princequillo 124. As it turned out, those were the last to finish, and Bolingbroke (118) was two and one-half lengths ahead of Princequillo at the wire, although Bolingbroke himself was not better than third behind lightweight Paperboy (103). Princequillo pulled up lame and did not race again.

Obviously, Campbell, whose professional opinion was unsurpassed at the time, thought that Princequillo was about eleven pounds or so below the best of his age, and Princequillo's performances at middle distances seemed to confirm that estimate.

Bull Hancock saw Princequillo win the Saratoga Cup at three and later remarked to his father, A.B. Hancock Sr.: "This is one horse we've got to have."

Later, Hancock said, "Mrs. Emory agreed to let us have a quarter-interest in him if we would stand him at our place (Ellerslie Stud) at Charlottesville, so we sent him there and stood him at $250.

"I couldn't get anybody much to breed to him. Mr. (C.T.) Chenery sent a mare, Mr. (William) Woodward agreed to send two mares, and my father sent four; he had all told, I think, about seventeen mares that first year. From them, he got Hill Prince (a champion and classic winner in America) and Prince Simon (classics-placed and champion in England). After that, we brought him to Kentucky (Claiborne Farm), raised him to a thousand, and he went right ahead."

"Right ahead" in the case of Princequillo meant leading the sire list twice, in 1957 and 1958, and siring sixty-five stakes winners, and eventually commanding a single season fee of at least $10,000. He never was syndicated in the usual sense of syndicate members owning equal shares, but his ownership broadened with his success. Luro sold his one-eighth interest as five one-fortieths, Prince Djordjadze's one-quarter interest was converted into ten lifetime seasons, and another one-eighth interest became four 1/32nd shares, at $8,000 each. Whitney Stone bought a one-eighth interest, and Hancock (Jr.) owned a three-eighths interest. Princequillo remained at Claiborne until his death in 1964.

Princequillo got 13.4 percent stakes winners from a total of 479 named foals. In addition to champions Hill Prince and Prince Simon, they included champions Round Table (Horse of the Year, former world leading money earner, and leader of the general sire list in 1972), Dedicate, Misty Morn, and Quill, plus other distinguished winners such as Coaching Club American Oaks winners How, Cherokee Rose, and Quillo Queen, and Garden State Stakes winner and promi-

TURFOTOS

Misty Morn

nent sire Prince John. Princequillo's other stakes winners included Dotted Line, Happy Princess, Kingmaker, Third Brother, Misty Flight, Black Hills, Monarchy, Whodunit, Prince Blessed, Rose Bower, Firm Policy, Princessnesian, Blue Prince, Tambourine, and Crimea II.

Also, his sons bred on; Round Table sired more stakes winners (eighty-three) than his sire did, and Prince John sired fifty-five stakes winners. (Both are subjects of separate chapters in this book.)

Princequillo's daughters have compiled a distinguished record as producers. The stallion was the leading broodmare sire (in money won by daughters' progeny) eight times since 1966. Several of his daughters are among the best producers of recent years. They include Somethingroyal, dam of Triple Crown winner Secretariat plus major sire Sir Gaylord; Key Bridge, dam of champions Fort Marcy and Key to the Mint; and Misty Morn, dam of champions Bold Lad and Successor.

Princequillo mares produced 170 North American stakes winners, including Pocahontas, High Bid, Hurry to Market, Syrian Sea, High Echelon, and Sham.

Accounting for Princequillo's tremendous success as a sire in the United States is quite a problem. In the first place, the most successful U.S. sires in modern times—Bold Ruler (leading sire eight times), Nasrullah (five times), and Bull Lea (five times)—never won beyond ten furlongs. They all had first-class speed and early maturity, but evidently lacked extreme stoutness. As between speed and stamina, the leaning in each case was distinctly toward speed although each of them had good stout strains close up on the dam's side.

In Princequillo's case, on the other hand, we have an undistinguished two-year-old who once could have been claimed for $1,500, who matured late in his three-year-old year, and whose strong point was stamina. Furthermore, there was no high-class speed close up in his pedigree, and his dam did not run at all as a two-year-old. His sire was a very good horse at twelve furlongs and more, but had a pedigree crammed with plodders. Also, Princequillo's first three dams were sired by proven failures and, apart from his dam, the mares in the family close up had no racing merit.

Here then, was the wrong kind of horse in his racing record, backed by the wrong kind of pedigree for America. Yet, in the face of a poor initial opportunity at stud, he was, as Bull Hancock suspected he would be, triumphant as a first-class sire. What is the explanation?

CHAPTER SEVENTY-FOUR

PRINCE JOHN

Whenever a high-class two-year-old with a stout pedigree appears, it often is observed that a good stud career is in the offing. Such a colt represents achievement of the ideal of Thoroughbred breeders—to produce an animal that possesses both speed and stamina. Hyperion and Blenheim II were examples of such a combination in Europe, and Man o' War was the American summit of such ambition.

It is easy enough to produce animals with pure speed and no stamina; High Time and Wise Counsellor were prepotent in this respect in the United States, as was Panorama in Ireland. At the other end of the spectrum, it is fairly easy to produce animals that have great stoutness but that are deficient in speed; Bruleur in France and Son-in-Law in England were dominant sires of that type.

Thus, when Prince John in the fall of 1955 demonstrated sufficient speed to win a major two-year-old race, his prospects as a sire took on a favorable aspect. He was sired by the stayer Princequillo and produced from a mare by Count Fleet (Belmont Stakes, etc.), and the second dam was by Blue Larkspur (Belmont Stakes). Before his racing, Prince John's pedigree well might have raised doubts as to his speed but not his stamina.

Prince John was bred by Mrs. John D. Hertz and was sold by her at the 1954 Keeneland summer yearling sale. Maxwell Gluck two years earlier had purchased the central portion of historic Elmendorf Farm near Lexington, and the New York clothing manufacturer had taken the name Elmendorf for his racing stable, which he then was in the process of building. (The next year, he singly bid $1,200,000 by sealed bid for Nashua, narrowly losing to a syndicate bid.)

Gluck purchased Prince John for $14,300, and the colt was turned over to Walter Kelley. As he was a big, spirited youngster, Prince John was not started until July 18, when he was fourth in a field of ten maidens in a five and one-half-furlong race at Jamaica. Prince John won his next race, another five and one-half-furlong maiden event, at Saratoga on August 9, and thereafter he was thought fit

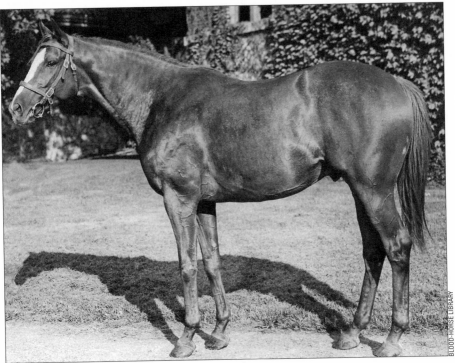

Prince John

enough for stakes competition.

In the Sanford Stakes, the colt with the staying pedigree ran with the pace all the way and, although perhaps tiring as he lugged in, he was overtaken only by favored Head Man, who beat him by a half-length. Kelley bypassed other stakes at Saratoga and sent Prince John to Chicago to prepare for the Washington Park Futurity on September 3.

One of fourteen starters for the six-furlong Washington Park Futurity, Prince John was sent off at 21-1. He finished second, beaten three and one-half lengths by the classy Swoon's Son. As Swoon's Son was giving the runner-up nine pounds, the result made Prince John out to be about twenty pounds behind Swoon's Son at the distance. Still, he had run better than a 21-1 shot might be expected to run, and the $30,000 he earned for second placed him onto the bargain-purchase rack.

Returned to New York, Prince John met Sanford winner Head Man again in a prep race for the Futurity. Carrying 113 pounds and receiving nine from Head Man, Prince John ran a very good race, getting six furlongs down the old, straight Widener Chute in 1:09 2/5 and winning by two lengths.

In the Futurity on October 8, Prince John and fourteen others raced down the

Widener Chute for six and one-half furlongs, Nail winning from Head Man, with Polly's Jet third. Prince John ran a creditable race in the slop, finishing fourth while beaten three lengths.

The Futurity then had not been overshadowed by the Champagne as New York's climactic juvenile race, but the super-rich Garden State Stakes had come along a few years earlier, and it was that test which became the next target of the leading two-year-olds. Kelley gave Prince John a prep, over the full Garden State Stakes distance of one and one-sixteenth miles, but the colt gave Angel Valenzuela trouble in the gate and was handled roughly by an assistant starter. He turned in a dull race, finishing fifth behind Career Boy.

A field of twelve turned out for the October 29 Garden State Stakes, worth a then-record $157,918 to the winner. Although his recent form prior to the prep had found Prince John able to run against the best without being outclassed, the overall strength of the field, plus his dismal prep, sent him off at 24-1.

Prince John raced close to early leaders Polly's Jet and Nail, and when they began to fall back after six furlongs, he moved up to take command turning for home. Under left-hand whipping, Prince John veered out, but he managed to hold off Career Boy and win by a nose. Favored Needles was a length back in third.

					Persimmon
				Prince Palatine, 1908	Lady Lightfoot
			Rose Prince, 1919		Perth
				Eglantine, 1906	Rose de Mai
		Prince Rose, 1928			Bayardo
				Gay Crusader, 1914	Gay Laura
			Indolence, 1920		Grey Leg
				Barrier, 1910	Bar the Way
Princequillo, 1940					Rock Sand
				Tracery, 1909	Topiary
			Papyrus, 1920		Marcovil
				Miss Matty, 1914	Simonath
		Cosquilla, 1933			Gallinule
				White Eagle, 1905	Merry Gal
			Quick Thought, 1918		Minoru
PRINCE JOHN				Mindful, 1913	Noble Martha
					Sundridge
				Sunreigh, 1919	Sweet Briar
			Reigh Count, 1925		Count Schomberg
				Contessina, 1909	Pitti
		Count Fleet, 1940			Maintenant
				Haste, 1923	Miss Malaprop
			Quickly, 1930		Stefan the Great
				Stephanie, 1925	Malachite
	Not Afraid, 1948				Black Toney
				Black Servant, 1918	Padula
			Blue Larkspur, 1926		North Star III
				Blossom Time, 1920	Vaila
		Banish Fear, 1932			Spearmint
				Over There, 1916	Summer Girl
			Herodiade, 1923		The Tetrarch
				Herodias, 1916	Honora

The time was 1:42 3/5, which was three-fifths of a second slower than the track record.

Prince John was returned to New York for what proved his final race, the one and one-sixteenth-mile Remsen Stakes at Jamaica on November 11. Again the track was sloppy, and Nail dashed home by two lengths, clinching the juvenile title. Prince John had trouble early and made up about five lengths in the final two furlongs after finally getting free to run.

The 1955 two-year-old crop had gone through the season without any individual rising to a clear leadership. Nail was voted the championship in two of three polls, but Needles won in the other poll, while on the Experimental Free Handicap, Career Boy was weighted at the top, one pound above the co-champions. Prince John was assigned 124 pounds, two pounds below Career Boy on the handicap. (The next year Barbizon scored a narrow victory in an upset in the Garden State, his only stakes and final race of the year, and was both the champion and the handicap topweight, so Prince John's race in the Remsen might have cost him high honors.)

YEAR	AGE	STS	1ST	2ND	3RD	EARNED
1955	at 2	9	3	3	0	$212,818
Lifetime		9	3	3	0	$212,818

Prince John, naturally, was regarded as among the best of the classics contenders for 1956, but after being sent to Hialeah, he broke a halter shank one morning, ran off, and fractured a pedal bone. He never raced again, although he did not stand his first season at stud until 1957.

Because of his pedigree, and his development at two, and his later stud career it remains tempting to speculate as to how Prince John would have measured up at three. Needles proved a classic colt of a high order, winning two-thirds of the Triple Crown, but Career Boy only occasionally showed his promised form, while Nail proved a non-stayer. Swoon's Son was a brilliant campaigner for several seasons but rarely ventured out of the Midwest.

Certainly, as a consistent progenitor of high-class horses, Prince John has been more successful than the best of his juvenile competitors of twenty-one seasons back. He entered stud at Elmendorf and later was syndicated and moved to Leslie Combs II's Spendthrift Farm near Lexington.[1]

Generally, stallions do not get better as they get older, the strong pattern of the breed being for the best runners to appear in the earlier crops of a stud's progeny. In terms of number of stakes winners, Prince John's progeny conformed to that pattern to some degree: He had four stakes winners in his first and third crops, although he got only one in his second; he then got five stakes winners in his

TONY LEONARD

Speak John

fourth crop, but not until his fourteenth crop did he again sire five stakes winners, matching his highest number to 1976.

In terms of when he sired the very best of his stakes winners, however, Prince John contradicted the breed pattern of early-is-best. Although he had gotten a number of nice stakes winners prior to 1965, it was in the foal crop of that year—his eighth crop—that Prince John got his first champion, Stage Door Johnny, winner of the Belmont Stakes in 1968 and named champion on some polls.

The next year, in 1966, Prince John's foal crop included Typecast, who became one of the stoutest mares of recent years, often defeating males at long distances, and who was named handicap mare champion of 1972.

Prince John's first two champions sired thus were stayers, but he was no specialist. His next outstanding runner, foaled in 1967, was Silent Screen, brilliant in 1969 as the two-year-old champion. Protagonist, a Prince John colt foaled in 1971, was not so quick to mature nor so brilliantly fast as was Silent Screen, but like the sire he came on late in the year; Protagonist won several major fall stakes and became the stallion's second juvenile colt champion. (Speak John, from Prince John's first crop, sired that season's two-year-old filly champion, Talking Picture, giving Elmendorf a juvenile-champion monopoly for 1973.)

Others among the fifty-five stakes winners sired by Prince John have exhibited a similar range of speed and stamina, some having their best years at two, others developing later. They include pronounced stayers such as Coaching Club American Oaks winner Magazine, plus Specious, Arbitrage, Jean-Pierre, and Princess Pout, and also Deceit, who was a brilliantly fast sprinter at two, yet won major races at middle distances at three. His other stakes winners include Rash Prince, Nevada P.J., Fairway Fun, Marry the Prince, Selari, Glossary, Jack Sprat, and Lefty. Several of Prince John's sons have become prominent sires.[2]

The ability to produce runners with speed as well as stamina was shown elsewhere by Prince John's forebears. Not only did Princequillo sire speed horses and stayers but Prince John's dam, Not Afraid, demonstrated the same versatility. An unraced mare who had shown high promise before being injured, Not Afraid produced a Nasrullah colt, Rulership, who showed such brilliance in his first start at two in 1957 that an offer of $150,000 was made. (Rulership later became a leading sire in Mexico.) On the other hand, Not Afraid later produced another Princequillo colt, Brave Lad, whose only stakes triumph came at four in the Display Handicap at two miles and whose other stakes placings were achieved going long.

Not Afraid's dam, Banish Fear, also produced Cosmic Bomb, who won the Arlington Futurity and other stakes at two, then stayed well enough to win the Lawrence Realization among his five stakes triumphs at three. Banish Fear's other foals included Hollywood Lassie Stakes winner Fleet Rings, and other stakes winners descending from Banish Fear include champion filly Lamb Chop.

End Notes:

1. Prince John stood at Elmendorf until 1962, when a syndicate composed of Leslie Combs II, Harry F. Guggenheim, and John Hanes purchased the stallion and moved him to Combs' Spendthrift Farm. On January 26, 1969, Prince John fractured a leg in his paddock and was euthanized. He was twenty-six years old.

2. Prince John's successful sons at stud included Speak John, Silent Screen, and Stage Door Johnny. The tail-male line of Prince John hangs by a thread today, that of his son Speak John, whose grandsons Greenwood Lake, Meadow Monster, Medford, and Thunder Rumble are among those who represent the line. Prince John also made his mark as a broodmare sire, leading the list in 1979, 1980, 1982, and 1986. His son Speak John led the list in 1985.

CHAPTER SEVENTY-FIVE

ROUND TABLE

R acing men and breeders love to argue about the class of great horses they have seen or read about. This enjoyable pastime usually boils down to a number of factors: (A) How many time records did a horse make (either track records or world records)? (B) What did he ever beat? (C) What weight could he carry and still win? (D) How far could he go? (E) How game was he?

Under all the headings above except (B), Round Table was one of the best racers on record. He was extremely sound, game, and consistent, and he could pack the weight. It was only when he tackled the New York horses that he began to seem something less than invincible, but there were extenuating circumstances on several occasions. He was a good one, and no mistake.

As a two-year-old, Round Table raced under the colors of his breeder, Claiborne Farm (A.B. Hancock Jr.). At that age, he won half of his ten races, including the Breeders' Futurity and Lafayette Stakes at Keeneland. There was nothing sensational about him, and Round Table was ranked eight pounds below Barbizon, the top weight on the Experimental Free Handicap. This is, indeed, the weight range from which many of the best classic and handicap horses have emerged.

On February 9, 1957, Round Table was sold, while on the way to the post in an allowance race at Hialeah. Joe Hernandez and Dr. John Peters bought him, acting for Oklahoma oilman Travis M. Kerr. Round Table had run tenth in the Hibiscus Stakes, and his prospects did not seem overwhelming to Hancock. The price was $145,000, but Hancock retained a 20 percent interest in the breeding rights.

The day he was sold, Round Table ran sixth in a seven-horse field, the winner being Iron Liege, who that year won the Kentucky Derby.

Round Table was sent to trainer Willie Molter in California and made a supplementary entry for the Santa Anita Derby. After winning an overnight race, he finished third in the Derby, beaten a head and a nose. In the San Bernardino, run over a heavy track, Round Table was only fifth. This convinced Molter of something that he already suspected—that Round Table was many pounds worse on

Round Table

an off track than he was on fast going. Molter took Round Table to Bay Meadows, where the competition generally is not as stiff as at Santa Anita, and there won the Bay Meadows Derby at the beginning of April.

That victory made owner Kerr eager to go to Kentucky for the Derby, but Molter was less enthusiastic. He had been wrong before, when he won the race with Determine after opposing the trip to Kentucky. So, Round Table went to Kentucky. Molter's method of training was to give his horse a prep race before a big event. The race chosen was the Blue Grass Stakes, which Round Table won by six lengths in record time. In the Kentucky Derby, he was only third, three lengths off Iron Liege and Gallant Man but ahead of favored Bold Ruler.

Back in California, Round Table (105 pounds) finished one and one-half lengths behind older Social Climber (119) in the Californian. Round Table, much like his sire, Princequillo, at a similar stage of his three-year-old career, was coming to his best form. He won eleven races in a row, including five features at Hollywood Park. In the Gold Cup there, Round Table (109) covered the ten furlongs in 1:58 3/5; this matched the record of Swaps in the same event and was the fastest ten furlongs ever recorded by a three-year-old to that point.

Despite his having won three races in July, when Round Table was shipped to Chicago for the American Derby, he was given the inevitable prep race before the big event. He won both races easily. Shipped east to Atlantic City, Round Table showed that he was, if anything, better on grass than he was on dirt. He won the United Nations Handicap from Tudor Era and Find. Back in Chicago, after another prep race that he won, Round Table (121) beat Swoon's Son easily in the Hawthorne Gold Cup.

His next stakes race, the ten-furlong Trenton Handicap, should have been the most revealing of the year because Round Table came up against both Gallant Man and Bold Ruler. He was only third favorite in a field of three.

The track was heavy, putting Round Table at a disadvantage, and it seems probable that it was a false-run race in any case. The way to beat Bold Ruler was to make him run the first six furlongs at a cracking pace. John Nerud had done this in the Belmont Stakes, putting in a pacemaker for Gallant Man, to force Bold Ruler to a fast pace in the early part of it. The result had been that when Bold Ruler cracked, Gallant Man beat him out of sight.

In the Trenton, there was no pacemaker for Gallant Man, and Bill Shoemaker

ROUND TABLE				
Princequillo, 1940	Prince Rose, 1928	Rose Prince, 1919	Prince Palatine, 1908	**Persimmon** / Lady Lightfoot
			Eglantine, 1906	Perth / Rose De Mai
		Indolence, 1920	Gay Crusader, 1914	Bayardo / Gay Laura
			Barrier, 1910	Grey Leg / Bar the Way
	Cosquilla, 1933	Papyrus, 1920	Tracery, 1909	Rock Sand / Topiary
			Miss Matty, 1914	Marcovil / Simonath
		Quick Thought, 1918	White Eagle, 1905	**Gallinule** / Merry Gal
			Mindful, 1913	Minoru / Noble Martha
Knight's Daughter, 1941	Sir Cosmo, 1926	The Boss, 1910	Orby, 1904	Orme / Rhoda B.
			Southern Cross, 1897	Meteor / Resplendent
		Ayn Hali, 1913	Desmond, 1896	St. Simon / L'Abbesse de Jouarre
			Lalla Rookh, 1904	Hackler / Lady Gough
	Feola, 1933	Friar Marcus, 1912	Cicero, 1902	Cyllene / Gas
			Prim Nun, 1906	**Persimmon** / Nunsuch
		Aloe, 1926	Son-in-Law, 1911	Dark Ronald / Mother-in-Law
			Alope, 1909	**Gallinule** / Altoviscar

was fearful of testing Bold Ruler's speed in the early going on a proven stayer like Gallant Man. The result was that Bold Ruler was allowed to go his own pace, without forcing, and Gallant Man never got close while Round Table could not handle the footing and ran a poor race, to be last.

As a four-year-old, Round Table won fourteen of twenty starts and was voted Horse of the Year. Starting at Santa Anita, he took the Malibu Stakes three days before he turned four, then won the San Fernando and the Santa Anita Maturity. Round Table (130) next won the nine-furlong San Antonio in 1:46 4/5, equaling the world's record.[1] He also won the Santa Anita Handicap of ten furlongs, establishing a new track record of 1:59 4/5. Going to Florida, he equaled that time in the Gulfstream Park Handicap, matching the track record of Coaltown.

Agua Caliente put up $50,000 in an effort to revive the Caliente Handicap, and the traveling Round Table won that one too, against modest opposition.

YEAR	AGE	STS	1ST	2ND	3RD	EARNED
1956	at 2	10	5	1	0	$ 73,326
1957	at 3	22	15	1	3	$ 600,383
1958	at 4	20	14	4	0	$ 662,780
1959	at 5	14	9	2	2	$ 413,380
Lifetime		66	43	8	5	$1,749,869

Round Table had been a model of consistency, winning nineteen of his last twenty starts. He then unexpectedly lost the Californian to Seaneen and barely won the Argonaut Handicap (under 132 pounds) from How Now. Returning to Chicago, Round Table twice beat Clem, giving away twenty and twenty-one pounds. Then Clem turned around and beat Round Table three times, twice with major weight concessions, but the last time, in the Woodward Stakes, at level weights. There was some excuse for Round Table in the Woodward as the track was sloppy and it was known he could not cope with it.

Back in Chicago again, Round Table gave Swoon's Son three pounds and beat him in the Hawthorne Gold Cup, setting a new track record of 1:59 4/5. There was not much of a let up on Round Table, as he was sent back to Santa Anita again for the winter racing.

After going under by a head to Hillsdale in the seven-furlong San Carlos Handicap, while conceding seventeen pounds, Round Table at five went back to his favorite distance of ten furlongs in the San Marcos Handicap. There, under 132 pounds, Round Table won in the astonishing time of 1:58 2/5, a world record on grass. In the Washington's Birthday Handicap, however, Round Table (134) again showed that he could not master soft going, even on the turf, and was unplaced. This loss of form was only temporary.

In Chicago, Round Table started in a big race without a prep. Carrying 130

Round Table's dam, Knight's Daughter

pounds, he went a mile in the Citation Handicap in 1:33 2/5, beating Etonian (104) a neck. Round Table (132) produced another course record on the grass in Washington Park's Stars and Stripes Handicap, but then was defeated, on an off track again, in the Equipoise Mile. He soon took the Arlington Handicap on grass, putting up another American time record of 1:53 2/5 for one and three-sixteenths miles.

His next two races may have been his greatest. In the Washington Park Handicap, Round Table (132) gave Dunce eighteen pounds and won by six and one-half lengths in 1:47 1/5, a new track record. Then, in the United Nations Handicap, he won handily under 136 pounds.

Round Table tried the weight-for-age Woodward Stakes again but was third to Sword Dancer and Hillsdale. He later showed that he could go beyond ten furlongs when, with 132 pounds up, he won the one and five-eighths-mile Manhattan Handicap from Bald Eagle (122).

Round Table then went under to Sword Dancer again in the weight-for-age Jockey Club Gold Cup of two miles, beaten seven lengths.

Against stakes horses, Round Table had turned in a succession of wonderful

ALEC RUSSELL

Apalachee

performances; but we must not forget that he lost when he faced the best of his contemporaries, Gallant Man, Bold Ruler, and the younger Sword Dancer. The net conclusion is that Round Table, despite his succession of track and world records, was no super horse. Rather, he was a first-class performer in one of the best foal crops in Turf history, and was up to extraordinary weights for such a small specimen—all honor to him for his soundness, gameness, and consistency.

Round Table's pedigree deserves some comment. His sire, Princequillo, is the subject of a chapter in this book. His dam, Knight's Daughter, ran in England during World War II. She started only four times, all as a two-year-old and won her first three races. She was a pretty smart filly and was assigned 117 pounds on the Free Handicap. That put her six pounds below Garden Path, who became one of the few fillies to win the Two Thousand Guineas, and also six pounds below Honeyway, who became the champion sprinter of his time in England.

Knight's Daughter was by Sir Cosmo, who was also the best sprinter of his time in England. Knight's Daughter may have had character problems, as she was observed to swish her tail ominously when coming under pressure in one of her races.

Her dam, Feola, was a high-class mare who ran second in the One Thousand

Guineas and third in the Oaks. The surprising thing is that Feola's sire, Friar Marcus, was a sprinter and sired sprinters, with very few exceptions. Perhaps the explanation is that the next dam [Aloe] was sired by Son-in-Law, at one time the best sire of stamina in England. The next dam, Alope, was by Gallinule (a good sire), and also ran second in the One Thousand Guineas. (Incidentally, Alope was twenty-five years younger than her sire. Feola, the dam of Knight's Daughter, was twenty-one years younger than her sire.)

Round Table, then, came from a line of mares that had shown consistently high form on the Turf, and with the speed of these first two dams and their sires added to the stoutness of Princequillo, an outstanding stud career was to be expected of the world-leading money winner at the time. This expectation has been fulfilled amply.

For his stud career, Round Table, returned to Claiborne near Paris, Kentucky, where he had been foaled on April 6, 1954, on the same date as Bold Ruler. (The horoscopes were good for great racehorses and splendid sires that day.)

Round Table sired eighty-three stakes winners and led the sire list in 1972.

One of Round Table's first stakes winners in his first crop was Baldric, who won the classic Two Thousand Guineas in England, and a number of his other best runners also raced abroad. These include two-year-old champions Apalachee and Targowice.

At home, Round Table's best runners included the grand mare Drumtop, frequent winner over colts, plus Duel, Knightly Manner, Advocator, He's a Smoothie, Poker, Morgaise, Beau Brummel, Tell, Rondeau, Upper Case, King's Bishop, Bicker, and Royal Glint, the last-named winner of six $100,000 races.

End Notes:

1. Round Table shared this world record with Noor (1950), Alidon (1955), Swaps (1956), and Gen. Duke (1957).

CHAPTER SEVENTY-SIX

PRINCE BIO

D uring the German occupation of France in World War II, racing was continued at the Paris courses. Thus, French breeders had an opportunity to sort out their best colts and fillies of each crop, despite the war.

One of the beneficiaries of this program was Prince Bio, who needed a racing career in order to have much of a chance at a stud career. Prince Bio's pedigree at the time seemed most unlikely to produce a colt of classic standard. His sire, Prince Rose, had been an inexpensive Newmarket yearling that was imported into Belgium. Prince Rose himself had an unattractive pedigree, being by the plodder Rose Prince and out of a poor race mare whose sire was Gay Crusader, a crack racehorse who was a failure at stud.

Prince Rose, nevertheless, proved the best horse ever to race in Belgium, also proved a notable runner in France, and became an influential sire. He got sons that were important in three countries—Princequillo in the United States, Prince Chevalier in England, and Prince Bio in France. Princequillo and his sons Round Table and Prince John have been subjects of other chapters in this book; we turn now to Prince Bio.

Biologie, dam of Prince Bio, had a pedigree even more unconventional for a top producer than did Prince Rose. She was bred by Baron Edouard de Rothschild, evidently in an experiment. Her sire, Bacteriophage, had made only one start in his life, that as a two-year-old. While he was only fourth in an ordinary race among a field of twenty, he must have been tried highly at home, for he was a warm favorite at 12-5.

Judging from Bacteriophage's pedigree, it seems certain that Rothschild looked upon him as a possible vehicle for introducing speed into his stud. The colt was by Tetratema, the premier speed sire in England, and was from Pharmacie, a high-class two-year-old.

This quest for more speed was understandable, for Rothschild had won the Grand Prix de Paris at nearly two miles on numerous occasions, but never had

BLOOD-HORSE LIBRARY

Prince Bio

won the French Derby at one and one-half miles. He kept Bacteriophage as a sire, but bred very few foals from him. In fact, the horse got fewer than ten foals.

Biologie, one of the few Bacteriophage foals, was a chestnut filly whom Rothschild put into training—without success. The filly started once as a two-year-old and was unplaced, then ran fourteen times at three. After once running second in a four-horse field for her breeder, Biologie was sold to run under the colors of R. Hakim, for whom she once finished fourth, but never closer. Later, Biologie was acquired by Willy Head, who bred Prince Bio from her. The colt raced in the name of C. Herbline.

Biologie's dam was Eponge, another Rothschild product, she sired by Cadum. The latter was a typical Rothschild plodder, whom the author often backed successfully in French marathon races, but who was not a success at stud. The next dam was Sea Moss, who was sired by William the Third, another Cup horse and only moderately successful at stud.

Thus, the third generation of Prince Bio's pedigree was made up in three-quarters by stout animals and in one-quarter by speed ancestors.

Taking his pedigree into account, it is not surprising that Prince Bio did not show much class early on. In fact, the surprising thing is that he showed anything as a two-year-old at all, even late in the year.

His first start was in May, and he was 60-1 and ran as expected. He did not race again until September, when he once again ran to his odds—75-1. During the remainder of the season, though, he never was unplaced.

Late in September, he was sent out for a seven-furlong handicap at Le Tremblay and won by four lengths in a field of seventeen at odds of about 19-1. Next he ran in a five-furlong race over the straight course at Maisons-Laffitte and was beaten by a half-length, after which he won another seven-furlong handicap by six lengths.

Prince Bio then came up against a really fast colt going seven furlongs, Le Volcan, and was beaten by three and one-half lengths. He concluded his two-year-old campaign at Auteuil in November, winning a mile race. In summary, Prince Bio at two made an abnormal improvement from spring to late fall, but the only time he came up against a really good colt, he went under. Aside from Le Volcan, he did not meet the cracks of his age, which included Ardan and Priam.

Prince Bio began his brief three-year-old campaign on April 10, 1944, at Maisons-Laffitte in the one and five-sixteenths-mile Prix de Fontainebleau. There was not much else of quality in the field, and he was even money, but he won by only a neck in a four-horse battle through the stretch. In the more important Prix Jean Prat at ten furlongs, Prince Bio was considered to be no match for Laborde,

				Persimmon, 1893	**St. Simon** Perdita
			Prince Palatine, 1908		
		Rose Prince, 1919		Lady Lightfoot, 1900	Isinglass Glare
			Eglantine, 1906	Perth, 1896	War Dance Primrose Dame
Prince Rose, 1928				Rose de Mai, 1900	Callistrate May Pole
			Gay Crusader, 1914	Bayardo, 1906	Bay Ronald Galicia
		Indolence, 1920		Gay Laura, 1909	Beppo Galeottia
			Barrier, 1910	Grey Leg, 1891	Pepper and Salt Quetta
PRINCE BIO				Bar the Way, 1901	Right-Away Barrisdale
			Tetratema, 1917	The Tetrarch, 1911	Roi Herode Vahren
		Bacteriophage, 1929		Scotch Gift, 1907	Symington Maund
			Pharmacie, 1918	Charles O'Malley, 1907	Desmond Goody Two-Shoes
Biologie, 1935				Prescription, 1912	Dinneford M.S.
			Cadum, 1921	Sans Souci, 1904	Le Roi Soleil Sanctimony
		Eponge, 1929		Spring Cleaning, 1915	Neil Gow Spring Night
			Sea Moss, 1917	William the Third, 1898	**St. Simon** Gravity
				Seadune, 1908	Ayrshire Seadown

Prince Taj

who was 1-10 and duly beat Prince Bio by four lengths.

In his next race, the one and five-sixteenths-mile Prix Daru-Noailles, Prince Bio was favored at 17-10 and won by two lengths. That race completed his pre-classic competition, for he next appeared for the one-mile Poule d'Essai des Poulains, the French equivalent of the Two Thousand Guineas. There were eight horses in the field, and apparently there was not much class in the race aside from Prince Bio, who won by two lengths.

Unfortunately, Prince Bio split a pastern during the running and never raced again, so we are left in something of a quandary as to his true racing class. He had won three of four starts at three and seemed to be improving with age—as his pedigree would suggest he should—but there was no evidence that he was a colt of extraordinary class, since he had not met either Ardan or Priam, the best of the generation. (It was, perhaps, an accident that Ardan and Priam were disappointing at stud, while Prince Bio—who had a less-appealing pedigree than did the others—was a considerable success.)

For a time after the Poule d'Essai, it was feared that Prince Bio's injury would force his destruction, but he was saved for stud duty and stood until 1966, when he died at Haras de Quetieville. After his racing career, he was acquired by Prince Aly Khan.

Physically, Prince Bio was a small, lop-eared, plain stallion, but his appearance did not stop him from being a major sire. He led the French sire list in 1951, and he sired two other horses who led the list, Sicambre and Prince Taj.

Sicambre, who also became the maternal grandsire of Sea-Bird, was a brilliant racehorse, best of his crop at two and winner of the French Derby and Grand Prix de Paris at three in 1951. Sicambre sired seven classic winners, including 1960 Belmont Stakes winner Celtic Ash.[1]

YEAR	AGE	STS	1ST	2ND	3RD	EARNED
1943	at 2	7	3	1	1	410,225 Fr
1944	at 3	4	3	1	0	1,108,650 Fr
Lifetime		11	6	2	1	1,518,875 Fr

Prince Taj, who was imported to Florida in 1966, led France's sire list in 1967 and 1968. His get included Astec, Taj Dewan, Rajput Princess, La Sarre, and Petrone.

Other sons of Prince Bio included Northern Light, another Grand Prix de Paris winner; Le Petit Prince, another French Derby winner; Sedan, a champion in Italy; and Rose Royale, winner of the One Thousand Guineas in England.

End Notes:

1. The sire line of Prince Bio still survives in the United States. Siphon, the sire of grade I winner Siphonic, is a fifth-generation descendant of Prince Bio through Sicambre, Shantung, Felicio, and Itajara.

PRINCE CHEVALIER

W hen Prince Chevalier made his first appearance as a two-year-old, on May 27, 1945, at Longchamp, in a five-furlong race not restricted to maidens, not much could have been expected of him, since his starting price was 25-1 in a field of eight. Nevertheless, he won by three-quarters of a length. Then, in a minor stakes called the Poule de Deux Ans, also at Longchamp, on June 4, he was only fourth.

In the middle of July, Prince Chevalier was sent after the first of the major two-year-old races in France, the Prix Robert Papin over five and one-half furlongs at Maisons-Laffitte. There, he ran into Nirgal, who was an odds-on choice at 1-2, in a field of five. Prince Chevalier was 20-1 and ran third to Nirgal, beaten four lengths. Skipping Deauville, Prince Chevalier did not come out again until September 23, for the Prix de la Salamandre of seven furlongs. That is the two-year-old race ranking next to the Grand Criterium in prestige in the French autumn program. Prince Chevalier still was not too highly regarded, as he went off at the generous price of 11-1 in a field of seven, but he won convincingly, by a length from the odds-on Tourville.

The victory obviously entitled Prince Chevalier to a chance in the Grand Criterium, a test of one mile that in most years establishes the French juvenile championship. Nirgal was a top-heavy favorite at 2-5 and well deserved to be, since he had won both the Robert Papin and the Prix Morny. Prince Chevalier was the only colt seriously backed to beat him, at 9-1, but they ran according to form, Nirgal winning by two lengths.

Prince Chevalier was given one more race as a two-year-old, in the one and one-quarter-mile (yes, ten furlongs for a two-year-old) Prix de Conde. His form in the Salamandre and the Grand Criterium made him a warm favorite, at 6-5, and he justified it, winning by three-quarters of a length. On the two-year-old handicap, Nirgal was assigned 133 pounds, and Prince Chevalier 128, which seemed a fair assessment on the public form.

CH. RECOUPE

Prince Chevalier

Prince Chevalier's form at three closely followed that of Tourbillon back in 1931. He began with an easy victory in the one and five-sixteenths-mile Prix Greffuhle, the first of the important spring tests for classics colts. He won by two lengths at the nice price of 7-1. The reason for the attractive odds was that Nirgal was among those present, at a price of 1-5. Nirgal finished second, and he came down with a serious illness the next day and was out of Prince Chevalier's path for some time to come.

In the Prix Daru-Noailles at the same distance, Prince Chevalier was only 1-10, and won by a length. In the last and most important of the pre-classic races, the Prix Lupin, still at the same distance, Prince Chevalier was again odds-on, at 7-10. He won by two lengths. By that time, with Nirgal out of the way, Prince Chevalier was regarded as invincible, and he started for the French Derby (Prix du Jockey-Club), run at Longchamp instead of Chantilly, its true home, over its usual distance of one and one-half miles. Prince Chevalier was 3-5 in a field of fifteen but only staved off Elseneur to win by a neck.

The next major race in France was the one and seven-eighths-mile Grand Prix de Paris, run at the end of June. While Prince Chevailer was second favorite at 2-1 in a field of eighteen (Nirgal was back again, at odds of 19-10), there was a new rival called Souverain, at odds of 107-2, who turned out to be a first-class horse over long courses. Prince Chevalier beat Nirgal easily, but Souverain in turn beat Prince Chevalier a short head.

That severe race may have taken something out of Prince Chevalier, because when he went to Ostend (Belgium) for the one and one-half-mile Grand Prix d'Ostende, he was beaten two lengths by Bouton Rose (also by Prince Rose). Returning to France, Prince Chevalier met Souverain again in the Prix Royal-Oak (French St. Leger), run over the same course as the Grand Prix de Paris. That time, Souverain beat Prince Chevalier by three-quarters of a length instead of by a short head.

The last start for Prince Chevalier was in the one and one-half-mile, weight-for-age Prix de l'Arc de Triomphe. There he met Marcel Boussac's pair, Caracalla and Ardan, who were odds-on at 3-10. Caracalla was a four-year-old who never had been beaten. After the race, he remained unbeaten, but he only got the better of Prince Chevalier by a head, with five-year-old Ardan fourth.

His spring form, coupled with his fine race in the Arc de Triomphe, pointed to Prince Chevalier as a three-year-old well up to classic standard. Because at that time, the French form was distinctly superior to the English form, Prince

				Persimmon, 1893	St. Simon
PRINCE CHEVALIER					Perdita
	Prince Rose, 1928	Rose Prince, 1919	Prince Palatine, 1908	Lady Lightfoot, 1900	Isinglass
					Glare
			Eglantine, 1906	Perth, 1896	War Dance
					Primrose Dame
				Rose de Mai, 1900	Callistrate
					May Pole
		Indolence, 1920	Gay Crusader, 1914	Bayardo, 1906	Bay Ronald
					Galicia
				Gay Laura, 1909	Beppo
					Galeottia
			Barrier, 1910	Grey Leg, 1891	Pepper and Salt
					Quetta
				Bar the Way, 1901	Right-Away
					Barrisdale
	Chevalerie, 1933	Abbot's Speed, 1923	Abbots Trace, 1917	Tracery, 1909	Rock Sand
					Topiary
				Abbots Anne, 1899	Right-Away
					Sister Lumley
			Mary Gaunt, 1912	John o' Gaunt, 1901	Isinglass
					La Fleche
				Quick, 1902	Cherry Tree
					Strike-a-Light
		Kassala, 1926	Cylgad, 1909	Cyllene, 1895	Bona Vista
					Arcadia
				Gadfly, 1896	Hampton
					Merry Duchess
			Farizade, 1921	Sardanapale, 1911	Prestige
					Gemma
				Diavolezza, 1911	Le Sagittaire
					Saint Astra

Chevalier had strong attraction for British breeders who hoped to re-introduce the great line of St. Simon into British breeding again. He was bought for a syndicate of British breeders through the British Bloodstock Agency. The colt was acquired from P. Boyriven, who had purchased him as a yearling from his breeder, R. de Beauregard.

Although he had shown good racing form and consistency, Prince Chevalier left something to be desired in the matter of pedigree. Still, his dam had better bloodlines than did the dams of Princequillo and Prince Bio, the two other sons of Prince Rose that largely were responsible for making the line fashionable and successful.

Prince Chevalier's dam, Chevalerie, was a winner, but that was about all. At two, her best effort in three races was to run third in a four-horse field in the provinces. At three, she did manage to win two tiny races at provincial courses, but she never tried to compete on the Paris circuit. Chevalerie's sire was Abbot's Speed,

YEAR	AGE	STS	1ST	2ND	3RD	EARNED
1945	at 2	6	3	1	1	591,350 Fr
1946	at 3	8	4	4	0	3,389,700 Fr
Lifetime		14	7	5	1	3,981,050 Fr

a moderate handicapper in England whose two best efforts were to win a handicap at three under 103 pounds and the Kempton Great Jubilee Handicap at four under 110 pounds. That form placed him about sixteen pounds below top-class horses, and he did not have much success as a sire.

Chevalerie, however, produced the good filly Legende, in addition to Prince Chevalier.

Kassala, second dam of Prince Chevalier, produced Pappageno II (also by Prince Rose), who won seven races, including the Manchester November Handicap. Pappageno II was a successful stallion, and although he himself was a stayer, his get included the brilliant sprinter Pappa Fourway.

Kassala was sired by Cylgad, who may have been up to classic standard, but who broke down early in his three-year-old season. The astute judge Federico Tesio did not hesitate to buy daughters of Cylgad for his stud, and he had great success with Try Try Again.

Prince Chevalier's third dam, Farizade, was a daughter of Diavolezza, daughter of the crack filly Saint Astra, who won the French Oaks and became the granddam of the noted broodmare sire Asterus.

Prince Chevalier was a horse of very high quality, solid bay in color, absolutely sound, and standing exactly sixteen hands high. He never led the English sire list, but ranked in the top ten there three times and led the French list once, in 1960.

CH. RECOUPE

Prince Chevalier winning the Prix Greffulhe at Longchamp

His best sons raced in England included Arctic Prince, winner of the Epsom Derby and later imported to America, where his get included Parka.

Prince Chevalier also sired Charlottesville, who won the Grand Prix de Paris and French Derby and who led England's sire list in 1966. Charlottesville sired Charlottown, who won the Derby in 1966, defeating Pretendre. The latter was by another Prince Chevalier horse, Doutelle. Pretendre later sired Canonero II, winner of the Kentucky Derby and Preakness in 1971.

Another son of Prince Chevalier to lead the English sire list was Court Harwell, who topped the list in 1965, largely off the winnings of his classic-winning son Meadow Court. Court Harwell later was sent to Argentina and became a champion sire there, too.

In addition to Pretendre's siring Canonero II, another instance of Prince Chevalier male-line influence in this country came through Pampered King II. A stakes-winning English son of Prince Chevalier, Pampered King II sired Czar Alexander, who was a major winner on grass in this country before being placed in stud here.

Other sons of Prince Chevalier included Flaneur II (broodmare sire of 1971 Belmont Stakes winner Pass Catcher), Chivalry, Pirate King, and Beau Prince (in France).

To the author, Prince Rose is an unsolved mystery. Very few sires have begotten three influential stallions in four crops, as he did (Princequillo, Prince Bio, Prince Chevalier). Furthermore, not one of those three stallions was out of a mare with good credentials.

We call attention to a curious series of facts:

(1) Prince Rose was out of a mare by Gay Crusader, a Triple Crown winner who the great jockey Steve Donoghue said was the best horse he ever rode.

(2) The dam of Djebel (Arc de Triomphe, four-time leading sire in France) was by Gay Crusader.

(3) El Greco, maternal grandsire of Ribot, was out of a mare by Gay Crusader.

Gay Crusader was a failure at stud, despite having the best of opportunities, and all three Gay Crusader mares involved above were valueless as race mares. In England, it generally was believed that the stock of Gay Crusader tended not to be genuine. Gay Crusader, however, was inbred with two free generations to the high-spirited sire Galopin, and there seems to have been a marked residue of unusual ability here.

CHAPTER SEVENTY-EIGHT

BOIS ROUSSEL

When Bois Roussel won the Epsom Derby in 1938, the author noted that his dam had been twenty-three years old when he was foaled, and we presumed that to be a record age for the dam of a classic winner. This turned out not to be so, for Horatia, the dam of 1806 Derby winner Paris, had been twenty-five years old when that colt was foaled. Furthermore, Horatia had foaled an earlier Derby winner, Archduke, when she was eighteen.

Nevertheless, Bois Roussel's dam, Plucky Liege, achieved distinctions that seem virtually unmatchable. She produced four sons (Sir Gallahad III, Bull Dog, Admiral Drake, and Bois Roussel) that led sire lists in major countries and that also became leading broodmare sires. The aggregate of such sire-list championships for Plucky Liege's sons was twenty-seven.

Bois Roussel's sire, Vatout, was by Prince Chimay, he by St. Simon's son Chaucer. Prince Chimay scored a stunning upset of Gainsborough in the 1918 Jockey Club Stakes, but aside from begetting Vatout he sired little of significance during his stud career in France.

Vatout began public life in claiming races and was haltered by Jefferson Davis Cohn, in whose colors he was to win the Poule d'Essai des Poulains (French Two Thousand Guineas) and run a good second to Double Life in the Cambridgeshire in England. The horse also was a good handicap winner in England. Vatout went to stud in 1931 and died six years later. He was in the useful category, both on the Turf and in the stud, but was not really first-class in either department. In addition to Bois Roussel, he sired Vatellor, who, in turn, got two consecutive Derby winners in Pearl Diver (1947) and My Love (1948).

The active story of Bois Roussel began with the ten-furlong Prix Juigne at Longchamp. The race is reserved for three-year-olds that never have raced, and numerous classic winners have made their debuts in the event. It happened that the Honorable Peter Beatty was present on the occasion of the 1938 Juigne, having gone to France with the hope of finding a colt that could win some good races

W.A. ROUCH

Bois Roussel

at home in England. Beatty attended the races with Prince Aly Khan and a leading English trainer, Fred Darling.

After Bois Roussel won the Prix Juigne by a neck from Joseph E. Widener's Astrologer, Beatty made an offer of 4,000 pounds to Leon Volterra, the colt's breeder and owner. Beatty's offer was refused, but he was spurred on by Prince Aly (who loved horse trading), and he upped his offer to 5,000 pounds. This price also was turned down, but it was well known that Volterra adopted the view that everything in his barn had a price, and Beatty again upped his figure.

Volterra's price was 8,000 pounds, and after an offer of 6,000 pounds, Beatty met the asking price.

Bois Roussel thus was sent to Beckhampton in England to be trained for the Epsom Derby by Darling. The latter already had trained four Derby winners, and in Bois Roussel's year he had the favorite in his yard in Pasch, winner of the Two Thousand Guineas. Bois Roussel did not thrive immediately upon his arrival at Beckhampton, and Darling did not take his chance of winning the Derby very seriously. Darling told the author that, after getting Bois Roussel into strong work, he found that the colt did not have much of a turn of speed but appeared to stay well. Still, it never occurred to the trainer that Bois Roussel was likely to beat Pasch at Epsom.

One day, as the Derby neared, Beatty arrived at Beckhampton with the news that he had bet 1,000 pounds on Darling's behalf that Bois Roussel would win the classic. Darling thanked him but cautioned him to curtail his enthusiasm, as the colt really had little chance. (When Darling's estate was settled in 1953, the amount listed was 60,000 pounds. The winnings from the bet made by Beatty in 1938 on Bois Roussel must have equaled about half of that amount.)

Since Gordon Richards, the champion jockey, was required for Pasch, Darling had to find another jockey for Bois Roussel. His choice was Charlie Elliott, who then was riding in France but who had won the Derby on Call Boy in 1927 and the Oaks on Brulette in 1931.

Elliott told the author that Bois Roussel (20-1) had been last for a long way, and that when he began to "niggle at him" to improve his position, he was unable to do so. It was not until they were beginning the descent to Tattenham Corner that Elliott, in desperation, gave Bois Roussel a good whack with his whip. The colt began to wake up and passed several horses on the downhill run to Tattenham Corner. Still, when they came into the stretch, Bois Roussel was a good twelve

Vatout, 1926	Prince Chimay, 1915	Chaucer, 1900	**St. Simon**, 1881	Galopin St. Angela
			Canterbury Pilgrim, 1893	Tristan Pilgrimage
		Gallorette, 1907	Gallinule, 1884	Isonomy Moorhen
			Orlet, 1891	Bend Or Ruth
	Vasthi, 1921	Sans Souci, 1904	Le Roi Soleil, 1895	Heaume Mlle De La Valliere
			Sanctimony, 1896	St. Serf Golden Iris
		Vaya, 1909	Beppo, 1903	Marco Pitti
BOIS ROUSSEL			Waterhen, 1894	Gallinule Gipsy Queen
	Spearmint, 1903	Carbine, 1885	Musket, 1867	Toxophilite W. Australian Mare
			Mersey, 1874	Knowsley Clemence
		Maid of the Mint, 1897	Minting, 1883	Lord Lyon Mint Sauce
Plucky Liege, 1912			Warble, 1884	Skylark Coturnix
	Concertina, 1896	**St. Simon**, 1881	Galopin, 1872	Vedette Flying Duchess
			St. Angela, 1865	King Tom Adeline
		Comic Song, 1884	Petrarch, 1873	Lord Clifden Laura
			Frivolity, 1867	Macaroni Miss Agnes

lengths back of the leaders and was not gaining on them.

Elliott began to ride vigorously again, and to his surprise Bois Roussel suddenly began picking up one horse after another. He was coming on the outside of the field and with an eighth-mile to go, only Pasch and Scottish Union were in front of him. Richards asked Pasch to go on and win his race but found that Scottish Union was too much for him. At that moment, Bois Roussel swept past Pasch in a couple of strides, and then collared Scottish Union with equal ease. The final margin in the first Derby televised was four lengths, with Scottish Union second. Elliott said that if the race had been another furlong Bois Roussel would have won by "half a furlong."

The time of 2:39 1/5, however, on good going, was the worst in twelve years with one exception. The field must have been made up of the most pronounced lot of non-stayers in the Derby for many a year. The other beaten jockeys were exclaiming about what a wonderful challenge Bois Roussel had made, but in fact, the rest of the field must have been stopping badly. This is not always an easy matter to judge when watching an actual race. The author well remembers watching a recent champion run in a long-distance race in New York. We were in the company of one of the best-known trainers, who was pointing out what a long time it took the horse "to get moving." In breaking the race down into its time fractions by quarters, the author discovered that the winner did not, in fact, "get moving." He ran the last half-mile in about 50 seconds, while his opponents took about three seconds more. It was his opponents who "got stopping."

YEAR	AGE	STS	1ST	2ND	3RD	EARNED
1938	at 3 (in Eng)	1	1	0	0	£9,228
In England		1	1	0	0	£9,228
1938	at 3 (in Fr)	2	1	0	1	205,600 Fr
In France		2	1	0	1	205,600 Fr

Bois Roussel kept his engagement for the one and seven-eighths-mile Grand Prix de Paris at the end of June. Federico Tesio sent his unbeaten Nearco from Italy for the race. Tesio did not have a good line to compare Italian form with French form, and he was not very confident about Nearco until the race preceding the Grand Prix was won by another one of his horses. Knowing what Nearco could do at home to this winner of a good race at Longchamp, Tesio suddenly realized that Nearco must have a very good chance. He knew that Nearco was not, as he put it, "a true stayer," but he also knew that the colt's brilliance was so extreme, that if he could be held up before being asked for much of an effort, his burst of speed was likely to carry him to victory, even at one and seven-eighths miles.

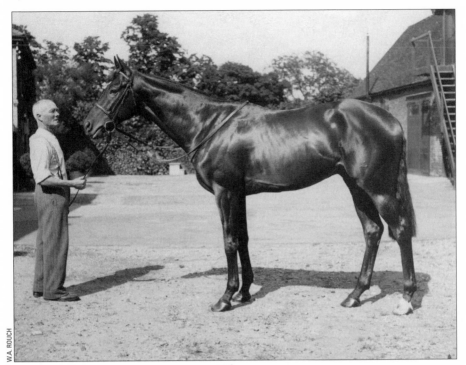

W.A. ROUCH

Tehran

That is exactly what happened. Nearco ran over everything in the last one-hundred yards and won by one and a half lengths. W.R. Johnstone was riding Canot, as he put it, "for a place." This was a technique he used on horses he did not think could win; it consisted in letting his mount stay tailed off until very late and then riding him through a field of exhausted horses. Johnstone did not expect to win a big race this way, but frequently got place money in big races using the method. Johnstone said that he did not have much belief in Canot and having finished second in the Grand Prix, riding in this fashion and beating Bois Roussel a length, he did not entertain a very high opinion of the Derby winner.

Gordon Richards, on the other hand, reported that he had been balked on Bois Roussel and believed that with a clear run, he would have won. Richards was not the sort of jockey to indulge in fantasies. Hence, there is little doubt, that under more favorable openings, Bois Roussel could have been closer. Since it was the last start for Bois Roussel, we are left with only three races on which to estimate his racing class.

On the whole, it seems most sensible to accept the view of Darling and Elliott that Bois Roussel did not have much in the way of a burst of speed but stayed

561

R. ANSCOMB

Petite Etoile, a granddaughter of Bois Roussel, with Lester Piggott up

thoroughly well. This characteristic would take us back to the Spearmint (maternal grandsire) quarter of his pedigree, and looking back on his stud career, it is pretty much the way his stock raced.

In winning the Derby, Bois Roussel had become the first member of the St. Simon male line to land the classic since Durbar II in 1914. Accordingly, when he went to stud, it was hoped that Bois Roussel would revive the once flourishing St. Simon line in England. Bois Roussel certainly could not be labeled a failure at stud, but when the St. Simon revival came, it came from other sources.

Bois Roussel was sold by Beatty to Prince Aly Khan in 1946, and the horse was syndicated later that year. He suffered from laminitis late in his life and was destroyed in 1955.

Bois Roussel led the English sire list in 1949, but his reputation suffered throughout his stud career from the tendency of so many of his sons and daughters to be difficult to train. His best stock included Migoli, who won the Prix de l'Arc de Triomphe and Eclipse Stakes and who later sired Gallant Man. Bois

Roussel also sired two English St. Leger winners, Tehran and Ridge Wood; the former was the sire of the brilliant Tulyar. Other sons of Bois Roussel included two Irish Derby winners, Fraise du Bois and Hindostan, the latter a major sire in Japan. Bois Roussel also got Swallow Tail, who was third in the Derby.

Bois Roussel's daughters compiled a distinguished record as broodmares, their produce including the great mare Petite Etoile, plus Epsom Derby winner St. Paddy and St. Leger winner Cantelo.

Bois Roussel was not a very impressive horse physically, being rather plain in appearance and lacking the magnetism and signs of vitality showed so plainly by many top horses. Bois Roussel's coat displayed a plentiful sprinkling of white hair, which is unusual in brown horses, but is found frequently in chestnuts. Such white hairs in the coat usually are associated with descent from Irish Birdcatcher, who was foaled in the 1830s. Since virtually all Thoroughbreds carry many crosses of Irish Birdcatcher, the reappearance of the white hairs is not a genetic miracle.

CHAPTER SEVENTY-NINE

MIGOLI

A s a general rule in Thoroughbred breeding, when the opposites—stamina and speed—are mated, the resulting offspring favors one characteristic or the other. Granted, the author has no comprehensive data to support this dictum, but it is the impression resulting from experience gathered over many years.

In the case of the Aga Khan's Migoli, the desired middle ground was achieved. His sire and dam represented the opposite ends of the spectrum, ranging from stoutness to speed. His sire, Bois Roussel, was well endowed with stamina but lacked a burst of speed, and most of his stock took after him in these respects. Migoli's dam, Mah Iran, won two races as a two-year-old and three more as a three-year-old at five and six furlongs. She was thought by some jockeys to be the fastest filly of her time, though her actual racing record does not quite endorse this lofty opinion.

Mah Iran was by Bahram, whose stock stayed very well and who stayed well himself. The next dam was Mah Mahal, the dam of the Derby winner Mahmoud and other winners. Mah Mahal was a modest winner over five furlongs, though her sire was the stout Gainsborough. The third dam was the flying filly Mumtaz Mahal, thought by many racing men to have been the speediest filly ever seen in England. (She also was the second dam of Nasrullah and third dam of Royal Charger.) Mumtaz Mahal's first three dams were all very speedy. It seems fair to say, in fact, that this line of mares was the speediest in the *General Stud Book*.

When Migoli first came out at York in the middle of May as a two-year-old, he was described as extremely backward, and he ran as expected. A month later, he ran in the important New Stakes at Ascot, and was third, beaten eight lengths by the winner, the speedy Petition (who later became a leading sire). His next race was also at Ascot, at a later meeting. This was in the National Breeders' Produce Stakes. While Migoli was only fourth to winner Tudor Minstrel, he showed in that race that he had distinct possibilities, as he was running on in very stout fashion

BLOOD-HORSE LIBRARY

The Aga Khan (left) with Prince Aly Khan (right)
and Laurel Park's John D. Schapiro

at the end of the race. He had been unable to go the pace in the early part of the running.

He ran again at the September meeting at Doncaster but failed to "accelerate," as the British Turf writers put it, and was unplaced.

Migoli showed his best efforts as a two-year-old in the seven-furlong Dewhurst Stakes at Newmarket. He was the only colt seriously backed to beat Marcel Boussac's Sandjar (who won the French Derby the following year). Knowing that his colt lacked a burst of speed, jockey Gordon Richards sent him into the lead at The Bushes, a quarter-mile from home, and let him stride along at his best pace. Sandjar could never get on terms with Migoli, who won by one and a half lengths. The figures in Phil Bull's *Best Horses of 1946* would have put Migoli into the Free Handicap with about 126 pounds (top weight, 133 pounds). Mr. Freer, the handicapper for the Jockey Club, did not take such a favorable view of Migoli, putting him in at 121 pounds. The next year's racing showed that Bull's estimate was considerably nearer the mark than was the official handicapper's. Migoli's weight was in the range on the Free Handicap that has supplied many classic winners from the stout, as opposed to the speedy, two-year-olds.

As a three-year-old, Migoli began his campaign in the one-mile Craven Stakes at Newmarket, and though still backward in condition, he gave thirteen pounds and a beating to a moderate animal called White Horses. A week before the Derby, he won the Royal Standard Stakes of ten furlongs at Manchester. In the Derby itself, he finished second but was running through a lot of beaten and exhausted colts, including the third finisher, Sayajirao, who afterward won the Irish Derby and the English St. Leger. He never came close to coming to grips with the winner Pearl Diver (really a pretty poor classic winner).

At Ascot, there was not much for Migoli to beat in the King Edward VII Stakes. For the ten-furlong Eclipse Stakes at Sandown Park, it was a different story. There Migoli came up against Tudor Minstrel, generally regarded as the fastest miler seen in England for a generation. It was, in fact, Tudor Minstrel's sheer speed that enabled Migoli to win. Tudor Minstrel was a tear away kind of colt that could not be taught to relax. Running in this style, he kept Migoli on full stretch to stay within touch for a mile. There was no question of "accelerating," as Migoli was doing his best. At the end of a mile, Tudor Minstrel had reached the end of his stamina reserves, and Migoli, continuing at much the same pace, won fairly easily.

The race for the St. Leger perplexed the Turf critics as well as the jockeys that rode in the race. Richards, on Migoli, reported that the pace was poor until well into the stretch, where the speed was turned on very suddenly. Migoli was unable to accelerate quickly, and in fact lost his action and began to climb when asked for a sudden effort.

Bull finally came to the conclusion that Migoli did not really stay more than ten furlongs. The Champion Stakes of ten furlongs at Newmarket in October did something to confirm this view. There Migoli followed the Aga Khan's other start-er, Claro, at a good pace, and then ran on to beat Marcel Boussac's Nirgal, who car-

MIGOLI					
Bois Roussel, 1935	Vatout, 1926	Prince Chimay, 1915	Chaucer, 1900	St. Simon / **Canterbury Pilgrim**
			Gallorette, 1907	Gallinule / Orlet
		Vasthi, 1921	Sans Souci, 1904	Le Roi Soleil / Sanctimony
			Vaya, 1909	Beppo / Waterhen
	Plucky Liege, 1912	Spearmint, 1903	Carbine, 1885	Musket / Mersey
			Maid of the Mint, 1897	Minting / Warble
		Concertina, 1896	St. Simon, 1881	Galopin / St. Angela
			Comic Song, 1884	Petrarch / Frivolity
Mah Iran, 1939	Bahram, 1932	Blandford, 1919	Sywnford, 1907	John o' Gaunt / **Canterbury Pilgrim**
			Blanche, 1912	White Eagle / Black Cherry
		Friar's Daughter, 1921	Friar Marcus, 1912	Cicero / Prim Nun
			Garron Lass, 1917	Roseland / **Concertina**
	Mah Mahal, 1928	Gainsborough, 1915	Bayardo, 1906	Bay Ronald / Galicia
			Rosedrop, 1907	St. Frusquin / Rosaline
		Mumtaz Mahal, 1921	The Tetrarch, 1911	Roi Herode / Vahren
			Lady Josephine, 1912	Sundridge / Americus Girl

Migoli winning the 1948 Arc de Triomphe

ried the full confidence of his stable. His last race of the year brought him another victory, in the one and five-eighths-mile Aintree Derby. Observers thought that, while he won, Migoli had done about all he could when the winning post was reached.

Migoli was kept in training as a four-year-old, and the Aga Khan was well rewarded for that decision. The colt's first appearance was in the fourteen-furlong Ormonde Stakes at Chester, on May 6, when he was beaten a neck and a length by Goyama and the high-class staying filly Mombasa. Chester is a saucer-shaped course, most unsuitable for a colt of Migoli's long-striding, steady way of racing.

A more suitable place was Hurst Park, where Migoli won the White Rose Stakes of nearly two miles by two lengths from an undistinguished field. In the one and a half-mile Coronation Cup at Epsom, where Migoli had been second in the Derby, he was second again, to Goyama, this time beaten a neck. They were the only two horses of much class in the race.

Migoli tried the ten-furlong Eclipse Stakes, which he had won the year before in a fast-run race, but this time he turned in a poor effort. The winner was Petition, who had been a much better two-year-old than Migoli had been; second was Sayajirao, and third was Noor, later conqueror of Citation in the United States.

Another victory but an unimportant one for Migoli came in a two-horse race for the Great Midland Breeders' Foal Plate of ten furlongs at Nottingham.

At the York August meeting, Migoli took the Rose of York Sweepstakes of one mile from Djelal by a head. This unexpectedly good form over a distance as short as a mile was some confirmation of Phil Bull's belief that Migoli was not an out-and-out stayer. There is a long run-in at York, and Migoli undoubtedly was sent along at full stretch for the last half-mile or so.

Migoli next was sent over to Paris for the one and a half-mile Prix de l'Arc de Triomphe, Europe's most important weight-for-age race. He won it by one and a half lengths from Nirgal, whom he had defeated the year before in the Champion Stakes. Third was favored Bey, the winner of the French Derby. Prince Aly Khan told the author that he was not in the least surprised (though we think a few of his bookmakers may have been), since he thought that Migoli was the best four-year-old in Europe. Prince Aly's favorite jockey, "Cheeky" Charlie Smirke, was the rider instead of Gordon Richards.

The hard race and the journey back and forth to Paris may have taken something out of Migoli, as his form in the Champion Stakes at Newmarket, which he attempt-

YEAR	AGE	STS	1ST	2ND	3RD	EARNED*
1946	at 2	5	1	0	1	£ 1,002
1947	at 3	8	6	1	1	£17,215
1948	at 4	7	3	1	1	£ 4,733
In England		**20**	**10**	**2**	**3**	**£22,950**
1948	at 4 (in Fr)	1	1	0	0	5,209,500 Fr
In France		**1**	**1**	**0**	**0**	**5,209,500 Fr**
* First-place money only						

ed to win for the second time, was poor. Migoli, ridden by Gordon Richards again, was unplaced, while Nirgal, whom Migoli had beaten twice, was second to Solar Slipper, regarded by some shrewd racing men as the best three-year-old in England that autumn. Solar Slipper's margin over Nirgal was three lengths, which is greater than Migoli's had been.

When races were run to suit him and Migoli was not required to make a sudden spurt, he was a pretty high-class colt, but he was not adaptable and was at the mercy of speedier horses, such as Petition, when the pace was such that his rivals had something left for a final effort.

Like most horses of this "one-pace" character, Migoli did not make a particularly good sire.

His best runners in Europe included Yla, winner of the French One Thousand Guineas equivalent (Poule d'Essai des Pouliches). He also got Cobetto and Induna, stakes winners in England, plus La Coquenne, who won stakes in France and placed in filly classics in France and Ireland, and also Audran, who won stakes and was classic-placed in Italy.

Migoli's major contribution as a stallion was to sire Gallant Man, a first-class and versatile colt who raced in the United States and who is the subject of a separate chapter. In 1959, two years after Gallant Man set a record in the Belmont Stakes, Migoli was imported to the United States. He was standing at John Leal's Corona Ranch in California at the time of his death, in 1963.

Migoli was represented by five stakes winners in America, in addition to Gallant Man.

Physically, Migoli was somewhat plain, like most of the stock sired by Bois Roussel, and he was faulted for being straight in the shoulder. His action when racing was "round," and when he was tired, he tended to "climb" even more.

CHAPTER EIGHTY

GALLANT MAN

Texas oilman Ralph Lowe in 1955 asked Humphrey Finney of the Fasig-Tipton Company to find him a high-class lot of yearlings that he could buy as a block. Finney got in touch with the representatives of the Aga Khan and found that the Aga Khan indeed would be willing to sell a group of his yearling colts, for $300,000.[1] Finney duly flew to Ireland, inspected the yearling colts, and concluded the deal. Of the nine colts included, only one turned out to be a very good one—Gallant Man. Actually, Finney told the author Gallant Man was only his fourth choice in the lot. (It is good to know that there are still some men connected with the Turf who do not claim omniscience.)

There are times, no matter what Colonel Phil Chinn and other renowned practical horsemen held, when it pays to know something about pedigrees. Gallant Man opened his racing career on May 18 as a two-year-old in a five-furlong maiden race at Hollywood Park. His odds were 31-1, and he finished tenth in a field of eleven. On May 29, he ran about the same way, finishing ninth in a field of twelve. He was beginning like a true son of Migoli, who only began to show he was a racehorse in late October of his two-year-old year.

On June 13, Gallant Man won a maiden race of five furlongs by three-quarters of a length from eleven others in :58 3/5. The odds were 49-1. Was this an old-fashioned betting coup? The owner is dead, so we would have to move into another place to ask him.

Gallant Man next had to move into the non-winners of two races class on July 11, and he ran sixth in a field of twelve. By October 3, Lowe had changed trainers, and Gallant Man was under the care of John Nerud in New York. Nerud described Gallant Man to the author as "just a fat little horse" when he came into his stable. He was not particularly surprised when Gallant Man ran ninth in a field of twelve for non-winners except in maiden or claiming races, at odds of 60-1. Just the same, it is a little startling to find that Gallant Man won his next start, over six furlongs, two weeks later in 1:10 1/5 at odds of 46.95-1.

Gallant Man

There was no more racing for Gallant Man until Christmas Day, when he won "non-winners of two races except maiden or claiming" at Tropical Park in Florida, at the more reasonable odds of 4-1.

It will be noted that Gallant Man was no whirlwind as a two-year-old on his overall form, but he certainly did win at some cheerful odds. In his seven starts at two, he never did meet a first-class two-year-old, and on his public form was not entitled to serious consideration for the three-year-old classics. All this, however, was about to change.

On January 3, 1957, Gallant Man came out in a field of twelve for a six-furlong race for "non-winners of a race of $2,750, except maiden or claiming" at Tropical Park. Gallant Man was odds-on at 0.95-1, and he won by six lengths in 1:09 2/5, setting a new track record. Second was Gen. Duke, from Calumet Farm, who shortly was to show that there was little between himself and Bold Ruler. On January 19 at Hialeah, Gallant Man won the six-furlong Hibiscus Stakes (his first stakes victory) by a half-length, but on January 30, he could do no better than fourth in the seven-furlong Bahamas Stakes, trailing Bold Ruler, Gen. Duke, and Federal Hill, while beaten eight lengths. The time of 1:22 equaled the track record.

Moving north to New York, Gallant Man was again fourth in the six-furlong Swift Stakes, to King Hairan, Missile, and Clem. The important trials for the great classic races were beginning, and on April 20, in the nine-furlong Wood Memorial, Gallant Man ran Bold Ruler to a nose in track-record time of 1:48 4/5. He actually headed Bold Ruler for a stride or two in the stretch.

This was the tune-up for the Kentucky Derby on May 4. There Gallant Man went under to Calumet's Iron Liege by a nose, with Round Table third and Bold Ruler fourth. Bill Shoemaker on Gallant Man mistook the sixteenth-mile pole for the winning post and stopped riding his colt briefly, and many thought it cost Gallant Man the race.

Back in New York, Gallant Man (124 pounds) was one of six starters for the nine-furlong Peter Pan Handicap. He was asked to concede from ten to sixteen pounds to his rivals and was regarded as a sure thing, at 1-2. He won readily enough, by two and a half lengths from Promised Land, a pretty good colt.

The one and a half-mile Belmont Stakes that year was run on June 15. There were only six starters, and John Nerud's problem was how to beat Bold Ruler, who was favored at 0.85-1, having taken the Preakness after his setback in the Kentucky Derby. Nerud knew that Bold Ruler was, by temperament, a front-runner. Very well,

				Chaucer
			Prince Chimay, 1915	Gallorette
		Vatout, 1926		Sans Souci
			Vasthi, 1921	Vaya
	Bois Roussel, 1935			Carbine
			Spearmint, 1903	Maid of the Mint
		Plucky Liege, 1912		St. Simon
			Concertina, 1896	Comic Song
Migoli, 1944				Swynford
			Blandford, 1919	Blanche
		Bahram, 1932		Friar Marcus
			Friar's Daughter, 1921	Garron Lass
	Mah Iran, 1939			Bayardo
			Gainsborough, 1915	Rosedrop
		Mah Mahal, 1928		The Tetrarch
			Mumtaz Mahal, 1921	Lady Josephine
GALLANT MAN				Swynford
			Blandford, 1919	Blanche
		Blenheim II, 1927		Charles O'Malley
			Malva, 1919	Wild Arum
	Mahmoud, 1933			Bayardo
			Gainsborough, 1915	Rosedrop
		Mah Mahal, 1928		The Tetrarch
			Mumtaz Mahal, 1921	Lady Josephine
Majideh, 1939				Sundridge
			Sunstar, 1908	Doris
		Buchan, 1916		Torpoint
			Hamoaze, 1911	Maid of the Mist
	Qurrat-al-Ain, 1927			Isinglass
			Louvois, 1910	Saint Louvaine
		Harpsichord, 1918		Llangibby
			Golden Harp, 1914	Goldscleugh

573

let him be in front, Nerud thought, but send something with him to force such a fast pace that Bold Ruler's stamina, which was suspect, would betray him near the end. With this in mind, Nerud put Bold Nero in the race, with instructions to take Bold Ruler as fast as he could for as far as he could. The fractions tell the story of what happened; six furlongs, 1:10 2/5; one mile, 1:35 3/5; ten furlongs, 2:01 2/5. At that point, Bold Ruler was still in front, but Gallant Man was closing on him. The final time was 2:26 3/5, a new American record, Gallant Man beating Bold Ruler twelve lengths. Nerud's strategy had paid off perfectly.

Moving to Saratoga, Gallant Man's target was the historic Travers, at ten furlongs. As a tune-up, he took a seven-furlong purse race of six starters by four lengths. In the Travers itself, with Bold Ruler absent, Gallant Man's price was only 3-20 against four rivals. He had to concede from ten to fourteen pounds but won anyway.

Moving back to New York, Gallant Man faced the highest-class racing in his life, over a period of two months, since his rivals included older horses as well as three-year-olds. On September 18 he took the Nassau County Handicap at nine furlongs by a neck from older Dedicate. To do it, he had to post a new track record of 1:47 1/5 for the distance, showing that Dedicate (126) was no slouch. Ten days later, the ten-furlong Woodward

YEAR	AGE	STS	1ST	2ND	3RD	EARNED
1956	at 2	7	3	0	0	$ 7,075
1957	at 3	14	8	4	0	$298,280
1958	at 4	5	3	0	1	$205,000
Lifetime		26	14	4	1	$510,355

Stakes was run, with only four starters. The conditions were weight-for-age, and the result came as something of a shock. The winner was Dedicate, by one and a half lengths; second was Gallant Man at odds of 3-5, two lengths in front of Bold Ruler, at odds of 2-1, and last was Reneged. The time was 2:01, with the last quarter-mile run in :25. The odds showed that the public by then accepted Gallant Man as superior to Bold Ruler, even at ten furlongs.

On October 12, the two-mile weight-for-age Jockey Club Gold Cup attracted a field of five. Gallant Man was regarded as a sure thing for this, as his price was only 3-10. He won going away, but his time was nearly three seconds slower than the record set by Nashua in 1956.

The Trenton Handicap of ten furlongs on November 9 at Garden State should have been one of the races of the century, as three of the four best colts of the brilliant 1954 foal crop were there in a three-horse field. The views of the handicapper for the race are revealing. The weights were Gallant Man, 124; Round Table, 124; Bold Ruler, 122. The race itself was something of a disappointment, since it

Gallant Romeo

was run on an off track, this in effect lowering the chances of Round Table in that class of competition since he was known to be many pounds below his best on anything but a fast surface. The net result was that it was a match race between Gallant Man and Bold Ruler. This time, John Nerud did not repeat his strategy that had been so successful in the Belmont; he did not put in a pacemaker for Gallant Man to force Bold Ruler to set a scorching pace for the first six furlongs.

Shoemaker chose not to make a front-running race against Bold Ruler, with the result that Eddie Arcaro and Bold Ruler got in front without being pressed. Arcaro kept his colt there throughout the race. The fractions of the race tell their own story: a mile in 1:36 4/5, nine furlongs in 1:49 3/5, ten furlongs in 2:01 3/5.

Arcaro had been able to conserve Bold Ruler enough so that the last furlong was run in 12 seconds flat. Nobody is going to run past a colt doing that after nine furlongs; all credit to Arcaro, and his delicate sense of pace. He was a Toscanini of the reins that day.

Technically, since Gallant Man was conceding two pounds to Bold Ruler and lost by two and a quarter lengths, he did not come out too far behind Bold Ruler on the handicapping figures. Round Table was eight and a half lengths behind

Gallant Man, but nobody took that result as a true bill, owing to the condition of the track.

One further comment about the race may be appropriate. Gallant Man's previous race had been in the two-mile Jockey Club Gold Cup, which he had won. To drop a colt back from racing at two miles to ten furlongs in the highest company is something that very few colts have attempted with success in Europe. When Golden Myth won the Ascot Gold Cup of two and a half miles and then the Eclipse Stakes of ten furlongs, it was regarded as a tremendous feat by British racing men, but in the United States there was less comment on the change in distance in Gallant Man's program.

As a four-year-old, Gallant Man first came out in the May 30 Carter Handicap of seven furlongs, where he encountered his old foe Bold Ruler again. That time, the weights were 135 on Bold Ruler and 128 on Gallant Man. Bold Ruler was 4-5. In other words, the handicapper thought Bold Ruler was seven pounds the better of the pair over the distance, and the public thought he was even more than that. The public turned out to be right, as Bold Ruler beat Gallant Man by three lengths.

About two weeks later, Gallant Man (130), priced at 3-1, beat Bold Ruler (135) two lengths in the one-mile Metropolitan Handicap. That time, the public was wrong, as it made Bold Ruler favorite at 19-20. At the weights, Bold Ruler still came out slightly the better.

A month later, Gallant Man went to California, for the ten-furlong Hollywood Gold Cup. Carrying 130 pounds and conceding up to twenty-two pounds to his four opponents, Gallant Man at odds of 2-5 won by a half-length. He stayed on to contest the one and five-eighths-mile Sunset Handicap, where he was asked to pick up 132 pounds in a field of six. Although he was conceding up to twenty-six pounds, there was not another high-class horse in the field, and Gallant Man went off at 1-2. He won about that way, coasting home by four lengths.

On September 6, Gallant Man was back at Belmont for the Sysonby Handicap of one mile. His weight was 134 pounds, and he was odds-on again at 2-3. He only finished fifth to Cohoes (116), later turned up lame, and never started again.

There is no doubt that the 1954 foal crop was one of the best on record having Bold Ruler, Round Table (both of whom became leading sires), Gallant Man, Iron Liege, Gen. Duke, Vertex, etc. Between Bold Ruler and Gallant Man the score was even with four victories each, but they were colts of a different style. Bold Ruler was the faster and had been much the better two-year-old, an age at which Gallant Man showed comparatively little. Gallant Man was much the stouter, as

JIM RAFTERY/TURFOTOS

Gallant Bloom

he showed in the Belmont Stakes. Round Table went under to Gallant Man both times they met, but the first time was in the Kentucky Derby, before Round Table had come to his full powers, and the second time was in the Trenton Handicap, when Round Table was at a marked disadvantage owing to the off track. Round Table was also a better two-year-old than was Gallant Man, though by no means remarkable at that age.

Taking it all in all, one can say that Gallant Man was in the very first flight of a group of remarkable horses. He was probably a better colt than his sire Migoli, in that he showed better form over shorter courses (the one-mile Metropolitan) and equally good form over two miles (the Jockey Club Gold Cup).

Migoli was an indifferent stallion, with a good pedigree, and good, if late-maturing, performance. Gallant Man's dam, Majideh, was the best filly of her year in Ireland, winning both the Irish One Thousand Guineas and Irish Oaks. In addition to Gallant Man, she became the dam of Masaka, winner of the English and Irish Oaks. As the dam of two classic winners, Majideh must be rated as an exceptionally high-class broodmare. Her dam, Qurrat-al-Ain, was a winner of the Queen Mary Stakes and the Coronation Stakes at Ascot.

With these credentials, Gallant Man went to stud [at Leslie Combs' Spendthrift Farm near Lexington, Kentucky] with prospects that were good, but not overwhelming in the United States, where so much emphasis is placed on early maturity and speed at the expense of stamina. While neither he nor any other horse of recent times matched the stud performance of Bold Ruler, Gallant Man became a marked success at stud. If his long-distance elements could be said to be a disadvantage, he overcame it. He sired fifty-one stakes winners, and he three times ranked among the leading ten sires on the general sire list.[2]

The best of his get includes champion filly Gallant Bloom, plus stakes winners Pattee Canyon, War Censor, Spicy Living, Gallant Romeo [sire of champion sprinters My Juliet and Gallant Bob], My Gallant, Coraggioso, Ring Twice, and April Dawn.[3]

End Notes:

1. This figure is reported as $220,000 in some references in *The Blood-Horse*.

2. Gallant Man was pensioned in 1981 and died on September 7, 1988, at age thirty-four.

3. Gallant Man also is the broodmare sire of 1980 Kentucky Derby winner Genuine Risk, champions Lord Avie and Guilty Conscience, and millionaire Stephan's Odyssey.

CHAPTER EIGHTY-ONE

MCGEE

M cGee presents one of those strange and fascinating cases of a high-class sire that no self-respecting stud farm should have allowed on the place.

To begin with, he was sired by White Knight who, owing to lack of ability or to unsoundness (or both), never started. This White Knight is not to be confused with a younger horse called The White Knight, who was a very high-class stayer. White Knight, the sire of McGee, was the equine equivalent of "single speech Hamilton," whose sole contribution to oratory during a very long term as a member of Parliament was: "Shut that window!" After the mating that produced McGee, White Knight was castrated, so McGee was his only offspring.

Certainly, it cannot be argued that White Knight was the worst sire that ever lived, since his sole representative, McGee, was a pretty fair racer. The ratio of winning produce to total num-ber of foals was 100 percent. It is too late at this date to learn why White Knight ever was allowed to serve a mare, let alone a mare with the beautiful pedigree of Remorse.

YEAR	AGE	STS	1ST	2ND	3RD	EARNED
1902	at 2	2	0	1	0	$ 350
1903	at 3	18	9	5	2	$ 6,370
1904	at 4	33	15	8	3	$11,730
Lifetime		53	24	14	5	$18,450

The only thing to recommend White Knight was that his dam, Whitelock, had stood training for five seasons and had won 4,507 pounds in thirty-five starts. Whitelock, though, failed to breed a winner among her eight foals. Her dam, White Heather, bred fifteen foals, of which four in addition to Whitelock were tiny winners. White Heather herself won 100 pounds. If we turn to Sir Hugo, the sire of White Knight, we are not much better off. It is true that he won the Derby, but this was owing to a very ill-judged ride by George Barrett on the great race mare La Fleche, who slammed him in the St. Leger. In any case, Sir Hugo was a failure as a sire.

Things are somewhat different when we turn to Remorse, the dam of McGee.

McGee

She was by Hermit, who led the sire list in England for seven years in succession and whose mares were unsurpassed in their era as broodmares. Remorse had been a small winner, had produced twelve foals, the last one being McGee, at the age of twenty-four. Perhaps this age factor was the reason she was bred to White Knight; nobody thought she would get in foal anyway. The next dam was Vex, a full sister to Galopin, whose blood together with that of his son St. Simon flooded through the *General Stud Book* much as the blood of Lexington did in the *American Stud Book*.

Vex herself was an interesting mare, breeding ten foals, of which five were winners. She was in training for six seasons, starting forty-seven times, and winning almost 3,000 pounds. She had good speed, winning the six-furlong Stewards' Cup at Goodwood and winning at up to twelve furlongs elsewhere. She even started fourteen times as a two-year-old, something almost unheard of for a filly in England.

It seems probable that McGee inherited his extreme soundness and toughness from either one or both of his granddams, Whitelock and Vex.

McGee was bred in England by Lord Bradford. His dam died during August of the year he was foaled. The youngster was sold for $125 as a yearling to Ed Corrigan and was imported at two along with eleven other horses Corrigan had acquired. (This shipment included Brantome and the dam of Roamer.)

Corrigan named the White Knight colt for Thomas McGee, who for a time was Corrigan's secretary and who later became involved in the insurance business in Kansas City. McGee made only two starts at two, placing once, then at three and four, he started fifty-one times, winning twenty-four races. The revealing facts are where he raced and the quality of his opposition. His home grounds were on the Chicago tracks, and he was sent on trips to such places as Kansas City and Memphis. Among the local allowance horses, he was something of a Triton among minnows, but when he took on a fairly good handicap horse like Dick Welles, McGee simply was not there. Dick Welles gave him weight and beat him in both the Premier Stakes and the Drexel Stakes. McGee did seem to be possessed of some speed, as he won the Fleetfoot Handicap and set an American record of 1:05 1/5 for five and a half furlongs, but a review of all his races does not give the impression that he was of stakes quality.

So here, at the end of his four-year-old year, we had a stud candidate with little to recommend him beyond soundness, toughness, a fair-to-good turn of speed,

White Knight, 1895	Sir Hugo, 1889	Wisdom, 1873	Blinkhoolie, 1864	Rataplan / Queen Mary
			Aline, 1862	Stockwell / Jeu d'Esprit
		Manoeuvre, 1874	Lord Clifden, 1860	**Newminster** / The Slave
			Quick March, 1863	Rataplan / Qui Vive
	Whitelock, 1881	Wenlock, 1869	Lord Clifden, 1860	**Newminster** / The Slave
			Mineral, 1863	Rataplan / Manganese
		White Heather, 1874	Blair Athol, 1861	Stockwell / Blink Bonny
			May Bell, 1853	Hetman Platoff / Sultan Mare
MCGEE				
Remorse, 1876	Hermit, 1864	**Newminster**, 1848	Touchstone, 1831	Camel / Banter
			Beeswing, 1833	Dr. Syntax / Ardrossan Mare
		Seclusion, 1857	Tadmor, 1846	Ion / Palmyra
			Miss Sellon, 1851	Cowl / Belle Dame
	Vex, 1865	Vedette, 1854	Voltigeur, 1847	Voltaire / Martha Lynn
			Mrs. Ridgway, 1849	Birdcatcher / Nan Darrell
		Flying Duchess, 1853	The Flying Dutchman, 1846	Bay Middleton / Barbelle
			Merope, 1841	Voltaire / Juniper Mare

KEENELAND-COOK

Exterminator

and an intriguing female line.

McGee only started once in a race with as much as $5,000 added, when he was not in the first three, and he only started once at a distance as long as ten furlongs, when he was unplaced. Nearly all his racing was at six furlongs to a mile. Yet he sired one of the greatest stayers ever seen on the American Turf—Exterminator. On any list of sires whose performance at stud far surpassed their performance on the track, McGee should be accorded a prominent place.

None of the major breeders would be interested in a horse such as McGee at the start of his career at stud, so he had to make it on his own. Moreover, when first retired to Corrigan's Freeland Stud near Lexington, McGee acquired a reputation for viciousness. It developed later that his apparent meanness was owing to his being confined in close quarters. In 1908 he was included in the Corrigan dispersal and was sold for $1,300 to C.W. Moore, who stood him for the rest of his life at Mere Hill Stud near Lexington, where McGee gave no further problems of temperament.

Moore stood the horse at first for $50, but McGee soon proved worth much more. By 1913 he had risen to fifth on the general sire list, and he was out of the top seven only once in the next ten years despite having far fewer runners than did many competing sires. He led the list in 1922, largely off the season earnings of Exterminator.

Winner of half of his one hundred starts and still regarded as one of the best geldings ever to have raced, Exterminator was the leading earner by McGee, accounting for $252,996 in eight seasons (during which he had nine trainers). Exterminator won the Kentucky Derby in 1918, and another gelding by McGee, Donerail, won it in 1913 at 91-1.

McGee sired 321 named foals in twenty-six crops, of which 9 percent (twenty-eight) won stakes. In addition to Exterminator and Donerail, McGee's stakes winners included In Memoriam, a high-class horse that beat Zev, and Viva America, who won the Kentucky Oaks in the same year Exterminator won the Derby.

McGee lived at Mere Hill to the age of thirty-one, at which time he was said to be the oldest stallion in Kentucky. He did not serve any mares during the last two years of his life.

CHAPTER EIGHTY-TWO

SPEARMINT

The Duke of Portland made the fabulously lucky purchase of St. Simon as a two-year-old in 1883 and bred and raced Donovan (like St. Simon, a son of Galopin) to win the Derby and St. Leger and to achieve the then-highest stakes total in the history of the British Turf. In 1895, the duke decided that he needed another sire at his stud as an outcross for his St. Simon and Donovan fillies. For this purpose, he imported Carbine, probably the best racer in the history of the Australian Turf.

Carbine had won the two-mile Melbourne Cup in record time, with 145 pounds up, and he covered the last five furlongs in 1:02. He was the idol of the Australian public and had made a fair start as a sire at the time of his sale. The enthusiasm of Australians for a great horse was such that a large delegation of admirers went to the dock to wave goodbye to Carbine as his ship left the pier for England.

To some extent, the Duke of Portland's consistent good luck deserted him in the purchase of Carbine. In England, Carbine was the sire of a good many winners, but Spearmint was the only really high-class colt among his British produce, and the Duke of Portland neither bred nor owned Spearmint. It seemed the Duke of Portland's good-luck fairy, after working for him overtime for more than twenty years, came in conflict with another good-luck fairy, who was fresh at the task of attending to the Turf affairs of Major Eustace Loder.

In the spring of 1902, Sir Tatton Sykes, owner of the famous Sledmere Stud in Yorkshire, was visiting the Duke of Portland's Welbeck Stud to inspect two of his mares that were to be covered by St. Simon and Carbine. Sir Tatton was then an old man but was in the market for another mare. He inquired of Welbeck stud groom John Huby if he knew where a nice mare could be bought. Huby replied that Sir James Duke had what he thought was the finest young mare in England at Welbeck for the stud season—Maid of the Mint.

Despite atrocious weather of cold wind and rain, Sir Tatton insisted on going to the somewhat distant paddock to inspect Maid of the Mint. Evidently she

Spearmint's sire, Carbine

CLARENCE HAILEY, NEWMARKET

pleased him, as he followed Huby's recommendation to offer 1,000 pounds for her. This did not quite suit Sir James Duke, who finally agreed to sell for 1,500 pounds, with 500 pounds additional to be paid if the mare had a colt in 1903 from her cover by Carbine. This was a pretty stiff price for a mare that was not a winner and had not yet bred a winner, but Sir Tatton paid the 1,500 pounds, and 500 pounds extra when Maid of the Mint foaled Spearmint in 1903.

In 1904, Maj. Loder's good fairy reached the peak of her form. She induced him to stay at Harrogate, a holiday resort on the Yorkshire coast, and to invite Noble Johnson, the manager of his Irish stud to stay with him. Shortly before the Doncaster sales in September, Loder and Johnson motored over from Harrogate to Sledmere to inspect the yearlings coming up for sale. (How many people in 1904 owned a motor car, especially one that could be counted on to get to Sledmere from Harrogate without breaking down, and equally important, get safely back again?)

After inspecting the Sledmere team of nine yearlings, Loder and Johnson decided that they would bid for the Carbine—Maid of the Mint colt, as the most promising of the lot. Their judgment proved to be correct, as they bought Spearmint for 300 guineas, he the cheapest of all the nine Sledmere yearlings, which averaged nearly 1,200 guineas. Score one for the philosophic school of contrary opinion: The majority is always wrong. The only cheaper Derby winner was Hard Ridden (1958), bought for 270 guineas.

Spearmint was sent to be trained by P.P. Gilpin at Newmarket. Shortly after his arrival, Spearmint became seriously ill, and it took him five months to recover. By July 1905, he was ready to run, and he made his first start in the Great Foal Plate at Lingfield. He must have been showing Gilpin something better than average on the training grounds, as he started at 9-4 in a field of ten. He won, but only by a head from Succory (received four pounds).

His next outing was at Derby, where Black Arrow, a brilliant two-year-old, gave him three pounds and a three-length beating. In the autumn, Spearmint was unplaced in a nursery handicap at Newmarket, where he was giving from ten to forty-five pounds to his competitors. Taking a line through Black Arrow, it seems probable that Spearmint was twelve to fifteen pounds behind the best of his age as a two-year-old.

The plan for Spearmint's three-year-old season was to train him for the Grand Prix de Paris. As he was a son of the great stayer Carbine, Gilpin believed that Spearmint would be well suited by a distance of one and seven-eighths miles in June, with 128 pounds up. Furthermore, Spearmint's maternal grandsire, Minting, had won the race in 1886, and no British colt had won the race in the intervening twenty years.

Gilpin's Derby candidate was the filly Flair, who had won the One Thousand Guineas so easily that she had become the favorite for the Derby. About three weeks before the Derby, run that year on May 30, Flair suffered an accident—a British euphemism for "broke down"—and could not run. This left Spearmint as the Gilpin stable's only candidate for the Derby, and as his preparation for the Grand Prix was well advanced, only a couple of gallops were required to make

Carbine, 1885	Musket, 1867	Toxophilite, 1855	Longbow, 1849	Ithuriel	Miss Bowe
			Legerdemain, 1846	Pantaloon	Decoy
		West Australian mare, 1857	West Australian, 1850	**Melbourne**	Mowerina
			Brown Bess, 1844	Camel	Brutandorf mare
	Mersey, 1874	Knowsley, 1859	**Stockwell**, 1849	The Baron	**Pocahontas**
			Orlando mare, 1853	**Orlando**	Brown Bess
		Clemence, 1865	Newminster, 1848	Touchstone	Beeswing
			Eulogy, 1843	Euclid	Martha Lynn
SPEARMINT	Minting, 1883	Lord Lyon, 1863	**Stockwell**, 1849	The Baron	**Pocahontas**
			Paradigm, 1852	Paragone	Ellen Horne
		Mint Sauce, 1875	Young Melbourne, 1855	**Melbourne**	Clarissa
			Sycee, 1864	Marsyas	Rose of Kent
Maid of the Mint, 1897	Warble, 1884	Skylark, 1873	King Tom, 1851	Harkaway	**Pocahontas**
			Wheat Ear, 1867	Young Melbourne	Swallow
		Coturnix, 1871	Thunderbolt, 1857	**Stockwell**	Cordelia
			Fravolina, 1862	**Orlando**	Apricot

him fighting fit for the Derby.

It was decided to work Spearmint with Maj. Loder's famous mare Pretty Polly, a five-year-old winner of twenty of twenty-one starts at that time (including the One Thousand Guineas, Oaks, St. Leger, and Coronation Cup). The weights carried in the trial were 125 pounds for Pretty Polly, 103 pounds for the three-year-old Spearmint, and 117 pounds for Hammerkop, a six-year-old who had won the 1905 Cesarewitch.

This meant that at one and one-half miles, Pretty Polly was giving six pounds more than the weight-for-age scale called for, taking into account the sex allowance. The first of three such trials took place on May 13 and the last on May 25. In the first gallop, Spearmint was described as "going wonderfully well," and in the last one he went considerably better than did Pretty Polly.

Gilpin tried to hoodwink the touts at Newmarket, and he even succeeded in deceiving his own stable jockey, Bernard Dillon. In June, Dillon had an interview with a correspondent of *The Sporting Life*, in which he said that as far as he knew, Pretty Polly never had been tried with Spearmint.

YEAR	AGE	STS	1ST	2ND	3RD	EARNED*
1905	at 2 (in Eng)	3	1	1	0	£ 835
1906	at 3 (in Eng)	1	1	0	0	£6,450
In England		**4**	**2**	**1**	**0**	**£7,285**
1906	at 3 (in Fr)	1	1	0	0	409,350 Fr
In France		**1**	**1**	**0**	**0**	**409,350 Fr**
* First-place money only						

One man at Newmarket was not hoodwinked. Archy Falcon had been a Newmarket correspondent for the racing press, and after developing his skills as a handicapper had launched into a career as a professional backer, relying on his own observations and handicapping. He made it his business to watch Gilpin's horses, and when he saw that the great mare Pretty Polly could not go with Spearmint at the end of a one and one-half-mile gallop, he knew his chance had come as a backer.

So much money went on Spearmint that he started second favorite for the Derby at 6-1. (Lally was favorite at 4-1.) The stable jockey, Dillon, was not given the mount on Spearmint, who was ridden by the great American jockey, Danny Maher. Spearmint won easily, by one and one-half lengths from Picton, with Troutbeck—who later won the St. Leger—two lengths farther back. The time, 2:36 4/5, was a new record for the race. Danny Maher then had ridden three of the last four Derby winners, and yet his British detractors claimed that he was no good at Epsom.

Was taking the stable jockey off Spearmint for the Derby part of Gilpin's betting coup strategy? Dillon was not given a chance to know how good Spearmint was, as he never rode in Spearmint's trials. Perhaps Maher did not know, either. In

Spearmint

any case, eleven days after the Derby, Dillon had the mount on Spearmint for the Grand Prix de Paris at Longchamp. The odds were slightly less than even money, and he beat Brisecoeur a half-length.

In the Grand Prix, Spearmint led from start to finish, something that rarely had been accomplished and that only a thoroughly good stayer could accomplish. Still, the riding tactics may have been a measure of prudence on the part of Dillon; French jockeys were known to be somewhat more than rough at times to English horses and jockeys.

Spearmint's legs went bad following the Grand Prix, and he could not run again, though he was kept in training until the following summer in the hope he could be gotten sound.

He went to stud at his owner's Old Connell Stud near The Curragh in Ireland. His fee was 250 pounds, where it remained until after the death of his owner, Maj. Loder, in 1914. From 300 guineas in 1915, it fell by stages to 95 guineas in 1920, when Spearmint's son, Spion Kop, won the Derby. It was raised to 200 guineas in 1921 and remained there.

Spearmint died of colic in the summer of 1924 at the Old Connell Stud.

A discussion of Spearmint's pedigree has been withheld in deference to the taste of Dr. Sam Johnson, the great lexicographer and "great panjandrum" of English

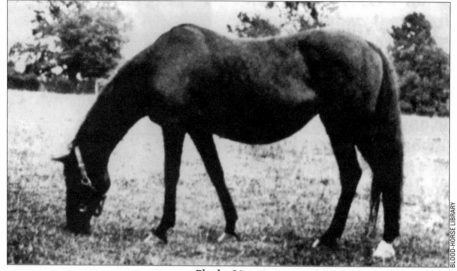

Plucky Liege

literature in the eighteenth century, who stated that he could not stand biographies which started with a pedigree and ended with a funeral.

Having gotten past Spearmint's death, we may turn now to his bloodlines.

While Spearmint was regarded as well above average among Derby winners, his pedigree was by no means remarkable. His sire, Carbine, had been only a qualified success in England, if that. His dam, Maid of the Mint, was by Minting, who was a very high-class runner but not a good sire. The mare was a non-starter and bred four other foals in addition to Spearmint, of which three were minor winners, although all were sired by top-class stallions.

The next dam, Warble, was by Skylark (not a good stallion). She won two races out of thirteen starts as a two-year-old and bred nine foals, of which three were winners; they included Wargrave (also by Carbine), who won the Cesarewitch as a six-year-old. Honey Bird, a minor winning daughter of Warble, bred Honeywood, who won the Cambridgeshire of 1914.

Warble's dam, Coturnix, was by Thunderbolt (again, not a good stallion). She won three races at three and four, for a total of 220 pounds. Before going to France (aged eighteen), she bred six foals, of which four were minor winners.

The next dam, Fravolina, was sired by Orlando (a high-class stallion and a son of the great sire Touchstone). She only won 25 pounds but bred thirteen foals, including six winners. Two of them, The Quail (2,351 pounds) and The Shaker (3,546 pounds), were each in training five seasons or more and won a lot of small races.

Thus, none of these first four dams had much racing or breeding merit, until Spearmint came along. It is not until the fourth generation that even a good sire appears. From a pedigree of this sort, a colt of Spearmint's class was most unlikely to emerge. He was not quite as much of a genetic freak as The Tetrarch or Hurry On, however, but neither was Spearmint quite as good a racehorse or as good a sire as either of them.

Spearmint was inbred to the great stallion Stockwell, and Spearmint's sire, Carbine, was inbred to the mare Brown Bess. The latter foaled the dam of Musket (Carbine's sire) and also produced the dam of Knowsley (Carbine's maternal grandsire).

The average distance of races won by Spearmint's stock was slightly longer than ten and a half furlongs. This figure might hint that his stock stayed, stayed so well that they lacked the speed generally necessary to win a classic. Nevertheless, he sired two English classic winners, two Irish classic winners, and an Italian Derby winner.

At the time of his death, Spearmint had sired ninety-three winners, of which forty-one had won at two, so the stamina of his get in fact did not overwhelm to the degree that they were plodders.

Spearmint's classic-winning colts were Spion Kop, winner of the Epsom Derby in 1920; Royal Lancer, winner of the English St. Leger in 1922; Zionist, winner of the Irish Derby (and second in the Epsom Derby) in 1925; and Spike Island, winner of the Irish Derby and Irish Two Thousand Guineas in 1922. [His Italian Derby winner was Fausta in 1914.]

Spearmint's chief contribution as a stallion, though, was siring Plucky Liege, a filly who at two was within one pound of Lady Josephine. Both Plucky Liege and Lady Josephine became producers of extraordinary merit. (The former produced Mumtaz Mahal and Lady Juror, from whom came many high-class descendants.)

Plucky Liege was one of the best broodmares of this century, as she was the dam of three major winners: Sir Gallahad III (French Two Thousand Guineas), Admiral Drake (Grand Prix de Paris), and Bois Roussel (Epsom Derby); the last-named was foaled when Plucky Liege was twenty-three years old. In addition, Plucky Liege produced Bull Dog, who like Sir Gallahad III was a leading stallion in the United States and a lasting influence.

CHAPTER EIGHTY-THREE

THE FINN

In 1910, when the New York tracks were forced to close because of anti-betting legislation, the Great Depression of the American Turf began. Arthur Hancock Sr. was taking mares from his Ellerslie Stud at Charlottesville, Virginia, to sell at county fairs as saddle horses, and many American Thoroughbreds were being shipped by the boatload to Europe and South America to be sold for whatever they would fetch.

In the midst of all this gloom, there were a few stalwarts who refused to panic and were determined to keep their breeding operations going, and, if necessary, to race their own stock. Most important among the commercial breeders in this group was John E. Madden, master of Hamburg Place near Lexington. He refused to quit, not hesitating to race and train the stock produced annually at Hamburg Place. In point of numbers, his operation was huge, so this program took an iron nerve and complete confidence in his judgment to carry it out.

Madden's two chief stallions during this bleak period were the imported horses Ogden and Star Shoot, both of whom he had bought. In 1912, the year before racing was resumed in New York, a black colt was foaled at Hamburg Place sired by Ogden and out of Livonia, by Star Shoot. That foal, The Finn, was put into training along with the other Madden-breds. The Finn first came to the races at Belmont Park on June 5 as a two-year-old in a five-furlong allowance race having five starters and a purse of $400. The Finn ran third, beaten about three lengths, and earned $30. In a similar race on June 8, The Finn finished last of eight. On June 12, over five and one-half furlongs, he was second, beaten by only a nose.

At the end of the month, racing had shifted to the old Aqueduct track. There Madden sent out The Finn in a five-furlong maiden race. The returns look as though Madden had a pretty good go at the bookmakers. The Finn was only even money in a field of seven, and he won easily, breaking the track record when he recorded the time of :59 2/5. Now the cat was out of the bag, and the betting opportunities were gone, for the time being.

The Finn won his next start, a handicap, against only three others at odds of only 7-10. He then lost an allowance race at Saratoga by a half-length, and he also lost his following race, a handicap of five and one-half furlongs at Saratoga. What the handicapper thought is pretty clear: The Finn (under 120 pounds) was asked to concede from six to eighteen pounds to five others, and he only failed by a length to beat Solly. The next handicap, of five and one-half furlongs over a sloppy track, The Finn won, with 119 pounds up, at odds of only 2-5.

At that point, Madden sold The Finn to Louis Winans, who had bought champion two-year-old Sir Martin (by Ogden) from him in 1908 for $75,000, for the purpose of winning the following year's English Derby. Sir Martin started favorite for the race but fell in the running, permitting King Edward VII's Minoru to win. (Winans' English trainer was Vivian Gooch, who in 1915 visited Hamburg Place and gave Madden a half-interest in the foal a Hanover mare named Lady Sterling was carrying. The following April, Lady Sterling produced a chestnut colt, by Star Shoot, and Madden bought Gooch's interest after the colt was weaned. Madden sold the colt for $10,000 after he failed to win in four starts at two. The colt was Sir Barton, who remained a maiden until he won the Kentucky Derby and who subsequently became America's first Triple Crown winner.)

Winans raced The Finn only once, in the Futurity on August 29 at Saratoga, and had no better luck in that race than he had had with Sir Martin in the Epsom Derby. Starting at 13-5 under 119 pounds, The Finn raced well back early, and he was closing fast on the outside in the final quarter-mile when he swerved into the fence and lost his rider.

That could not have pleased Winans too much, and when The Finn reappeared as a three-year-old, he carried the colors of H.C. Hallenbeck. The colt's first race at three came on May 25, at Belmont Park in the five and a half-furlong Littleneck Handicap. The Finn, though bumped, made a good effort to be second. That race evidently was a prep for the one-mile Withers, then regarded as the American equivalent of the English Two Thousand Guineas. The Finn led four rivals all the way to win easily, but the time was a poor 1:39 2/5 over a fast track.

The Finn's next race was a three-horse affair for the Belmont Stakes, then run at a distance of one and three-eighths miles. The Finn took that one in a canter by four lengths.

There is no record known to the author of the price Winans paid Madden for The Finn (Hallenbeck reportedly got the colt for $15,000). Nor are there records of the levels of blood pressure achieved by Winans and Madden after The Finn won both the Withers and the Belmont. In all probability, Madden was very pleased because his business was developing horses at the track and selling them. (In addition to Sir Martin, he had sold Irish Lad to H.P. Whitney and Herman Duryea. It was the latter who took Irish Lad to France, where he sired Banshee, second dam of Tourbillon, the foundation sire of Marcel Boussac's great stud.)

The Finn next took the Southampton Handicap easily under top weight of 126 pounds, and he also won the Hamilton Derby in Ontario, Canada. In Fort Erie's ten-furlong Canadian Derby, however, he failed by a head to concede eight pounds to Waterblossom. Back in New York at the end of July, he was fourth (with top weight) in the Knickerbocker Handicap, then at Saratoga he finished last in the nine-furlong Champlain Handicap and fourth with 126 pounds up in the one-mile Saranac Handicap, won by Regret (123). The track must have been slow in those days, because the time, with the going listed as good, was 1:42.

The Finn then won the one and three-sixteenths-mile Huron Handicap under top weight (122 pounds). Four-year-old Stromboli, one of the first of many high-class horses sired by Fair Play, then beat The Finn by about one and one-half lengths in the nine-furlong Belmont Park Autumn Handicap. That was a fairly interesting result, since The Finn had slightly the worst of the weights on a weight-for-age basis, he carrying 112 pounds to Stromboli's 118. Stromboli was

THE FINN				
Ogden, 1894	Kilwarlin, 1884	Arbitrator, 1874	Solon, 1861	West Australian / Birdcatcher mare
			True Heart, 1864	Musjid / Mary Jane
		Hasty Girl, 1875	Lord Gough, 1869	Gladiateur / Battaglia
			Irritation, 1862	King of Trumps / Patience
	Oriole, 1887	Bend Or, 1877	Doncaster, 1870	Stockwell / Marigold
			Rouge Rose, 1865	Thormanby / Ellen Horne
		Fenella, 1869	Cambuscan, 1861	**Newminster** / The Arrow
			La Favorite, 1863	Monarque / Constance
Livonia, 1907	Star Shoot, 1898	Isinglass, 1890	Isonomy, 1875	Sterling / Isola Bella
			Dead Lock, 1878	Wenlock / Malpractice
		Astrology, 1887	Hermit, 1864	**Newminster** / Seclusion
			Stella, 1879	Brother to Strafford / Toxophilite mare
	Woodray, 1897	Rayon d'Or, 1876	Flageolet, 1870	Plutus / **La Favorite**
			Araucaria, 1862	Ambrose / Pocahontas
		Wood Nymph, 1891	Magnetizer, 1885	The Ill-Used / Magnetism
			Woodbine, 1869	Kentucky / Fleur des Champs

L.S. SUTCLIFFE

The Finn

a good racer, though not outstanding, and the Autumn Handicap indicated that The Finn was in about the same class.

The colt's program now was made up altogether of handicaps. In the one and one-sixteenth-mile Baltimore Handicap, seven-year-old Short Grass, a first-class handicapper, was set to give The Finn twelve pounds over a heavy track. The Finn, at those weights, literally lost Short Grass. The Finn could not concede seven pounds to a modest four-year-old called Gainer, though, in the nine-furlong Washington Handicap at Laurel.

In the Ellicott City Handicap for three-year-olds, The Finn (123) beat Trial by Jury (126) six lengths over a sloppy track.[1] In his last race of the year, The Finn won the Dixie Handicap of ten furlongs in heavy going, under top weight. It seems clear that he stayed well and loved the heavy going.

As a four-year-old, The Finn, like all horses of that age in the United States at the time, was in the hands of the handicappers. Thus, going over his record is like unwinding the spool of movie film. One can see almost exactly what his capacities were, at different seasons of the year.

He first came out in the six-furlong Paumonok Handicap with top weight and was nowhere. His next effort was in the Kings County Handicap, in which the great gelding Roamer, aged five, was asked to concede The Finn thirteen pounds. With 133 pounds up, Roamer was unplaced; The Finn (120) was second.

The Finn then won the Metropolitan with 120 pounds up, beating Stromboli

(122) by three-quarters of a length. At that stage, they were about even. In the ten-furlong Suburban, The Finn (127) was asked to give Stromboli (123) four pounds and could not do it; three-year-old Friar Rock (101) beat them both easily.[2]

In the one-mile Delaware Handicap at Saratoga, Pennant (127) beat Stromboli (125) by two lengths, with The Finn (119) unplaced, but Pennant under 130 pounds could not give The Finn thirteen pounds, nor could Stromboli give him six pounds, in the Champlain Handicap, which The Finn won in 1:52 4/5 for the nine furlongs. At that stage, The Finn was about ten pounds behind Pennant. In Saratoga's Merchants' and Citizens' Handicap of one and three-sixteenths miles, Roamer (127) could not give The Finn (123) four pounds, and The Finn equaled the track record of 1:58. In the one and three-quarters-mile Saratoga Cup, at

YEAR	AGE	STS	1ST	2ND	3RD	EARNED
1914	at 2	9	3	3	1	$ 1,425
1915	at 3	20	9	4	2	$17,985
1916	at 4	14	6	2	1	$15,630
1917	at 5	7	1	1	2	$ 3,925
Lifetime		50	19	10	6	$38,965

weight-for-age, neither Roamer nor The Finn was any match for Friar Rock. That race may have been the basis for Sam Hildreth's remark that "Friar Rock was the best I ever saw over a distance of ground."

In Maryland, The Finn beat both Roamer and Stromboli at level weights in the Chesterbrook Handicap. The handicappers then thought that The Finn was the best horse in the country (Pennant having been sidelined). The Havre de Grace Handicap was at nine furlongs, and The Finn (129) beat Spur (a three-year-old carrying 117 1/2), Borrow (118), Stromboli (123), and Roamer (126).

As a five-year-old, The Finn was out seven times, winning once and placing three times. His lone victory that year came in the one and one-eighth-mile Long Beach Handicap, in which he beat George Smith and three others, equaling the track record of 1:52.

Any colt that could establish a track record at Aqueduct for five furlongs at two, win the Withers and Belmont at three, and at four equal a track record at Saratoga, win the Metropolitan, then give weight and a beating to the best handicap horses left in training in the autumn has to be accounted a good racehorse. The Finn was not, however, an extraordinary horse. He was, in fact, about ten pounds behind Pennant, who made a better sire than did The Finn. It should be borne in mind, however, that although Pennant was a much better two-year-old than was The Finn, the latter stayed one and three-eighths miles well, while Pennant's limit was about one mile.

From the standpoint of pedigree, The Finn was only fairly strong. His dam,

Flying Ebony

Livonia, was a stakes winner of six races as a two-year-old. It is not until the fourth dam, Woodbine, is reached that one finds a really good race mare. The intervening mares produced some winners and a couple of unimportant stakes winners.

The Finn's sire, Ogden, did well for Madden but broke no records. A son of St. Leger winner Kilwarlin, Ogden was foaled in England in 1894 and later that year was brought to this country along with his dam, Oriole, by Marcus Daly. Turf historians consider Ogden the best of his division at two, when he beat Ornament in the Futurity and Great Eastern Stakes. Ogden beat other good horses, winning fifteen of his twenty-eight career starts, and generally was regarded as an animal of excellent speed, but a middle-distance performer at best.

When Daly died late in 1900, Ogden was included in a dispersal of his Bitter Root Stud held in January. Ogden had been retired after his four-year-old campaign (1898) and had spent two seasons at stud, but he was put back into training in 1901 by Billy Lakeland, who had handled Ogden for Daly at four and bought him at the Bitter Root dispersal for $5,000. Ogden lost his first three races at seven, then won six straight, two of them on the same day (on September 2 at Coney Island).[3] Madden came looking for him after that feat, purchased him privately, and sent him to Hamburg Place.

So far as the author is aware, there currently is no surviving male line tracing to Ogden, and thus to The Finn. Ogden never led the sire list, but he ranked among the top twenty on twelve occasions, being second in 1908 and 1913, third in 1915 and 1916, and fourth in 1914. The best of Ogden's sons were The Finn, Sir Martin, and Fayette. The last-named was an unimportant sire; Sir Martin got some useful runners but left no good sons to carry on the line.

The Finn became leading sire in 1923 due to the then-record $272,008 earnings of his son, Zev, hero of the ill-starred match with English Derby winner Papyrus. After 1923, The Finn never again ranked among the first ten leading sires, and only twice was he in the first twenty. His opportunity was pretty good, since he stood at W.R. Coe's Shoshone Stud near Lexington, where the quality of mares was fairly high. (He spent his first years at stud at Hamburg Place, Madden having repurchased him after retirement. Madden sold the horse in 1923 to Coe for a reported $110,000.)

Zev, considered the best horse in training in 1923, was an almost complete failure at stud, siring only the minor stakes winners Zevson and Zida. The Finn's son Flying Ebony, winner of the 1925 Kentucky Derby, twice ranked among the top ten sires and was in the top twenty one other time. The chances of survival of the line, however, were lessened dramatically in 1934, when Flying Ebony's best son, Dark Secret, was destroyed after gallantly racing to victory with a broken leg in the Jockey Club Gold Cup.

Stakes winners sired by The Finn also included Nurmi, Euclid, Finite, Sankari, Seventeen Sixty, Paavo, Igloo, Begorra, Torpointer, and Silver Finn. The Finn died at Shoshone Stud near Lexington at the age of thirteen.

End Notes:

1. The Finn beat Distant Shore by a head. Trial by Jury was six lengths behind Distant Shore.

2. Friar Rock won by two and a half lengths over Short Grass, who was three lengths clear of Stromboli. The Finn was a length back in fourth.

3. Ogden won the second race on the card, a six-furlong allowance race by one length in 1:13 1/5. He carried 130 pounds. In the sixth race on the card, Ogden carried 126 pounds to a one-length win in a turf handicap at one and one-sixteenth miles.

CHAPTER EIGHTY-FOUR

BEAU PERE

T here is a never-ending argument among breeders and racing men as to the relative importance of performance and pedigree in assessing the prospects of a stallion when he first goes to stud. This is never likely to be settled to the satisfaction of all parties, since there are so many examples at each end of the spectrum, and they are by no means uniform in their results.

When you have both, top performance coupled with top pedigree, it is reasonable to forecast optimum stud performance, as in the cases of Hyperion, Nearco, and Tourbillon, who were the best sires in England and France up to about 1950, but it is not always so. Citation was one of the best performers on record and was backed by a very good pedigree, yet was a relative disappointment at stud.

Alsab was a performer of the highest class, backed by a poor pedigree, and while he sired a few good animals, was nothing like as good a sire as he had been a racehorse. Nasrullah and Heliopolis were just below classic standard (with Nasrullah the more talented racer of the pair), backed by very fine pedigrees, and both made excellent sires.

YEAR	AGE	STS	1ST	2ND	3RD	EARNED*
1929	at 2	unraced				
1930	at 3	7	1	1	0	£261
1931	at 4	4	2	0	0	£713
Lifetime		11	3	1	0	£974

The greater gamble, of course, is to take a horse with known poor racing form, but backed by a very high-class pedigree, and see what happens at stud. This was done with Tredennis, who was so useless in training that he was bought for a hundred pounds. He sired Bachelor's Double and a good many other high-class racers, including the dam of the Derby and St. Leger winner Coronach. In this same category, but with a little better performance record, was Beau Pere.

Beau Pere did not start at two and ran seven times at three, for one win and one second and total first-place winnings of 261 pounds. At four, he started four times, winning two races, total value 713 pounds. His winning races were the Norfolk and Suffolk Handicap of one mile at three and the Swaffham Plate

Beau Pere

Handicap and Chesterfield Plate, each of one and three-quarters miles, at four. These are third- or fourth-class events. The author's guess is that on a handicapping basis this racing record would put Beau Pere more than thirty pounds below the top form of his age.

Nevertheless, Sir John Jardine, his breeder and owner, put him to stud in England. He made the seasons of 1932 and 1933 there, siring a total of six foals, of which two were obscure winners. At this point, Beau Pere was sold for five hundred pounds to New Zealand as a stallion. Breeders in that country had experienced good luck importing well-bred English stallions with poor racing credentials. Tea Tray (by The Tetrarch), who never ran, had turned out well, and Foxbridge (by Foxlaw) led the New Zealand sire list eleven years in succession.

Beau Pere stood in New Zealand for three seasons and became the leading sire in that country for the 1938–39 and 1939–40 seasons. He was the leading two-year-old sire the first season his stock appeared there. He was then bought for Australia. There, he also became leading sire for three successive years. At that point, he was bought by Louis B. Mayer of Hollywood, California, as the foundation sire for the stud Mayer was assembling.

Beau Pere's first U.S. foals arrived in 1942, and he was a success from the beginning. Among his stakes winners were the first-class mare Honeymoon (Hollywood Oaks, Hollywood Derby, etc.), plus Father Neptune, Pater, Grandpere, Bellesoeur, Judy-Rae, Stepfather, Bridal Shower, and U Time. His daughter, Iron Reward, became the dam of one of the best racers seen on the American Turf, Swaps.

Beau Pere was even more remarkable as a sire of two-year-olds. In 1943, he sired fourteen winners from sixteen foals to be co-leader in number of winners, and in 1948 he was the leading sire in number of two-year-old winners, with fourteen from twenty-eight foals.

On the general sire list, he was in the top twenty on five occasions. In other words, Beau Pere was a consistently high-class sire in New Zealand, Australia, and the United States. He sired a total of forty-nine stakes winners, of which twenty-one were foaled in this country.

In his old age, he was transferred to Leslie Combs II's Spendthrift Farm near Lexington, Kentucky, but he died before he could make a season there. Physically, Beau Pere was not a very attractive horse, being big, somewhat on the leg, and coarse. Both his sire and dam were Thoroughbreds of high quality, but he did not take after either one of them in looks.

BEAU PERE				
Son-in-Law, 1911	Dark Ronald, 1905	Bay Ronald, 1893	**Hampton**, 1872	Lord Clifden / Lady Langden
			Black Duchess, 1886	Galliard / Black Corrie
		Darkie, 1889	Thurio, 1875	Cremorne / Verona
			Insignia, 1882	Blair Athol / Decoration
	Mother-in-Law, 1906	Matchmaker, 1892	Donovan, 1886	**Galopin** / Mowerina
			Match Girl, 1882	Plebeian / Fusee
		Be Cannie, 1891	Jock of Oran, 1869	Blair Athol / Tunstall Maid
			Reticence, 1874	Vespasian / Seclusion
Cinna, 1917	Polymelus, 1902	Cyllene, 1895	Bona Vista, 1889	Bend Or / Vista
			Arcadia, 1887	Isonomy / Distant Shore
		Maid Marian, 1886	**Hampton**, 1872	Lord Clifden / Lady Langden
			Quiver, 1872	Toxophilite / Y. Melbourne Mare
	Baroness La Fleche, 1900	Ladas, 1891	**Hampton**, 1872	Lord Clifden / Lady Langden
			Illuminata, 1877	Rosicrucian / Paraffin
		La Fleche, 1889	St. Simon, 1881	**Galopin** / St. Angela
			Quiver, 1872	Toxophilite / Y. Melbourne Mare

Iron Reward

What, then, was the explanation of his success as a sire, starting with his poor known racing class? Especially, what was the explanation of his proven ability to sire good two-year-olds, considering that he was by Son-in-Law, whose stock matured late and who was the best source of stamina in the British Isles? (Beau Pere himself did not even run as a two-year-old.)

The answer must be that, genetically, he did not transmit much of Son-in-Law. Turning to his dam Cinna, what was to be found? Cinna had been a first-class racer, though not a great one. In three starts as a two-year-old, she had been a winner, and she was second in the important New Stakes at Ascot and in the less-important Bretby Post Stakes at Newmarket. As a three-year-old, she won the One Thousand Guineas and the Coronation Stakes at Ascot and was second in the Oaks. Her sire was Polymelus, the best stallion of his time in England.

The next dam, Baroness La Fleche, was also a high-class filly. Her dam was La Fleche, one of the very best race mares ever seen on the English Turf. So, here we have a female line with three straight stakes winners, two of which were classic winners. One additional feature of the pedigree is that Cinna was inbred to the great broodmare Quiver with two free generations. Quiver produced La Fleche and her full sister Memoir (Oaks and St. Leger) and was the granddam of Polymelus (five-time leading sire in England) and Grafton (four-time leading sire in Australia).

Cinna was also the dam of Buckler and Mr. Standfast, who showed little racing form but both made good sires in Australia.

Beau Pere, then, transmitted the high racing class and lovely pedigree of his dam Cinna, instead of his own poor racing class and the late-maturing, plodding characteristics of his sire Son-in-Law.

CHAPTER EIGHTY-FIVE

COUNT FLEET

O ur two favorite entries in the deflated pomposity stakes were the late Lord Curzon, Viceroy of India during Queen Victoria's reign, and the late Willis Sharpe Kilmer, master of Court Manor Stud at Newmarket, Virginia, and avid promoter of the medicinal remedy Swamproot. (The latter, which was said to be well laced with alcohol, sold particularly well during the Prohibition Era.)

Lord Curzon was demonstrating his bent for pomposity in an address to the House of Lords, and looking at him with evident dislike across the aisle was a twenty-one-year-old peer, who had just been admitted to take his seat in the House. Gazing up at the vaulted ceiling, Lord Curzon said: "My Lords, I ask myself this question." The twenty-one-year-old replied, "And a damned silly answer you'll get."

Kilmer was another fitting target for the same sort of riposte. In 1916, he had gone to Saratoga, where he had bought a yearling colt by Sundridge—Sweet Briar, imported from France. A really gorgeous pair of ringbones possessed by the colt had escaped the Kilmer eye; nevertheless, the colt, named Sun Briar, turned out to be about the best two-year-old of 1917.

When the time came to prepare Sun Briar for the Kentucky Derby, Kilmer was ready with a pontifical statement to his trainer: "McDaniel, you must not run Sun Briar in the Kentucky Derby unless you can guarantee he will win."

Henry McDaniel replied: "If I could guarantee a horse would win any race, I would run a three-horse parlay, and then I wouldn't have to be bothered with you."

Still, Kilmer enjoyed the last laugh in this exchange. As a work horse for Sun Briar, Kilmer was persuaded to buy a lanky, chestnut gelding. Named Exterminator and affectionately known as Old Bones, the latter won the Kentucky Derby in place of Sun Briar and became something of a folk hero, winning fifty out of a hundred starts and about $250,000.

Kilmer was so impressed with Sun Briar that he bought his full brother,

Sunreigh, whom he imported from Europe; Sunreigh, however, never won a race. Nevertheless, Kilmer used him as a stallion and bred him to an imported mare named Contessina, who also had failed to win a race. Contessina was by a

poor stallion named Count Schomberg, who had been a very tough racehorse and had run over fences as well as on the flat.

The result of this concentration of failure was Reigh Count, who turned out to be the best colt of the 1925 crop. It was at Saratoga that John D. Hertz was attracted to Reigh Count in a maiden race. In the last sixteenth-mile, Reigh Count reached over and bit a competing colt on the neck. Reigh Count's apparent desire to win thus exhibited, so

Count Fleet's sire, Reigh Count

impressed Hertz that he visited Kilmer with a view to purchase. Hertz told the author that Kilmer "hemmed and hawed" about it—perhaps he would sell, and perhaps he would not.

Hertz, who had grown up in a tough part of Chicago, was not the man to put up with Kilmer's whimsical dillydallying. He took a check out of his pocket, duly signed it, and said, "you have ten minutes to accept it." Kilmer accepted.

Racing in the colors of Mrs. Hertz, Reigh Count ran second in the Belmont Futurity to the same stable's great filly Anita Peabody. Hertz told the author that if Reigh Count had been asked for a serious effort, he might have won.

(The author became personal friends with Hertz and was impressed by the genuine interest Hertz had in Thoroughbreds and by the affection he had for his own horses. One day, at Belmont Park, while we were walking together from the Turf and Field Club to the saddling enclosure, on impulse we asked him: "Do you really like this racing?"

He answered with a smile: "The day I sold the Yellow Cab Co. for $40,000,000, I felt pretty good—but not the way I felt the day I won the Futurity with Anita

Peabody, bred by Fannie and me.")

As a three-year-old, Reigh Count won the Kentucky Derby and proved to be a very high-class colt. As a four-year-old, Reigh Count was sent to England, accompanied by his trainer and by jockey Chick Lang. After a few races in which Reigh Count finished unplaced, Lang approached the owner and said: "Mr. Hertz, you are going to have to take me off Reigh Count."

"But why, Chick? You always have ridden him."

"I have been watching these English jockeys, and the way they ride on these rolling courses, where there are hills and dips," the jockey said. "They all ride with a much longer rein than we do in America, and this allows the horse freedom to move his head so that he can balance himself according to the gradient. Now, Mr. Hertz, I have ridden with a very short rein all my life, and I simply can't adjust to these changed conditions.

"You get one of the top English jockeys for Reigh Count, and you will see the difference."

Acting on Lang's advice, Hertz obtained Joe Childs, one of the best English riders, particularly in distance races, and Reigh Count won the one and a half-mile Coronation Cup at Epsom. For the two and a half-mile Ascot Gold Cup, Lord

Reigh Count, 1925	Sunreigh, 1919	Sundridge, 1898	Amphion, 1886	Rosebery Suicide
			Sierra, 1889	Springfield Sanda
		Sweet Briar II, 1908	St. Frusquin, 1893	St. Simon Isabel
			Presentation, 1898	Orion Dubia
	Contessina, 1909	Count Schomberg, 1892	Aughrim, 1883	Xenophon Lashaway
			Clonavarn, 1885	Baliol Expectation
		Pitti, 1898	St. Frusquin, 1893	St. Simon Isabel
			Florence, 1880	Wisdom Enigma
COUNT FLEET				
Quickly, 1930	Haste, 1923	Maintenant, 1913	Maintenon, 1903	Le Sagittaire Marcia
			Martha Gorman, 1902	Sir Dixon Sallie McClelland
		Miss Malaprop, 1909	Meddler, 1890	St Gatien Busybody
			Correction, 1888	Himyar Mannie Gray
	Stephanie, 1925	Stefan the Great, 1916	The Tetrarch, 1911	Roi Herode Vahren
			Perfect Peach, 1907	Persimmon Fascination
		Malachite, 1913	Rock Sand, 1900	Sainfoin Roquebrune
			Miss Hanover, 1897	Hanover Miss Dawn

Count Fleet

Harewood exercised a prior claim that he had on Childs for a horse that had no chance (reportedly so that the jockey could not ride Reigh Count). Hertz then got Harry Wragg to ride Reigh Count, and they finished second. Wragg, who previously never had ridden Reigh Count, said to Hertz after the race that had he understood the colt better he thought he could have won.

When Hertz retired Reigh Count to stud, the colt spent his first six seasons through 1935 at his owner's Leona Heights Stock Farm in Cary, Illinois, where his opportunities necessarily were limited. In 1936 Reigh Count was shifted to A.B. Hancock's Claiborne Stud near Paris, Kentucky, and he remained there through 1939, the year he begot Count Fleet.

Reigh Count was not exactly a fashionable stallion at the time, nor was he a total failure, having ranked in the leading twenty sires five years in succession. In 1940 Reigh Count was moved to his owner's new establishment, the Stoner Creek Stud, very near Claiborne.

Hertz had been purchasing mares to mate with Reigh Count and told the author that he was very partial to the gray line of blood descending from the great French sire Le Sancy. Hertz' filly Anita Peabody had been out of a daughter of that gray marvel The Tetrarch. So, acting on this belief, he bought the mare Quickly, whose pedigree carried two crosses of Le Sancy, one through The Tetrarch and one through Maintenon.

Quickly was a hardy mare and a sound one, having won thirty-two of eighty-five starts, with fourteen seconds and thirteen thirds. She generally ran at six furlongs but had once won at a mile. In class, she ran for as little as a $2,000 claiming price. Her sire, Haste, had been a fair miler, winning the one-mile Withers Stakes, but he had proved to be an indifferent sire. Quickly's dam, Stephanie, made only three starts, winning a maiden race in her first attempt, then finishing fourth, and next running unplaced in the Spinaway Stakes. Stephanie was by Stefan the Great, labeled by the caustic tongue of Henry McDaniel "Stop 'em the Great." He

YEAR	AGE	STS	1ST	2ND	3RD	EARNED
1942	at 2	15	10	4	1	$ 76,245
1943	at 3	6	6	0	0	$174,055
Lifetime		21	16	4	1	$250,300

was a poor sire both in this country and in England. Nevertheless, Stephanie bred two stakes winners, Crout Au Pot and Silver Spear, among her six foals. The next dam, Malachite, was a good race mare, winning the fillies' ten-furlong traditional Alabama Stakes. She was by Rock Sand, and her dam was by Hanover.

Thus, Count Fleet's ancestry represented a mixture of stoutness (in Reigh Count) and speed (in Quickly through her immediate ancestors, reinforced by stoutness again after two removes). Like many colts that stay well and continue developing, Count Fleet was not overwhelming in his first efforts. On June 1, 1942, he was second at Belmont Park, and he again was second on June 15. In his third start, on June 19, however, he won a maiden race by four lengths; then he won again on July 4 and followed with a second in the East View Stakes. It was not until July 22 that Count Fleet scored his first stakes victory, that in the Wakefield at the old Empire City track.

Count Fleet then was sent to Chicago to try for the Washington Park Futurity. There, Occupation, then the crack two-year-old on the Chicago tracks, was set to concede Count Fleet five pounds. Count Fleet was not then a fast breaker and did not get a very clear run. He emerged from the pack too late to win, but he was charging at the finish and went under by only a neck.

Both colts subsequently were shipped to New York with the Futurity as their joint objective. Count Fleet won a couple of overnight allowance races, and then four days before the Futurity turned in what may be the most extraordinary time trial on record for a two-year-old, over six furlongs—three furlongs in :33, four in :44 4/5, five in :56, and six in 1:08 1/5.

That was Count Fleet's race, and trainer Don Cameron did not deserve any medals for submitting any two-year-old to such a scorching ordeal so close to a big race.

When the Futurity was run, Occupation conceded seven pounds to Count Fleet and won by five lengths, going the first six furlongs in 1:08 3/5 and the six and a half furlongs in 1:15 1/5. Second was the filly Askmenow, a head in front of Count Fleet. (Hertz thought that Count Fleet had an amatory interest in Askmenow and was unwilling to pass her.) Anyway, Count Fleet never was beaten again, his late-maturing staying blood then asserting itself.

The next week, he won the one-mile Champagne Stakes in 1:34 4/5, breaking the track record at Belmont Park (including older horses) and establishing a two-year-old mark that was not bettered for twenty-three years.

His next big race was the Pimlico Futurity, at one and one-sixteenth miles. Occupation was the public favorite, since he twice had defeated Count Fleet, conceding weight each time. That time, Occupation was asked to concede three pounds to Count Fleet. The pair raced together for five furlongs, and then Count Fleet came away to win by five lengths in 1:43 3/5, equaling the track record. Only one more start remained for Count Fleet as a two-year-old—the Walden Stakes, which he took by an estimated thirty lengths.

In the Experimental Free Handicap, the late John B. Campbell paid Count Fleet the highest tribute in all of his years as handicapper. He assigned Count Fleet 132 pounds, six above normal scale and two more than he gave the extraordinary two-year-olds Alsab (1941) and Native Dancer (1952).

Count Fleet's three-year-old campaign was simply a series of triumphs. First came a victory in an overnight allowance race at a mile and seventy yards, then a win in the one and one-sixteenth-mile Wood Memorial, in which he beat Blue Swords three and a half lengths. He then won the Kentucky Derby easily by three lengths from Blue Swords and scored another victory over Blue Swords in the Preakness, that time by eight lengths. Next in New York, he took the one-mile Withers by five lengths, and in the one and a half-mile Belmont Stakes, he won by twenty-five lengths. During the latter race, however, he struck his right front ankle, and he did not start again.

Count Fleet was the only three-year-old, except Sir Barton, to win all three spring classics plus the Withers.

Physically, Count Fleet did not look the part of a great racehorse. He was narrow, light-waisted, and flat-muscled. Furthermore, he ran with a good deal of knee action, and frequently his ears were laid back on his neck, giving him an

BELMONT PARK

Counterpoint with owner C.V. Whitney

ungenerous appearance, but he was the embodiment of driving will power.

His best performances suggested that he was the best racer seen since Man o' War. The only doubt concerning this was that his true class was not revealed until late autumn as a two-year-old. If a case can be made that Man o' War was twenty-one pounds better than the next best three-year-old of his year, then it can be argued that Count Fleet was at least ten to twelve pounds better than Blue Swords, the next best three-year-old of 1943. He was a tear away sort, and nothing could live with him.

Count Fleet was somewhat irregular in the quality of his stud performances. His Average-Earnings Index was 2.29, that being in the top 4 percent of all sires. He was the sire of 267 winners racing in America and of thirty-nine stakes winners, but he ranked only in the top twenty leading sires seven times, although he lived to be thirty-three years old.

Leading sire in 1951, he sired that season's Horse of the Year, Counterpoint, as well as the 1952 Horse of the Year, One Count, plus the champion filly Kiss Me Kate.

When Count Turf won the 1951 Kentucky Derby, it completed the first three-generation sire chain in the history of the race—Reigh Count, Count Fleet, Count Turf.[1] (As the great breeder Federico Tesio pointed out, no chain has gone further than three in the Epsom Derby—Doncaster, Bend Or, Ormonde.)

None of Count Fleet's sons scored a solid success at stud. Counterpoint had a higher earnings index than his sire, but he was not very fertile. Some of Count Fleet's daughters have produced well; the great gelding Kelso and the champion filly Lamb Chop each were out of Count Fleet mares. Count Fleet was the leading broodmare sire in 1963.

Of the eight colts that won the Triple Crown before Secretariat, only two, Count Fleet and War Admiral, ever became the leading sire, and these two led only for one year each.[2] Is there a disturbing thought here for those dogmatists who rely on racing class as the sole guide to a horse's prospects as a future stallion?

End Notes:

1. A second three-generation sire chain was formed by Pensive (1944), Ponder (1949), and Needles (1956).

2. This was, of course, written in 1976 prior to the advent of 1977 Triple Crown winner and leading sire Seattle Slew.

CHAPTER EIGHTY-SIX

RIBOT

There is a substantial body of opinion throughout the whole international world of racing—embracing breeders, owners, trainers, jockeys, and students of the Thoroughbred—that Ribot was the greatest Thoroughbred bred to date in the twentieth century. This opinion would include both his career on the Turf and his career at stud. Thus, it is incumbent upon us to deal with his history with the utmost care, but this is somewhat difficult, since some of the best students the author knows have expressed complete bewilderment as to the true source of Ribot's greatness. Ribot was bred by the most influential breeder of the twentieth century on an international basis, Federico Tesio, of the Dormello Stud in Italy; considering the limited means at his disposal and the small number of foals he bred annually (about twelve), there will be few to dispute his exalted ranking. Following Tesio's death in 1954, his stud went downhill to some extent, as there was no one to replace his first-class intelligence, coupled with the artistic sense about the Thoroughbred character and conformation. Indeed, who could have?

In one sense, Ribot was typical of the methods Tesio had used for many years; in other ways he was not. Tesio liked to start with a mare tracing to a first-class race mare, and a good taproot, even if the mare herself was of very little use on the racecourse. For instance, in the case of the great racer and sire Nearco, Tesio bought his granddam, Catnip, for 75 pounds, she having won no more than 100 pounds. Note, however, that (A) Catnip was by Spearmint, a winner of the Epsom Derby and Grand Prix de Paris, out of Sibola, winner of the One Thousand Guineas and nearly winner of the Oaks, when breaking down, and (B) that Sibola traced to the first-class taproot Maiden, a winner of the Travers Stakes, by Lexington. Now, the Tesio pattern was to breed up from Catnip. This he did by sending her to Havresac II, the outstanding sire in Italy, where he headed the leading sire's list ten times, nine of which were successive. From this mating, he bred the filly Nogara, who had first-class speed, winning both the One Thousand and Two Thousand Guineas in Italy.

Nogara was sent to Pharos, a horse with first-class speed and about the best sire in Europe at the time. Again, note that Pharos was not a sprinter. (Tesio did not patronize sprinters.) His best distance was ten furlongs, and he was only beaten a length in the Derby. From this mating came Nearco, who thus had a pedigree combining first-class speed and first-class stamina. In addition, Havresac II carried strong inbreeding to St. Simon, and Pharos was inbred also to St. Simon. Tesio told the author that he was a staunch believer in accumulating St. Simon blood in his pedigrees.

It is all very easy to explain after the event. Nevertheless, these were the steps that Tesio took that resulted in Nearco.

Similarly, in the case of Donatello II (sire of Crepello and Alycidon), Tesio started with the purchase of a yearling filly, that one by the unfashionable sire Bridge of Earn; the price was 160 guineas. The filly was a granddaughter of the wonderful race mare Pretty Polly (who had a poor pedigree herself). The filly, Duccia di Buoninsegna, turned out to be a very high-class racer on the Italian Turf and was bred up to Clarissimus, a high-class winner of the English Two Thousand Guineas and then standing in France.[1] From this mating came Delleana, a winner of eight races, including the Gran Premio d'Italia. That mare was mated with Blenheim II, a colt of first-class speed who also stayed well. From that mating came Donatello II.

YEAR	AGE	STS	1ST	2ND	3RD	EARNED
1954	at 2 (in Ity)	3	3	0	0	5,120,000 lire
1955	at 3 (in Ity)	5	5	0	0	11,400,000 lire
1956	at 4 (in Ity)	5	5	0	0	13,860,000 lire
In Italy		**13**	**13**	**0**	**0**	**30,360,000 lire**
1955	at 3 (in Fr)	1	1	0	0	30,365,000 Fr
1956	at 4 (in Fr)	1	1	0	0	29,515,000 Fr
In France		**2**	**2**	**0**	**0**	**59,880,000 Fr**
1956	at 3 (in Eng)	1	1	0	0	£23,727
In England		**1**	**1**	**0**	**0**	**£23,727**

While the above two cases seem fairly clear in their pattern, and even similar in their results, the case of Ribot differs in important aspects. In the first place, there was no first-class race mare at the base of the female line. The fourth dam, Volcanic, was only a fair race mare, having earned 2,261 pounds. Her best race was the Lavant Stakes, a second- or third-class affair. She bred five winners from eleven foals, the best of them being Cyclonic, winner of 10,402 pounds, including the Jockey Club Stakes. This was some way below classic form.

Ribot's third dam, Bucolic (by Buchan, a pretty good sire of mares), won only a maiden race, value 326 pounds, as a two-year-old. In 1936 Bucolic had a filly by Mannamead, who was sold as a yearling for 470 guineas, and in 1936 Bucolic had a colt by Papyrus (a full brother to the second dam of Ribot) that won a single selling race and was sold to Germany. Bucolic's colt by Obliterate was sold to Panama, and Bucolic herself was sold for 80 guineas at the December sales.

Ribot's second dam, Barbara Burrini, was bought as a foal by Tesio at the December sales for 350 guineas. She was another of Bucolic's foals by Papyrus. The latter was by no means a fashionable sire, but he had won the Derby and was the best son of Tracery, to whose blood Tesio was very partial. Taken to Italy, Barbara Burrini won six races at three and four at from seven to fifteen furlongs. In other words, she stayed well but was not precocious, and she must have been somewhat lacking in speed, as none of these races were of importance.

Tesio then mated Barbara Burrini with El Greco, a stallion he had bred, owned, and raced himself. El Greco was a high-class racer, ranked only one pound below Donatello II in the Handicap Optional (free handicap) for two-year-olds. He was unbeaten at two and won the Premio Chiusura, an all-aged event of great prestige in Italy. El Greco won that race by ten lengths! The next year it was won by Nearco.

As a three-year-old, El Greco played second fiddle to his more famous stable companion, Donatello II, but nevertheless won six races, including the St. Leger

			Cavaliere d'Arpino, 1926	Havresac II, 1915	Rabelais / Hors Concours
		Bellini, 1937		Chuette, 1916	Cicero / Chute
			Bella Minna, 1923	Bachelor's Double, 1906	Tredennis / Lady Bawn
Tenerani, 1944				Santa Minna, 1915	Santoi / Minnow
			Apelle, 1923	Sardanapale, 1911	Prestige / Gemma
		Tofanella, 1931		Angelina, 1913	St. Frusquin / Seraphine
			Try Try Again, 1922	Cylgad, 1909	Cyllene / Gadfly
RIBOT				Perseverance, 1904	Persimmon / Reminiscence
			Pharos, 1920	Phalaris, 1913	Polymelus / Bromus
		El Greco, 1934		Scapa Flow, 1914	Chaucer / Anchora
			Gay Camp, 1923	Gay Crusader, 1914	Bayardo / Gay Laura
Romanella, 1943				Parasol, 1917	Sunstar / Cyclamen
			Papyrus, 1920	Tracery, 1909	Rock Sand / Topiary
		Barbara Burrini, 1937		Miss Matty, 1914	Marcovil / Simonath
			Bucolic, 1926	Buchan, 1916	Sunstar / Hamoaze
				Volcanic, 1918	Corcyra / La Soufriere

Italiano, and he was second to Nearco in the Premio Chiusura. As a four-year-old, El Greco again was unbeaten, his races including France's Omnium. El Greco undoubtedly was a very high-class colt. In fact, when the negotiations were under way for the sale of Nearco to England, it was stipulated by the Italian government, that if Nearco went abroad, El Greco could not also be sold abroad.

Mated with El Greco, Barbara Burrini produced Romanella, who turned out to be the best two-year-old filly of her year in Italy, winning five races. At the end of her juvenile season, Romanella turned somewhat sour and would no longer exert herself, even in home gallops. In addition, she began to develop a ring bone. For these reasons, Tesio decided to retire her from racing and bred her as a three-year-old.

Romanella bred sixteen foals, of which nine were winners and three were classic winners. Two of her foals died. She must be regarded as an exceptionally high-class broodmare, and the way in which Tesio regarded her is evident from the matings he arranged:

(1) Rovezzana, filly by Niccolo Dell'Arca, a stout horse who won the Italian Derby by twenty lengths. Rovezzana, who was not tried at two, won three races at six furlongs at three.

(2) Rosalba Bernini, filly by Niccolo Dell'Arca. Won three races.

(3) Colt by Traghetto. Died as foal.

(4) Rabirio, colt, by Airborne (Epsom Derby and St. Leger, a plodder). Won a handicap as a four-year-old.

(5) Radowska, filly also by Airborne. Won twelve races.

(6) Ribot, colt by Tenerani. Unbeaten winner of sixteen races.

(7) Raffaellina, filly by Tenerani—full sister to Ribot. Unraced. [Died as a two-year-old.]

(8) Roderiga, filly by My Love, a plodder. Unraced.

(9) Rodin II (after mare was barren for a year), colt by Supreme Court, a stout horse who won the King George VI and Queen Elizabeth Stakes. Only placed in modest races.

(10) Rossellina, filly by Tenerani—full sister to Ribot. Won three races, including the Italian One Thousand Guineas.

(11) Rousseau II, colt by Owen Tudor. Modest winner.

(12) Colt by Botticelli. Died early.

(13) Romagnola, filly by Tenerani—full sister to Ribot. Unraced.

(14) Romney, colt by Shantung, who placed in the Epsom Derby and Grand Prix de Saint-Cloud. Winner of three races at three.

(15) Raeburn II, colt by Botticelli, a winner of the Italian Derby and the Ascot

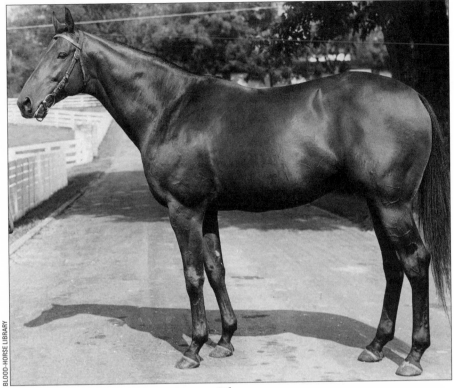

Ribot

Gold Cup. Won Italian Two Thousand Guineas and second in Italian Derby. Not a success at stud; exported to Japan.

(16) Remondina, filly by Antelami, an Italian Derby winner. Unplaced at two.

Since all of the above stallions used had good distance capacity, including the Cup winners Owen Tudor and Botticelli, it seems clear that Tesio was convinced that the early maturing and first-class speed of Romanella required the assistance of stout blood in her mates. Two of Romanella's three classic winners were by Tenerani, which was certainly stout enough.

Tenerani had been an indifferent two-year-old, winning three modest races in seven starts. As a three-year-old, he improved out of all recognition, winning the Italian Derby, the Gran Premio di Milano, the St. Leger Italiano (by twelve lengths), the Gran Premio d'Italia, and the Gran Premio del Jockey Club. At four, he was seemingly still better, winning six good races in Italy and then going on to England to win the Goodwood Cup and the Queen Elizabeth Stakes from Black Tarquin. According to his connections, Tenerani was a sound horse but lacked a burst of finishing speed.

At stud, Tenerani was not the failure (apart from Ribot), which is generally thought to be the case. In addition to Ribot, he sired Tissot (1953), who was the best of his generation in Italy and led the sire list three times.

Tenerani was sired by Bellini, who was a very good racehorse, also bred in Italy by Tesio. Bellini raced from two to four and won fifteen races, never being out of the money. On the two-year-old Handicap Optional, Bellini shared top weight with Sabla. Tesio observed that Bellini had an exceptional burst of speed and that if he could be held up until the last fifty to one hundred yards of a race, he always won.

Unfortunately, Bellini's stud career began in World War II, and he only sired thirteen foals in three stud seasons, when he was traded to the German SS for fodder that Tesio could not otherwise obtain. Eleven of his thirteen foals were winners.

Bellini's sire was Cavaliere d'Arpino, whom Tesio named as the best racer he had ever bred, despite his having bred both Donatello II and Nearco. Unfortunately, Cavaliere d'Arpino was very unsound, having knee and tendon problems. He did not start at two and started only once at three. He then ran four times at four and made hacks of his rivals in such races as the Omnium, the Premio Ambrosiano, and the Gran Premio di Milano. He could put on a devastating burst of speed wherever and whenever called upon.

It is significant that, despite the horse's unsoundness, Tesio bred to him, and through the judicious selection of mares bred his unsoundness out of the strain. Ribot and Tenerani were particularly sound horses.

Tesio died in 1954, several months before the racing debut of what probably was his greatest horse. The colt was so small initially that he was not named to the classics, but it was reported that Tesio later watched Ribot at exercise in his early training, and muttered to himself: "I don't know; I don't know; there is something about him." Perhaps, he suspected what he had.

The colt's first race was a sprint at Milan on July 4, and he won by a length. Thereafter, he took the Criterium Nazionale by two lengths, then edged Gail by a head in the seven and one-half-furlong Gran Criterium at Milan. The latter was the only close race he ever experienced.

His juvenile activity confined to three races, Ribot was put away until the next March, when he came back to win the Premio Pisa by six lengths. He then dashed Gail by ten lengths in the Premio Emanuele Filiberto and next added the Premio Brembo and the Premio Besana (by ten lengths).

Unbeaten in seven races but not yet tested in international competition, Ribot

Graustark

then was sent out of Italy for the first time. His target was the Prix de l'Arc de Triomphe, already a race of major international prestige and one which he helped establish as the climactic test in Europe. Ribot was 9-1 but drew away in the straight to win by nearly three lengths.

By the time Ribot returned to Longchamp at four, he was an international star of the first order. After his 1955 Arc, he returned home to Italy (he actually was foaled in England) to win the Gran Premio del Jockey Club by fifteen lengths, completing a second season unbeaten. He began the next year at four by winning the Premio Guilio Venino by four lengths, then the Premio Vittuone four days later by twelve lengths.

Ribot next won the Premio Garbagnate and the one and seven-eighths-mile Gran Premio di Milano each by eight lengths. It was time then for another invasion, one to England, for the King George VI and Queen Elizabeth Stakes. In heavy going, Ribot was unsettled early but came away to win by five lengths.

Home again, he won the Premio Piazzale by eight lengths, preparatory to his final race, another Arc de Triomphe. That time, he was 3-5 against a crack field, and he raced brilliantly, winning by six lengths from Talgo, with Tanerko,

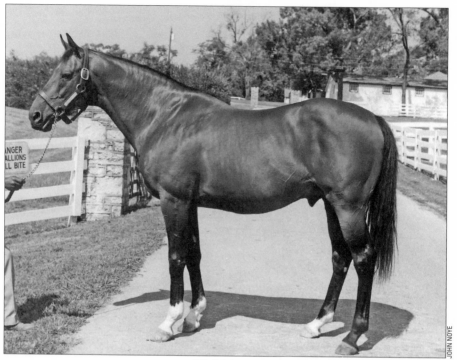

JOHN NOYE

His Majesty

America's Career Boy, and Master Boing next across the wire.

Ribot, unbeaten in sixteen races, entered stud in 1957. He stood one year in England and three in Italy, then was brought to the United States by John W. Galbreath, at whose Darby Dan Farm he stood until his death at twenty in 1972.

Physically, Ribot was not a very impressive horse. We were told he stood sixteen hands high at maturity, but there was nothing flashy or eye-catching about him. The most remarkable feature, according to the author's recollection, was the strong development of the thighs and gaskins. His driving power was unmistakable.

The United States would seem the worst possible country for Ribot as a stallion, as the emphasis on early maturity and sheer speed here is the exact opposite of the characteristics of many of Ribot's sons and daughters. A persistent characteristic of the strain was lateness in reaching maturity, although the record indicating late development may in part have been authored by owners and trainers simply choosing not to push the youngsters into early two-year-old racing. Many of the Ribots, including some of the best ones, exhibited their sire's sometimes erratic behavior.

Ribot did get some horses of precocity and brilliant speed. His son Graustark, although not tested against the best at two, had brilliant speed and took a reputation of potential greatness to stud; as a stallion, he became one of the many Ribot horses to reach a high level of success.

Ribot undoubtedly benefited from the realization of breeders and buyers that his stock was apt to be well-suited to European racing, and a number of his American-bred horses were sent abroad to race. The late Charles Engelhard, in particular, won major European races with a succession of Ribot yearling purchases, and one of them, Ribofilio, came to hand quickly enough to be the two-year-old champion of his year in England. Ribot also sired American-bred Filiberto, one of the top-ranked colts of his year at two in France. Certainly, his stock was not completely devoid of speed and precocity, but his best success was as the sire of classic horses.

Ribot was the leading sire in England three times and ranked high on lists in the United States, Italy, and France. His major winners in the British Isles included full brothers Ribero and Ribocco, who in successive years won both the Irish Sweeps Derby and the English St. Leger; Ragusa, winner of the King George VI and Queen Elizabeth Stakes as well as the family-owned Sweeps Derby–St. Leger double and sire of Epsom Derby winner Morston; Long Look, winner of the Epsom Oaks; Boucher, winner of the English St. Leger; Regal Exception, winner of the Irish Guiness Oaks; plus Romulus, Blood Royal, and Riboboy.

In Italy, Ribot was represented by Oaks winner Alice Frey and other major winners Prince Royal II and Molvedo. The latter pair, like their sire, invaded France to win the Prix de l'Arc de Triomphe.

Ribot's American-raced horses, in addition to Graustark, included Arts and Letters, winner of the Belmont, Jockey Club Gold Cup, etc., and Horse of the Year in 1969; Tom Rolfe, winner of the Preakness and champion three-year-old of 1965; plus Destro, Sir Ribot, Sette Bello, and His Majesty.

All told, Ribot is the sire of sixty-five stakes winners (15.7 percent of his named foals). Only seven horses to have stood in North America during this century have sired as many or more stakes winners.[2]

As mentioned above, many of Ribot's sons became major sires. Graustark's get includes Jim French, Key to the Mint, Avatar, Prove Out, and Caracolero; Tom Rolfe's get includes Hoist the Flag, Run the Gantlet, and Droll Role; Prince Royal II's get includes Unconscious; and Sir Ribot's get includes Two to Paris.[3]

Several of his other major winners are in early phases of their stud careers, and, as mentioned, Ribot's final foals were foaled in 1973.[4]

Some of the best students the author knows report that they have studied and studied Ribot's pedigree in an effort to explain his brilliance, on the Turf and at stud. They have arrived nowhere, and the author, too, is at the same spot. Explainable or not, though, Ribot was in all probability the most remarkable Thoroughbred of modern times.

End Notes:

1. Duccia di Buoninsegna also won the Premio Regina Elena (Italian One Thousand Guineas) in 1929 and became the first of four successive generations to win the Italian classic. Her daughter Delleana (Clarissimus) won in 1928. Dellana's daughter Dossa Dossi (Spike Island), in 1933. Dossa Dossi's daughter Dagherotipia (Manna), in 1939.

2. At that time of publication Ribot was the sire of sixty-five stakes winners. The seven ranking above him were Nasrullah, Court Martial, Broomstick, Mahmoud, Bold Ruler, Sir Gallahad III, and Princequillo. Ribot added two more stakes winners in subsequent years, giving him a lifetime total of sixty-seven.

3. The Ribot sire line in the United States is mainly extant due to His Majesty, a full brother to Graustark. From 655 foals, His Majesty sired fifty-nine stakes winners (9 percent). Among those were grade I winner Cormorant, sire of 1994 Kentucky Derby winner Go for Gin, and 1981 Kentucky Derby winner Pleasant Colony, who are the main conduits for the Ribot sire line. This and other branches of the Ribot line are represented throughout the world by such stallions as Java Gold (Graustark branch), Flemensfirth (Tom Rolfe branch), Denon (His Majesty branch), Law Society (Tom Rolfe branch), and Sportsworld (Tom Rolfe branch).

4. Ribot's final, abbreviated crop had one stakes winner, Riboboy, who won group races in England and France.

CONCLUSION

This series has included most of the key sires of the twentieth century and has been oriented toward their influence on North American racing. This latter qualification has resulted in the omission of such sires as Hurry On, Havresac II, and Dark Ronald of Europe, Congreve of Argentina, and Foxbridge of New Zealand.

Within the limits of the survey, then, what are its lessons?

There seem to be no absolute rules to which there are no exceptions, but there are a number of guidelines that are of good practical use.

The vast majority of the eighty-eight horses included were very high-class racers, but not all of them were. Alibhai never started, and Black Toney, High Time, McGee, Bull Dog, and Pilate had very moderate racing form.

Conversely, not all great racers make good sires. Epinard (1920) was a much better racehorse than his contemporary, Sir Gallahad III, but Epinard was an unsuccessful sire while Sir Gallahad III led the American sire list four times. Seabiscuit, Whirlaway, Citation, and Coaltown all were top-class racers but were not as good at stud.

In the main, however, high-class sires have been high-class racers before retiring to stud. They also benefit from much the best opportunities (initially) at stud.

Are there any significant differences between the type of racing performances of horses that make high-class sires and the type of racing performances of those sires that prove to be failures at stud? In this area, the guidelines seem to be fairly reliable. The only sires appearing in this survey of high-class sires that were late maturing and that could be classified as plodders were:

(1) Bruleur (1910 in France) did not run at two and his high-class form was at one and seven-eighths miles at three. His type of late-maturing stamina, and absence of early maturity and of good speed over a short course, was particularly suited to the French racing program of the time, when there were only about four or five stakes of importance for two-year-olds and a very limited number of stakes of one mile or less for older horses at distances. It is noteworthy that Bruleur's blood did not succeed outside France until it was crossed with a number of strains of much faster, earlier-maturing blood.

(2) Princequillo (1940) was a poor two-year-old, running in low-class claiming races at that age. As a three-year-old, however, he had very high form at distance from one and a quarter miles to two miles (Jockey Club Gold Cup). Moreover, Princequillo had no short-running, early-maturing blood within the first three removes of his pedigree. Hence his record as a very high-class sire in the United States of stock well-endowed with speed and early maturity was not in line with the normal expectations from his own Turf performances and his pedigree. Princequillo represents the most striking exception within the recollection of the author of the guideline that early maturity and good class over short courses are prime requisites for success at stud in the United States under the conditions of the current American racing program.

(3) Bois Roussel (1935) ran only as a three-year-old and then only started three times. He won at one and a quarter miles (Prix Juigne) and one and a half miles (Epsom Derby) and was third in the Grand Prix de Paris at one and seven-eighths miles. His jockey at Epsom, C.E. Elliott, stated that the colt was without speed and won because the others stopped badly. Most of Bois Roussel's stock were late to mature and stayed well. He headed the list of winning sires once in England and was an influential broodmare sire. The only impact of his male line in the United States is through a grandson, Gallant Man (1954), who was the result of crossing two successive mares of speed lines on the Bois Roussel male line.

What about very fast horses of limited distance capacity? There are not many of this type in our survey, either:

(1) Phalaris (1913) was regarded by his trainer, the Honorable George Lambton, as a sprinter but did win a race at one and a quarter miles. He could not, however, gain a place in the Two Thousand Guineas of one mile or the Cambridgeshire of nine furlongs. The average distance of the races won by the produce of Phalaris was slightly more than one mile, very different from the winning distance of the produce of the sires of virtually pure sprinters, such as Tetratema and Panorama.

The great success of Phalaris at stud was with the very stoutly bred mares in the Lord Derby stud, particularly the daughters of Chaucer. Outside of the Derby stud mares, Phalaris sired Manna (Guineas and Epsom Derby) from Waffles, an unraced daughter of Buckwheat, a very stout horse, the next dam a daughter of St. Simon (Ascot Gold Cup of two and a half miles, etc.); and Chatelaine (Epsom Oaks) from a stoutly bred mare from the Sledmere stud.

(2) High Time (1916) won only one race and that as a two-year-old. He had tremendous early speed but showed every sign of stopping badly and an inability to cope with any distance beyond a sprint. He was a bleeder and had an obstruc-

tion in his head which interfered with normal breathing. Still, an inference can be drawn that he was no more than a sprinter from the fact that his runners were generally best as two-year-olds. Sarazen was the only one of his get that succeeded in a high-class race at a distance as far as ten furlongs. High Time's blood has not carried on very well, the best channel being through Eight Thirty, whose dam was by High Time.

(3) Tetratema (1917) won the one-mile Guineas, but his chief fame was gained as an unbeaten two-year-old and as a sprinter. At stud, he was virtually a pure dominant as a sire of sprinters, and his blood has not carried on with much success in England, Ireland, or elsewhere.

(4) Roman (1937) was a high-class sprinter and a very good sire of two-year-olds. Hasty Road was the only one of his get that could cope with a classic race, which he did in winning the Preakness.

(5) Royal Charger (1942) could not win beyond seven furlongs and was also an exception to the guideline in that he was not a high-class two-year-old. He was an excellent sire, both in Ireland and the United States, and he did not have the pedigree of a complete sprinter. His sire, Nearco, got many colts and fillies that could win in the highest class at one and a half miles and beyond; his first dam (a nonstarter) was by Solario (St. Leger and Ascot Gold Cup) and his second dam was by Blenheim II (Epsom Derby).

A total of five sprinters out of eighty-eight stallions in the survey does not suggest that short-running sprinters are very good prospects to make sires of the highest class, even in the United States, where early maturity and short-distance speed capacity in racers are at a premium.

Thus, we have an aggregate of eight exceptions—three late-maturing horses excelling in stamina and deficient in speed, and five sprinters, deficient in stamina. This does not make a very imposing total out of a list of eighty-eight of the very best sires.

What about inbred as against outbred pedigrees in this group of high-class sires?

The average degree of inbreeding for any breed as a whole varies to some extent with the population. In the early stages of the development of a breed, when the population is small, inbreeding is bound to be far more frequent than it is after different strains become more abundant. In the days of Eclipse, Herod, and Herod's son Highflyer, there was not too much choice for very high-class blood outside those strains. (Matchem always played an inferior role.) Similarly, in the early days of the American Thoroughbred—though there was no *American Stud*

Book at the time—there were many reports of the outstanding sire Sir Archy being mated with his own daughters. (Such a cross is reported in the back pedigree of the great sire Nearco.)

In the group of sires covered by the present survey, there are only three sires that could be classed as inbred much more intensely than the average for the breed during the time period included in the survey:

(1) High Time—inbred to Domino with one free generation. High Time was a dominant sire for early maturity and good speed.

(2) Ksar (1918)—inbred to Omnium II with one free generation. Ksar was a dominant sire for both soundness and stamina. The best French sire of the twentieth century, Tourbillon, was by Ksar. Tourbillon's dam, Durban, however, was the best two-year-old of her year in France, and her first two dams showed first-class speed.

(3) Turn-to (1951)—inbred with two free generations to Pharos. Turn-to's overall record as a sire was not too consistent, but he did seem to excel as a sire of sires. Of his best sons, Sir Gaylord, Hail to Reason, and Cyane, all proved to be good sires, though none of them stood training for very long. Another crack son, First Landing, raced hard for three years. Turn-to himself broke down prior to the Kentucky Derby.

Turn-to is the only highly inbred sire the author has been able to find in the list of sires compiled by *The Blood-Horse* having an Average-Earnings Index of 3.00 or higher. This in itself is somewhat remarkable, as the devotees of inbreeding are constantly trying relatively close inbreeding crosses and patterns in their pedigrees. All that can be said with certainty at this time is that, to date, such inbreeding patterns have not succeeded well in producing sires of the highest class. (Turn-to was bred in Ireland and was inbred to a particularly sound, tough horse in Pharos, who stood training for four seasons without becoming unsound.)

What about the physical types of the sires included in the survey?

The sires ranged all the way from the exceptionally small to the exceptionally large. The small sires were rather large-bodied horses on short legs.

The great Italian breeder Federico Tesio had a prejudice against very large, heavy, burly sires; he liked refined, medium-sized to small horses that were good two-year-olds and then could show to advantage as three-year-olds at ten furlongs and, preferably, at twelve furlongs. (Using these standards, he would have rejected Bull Lea.)

What about a high charge of nervous energy, as contrasted with horses of placid temperament?

There does not appear to be any general rule in this area. Nearco and Tourbillon were both sires highly charged with nervous energy. It may be observed that such horses not infrequently sire high-class stock from mares of placid temperament, as with Nearco's sons Dante and Sayajirao, both classic winners in England from a mare of very modest racing class by a horse of a placid strain in Dark Legend.

In contrast with sires of this type are stallions like Bull Lea (1935), who give every appearance of placid temperament. Highly charged mares of good racing performance appear to be particularly well suited as mates for such sires. (Good race mares appear to do well with almost all sires.)

Lastly, is the actual appearance of the horse a reliable guide to his prospects as a sire? So often, one hears breeders say, "He is such a good-looking horse," in tones of admiration. It is clear beyond doubt that racing is not a beauty contest but a performance contest. Bull Lea and Prince Bio (in France) were homely horses, and this lack of quality undoubtedly told against their appeal in their early days at stud; Hyperion (1930), when he had grown his full winter coat, looked more like a highland pack pony than a racehorse; Man o' War had a Roman nose, in sharp contrast to the beautiful dished faces of the sires throwing back to their Arab ancestors.

The chief points of importance to note in the appearance of stallions seems to be structural defects. Tourbillon (1928), for instance, had markedly sickle hocks and transmitted them to many of his produce. If a breeder objects to sickle hocks, he probably should not breed to a horse like Tourbillon. Blandford (1919) was very upright in his pasterns and transmitted this defect to a fairly high proportion of his stock. He broke down midway in his three-year-old year, as did his son, Blenheim II, probably owing to this defect. Mated with sound strains, this fault could be bred out, with very sound stock resulting.

There are, alas, virtually no perfect horses, any more than there are many perfect people (who are bred with considerably less care than horses). The everlasting problems in selecting breeding stock are: What should we insist on in the way of conformation, performance, and pedigree, and what defects are we prepared to overlook?

Even Man o' War was not perfect. He had a weak female line and was a very undeveloped, thin, foalish-looking yearling, but can anyone truthfully say that even with these drawbacks, he would not like to have owned Man o' War both as a racer and as a sire?

ABOUT THE AUTHOR

Abram S. Hewitt was a veritable Renaissance man during his long and distinguished life. A native New Yorker, he was a grandson and namesake of a mayor of New York City. In 1925 he graduated from Oxford with honors in philosophy, politics, and economics, and then went on to earn a law degree from Columbia University, later teaching there and at Johns Hopkins University. A formidable international lawyer, he also worked in Washington, D.C., as part of President Franklin D. Roosevelt's New Deal, organizing the Farm Credit Administration and serving as counsel for various agencies.

On the equine side of things, Hewitt maintained a lifelong fascination for the Thoroughbred and first owned racehorses in the 1920s. Then, beginning in 1937, he bred a dozen stakes winners before selling his bloodstock in 1950. The best of these was Phalanx, a son of Pilate, a stallion Hewitt had acquired to stand at stud. Phalanx, raced in partnership with C.V. Whitney, won the 1947 Belmont Stakes and was champion three-year-old colt.

During the 1930s Hewitt became a regular contributor to *The Blood-Horse*, also sending reports to the *Morning Telegraph* from time to time. In 1973 he began work on *Sire Lines*, which appeared in serial form in *The Blood-Horse* before being published as a book in 1977. He also wrote *The Great Breeders and Their Methods*, published in 1982 by *The Thoroughbred Record*. He lived in Lexington, Kentucky, while he was writing *Sire Lines* and served as a pedigree adviser to Nelson Bunker Hunt. Hewitt also imported the Irish-bred Sirlad, who won the 1979 Sunset Handicap in Hewitt's colors.

Hewitt died in 1987. He was in his 80s.